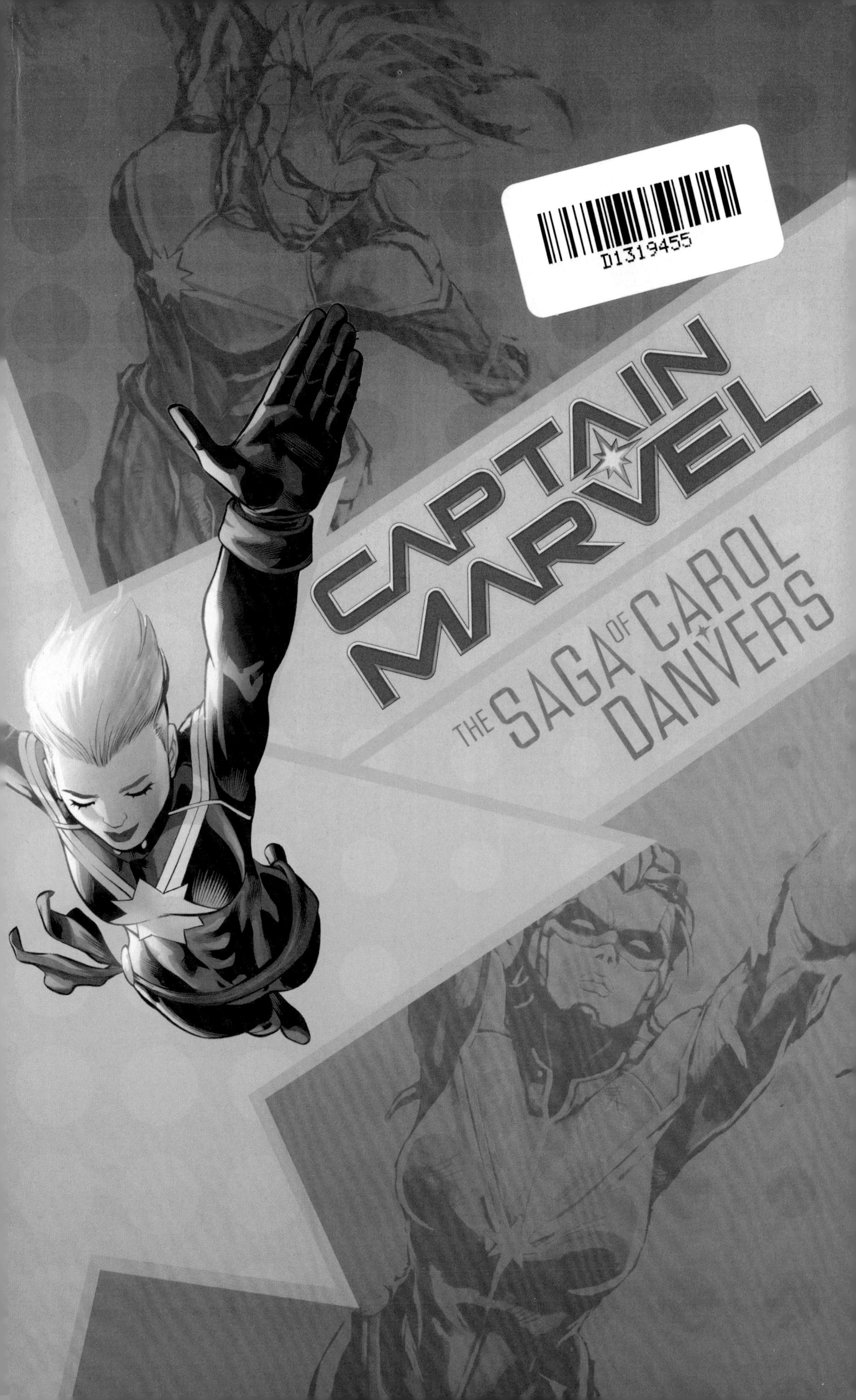
CAPTAIN MARVEL
THE SAGA OF CAROL DANVERS

CAPTAIN MARVEL
THE SAGA OF CAROL DANVERS

CAPTAIN MARVEL #1-4

WRITER **KELLY SUE DeCONNICK**
ARTISTS **DEXTER SOY** WITH
    RICHARD ELSON [#3 PP.17-18],
    KARL KESEL [#3 P.19] &
    AL BARRIONUEVO [#4 PP.16-20]
COLOR ARTISTS **DEXTER SOY** WITH **WIL QUINTANA**
    [#3 PP.17-18, #4 16-20] &
    JAVIER RODRIGUEZ [#3 P.19]
COVER ART **ED McGUINNESS, DEXTER VINES** &
    JAVIER RODRÍGUEZ

CAPTAIN MARVEL #5-6

WRITER **KELLY SUE DeCONNICK**
PENCILER **EMMA RIOS**
INKERS **EMMA RIOS** WITH **ÁLVARO LÓPEZ** [#6]
COLOR ARTIST **JORDIE BELLAIRE**
COVER ART **TERRY DODSON** & **RACHEL DODSON**

CAPTAIN MARVEL #7-8

WRITERS **KELLY SUE DeCONNICK** &
    CHRISTOPHER SEBELA
ARTIST **DEXTER SOY**
COLOR ARTISTS **DEXTER SOY** [#7] &
    VERONICA GANDINI [#8]
COVER ART **JAMIE McKELVIE** & **JORDIE BELLAIRE** [#7];
    DEXTER SOY [#8]

CAPTAIN MARVEL #17

WRITER **KELLY SUE DeCONNICK**
ARTIST **FILIPE ANDRADE**
COLOR ARTIST **JORDIE BELLAIRE**
COVER ART **JOE QUINONES**

LETTERER VC's **JOE CARAMAGNA**
ASSISTANT EDITORS **ELLIE PYLE** [#1-2] & **DEVIN LEWIS** [#17]
ASSOCIATE EDITOR **SANA AMANAT** [#1-3]
EDITORS **STEPHEN WACKER** [#1-3] & **SANA AMANAT** [#4-8, #17]
SENIOR EDITOR **STEPHEN WACKER** [#4-8, #17]

CAPTAIN MARVEL COSTUME DESIGN BY **JAMIE McKELVIE**
SPECIAL THANKS TO **MAKI YAMANE** & **SIGRID ELLIS**
ISSUE #4 DEDICATED TO ASTRONAUT **SALLY RIDE**

THE LIFE OF CAPTAIN MARVEL #1-5

WRITER **MARGARET STOHL**
PENCILER [PRESENT DAY] **CARLOS PACHECO**
INKER [PRESENT DAY] **RAFAEL FONTERIZ**
COLOR ARTISTS [PRESENT DAY] **MARCIO MENYZ** WITH
    FEDERICO BLEE [#5]

ARTIST & COLOR ARTIST **MARGUERITE SAUVAGE**
[#1-3 & #5 FLASHBACKS]
ARTIST [#4 FLASHBACKS] **ERICA D'URSO**
COLOR ARTIST [#4 FLASHBACKS] **MARCIO MENYZ**

LETTERER VC's **CLAYTON COWLES**
COVER ART **JULIAN TOTINO TEDESCO**

EDITOR **SARAH BRUNSTAD**
CONSULTING EDITOR **SANA AMANAT**
EXECUTIVE EDITOR **TOM BREVOORT**

KREE "KLEANER" DESIGN BY **JOSHUA JAMES SHAW**
SPECIAL THANKS TO **AXEL ALONSO** & **STEPHEN WACKER**

COLLECTION EDITOR **DANIEL KIRCHHOFFER**
ASSOCIATE MANAGER, TALENT RELATIONS **LISA MONTALBANO**
DIRECTOR, PRODUCTION & SPECIAL PROJECTS **JENNIFER GRÜNWALD**
VP PRODUCTION & SPECIAL PROJECTS **JEFF YOUNGQUIST**
RESEARCH **JESS HARROLD**
BOOK DESIGNER **STACIE ZUCKER**
MANAGER & SENIOR DESIGNER **ADAM DEL RE**
LEAD DESIGNER **JAY BOWEN**
SVP PRINT, SALES & MARKETING **DAVID GABRIEL**
EDITOR IN CHIEF **C.B. CEBULSKI**

CAPTAIN MARVEL: THE SAGA OF CAROL DANVERS. Contains material originally published in magazine form as CAPTAIN MARVEL (2012) #1-8 and #17, and THE LIFE OF CAPTAIN MARVEL (2018) #1-5. First printing 2023. ISBN 978-1-302-95181-8. Published by MARVEL WORLDWIDE, INC., a subsidiary of MARVEL ENTERTAINMENT, LLC. OFFICE OF PUBLICATION: 1290 Avenue of the Americas, New York, NY 10104. © 2023 MARVEL No similarity between any of the names, characters, persons, and/or institutions in this book with those of any living or dead person or institution is intended, and any such similarity which may exist is purely coincidental. **Printed in Canada.** KEVIN FEIGE, Chief Creative Officer; DAN BUCKLEY, President, Marvel Entertainment; DAVID BOGART, Associate Publisher & SVP of Talent Affairs; TOM BREVOORT, VP, Executive Editor; NICK LOWE, Executive Editor, VP of Content, Digital Publishing; DAVID GABRIEL, VP of Print & Digital Publishing; SVEN LARSEN, VP of Licensed Publishing; MARK ANNUNZIATO, VP of Planning & Forecasting; JEFF YOUNGQUIST, VP of Production & Special Projects; ALEX MORALES, Director of Publishing Operations; DAN EDINGTON, Director of Editorial Operations; RICKEY PURDIN, Director of Talent Relations; JENNIFER GRÜNWALD, Director of Production & Special Projects; SUSAN CRESPI, Production Manager; STAN LEE, Chairman Emeritus. For information regarding advertising in Marvel Comics or on Marvel.com, please contact Vit DeBellis, Custom Solutions & Integrated Advertising Manager, at vdebellis@marvel.com. For Marvel subscription inquiries, please call 888-511-5480. **Manufactured between 7/14/2023 and 8/15/2023 by SOLISCO PRINTERS, SCOTT, QC, CANADA.**

10 9 8 7 6 5 4 3 2 1

CAPTAIN MARVEL #1

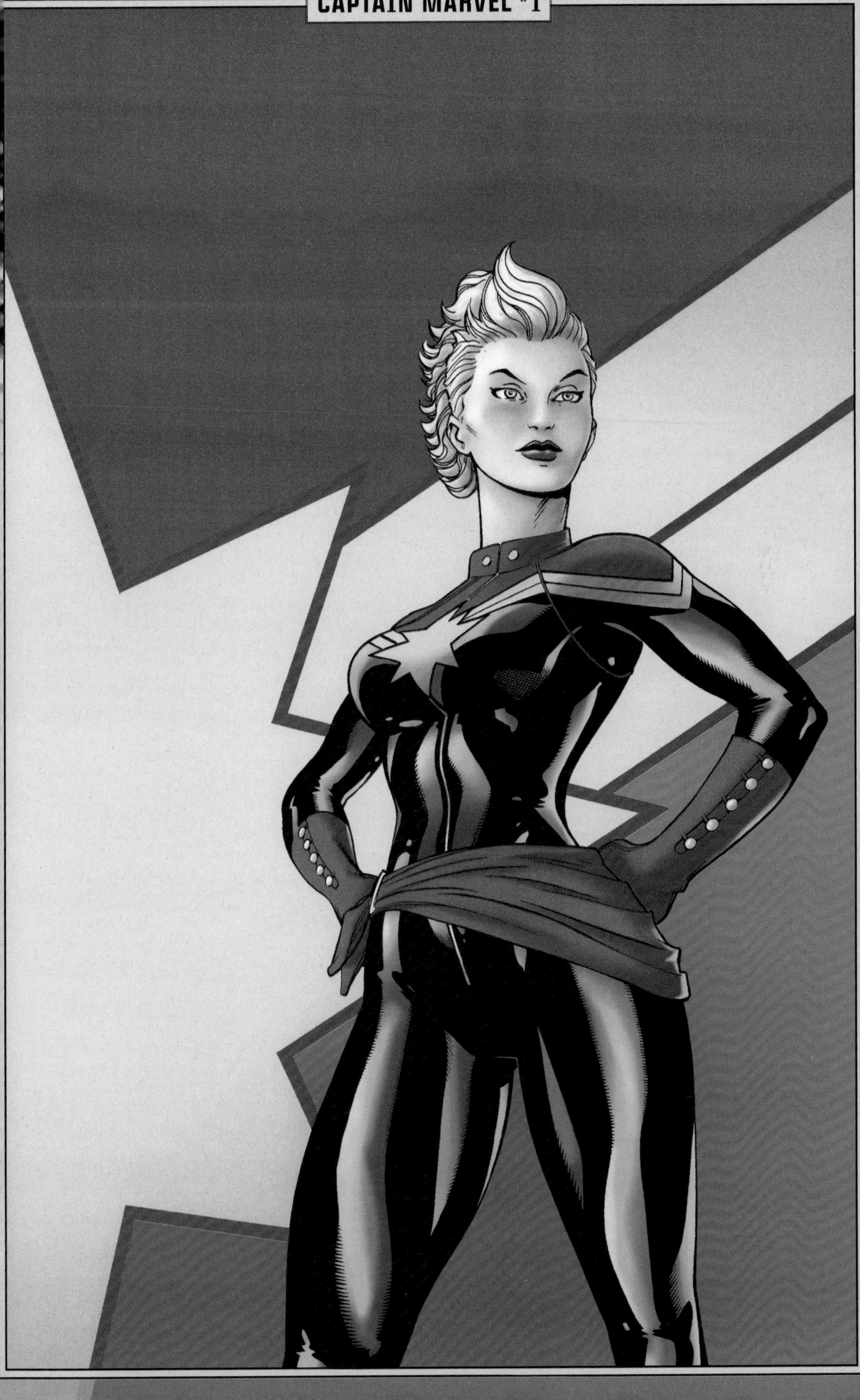

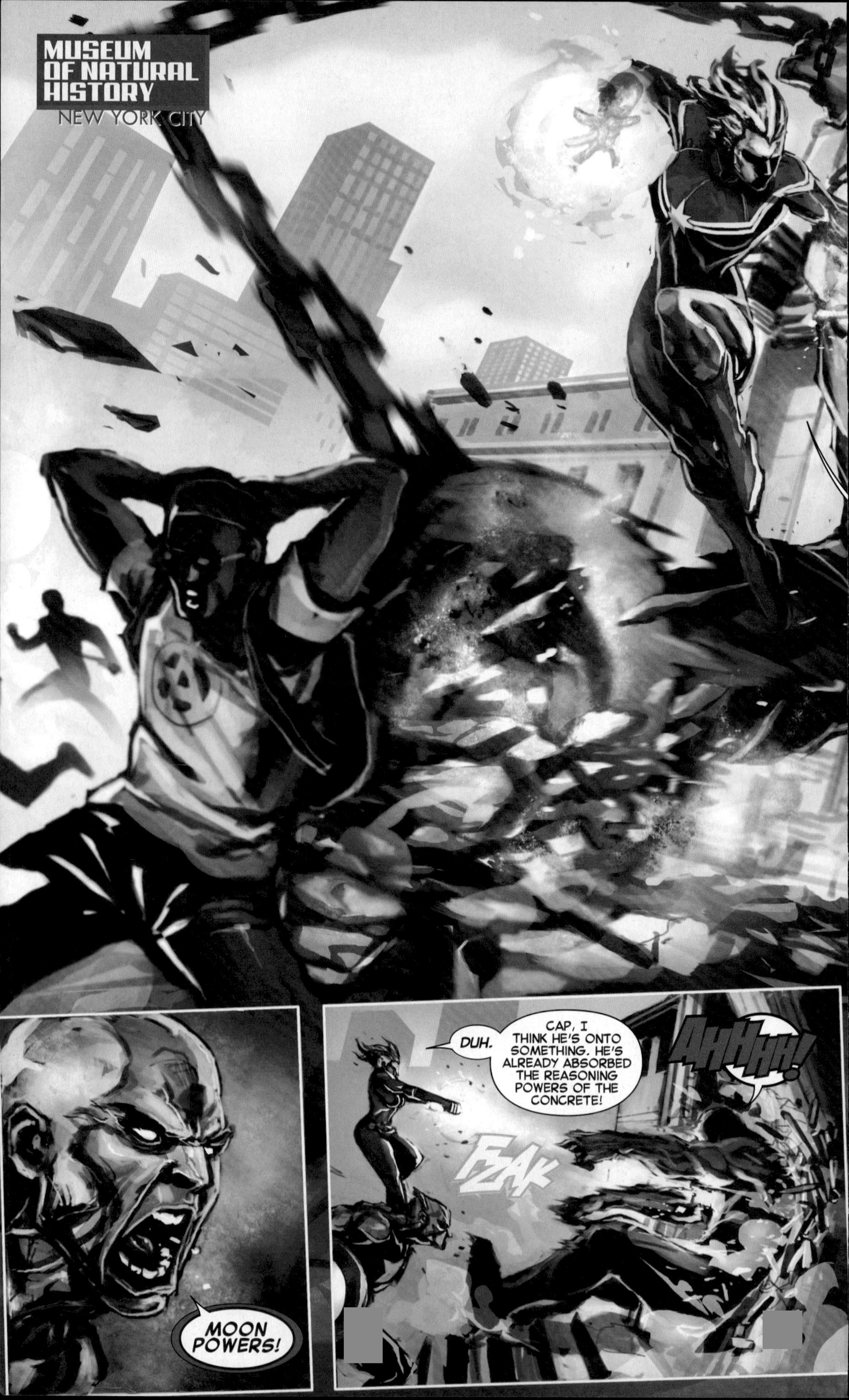
MUSEUM OF NATURAL HISTORY
NEW YORK CITY
MOON POWERS!
DUH.
CAP, I THINK HE'S ONTO SOMETHING. HE'S ALREADY ABSORBED THE REASONING POWERS OF THE CONCRETE!
AHHHH!
FZAK

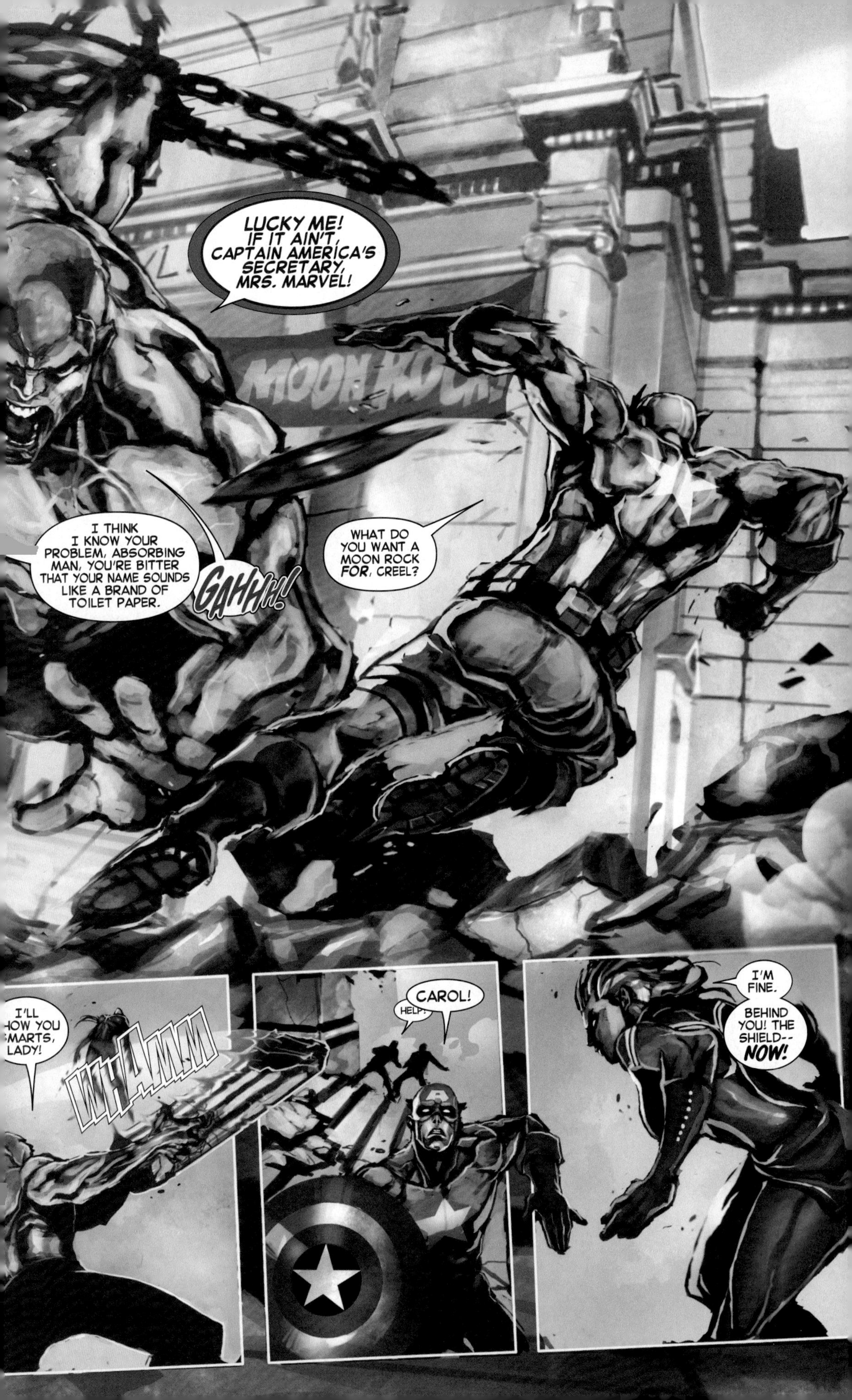
LUCKY ME! IF IT AIN'T, CAPTAIN AMERICA'S SECRETARY, MRS. MARVEL!
I THINK I KNOW YOUR PROBLEM, ABSORBING MAN, YOU'RE BITTER THAT YOUR NAME SOUNDS LIKE A BRAND OF TOILET PAPER.
GAHHH!
WHAT DO YOU WANT A MOON ROCK FOR, CREEL?
I'LL HOW YOU MARTS, LADY!
WHAMM
CAROL!
HELP!
I'M FINE.
BEHIND YOU! THE SHIELD-- NOW!

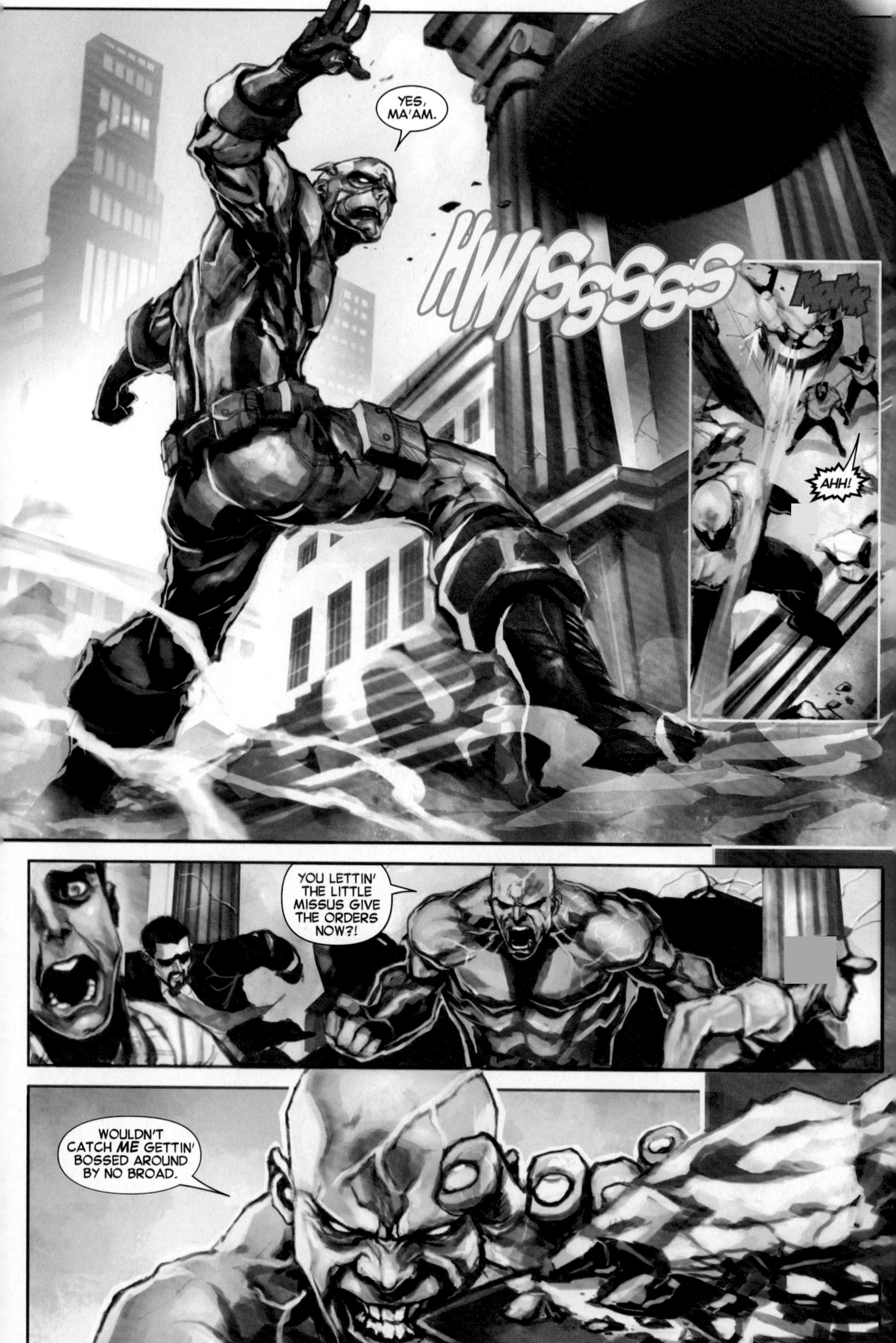
YES, MA'AM.
HWISSSSSS
AHH!
YOU LETTIN' THE LITTLE MISSUS GIVE THE ORDERS NOW?!
WOULDN'T CATCH *ME* GETTIN' BOSSED AROUND BY NO BROAD.

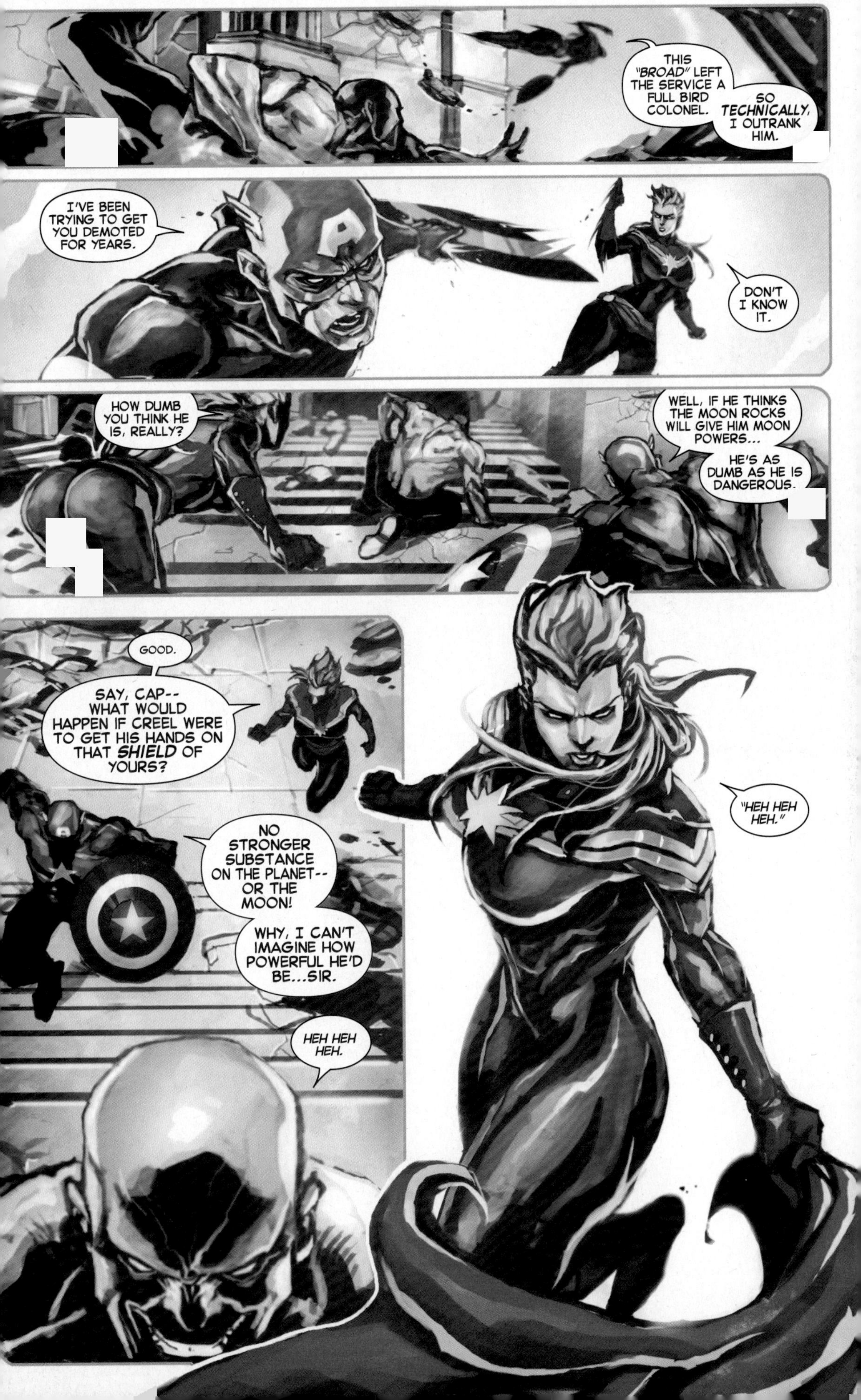
THIS "BROAD" LEFT THE SERVICE A FULL BIRD COLONEL.
SO TECHNICALLY, I OUTRANK HIM.
I'VE BEEN TRYING TO GET YOU DEMOTED FOR YEARS.
DON'T I KNOW IT.
HOW DUMB YOU THINK HE IS, REALLY?
WELL, IF HE THINKS THE MOON ROCKS WILL GIVE HIM MOON POWERS...
HE'S AS DUMB AS HE IS DANGEROUS.
GOOD.
SAY, CAP-- WHAT WOULD HAPPEN IF CREEL WERE TO GET HIS HANDS ON THAT SHIELD OF YOURS?
NO STRONGER SUBSTANCE ON THE PLANET-- OR THE MOON!
WHY, I CAN'T IMAGINE HOW POWERFUL HE'D BE...SIR.
HEH HEH HEH.
"HEH HEH HEH."

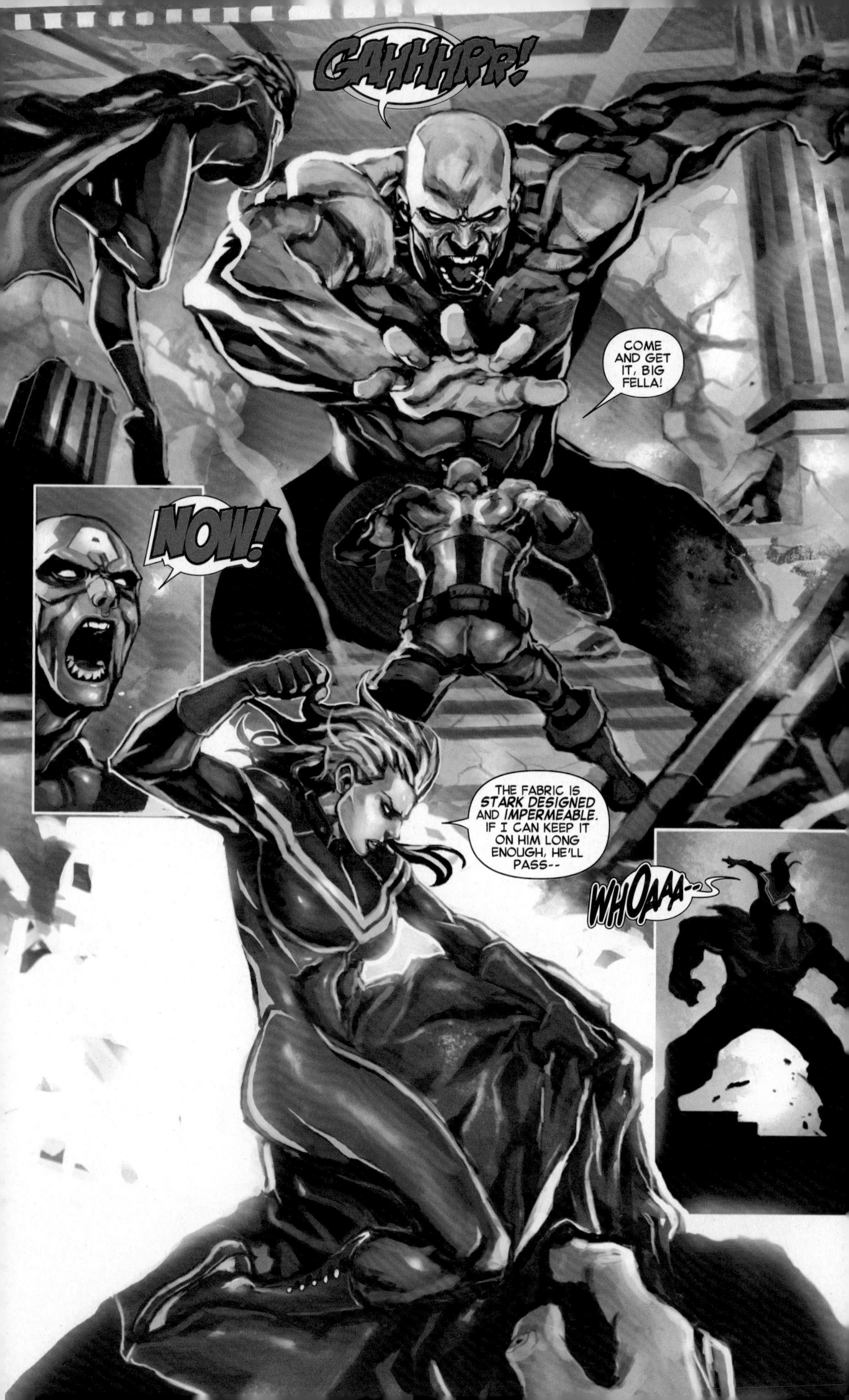
GAHHHRR!
COME AND GET IT, BIG FELLA!
NOW!
THE FABRIC IS STARK DESIGNED AND IMPERMEABLE. IF I CAN KEEP IT ON HIM LONG ENOUGH, HE'LL PASS--
WHOAAA--

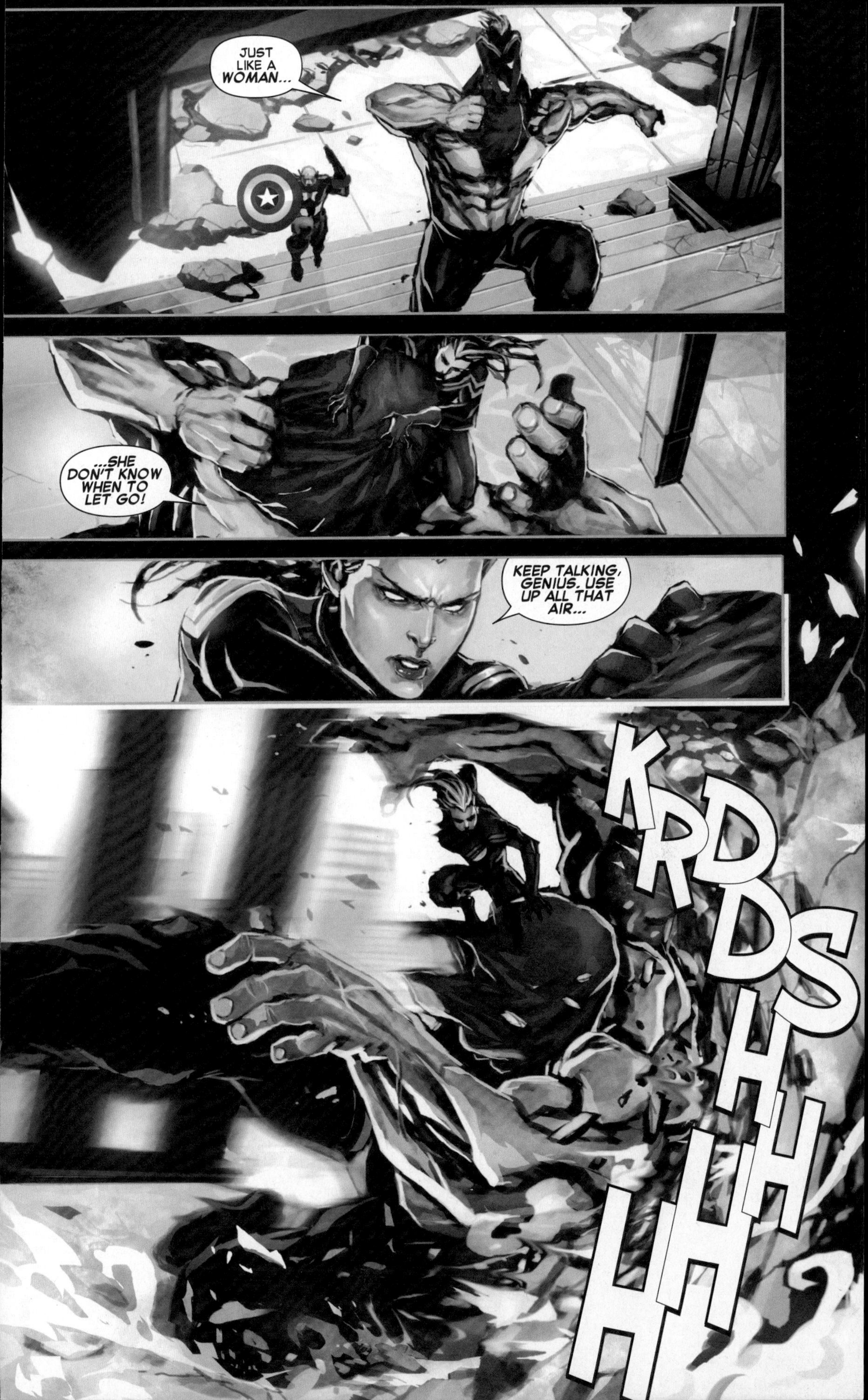
JUST LIKE A WOMAN...
...SHE DON'T KNOW WHEN TO LET GO!
KEEP TALKING, GENIUS. USE UP ALL THAT AIR...
KRDSHHHHH

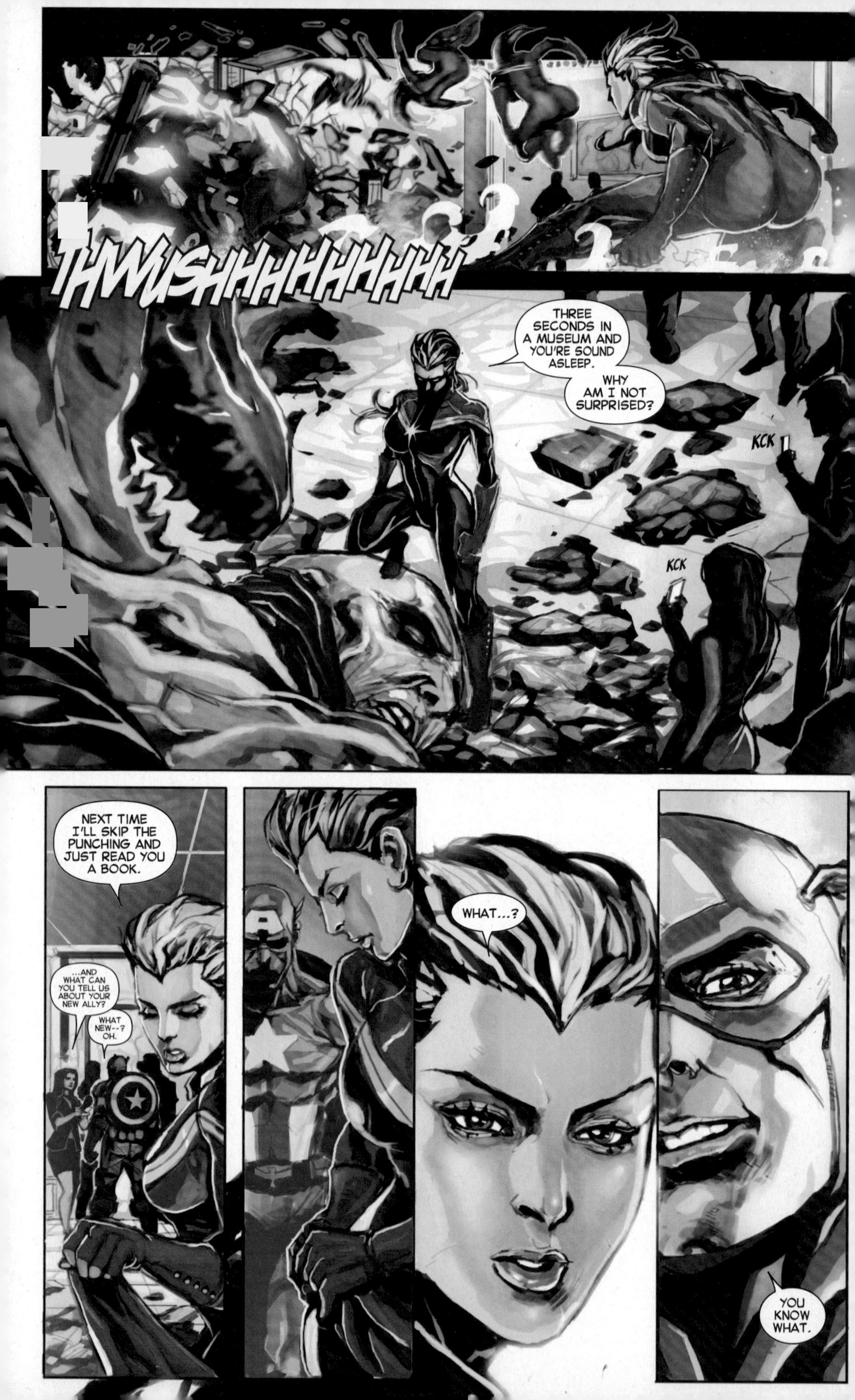
THWUSHHHHHHHHHH
THREE SECONDS IN A MUSEUM AND YOU'RE SOUND ASLEEP.
WHY AM I NOT SURPRISED?
KCK
KCK
NEXT TIME I'LL SKIP THE PUNCHING AND JUST READ YOU A BOOK.
...AND WHAT CAN YOU TELL US ABOUT YOUR NEW ALLY?
WHAT NEW--? OH.
WHAT...?
YOU KNOW WHAT.

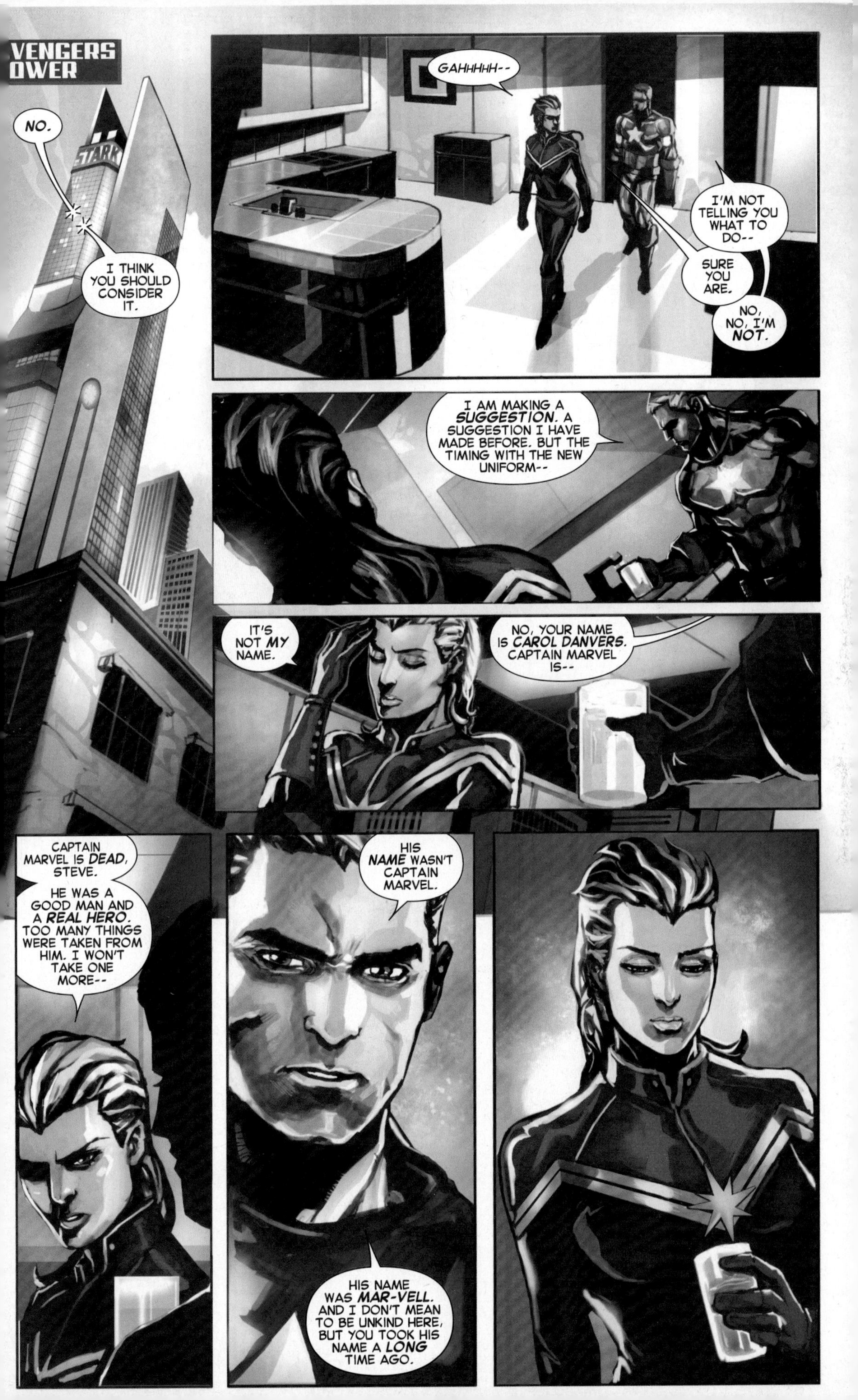
VENGERS
OWER
NO.
I THINK YOU SHOULD CONSIDER IT.
GAHHHHH--
I'M NOT TELLING YOU WHAT TO DO--
SURE YOU ARE.
NO, NO, I'M NOT.
I AM MAKING A SUGGESTION. A SUGGESTION I HAVE MADE BEFORE. BUT THE TIMING WITH THE NEW UNIFORM--
IT'S NOT MY NAME.
NO, YOUR NAME IS CAROL DANVERS. CAPTAIN MARVEL IS--
CAPTAIN MARVEL IS DEAD, STEVE.
HE WAS A GOOD MAN AND A REAL HERO. TOO MANY THINGS WERE TAKEN FROM HIM. I WON'T TAKE ONE MORE--
HIS NAME WASN'T CAPTAIN MARVEL.
HIS NAME WAS MAR-VELL. AND I DON'T MEAN TO BE UNKIND HERE, BUT YOU TOOK HIS NAME A LONG TIME AGO.

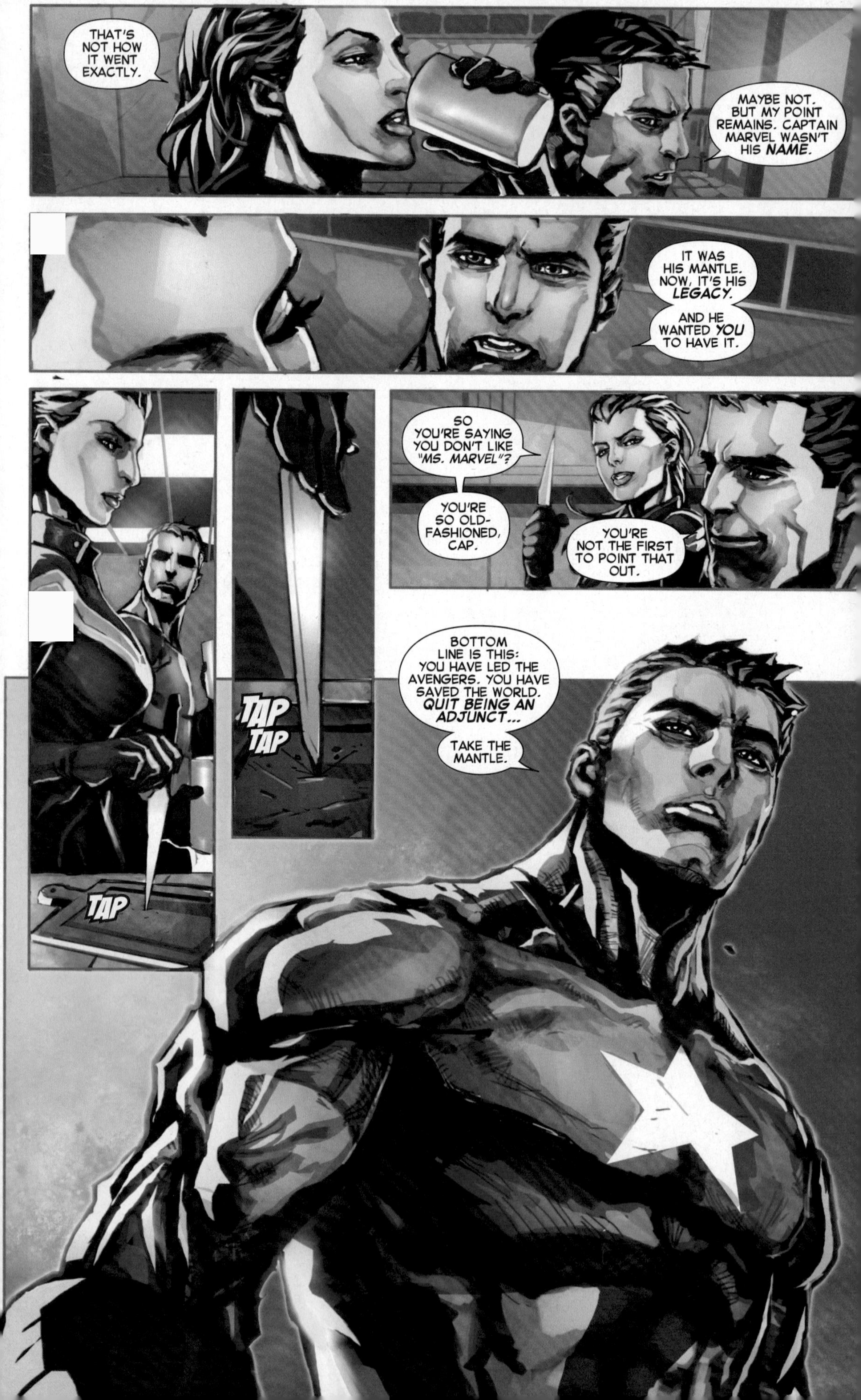
THAT'S NOT HOW IT WENT EXACTLY.
MAYBE NOT. BUT MY POINT REMAINS. CAPTAIN MARVEL WASN'T HIS NAME.
IT WAS HIS MANTLE. NOW, IT'S HIS LEGACY.
AND HE WANTED YOU TO HAVE IT.
TAP
TAP TAP
SO YOU'RE SAYING YOU DON'T LIKE "MS. MARVEL"?
YOU'RE SO OLD-FASHIONED, CAP.
YOU'RE NOT THE FIRST TO POINT THAT OUT.
BOTTOM LINE IS THIS: YOU HAVE LED THE AVENGERS. YOU HAVE SAVED THE WORLD. QUIT BEING AN ADJUNCT...
TAKE THE MANTLE.

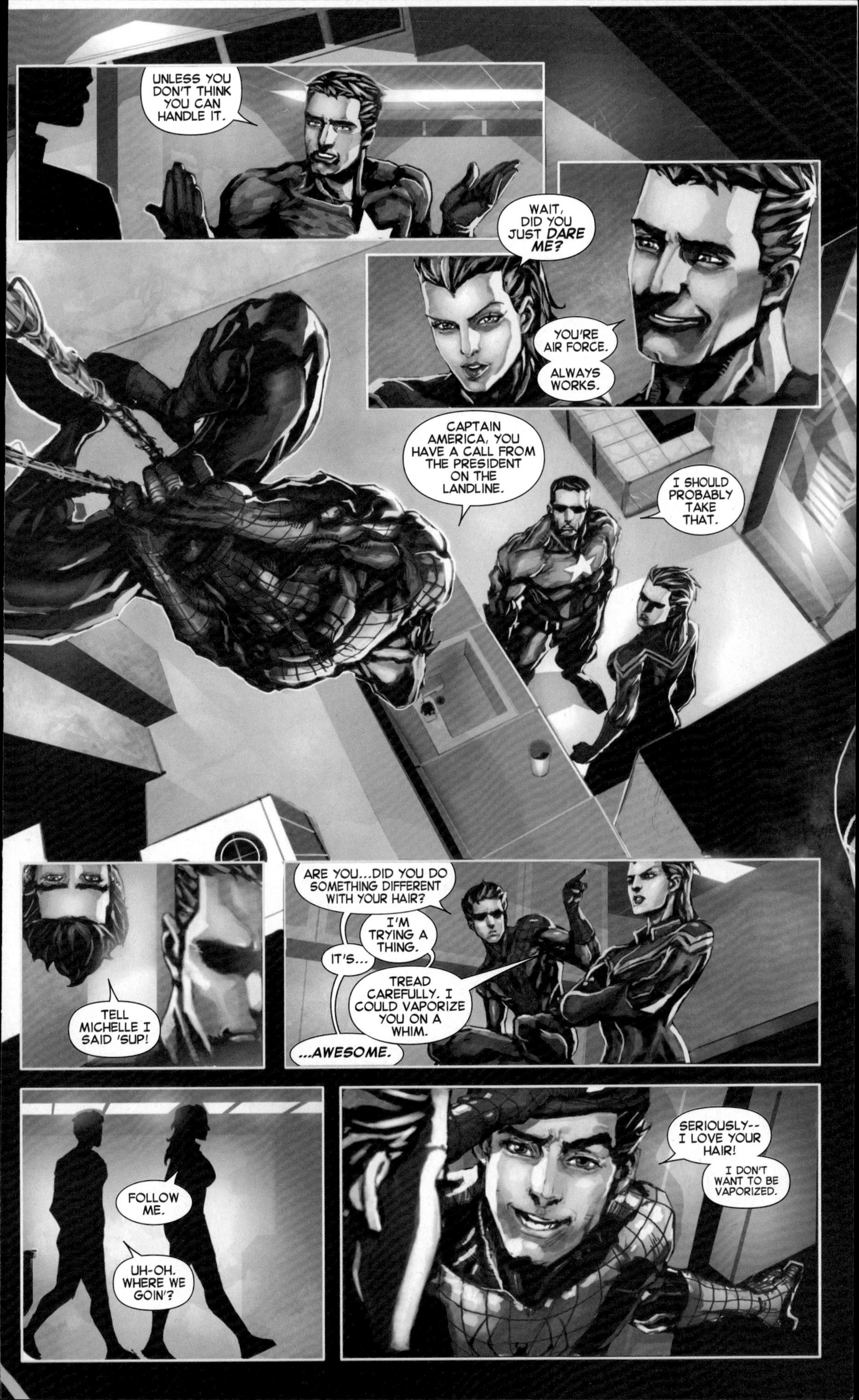
UNLESS YOU DON'T THINK YOU CAN HANDLE IT.
WAIT, DID YOU JUST DARE ME?
YOU'RE AIR FORCE.
ALWAYS WORKS.
CAPTAIN AMERICA, YOU HAVE A CALL FROM THE PRESIDENT ON THE LANDLINE.
I SHOULD PROBABLY TAKE THAT.
TELL MICHELLE I SAID 'SUP!
ARE YOU...DID YOU DO SOMETHING DIFFERENT WITH YOUR HAIR?
I'M TRYING A THING.
IT'S...
TREAD CAREFULLY. I COULD VAPORIZE YOU ON A WHIM.
...AWESOME.
FOLLOW ME.
UH-OH. WHERE WE GOIN'?
SERIOUSLY-- I LOVE YOUR HAIR!
I DON'T WANT TO BE VAPORIZED.

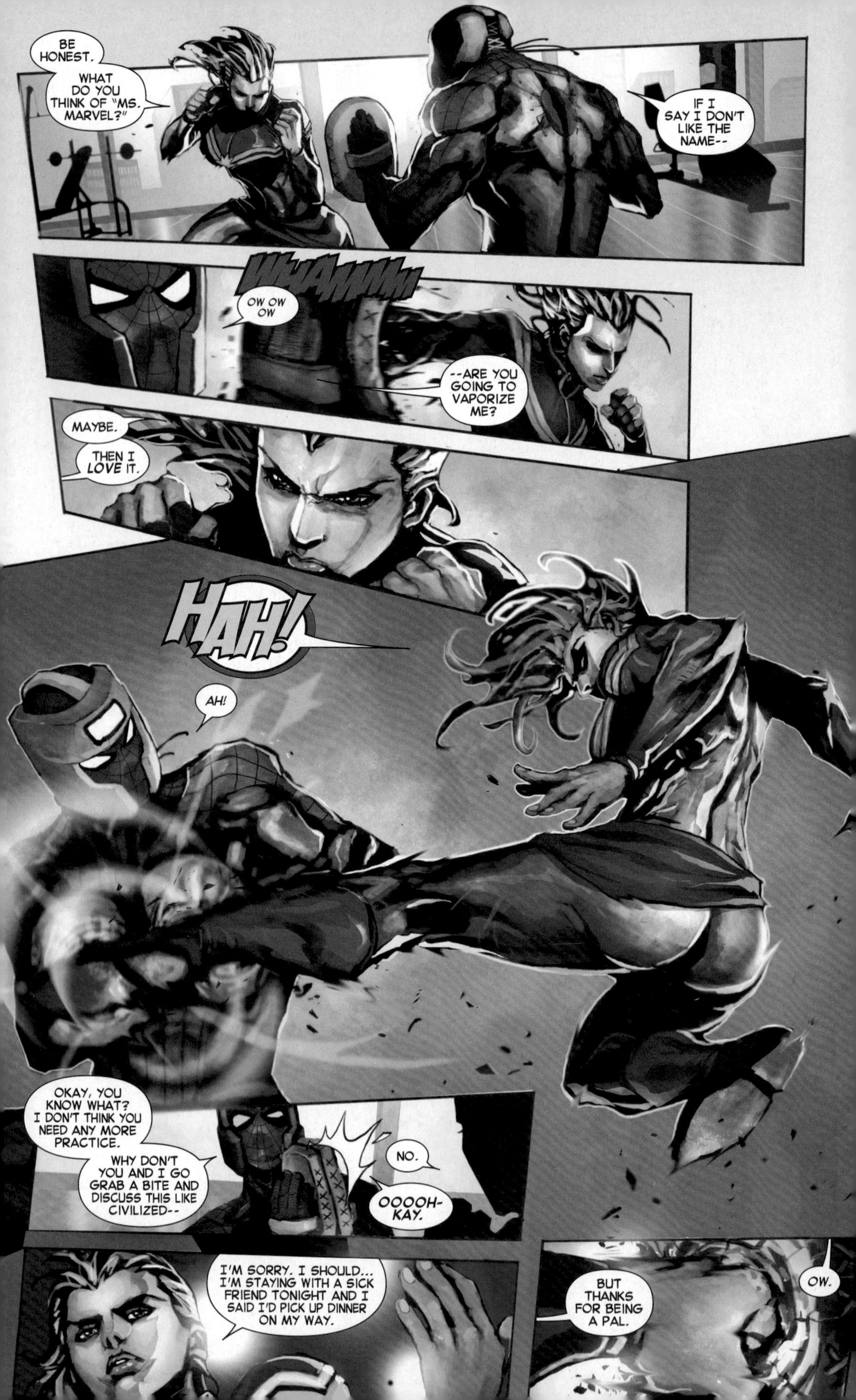

BE HONEST.
WHAT DO YOU THINK OF "MS. MARVEL?"
IF I SAY I DON'T LIKE THE NAME--
WHAAMMM
OW OW OW
--ARE YOU GOING TO VAPORIZE ME?
MAYBE.
THEN I LOVE IT.
HAH!
AH!
OKAY, YOU KNOW WHAT? I DON'T THINK YOU NEED ANY MORE PRACTICE.
WHY DON'T YOU AND I GO GRAB A BITE AND DISCUSS THIS LIKE CIVILIZED--
NO.
OOOOH-KAY.
I'M SORRY. I SHOULD... I'M STAYING WITH A SICK FRIEND TONIGHT AND I SAID I'D PICK UP DINNER ON MY WAY.
BUT THANKS FOR BEING A PAL.
OW.

I WAS A LUCKY KID BECAUSE I HAD TWO HEROES--MY DAD AND A PILOT NAMED HELEN COBB.

HELEN HELD FIFTEEN SPEED RECORDS WHEN SHE RETIRED.

FIFTEEN.

I'M NOT PRONE TO ENVY. BUT THOSE RECORDS...

I ENVY THOSE RECORDS.

I CAN FLY. FAST.

REAL FAST.

BUT THESE "ABILITIES" COME AT A COST. FOR ONE THING, I'LL NEVER BE ALLOWED TO HOLD A RECORD LIKE HELEN'S.

I CAN'T EVEN COMPETE. WOULDN'T BE A FAIR FIGHT.

I LOST MY SHOT WHEN I WAS CAUGHT IN THE BLAST OF THAT ALIEN PSYCHE-MAGNETRON DEVICE.

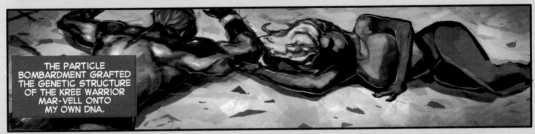

THE PARTICLE BOMBARDMENT GRAFTED THE GENETIC STRUCTURE OF THE KREE WARRIOR MAR-VELL ONTO MY OWN DNA.

IT'S A HELL OF A REWARD...BUT IT ERASED WHAT I LOVED MOST...

...THE RISK.

ONE MINUTE, FIFTY-EIGHT SECONDS FROM BROADWAY TO THE END OF OUR ATMOSPHERE, A NEW PERSONAL BEST.

LUCKY ME.

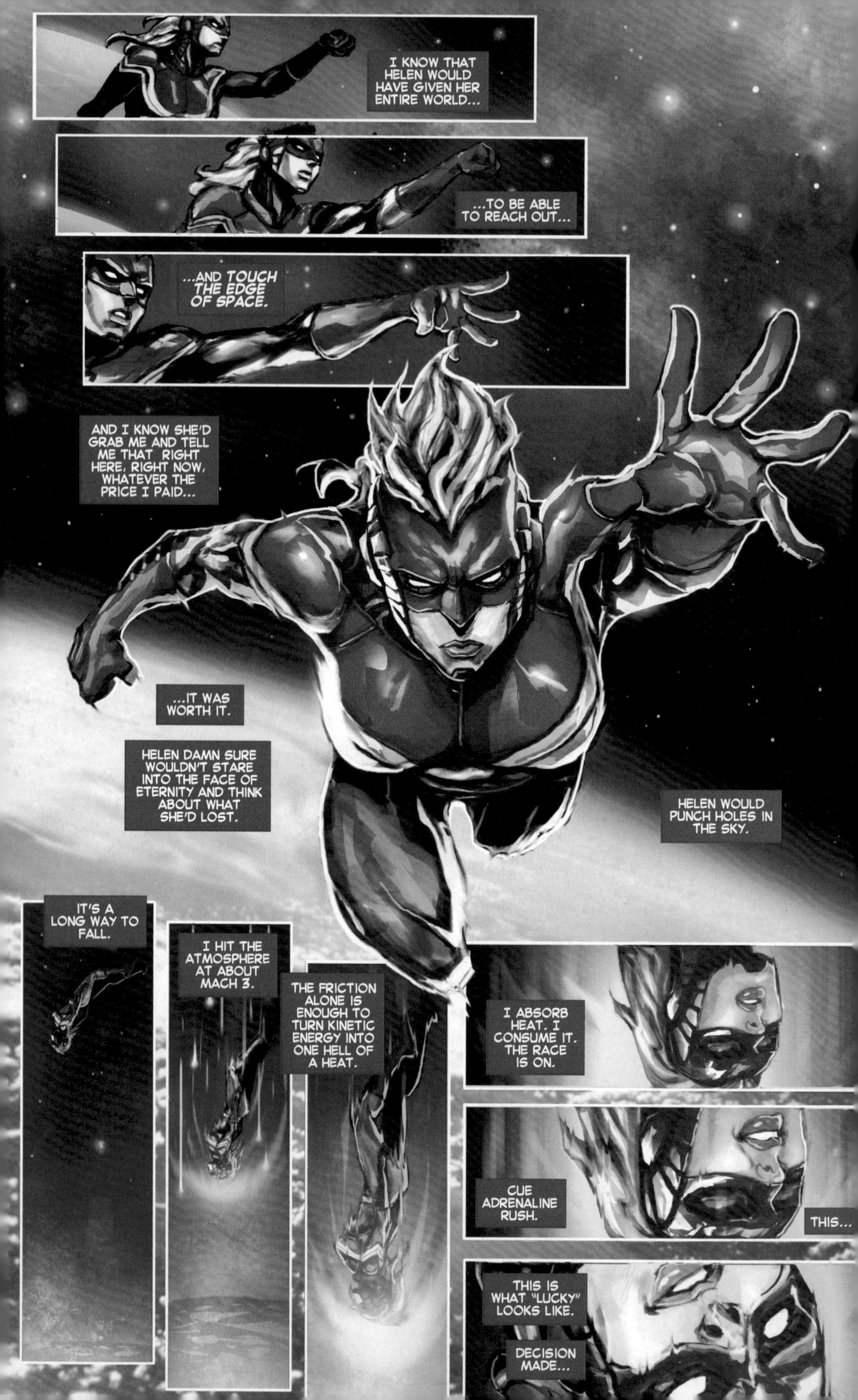
I KNOW THAT HELEN WOULD HAVE GIVEN HER ENTIRE WORLD...
...TO BE ABLE TO REACH OUT...
...AND TOUCH THE EDGE OF SPACE.
AND I KNOW SHE'D GRAB ME AND TELL ME THAT RIGHT HERE, RIGHT NOW, WHATEVER THE PRICE I PAID...
...IT WAS WORTH IT.
HELEN DAMN SURE WOULDN'T STARE INTO THE FACE OF ETERNITY AND THINK ABOUT WHAT SHE'D LOST.
HELEN WOULD PUNCH HOLES IN THE SKY.
IT'S A LONG WAY TO FALL.
I HIT THE ATMOSPHERE AT ABOUT MACH 3.
THE FRICTION ALONE IS ENOUGH TO TURN KINETIC ENERGY INTO ONE HELL OF A HEAT.
I ABSORB HEAT. I CONSUME IT. THE RACE IS ON.
CUE ADRENALINE RUSH.
THIS...
THIS IS WHAT "LUCKY" LOOKS LIKE.
DECISION MADE...

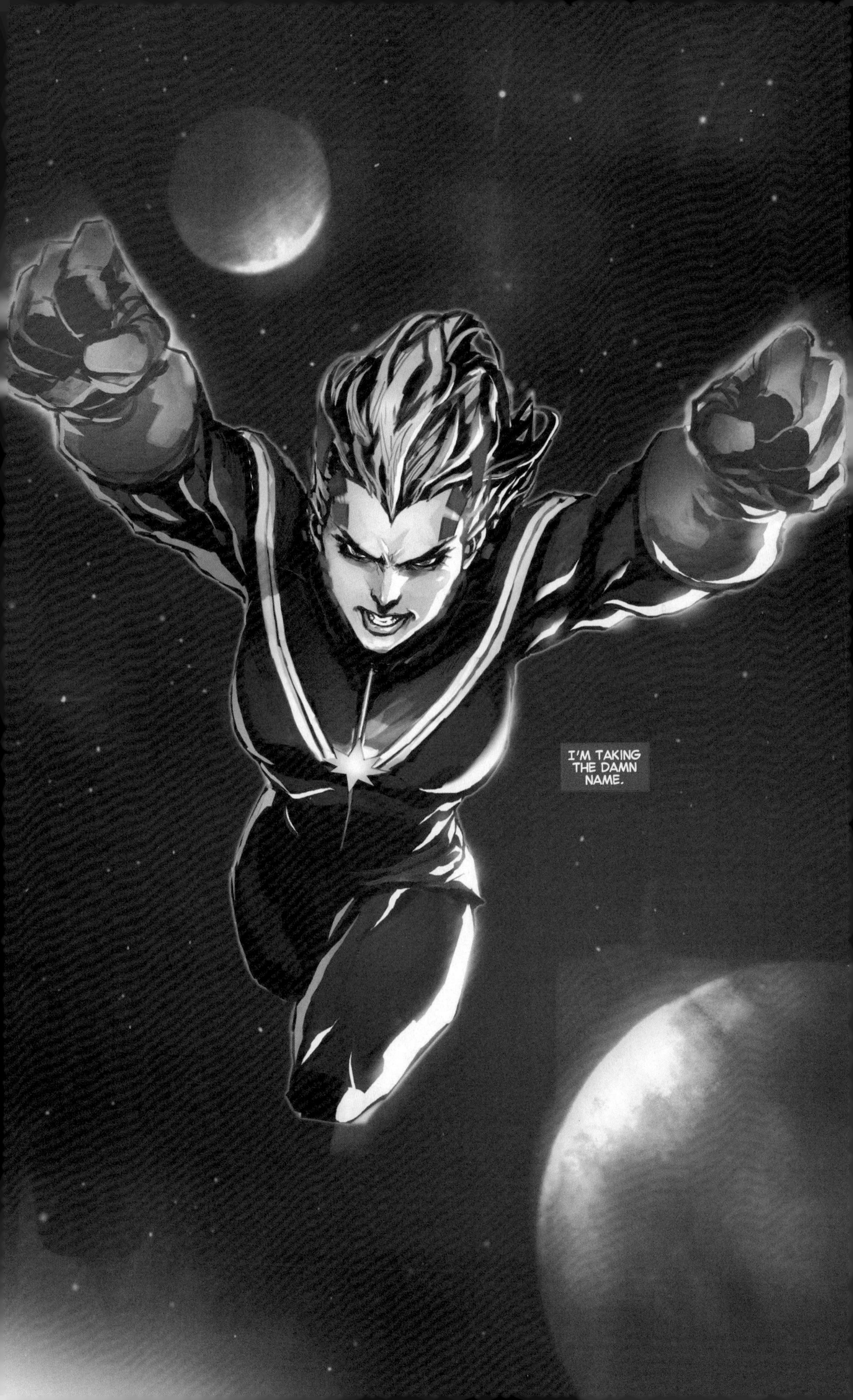
I'M TAKING THE DAMN NAME.

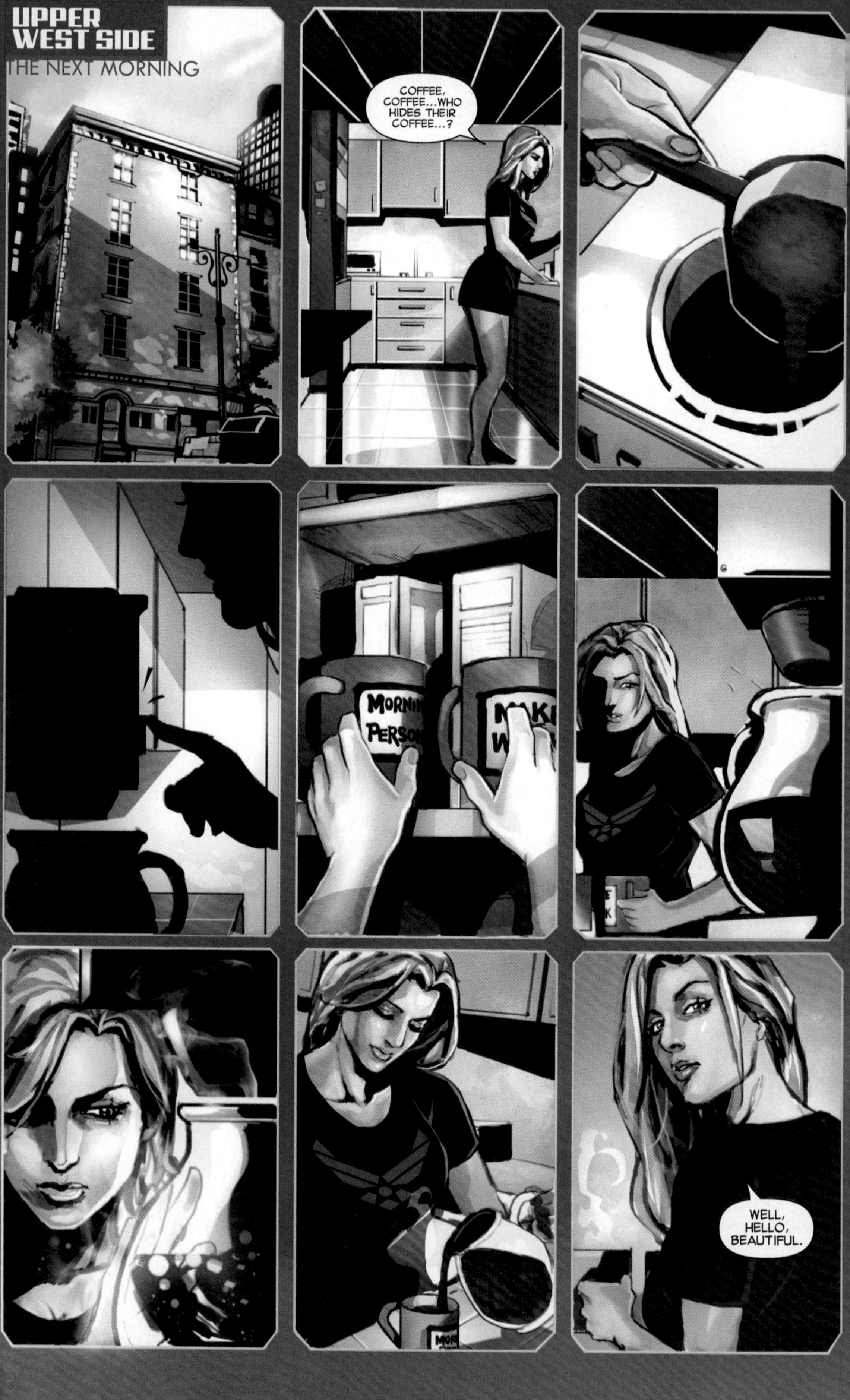
UPPER WEST SIDE
THE NEXT MORNING
COFFEE, COFFEE...WHO HIDES THEIR COFFEE...?
WELL, HELLO, BEAUTIFUL.

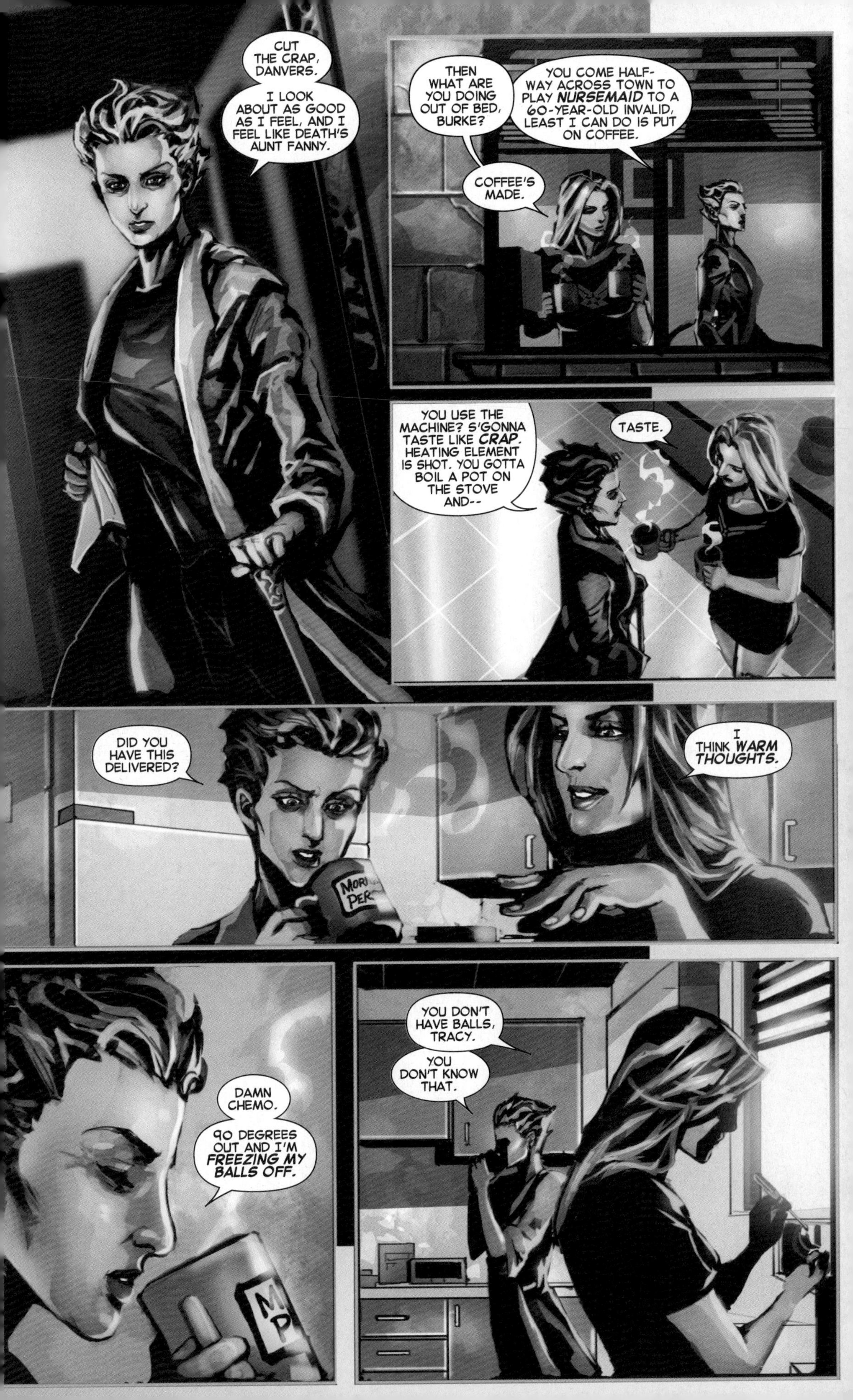
CUT THE CRAP, DANVERS.
I LOOK ABOUT AS GOOD AS I FEEL, AND I FEEL LIKE DEATH'S AUNT FANNY.
THEN WHAT ARE YOU DOING OUT OF BED, BURKE?
YOU COME HALF-WAY ACROSS TOWN TO PLAY **NURSEMAID** TO A 60-YEAR-OLD INVALID, LEAST I CAN DO IS PUT ON COFFEE.
COFFEE'S MADE.
YOU USE THE MACHINE? S'GONNA TASTE LIKE **CRAP**. HEATING ELEMENT IS SHOT. YOU GOTTA BOIL A POT ON THE STOVE AND--
TASTE.
DID YOU HAVE THIS DELIVERED?
I THINK **WARM THOUGHTS.**
DAMN CHEMO.
90 DEGREES OUT AND I'M **FREEZING MY BALLS OFF.**
YOU DON'T HAVE BALLS, TRACY.
YOU DON'T KNOW THAT.

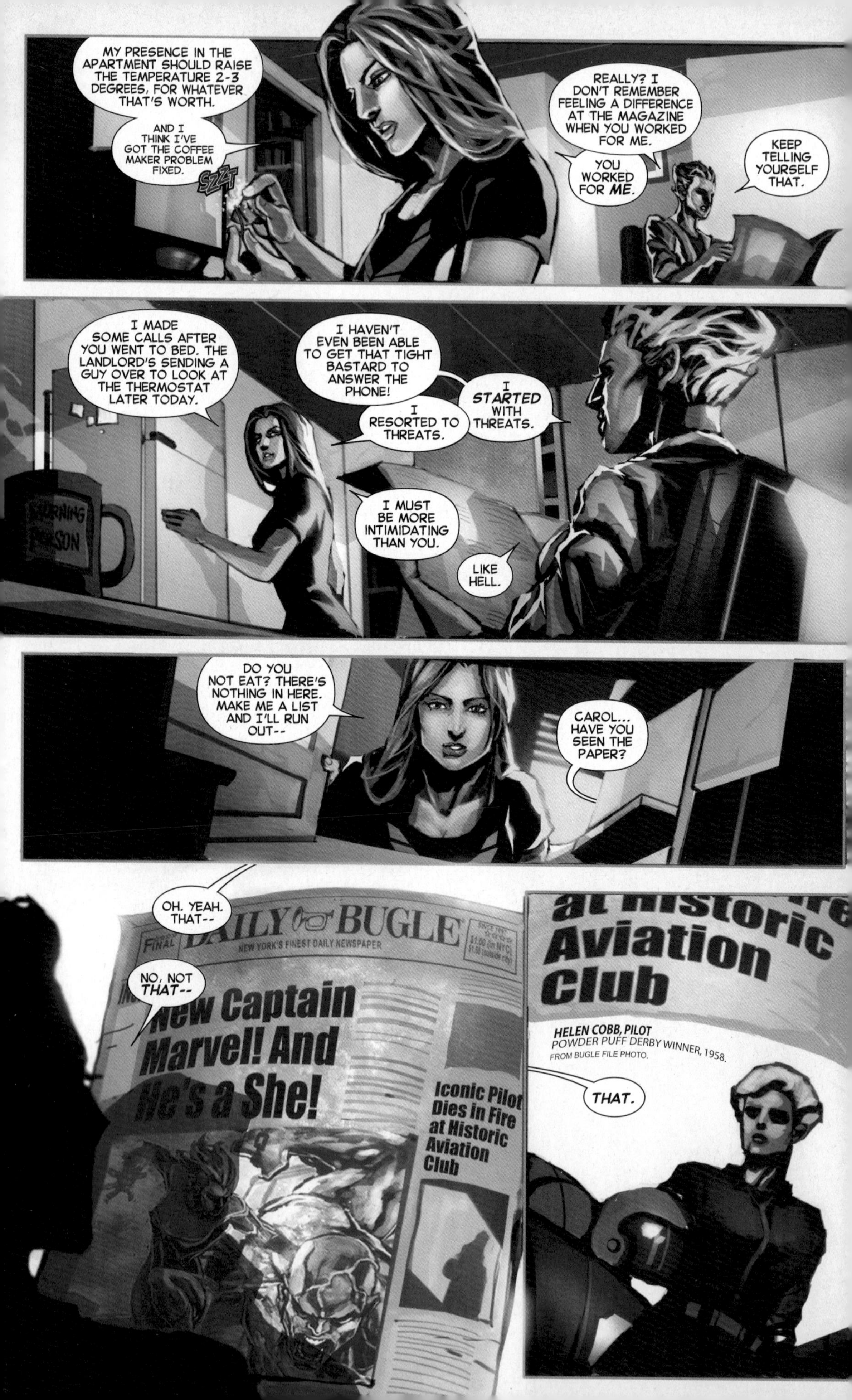

MY PRESENCE IN THE APARTMENT SHOULD RAISE THE TEMPERATURE 2-3 DEGREES, FOR WHATEVER THAT'S WORTH.
AND I THINK I'VE GOT THE COFFEE MAKER PROBLEM FIXED.
SZZT
REALLY? I DON'T REMEMBER FEELING A DIFFERENCE AT THE MAGAZINE WHEN YOU WORKED FOR ME.
YOU WORKED FOR *ME*.
KEEP TELLING YOURSELF THAT.
I MADE SOME CALLS AFTER YOU WENT TO BED. THE LANDLORD'S SENDING A GUY OVER TO LOOK AT THE THERMOSTAT LATER TODAY.
I HAVEN'T EVEN BEEN ABLE TO GET THAT TIGHT BASTARD TO ANSWER THE PHONE!
I RESORTED TO THREATS.
I *STARTED* WITH THREATS.
I MUST BE MORE INTIMIDATING THAN YOU.
LIKE HELL.
DO YOU NOT EAT? THERE'S NOTHING IN HERE. MAKE ME A LIST AND I'LL RUN OUT--
CAROL... HAVE YOU SEEN THE PAPER?
OH. YEAH. THAT--
DAILY BUGLE
FINAL
NEW YORK'S FINEST DAILY NEWSPAPER
NO, NOT *THAT*--
New Captain Marvel! And He's a She!
Iconic Pilot Dies in Fire at Historic Aviation Club
at Historic Aviation Club
HELEN COBB, PILOT
POWDER PUFF DERBY WINNER, 1958.
FROM BUGLE FILE PHOTO.
THAT.

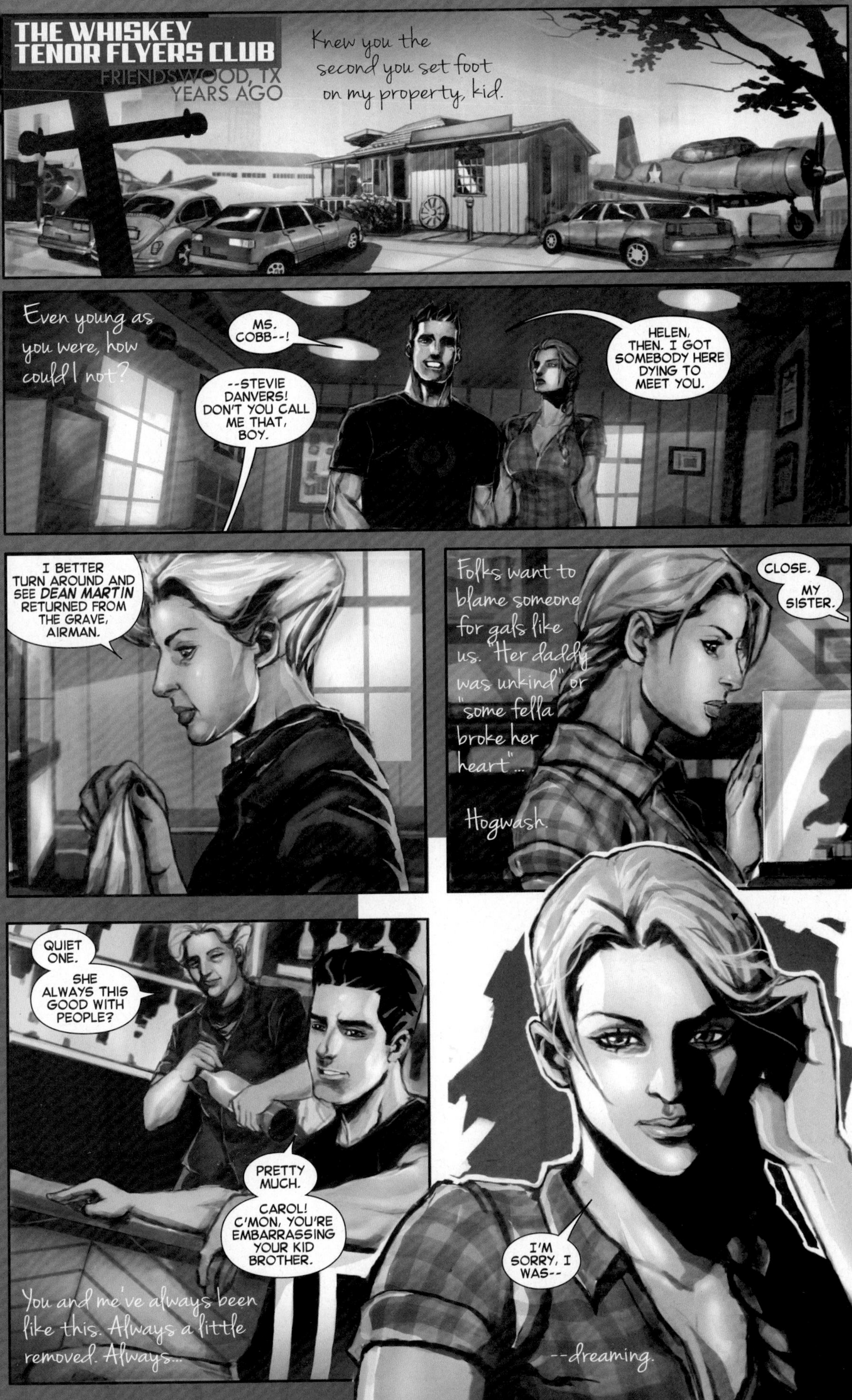

THE WHISKEY TENOR FLYERS CLUB
FRIENDSWOOD, TX
YEARS AGO
Knew you the second you set foot on my property, kid.
Even young as you were, how could I not?
MS. COBB--!
--STEVIE DANVERS! DON'T YOU CALL ME THAT, BOY.
HELEN, THEN. I GOT SOMEBODY HERE DYING TO MEET YOU.
I BETTER TURN AROUND AND SEE DEAN MARTIN RETURNED FROM THE GRAVE, AIRMAN.
Folks want to blame someone for gals like us. "Her daddy was unkind" or "some fella broke her heart"...
Hogwash.
CLOSE. MY SISTER.
QUIET ONE.
SHE ALWAYS THIS GOOD WITH PEOPLE?
PRETTY MUCH.
CAROL! C'MON, YOU'RE EMBARRASSING YOUR KID BROTHER.
You and me've always been like this. Always a little removed. Always...
I'M SORRY, I WAS--
--dreaming.

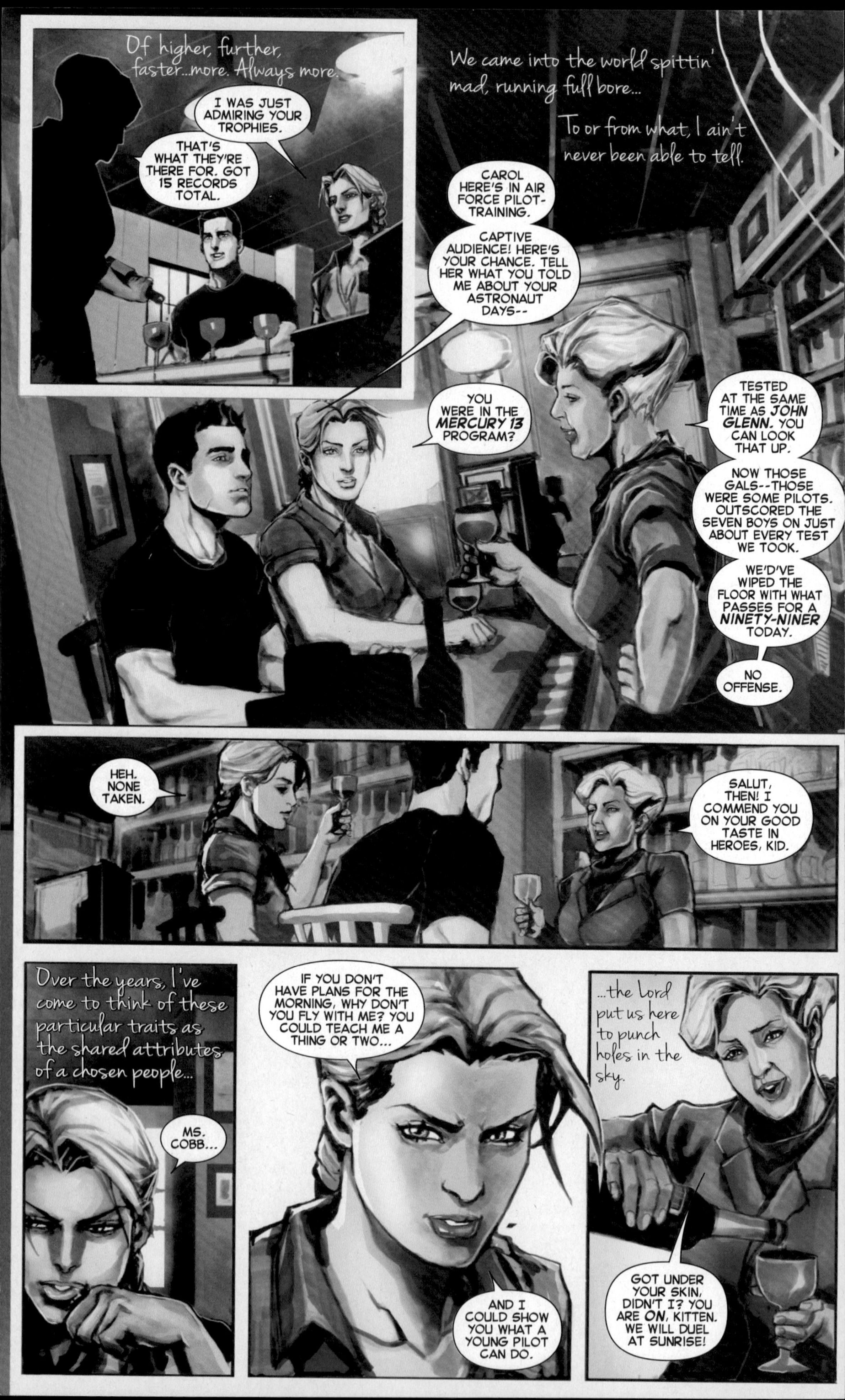
Of higher, further, faster...more. Always more.
I WAS JUST ADMIRING YOUR TROPHIES.
THAT'S WHAT THEY'RE THERE FOR. GOT 15 RECORDS TOTAL.
We came into the world spittin' mad, running full bore...
To or from what, I ain't never been able to tell.
CAROL HERE'S IN AIR FORCE PILOT-TRAINING.
CAPTIVE AUDIENCE! HERE'S YOUR CHANCE. TELL HER WHAT YOU TOLD ME ABOUT YOUR ASTRONAUT DAYS--
YOU WERE IN THE MERCURY 13 PROGRAM?
TESTED AT THE SAME TIME AS JOHN GLENN. YOU CAN LOOK THAT UP.
NOW THOSE GALS--THOSE WERE SOME PILOTS. OUTSCORED THE SEVEN BOYS ON JUST ABOUT EVERY TEST WE TOOK.
WE'D'VE WIPED THE FLOOR WITH WHAT PASSES FOR A NINETY-NINER TODAY.
NO OFFENSE.
HEH. NONE TAKEN.
SALUT, THEN! I COMMEND YOU ON YOUR GOOD TASTE IN HEROES, KID.
Over the years, I've come to think of these particular traits as the shared attributes of a chosen people...
MS. COBB...
IF YOU DON'T HAVE PLANS FOR THE MORNING, WHY DON'T YOU FLY WITH ME? YOU COULD TEACH ME A THING OR TWO...
AND I COULD SHOW YOU WHAT A YOUNG PILOT CAN DO.
...the Lord put us here to punch holes in the sky.
GOT UNDER YOUR SKIN, DIDN'T I? YOU ARE ON, KITTEN. WE WILL DUEL AT SUNRISE!

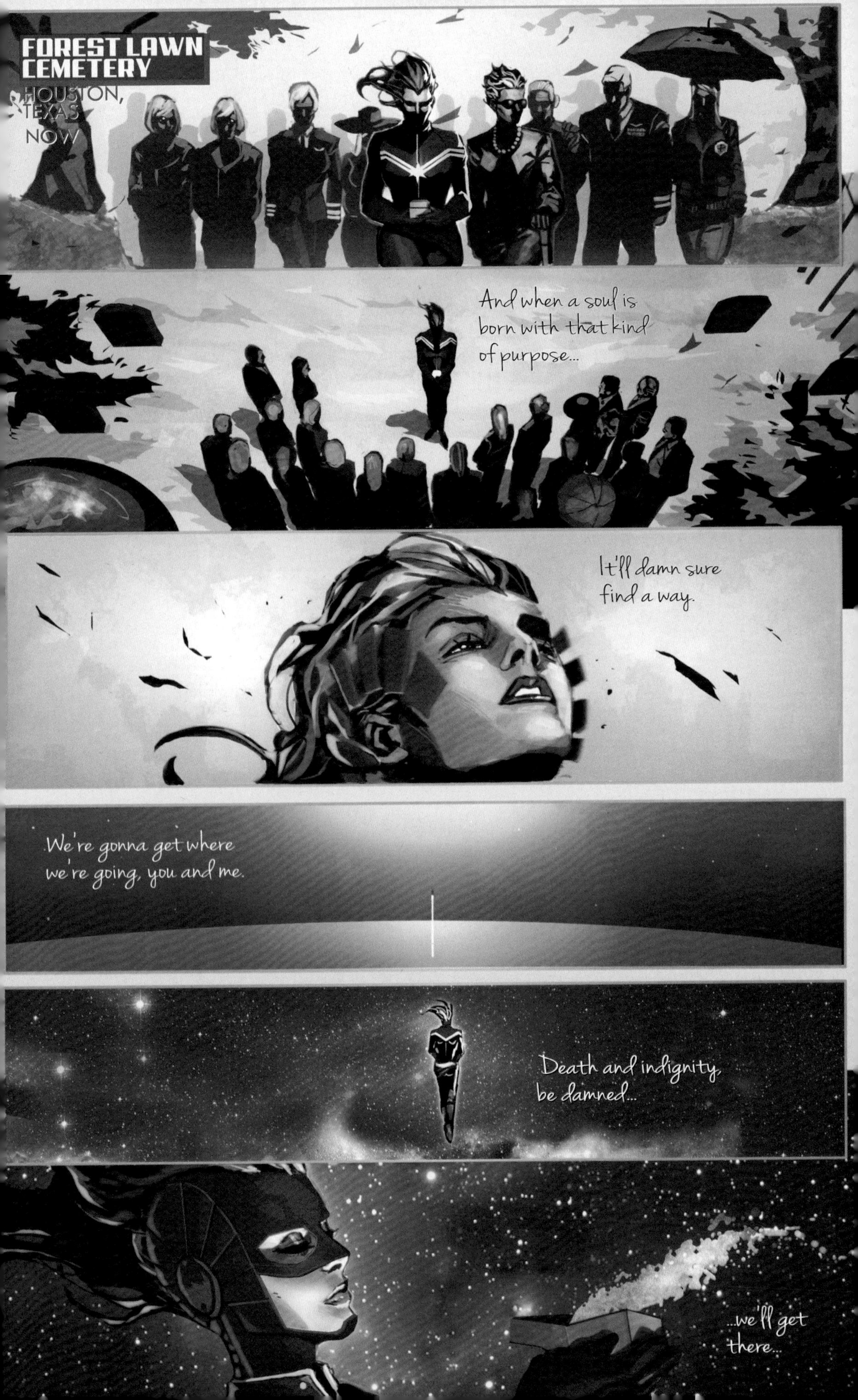
FOREST LAWN CEMETERY
HOUSTON, TEXAS
NOW
And when a soul is born with that kind of purpose...
It'll damn sure find a way.
We're gonna get where we're going, you and me.
Death and indignity, be damned...
...we'll get there...

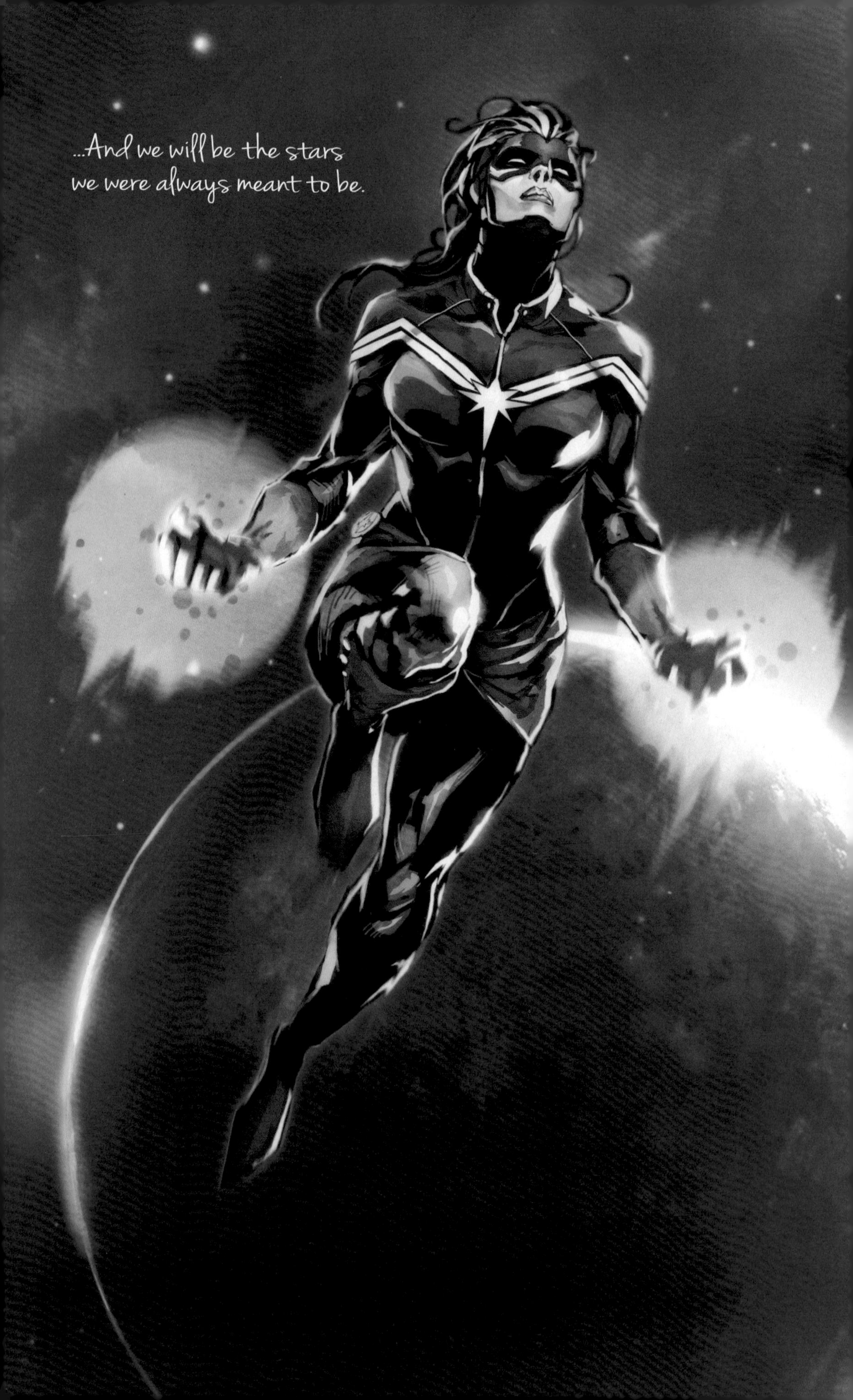
...And we will be the stars
we were always meant to be.

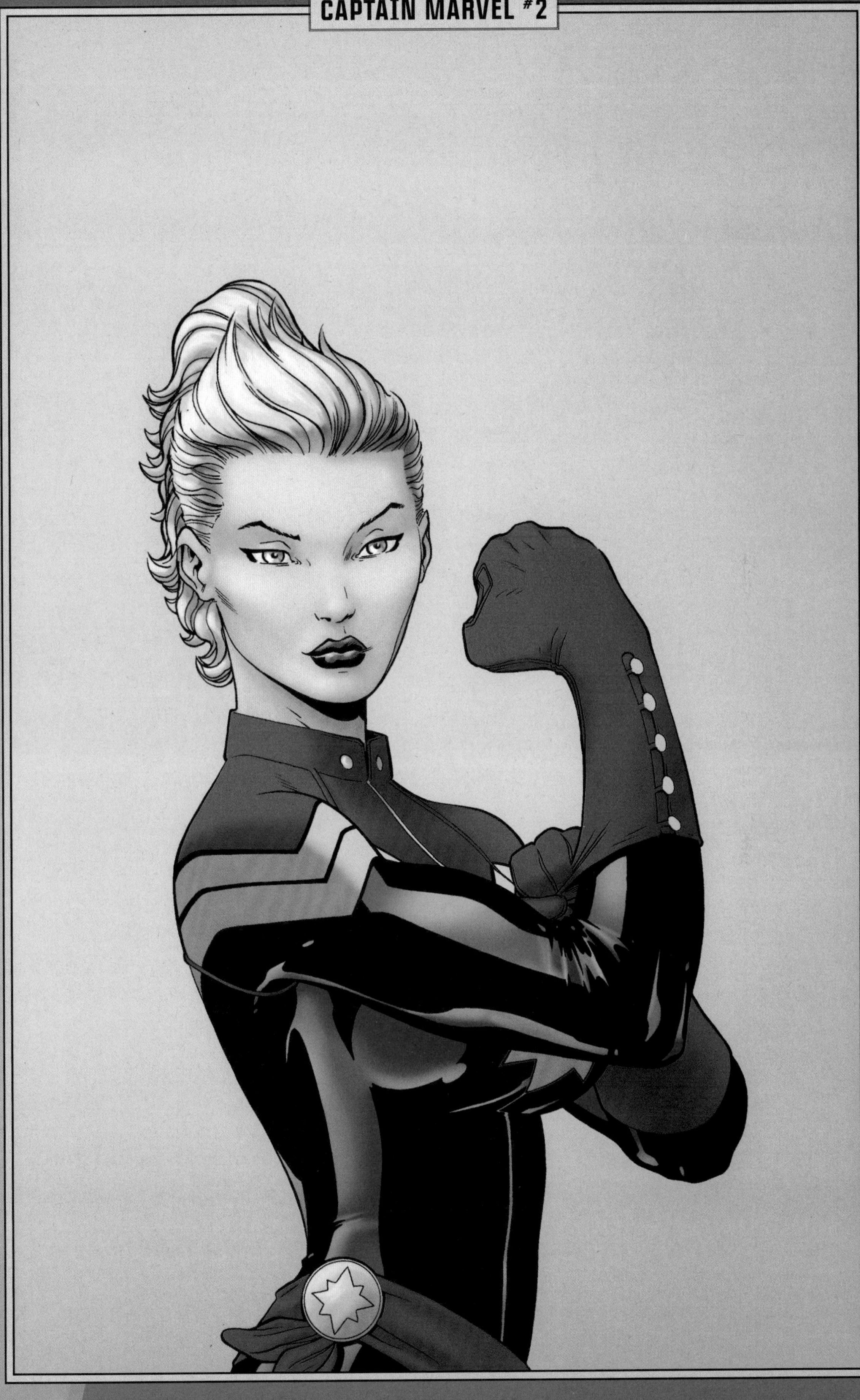

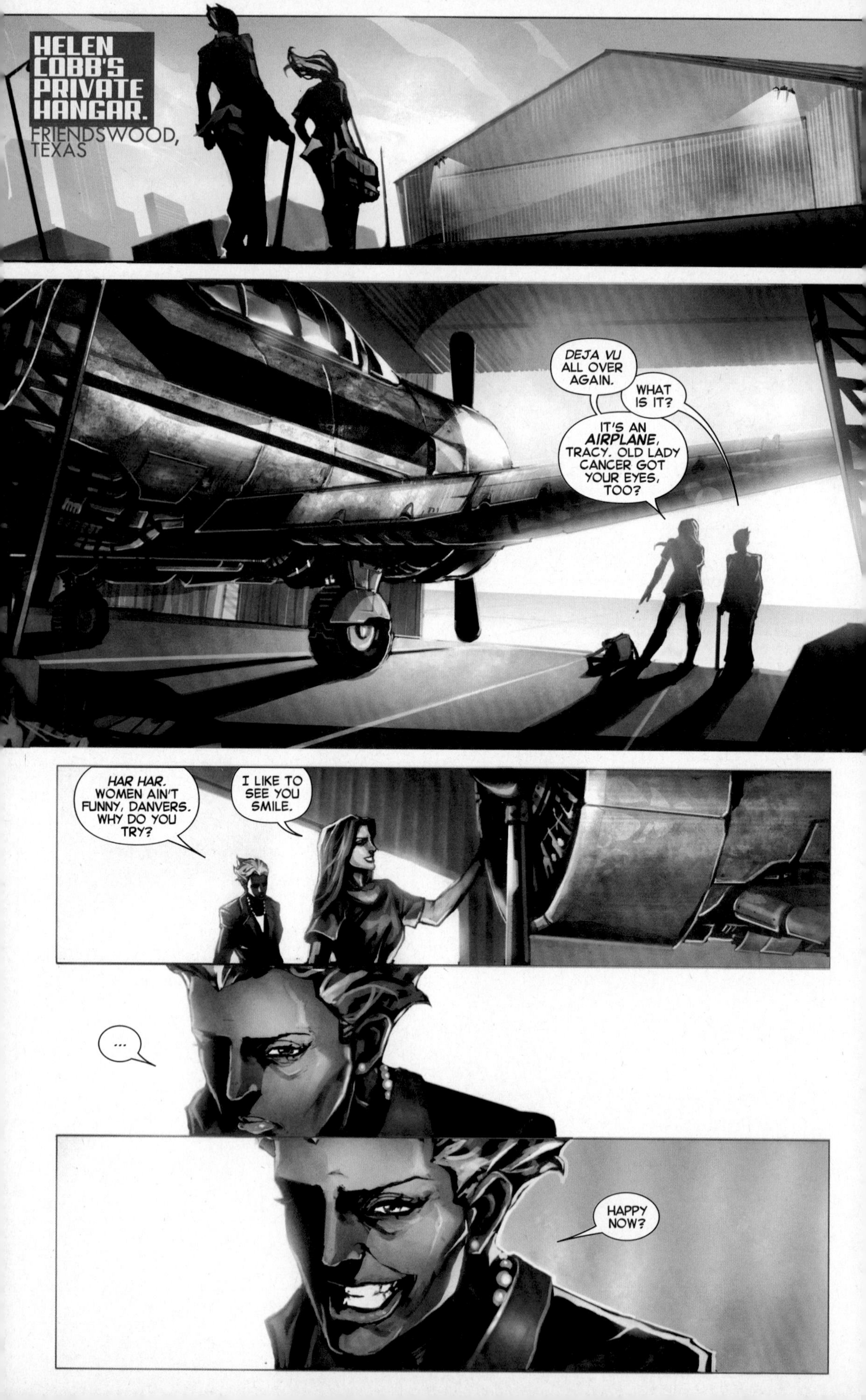
HELEN COBB'S PRIVATE HANGAR.
FRIENDSWOOD, TEXAS
DEJA VU ALL OVER AGAIN.
WHAT IS IT?
IT'S AN AIRPLANE, TRACY. OLD LADY CANCER GOT YOUR EYES, TOO?
HAR HAR. WOMEN AIN'T FUNNY, DANVERS. WHY DO YOU TRY?
I LIKE TO SEE YOU SMILE.
...
HAPPY NOW?

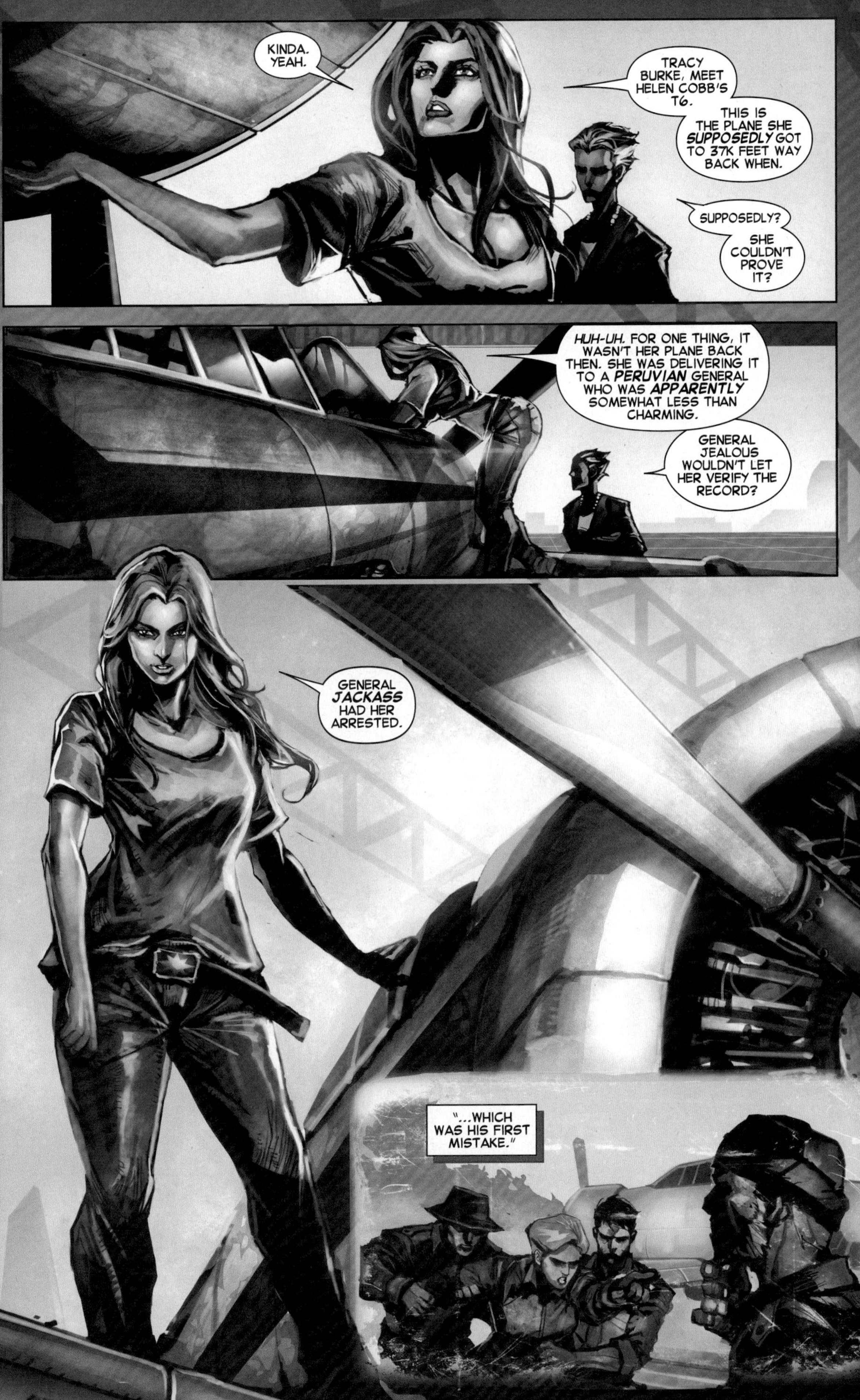
KINDA. YEAH.
TRACY BURKE, MEET HELEN COBB'S T6.
THIS IS THE PLANE SHE *SUPPOSEDLY* GOT TO 37K FEET WAY BACK WHEN.
SUPPOSEDLY?
SHE COULDN'T PROVE IT?
HUH-UH. FOR ONE THING, IT WASN'T HER PLANE BACK THEN. SHE WAS DELIVERING IT TO A *PERUVIAN* GENERAL WHO WAS *APPARENTLY* SOMEWHAT LESS THAN CHARMING.
GENERAL JEALOUS WOULDN'T LET HER VERIFY THE RECORD?
GENERAL *JACKASS* HAD HER ARRESTED.
"...WHICH WAS HIS FIRST MISTAKE."

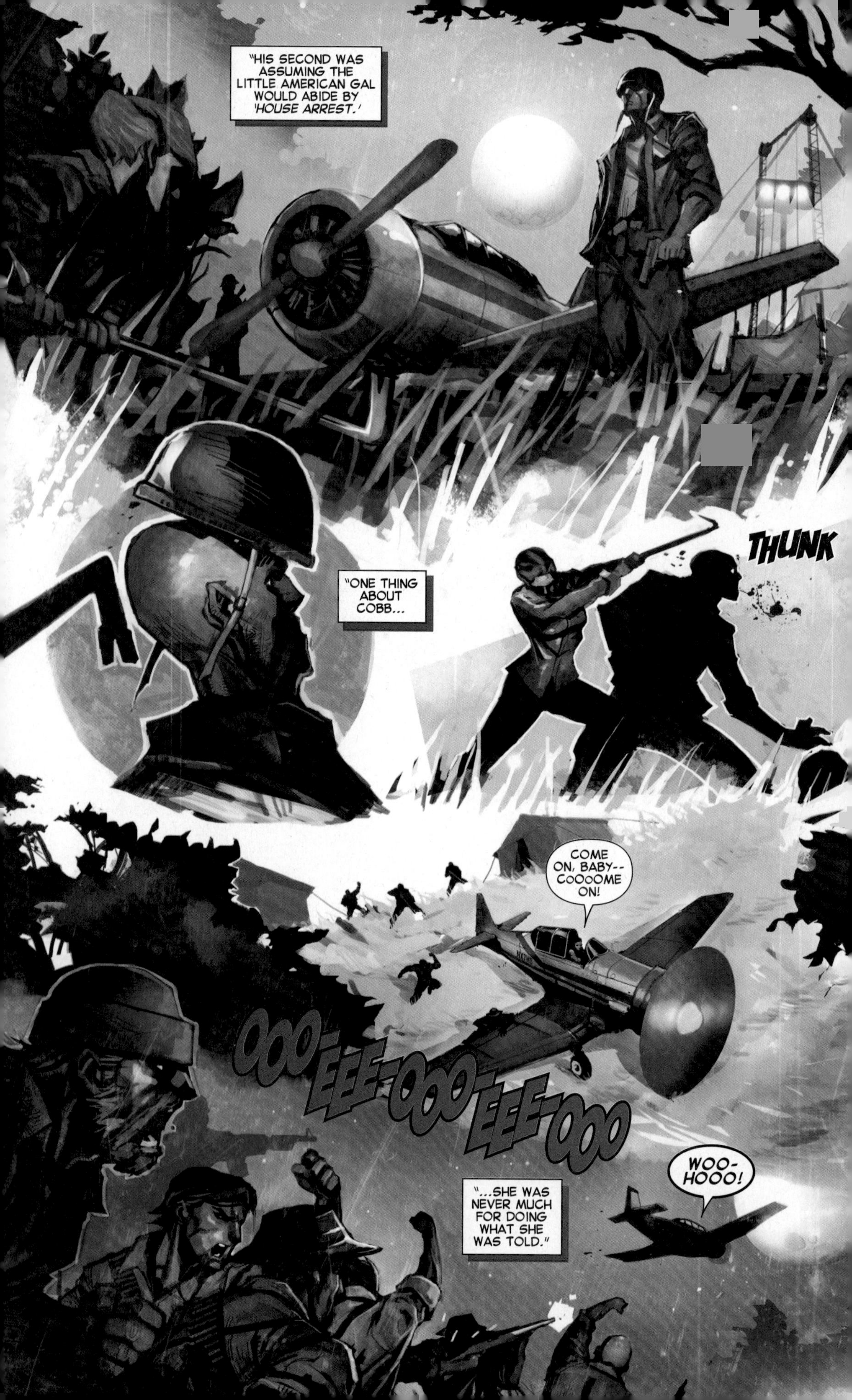
"HIS SECOND WAS ASSUMING THE LITTLE AMERICAN GAL WOULD ABIDE BY *'HOUSE ARREST.'*
"ONE THING ABOUT COBB...
THUNK
COME ON, BABY-- COOOOME ON!
OOO-EEE-OOO-EEE-OOO
WOO-HOOO!
"...SHE WAS NEVER MUCH FOR DOING WHAT SHE WAS TOLD."

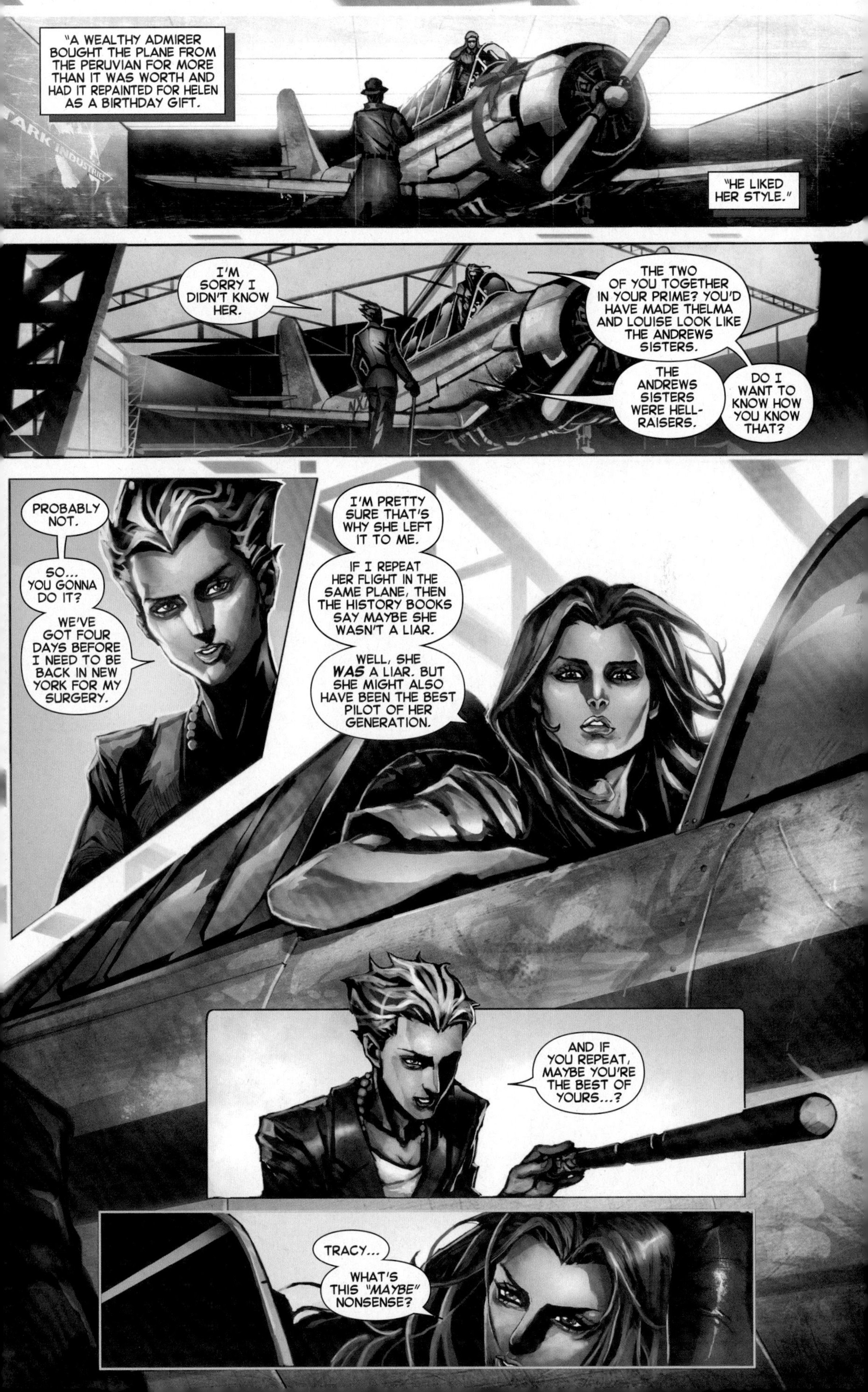
"A WEALTHY ADMIRER BOUGHT THE PLANE FROM THE PERUVIAN FOR MORE THAN IT WAS WORTH AND HAD IT REPAINTED FOR HELEN AS A BIRTHDAY GIFT.
"HE LIKED HER STYLE."
I'M SORRY I DIDN'T KNOW HER.
THE TWO OF YOU TOGETHER IN YOUR PRIME? YOU'D HAVE MADE THELMA AND LOUISE LOOK LIKE THE ANDREWS SISTERS.
THE ANDREWS SISTERS WERE HELL-RAISERS.
DO I WANT TO KNOW HOW YOU KNOW THAT?
PROBABLY NOT.
SO... YOU GONNA DO IT?
WE'VE GOT FOUR DAYS BEFORE I NEED TO BE BACK IN NEW YORK FOR MY SURGERY.
I'M PRETTY SURE THAT'S WHY SHE LEFT IT TO ME.
IF I REPEAT HER FLIGHT IN THE SAME PLANE, THEN THE HISTORY BOOKS SAY MAYBE SHE WASN'T A LIAR.
WELL, SHE *WAS* A LIAR. BUT SHE MIGHT ALSO HAVE BEEN THE BEST PILOT OF HER GENERATION.
AND IF YOU REPEAT, MAYBE YOU'RE THE BEST OF YOURS...?
TRACY...
WHAT'S THIS "*MAYBE*" NONSENSE?

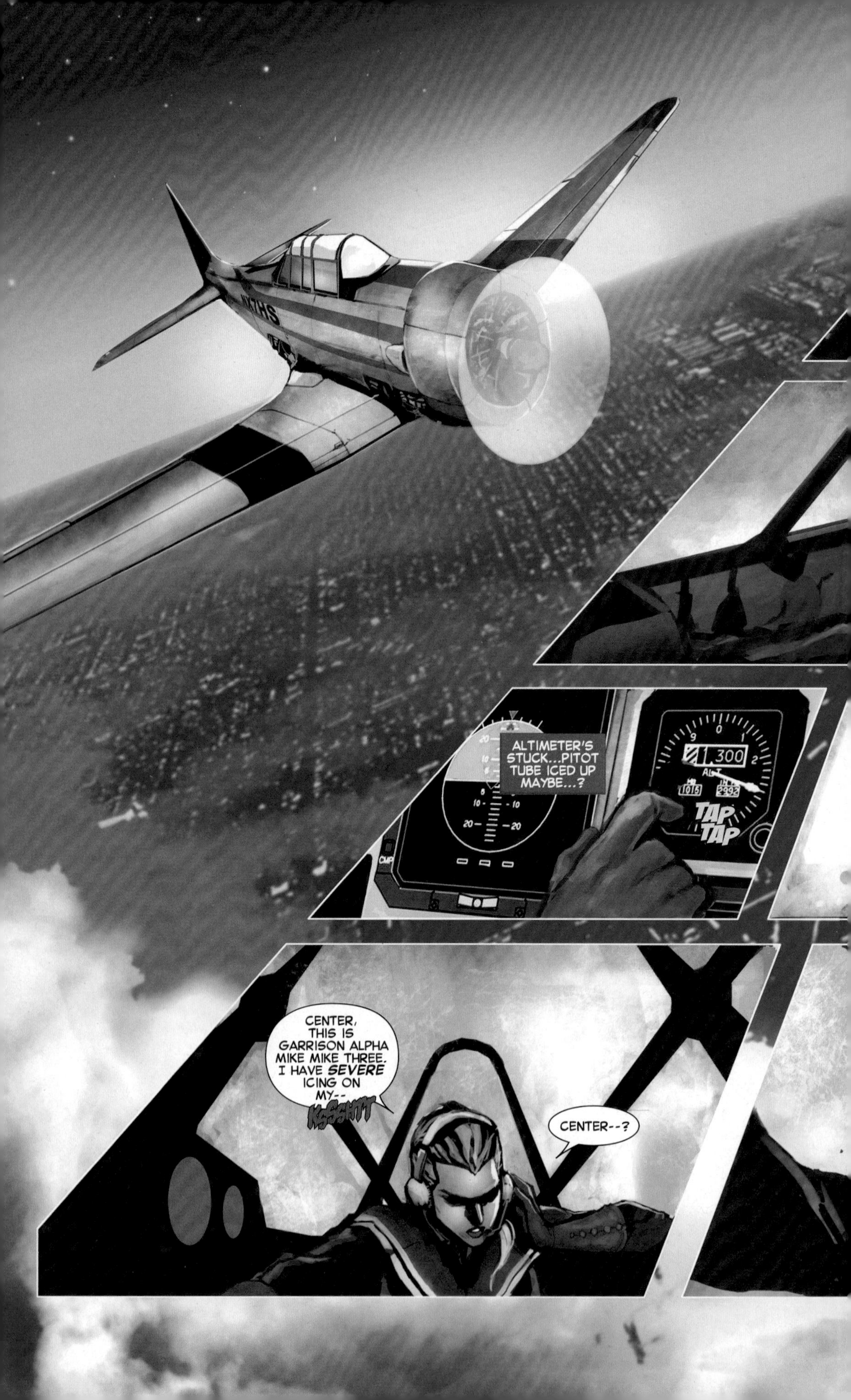
NX7HS
ALTIMETER'S STUCK...PITOT TUBE ICED UP MAYBE...?
TAP TAP
CENTER, THIS IS GARRISON ALPHA MIKE MIKE THREE. I HAVE *SEVERE* ICING ON MY--
KSSHHT
CENTER--?

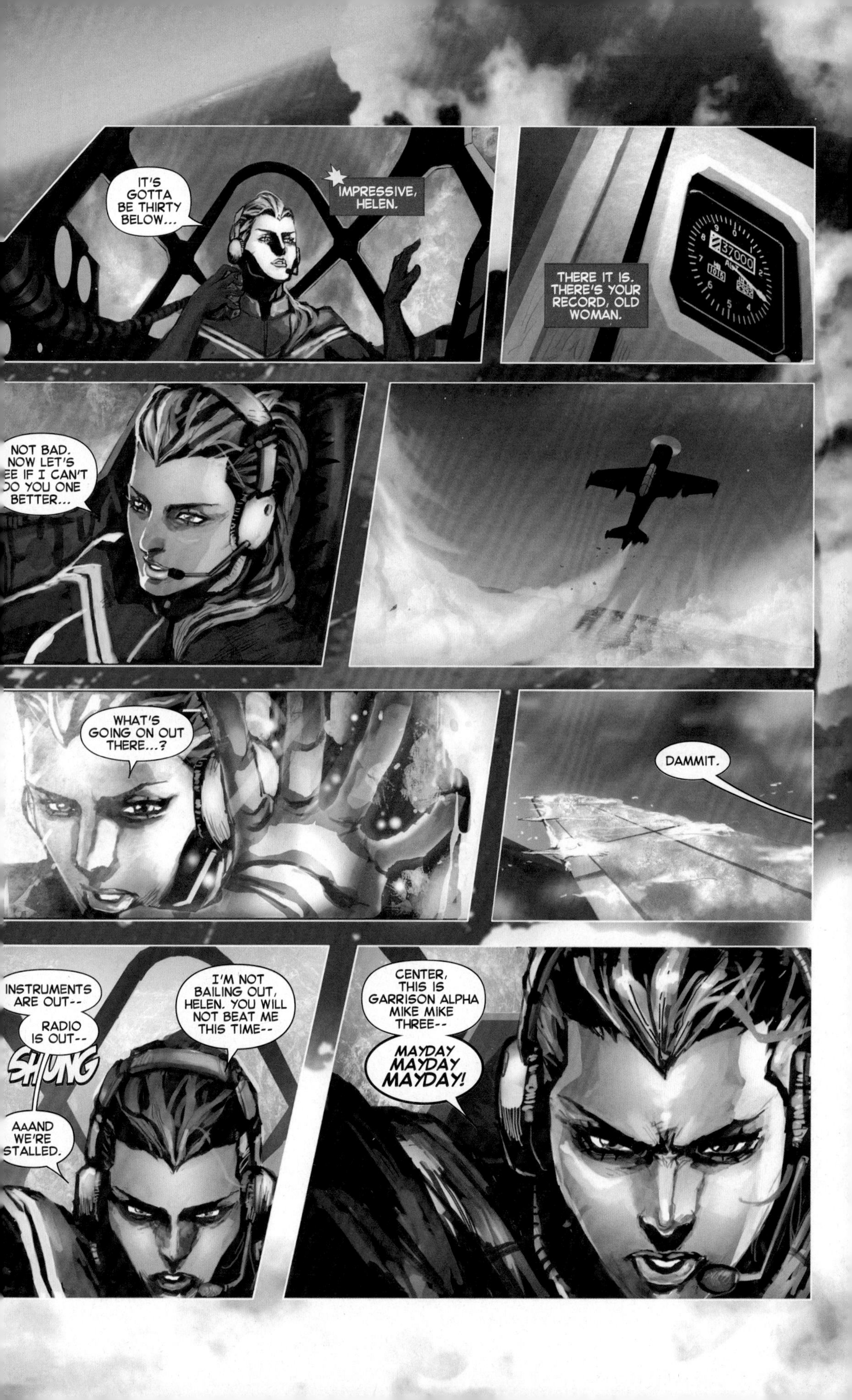
IT'S GOTTA BE THIRTY BELOW...
IMPRESSIVE, HELEN.
THERE IT IS. THERE'S YOUR RECORD, OLD WOMAN.
NOT BAD. NOW LET'S SEE IF I CAN'T DO YOU ONE BETTER...
WHAT'S GOING ON OUT THERE...?
DAMMIT.
INSTRUMENTS ARE OUT--
RADIO IS OUT--
SHUNG
AAAND WE'RE STALLED.
I'M NOT BAILING OUT, HELEN. YOU WILL NOT BEAT ME THIS TIME--
CENTER, THIS IS GARRISON ALPHA MIKE MIKE THREE--
MAYDAY MAYDAY MAYDAY!

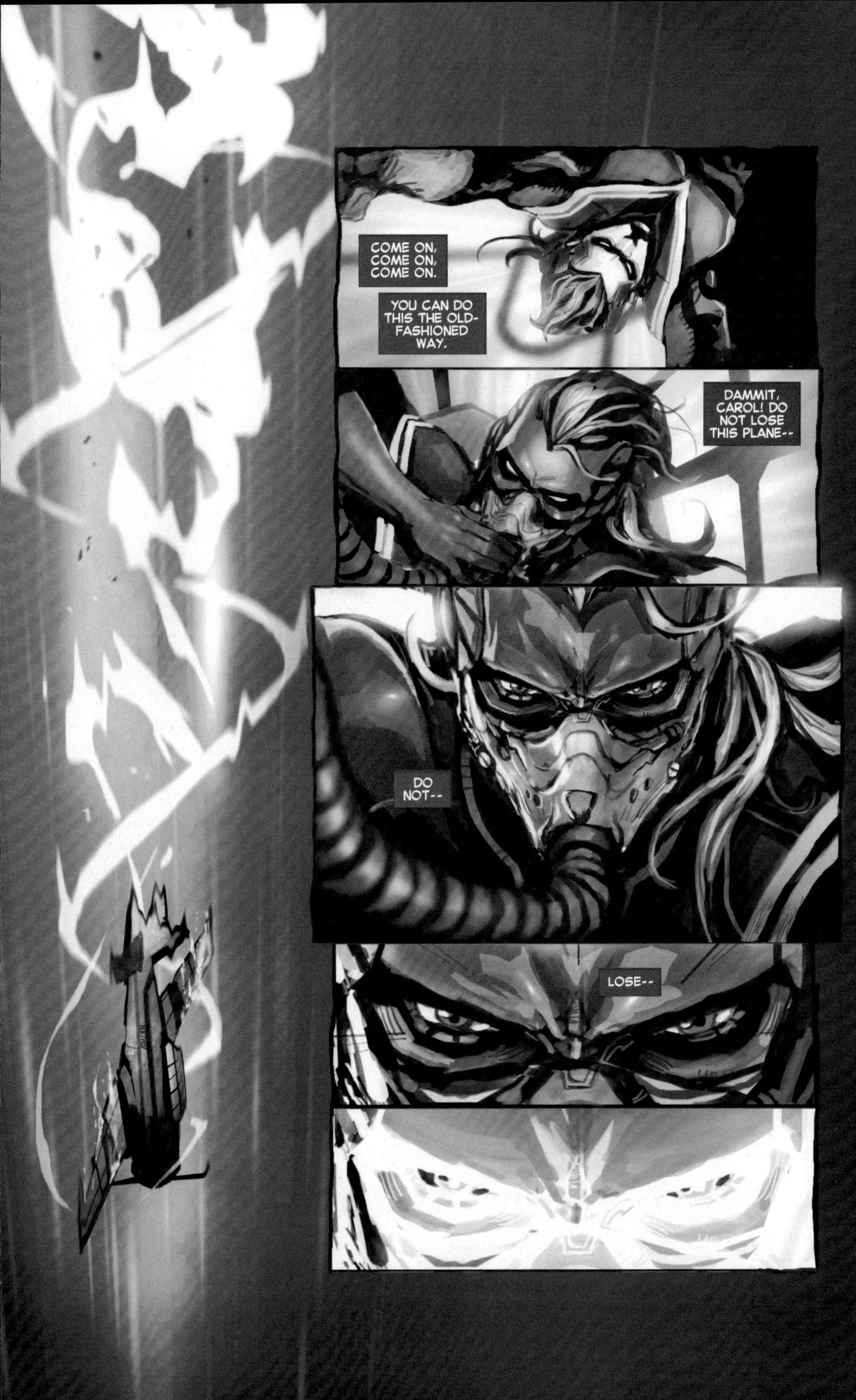
COME ON, COME ON, COME ON.
YOU CAN DO THIS THE OLD-FASHIONED WAY.
DAMMIT, CAROL! DO NOT LOSE THIS PLANE--
DO NOT--
LOSE--

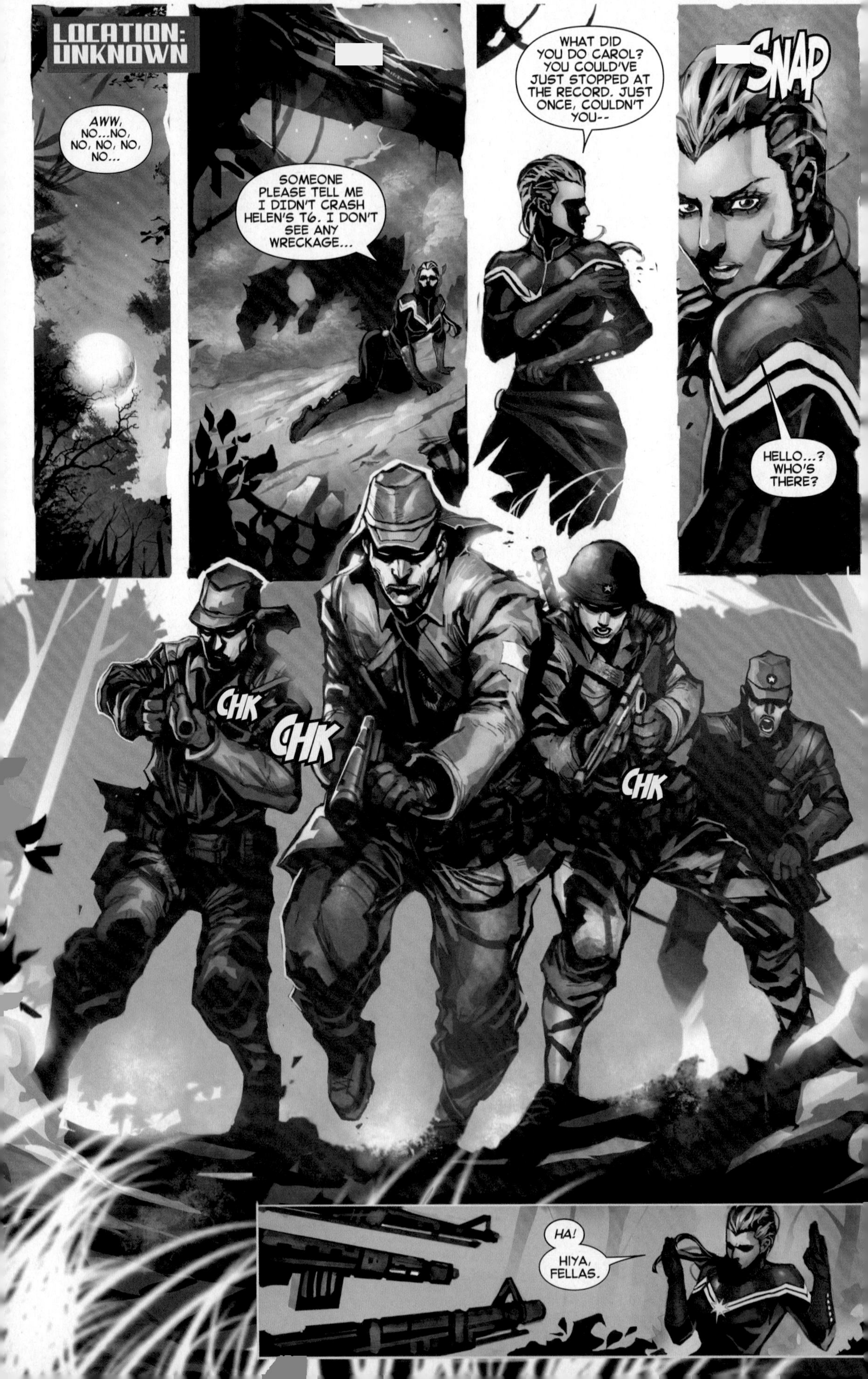
LOCATION: UNKNOWN
AWW, NO...NO, NO, NO, NO, NO...
SOMEONE PLEASE TELL ME I DIDN'T CRASH HELEN'S T6. I DON'T SEE ANY WRECKAGE...
WHAT DID YOU DO CAROL? YOU COULD'VE JUST STOPPED AT THE RECORD. JUST ONCE, COULDN'T YOU--
SNAP
HELLO...? WHO'S THERE?
CHK
CHK
CHK
HA!
HIYA, FELLAS.

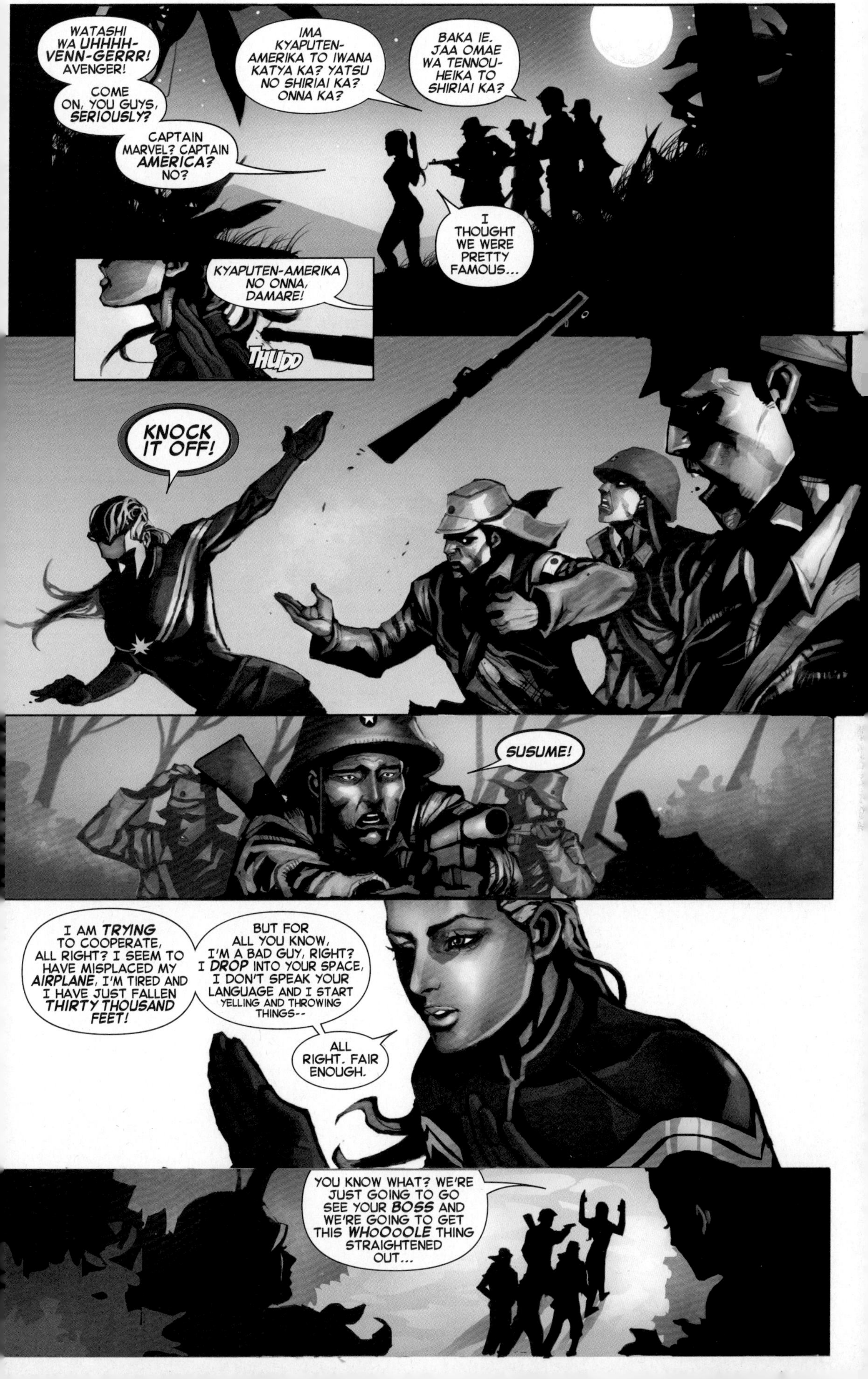
WATASHI WA UHHHH-VENN-GERRR! AVENGER!
COME ON, YOU GUYS, SERIOUSLY?
CAPTAIN MARVEL? CAPTAIN AMERICA? NO?
IMA KYAPUTEN-AMERIKA TO IWANA KATYA KA? YATSU NO SHIRIAI KA? ONNA KA?
BAKA IE. JAA OMAE WA TENNOU-HEIKA TO SHIRIAI KA?
I THOUGHT WE WERE PRETTY FAMOUS...
KYAPUTEN-AMERIKA NO ONNA, DAMARE!
THUDD
KNOCK IT OFF!
SUSUME!
I AM TRYING TO COOPERATE, ALL RIGHT? I SEEM TO HAVE MISPLACED MY AIRPLANE, I'M TIRED AND I HAVE JUST FALLEN THIRTY THOUSAND FEET!
BUT FOR ALL YOU KNOW, I'M A BAD GUY, RIGHT? I DROP INTO YOUR SPACE, I DON'T SPEAK YOUR LANGUAGE AND I START YELLING AND THROWING THINGS--
ALL RIGHT. FAIR ENOUGH.
YOU KNOW WHAT? WE'RE JUST GOING TO GO SEE YOUR BOSS AND WE'RE GOING TO GET THIS WHOOOOLE THING STRAIGHTENED OUT...

WHAT IS THIS...?

IS THIS-- IS THIS ONE OF THOSE ISLANDS THAT THINKS IT'S STILL WORLD WAR II?

BECAUSE I HAVE SOME GOOD NEWS AND SOME BAD NEWS FOR YOU GUYS--

EXCUSE ME, I'M SORRY, I FEEL REALLY BAD ASKING THIS--

BUT IS THERE ANYONE HE WHO SPEAK ENGLISH?

KYAPUTEN-
AMERIKA NO
ONNA! KISAMA WA
HORYO DE ARU!
YOTTE--

TKK

GURENE-DO?!

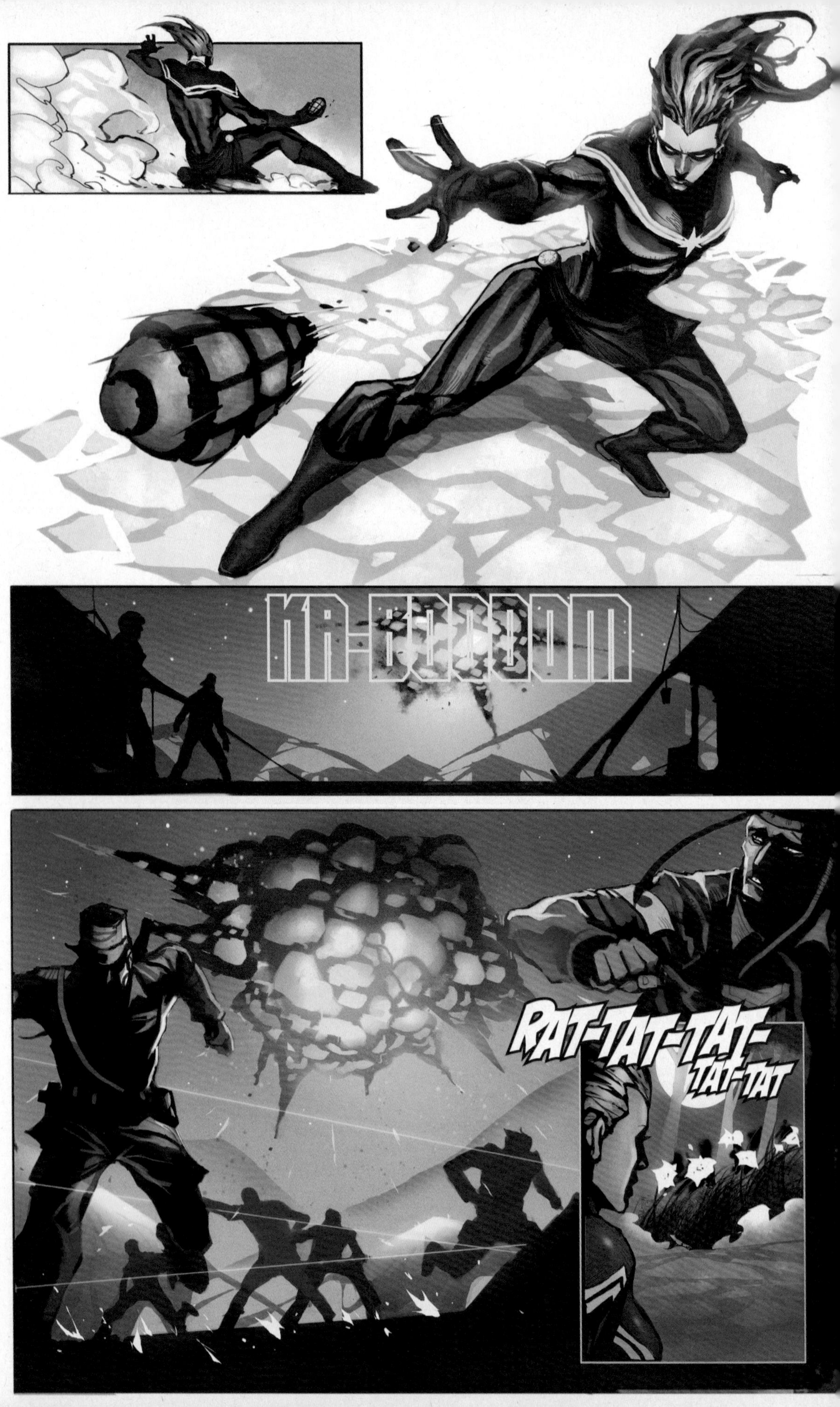
KA-BOOOOM
RAT-TAT-TAT-TAT-TAT

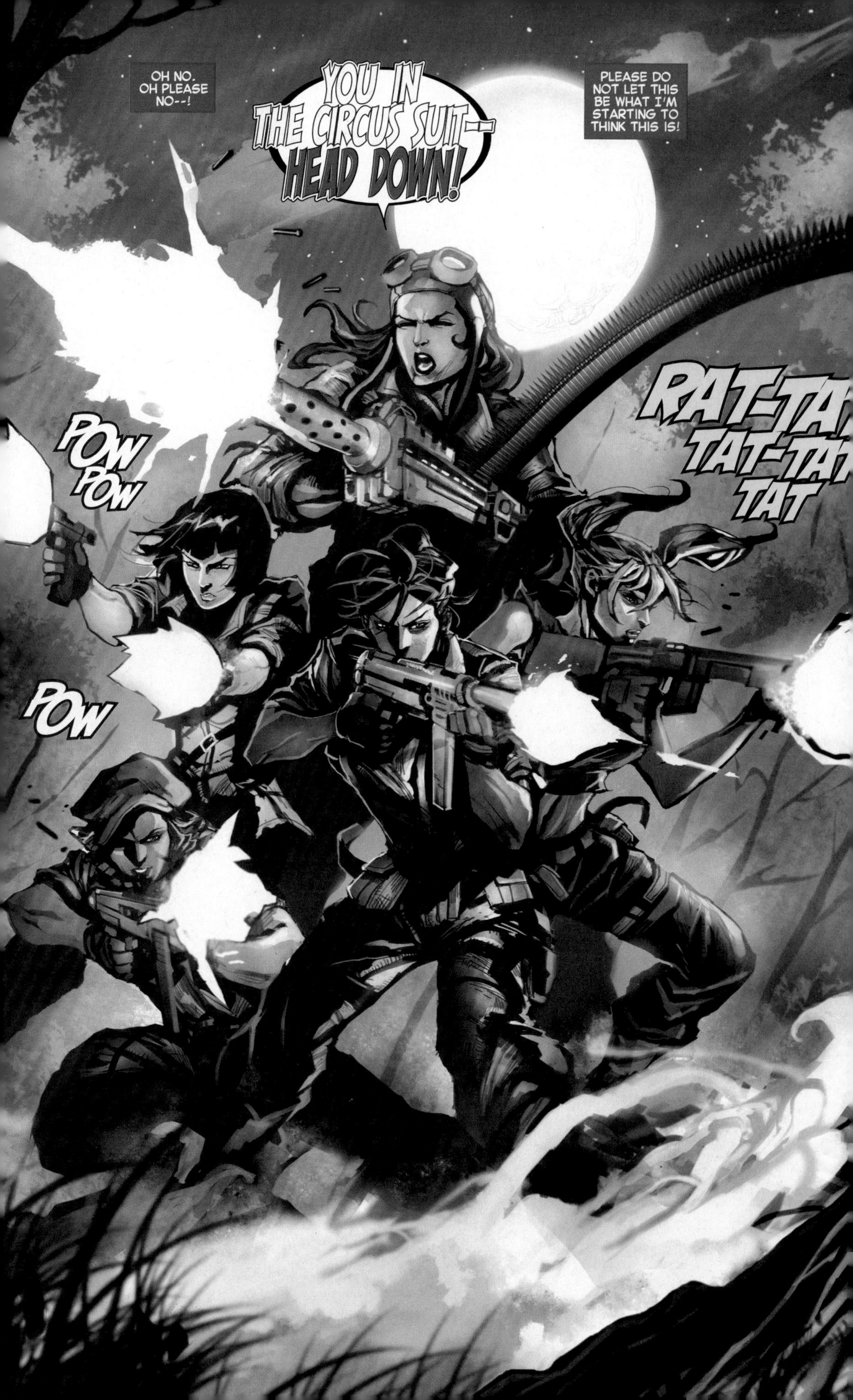
OH NO. OH PLEASE NO--!
YOU IN THE CIRCUS SUIT--HEAD DOWN!
PLEASE DO NOT LET THIS BE WHAT I'M STARTING TO THINK THIS IS!
POW POW
POW
RAT-TAT TAT-TAT TAT

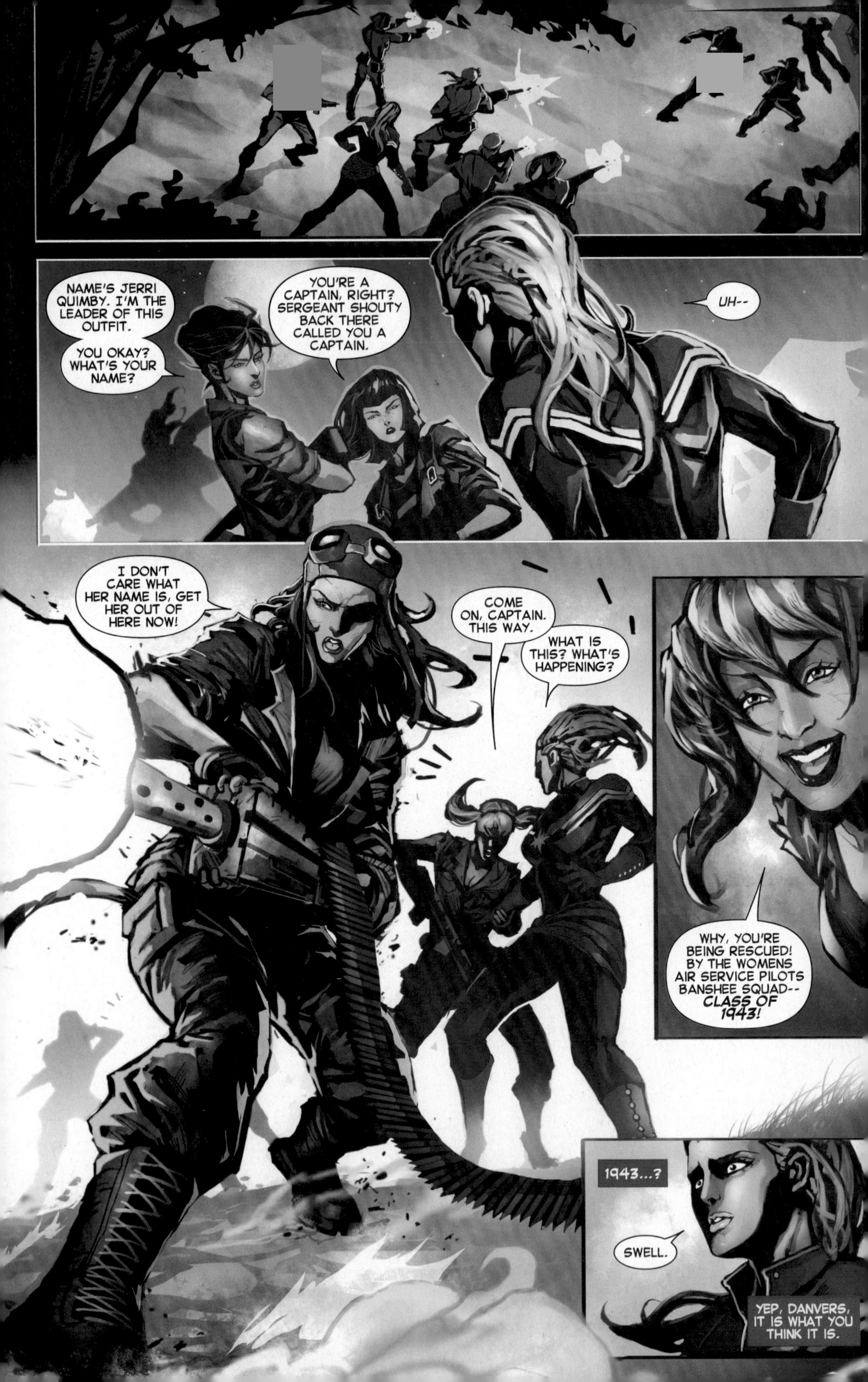

NAME'S JERRI QUIMBY. I'M THE LEADER OF THIS OUTFIT.
YOU OKAY? WHAT'S YOUR NAME?
YOU'RE A CAPTAIN, RIGHT? SERGEANT SHOUTY BACK THERE CALLED YOU A CAPTAIN.
UH--
I DON'T CARE WHAT HER NAME IS, GET HER OUT OF HERE NOW!
COME ON, CAPTAIN. THIS WAY.
WHAT IS THIS? WHAT'S HAPPENING?
WHY, YOU'RE BEING RESCUED! BY THE WOMENS AIR SERVICE PILOTS BANSHEE SQUAD-- CLASS OF 1943!
1943...?
SWELL.
YEP, DANVERS, IT IS WHAT YOU THINK IT IS.

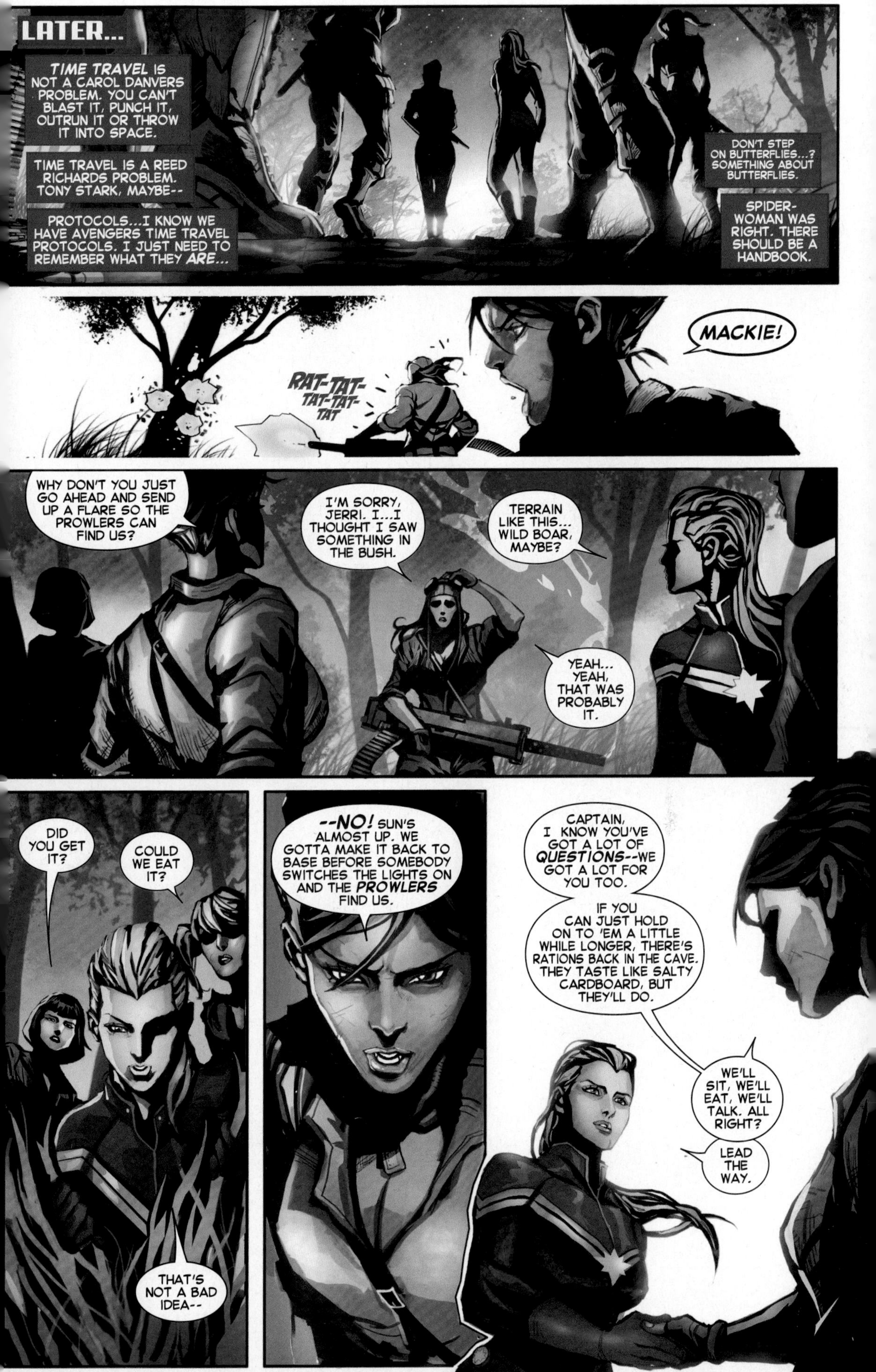

LATER...
TIME TRAVEL IS NOT A CAROL DANVERS PROBLEM. YOU CAN'T BLAST IT, PUNCH IT, OUTRUN IT OR THROW IT INTO SPACE.
TIME TRAVEL IS A REED RICHARDS PROBLEM. TONY STARK, MAYBE--
PROTOCOLS...I KNOW WE HAVE AVENGERS TIME TRAVEL PROTOCOLS. I JUST NEED TO REMEMBER WHAT THEY ARE...
DON'T STEP ON BUTTERFLIES...? SOMETHING ABOUT BUTTERFLIES.
SPIDER-WOMAN WAS RIGHT. THERE SHOULD BE A HANDBOOK.
RAT-TAT-TAT-TAT-TAT
MACKIE!
WHY DON'T YOU JUST GO AHEAD AND SEND UP A FLARE SO THE PROWLERS CAN FIND US?
I'M SORRY, JERRI. I...I THOUGHT I SAW SOMETHING IN THE BUSH.
TERRAIN LIKE THIS... WILD BOAR, MAYBE?
YEAH... YEAH, THAT WAS PROBABLY IT.
DID YOU GET IT?
COULD WE EAT IT?
THAT'S NOT A BAD IDEA--
--NO! SUN'S ALMOST UP. WE GOTTA MAKE IT BACK TO BASE BEFORE SOMEBODY SWITCHES THE LIGHTS ON AND THE PROWLERS FIND US.
CAPTAIN, I KNOW YOU'VE GOT A LOT OF QUESTIONS--WE GOT A LOT FOR YOU TOO.
IF YOU CAN JUST HOLD ON TO 'EM A LITTLE WHILE LONGER, THERE'S RATIONS BACK IN THE CAVE. THEY TASTE LIKE SALTY CARDBOARD, BUT THEY'LL DO.
WE'LL SIT, WE'LL EAT, WE'LL TALK. ALL RIGHT?
LEAD THE WAY.

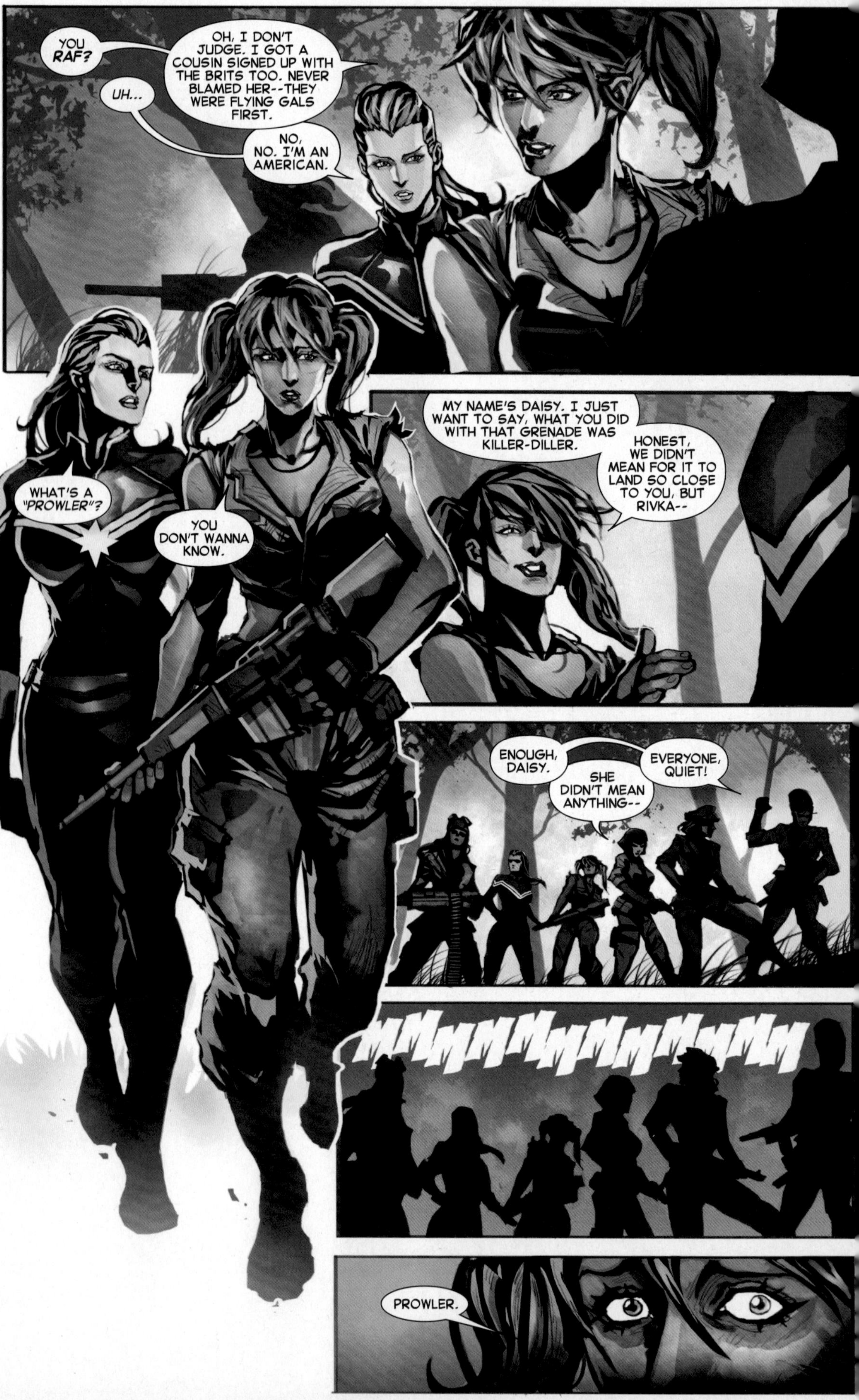
YOU RAF?
OH, I DON'T JUDGE. I GOT A COUSIN SIGNED UP WITH THE BRITS TOO. NEVER BLAMED HER--THEY WERE FLYING GALS FIRST.
UH...
NO, NO. I'M AN AMERICAN.
WHAT'S A "PROWLER"?
YOU DON'T WANNA KNOW.
MY NAME'S DAISY. I JUST WANT TO SAY, WHAT YOU DID WITH THAT GRENADE WAS KILLER-DILLER.
HONEST, WE DIDN'T MEAN FOR IT TO LAND SO CLOSE TO YOU, BUT RIVKA--
ENOUGH, DAISY.
SHE DIDN'T MEAN ANYTHING--
EVERYONE, QUIET!
MMMMMMMMMMMMMMMM
PROWLER.

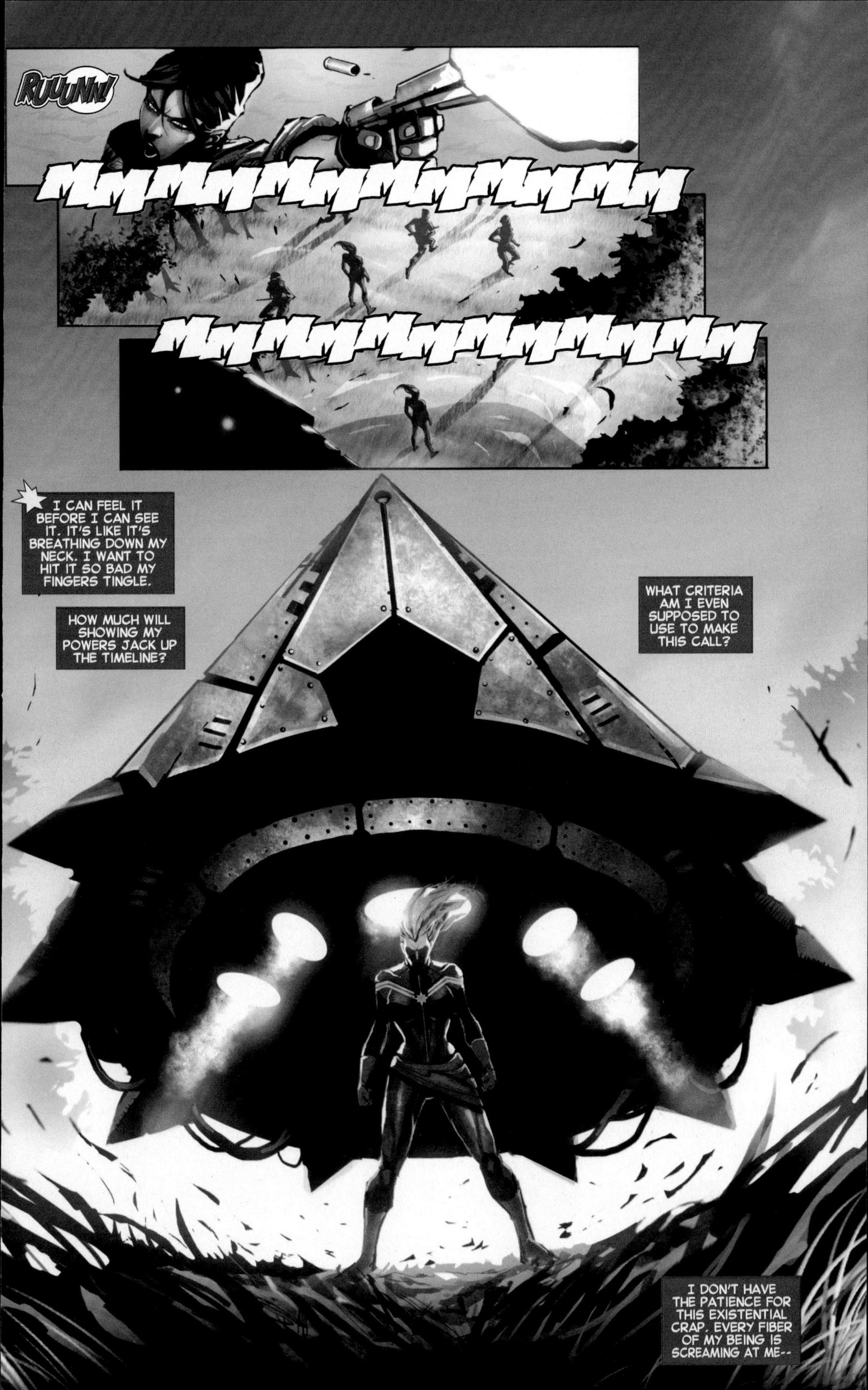
RUUUNN!
MMMMMMMMMMMMMMMMMMMM
MMMMMMMMMMMMMMMMMMMMMM
I CAN FEEL IT BEFORE I CAN SEE IT. IT'S LIKE IT'S BREATHING DOWN MY NECK. I WANT TO HIT IT SO BAD MY FINGERS TINGLE.
HOW MUCH WILL SHOWING MY POWERS JACK UP THE TIMELINE?
WHAT CRITERIA AM I EVEN SUPPOSED TO USE TO MAKE THIS CALL?
I DON'T HAVE THE PATIENCE FOR THIS EXISTENTIAL CRAP. EVERY FIBER OF MY BEING IS SCREAMING AT ME--

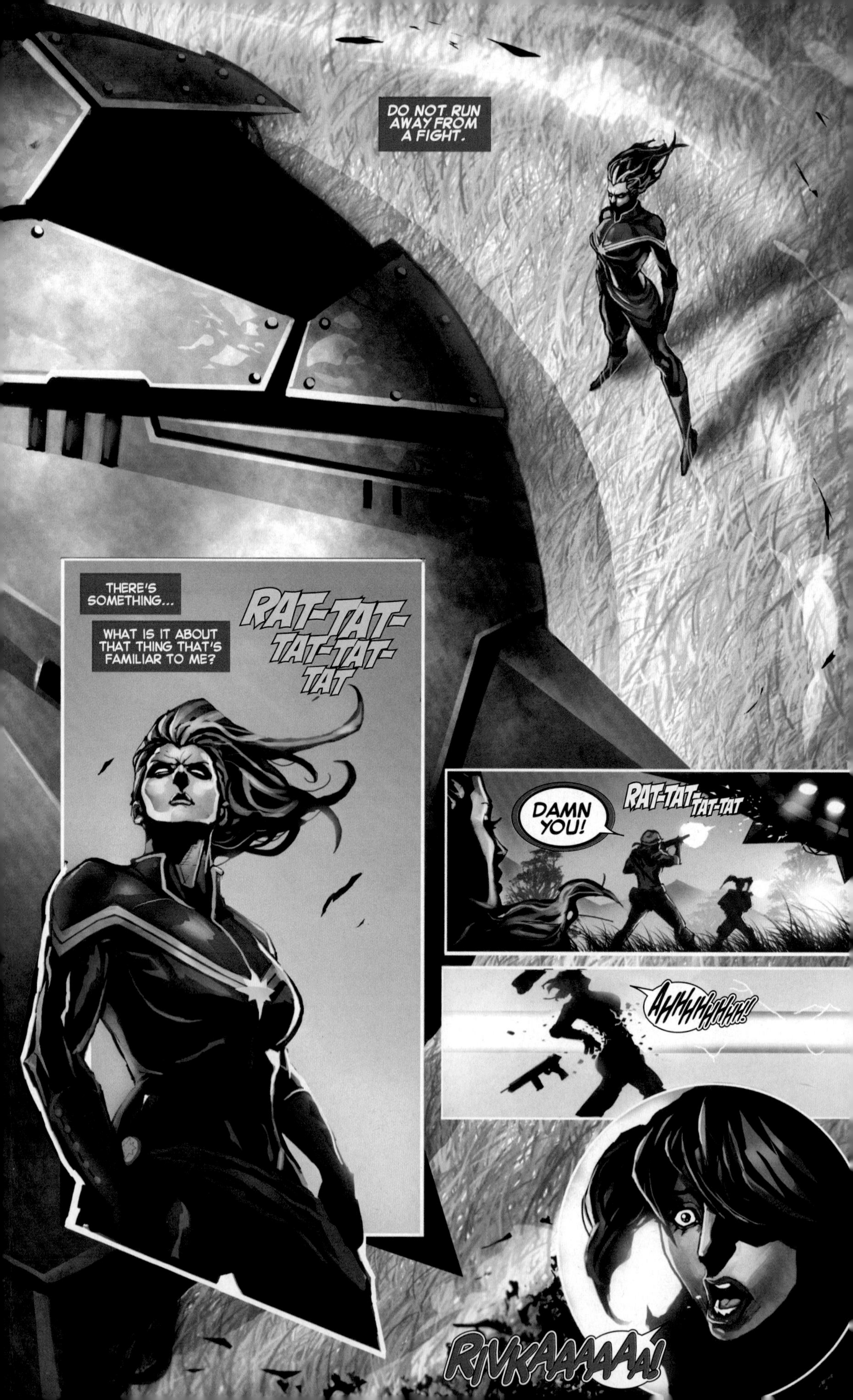
DO NOT RUN AWAY FROM A FIGHT.
THERE'S SOMETHING...
WHAT IS IT ABOUT THAT THING THAT'S FAMILIAR TO ME?
RAT-TAT-TAT-TAT-TAT
DAMN YOU!
RAT-TAT-TAT-TAT
AHHHHHHHH!
RIVKAAAAAA!

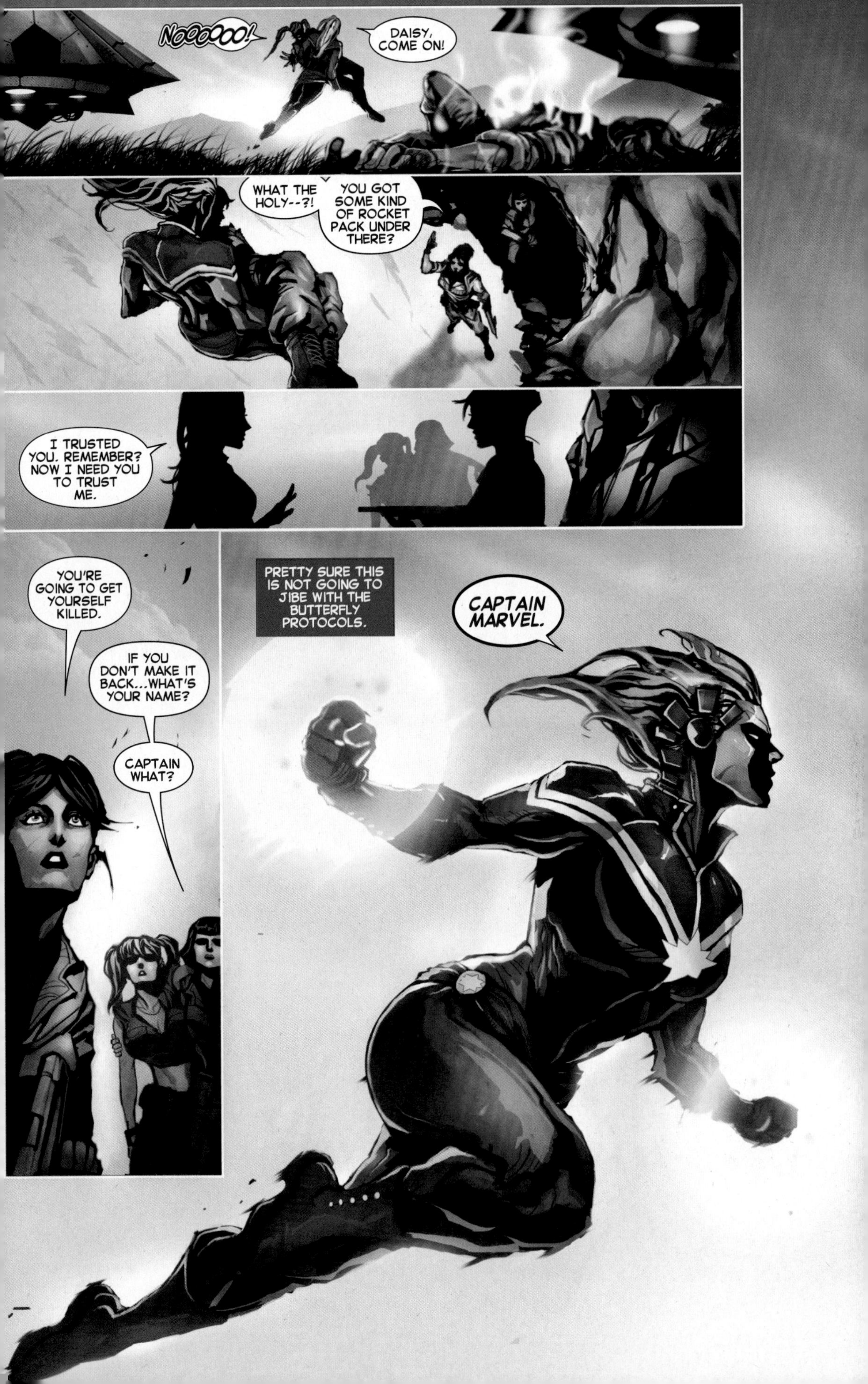
NOOOOOO!
DAISY, COME ON!
WHAT THE HOLY--?!
YOU GOT SOME KIND OF ROCKET PACK UNDER THERE?
I TRUSTED YOU. REMEMBER? NOW I NEED YOU TO TRUST ME.
YOU'RE GOING TO GET YOURSELF KILLED.
IF YOU DON'T MAKE IT BACK...WHAT'S YOUR NAME?
CAPTAIN WHAT?
PRETTY SURE THIS IS NOT GOING TO JIBE WITH THE BUTTERFLY PROTOCOLS.
CAPTAIN MARVEL.

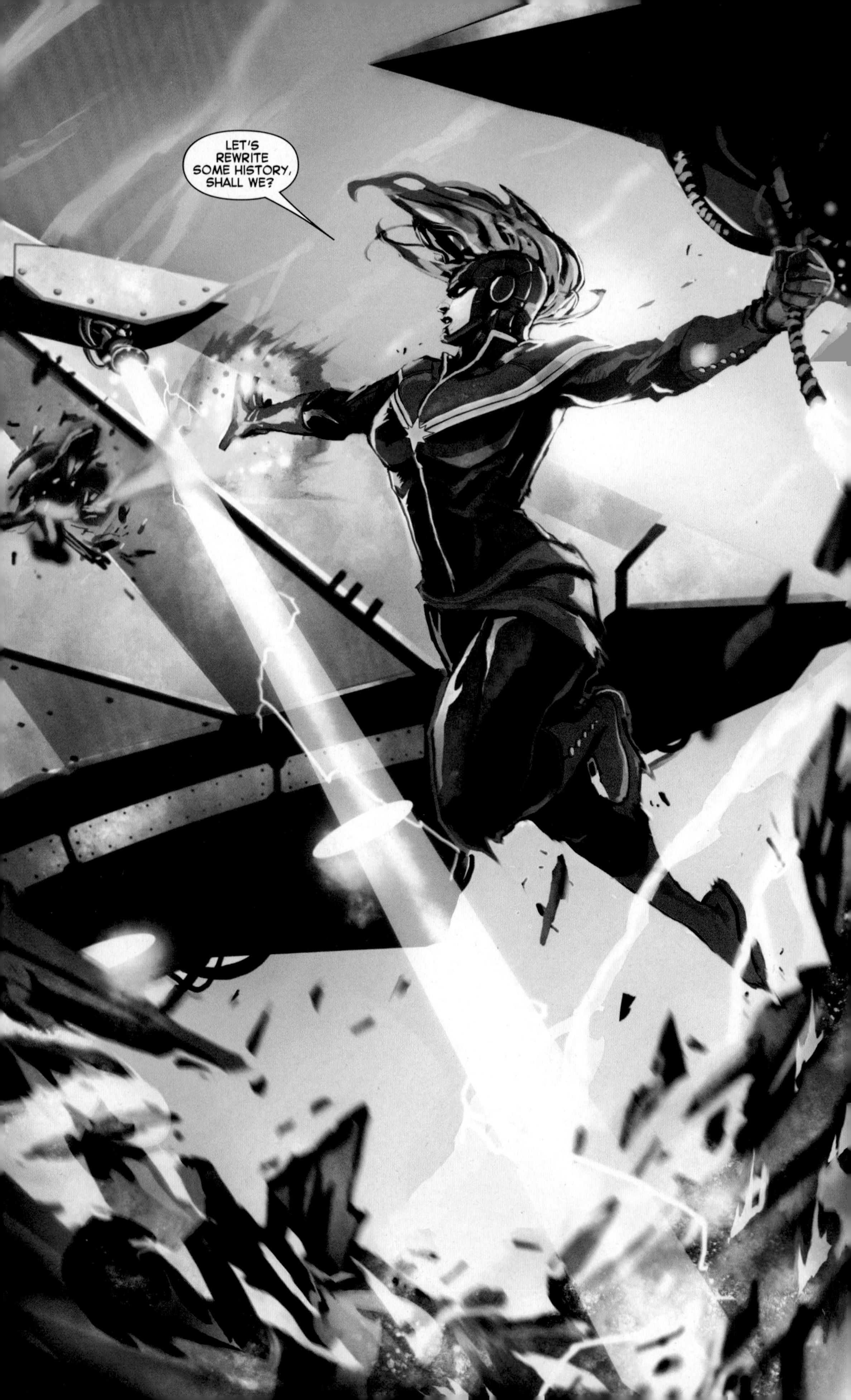
LET'S REWRITE SOME HISTORY, SHALL WE?

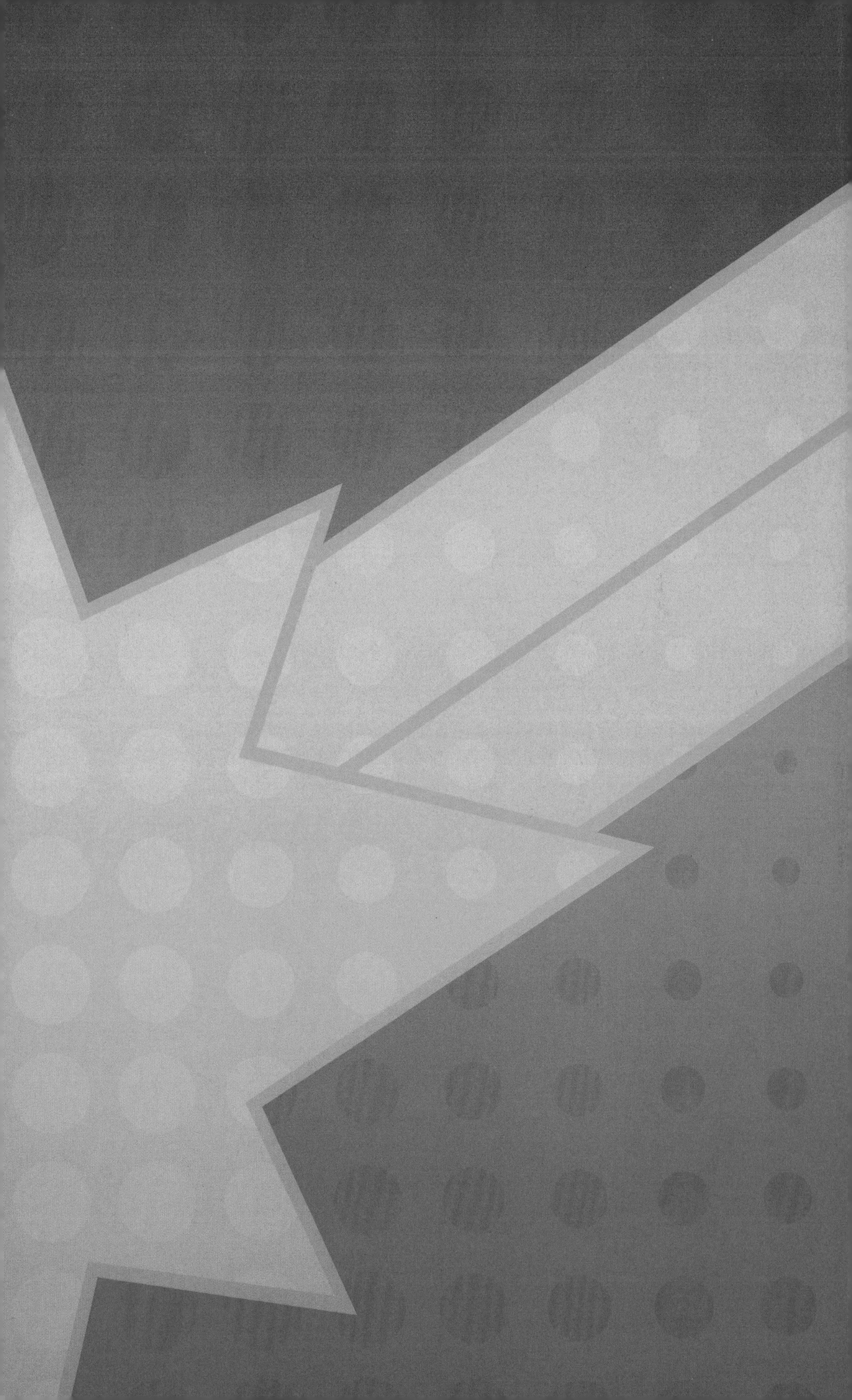

CAPTAIN MARVEL #3

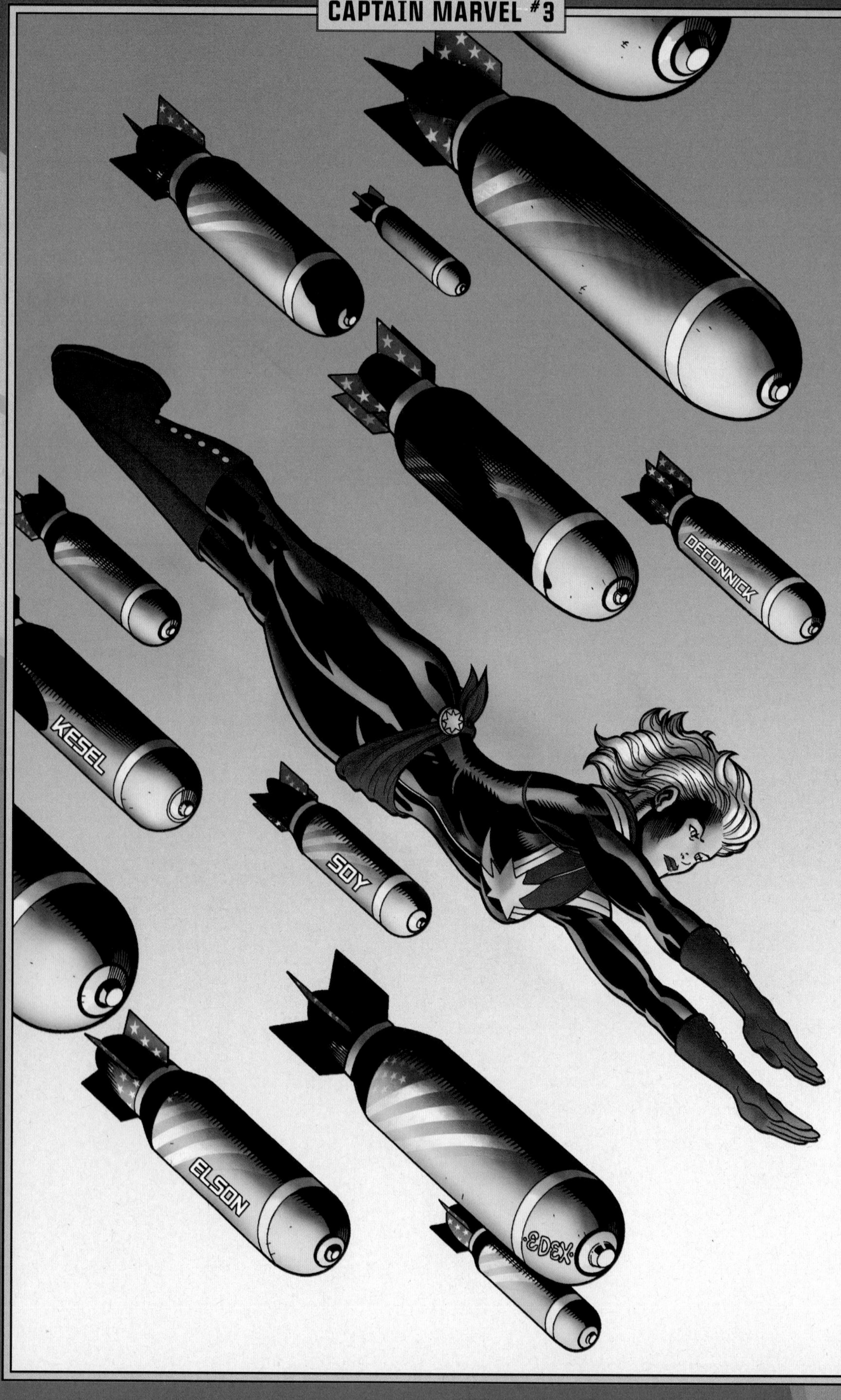
DECONNICK
KESEL
SOY
ELSON
EDEX

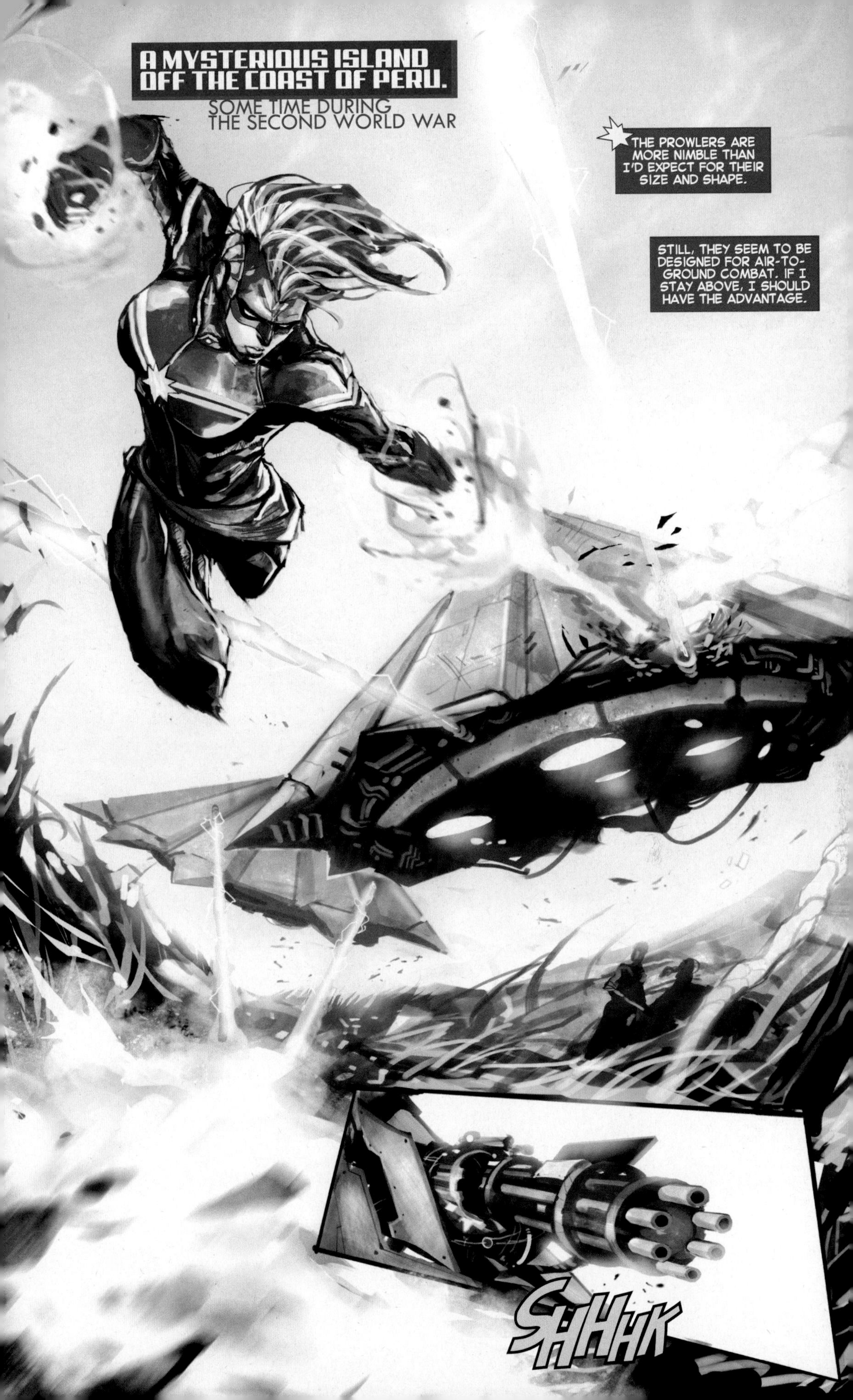
A MYSTERIOUS ISLAND OFF THE COAST OF PERU.
SOME TIME DURING THE SECOND WORLD WAR
THE PROWLERS ARE MORE NIMBLE THAN I'D EXPECT FOR THEIR SIZE AND SHAPE.
STILL, THEY SEEM TO BE DESIGNED FOR AIR-TO-GROUND COMBAT. IF I STAY ABOVE, I SHOULD HAVE THE ADVANTAGE.
SHHHK

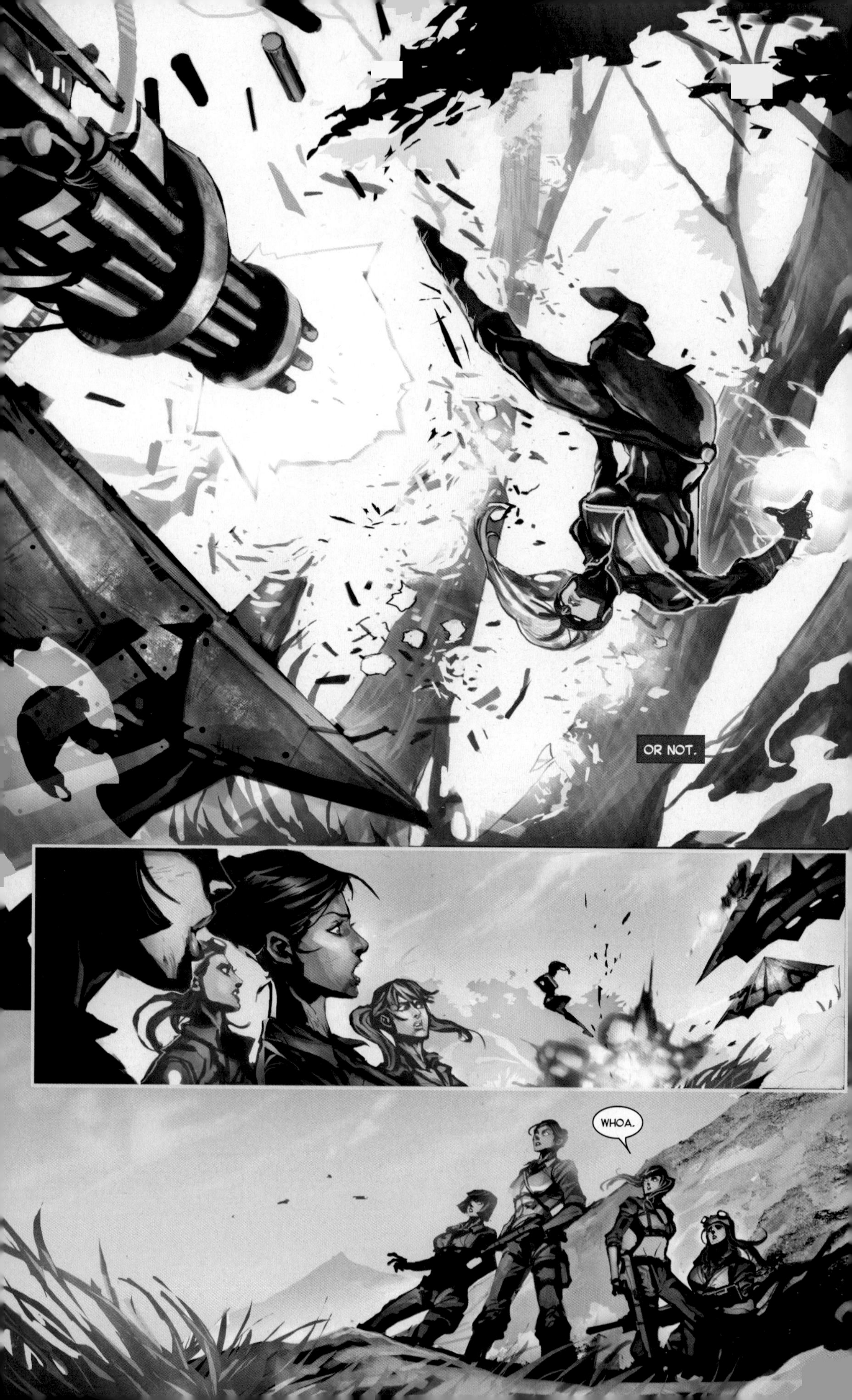
OR NOT.
WHOA.

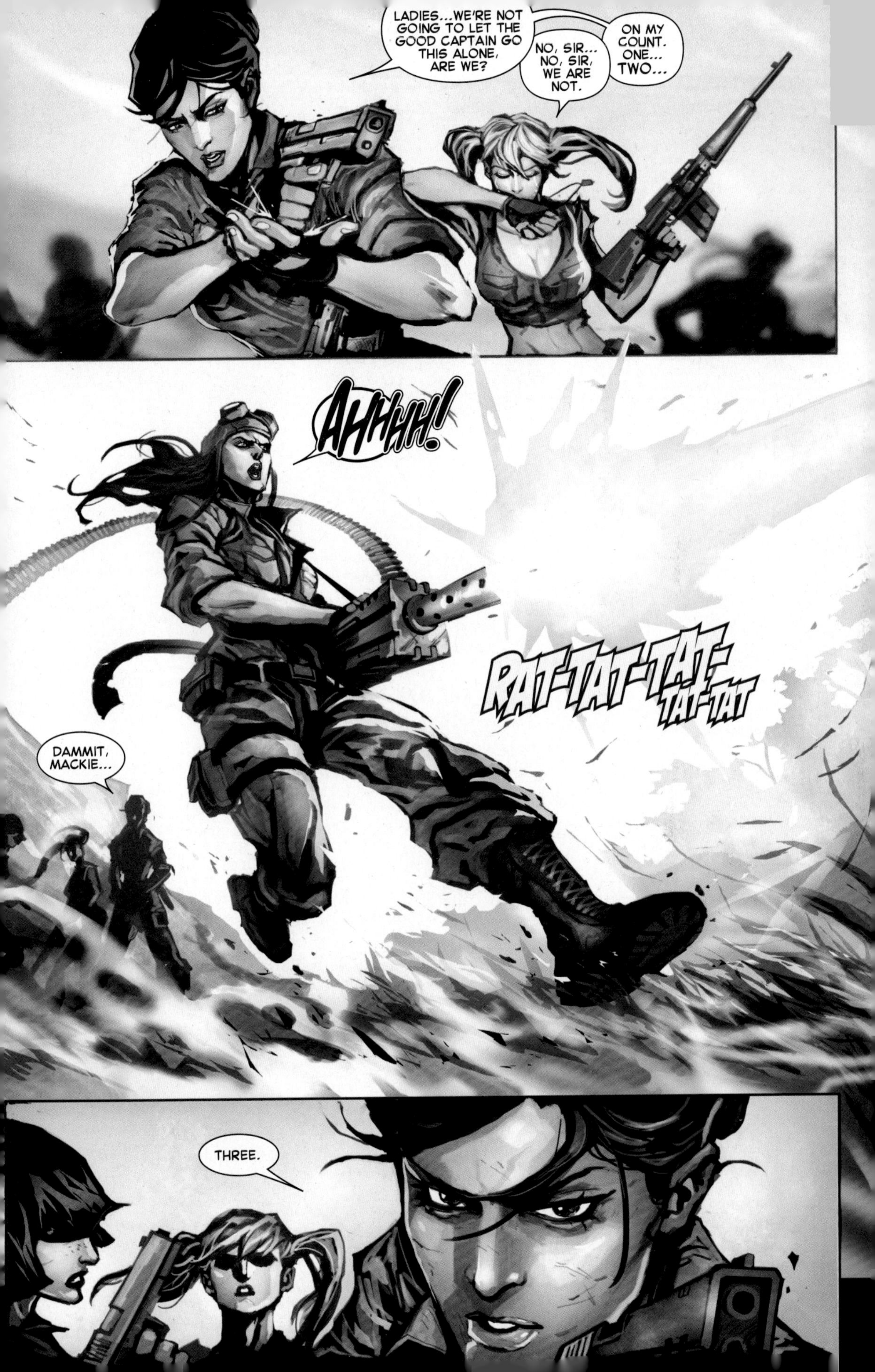
LADIES...WE'RE NOT GOING TO LET THE GOOD CAPTAIN GO THIS ALONE, ARE WE?
NO, SIR... NO, SIR, WE ARE NOT.
ON MY COUNT. ONE... TWO...
AHHHH!
RAT-TAT-TAT-TAT-TAT
DAMMIT, MACKIE...
THREE.

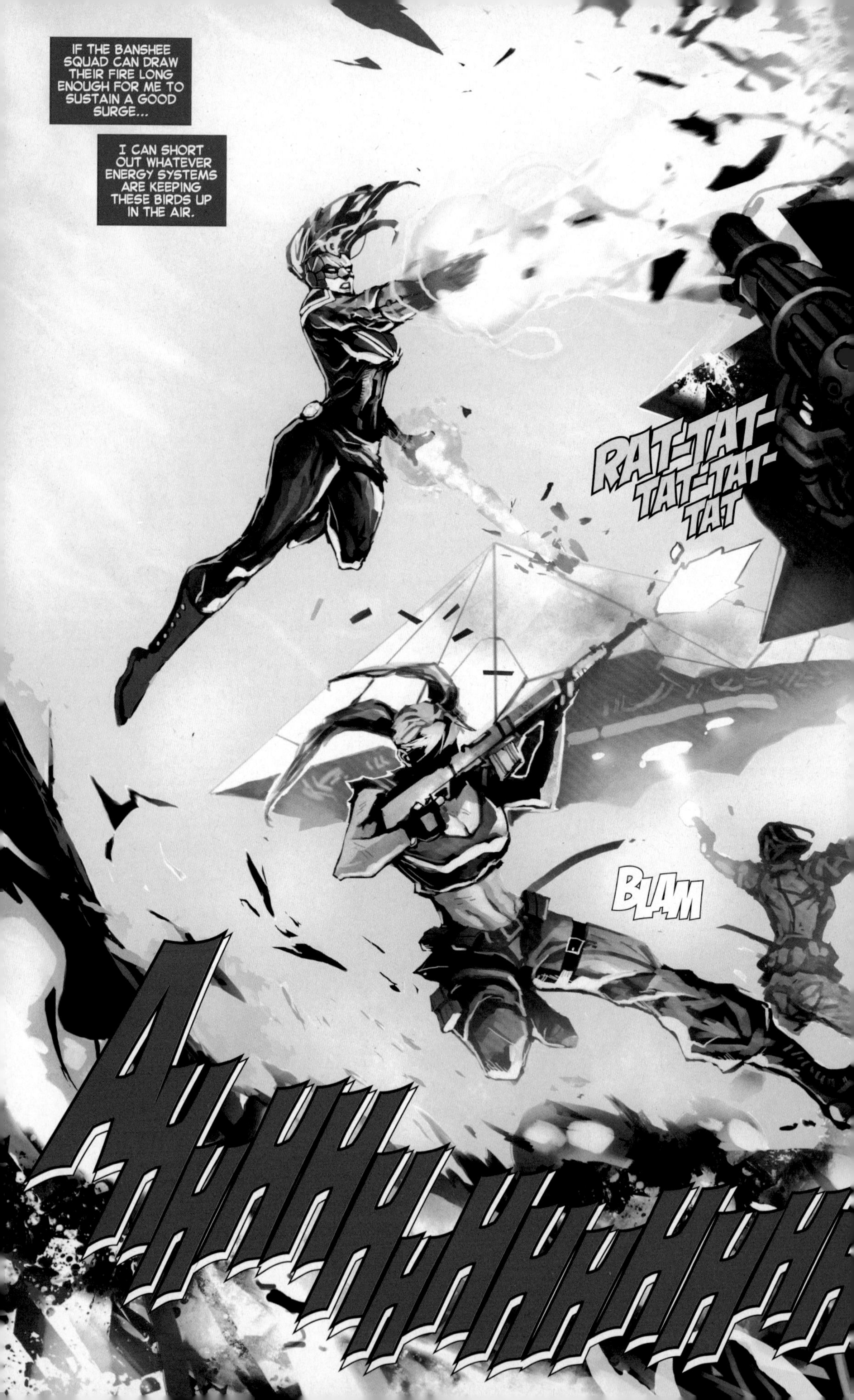
IF THE BANSHEE SQUAD CAN DRAW THEIR FIRE LONG ENOUGH FOR ME TO SUSTAIN A GOOD SURGE...
I CAN SHORT OUT WHATEVER ENERGY SYSTEMS ARE KEEPING THESE BIRDS UP IN THE AIR.
RAT-TAT-TAT-TAT-TAT
BLAM

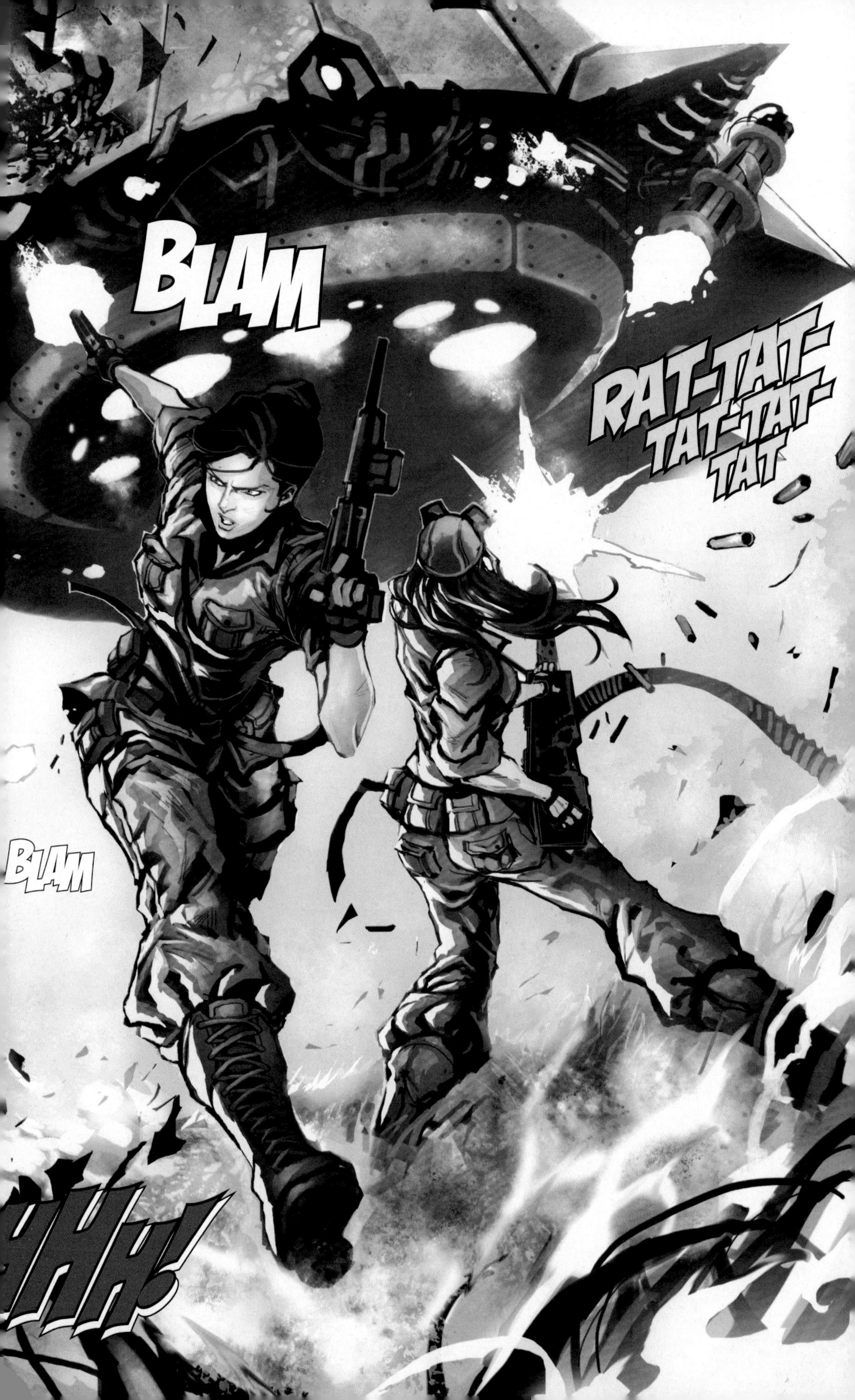
BLAM
RAT-TAT-TAT-TAT-TAT
BLAM

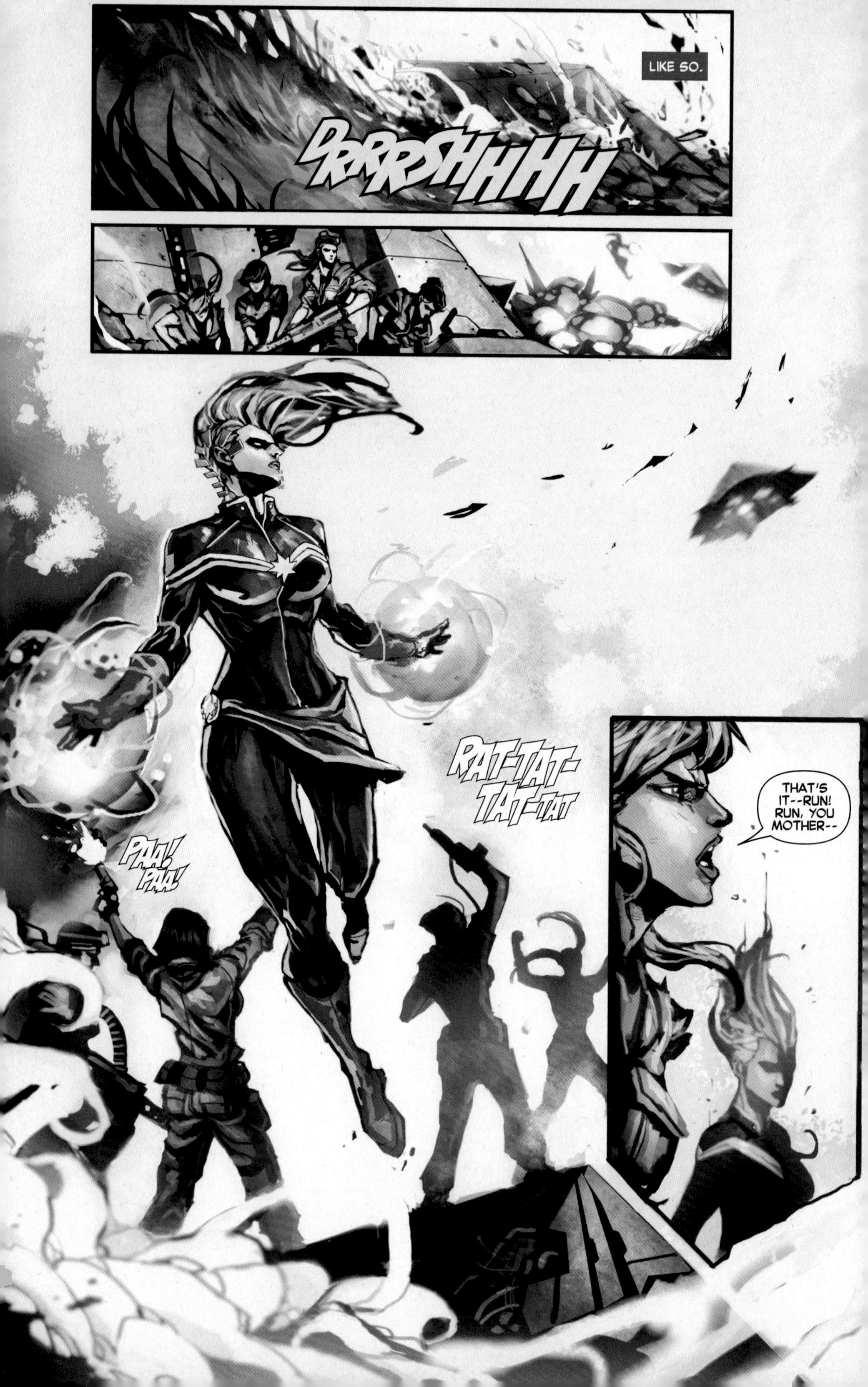
LIKE SO.
DRRRSHHHHH
RAT-TAT-TAT-TAT
PAA! PAA!
THAT'S IT--RUN! RUN, YOU MOTHER--

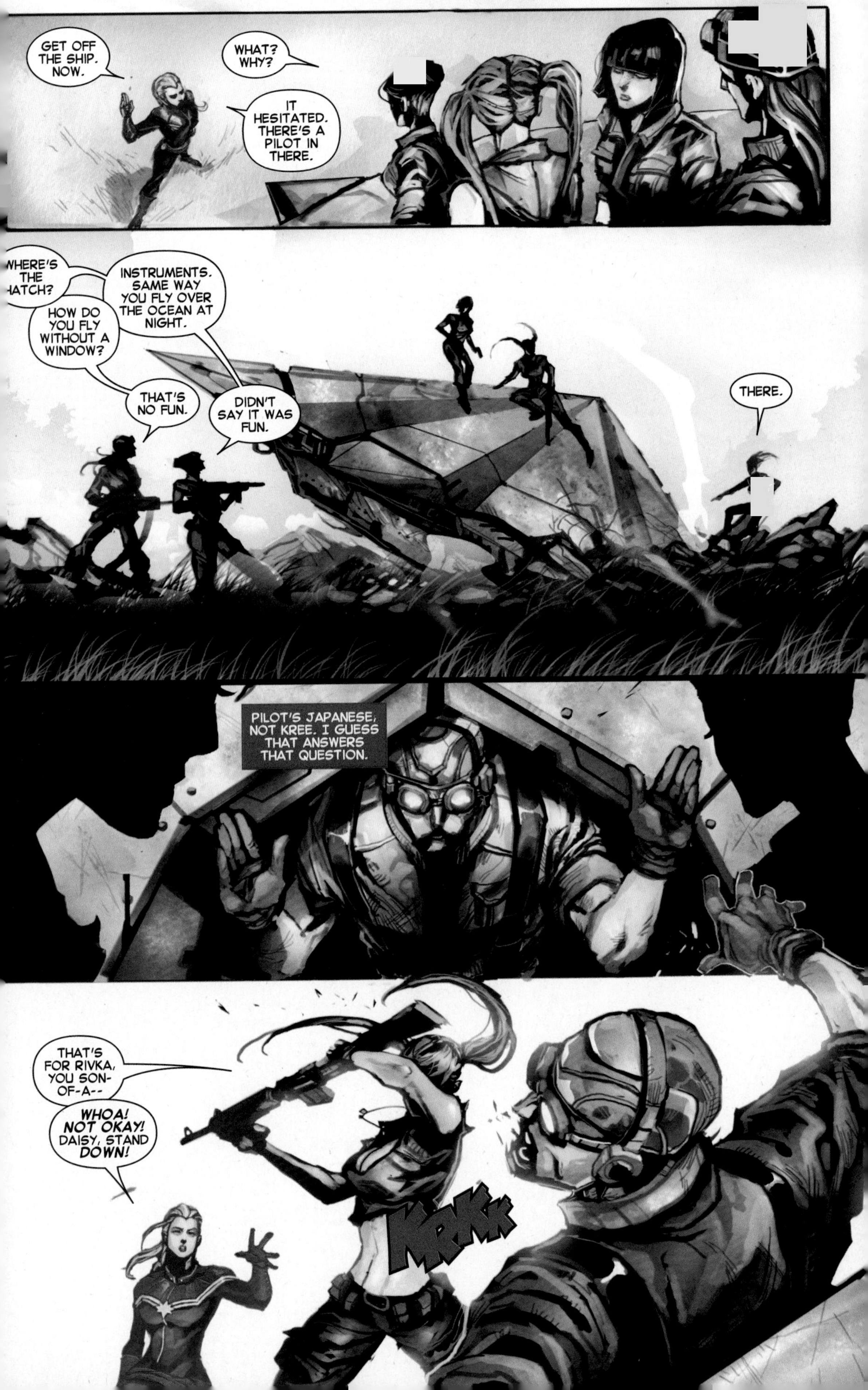
GET OFF THE SHIP. NOW.
WHAT? WHY?
IT HESITATED. THERE'S A PILOT IN THERE.
WHERE'S THE HATCH?
INSTRUMENTS. SAME WAY YOU FLY OVER THE OCEAN AT NIGHT.
HOW DO YOU FLY WITHOUT A WINDOW?
THAT'S NO FUN.
DIDN'T SAY IT WAS FUN.
THERE.
PILOT'S JAPANESE, NOT KREE. I GUESS THAT ANSWERS THAT QUESTION.
THAT'S FOR RIVKA, YOU SON-OF-A--
WHOA! NOT OKAY! DAISY, STAND DOWN!
KRRKK

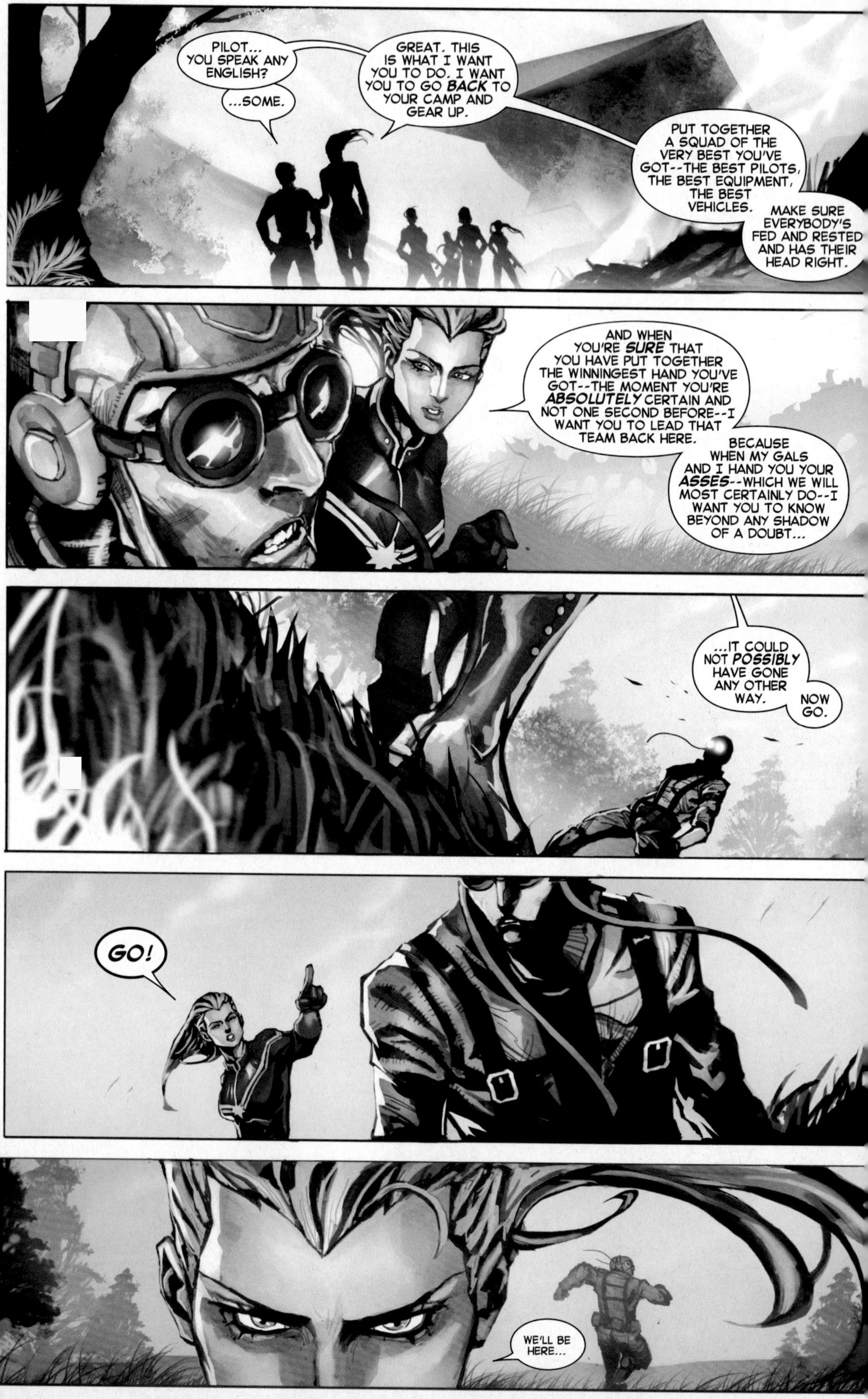
PILOT... YOU SPEAK ANY ENGLISH?
...SOME.
GREAT. THIS IS WHAT I WANT YOU TO DO. I WANT YOU TO GO BACK TO YOUR CAMP AND GEAR UP.
PUT TOGETHER A SQUAD OF THE VERY BEST YOU'VE GOT--THE BEST PILOTS, THE BEST EQUIPMENT, THE BEST VEHICLES.
MAKE SURE EVERYBODY'S FED AND RESTED AND HAS THEIR HEAD RIGHT.
AND WHEN YOU'RE SURE THAT YOU HAVE PUT TOGETHER THE WINNINGEST HAND YOU'VE GOT--THE MOMENT YOU'RE ABSOLUTELY CERTAIN AND NOT ONE SECOND BEFORE--I WANT YOU TO LEAD THAT TEAM BACK HERE.
BECAUSE WHEN MY GALS AND I HAND YOU YOUR ASSES--WHICH WE WILL MOST CERTAINLY DO--I WANT YOU TO KNOW BEYOND ANY SHADOW OF A DOUBT...
...IT COULD NOT POSSIBLY HAVE GONE ANY OTHER WAY.
NOW GO.
GO!
WE'LL BE HERE...

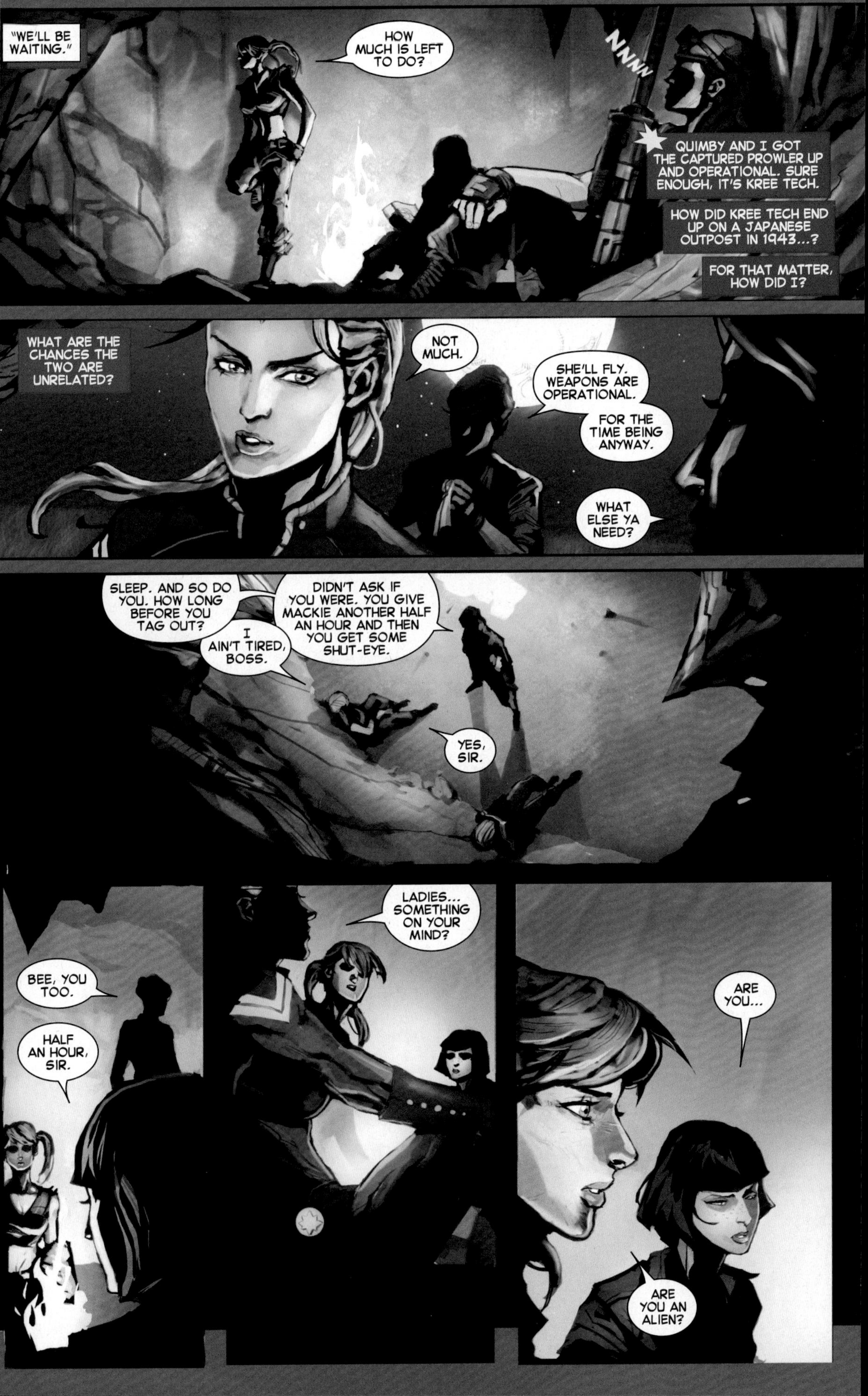
"WE'LL BE WAITING."
HOW MUCH IS LEFT TO DO?
NNNN
QUIMBY AND I GOT THE CAPTURED PROWLER UP AND OPERATIONAL. SURE ENOUGH, IT'S KREE TECH.
HOW DID KREE TECH END UP ON A JAPANESE OUTPOST IN 1943...?
FOR THAT MATTER, HOW DID I?
WHAT ARE THE CHANCES THE TWO ARE UNRELATED?
NOT MUCH.
SHE'LL FLY. WEAPONS ARE OPERATIONAL.
FOR THE TIME BEING ANYWAY.
WHAT ELSE YA NEED?
SLEEP. AND SO DO YOU. HOW LONG BEFORE YOU TAG OUT?
I AIN'T TIRED, BOSS.
DIDN'T ASK IF YOU WERE. YOU GIVE MACKIE ANOTHER HALF AN HOUR AND THEN YOU GET SOME SHUT-EYE.
YES, SIR.
BEE, YOU TOO.
HALF AN HOUR, SIR.
LADIES... SOMETHING ON YOUR MIND?
ARE YOU...
ARE YOU AN ALIEN?

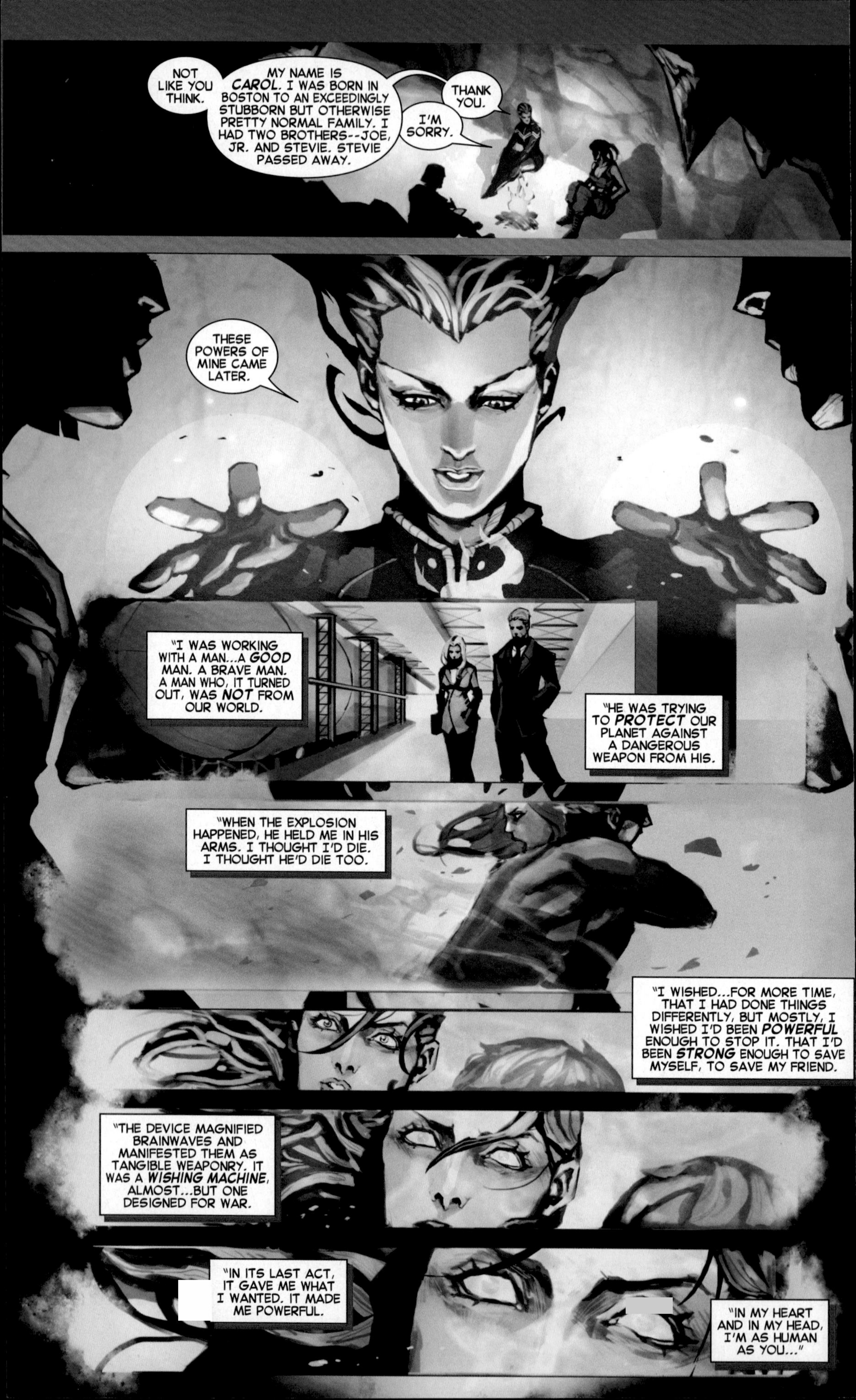
NOT LIKE YOU THINK.
MY NAME IS CAROL. I WAS BORN IN BOSTON TO AN EXCEEDINGLY STUBBORN BUT OTHERWISE PRETTY NORMAL FAMILY. I HAD TWO BROTHERS--JOE, JR. AND STEVIE. STEVIE PASSED AWAY.
THANK YOU.
I'M SORRY.
THESE POWERS OF MINE CAME LATER.
"I WAS WORKING WITH A MAN...A GOOD MAN. A BRAVE MAN. A MAN WHO, IT TURNED OUT, WAS NOT FROM OUR WORLD.
"HE WAS TRYING TO PROTECT OUR PLANET AGAINST A DANGEROUS WEAPON FROM HIS.
"WHEN THE EXPLOSION HAPPENED, HE HELD ME IN HIS ARMS. I THOUGHT I'D DIE. I THOUGHT HE'D DIE TOO.
"I WISHED...FOR MORE TIME, THAT I HAD DONE THINGS DIFFERENTLY, BUT MOSTLY, I WISHED I'D BEEN POWERFUL ENOUGH TO STOP IT. THAT I'D BEEN STRONG ENOUGH TO SAVE MYSELF, TO SAVE MY FRIEND.
"THE DEVICE MAGNIFIED BRAINWAVES AND MANIFESTED THEM AS TANGIBLE WEAPONRY. IT WAS A WISHING MACHINE, ALMOST...BUT ONE DESIGNED FOR WAR.
"IN ITS LAST ACT, IT GAVE ME WHAT I WANTED. IT MADE ME POWERFUL.
"IN MY HEART AND IN MY HEAD, I'M AS HUMAN AS YOU..."

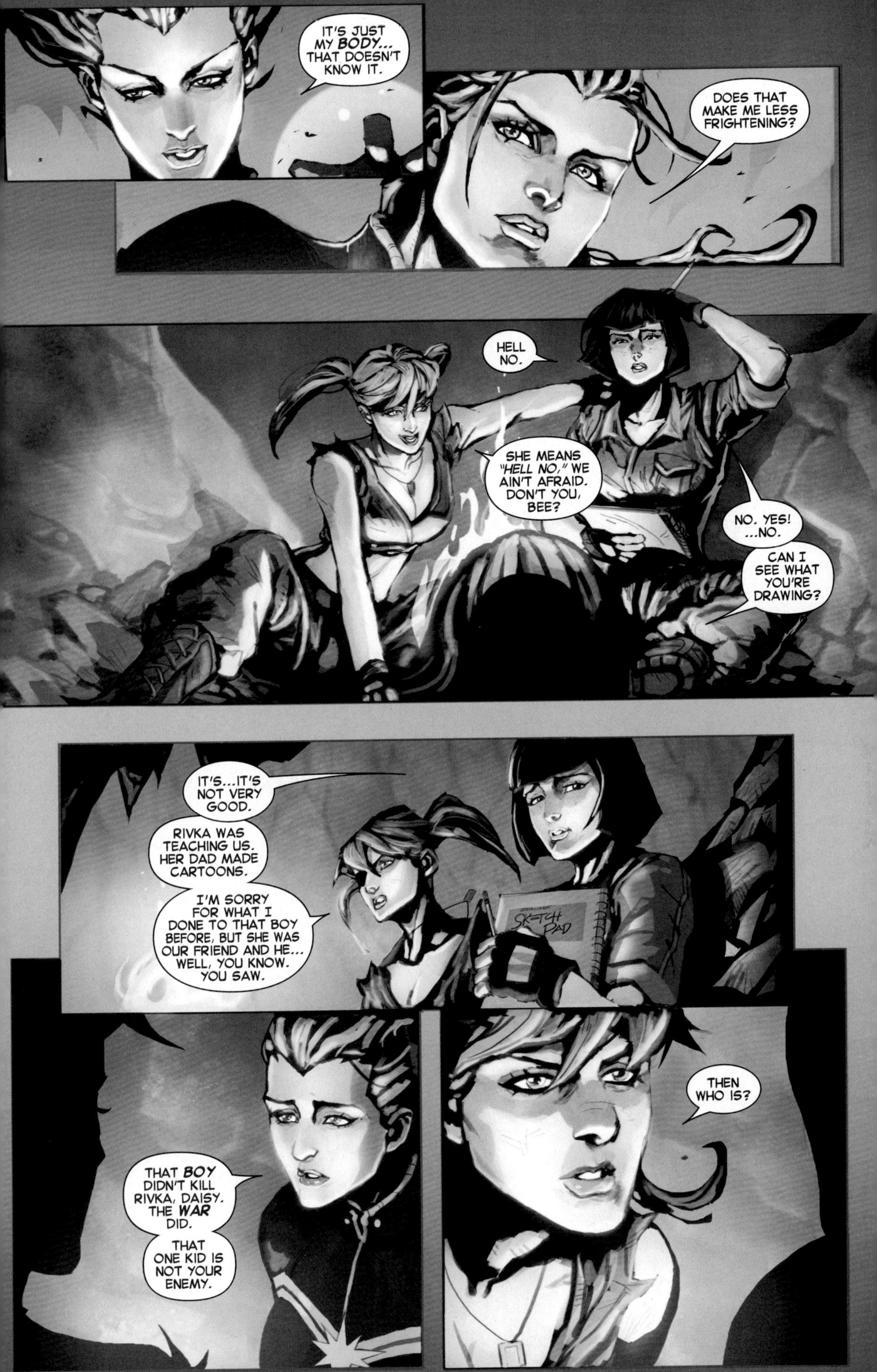
IT'S JUST MY BODY... THAT DOESN'T KNOW IT.
DOES THAT MAKE ME LESS FRIGHTENING?
HELL NO.
SHE MEANS "HELL NO," WE AIN'T AFRAID. DON'T YOU, BEE?
NO. YES! ...NO.
CAN I SEE WHAT YOU'RE DRAWING?
IT'S...IT'S NOT VERY GOOD.
RIVKA WAS TEACHING US. HER DAD MADE CARTOONS.
I'M SORRY FOR WHAT I DONE TO THAT BOY BEFORE, BUT SHE WAS OUR FRIEND AND HE... WELL, YOU KNOW. YOU SAW.
SKETCH PAD
THAT BOY DIDN'T KILL RIVKA, DAISY. THE WAR DID.
THAT ONE KID IS NOT YOUR ENEMY.
THEN WHO IS?

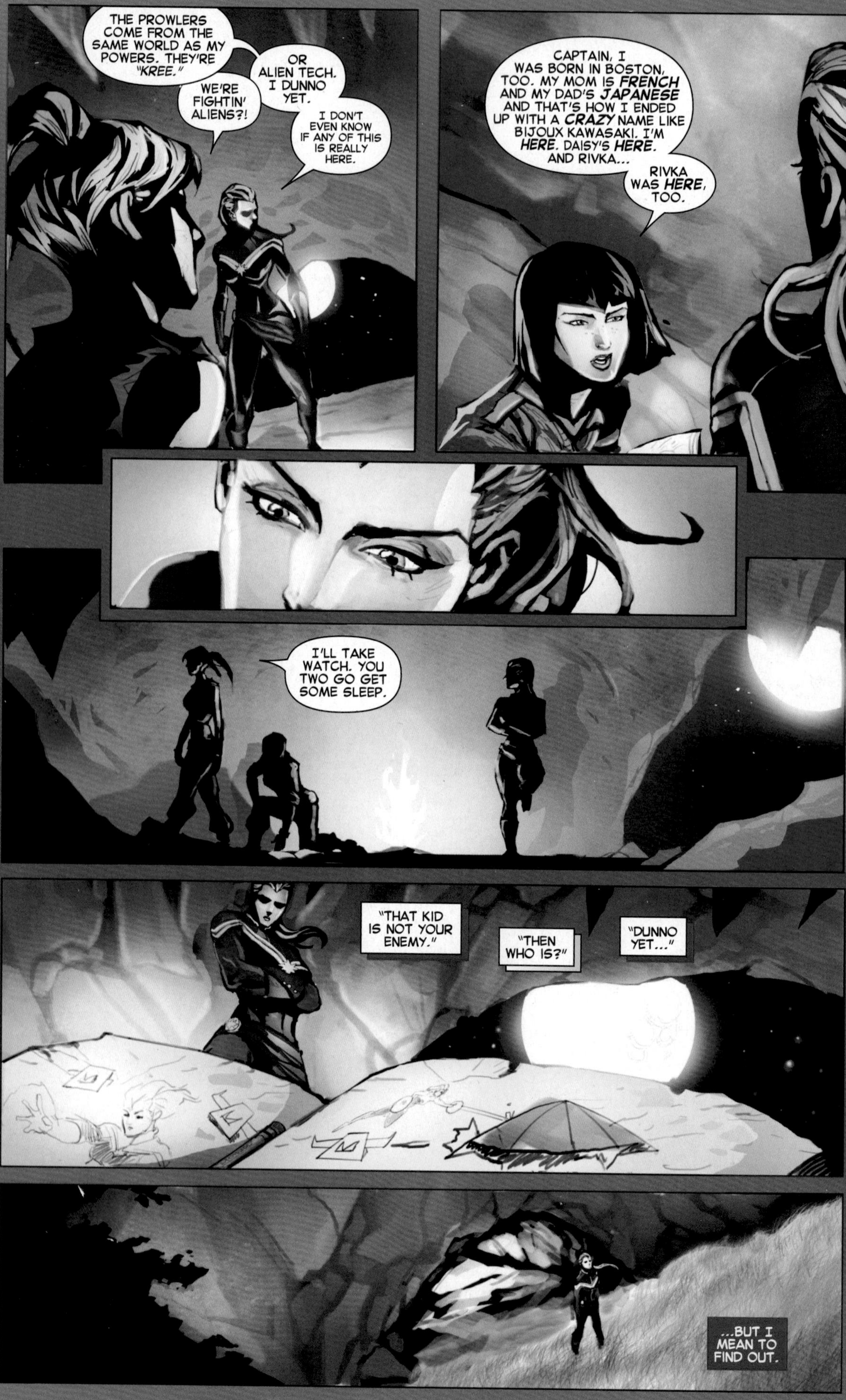
THE PROWLERS COME FROM THE SAME WORLD AS MY POWERS. THEY'RE "KREE."
WE'RE FIGHTIN' ALIENS?!
OR ALIEN TECH. I DUNNO YET.
I DON'T EVEN KNOW IF ANY OF THIS IS REALLY HERE.
CAPTAIN, I WAS BORN IN BOSTON, TOO. MY MOM IS FRENCH AND MY DAD'S JAPANESE AND THAT'S HOW I ENDED UP WITH A CRAZY NAME LIKE BIJOUX KAWASAKI. I'M HERE. DAISY'S HERE. AND RIVKA...
RIVKA WAS HERE, TOO.
I'LL TAKE WATCH. YOU TWO GO GET SOME SLEEP.
"THAT KID IS NOT YOUR ENEMY."
"THEN WHO IS?"
"DUNNO YET..."
...BUT I MEAN TO FIND OUT.

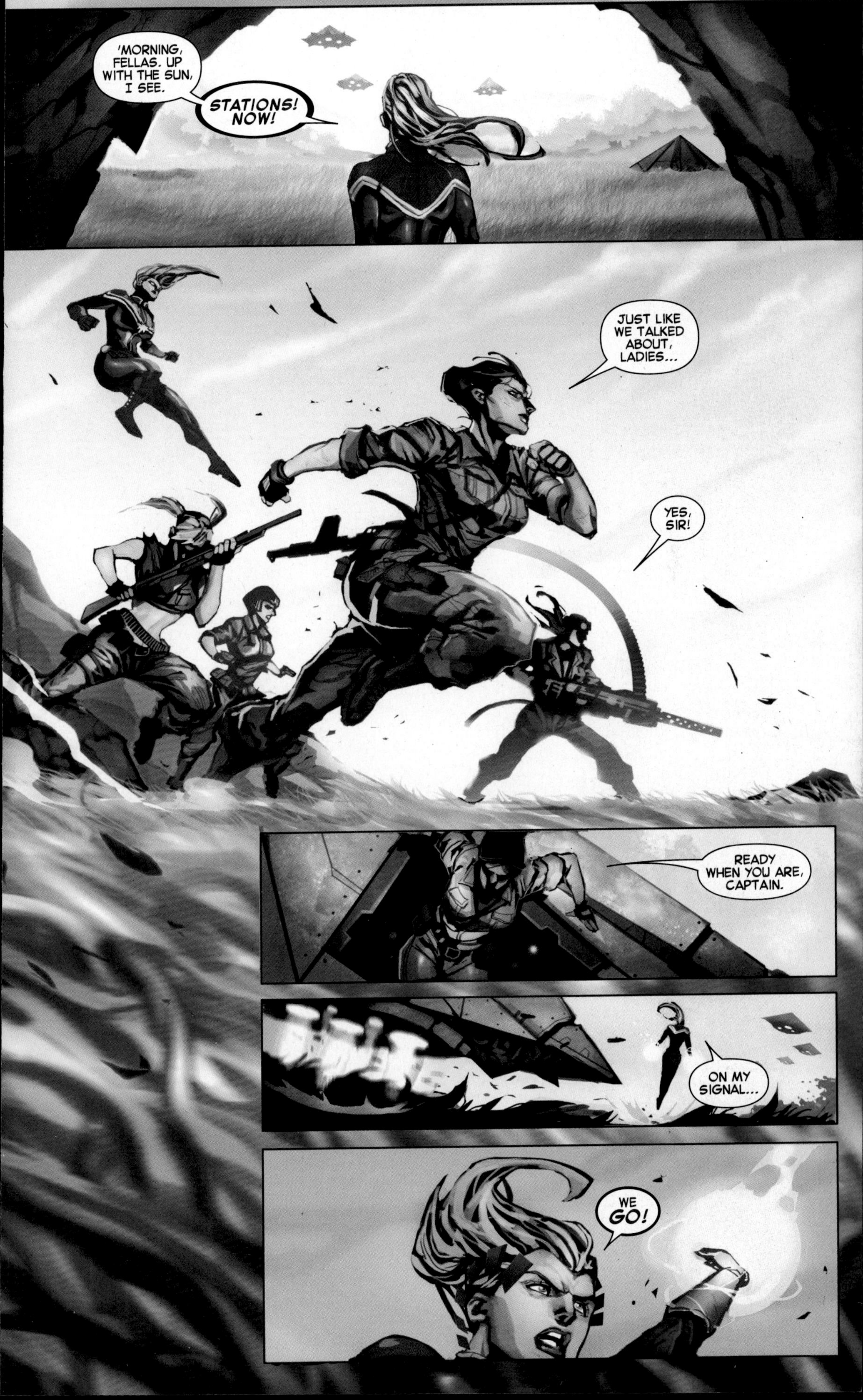
'MORNING, FELLAS. UP WITH THE SUN, I SEE.
STATIONS! NOW!
JUST LIKE WE TALKED ABOUT, LADIES...
YES, SIR!
READY WHEN YOU ARE, CAPTAIN.
ON MY SIGNAL...
WE GO!

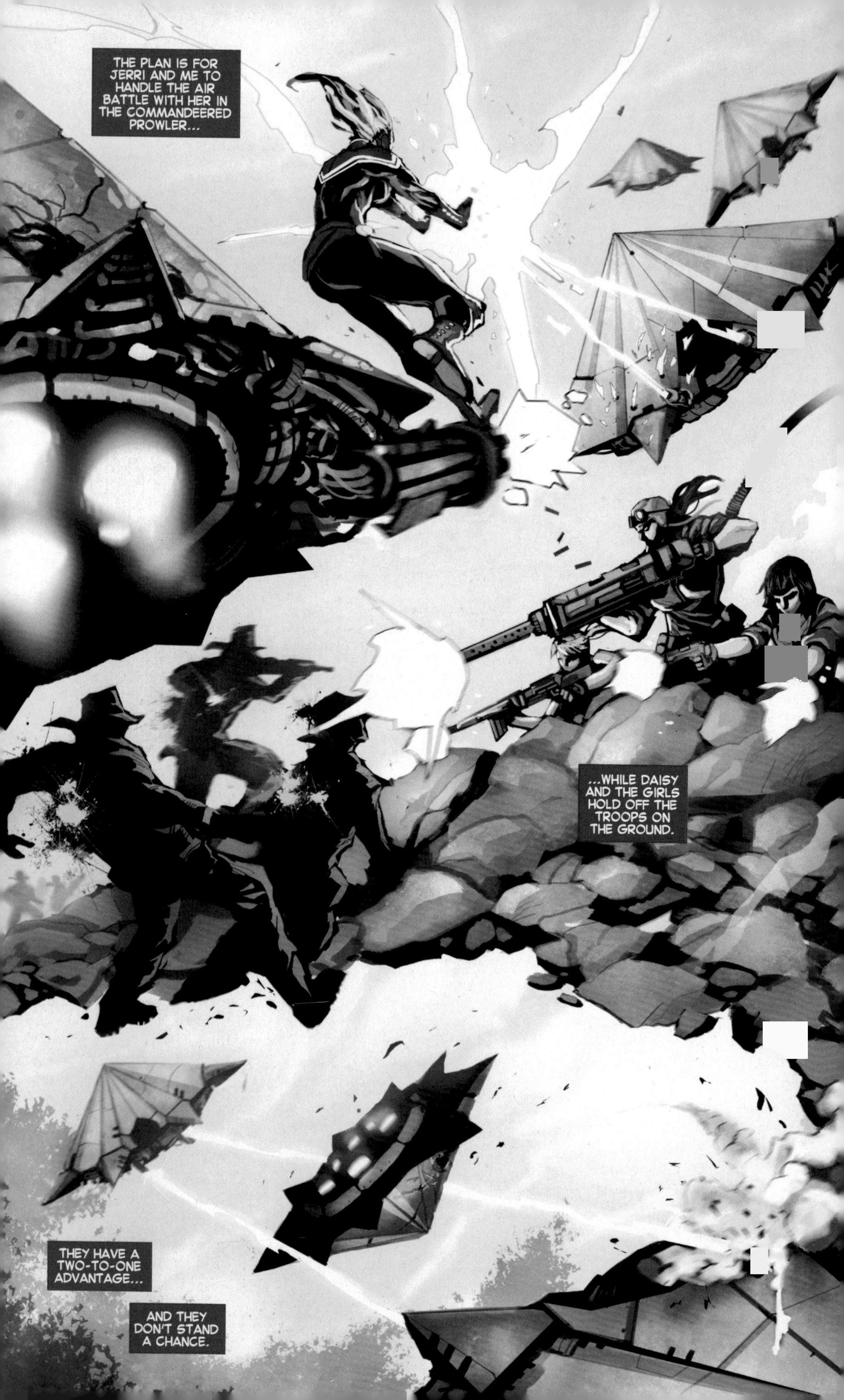
THE PLAN IS FOR JERRI AND ME TO HANDLE THE AIR BATTLE WITH HER IN THE COMMANDEERED PROWLER...
...WHILE DAISY AND THE GIRLS HOLD OFF THE TROOPS ON THE GROUND.
THEY HAVE A TWO-TO-ONE ADVANTAGE...
AND THEY DON'T STAND A CHANCE.

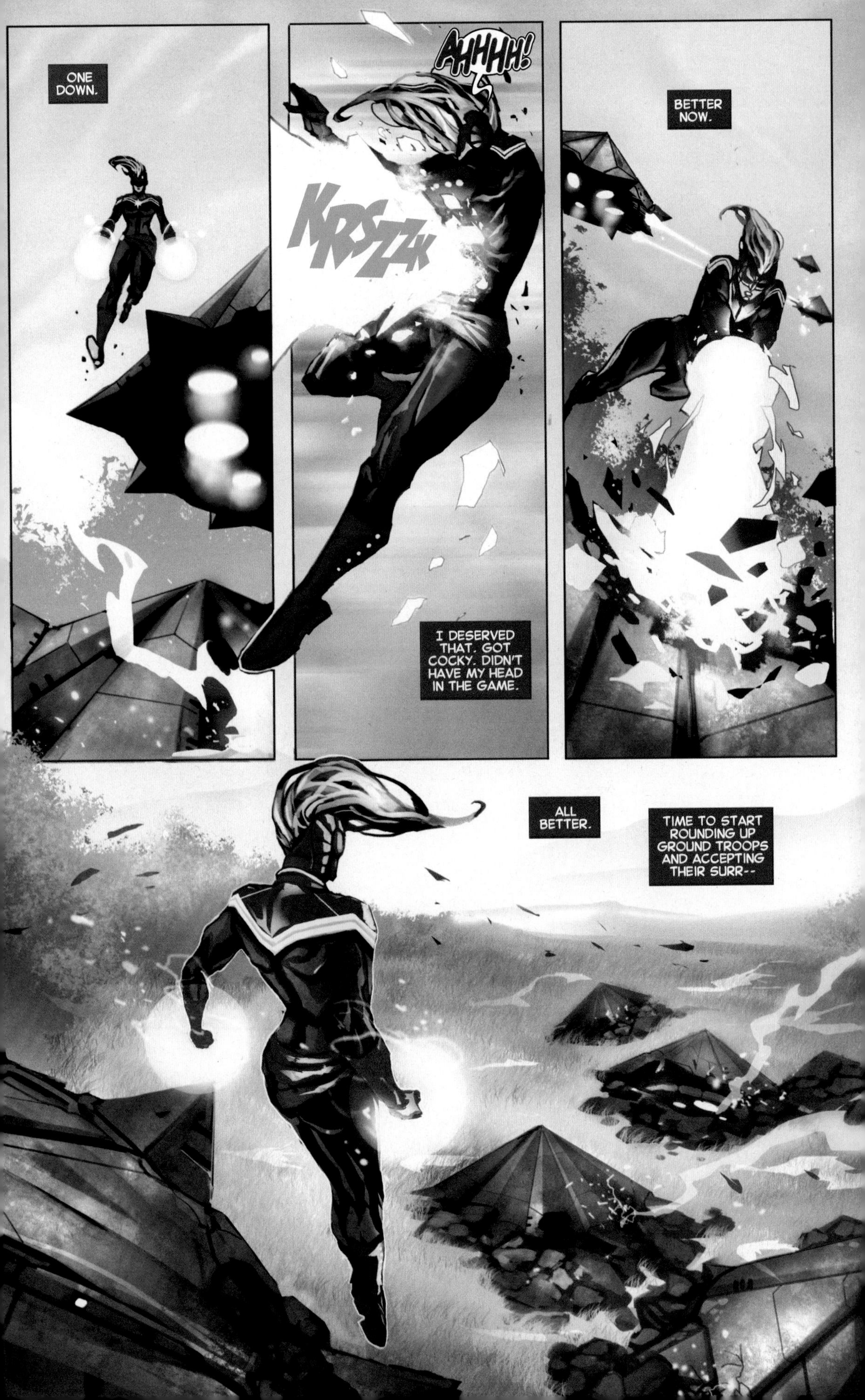
ONE DOWN.
AHHHH!
KRSZZK
I DESERVED THAT. GOT COCKY. DIDN'T HAVE MY HEAD IN THE GAME.
BETTER NOW.
ALL BETTER.
TIME TO START ROUNDING UP GROUND TROOPS AND ACCEPTING THEIR SURR--

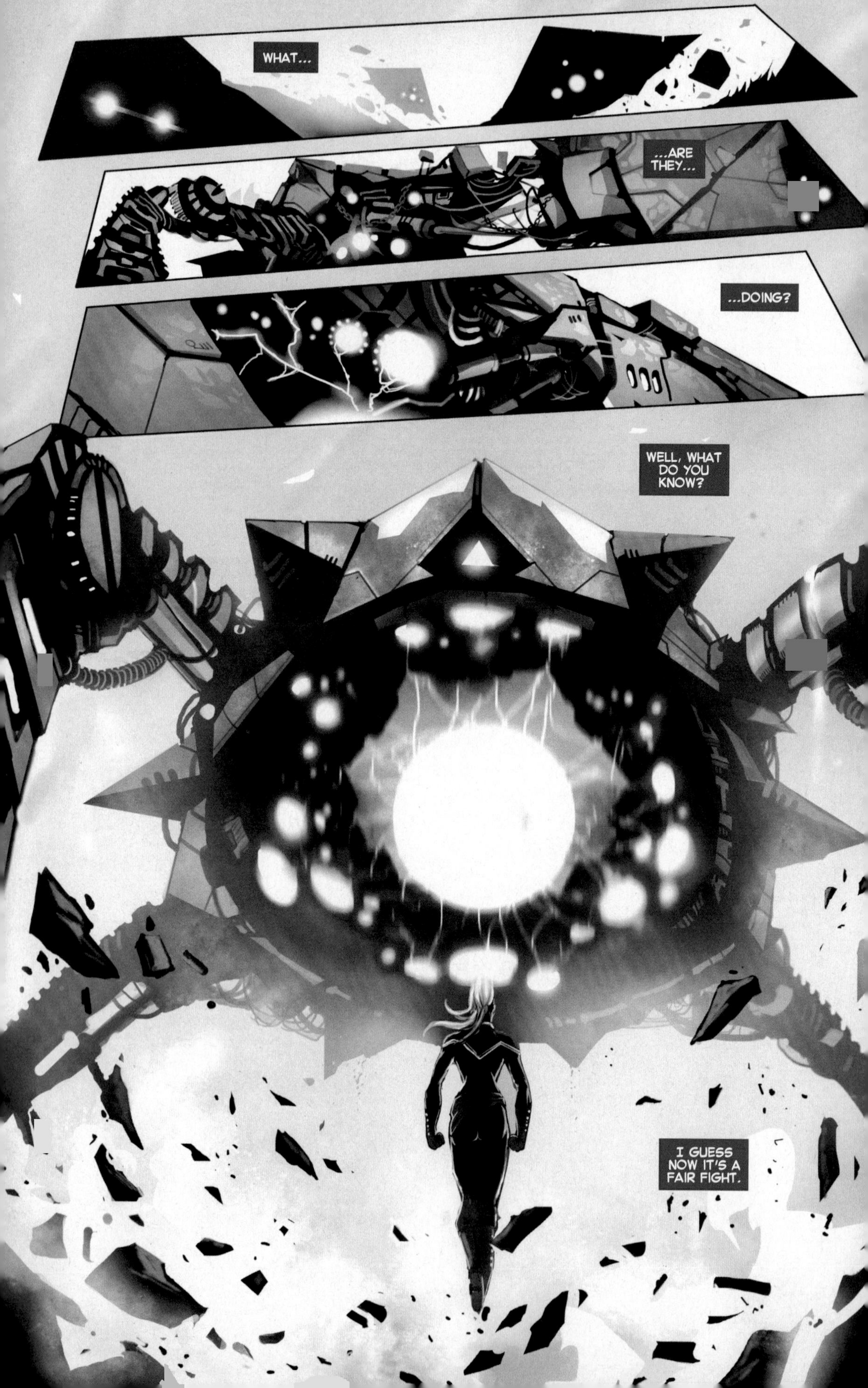
WHAT...
...ARE THEY...
...DOING?
WELL, WHAT DO YOU KNOW?
I GUESS NOW IT'S A FAIR FIGHT.

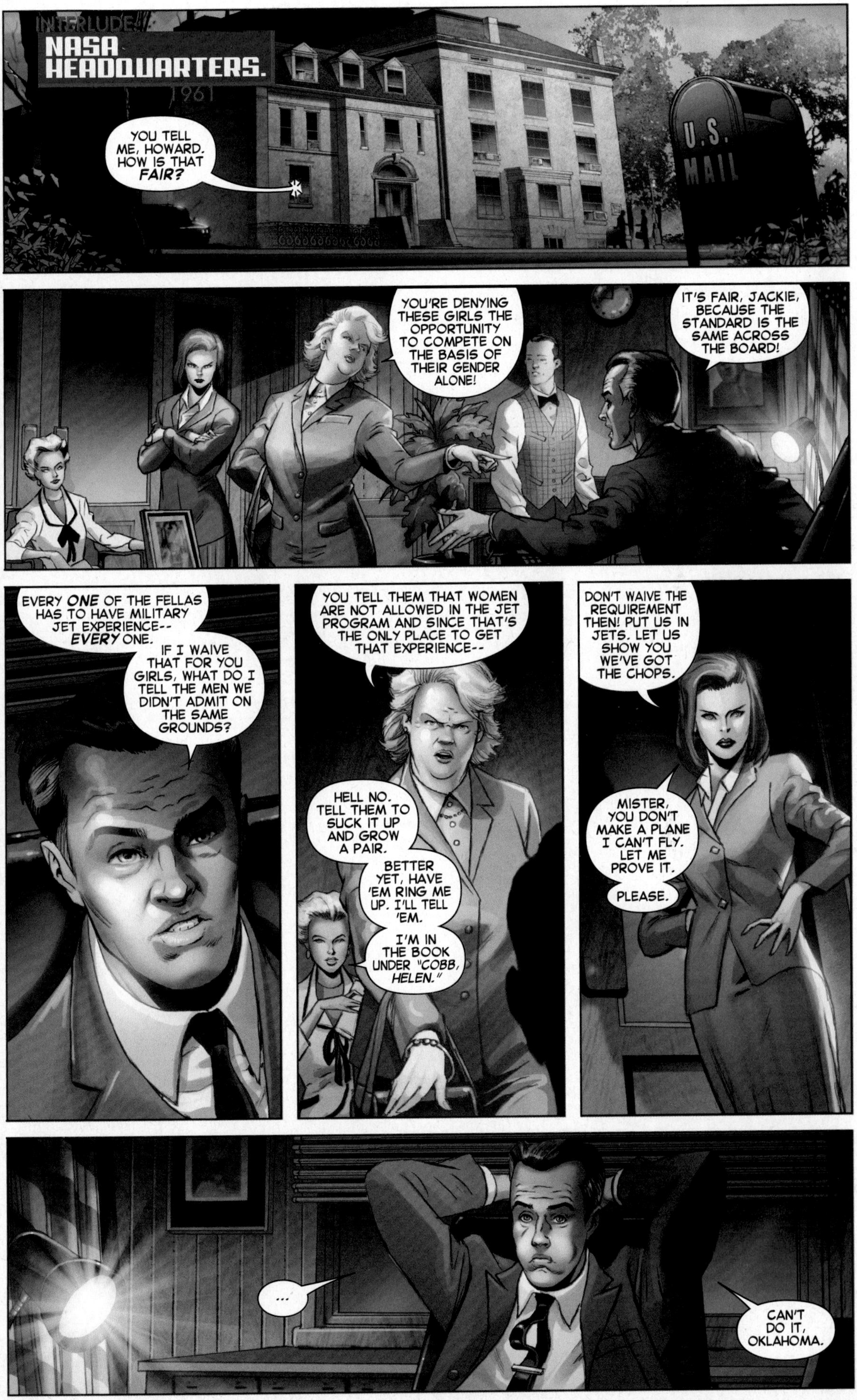
INTERLUDE:
NASA HEADQUARTERS.
1961
YOU TELL ME, HOWARD. HOW IS THAT FAIR?
U.S. MAIL
YOU'RE DENYING THESE GIRLS THE OPPORTUNITY TO COMPETE ON THE BASIS OF THEIR GENDER ALONE!
IT'S FAIR, JACKIE, BECAUSE THE STANDARD IS THE SAME ACROSS THE BOARD!
EVERY ONE OF THE FELLAS HAS TO HAVE MILITARY JET EXPERIENCE-- EVERY ONE.
IF I WAIVE THAT FOR YOU GIRLS, WHAT DO I TELL THE MEN WE DIDN'T ADMIT ON THE SAME GROUNDS?
YOU TELL THEM THAT WOMEN ARE NOT ALLOWED IN THE JET PROGRAM AND SINCE THAT'S THE ONLY PLACE TO GET THAT EXPERIENCE--
HELL NO. TELL THEM TO SUCK IT UP AND GROW A PAIR.
BETTER YET, HAVE 'EM RING ME UP. I'LL TELL 'EM.
I'M IN THE BOOK UNDER "COBB, HELEN."
DON'T WAIVE THE REQUIREMENT THEN! PUT US IN JETS. LET US SHOW YOU WE'VE GOT THE CHOPS.
MISTER, YOU DON'T MAKE A PLANE I CAN'T FLY. LET ME PROVE IT.
PLEASE.
...
CAN'T DO IT, OKLAHOMA.

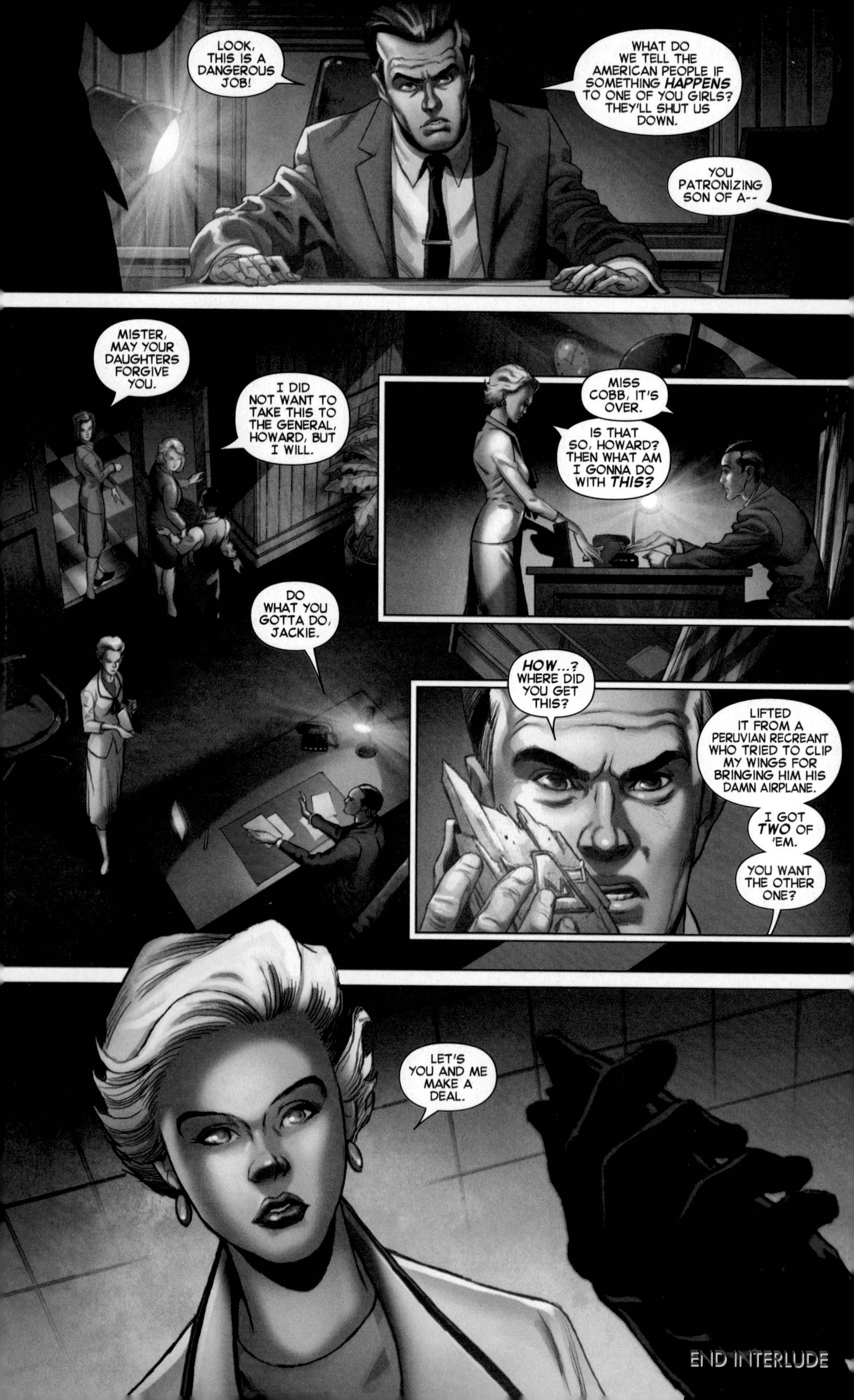
LOOK, THIS IS A DANGEROUS JOB!
WHAT DO WE TELL THE AMERICAN PEOPLE IF SOMETHING HAPPENS TO ONE OF YOU GIRLS? THEY'LL SHUT US DOWN.
YOU PATRONIZING SON OF A--
MISTER, MAY YOUR DAUGHTERS FORGIVE YOU.
I DID NOT WANT TO TAKE THIS TO THE GENERAL, HOWARD, BUT I WILL.
MISS COBB, IT'S OVER.
IS THAT SO, HOWARD? THEN WHAT AM I GONNA DO WITH THIS?
DO WHAT YOU GOTTA DO, JACKIE.
HOW...? WHERE DID YOU GET THIS?
LIFTED IT FROM A PERUVIAN RECREANT WHO TRIED TO CLIP MY WINGS FOR BRINGING HIM HIS DAMN AIRPLANE.
I GOT TWO OF 'EM.
YOU WANT THE OTHER ONE?
LET'S YOU AND ME MAKE A DEAL.
END INTERLUDE

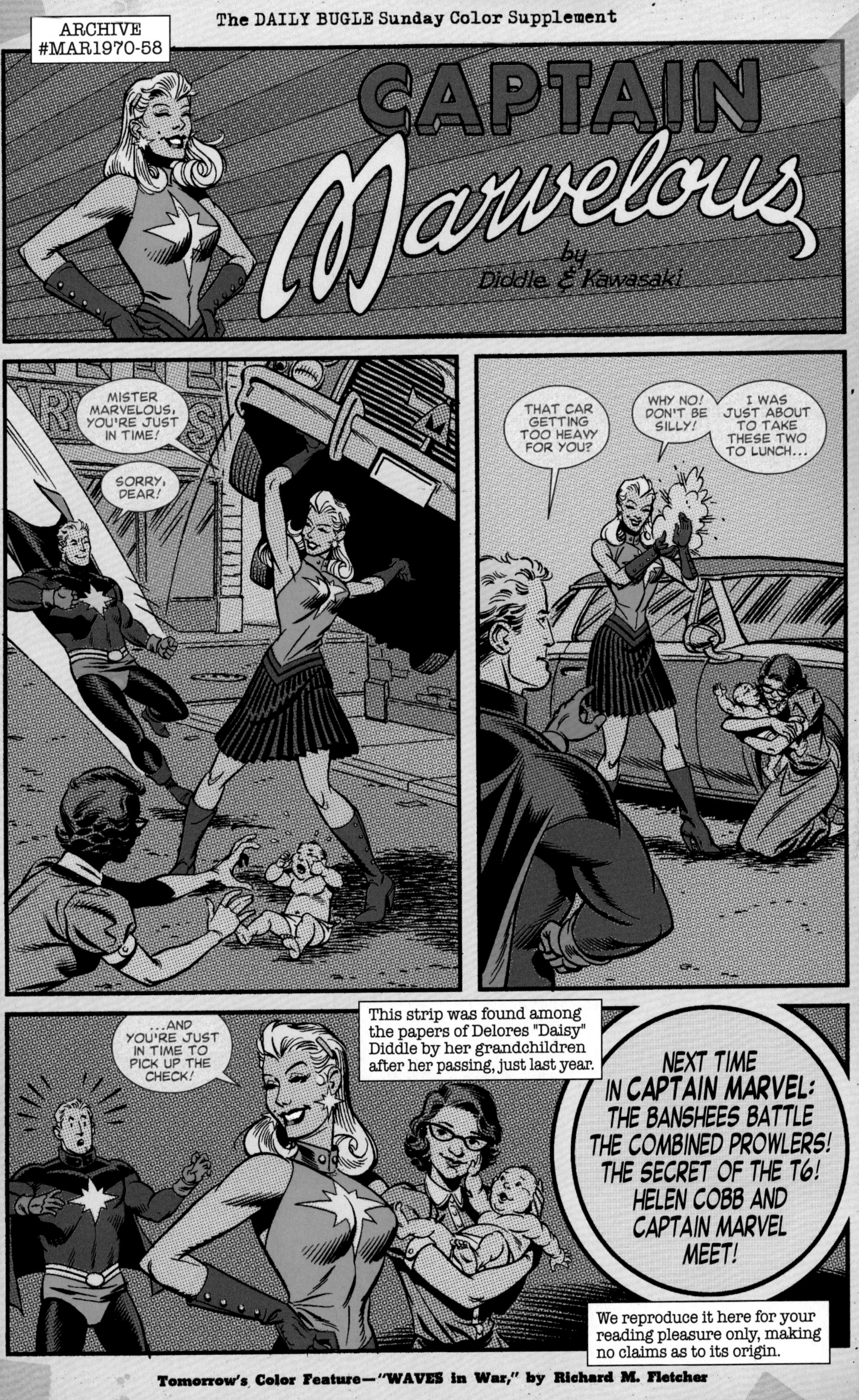
ARCHIVE
#MAR1970-58
The DAILY BUGLE Sunday Color Supplement
CAPTAIN Marvelous
by Diddle & Kawasaki
MISTER MARVELOUS, YOU'RE JUST IN TIME!
SORRY, DEAR!
THAT CAR GETTING TOO HEAVY FOR YOU?
WHY NO! DON'T BE SILLY!
I WAS JUST ABOUT TO TAKE THESE TWO TO LUNCH...
...AND YOU'RE JUST IN TIME TO PICK UP THE CHECK!
This strip was found among the papers of Delores "Daisy" Diddle by her grandchildren after her passing, just last year.
NEXT TIME IN CAPTAIN MARVEL: THE BANSHEES BATTLE THE COMBINED PROWLERS! THE SECRET OF THE T6! HELEN COBB AND CAPTAIN MARVEL MEET!
We reproduce it here for your reading pleasure only, making no claims as to its origin.
Tomorrow's Color Feature—"WAVES in War," by Richard M. Fletcher

CAPTAIN MARVEL #4

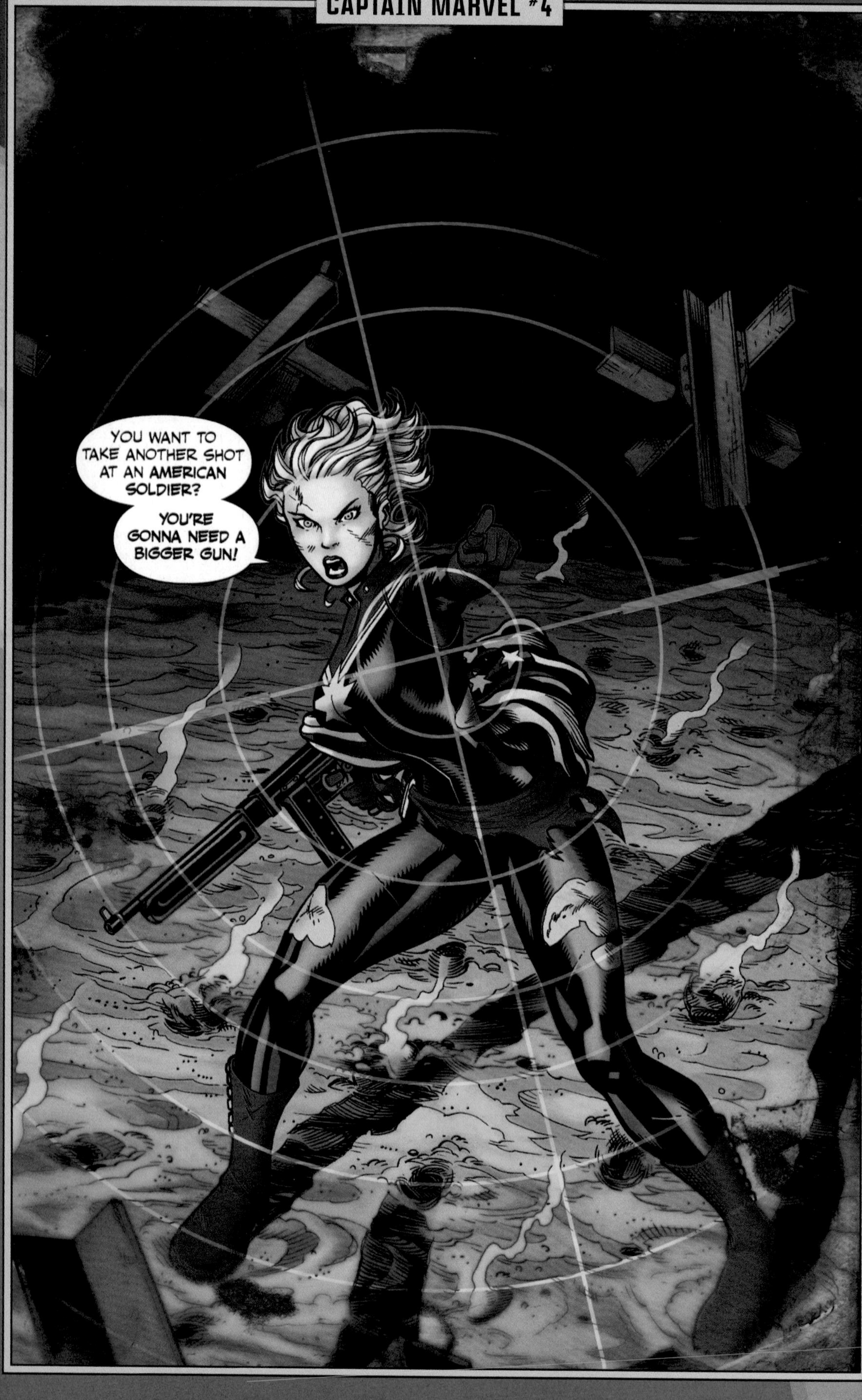
YOU WANT TO TAKE ANOTHER SHOT AT AN AMERICAN SOLDIER?
YOU'RE GONNA NEED A BIGGER GUN!

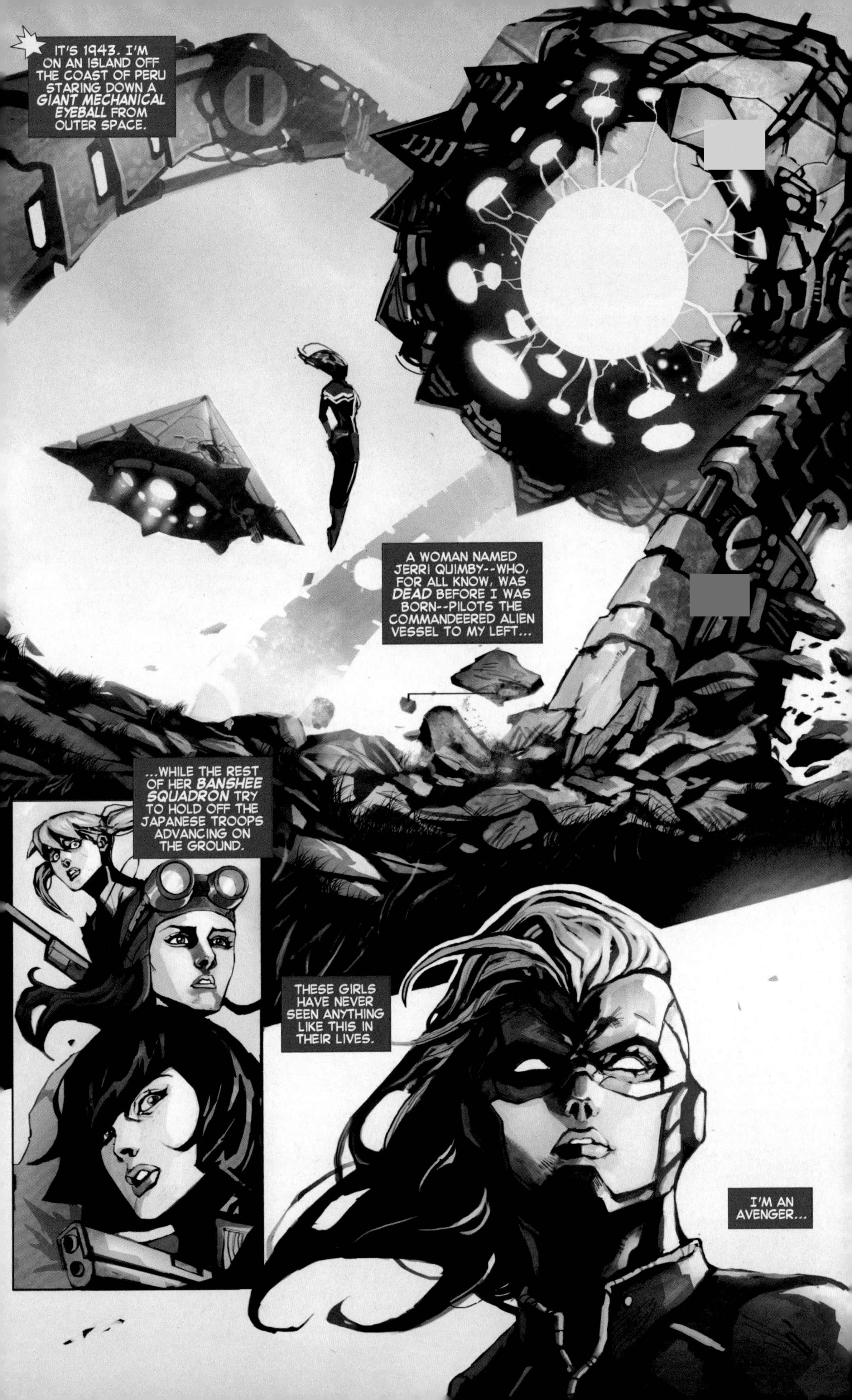
IT'S 1943. I'M ON AN ISLAND OFF THE COAST OF PERU STARING DOWN A *GIANT MECHANICAL EYEBALL* FROM OUTER SPACE.
A WOMAN NAMED JERRI QUIMBY--WHO, FOR ALL KNOW, WAS *DEAD* BEFORE I WAS BORN--PILOTS THE COMMANDEERED ALIEN VESSEL TO MY LEFT...
...WHILE THE REST OF HER *BANSHEE SQUADRON* TRY TO HOLD OFF THE JAPANESE TROOPS ADVANCING ON THE GROUND.
THESE GIRLS HAVE NEVER SEEN ANYTHING LIKE THIS IN THEIR LIVES.
I'M AN AVENGER...

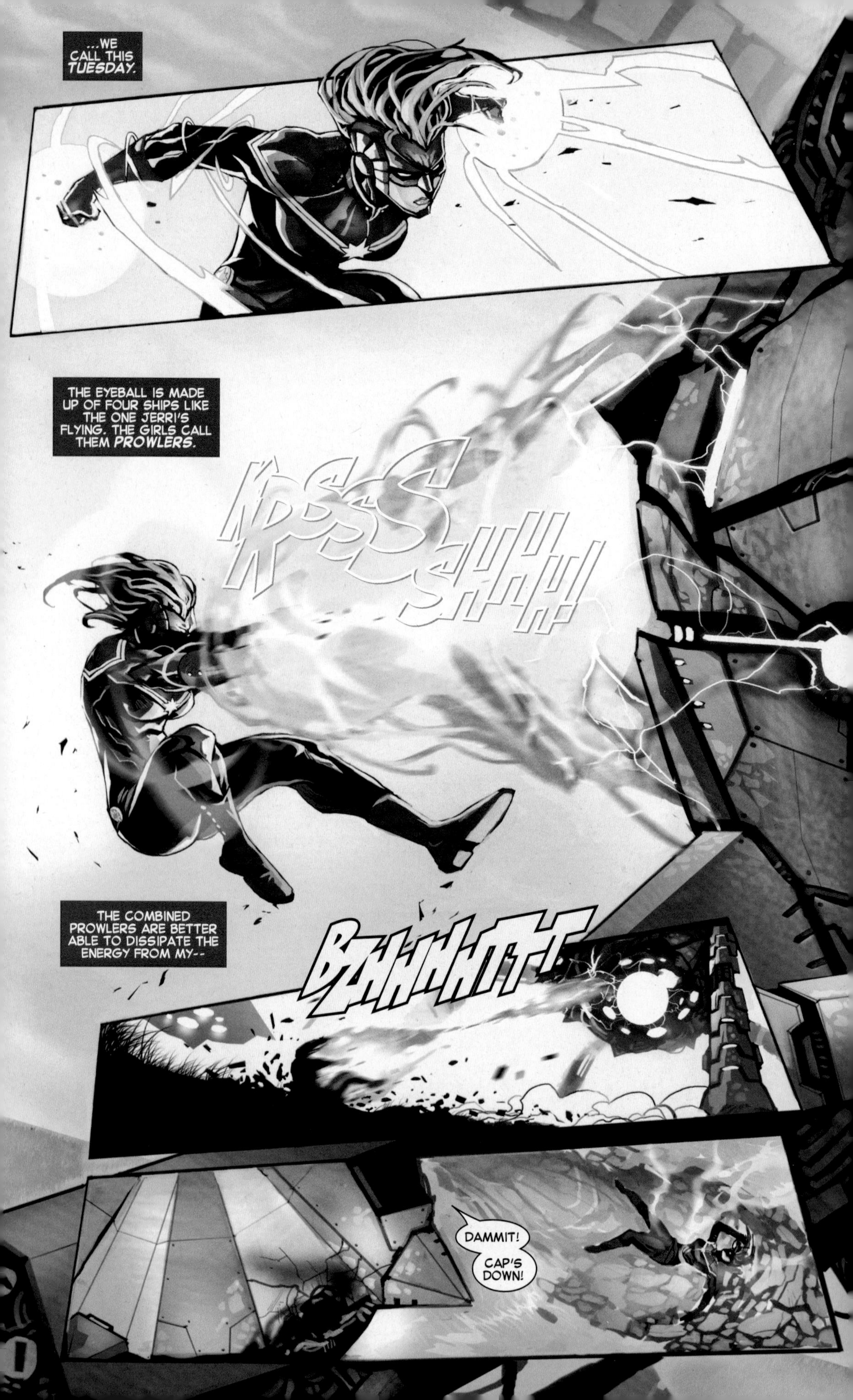
...WE CALL THIS *TUESDAY*.
THE EYEBALL IS MADE UP OF FOUR SHIPS LIKE THE ONE JERRI'S FLYING. THE GIRLS CALL THEM *PROWLERS*.
KRSSSSHHHH!
THE COMBINED PROWLERS ARE BETTER ABLE TO DISSIPATE THE ENERGY FROM MY--
BZHHHHTTT
DAMMIT!
CAP'S DOWN!

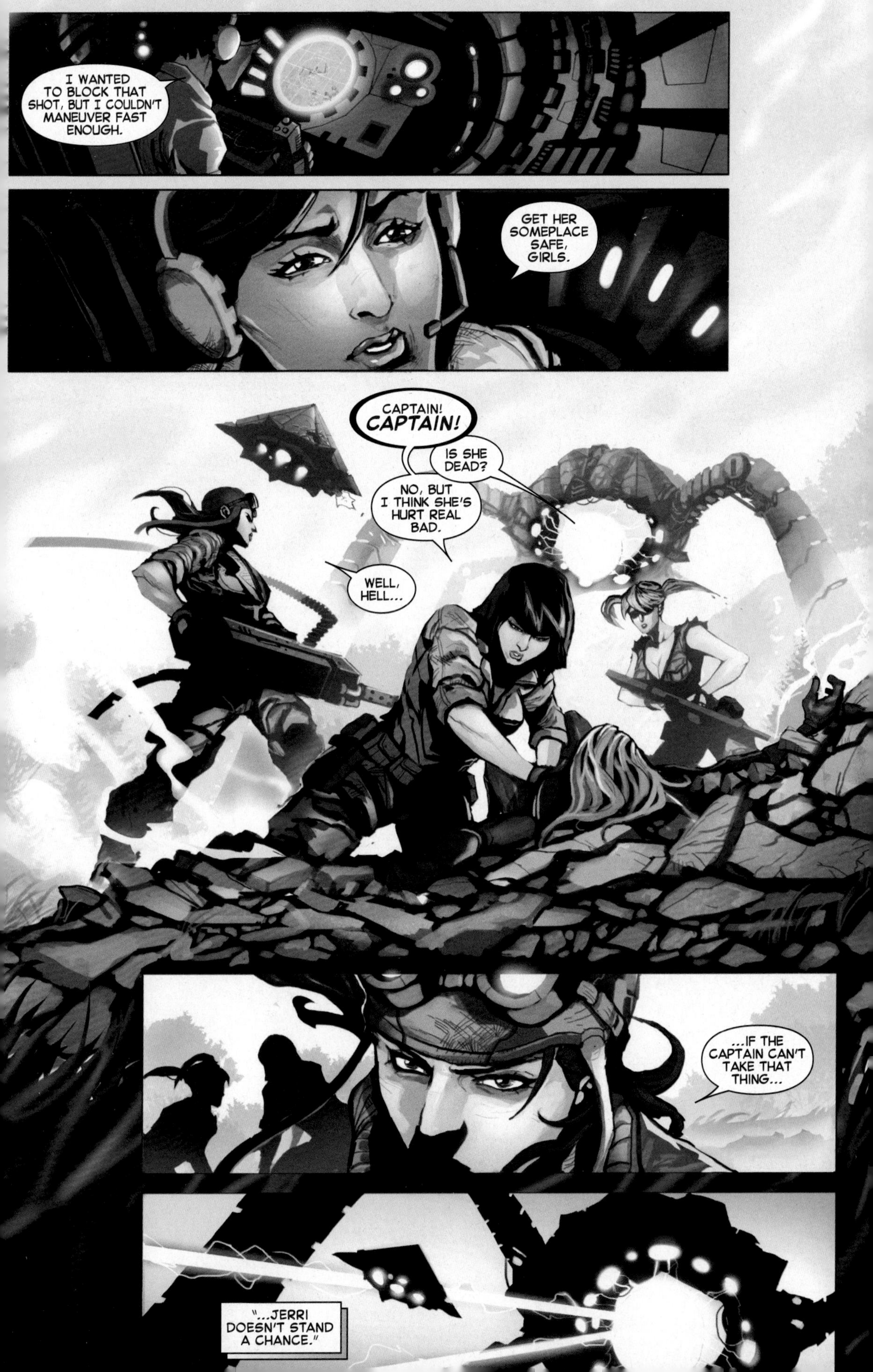
I WANTED TO BLOCK THAT SHOT, BUT I COULDN'T MANEUVER FAST ENOUGH.
GET HER SOMEPLACE SAFE, GIRLS.
CAPTAIN! CAPTAIN!
IS SHE DEAD?
NO, BUT I THINK SHE'S HURT REAL BAD.
WELL, HELL...
...IF THE CAPTAIN CAN'T TAKE THAT THING...
"...JERRI DOESN'T STAND A CHANCE."

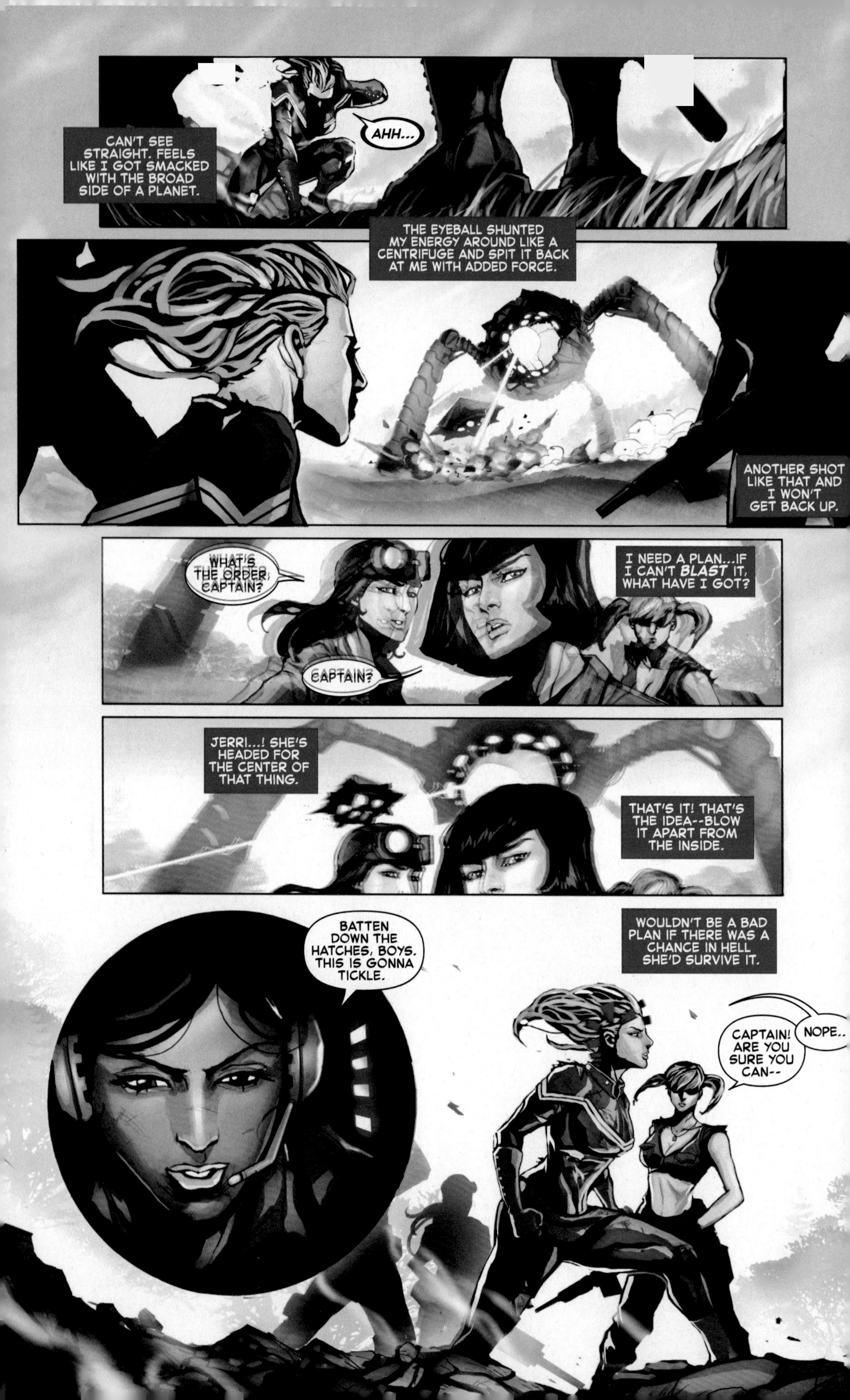
CAN'T SEE STRAIGHT. FEELS LIKE I GOT SMACKED WITH THE BROAD SIDE OF A PLANET.
AHH...
THE EYEBALL SHUNTED MY ENERGY AROUND LIKE A CENTRIFUGE AND SPIT IT BACK AT ME WITH ADDED FORCE.
ANOTHER SHOT LIKE THAT AND I WON'T GET BACK UP.
WHAT'S THE ORDER, CAPTAIN?
I NEED A PLAN...IF I CAN'T BLAST IT, WHAT HAVE I GOT?
CAPTAIN?
JERRI...! SHE'S HEADED FOR THE CENTER OF THAT THING.
THAT'S IT! THAT'S THE IDEA--BLOW IT APART FROM THE INSIDE.
BATTEN DOWN THE HATCHES, BOYS. THIS IS GONNA TICKLE.
WOULDN'T BE A BAD PLAN IF THERE WAS A CHANCE IN HELL SHE'D SURVIVE IT.
CAPTAIN! ARE YOU SURE YOU CAN--
NOPE..

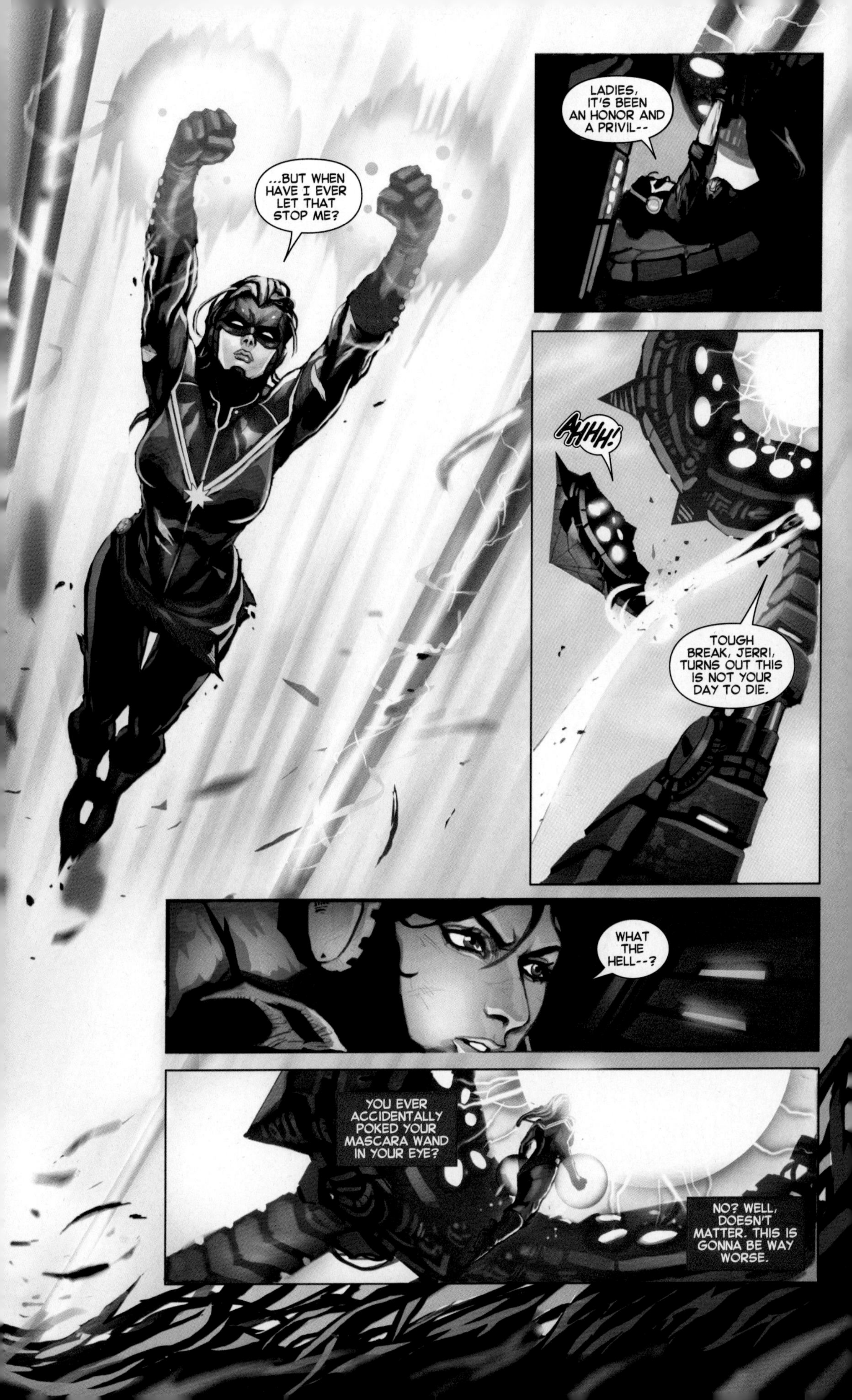
...BUT WHEN HAVE I EVER LET THAT STOP ME?
LADIES, IT'S BEEN AN HONOR AND A PRIVIL--
AHHH!
TOUGH BREAK, JERRI, TURNS OUT THIS IS NOT YOUR DAY TO DIE.
WHAT THE HELL--?
YOU EVER ACCIDENTALLY POKED YOUR MASCARA WAND IN YOUR EYE?
NO? WELL, DOESN'T MATTER. THIS IS GONNA BE WAY WORSE.

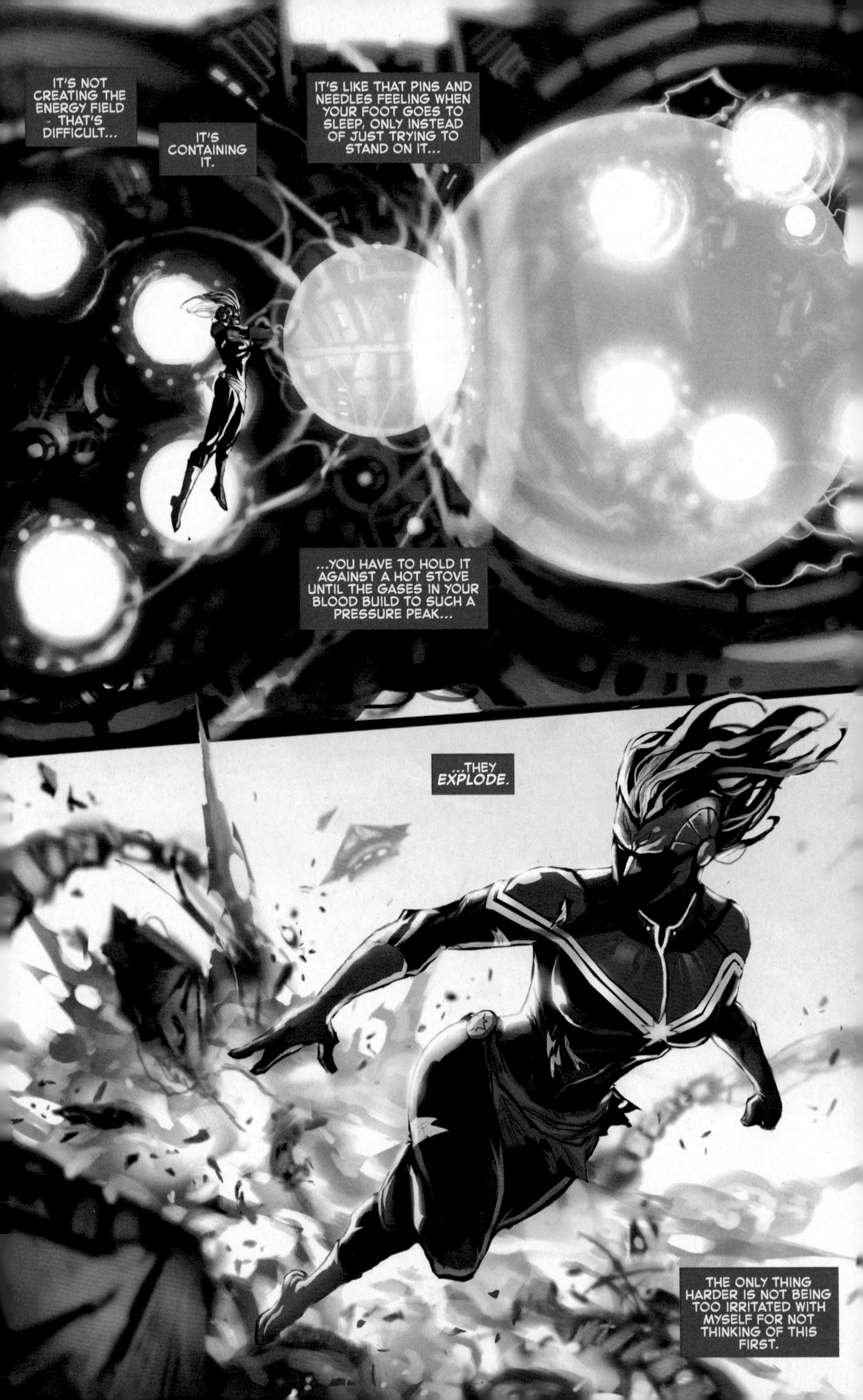
IT'S NOT CREATING THE ENERGY FIELD - THAT'S DIFFICULT...
IT'S CONTAINING IT.
IT'S LIKE THAT PINS AND NEEDLES FEELING WHEN YOUR FOOT GOES TO SLEEP, ONLY INSTEAD OF JUST TRYING TO STAND ON IT...
...YOU HAVE TO HOLD IT AGAINST A HOT STOVE UNTIL THE GASES IN YOUR BLOOD BUILD TO SUCH A PRESSURE PEAK...
...THEY *EXPLODE*.
THE ONLY THING HARDER IS NOT BEING TOO IRRITATED WITH MYSELF FOR NOT THINKING OF THIS FIRST.

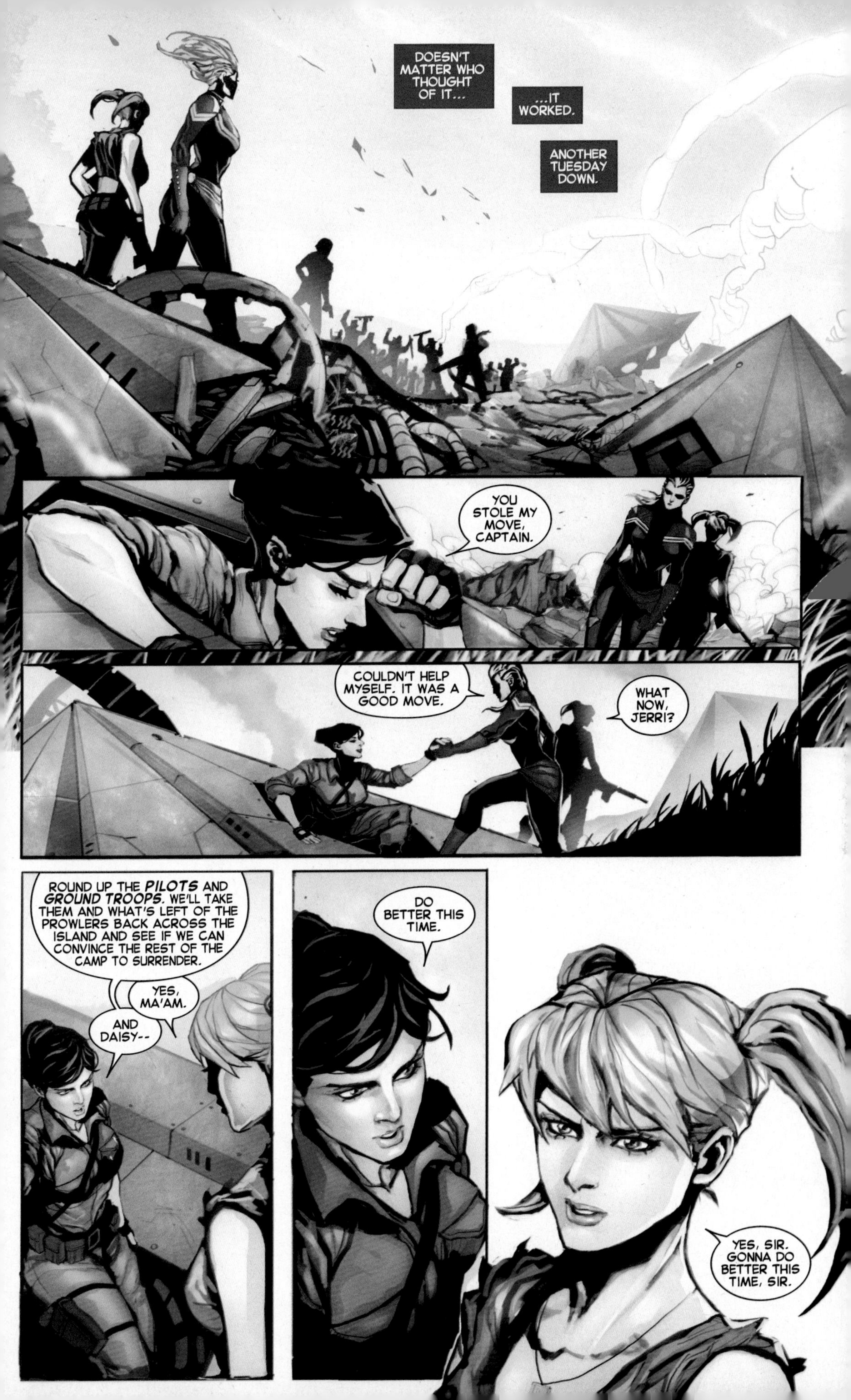
DOESN'T MATTER WHO THOUGHT OF IT...
...IT WORKED.
ANOTHER TUESDAY DOWN.
YOU STOLE MY MOVE, CAPTAIN.
COULDN'T HELP MYSELF. IT WAS A GOOD MOVE.
WHAT NOW, JERRI?
ROUND UP THE PILOTS AND GROUND TROOPS. WE'LL TAKE THEM AND WHAT'S LEFT OF THE PROWLERS BACK ACROSS THE ISLAND AND SEE IF WE CAN CONVINCE THE REST OF THE CAMP TO SURRENDER.
YES, MA'AM.
AND DAISY--
DO BETTER THIS TIME.
YES, SIR. GONNA DO BETTER THIS TIME, SIR.

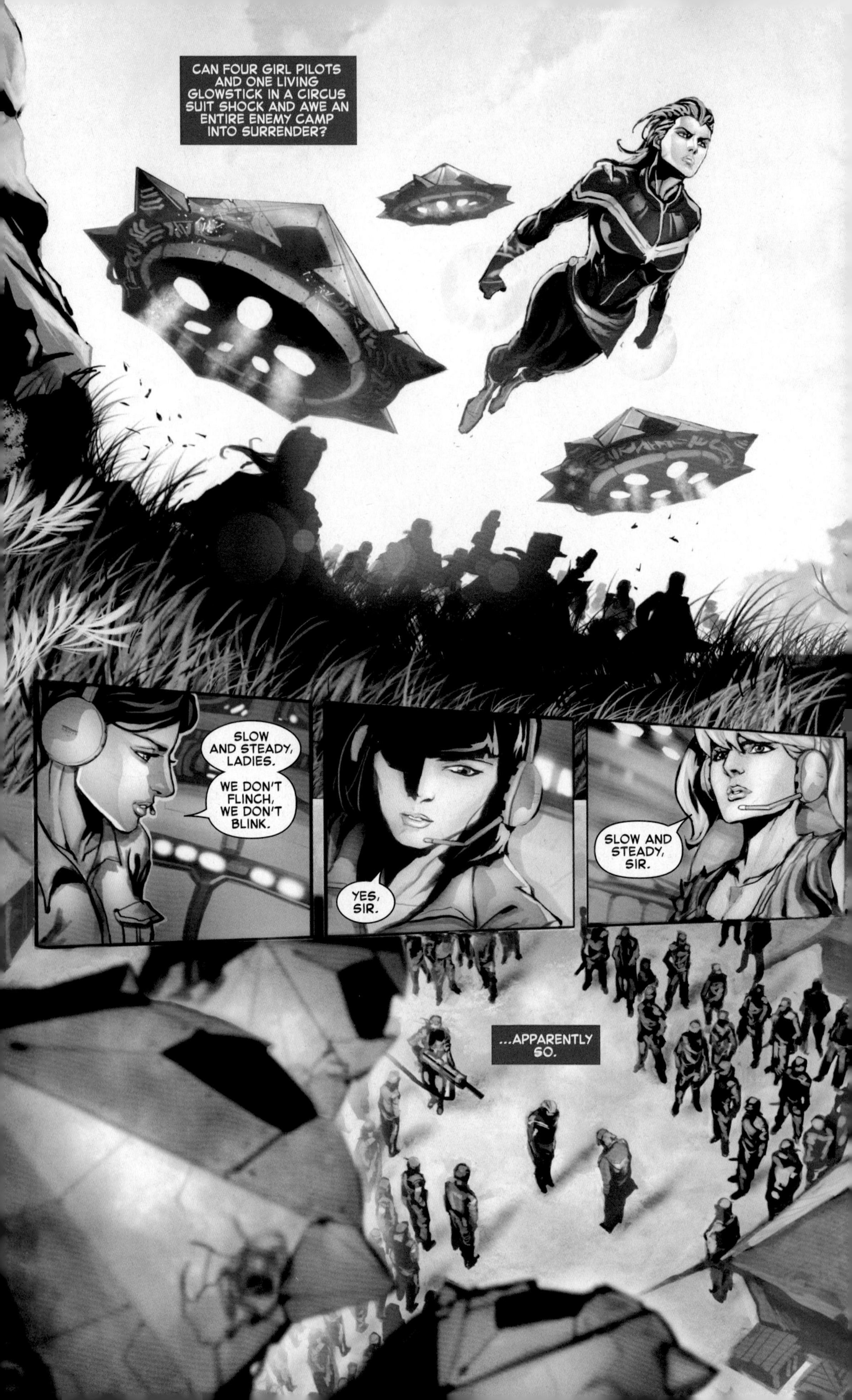
CAN FOUR GIRL PILOTS AND ONE LIVING GLOWSTICK IN A CIRCUS SUIT SHOCK AND AWE AN ENTIRE ENEMY CAMP INTO SURRENDER?
SLOW AND STEADY, LADIES.
WE DON'T FLINCH, WE DON'T BLINK.
YES, SIR.
SLOW AND STEADY, SIR.
...APPARENTLY SO.

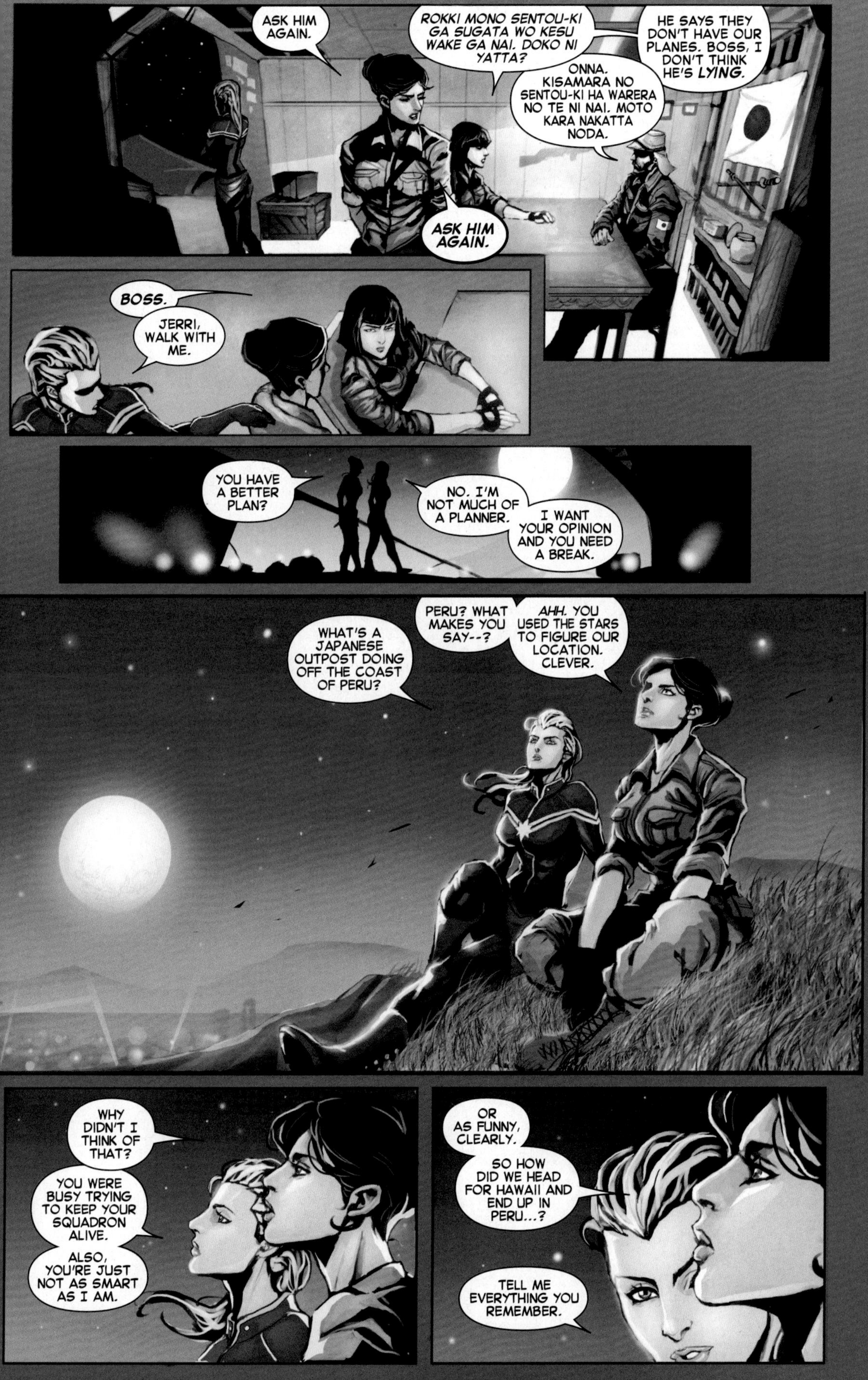
ASK HIM AGAIN.
ROKKI MONO SENTOU-KI GA SUGATA WO KESU WAKE GA NAI. DOKO NI YATTA?
HE SAYS THEY DON'T HAVE OUR PLANES. BOSS, I DON'T THINK HE'S LYING.
ONNA. KISAMARA NO SENTOU-KI HA WARERA NO TE NI NAI. MOTO KARA NAKATTA NODA.
ASK HIM AGAIN.
BOSS.
JERRI, WALK WITH ME.
YOU HAVE A BETTER PLAN?
NO. I'M NOT MUCH OF A PLANNER.
I WANT YOUR OPINION AND YOU NEED A BREAK.
WHAT'S A JAPANESE OUTPOST DOING OFF THE COAST OF PERU?
PERU? WHAT MAKES YOU SAY--?
AHH. YOU USED THE STARS TO FIGURE OUR LOCATION. CLEVER.
WHY DIDN'T I THINK OF THAT?
YOU WERE BUSY TRYING TO KEEP YOUR SQUADRON ALIVE.
ALSO, YOU'RE JUST NOT AS SMART AS I AM.
OR AS FUNNY, CLEARLY.
SO HOW DID WE HEAD FOR HAWAII AND END UP IN PERU...?
TELL ME EVERYTHING YOU REMEMBER.

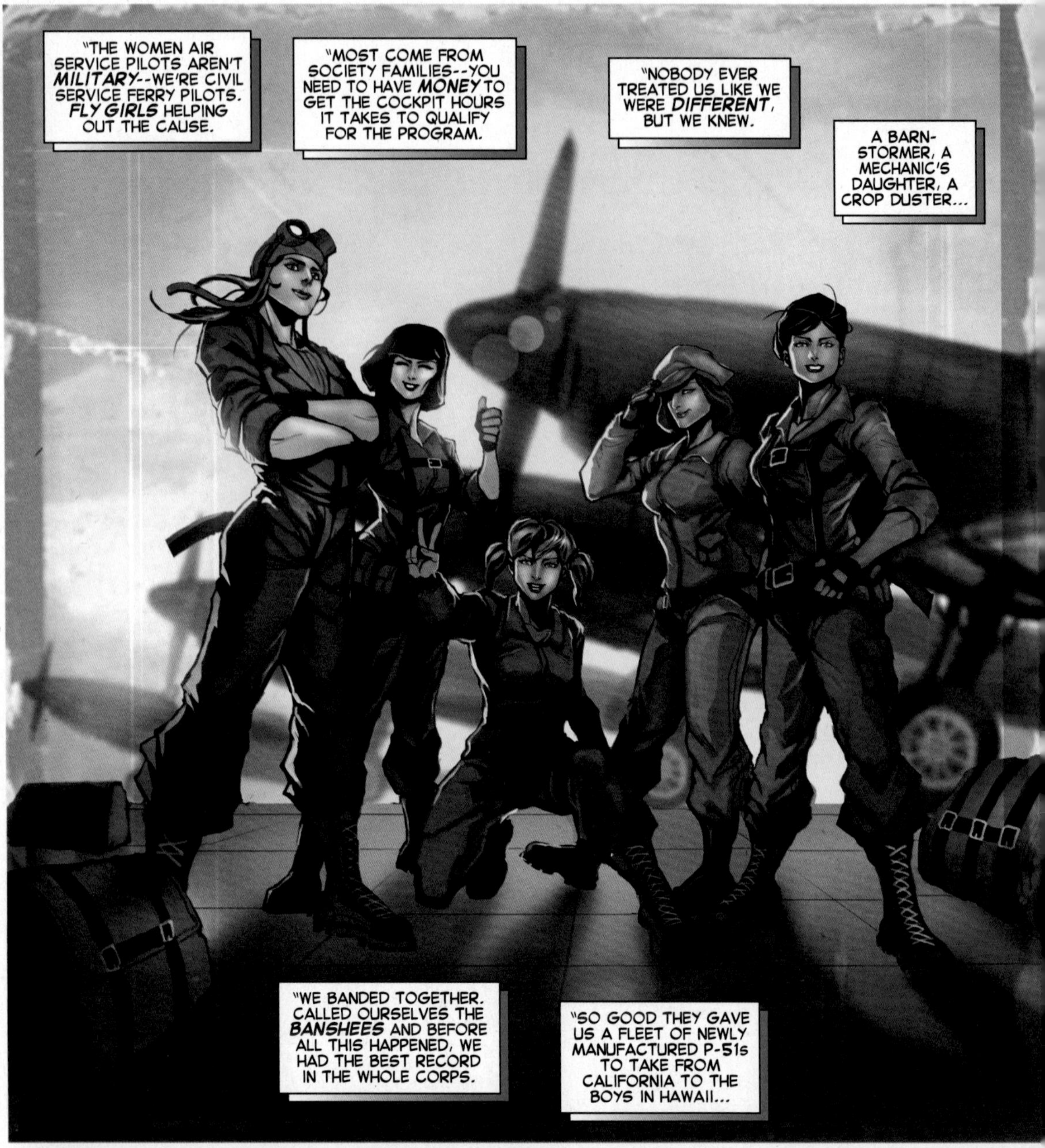
"THE WOMEN AIR SERVICE PILOTS AREN'T MILITARY--WE'RE CIVIL SERVICE FERRY PILOTS. FLY GIRLS HELPING OUT THE CAUSE.
"MOST COME FROM SOCIETY FAMILIES--YOU NEED TO HAVE MONEY TO GET THE COCKPIT HOURS IT TAKES TO QUALIFY FOR THE PROGRAM.
"NOBODY EVER TREATED US LIKE WE WERE DIFFERENT, BUT WE KNEW.
A BARN-STORMER, A MECHANIC'S DAUGHTER, A CROP DUSTER...
"WE BANDED TOGETHER. CALLED OURSELVES THE BANSHEES AND BEFORE ALL THIS HAPPENED, WE HAD THE BEST RECORD IN THE WHOLE CORPS.
"SO GOOD THEY GAVE US A FLEET OF NEWLY MANUFACTURED P-51s TO TAKE FROM CALIFORNIA TO THE BOYS IN HAWAII...

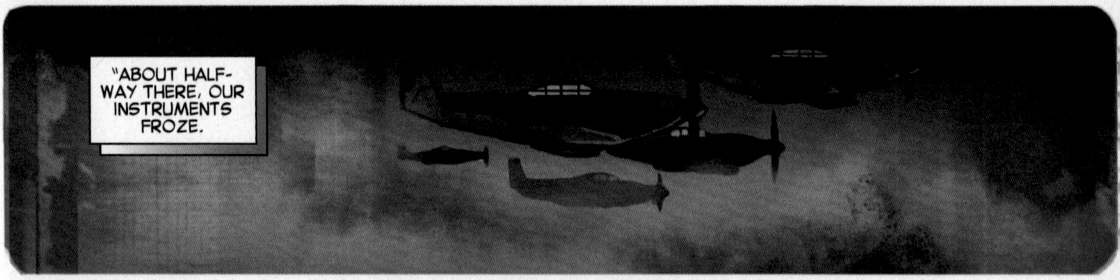
"ABOUT HALF-WAY THERE, OUR INSTRUMENTS FROZE.

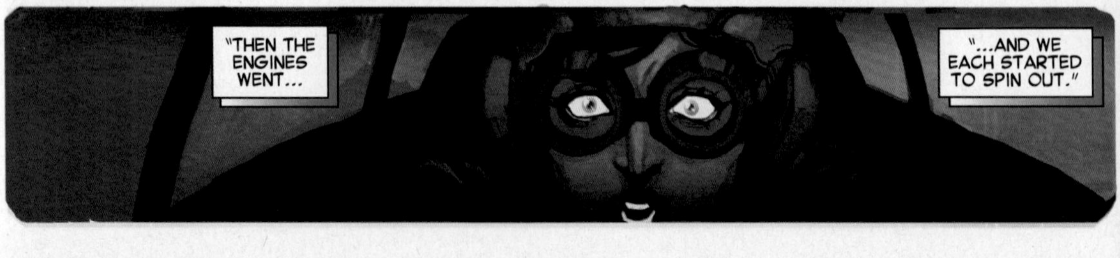
"THEN THE ENGINES WENT...
"...AND WE EACH STARTED TO SPIN OUT."

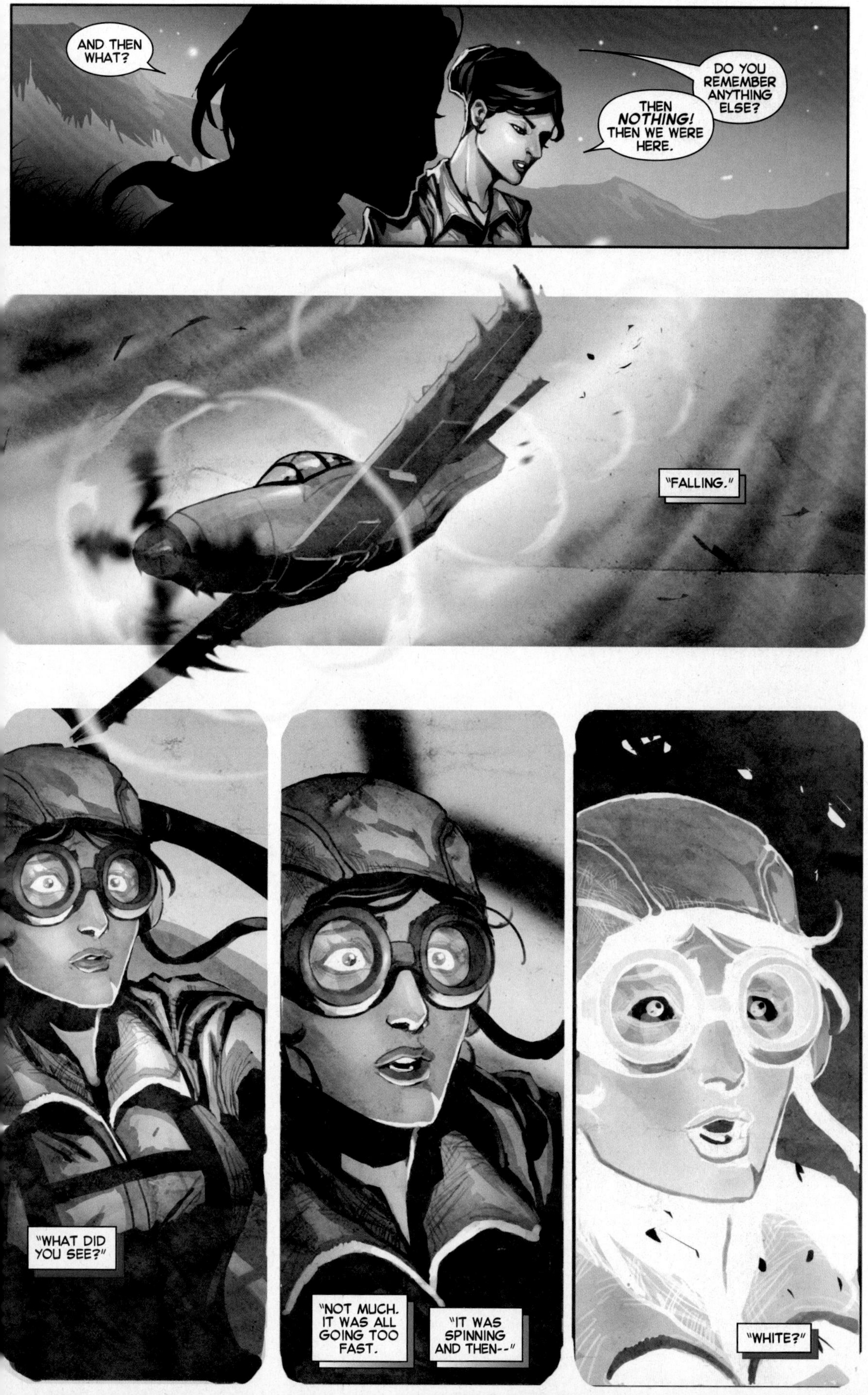
AND THEN WHAT?
DO YOU REMEMBER ANYTHING ELSE?
THEN *NOTHING!* THEN WE WERE HERE.
"FALLING."
"WHAT DID YOU SEE?"
"NOT MUCH. IT WAS ALL GOING TOO FAST.
"IT WAS SPINNING AND THEN--"
"WHITE?"

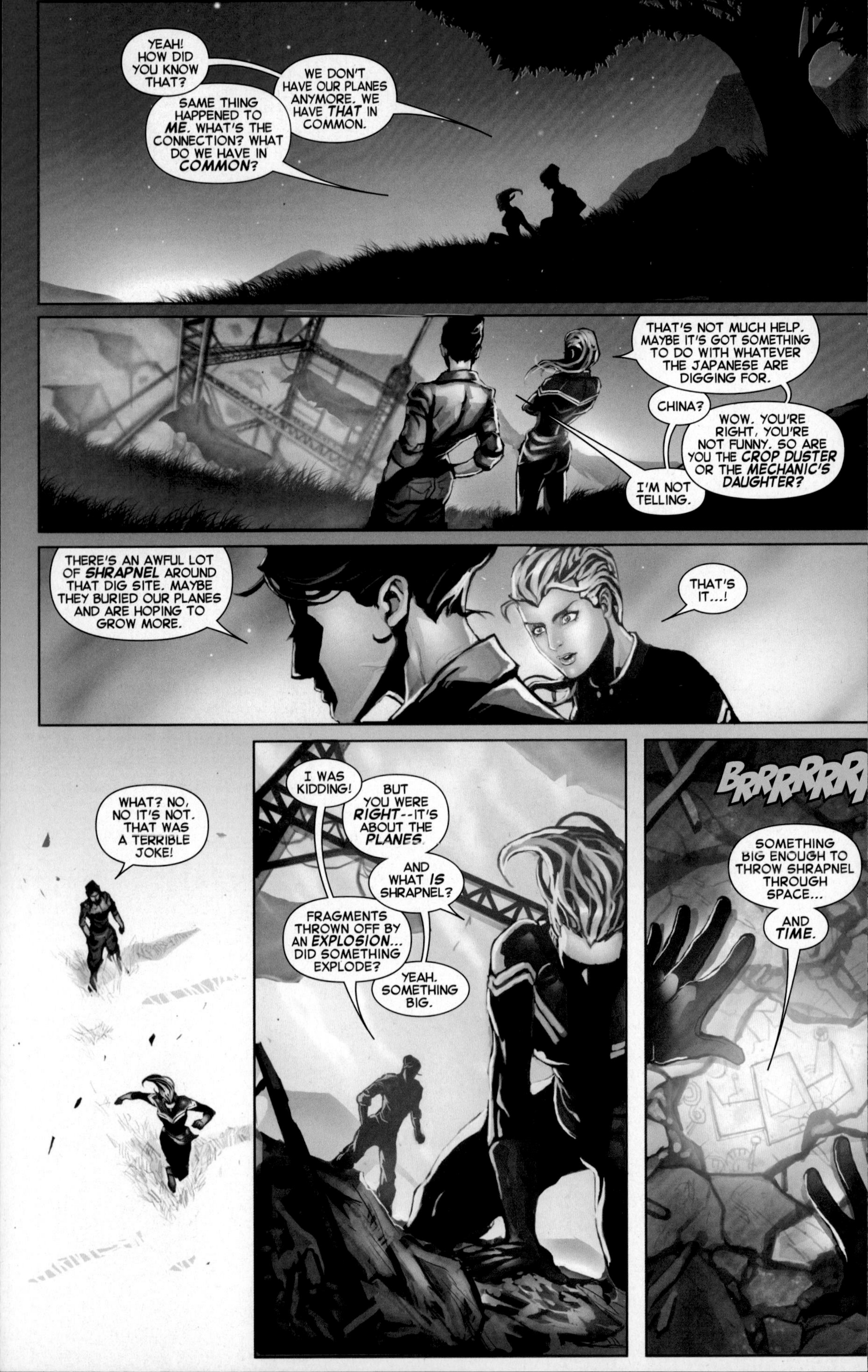
WE DON'T HAVE OUR PLANES ANYMORE. WE HAVE THAT IN COMMON.
YEAH! HOW DID YOU KNOW THAT?
SAME THING HAPPENED TO ME. WHAT'S THE CONNECTION? WHAT DO WE HAVE IN COMMON?
THAT'S NOT MUCH HELP. MAYBE IT'S GOT SOMETHING TO DO WITH WHATEVER THE JAPANESE ARE DIGGING FOR.
CHINA?
WOW. YOU'RE RIGHT, YOU'RE NOT FUNNY. SO ARE YOU THE CROP DUSTER OR THE MECHANIC'S DAUGHTER?
I'M NOT TELLING.
THERE'S AN AWFUL LOT OF SHRAPNEL AROUND THAT DIG SITE. MAYBE THEY BURIED OUR PLANES AND ARE HOPING TO GROW MORE.
THAT'S IT...!
WHAT? NO, NO IT'S NOT. THAT WAS A TERRIBLE JOKE!
I WAS KIDDING!
BUT YOU WERE RIGHT--IT'S ABOUT THE PLANES.
AND WHAT IS SHRAPNEL?
FRAGMENTS THROWN OFF BY AN EXPLOSION... DID SOMETHING EXPLODE?
YEAH. SOMETHING BIG.
BRRRRRR
SOMETHING BIG ENOUGH TO THROW SHRAPNEL THROUGH SPACE...
AND TIME.

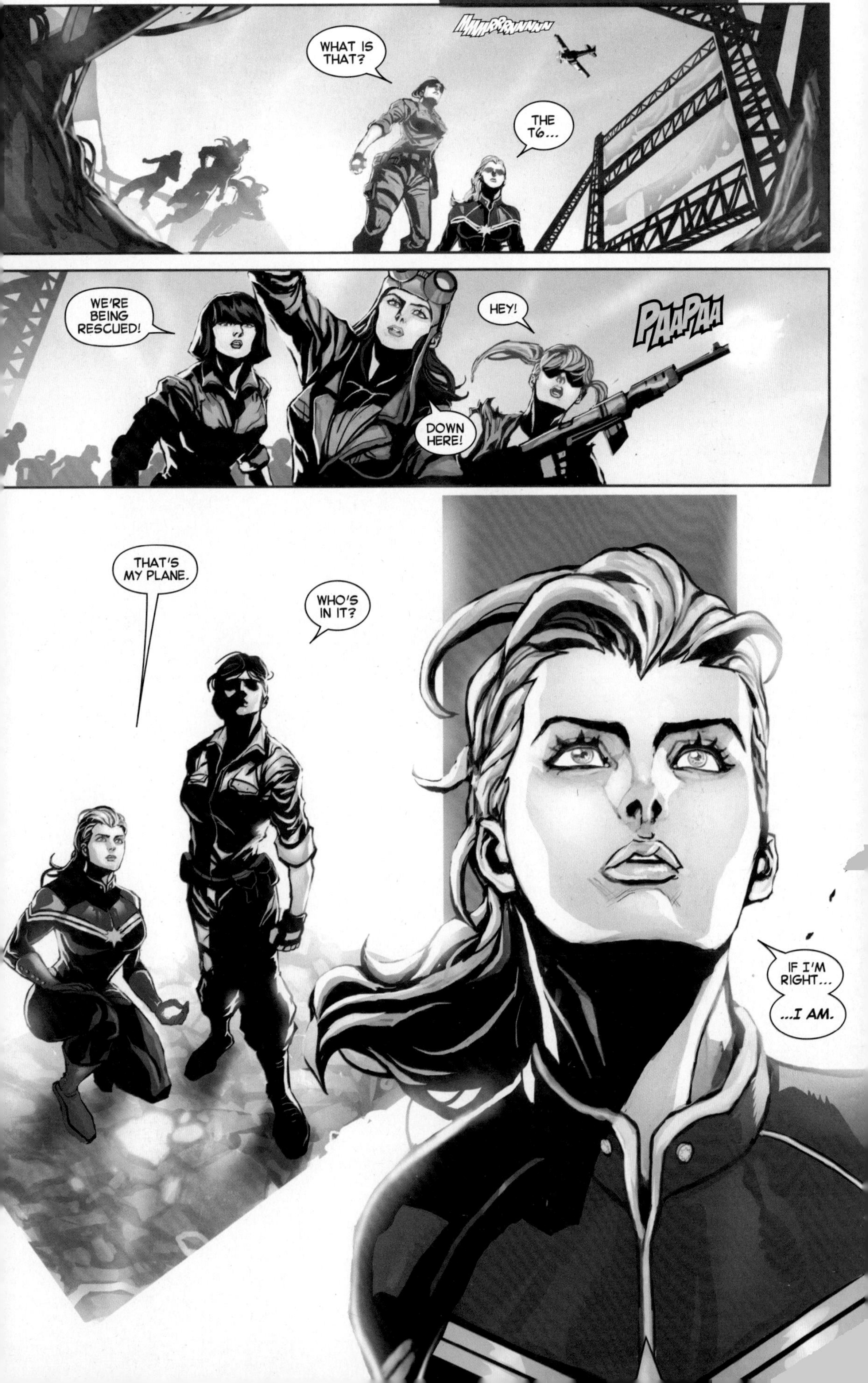
MMMRRRRNNNNN
WHAT IS THAT?
THE T6...
WE'RE BEING RESCUED!
HEY!
PAAPAA
DOWN HERE!
THAT'S MY PLANE.
WHO'S IN IT?
IF I'M RIGHT...
...I AM.

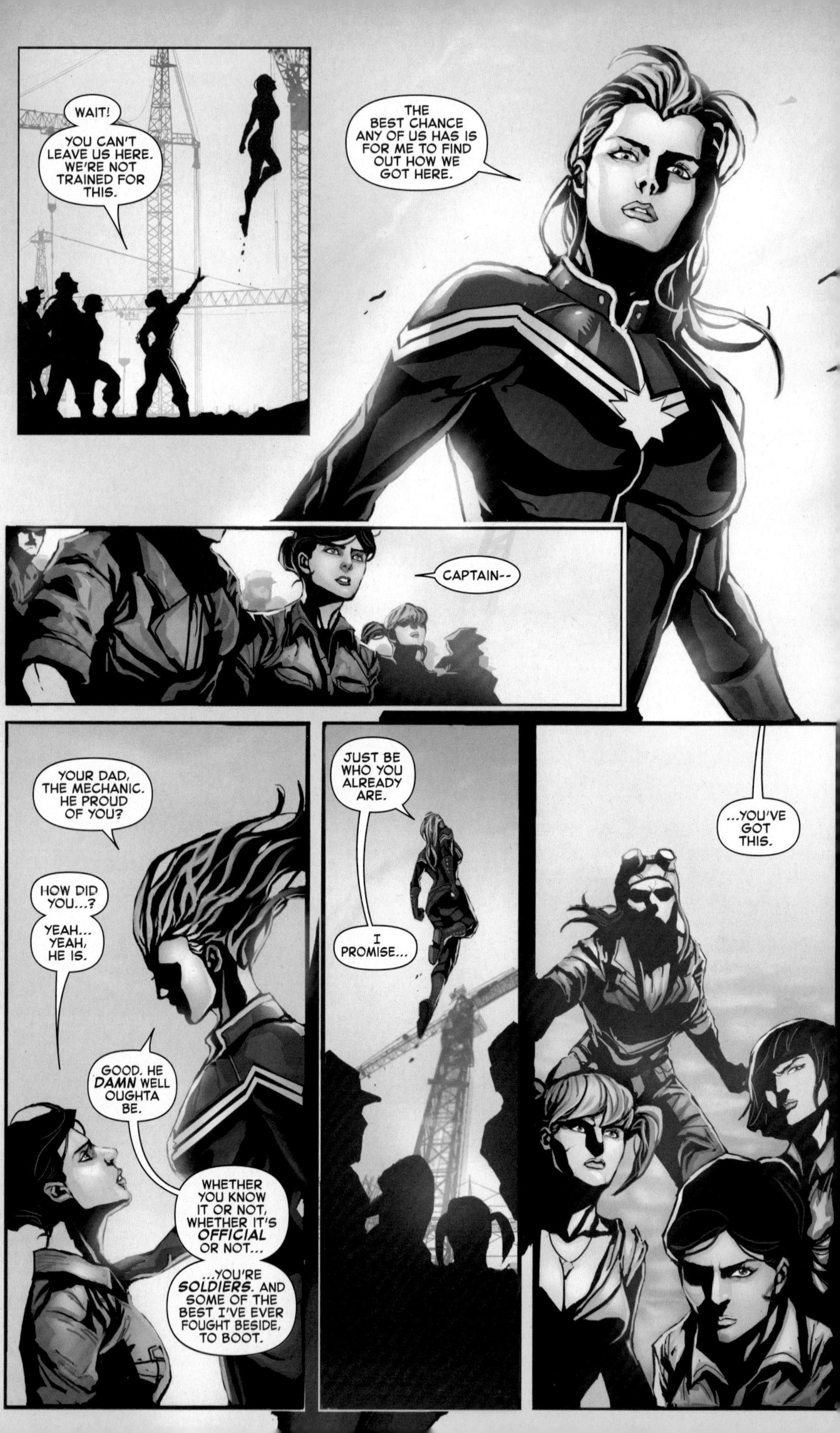
WAIT!
YOU CAN'T LEAVE US HERE. WE'RE NOT TRAINED FOR THIS.
THE BEST CHANCE ANY OF US HAS IS FOR ME TO FIND OUT HOW WE GOT HERE.
CAPTAIN--
YOUR DAD, THE MECHANIC. HE PROUD OF YOU?
HOW DID YOU...?
YEAH... YEAH, HE IS.
GOOD. HE DAMN WELL OUGHTA BE.
WHETHER YOU KNOW IT OR NOT, WHETHER IT'S OFFICIAL OR NOT...
...YOU'RE SOLDIERS. AND SOME OF THE BEST I'VE EVER FOUGHT BESIDE, TO BOOT.
JUST BE WHO YOU ALREADY ARE.
I PROMISE...
...YOU'VE GOT THIS.

HELEN COBB, WHAT KIND OF PANDORA'S BOX DID YOU LEAVE ME WHEN YOU LEFT ME YOUR PLANE?

WHAT'S THE SECRET HIDDEN INSIDE?

WHAT DID YOU DO TO ME...

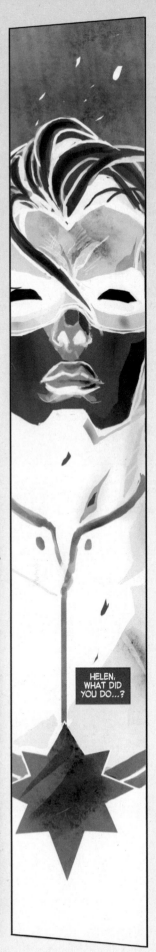

HELEN, WHAT DID YOU DO...?

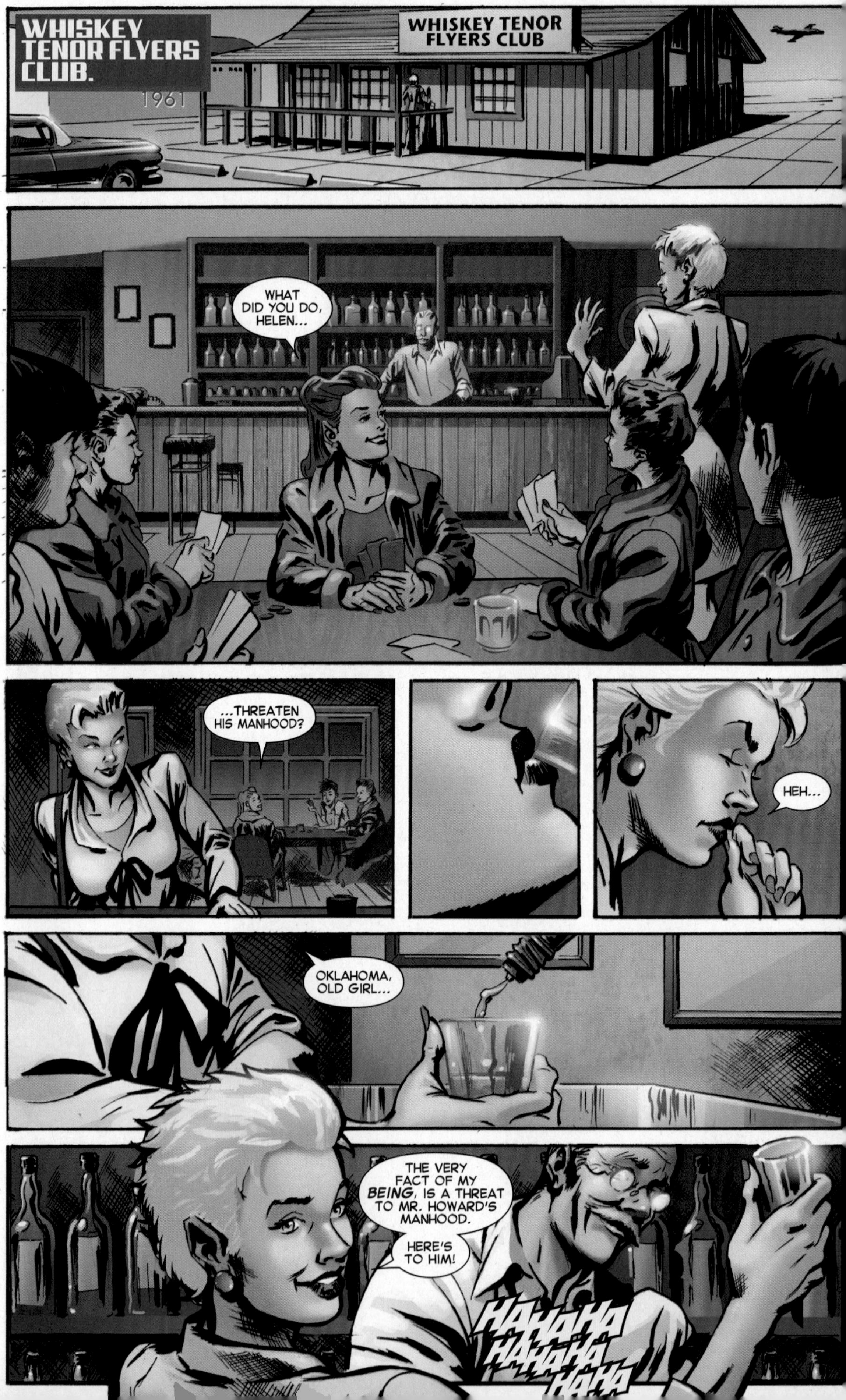
WHISKEY TENOR FLYERS CLUB.
1961
WHISKEY TENOR FLYERS CLUB
WHAT DID YOU DO, HELEN...
...THREATEN HIS MANHOOD?
HEH...
OKLAHOMA, OLD GIRL...
THE VERY FACT OF MY BEING, IS A THREAT TO MR. HOWARD'S MANHOOD.
HERE'S TO HIM!
HAHAHA HAHAHA HAHA

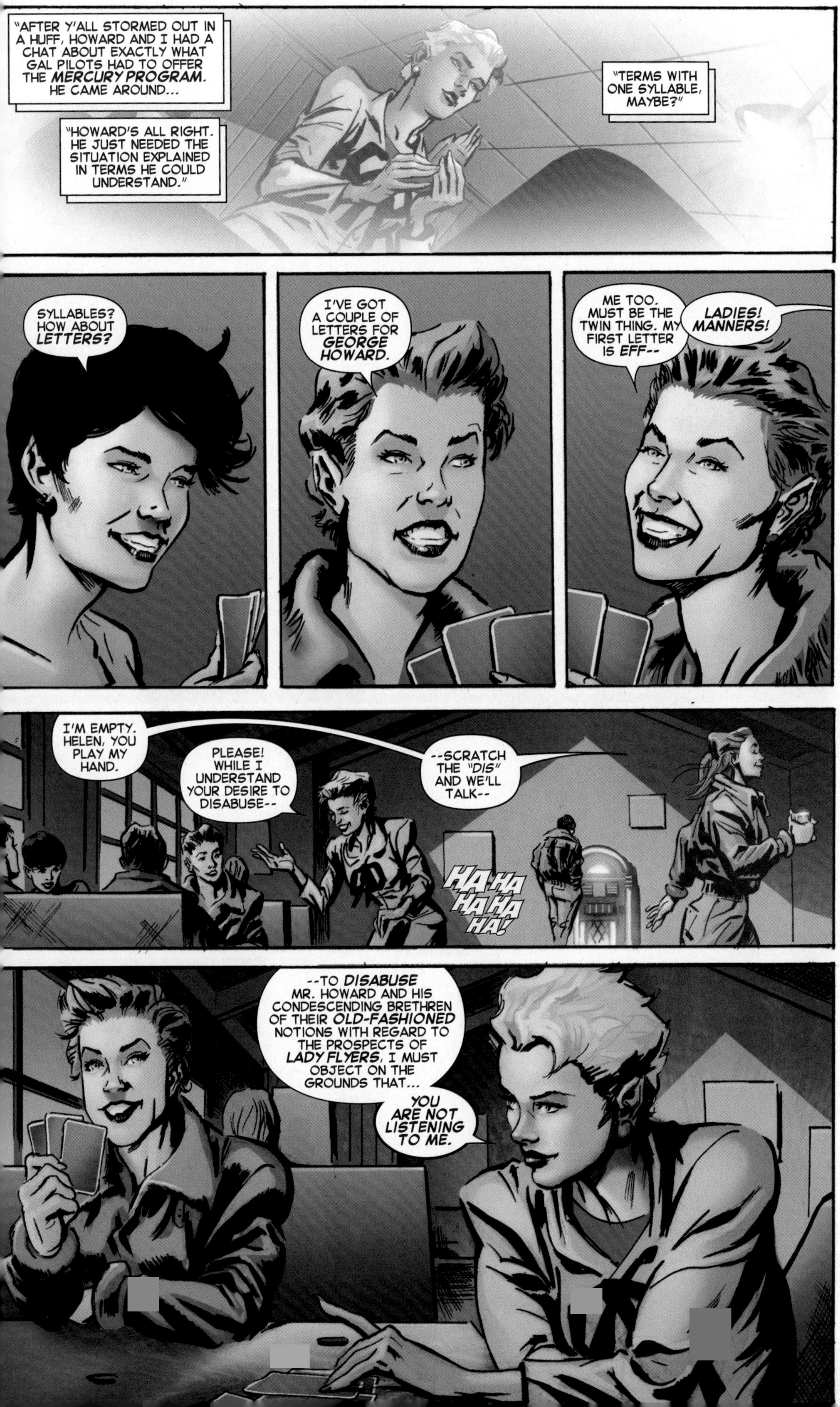
"AFTER Y'ALL STORMED OUT IN A HUFF, HOWARD AND I HAD A CHAT ABOUT EXACTLY WHAT GAL PILOTS HAD TO OFFER THE MERCURY PROGRAM. HE CAME AROUND...
"HOWARD'S ALL RIGHT. HE JUST NEEDED THE SITUATION EXPLAINED IN TERMS HE COULD UNDERSTAND."
"TERMS WITH ONE SYLLABLE, MAYBE?"
SYLLABLES? HOW ABOUT LETTERS?
I'VE GOT A COUPLE OF LETTERS FOR GEORGE HOWARD.
ME TOO. MUST BE THE TWIN THING. MY FIRST LETTER IS EFF--
LADIES! MANNERS!
I'M EMPTY. HELEN, YOU PLAY MY HAND.
PLEASE! WHILE I UNDERSTAND YOUR DESIRE TO DISABUSE--
--SCRATCH THE "DIS" AND WE'LL TALK--
HA-HA HA HA HA HA!
--TO DISABUSE MR. HOWARD AND HIS CONDESCENDING BRETHREN OF THEIR OLD-FASHIONED NOTIONS WITH REGARD TO THE PROSPECTS OF LADY FLYERS, I MUST OBJECT ON THE GROUNDS THAT...
YOU ARE NOT LISTENING TO ME.

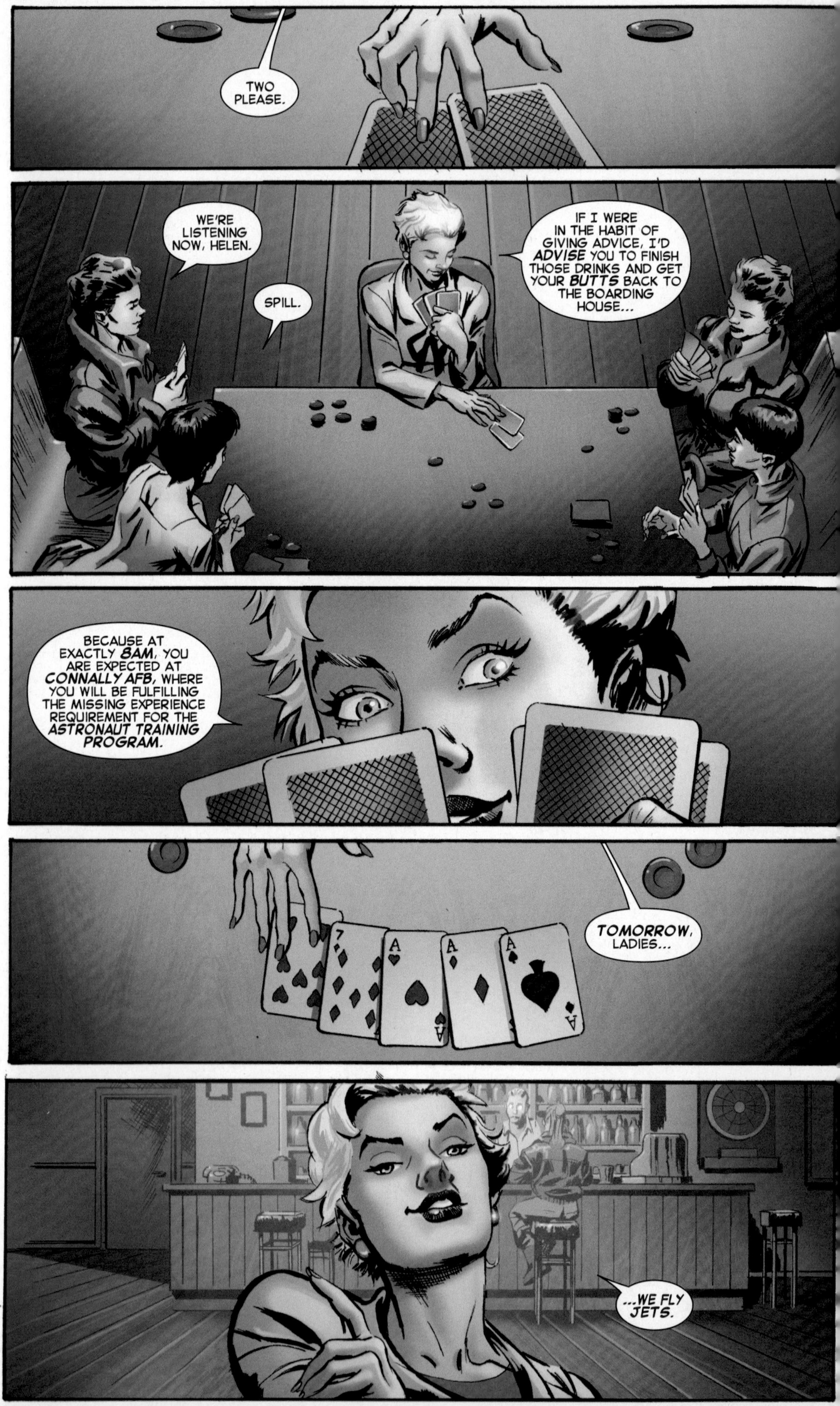
TWO PLEASE.
WE'RE LISTENING NOW, HELEN.
SPILL.
IF I WERE IN THE HABIT OF GIVING ADVICE, I'D ADVISE YOU TO FINISH THOSE DRINKS AND GET YOUR BUTTS BACK TO THE BOARDING HOUSE...
BECAUSE AT EXACTLY 8AM, YOU ARE EXPECTED AT CONNALLY AFB, WHERE YOU WILL BE FULFILLING THE MISSING EXPERIENCE REQUIREMENT FOR THE ASTRONAUT TRAINING PROGRAM.
TOMORROW, LADIES...
...WE FLY JETS.

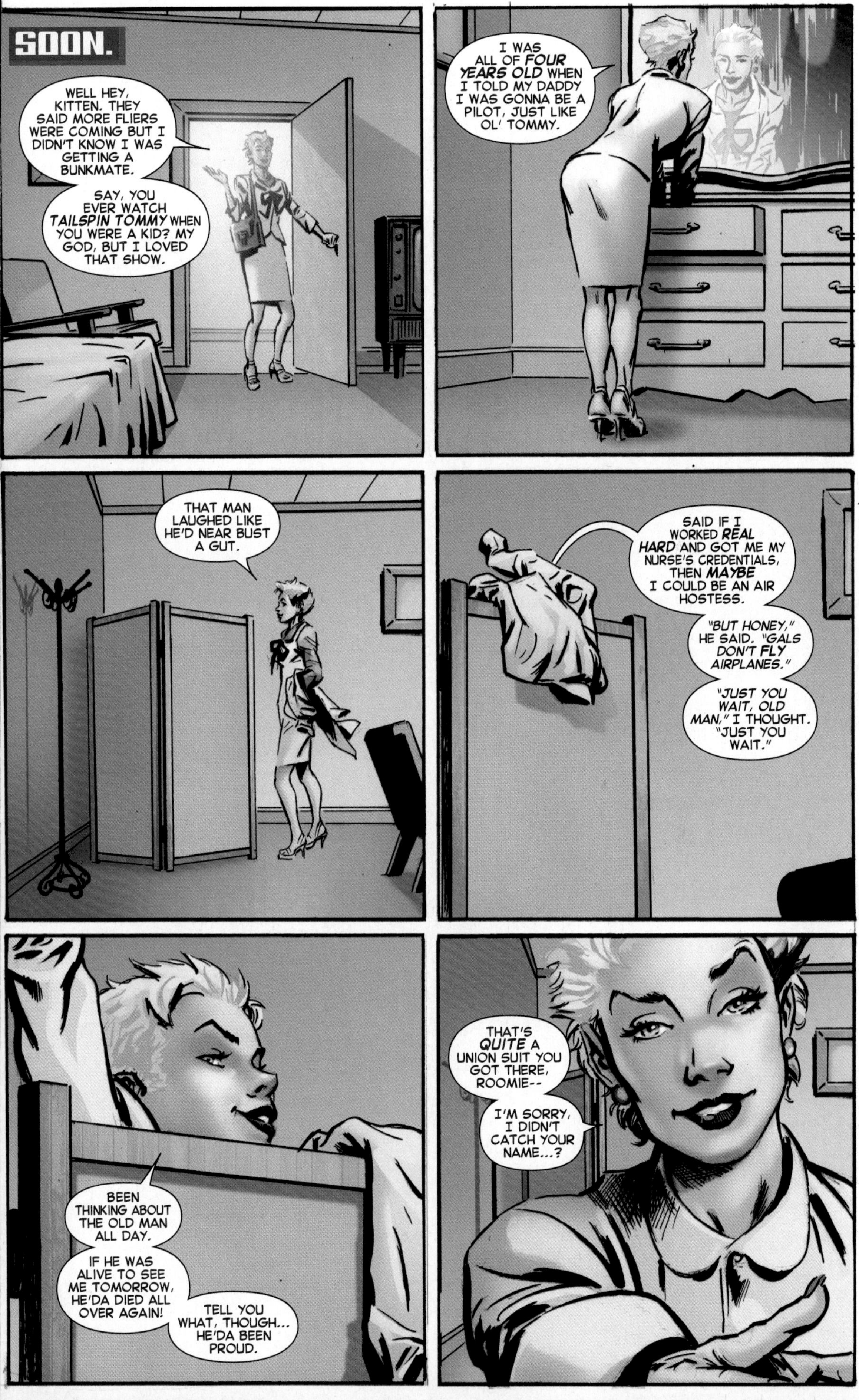
SOON.
WELL HEY, KITTEN. THEY SAID MORE FLIERS WERE COMING BUT I DIDN'T KNOW I WAS GETTING A BUNKMATE.
SAY, YOU EVER WATCH TAILSPIN TOMMY WHEN YOU WERE A KID? MY GOD, BUT I LOVED THAT SHOW.
I WAS ALL OF FOUR YEARS OLD WHEN I TOLD MY DADDY I WAS GONNA BE A PILOT, JUST LIKE OL' TOMMY.
THAT MAN LAUGHED LIKE HE'D NEAR BUST A GUT.
SAID IF I WORKED REAL HARD AND GOT ME MY NURSE'S CREDENTIALS, THEN MAYBE I COULD BE AN AIR HOSTESS.
"BUT HONEY," HE SAID. "GALS DON'T FLY AIRPLANES."
"JUST YOU WAIT, OLD MAN," I THOUGHT. "JUST YOU WAIT."
BEEN THINKING ABOUT THE OLD MAN ALL DAY.
IF HE WAS ALIVE TO SEE ME TOMORROW, HE'DA DIED ALL OVER AGAIN!
TELL YOU WHAT, THOUGH... HE'DA BEEN PROUD.
THAT'S QUITE A UNION SUIT YOU GOT THERE, ROOMIE--
I'M SORRY, I DIDN'T CATCH YOUR NAME...?

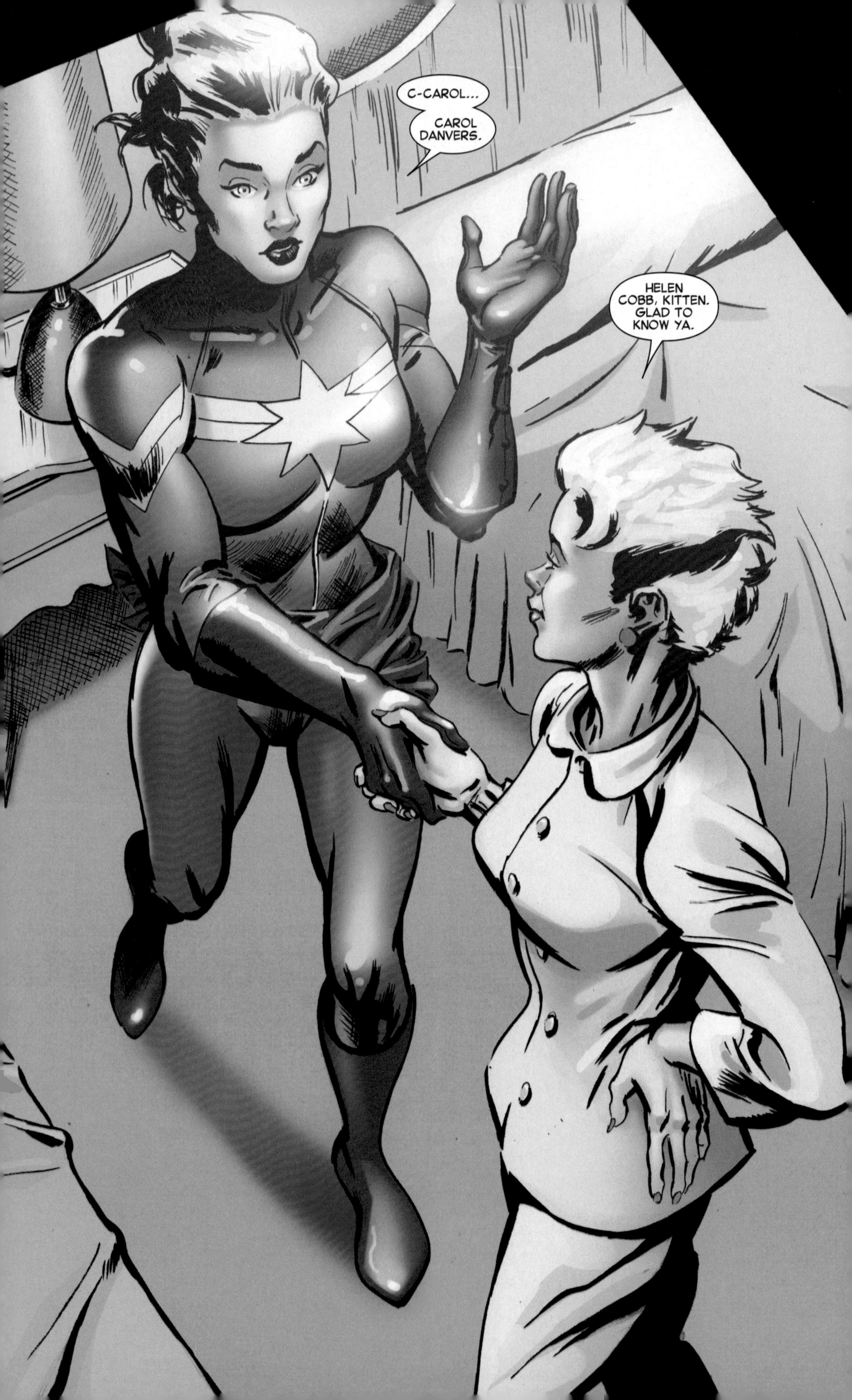
C-CAROL...
CAROL DANVERS.
HELEN COBB, KITTEN. GLAD TO KNOW YA.

CAPTAIN MARVEL #5

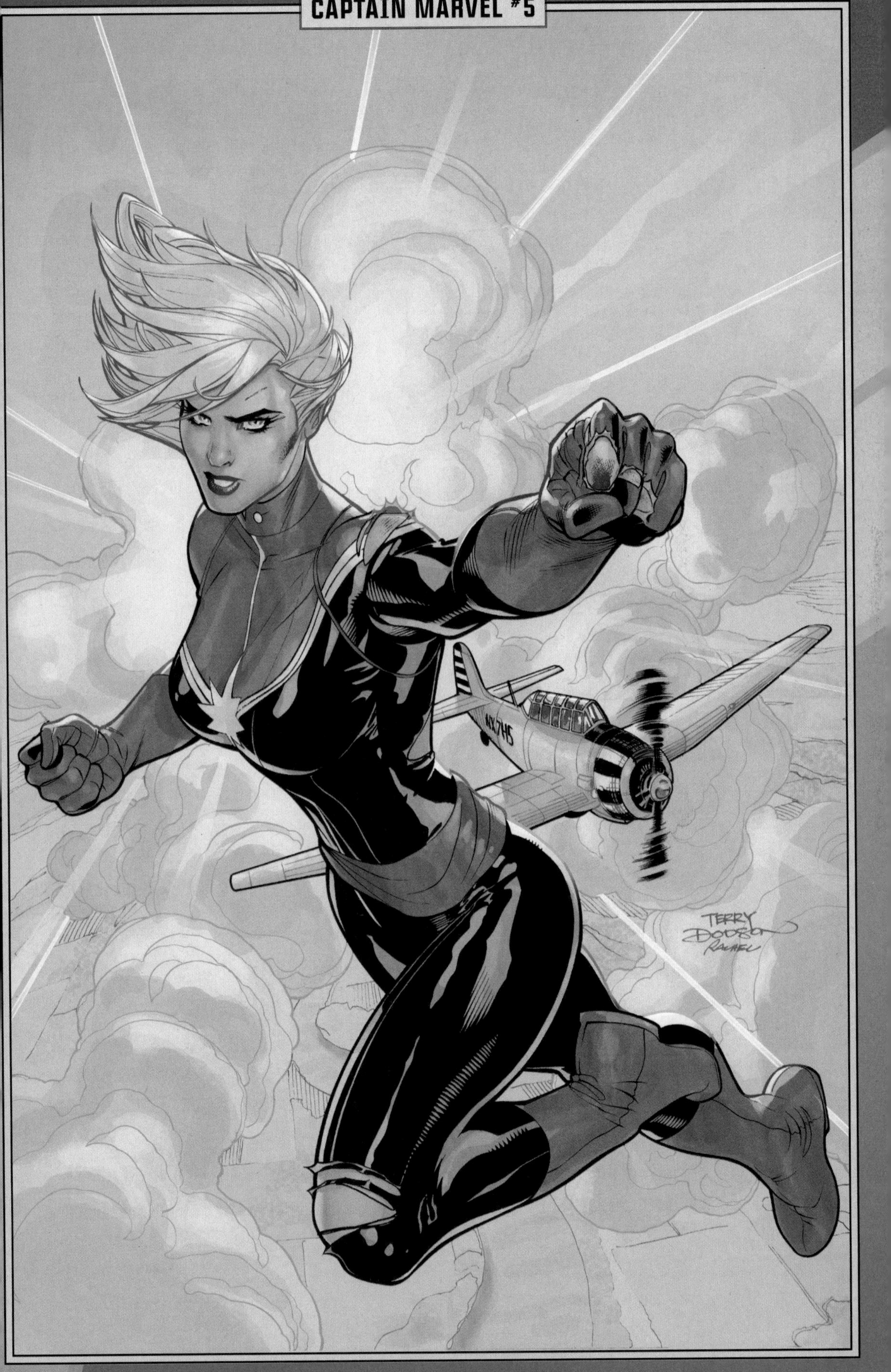
NX7H5
TERRY DODSON RACHEL

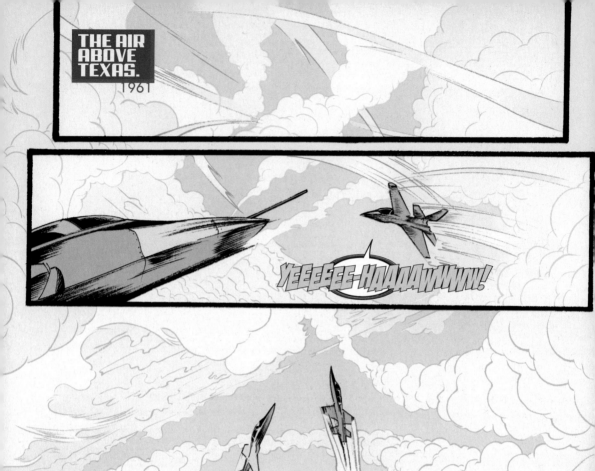

THE AIR ABOVE TEXAS. 1961

YEEEEEE-HAAAAWWWW!

I DO BELIEVE YOU'VE *GOT* ME, DANVERS.

THIS IS JUST FOR QUALIFYING JET EXPERIENCE, HELEN. IT'S *NOT* A RACE.

KEEP TELLING YOURSELF THAT.

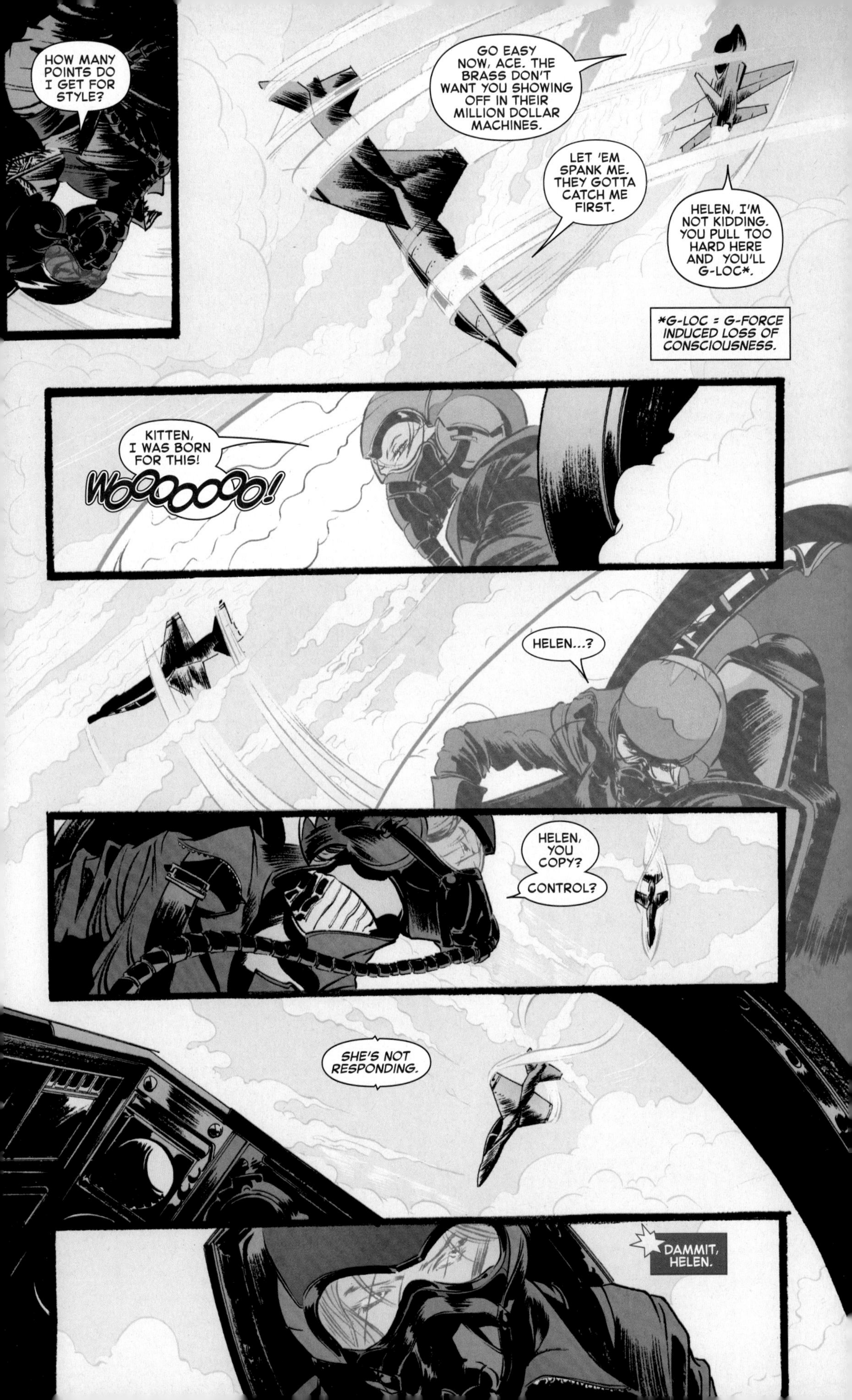
HOW MANY POINTS DO I GET FOR STYLE?
GO EASY NOW, ACE. THE BRASS DON'T WANT YOU SHOWING OFF IN THEIR MILLION DOLLAR MACHINES.
LET 'EM SPANK ME. THEY GOTTA CATCH ME FIRST.
HELEN, I'M NOT KIDDING. YOU PULL TOO HARD HERE AND YOU'LL G-LOC*.
*G-LOC = G-FORCE INDUCED LOSS OF CONSCIOUSNESS.
KITTEN, I WAS BORN FOR THIS!
WOOOOOOOO!
HELEN...?
HELEN, YOU COPY?
CONTROL?
SHE'S NOT RESPONDING.
DAMMIT, HELEN.

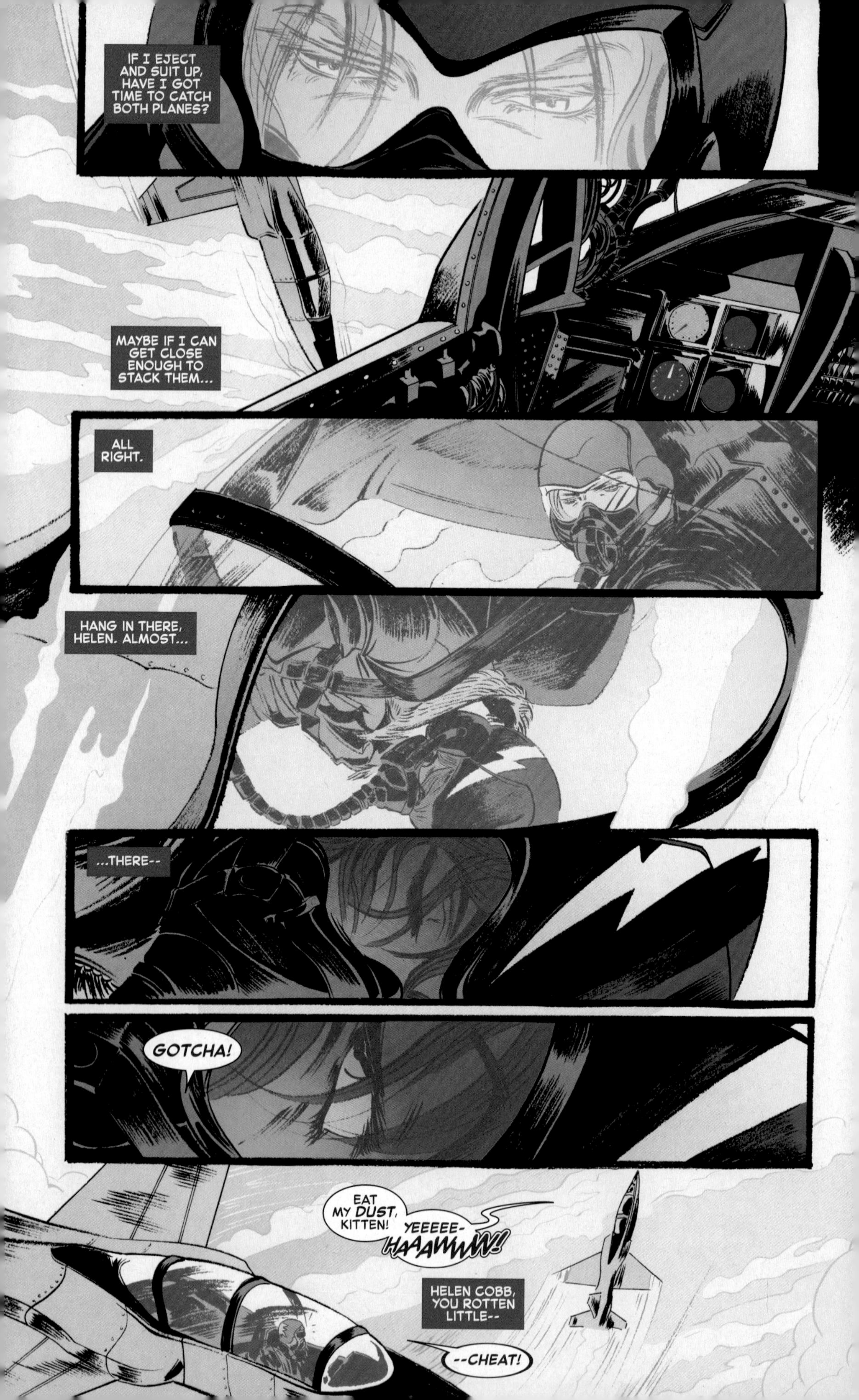
IF I EJECT AND SUIT UP, HAVE I GOT TIME TO CATCH BOTH PLANES?
MAYBE IF I CAN GET CLOSE ENOUGH TO STACK THEM...
ALL RIGHT.
HANG IN THERE, HELEN. ALMOST...
...THERE--
GOTCHA!
EAT MY DUST, KITTEN!
YEEEEE-HAAAWWW!
HELEN COBB, YOU ROTTEN LITTLE--
--CHEAT!

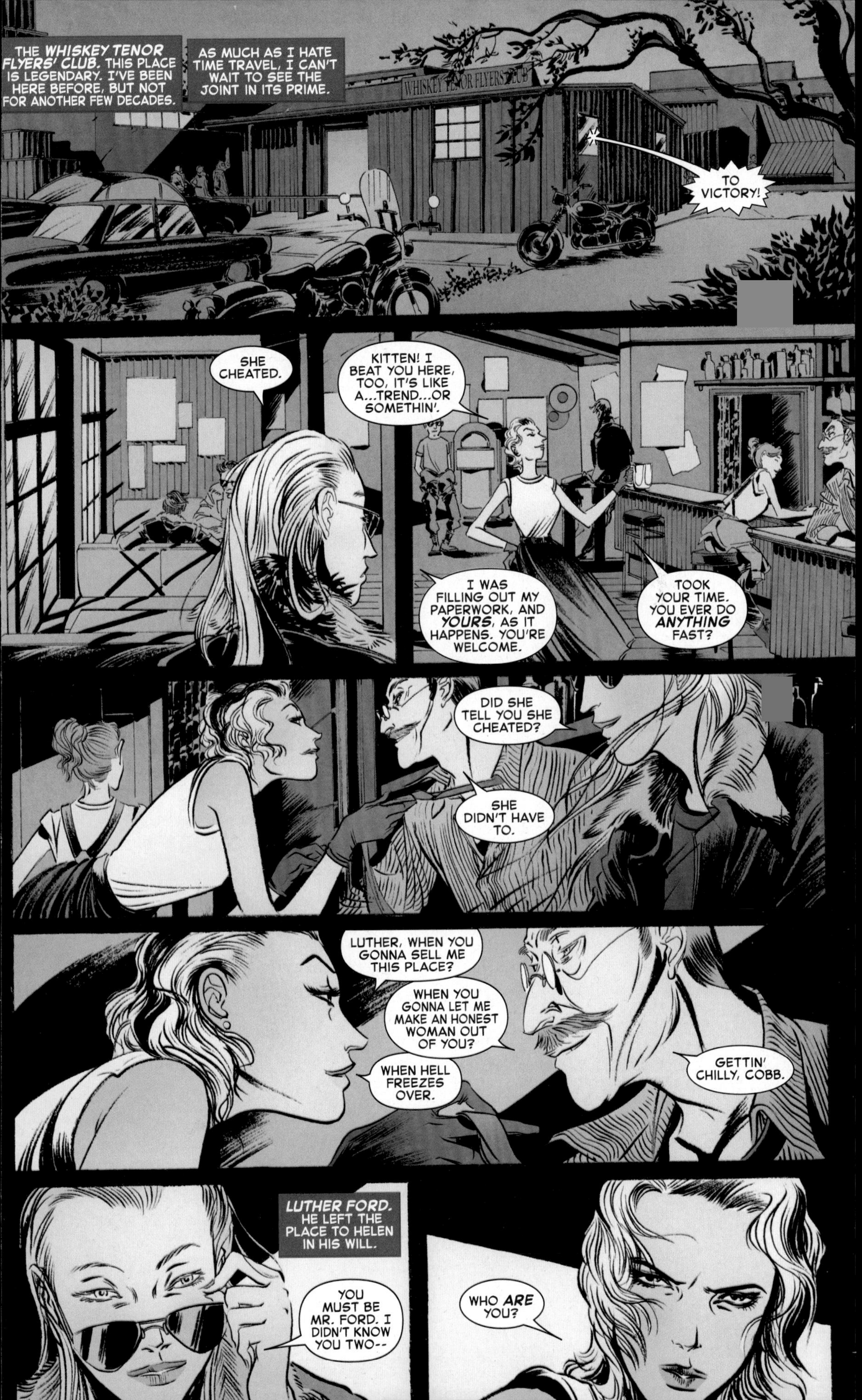
THE WHISKEY TENOR FLYERS' CLUB. THIS PLACE IS LEGENDARY. I'VE BEEN HERE BEFORE, BUT NOT FOR ANOTHER FEW DECADES.
AS MUCH AS I HATE TIME TRAVEL, I CAN'T WAIT TO SEE THE JOINT IN ITS PRIME.
WHISKEY TENOR FLYERS CLUB
TO VICTORY!
SHE CHEATED.
KITTEN! I BEAT YOU HERE, TOO. IT'S LIKE A...TREND...OR SOMETHIN'.
I WAS FILLING OUT MY PAPERWORK, AND YOURS, AS IT HAPPENS. YOU'RE WELCOME.
TOOK YOUR TIME. YOU EVER DO ANYTHING FAST?
DID SHE TELL YOU SHE CHEATED?
SHE DIDN'T HAVE TO.
LUTHER, WHEN YOU GONNA SELL ME THIS PLACE?
WHEN YOU GONNA LET ME MAKE AN HONEST WOMAN OUT OF YOU?
WHEN HELL FREEZES OVER.
GETTIN' CHILLY, COBB.
LUTHER FORD. HE LEFT THE PLACE TO HELEN IN HIS WILL.
YOU MUST BE MR. FORD. I DIDN'T KNOW YOU TWO--
WHO ARE YOU?

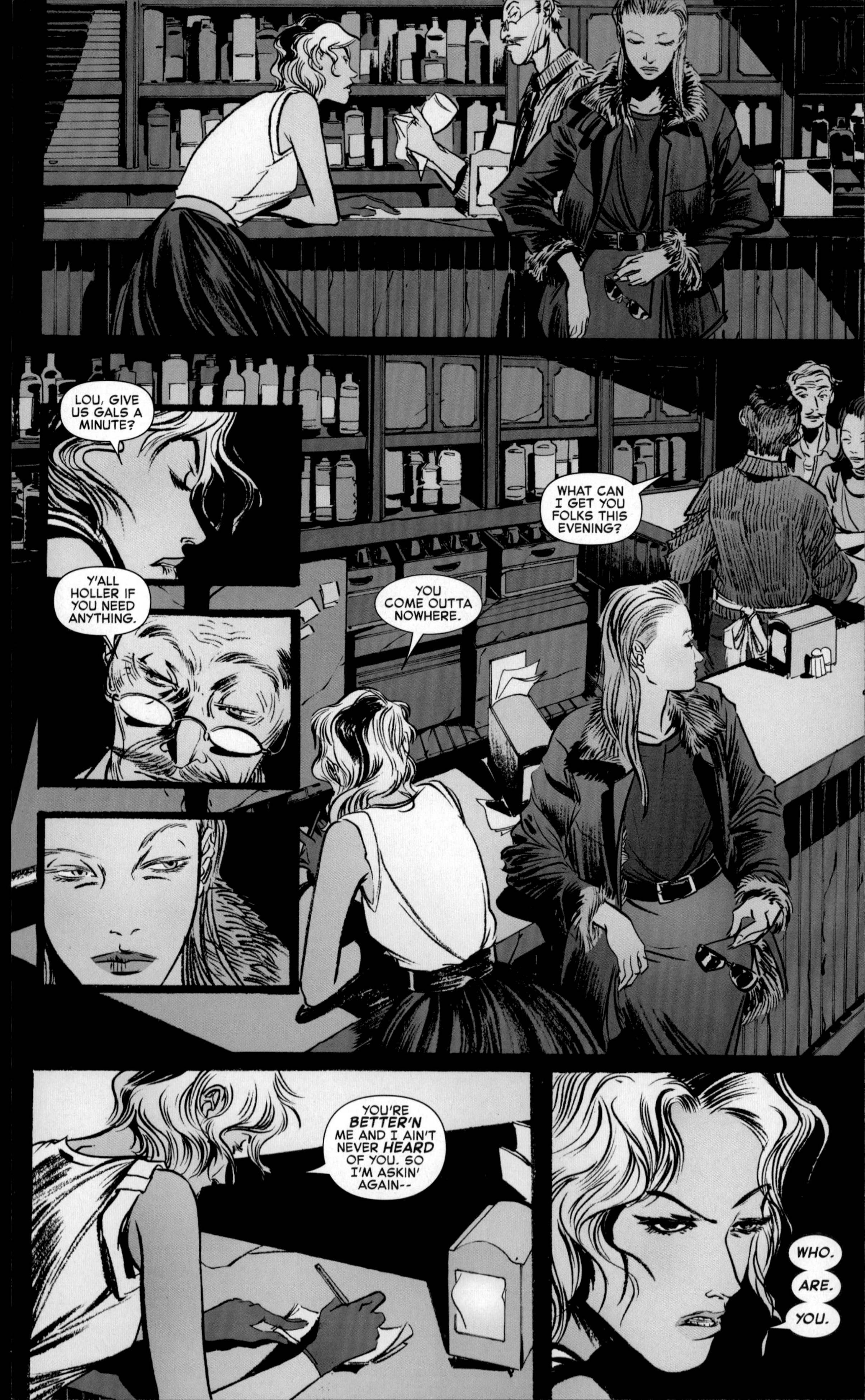
LOU, GIVE US GALS A MINUTE?
Y'ALL HOLLER IF YOU NEED ANYTHING.
YOU COME OUTTA NOWHERE.
WHAT CAN I GET YOU FOLKS THIS EVENING?
YOU'RE BETTER'N ME AND I AIN'T NEVER HEARD OF YOU. SO I'M ASKIN' AGAIN--
WHO.
ARE.
YOU.

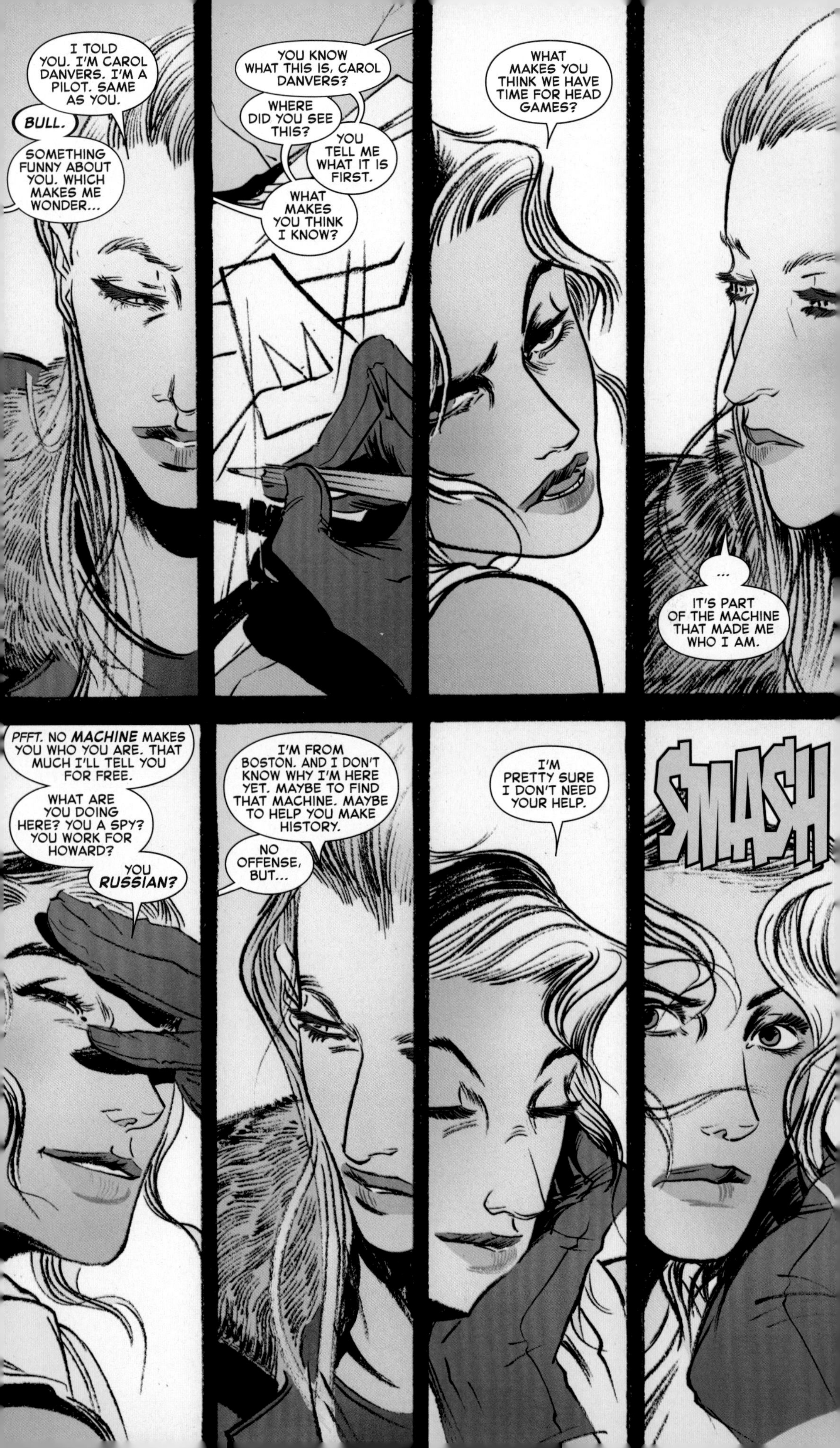
I TOLD YOU. I'M CAROL DANVERS. I'M A PILOT. SAME AS YOU.
BULL.
SOMETHING FUNNY ABOUT YOU. WHICH MAKES ME WONDER...
YOU KNOW WHAT THIS IS, CAROL DANVERS?
WHERE DID YOU SEE THIS?
YOU TELL ME WHAT IT IS FIRST.
WHAT MAKES YOU THINK I KNOW?
WHAT MAKES YOU THINK WE HAVE TIME FOR HEAD GAMES?
...
IT'S PART OF THE MACHINE THAT MADE ME WHO I AM.
PFFT. NO MACHINE MAKES YOU WHO YOU ARE. THAT MUCH I'LL TELL YOU FOR FREE.
WHAT ARE YOU DOING HERE? YOU A SPY? YOU WORK FOR HOWARD?
YOU RUSSIAN?
I'M FROM BOSTON. AND I DON'T KNOW WHY I'M HERE YET. MAYBE TO FIND THAT MACHINE. MAYBE TO HELP YOU MAKE HISTORY.
NO OFFENSE, BUT...
I'M PRETTY SURE I DON'T NEED YOUR HELP.
SMASH

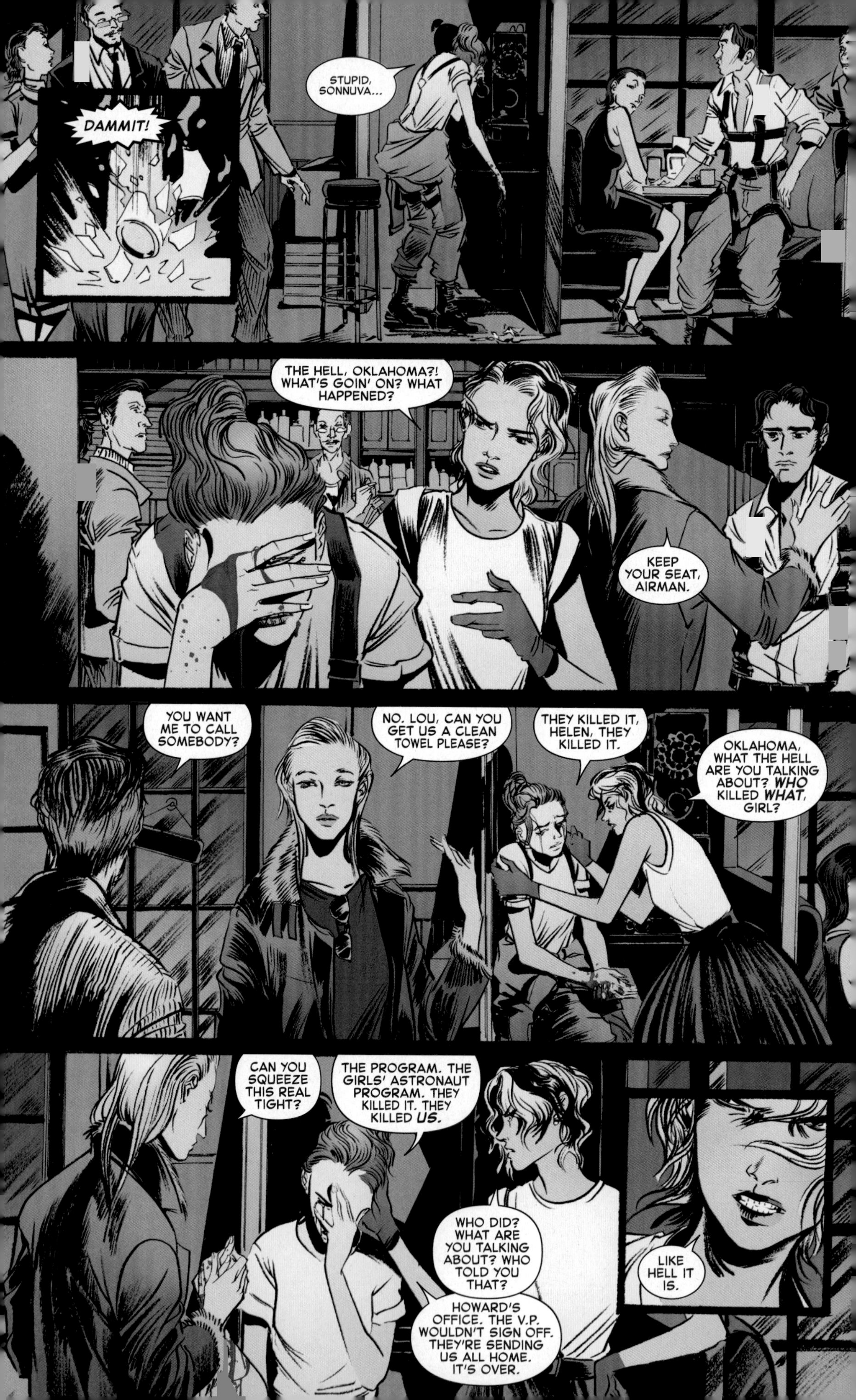
DAMMIT!
STUPID, SONNUVA...
THE HELL, OKLAHOMA?! WHAT'S GOIN' ON? WHAT HAPPENED?
KEEP YOUR SEAT, AIRMAN.
YOU WANT ME TO CALL SOMEBODY?
NO. LOU, CAN YOU GET US A CLEAN TOWEL PLEASE?
THEY KILLED IT, HELEN, THEY KILLED IT.
OKLAHOMA, WHAT THE HELL ARE YOU TALKING ABOUT? WHO KILLED WHAT, GIRL?
CAN YOU SQUEEZE THIS REAL TIGHT?
THE PROGRAM. THE GIRLS' ASTRONAUT PROGRAM. THEY KILLED IT. THEY KILLED US.
WHO DID? WHAT ARE YOU TALKING ABOUT? WHO TOLD YOU THAT?
HOWARD'S OFFICE. THE V.P. WOULDN'T SIGN OFF. THEY'RE SENDING US ALL HOME. IT'S OVER.
LIKE HELL IT IS.

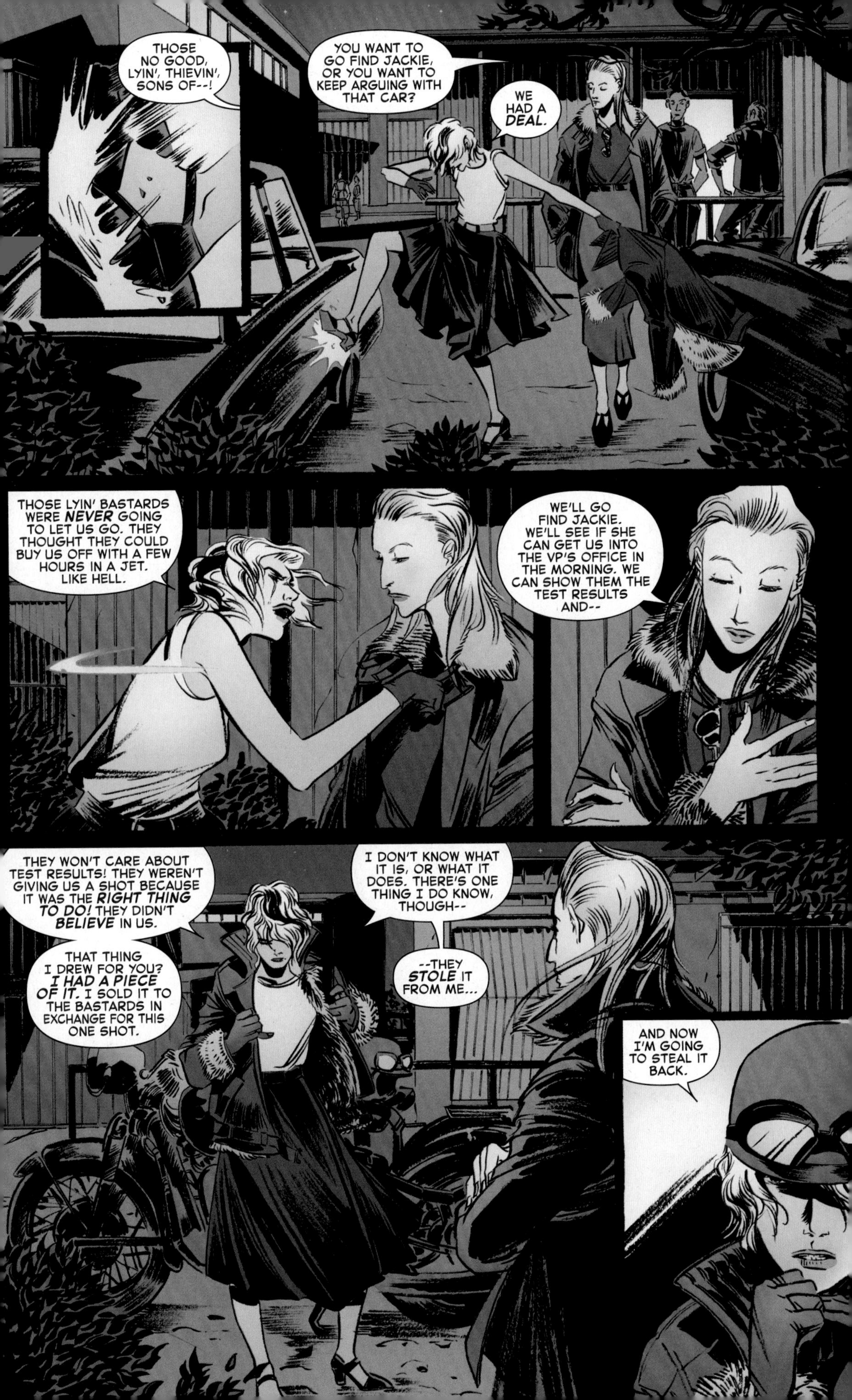
THOSE NO GOOD, LYIN', THIEVIN', SONS OF--!
YOU WANT TO GO FIND JACKIE, OR YOU WANT TO KEEP ARGUING WITH THAT CAR?
WE HAD A ***DEAL.***
THOSE LYIN' BASTARDS WERE ***NEVER*** GOING TO LET US GO. THEY THOUGHT THEY COULD BUY US OFF WITH A FEW HOURS IN A JET. LIKE HELL.
WE'LL GO FIND JACKIE. WE'LL SEE IF SHE CAN GET US INTO THE VP'S OFFICE IN THE MORNING. WE CAN SHOW THEM THE TEST RESULTS AND--
THEY WON'T CARE ABOUT TEST RESULTS! THEY WEREN'T GIVING US A SHOT BECAUSE IT WAS THE ***RIGHT THING TO DO!*** THEY DIDN'T ***BELIEVE*** IN US.
THAT THING I DREW FOR YOU? ***I HAD A PIECE OF IT.*** I SOLD IT TO THE BASTARDS IN EXCHANGE FOR THIS ONE SHOT.
I DON'T KNOW WHAT IT IS, OR WHAT IT DOES. THERE'S ONE THING I DO KNOW, THOUGH--
--THEY ***STOLE*** IT FROM ME...
AND NOW I'M GOING TO STEAL IT BACK.

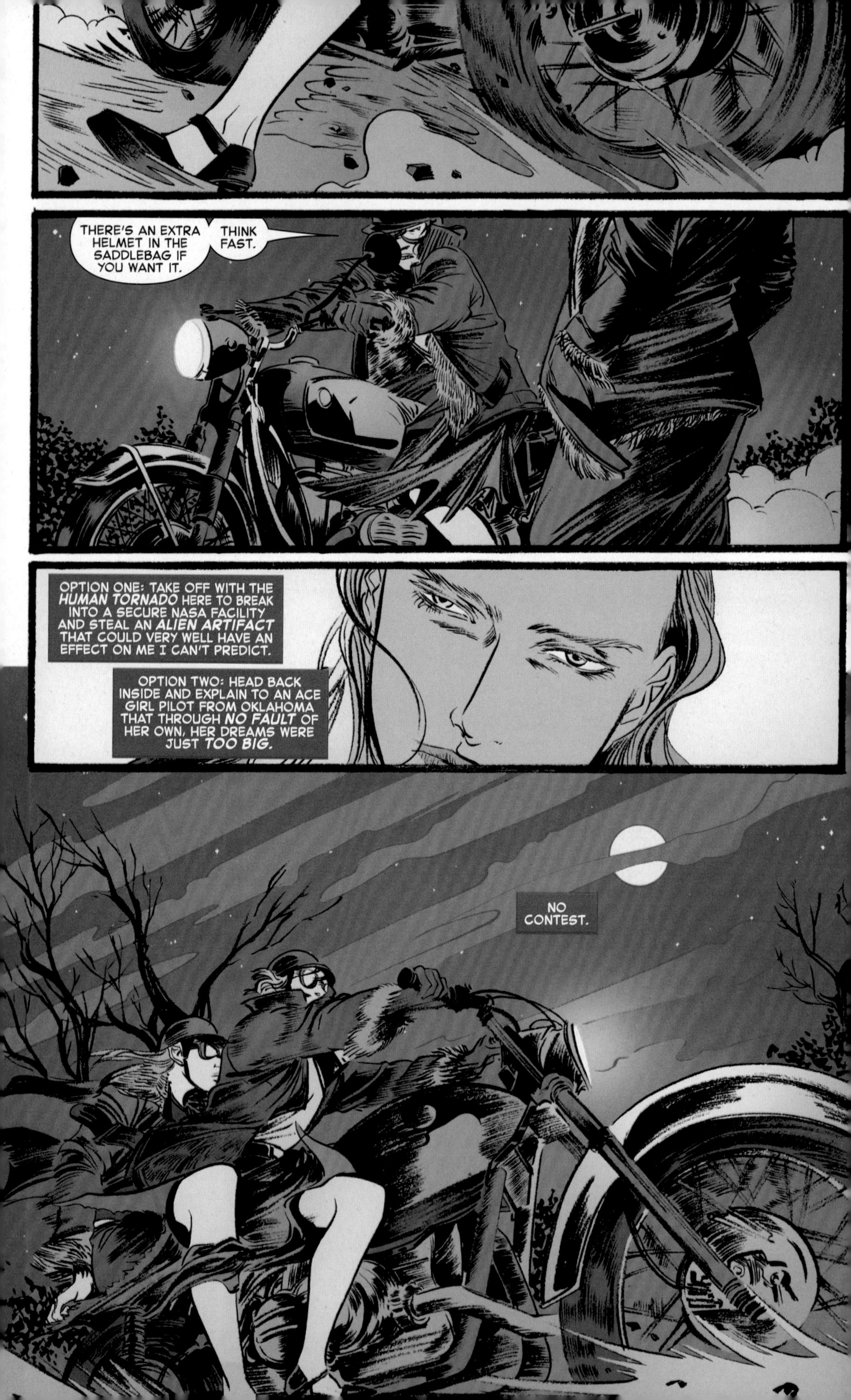

THERE'S AN EXTRA HELMET IN THE SADDLEBAG IF YOU WANT IT.
THINK FAST.
OPTION ONE: TAKE OFF WITH THE *HUMAN TORNADO* HERE TO BREAK INTO A SECURE NASA FACILITY AND STEAL AN *ALIEN ARTIFACT* THAT COULD VERY WELL HAVE AN EFFECT ON ME I CAN'T PREDICT.
OPTION TWO: HEAD BACK INSIDE AND EXPLAIN TO AN ACE GIRL PILOT FROM OKLAHOMA THAT THROUGH *NO FAULT* OF HER OWN, HER DREAMS WERE JUST *TOO BIG.*
NO CONTEST.

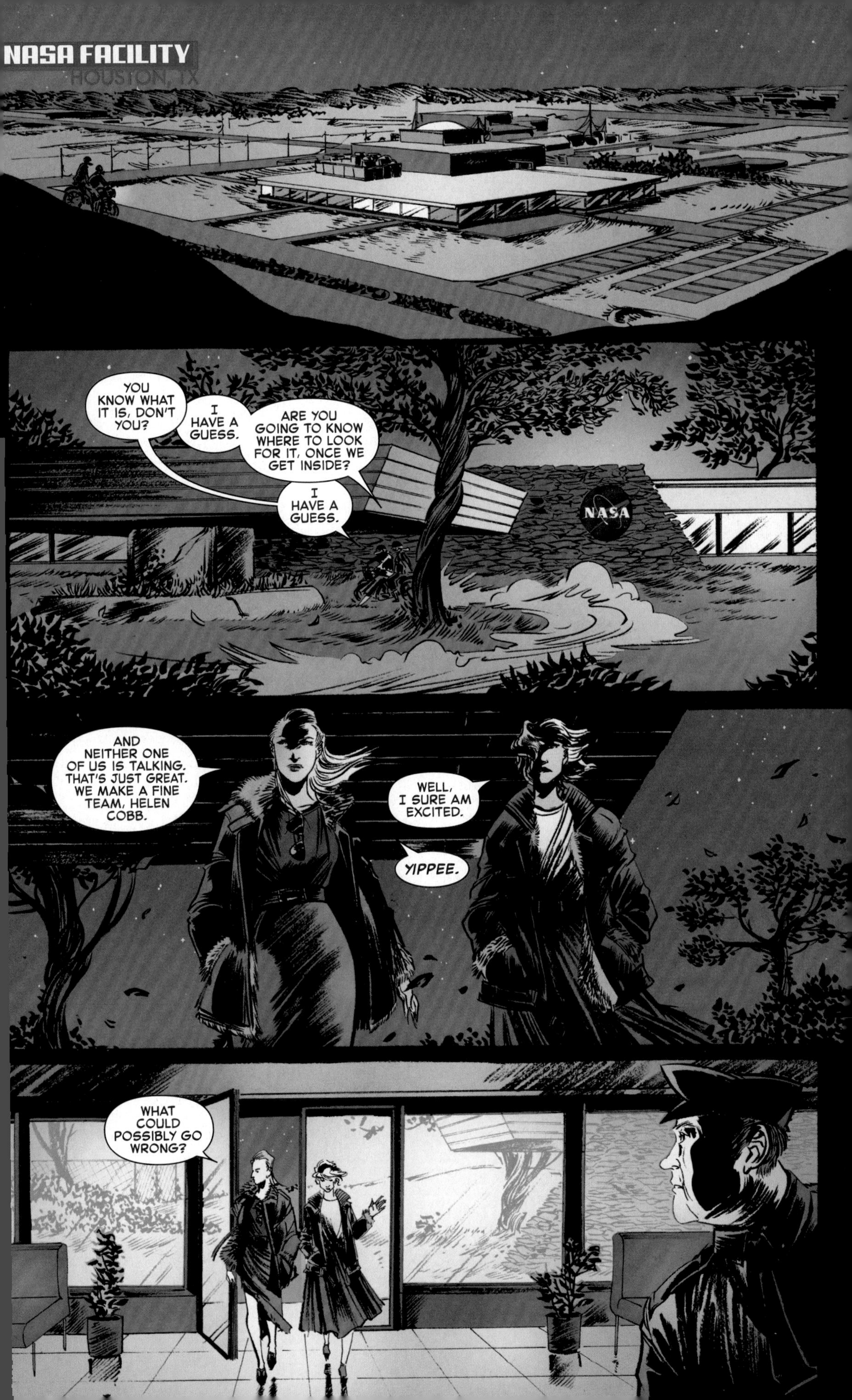
NASA FACILITY
HOUSTON, TX
YOU KNOW WHAT IT IS, DON'T YOU?
I HAVE A GUESS.
ARE YOU GOING TO KNOW WHERE TO LOOK FOR IT, ONCE WE GET INSIDE?
I HAVE A GUESS.
NASA
AND NEITHER ONE OF US IS TALKING. THAT'S JUST GREAT. WE MAKE A FINE TEAM, HELEN COBB.
WELL, I SURE AM EXCITED.
YIPPEE.
WHAT COULD POSSIBLY GO WRONG?

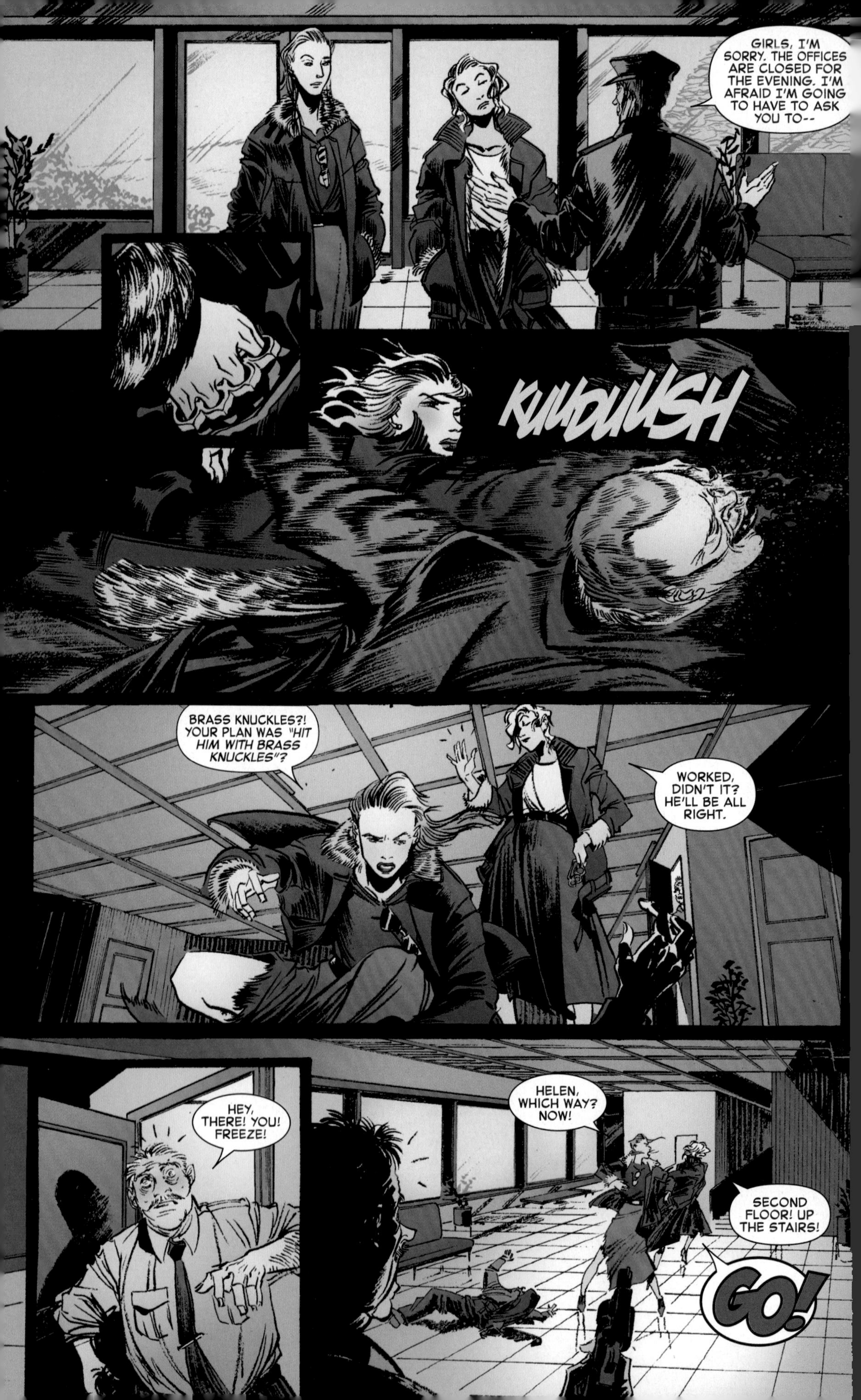
GIRLS, I'M SORRY. THE OFFICES ARE CLOSED FOR THE EVENING. I'M AFRAID I'M GOING TO HAVE TO ASK YOU TO--
KUUDUUSH
BRASS KNUCKLES?! YOUR PLAN WAS "HIT HIM WITH BRASS KNUCKLES"?
WORKED, DIDN'T IT? HE'LL BE ALL RIGHT.
HEY, THERE! YOU! FREEZE!
HELEN, WHICH WAY? NOW!
SECOND FLOOR! UP THE STAIRS!
GO!

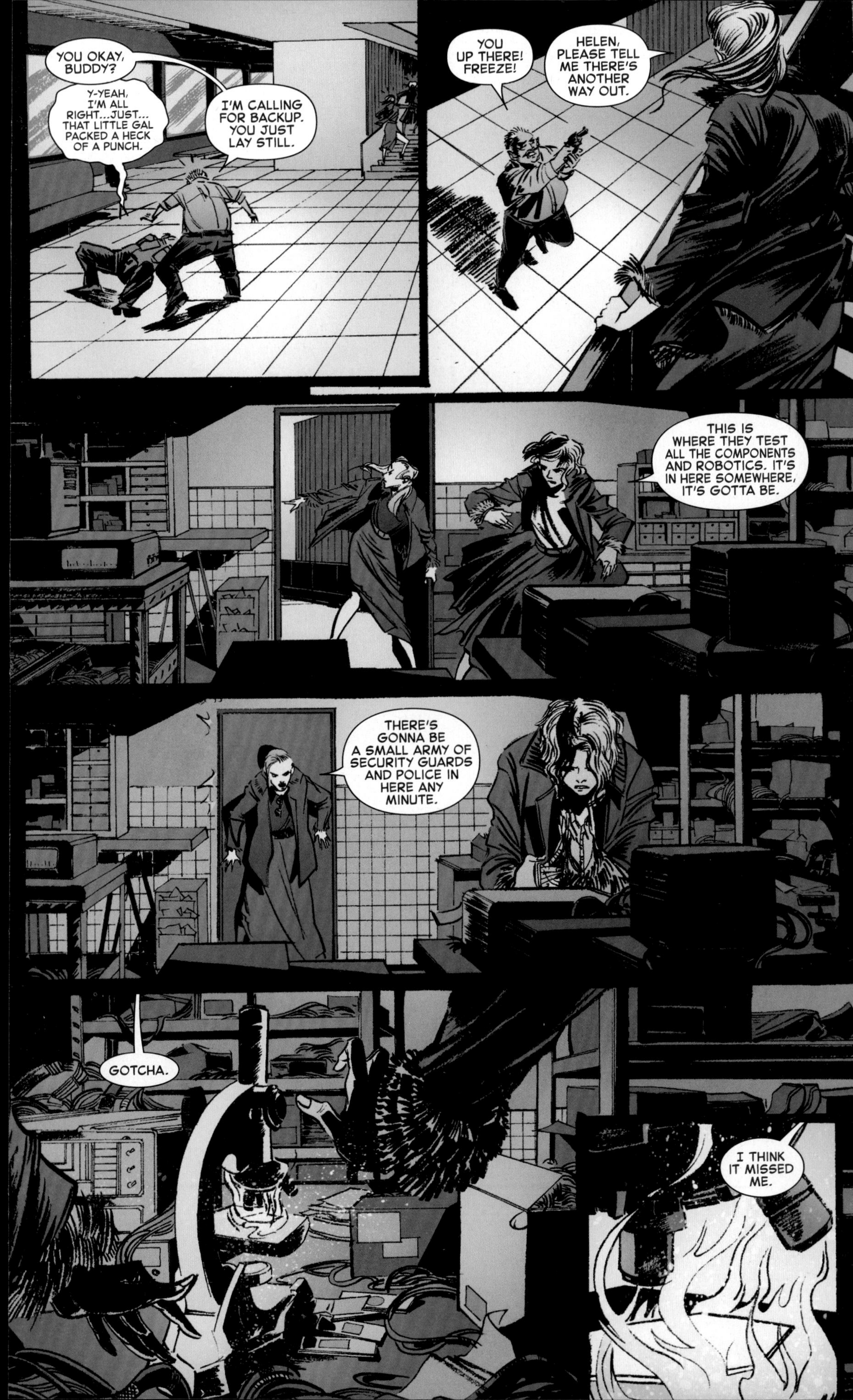
YOU OKAY, BUDDY?
Y-YEAH, I'M ALL RIGHT...JUST... THAT LITTLE GAL PACKED A HECK OF A PUNCH.
I'M CALLING FOR BACKUP. YOU JUST LAY STILL.
YOU UP THERE! FREEZE!
HELEN, PLEASE TELL ME THERE'S ANOTHER WAY OUT.
THIS IS WHERE THEY TEST ALL THE COMPONENTS AND ROBOTICS. IT'S IN HERE SOMEWHERE, IT'S GOTTA BE.
THERE'S GONNA BE A SMALL ARMY OF SECURITY GUARDS AND POLICE IN HERE ANY MINUTE.
GOTCHA.
I THINK IT MISSED ME.

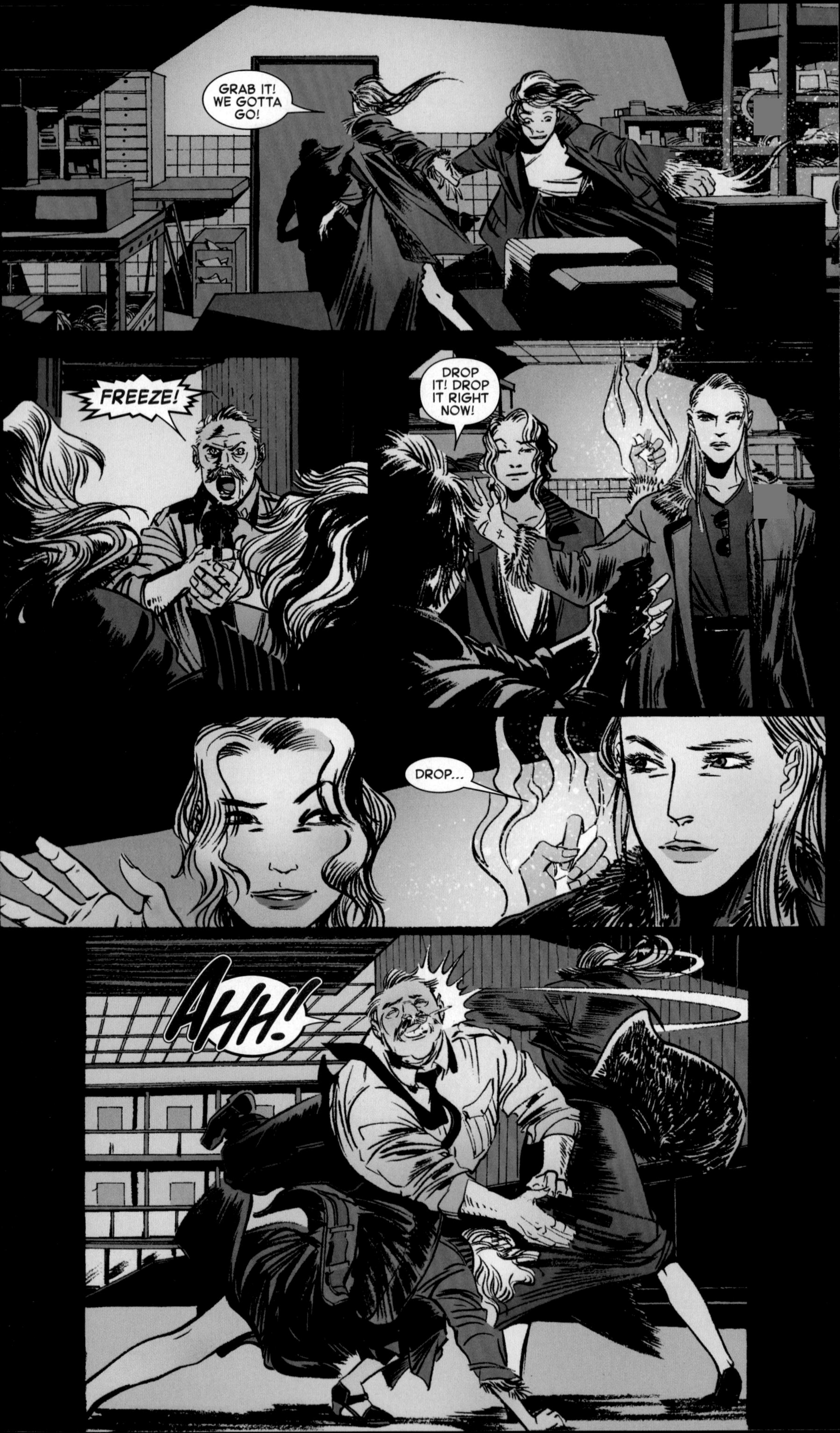
GRAB IT! WE GOTTA GO!
FREEZE!
DROP IT! DROP IT RIGHT NOW!
DROP...
AHH!

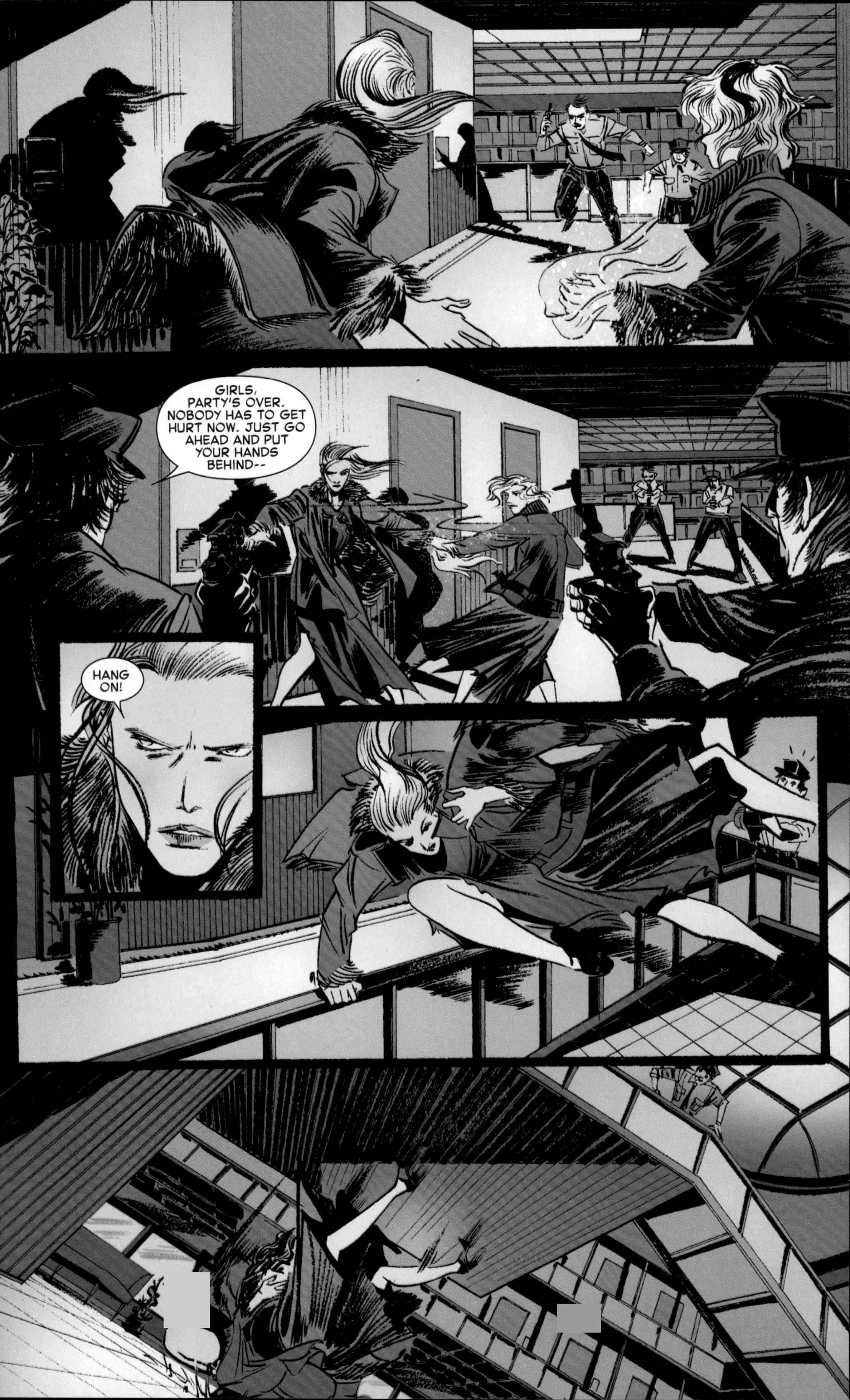
GIRLS, PARTY'S OVER. NOBODY HAS TO GET HURT NOW. JUST GO AHEAD AND PUT YOUR HANDS BEHIND--
HANG ON!

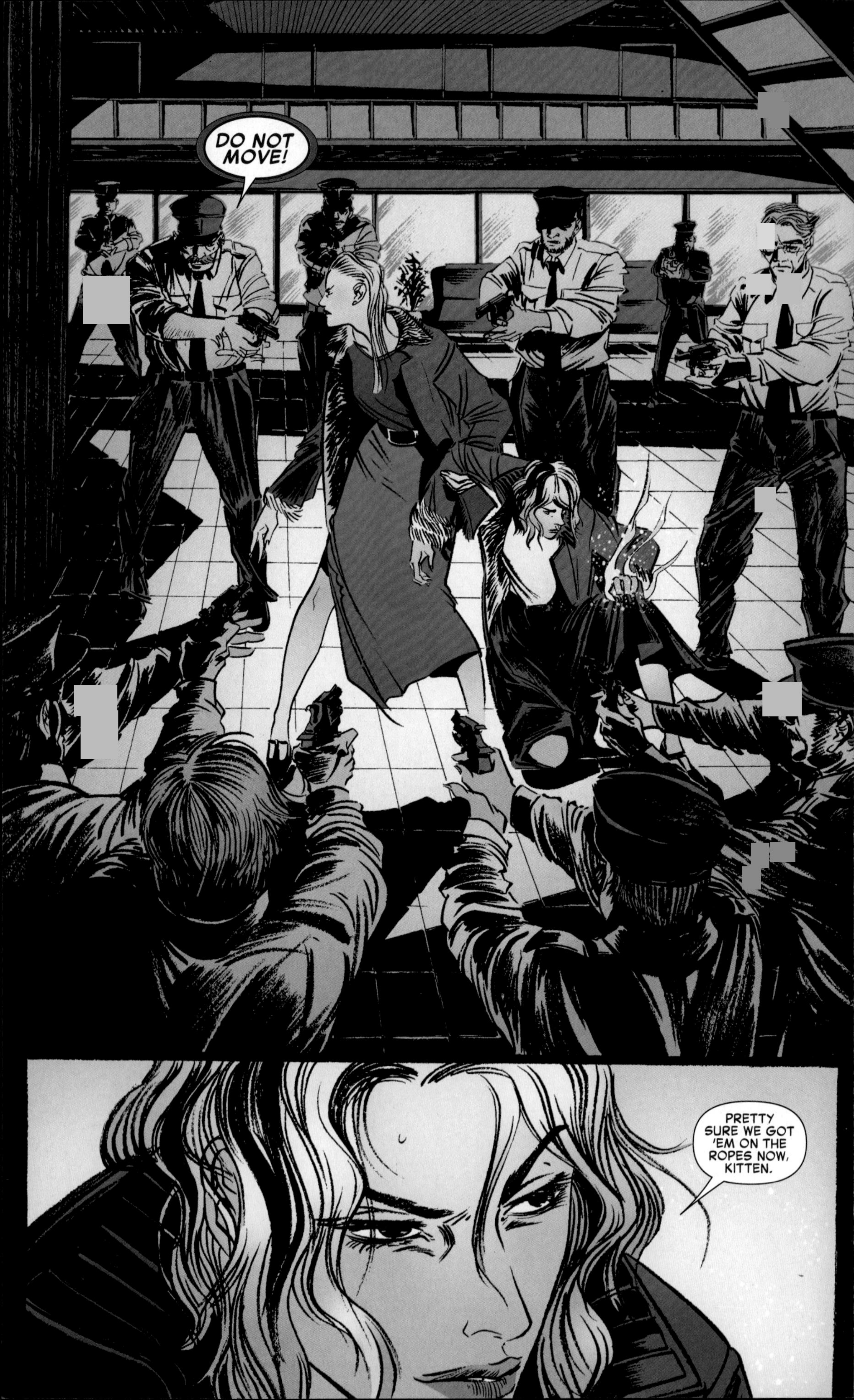
DO NOT MOVE!
PRETTY SURE WE GOT 'EM ON THE ROPES NOW, KITTEN.

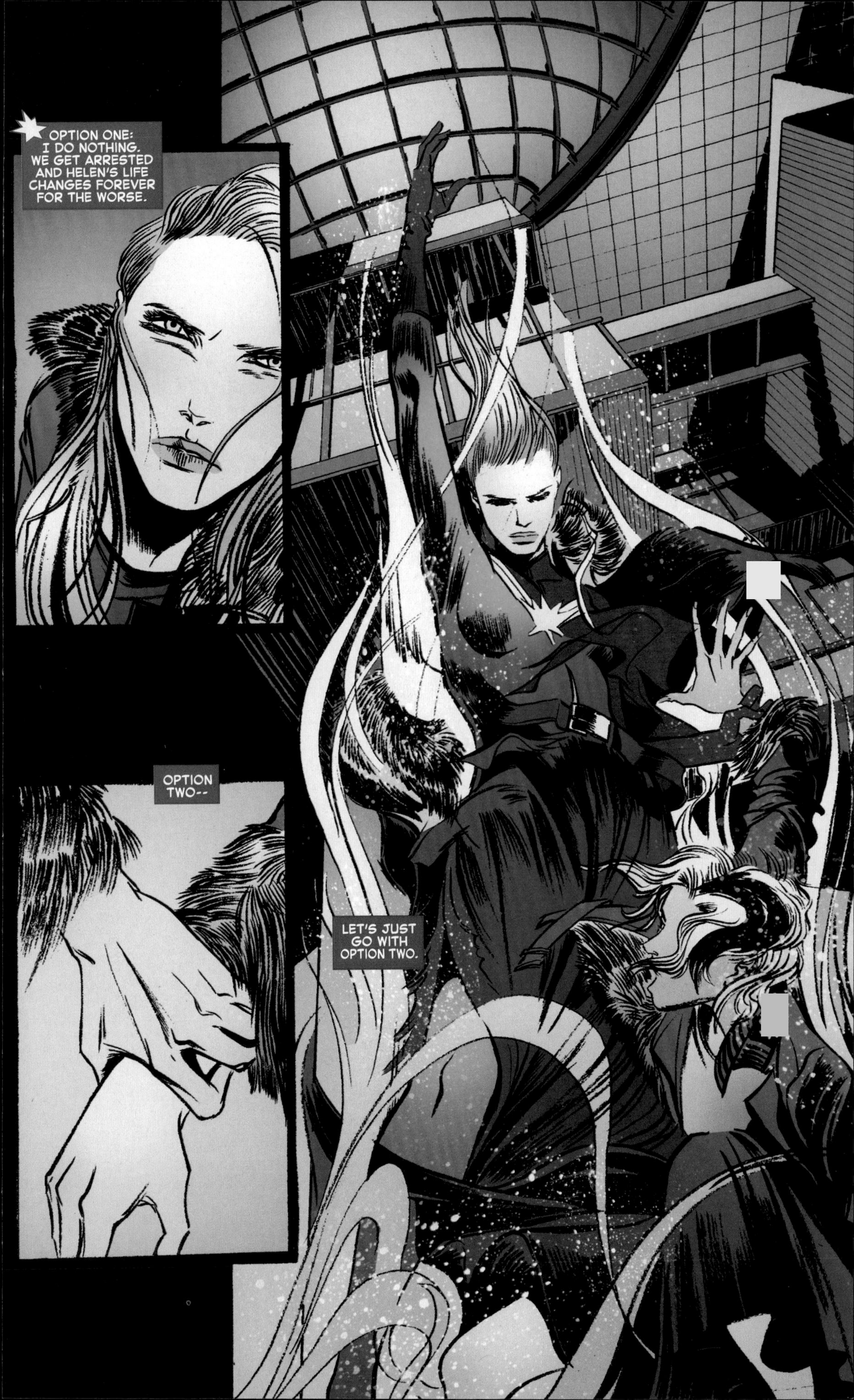
OPTION ONE: I DO NOTHING. WE GET ARRESTED AND HELEN'S LIFE CHANGES FOREVER FOR THE WORSE.
OPTION TWO--
LET'S JUST GO WITH OPTION TWO.

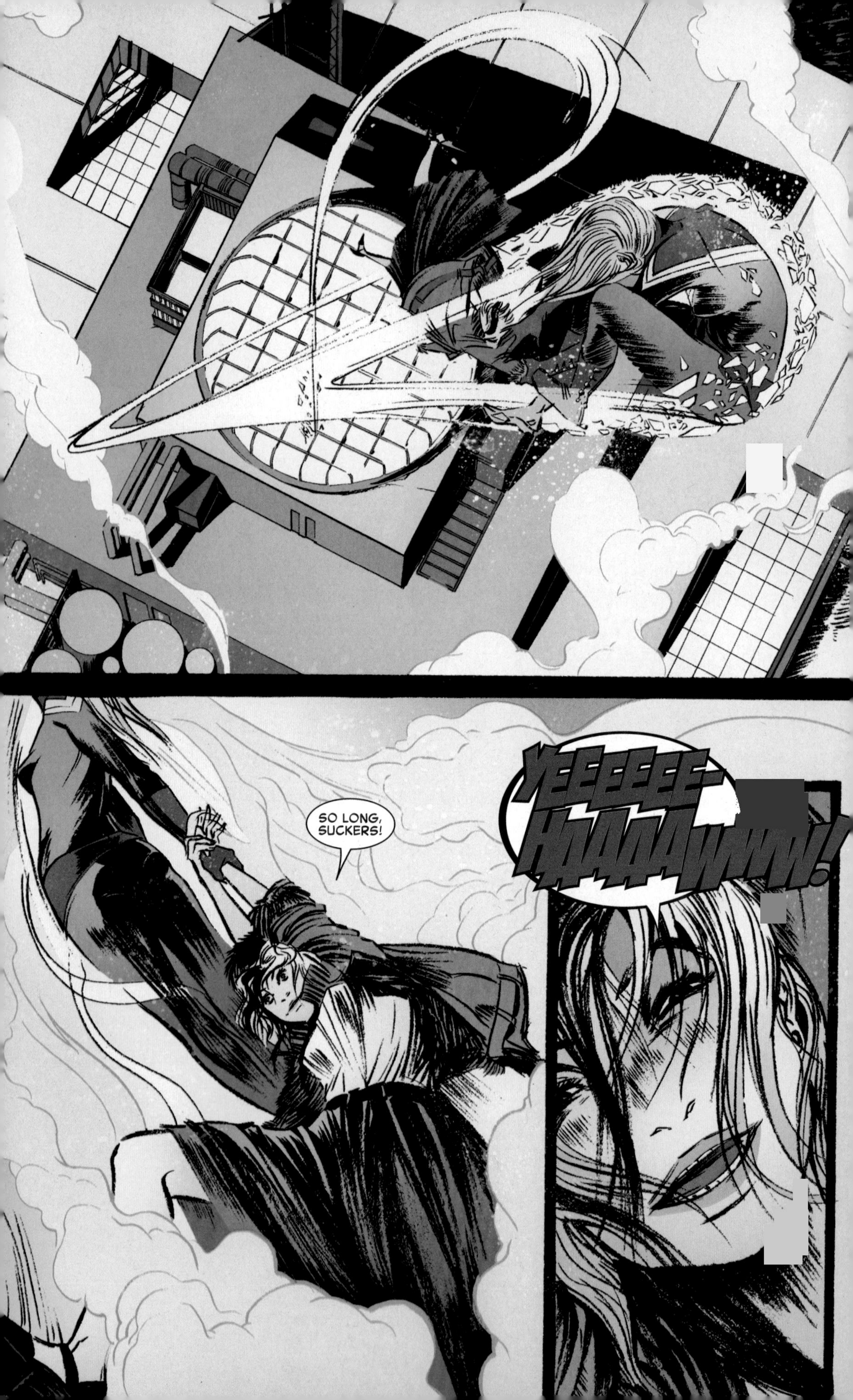
SO LONG, SUCKERS!
YEEEEEE-
HAAAAWWWW!

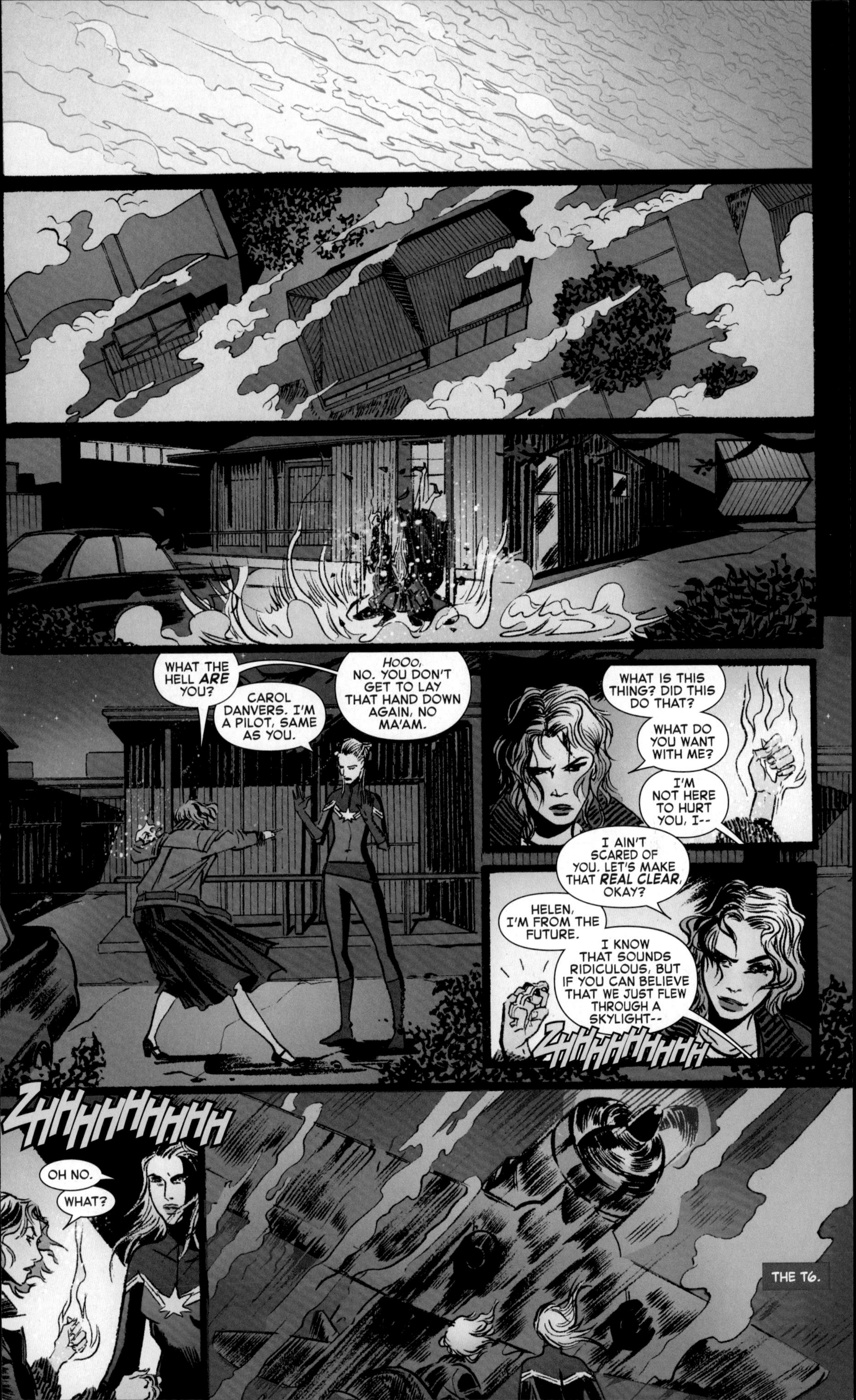
WHAT THE HELL ARE YOU?
CAROL DANVERS. I'M A PILOT, SAME AS YOU.
HOOO, NO. YOU DON'T GET TO LAY THAT HAND DOWN AGAIN, NO MA'AM.
WHAT IS THIS THING? DID THIS DO THAT?
WHAT DO YOU WANT WITH ME?
I'M NOT HERE TO HURT YOU, I--
I AIN'T SCARED OF YOU. LET'S MAKE THAT REAL CLEAR, OKAY?
HELEN, I'M FROM THE FUTURE.
I KNOW THAT SOUNDS RIDICULOUS, BUT IF YOU CAN BELIEVE THAT WE JUST FLEW THROUGH A SKYLIGHT--
ZHHHHHHHHHH
ZHHHHHHHHHH
OH NO.
WHAT?
THE T6.

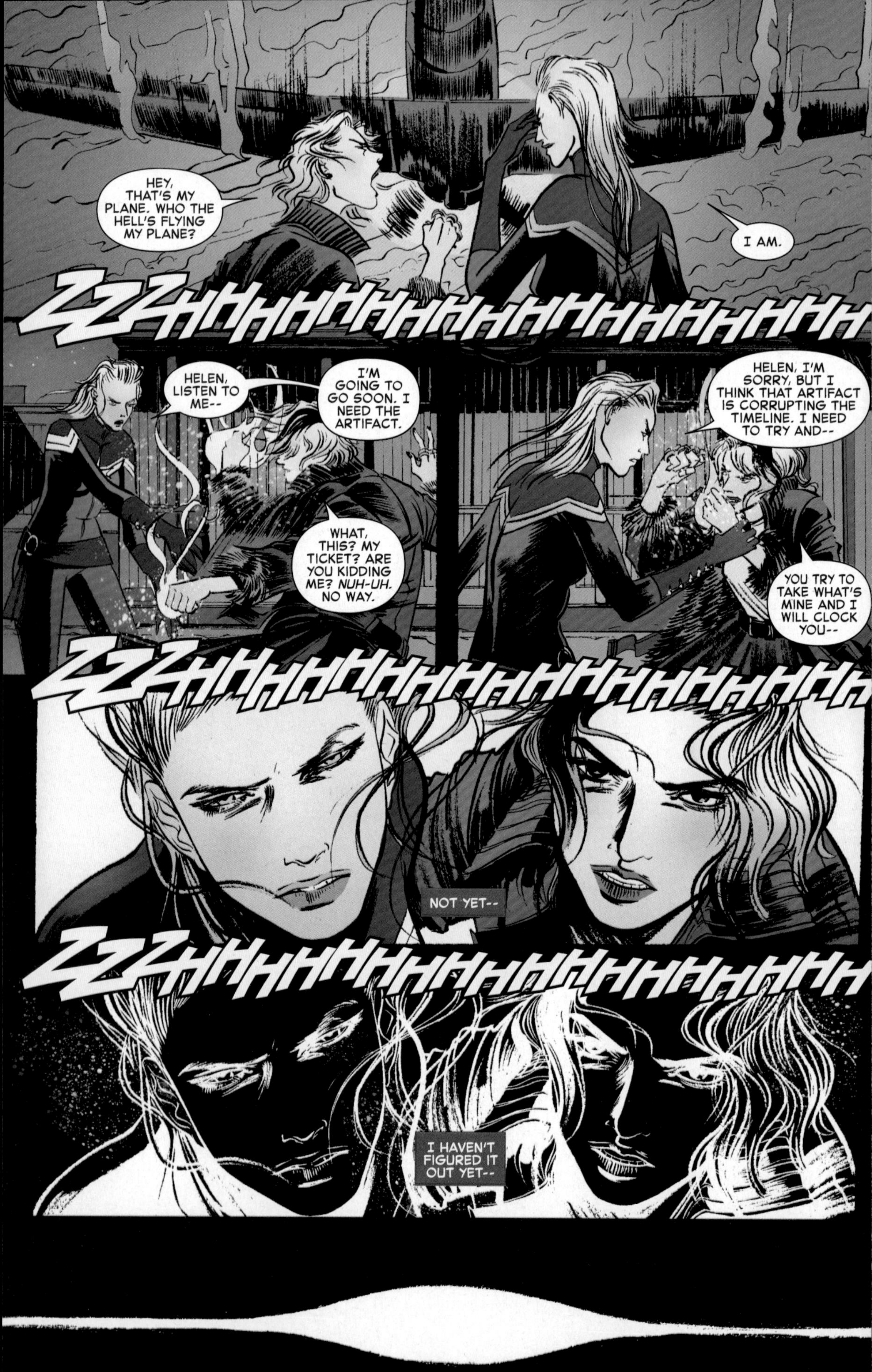
HEY, THAT'S MY PLANE. WHO THE HELL'S FLYING MY PLANE?
I AM.
ZZZHHHHHHHHHHHHHHHHHHHHHHHHHHHH
HELEN, LISTEN TO ME--
I'M GOING TO GO SOON. I NEED THE ARTIFACT.
WHAT, THIS? MY TICKET? ARE YOU KIDDING ME? NUH-UH. NO WAY.
HELEN, I'M SORRY, BUT I THINK THAT ARTIFACT IS CORRUPTING THE TIMELINE. I NEED TO TRY AND--
YOU TRY TO TAKE WHAT'S MINE AND I WILL CLOCK YOU--
ZZZHHHHHHHHHHHHHHHHHHHHHHHHHHHH
NOT YET--
ZZZHHHHHHHHHHHHHHHHHHHHHHHHHHHH
I HAVEN'T FIGURED IT OUT YET--

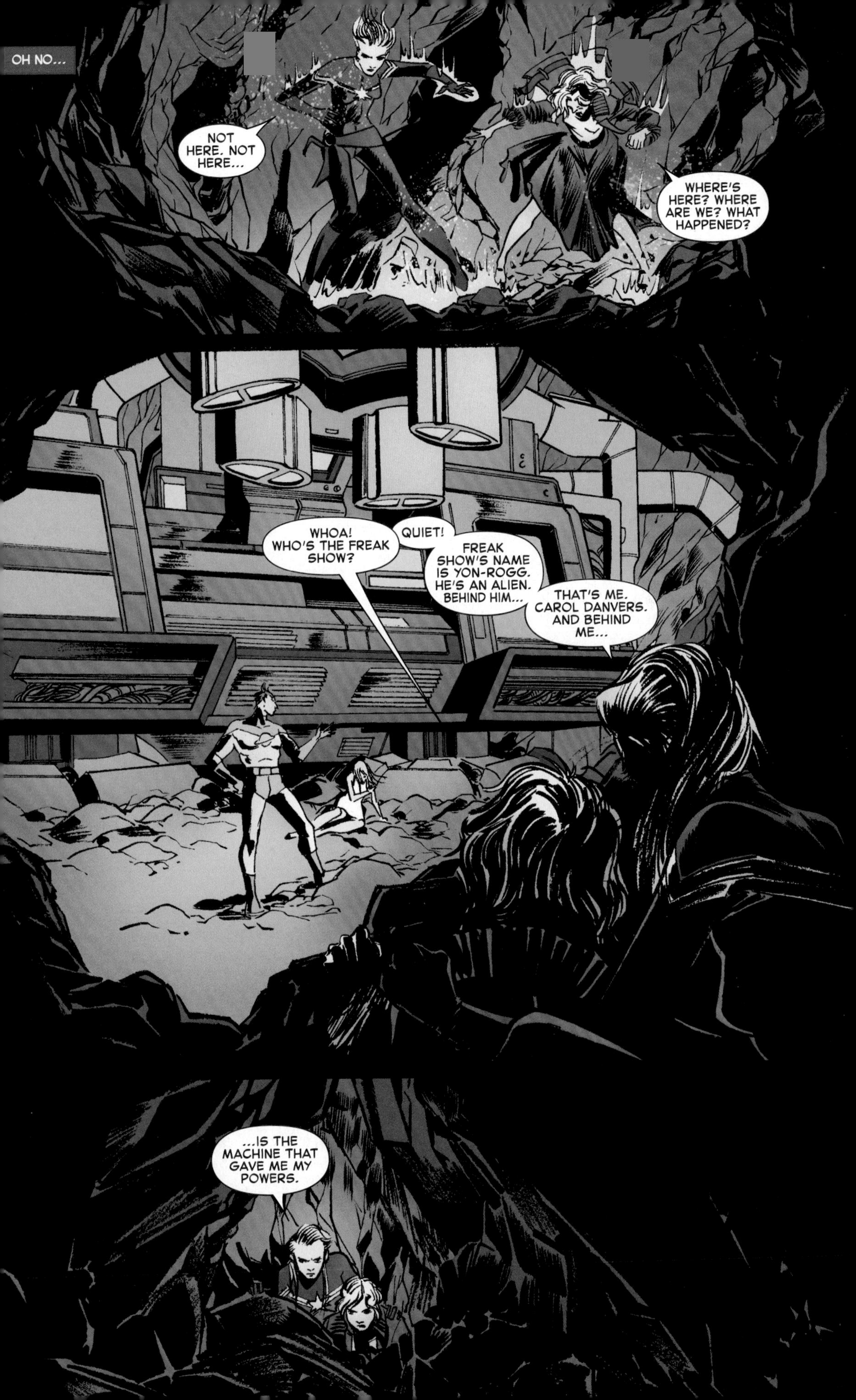
OH NO...
NOT HERE. NOT HERE...
WHERE'S HERE? WHERE ARE WE? WHAT HAPPENED?
WHOA! WHO'S THE FREAK SHOW?
QUIET!
FREAK SHOW'S NAME IS YON-ROGG. HE'S AN ALIEN. BEHIND HIM...
THAT'S ME. CAROL DANVERS. AND BEHIND ME...
...IS THE MACHINE THAT GAVE ME MY POWERS.

CAPTAIN MARVEL #6

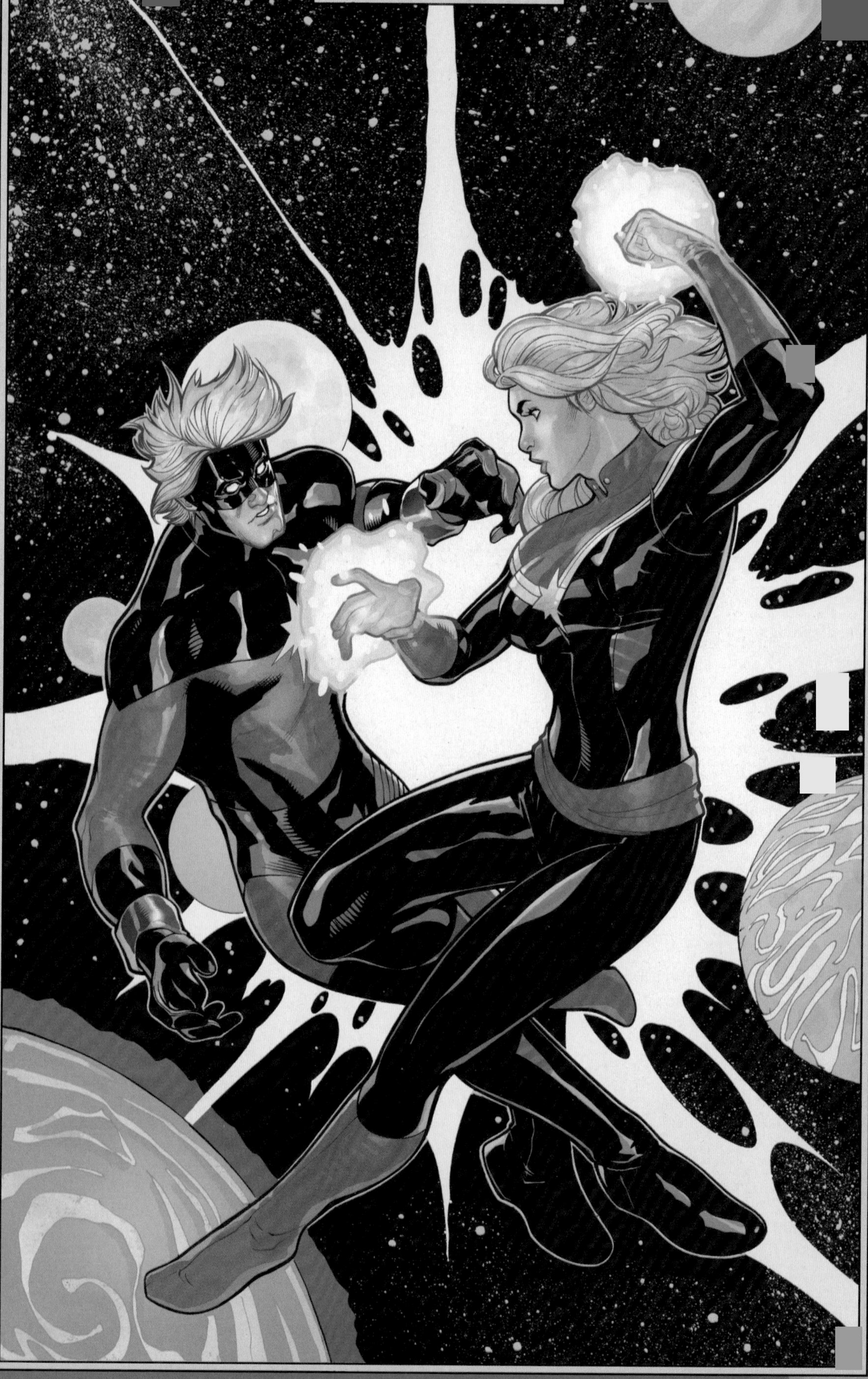

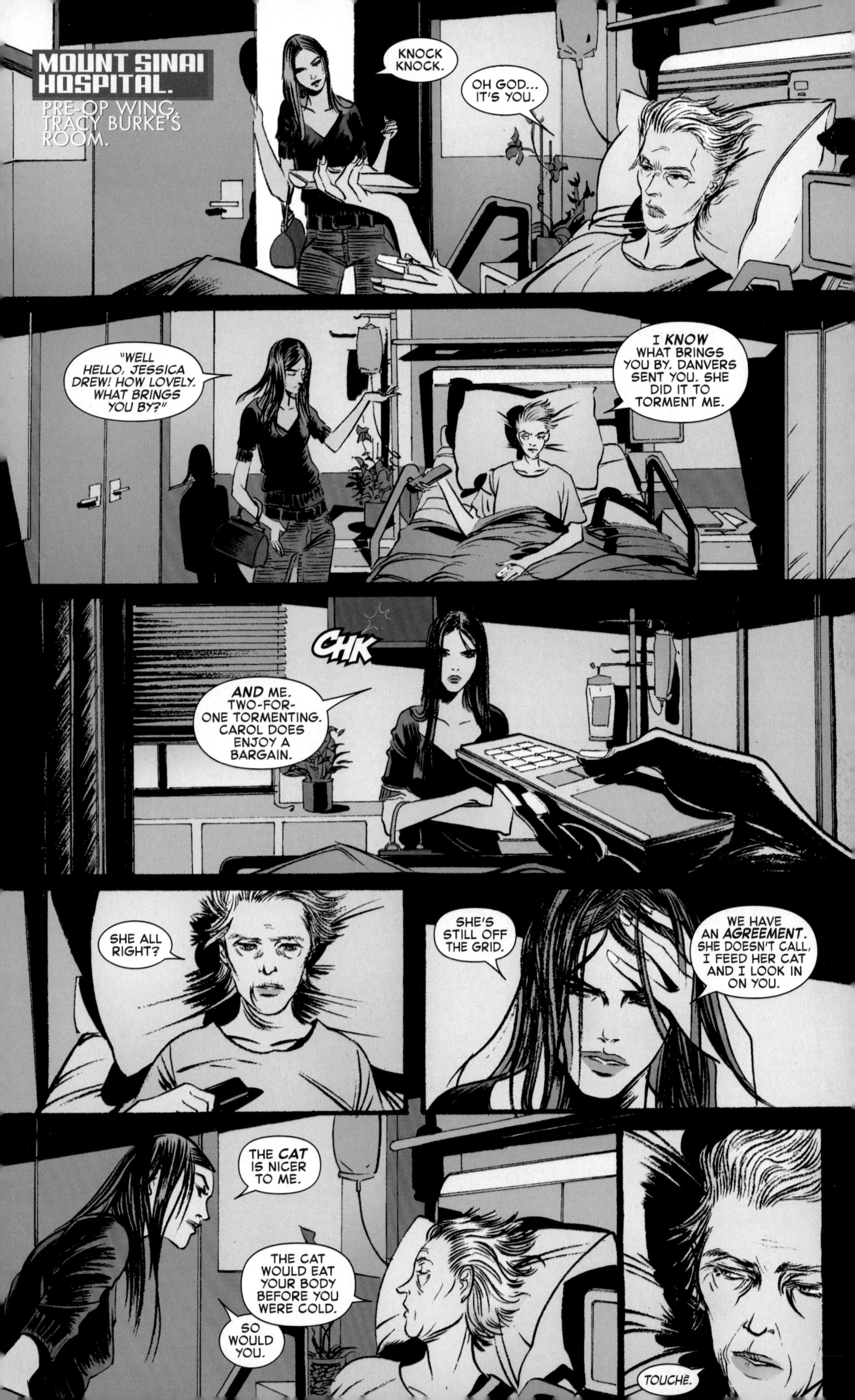
MOUNT SINAI HOSPITAL.
PRE-OP WING, TRACY BURKE'S ROOM.
KNOCK KNOCK.
OH GOD... IT'S YOU.
"WELL HELLO, JESSICA DREW! HOW LOVELY. WHAT BRINGS YOU BY?"
I KNOW WHAT BRINGS YOU BY. DANVERS SENT YOU. SHE DID IT TO TORMENT ME.
CHK
AND ME. TWO-FOR-ONE TORMENTING. CAROL DOES ENJOY A BARGAIN.
SHE ALL RIGHT?
SHE'S STILL OFF THE GRID.
WE HAVE AN AGREEMENT. SHE DOESN'T CALL, I FEED HER CAT AND I LOOK IN ON YOU.
THE CAT IS NICER TO ME.
THE CAT WOULD EAT YOUR BODY BEFORE YOU WERE COLD.
SO WOULD YOU.
TOUCHÉ.

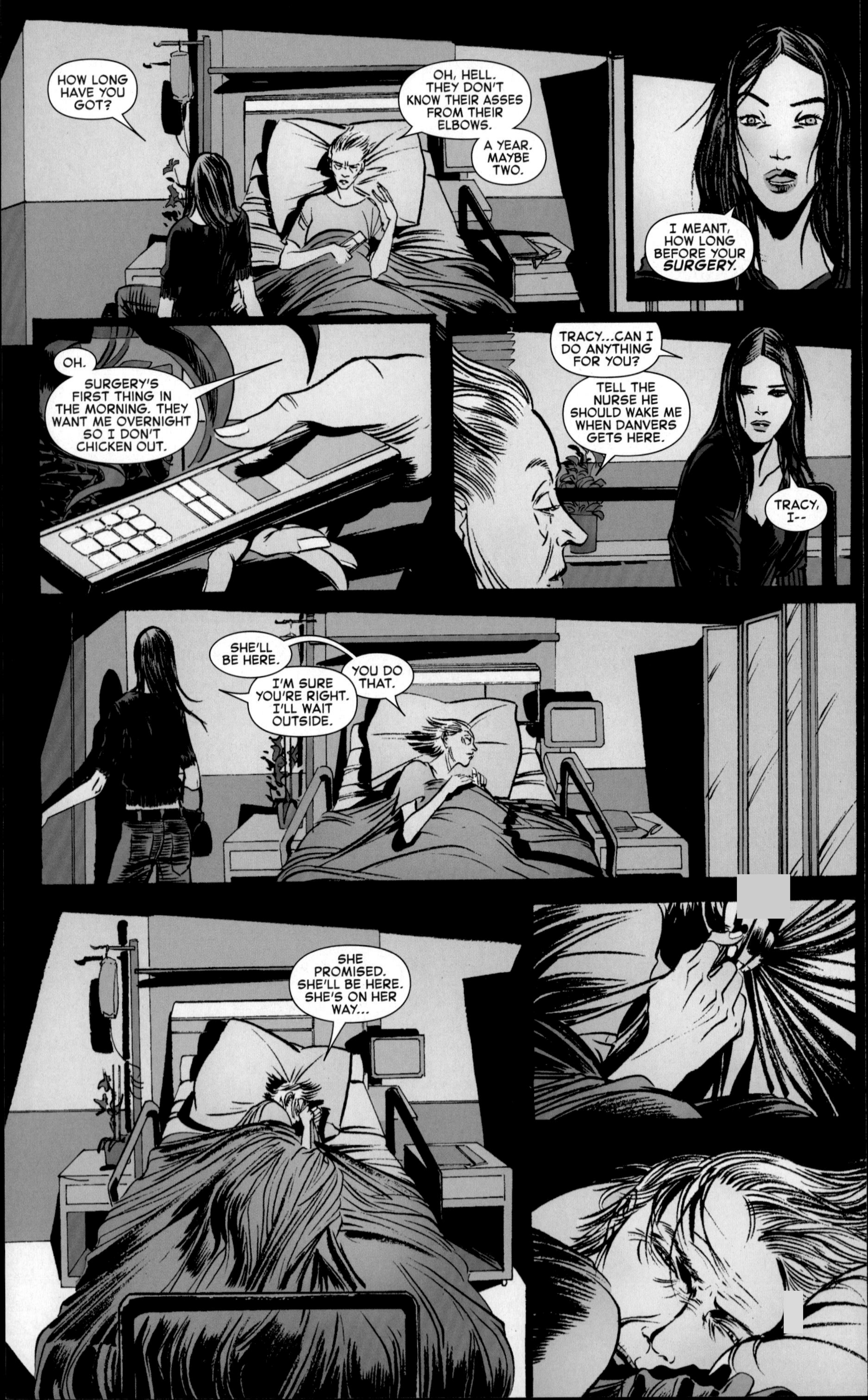
HOW LONG HAVE YOU GOT?
OH, HELL. THEY DON'T KNOW THEIR ASSES FROM THEIR ELBOWS.
A YEAR. MAYBE TWO.
I MEANT, HOW LONG BEFORE YOUR SURGERY.
OH.
SURGERY'S FIRST THING IN THE MORNING. THEY WANT ME OVERNIGHT SO I DON'T CHICKEN OUT.
TRACY...CAN I DO ANYTHING FOR YOU?
TELL THE NURSE HE SHOULD WAKE ME WHEN DANVERS GETS HERE.
TRACY, I--
SHE'LL BE HERE.
I'M SURE YOU'RE RIGHT. I'LL WAIT OUTSIDE.
YOU DO THAT.
SHE PROMISED. SHE'LL BE HERE. SHE'S ON HER WAY...

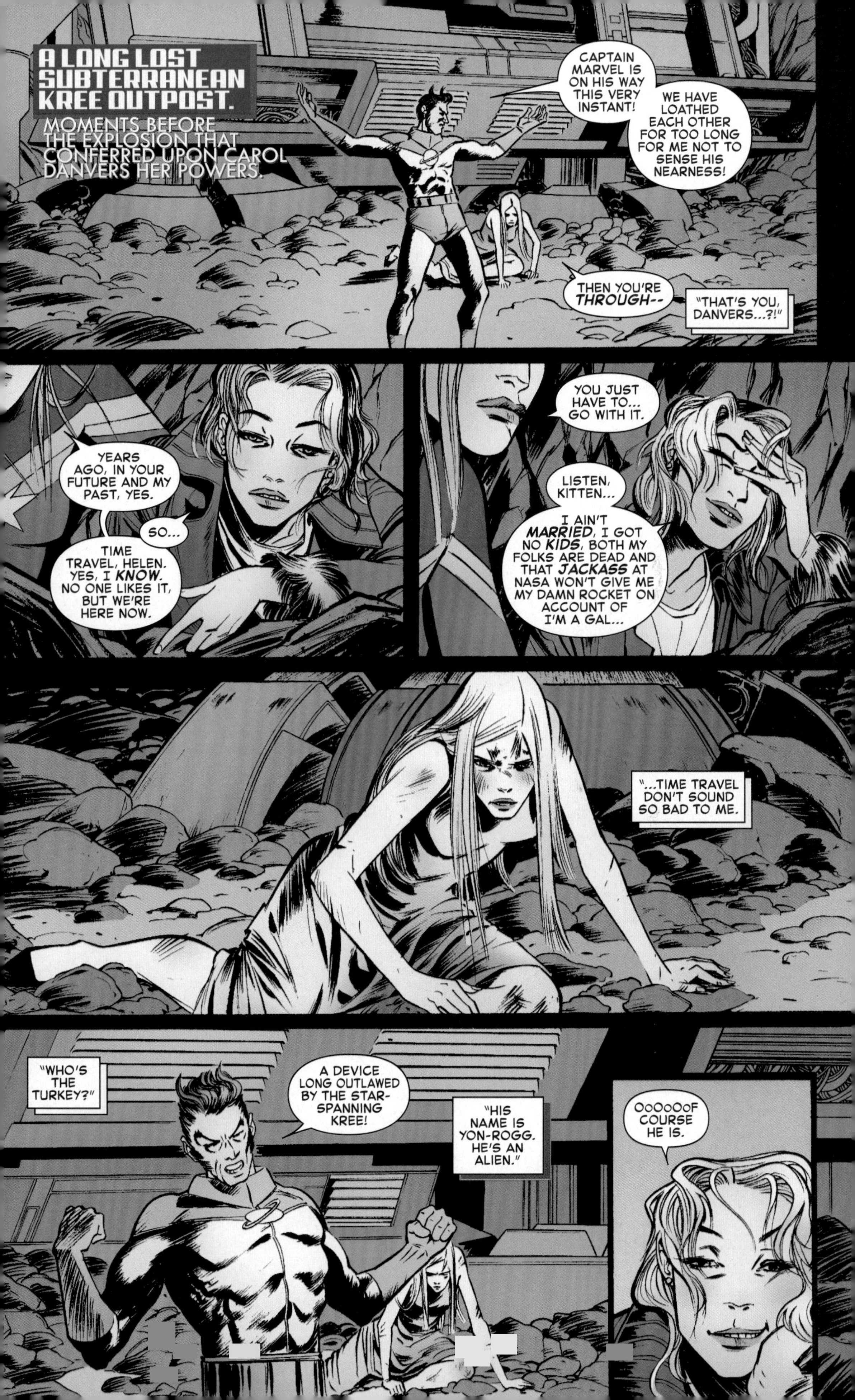
A LONG LOST SUBTERRANEAN KREE OUTPOST.
MOMENTS BEFORE THE EXPLOSION THAT CONFERRED UPON CAROL DANVERS HER POWERS.
CAPTAIN MARVEL IS ON HIS WAY THIS VERY INSTANT!
WE HAVE LOATHED EACH OTHER FOR TOO LONG FOR ME NOT TO SENSE HIS NEARNESS!
THEN YOU'RE THROUGH--
"THAT'S YOU, DANVERS...?!"
YEARS AGO, IN YOUR FUTURE AND MY PAST, YES.
SO...
TIME TRAVEL, HELEN. YES, I KNOW. NO ONE LIKES IT, BUT WE'RE HERE NOW.
YOU JUST HAVE TO... GO WITH IT.
LISTEN, KITTEN...
I AIN'T MARRIED, I GOT NO KIDS, BOTH MY FOLKS ARE DEAD AND THAT JACKASS AT NASA WON'T GIVE ME MY DAMN ROCKET ON ACCOUNT OF I'M A GAL...
"...TIME TRAVEL DON'T SOUND SO BAD TO ME.
"WHO'S THE TURKEY?"
A DEVICE LONG OUTLAWED BY THE STAR-SPANNING KREE!
"HIS NAME IS YON-ROGG. HE'S AN ALIEN."
OOOOOOF COURSE HE IS.

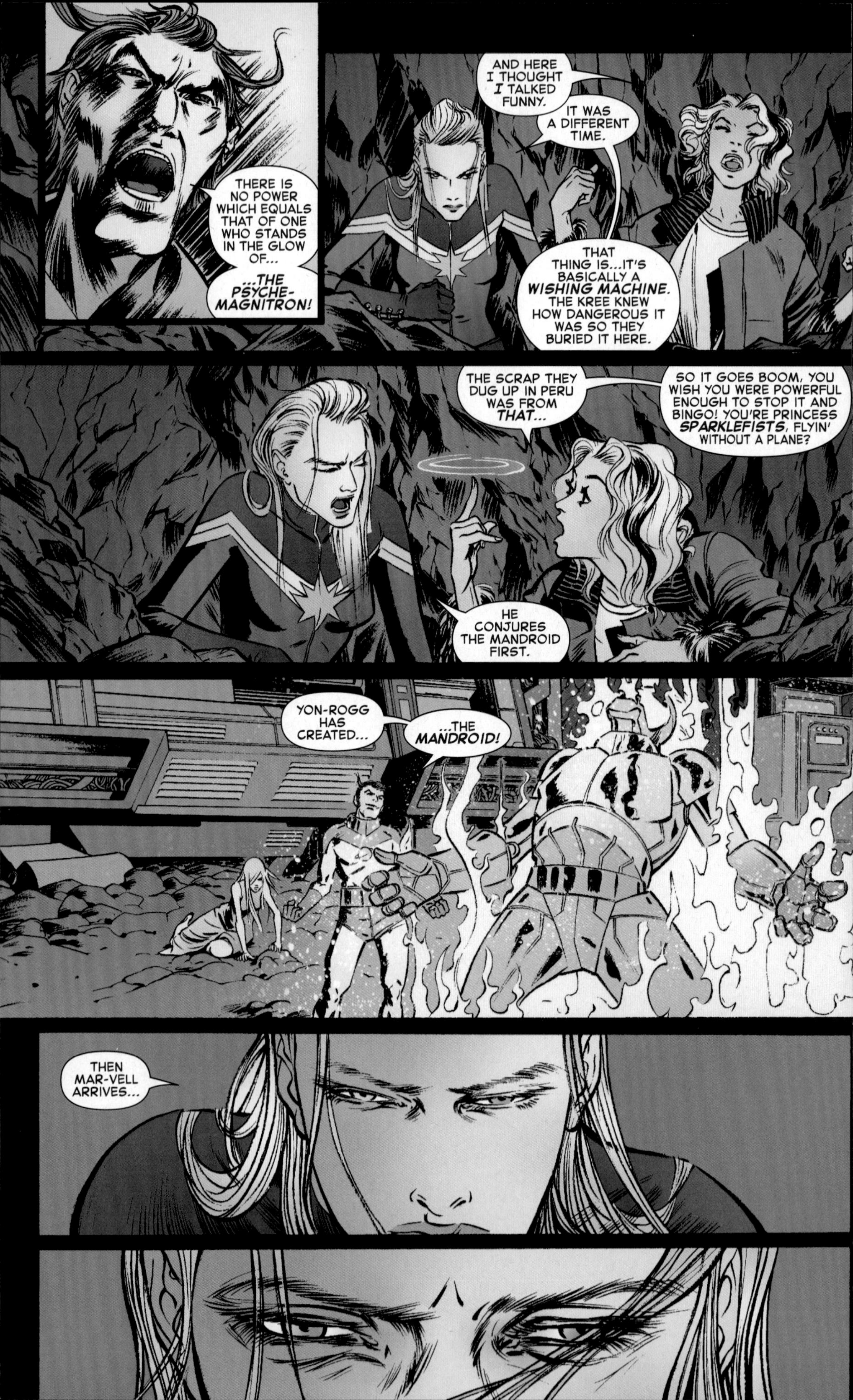
THERE IS NO POWER WHICH EQUALS THAT OF ONE WHO STANDS IN THE GLOW OF...
...THE PSYCHE-MAGNITRON!
AND HERE I THOUGHT I TALKED FUNNY.
IT WAS A DIFFERENT TIME.
THAT THING IS...IT'S BASICALLY A WISHING MACHINE. THE KREE KNEW HOW DANGEROUS IT WAS SO THEY BURIED IT HERE.
THE SCRAP THEY DUG UP IN PERU WAS FROM THAT...
SO IT GOES BOOM, YOU WISH YOU WERE POWERFUL ENOUGH TO STOP IT AND BINGO! YOU'RE PRINCESS SPARKLEFISTS, FLYIN' WITHOUT A PLANE?
HE CONJURES THE MANDROID FIRST.
YON-ROGG HAS CREATED...
...THE MANDROID!
THEN MAR-VELL ARRIVES...

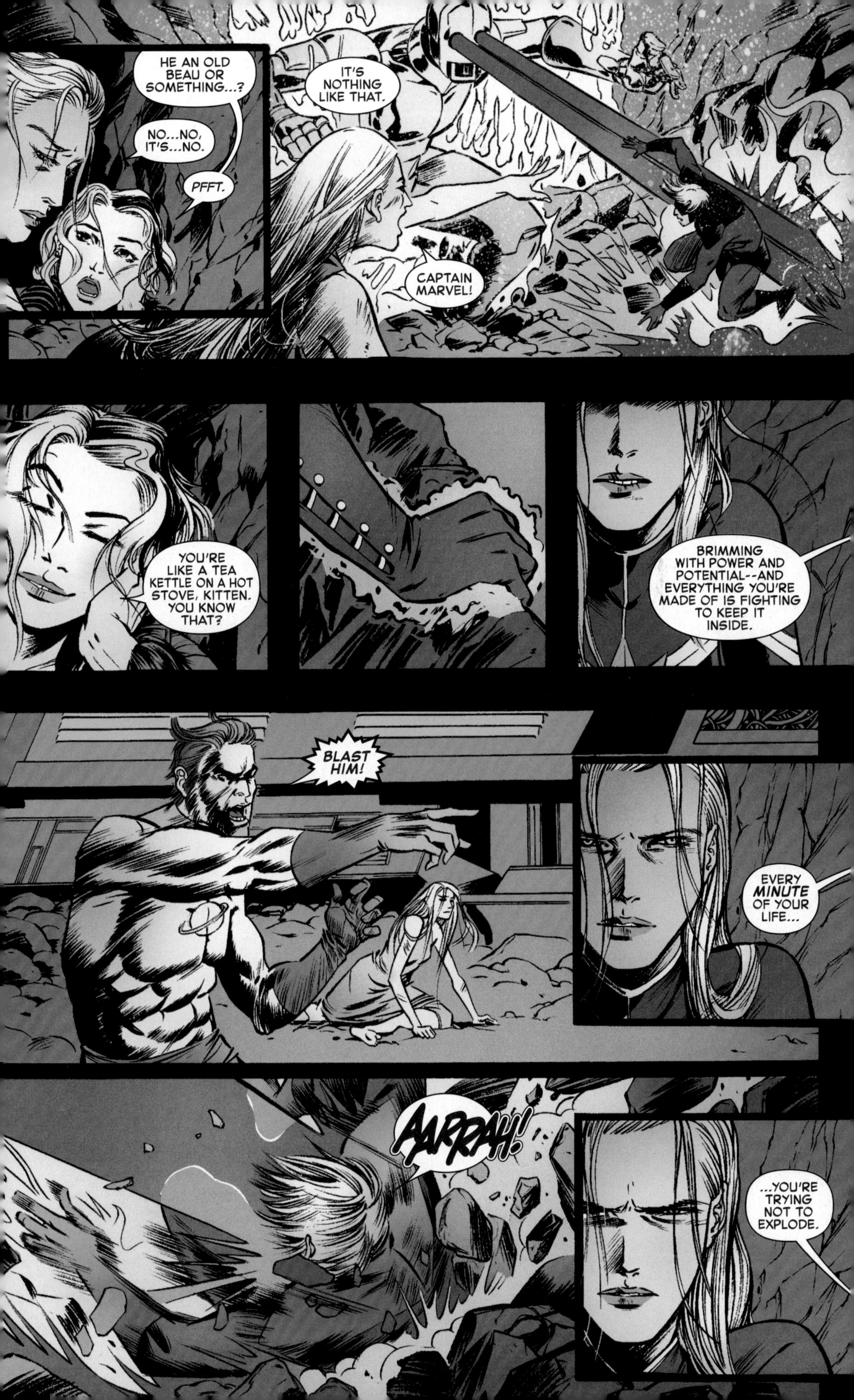

HE AN OLD BEAU OR SOMETHING...?
NO...NO, IT'S...NO.
PFFT.
IT'S NOTHING LIKE THAT.
CAPTAIN MARVEL!
YOU'RE LIKE A TEA KETTLE ON A HOT STOVE, KITTEN. YOU KNOW THAT?
BRIMMING WITH POWER AND POTENTIAL--AND EVERYTHING YOU'RE MADE OF IS FIGHTING TO KEEP IT INSIDE.
BLAST HIM!
EVERY MINUTE OF YOUR LIFE...
AARRAH!
...YOU'RE TRYING NOT TO EXPLODE.

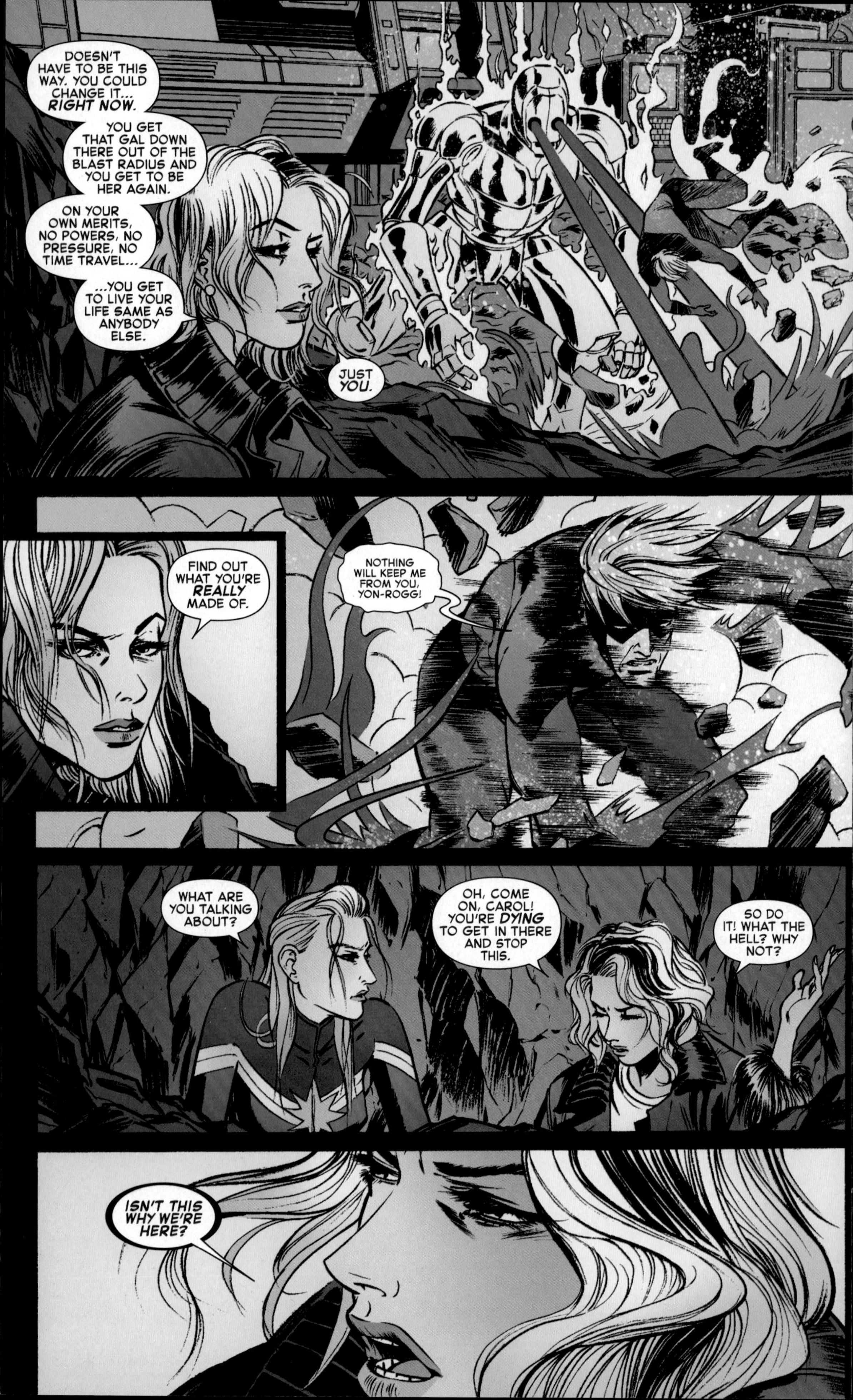

DOESN'T HAVE TO BE THIS WAY. YOU COULD CHANGE IT... *RIGHT NOW*.
YOU GET THAT GAL DOWN THERE OUT OF THE BLAST RADIUS AND YOU GET TO BE HER AGAIN.
ON YOUR OWN MERITS, NO POWERS, NO PRESSURE, NO TIME TRAVEL...
...YOU GET TO LIVE YOUR LIFE SAME AS ANYBODY ELSE.
JUST *YOU*.
FIND OUT WHAT YOU'RE *REALLY* MADE OF.
NOTHING WILL KEEP ME FROM YOU, YON-ROGG!
WHAT ARE YOU TALKING ABOUT?
OH, COME ON, CAROL! YOU'RE *DYING* TO GET IN THERE AND STOP THIS.
SO DO IT! WHAT THE HELL? WHY NOT?
ISN'T THIS WHY WE'RE HERE?

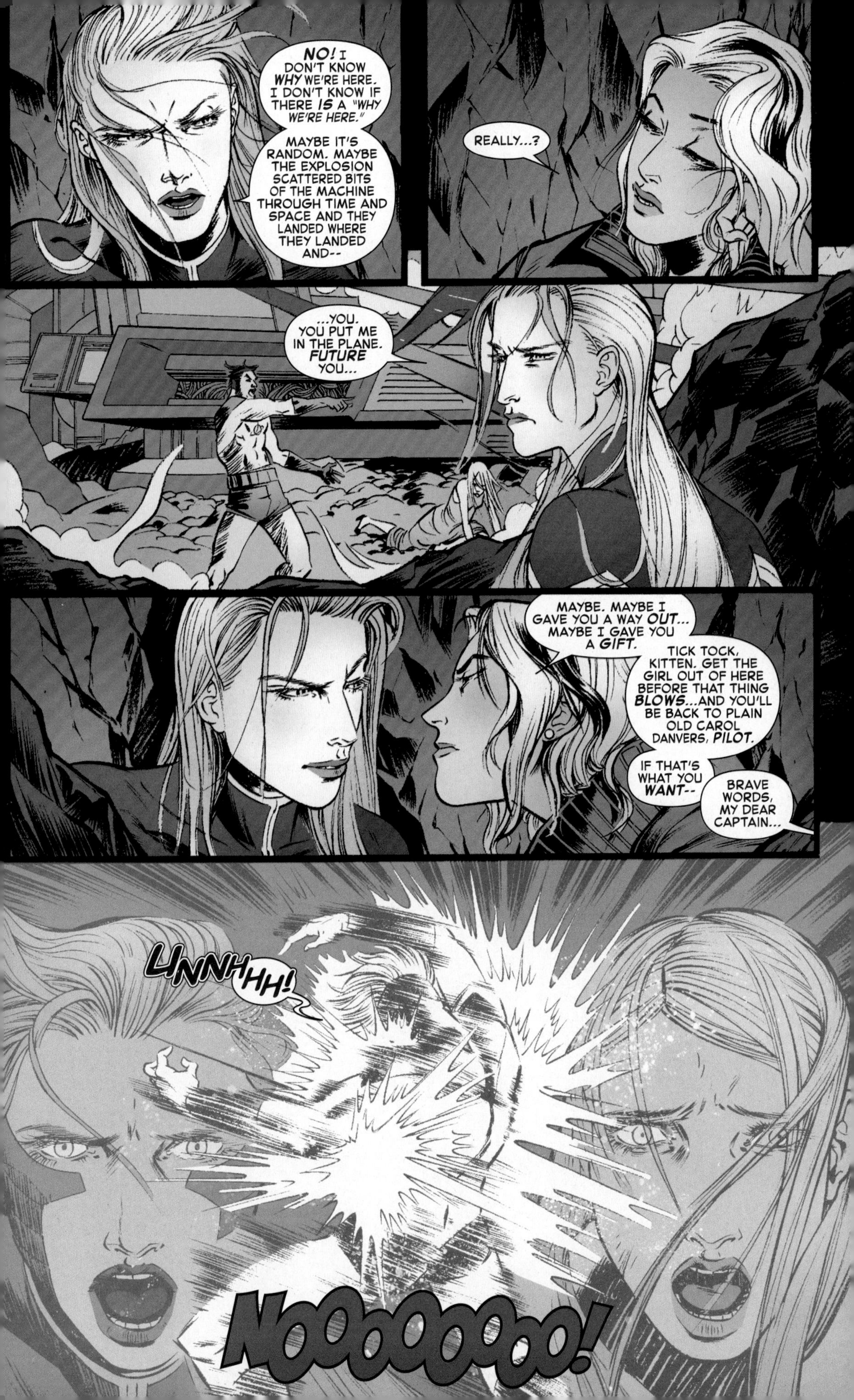
NO! I DON'T KNOW WHY WE'RE HERE. I DON'T KNOW IF THERE IS A "WHY WE'RE HERE."
MAYBE IT'S RANDOM. MAYBE THE EXPLOSION SCATTERED BITS OF THE MACHINE THROUGH TIME AND SPACE AND THEY LANDED WHERE THEY LANDED AND--
REALLY...?
...YOU. YOU PUT ME IN THE PLANE. FUTURE YOU...
MAYBE. MAYBE I GAVE YOU A WAY OUT... MAYBE I GAVE YOU A GIFT.
TICK TOCK, KITTEN. GET THE GIRL OUT OF HERE BEFORE THAT THING BLOWS...AND YOU'LL BE BACK TO PLAIN OLD CAROL DANVERS, PILOT.
IF THAT'S WHAT YOU WANT--
BRAVE WORDS, MY DEAR CAPTAIN...
UNNHHH!
NOOOOOOOO!

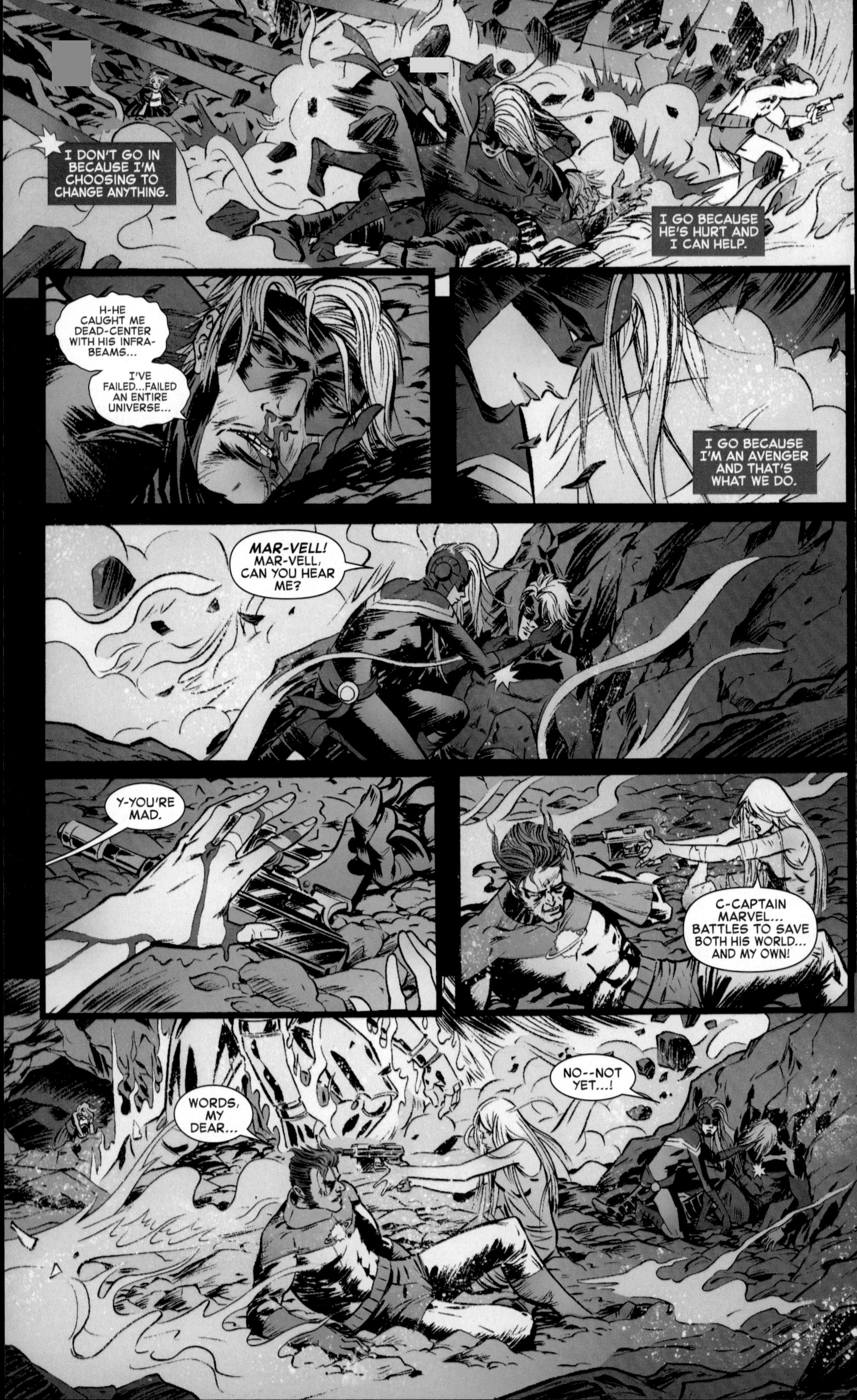
I DON'T GO IN BECAUSE I'M CHOOSING TO CHANGE ANYTHING.
I GO BECAUSE HE'S HURT AND I CAN HELP.
H-HE CAUGHT ME DEAD-CENTER WITH HIS INFRA-BEAMS...
I'VE FAILED...FAILED AN ENTIRE UNIVERSE...
I GO BECAUSE I'M AN AVENGER AND THAT'S WHAT WE DO.
MAR-VELL! MAR-VELL, CAN YOU HEAR ME?
Y-YOU'RE MAD.
C-CAPTAIN MARVEL... BATTLES TO SAVE BOTH HIS WORLD... AND MY OWN!
NO--NOT YET...!
WORDS, MY DEAR...

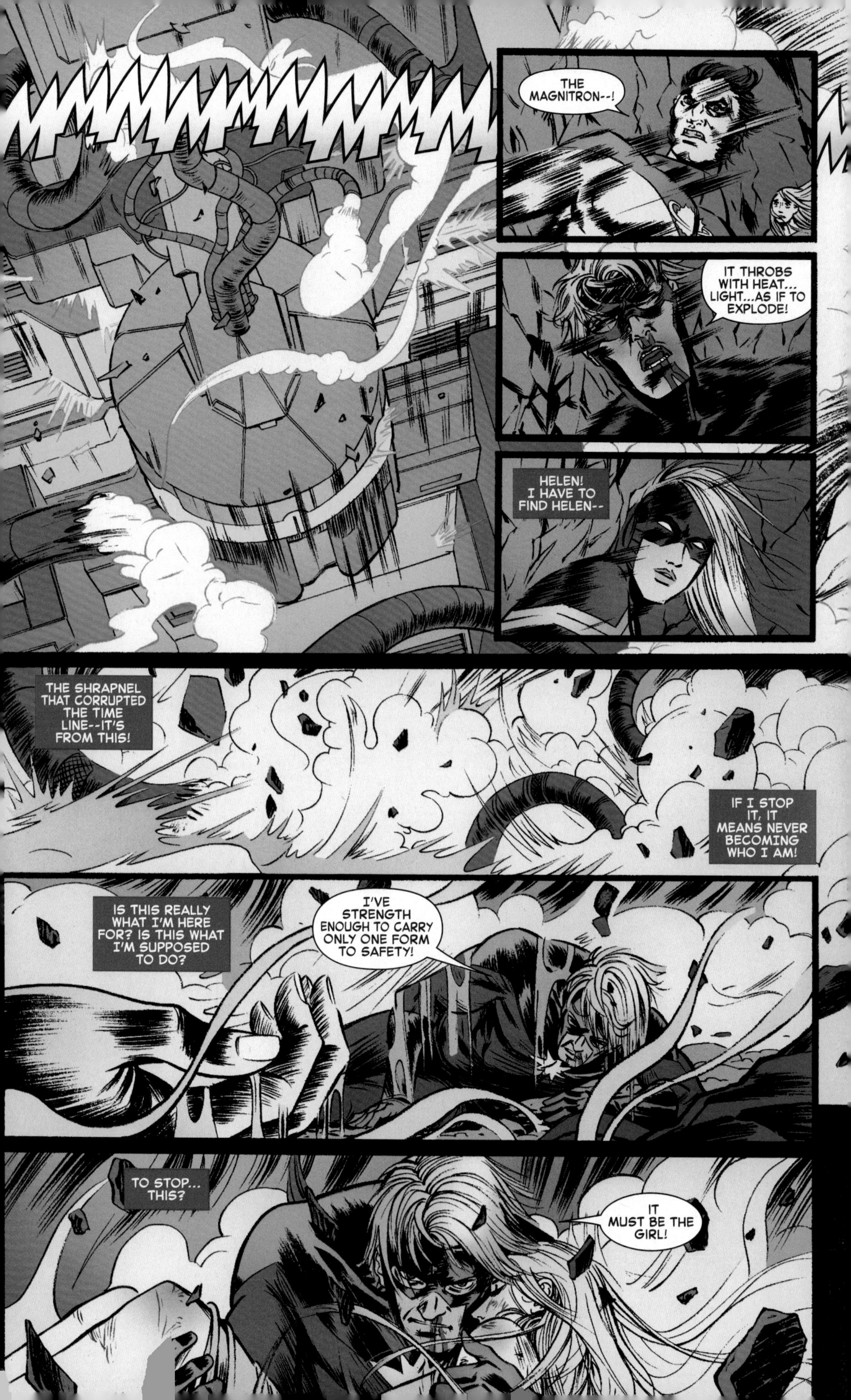
THE MAGNITRON--!
IT THROBS WITH HEAT... LIGHT...AS IF TO EXPLODE!
HELEN! I HAVE TO FIND HELEN--
THE SHRAPNEL THAT CORRUPTED THE TIME LINE--IT'S FROM THIS!
IF I STOP IT, IT MEANS NEVER BECOMING WHO I AM!
IS THIS REALLY WHAT I'M HERE FOR? IS THIS WHAT I'M SUPPOSED TO DO?
I'VE STRENGTH ENOUGH TO CARRY ONLY ONE FORM TO SAFETY!
TO STOP... THIS?
IT MUST BE THE GIRL!

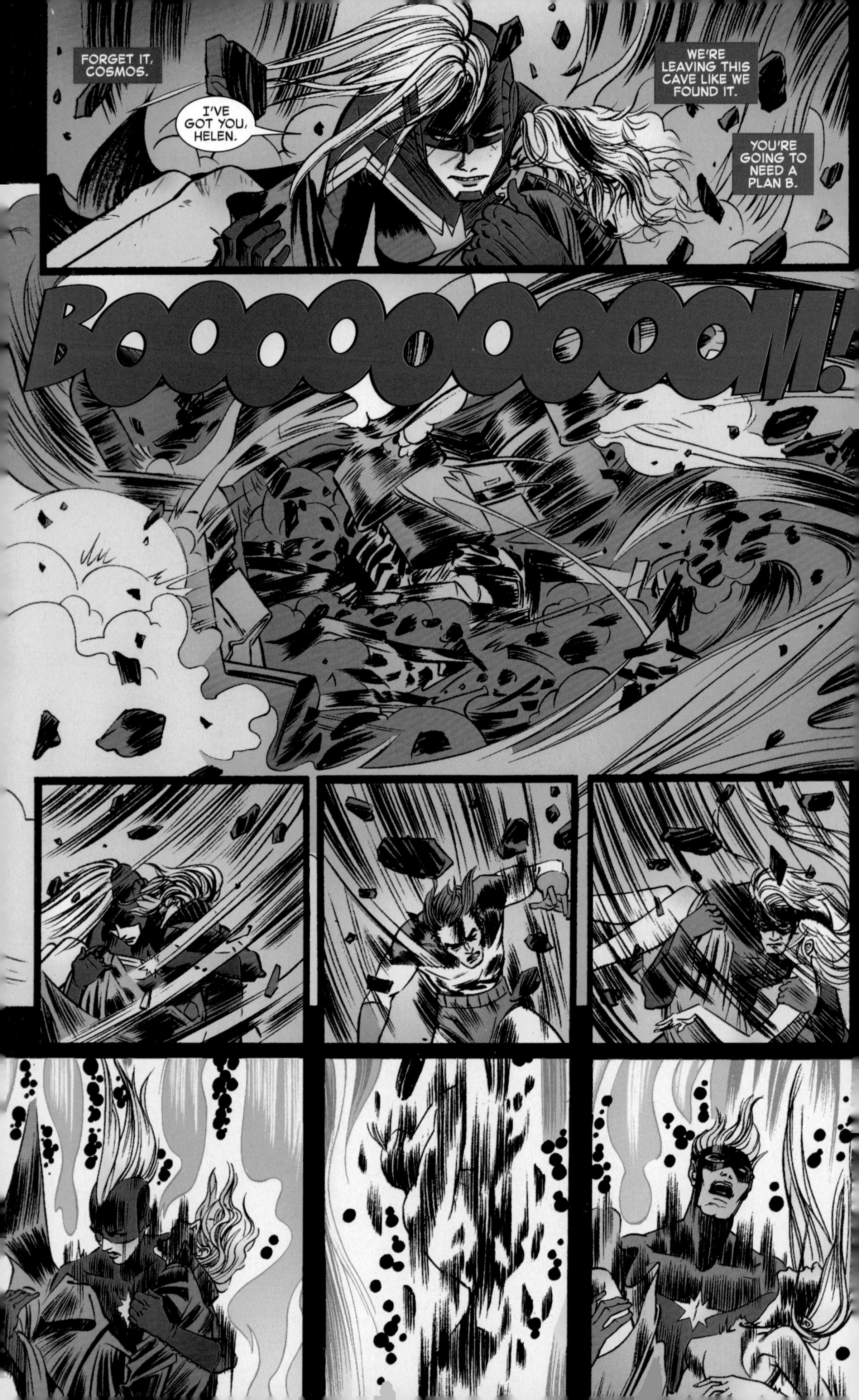
FORGET IT, COSMOS.
I'VE GOT YOU, HELEN.
WE'RE LEAVING THIS CAVE LIKE WE FOUND IT.
YOU'RE GOING TO NEED A PLAN B.
BOOOOOOOOOM!!

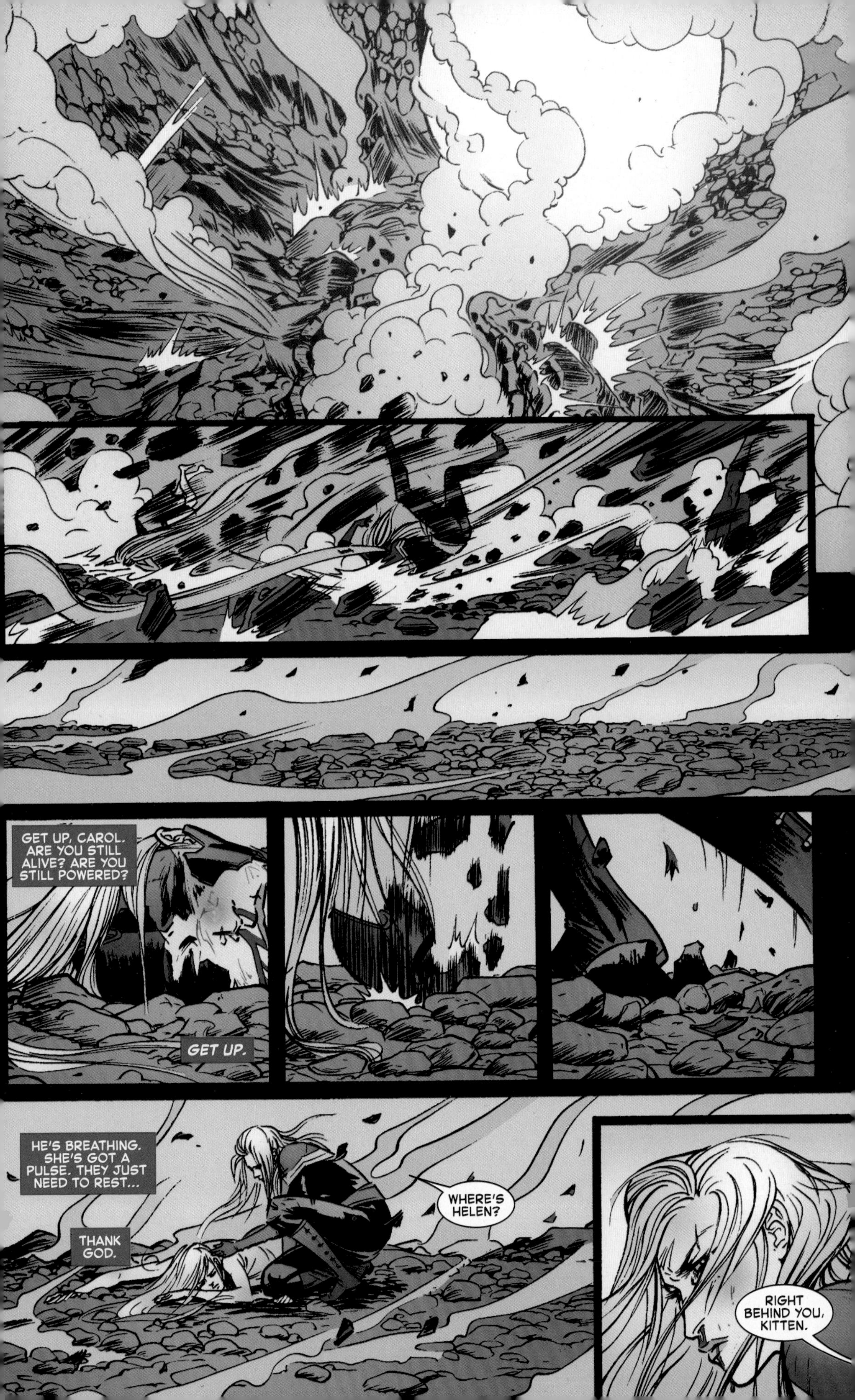
GET UP, CAROL. ARE YOU STILL ALIVE? ARE YOU STILL POWERED?
GET UP.
HE'S BREATHING. SHE'S GOT A PULSE. THEY JUST NEED TO REST...
THANK GOD.
WHERE'S HELEN?
RIGHT BEHIND YOU, KITTEN.

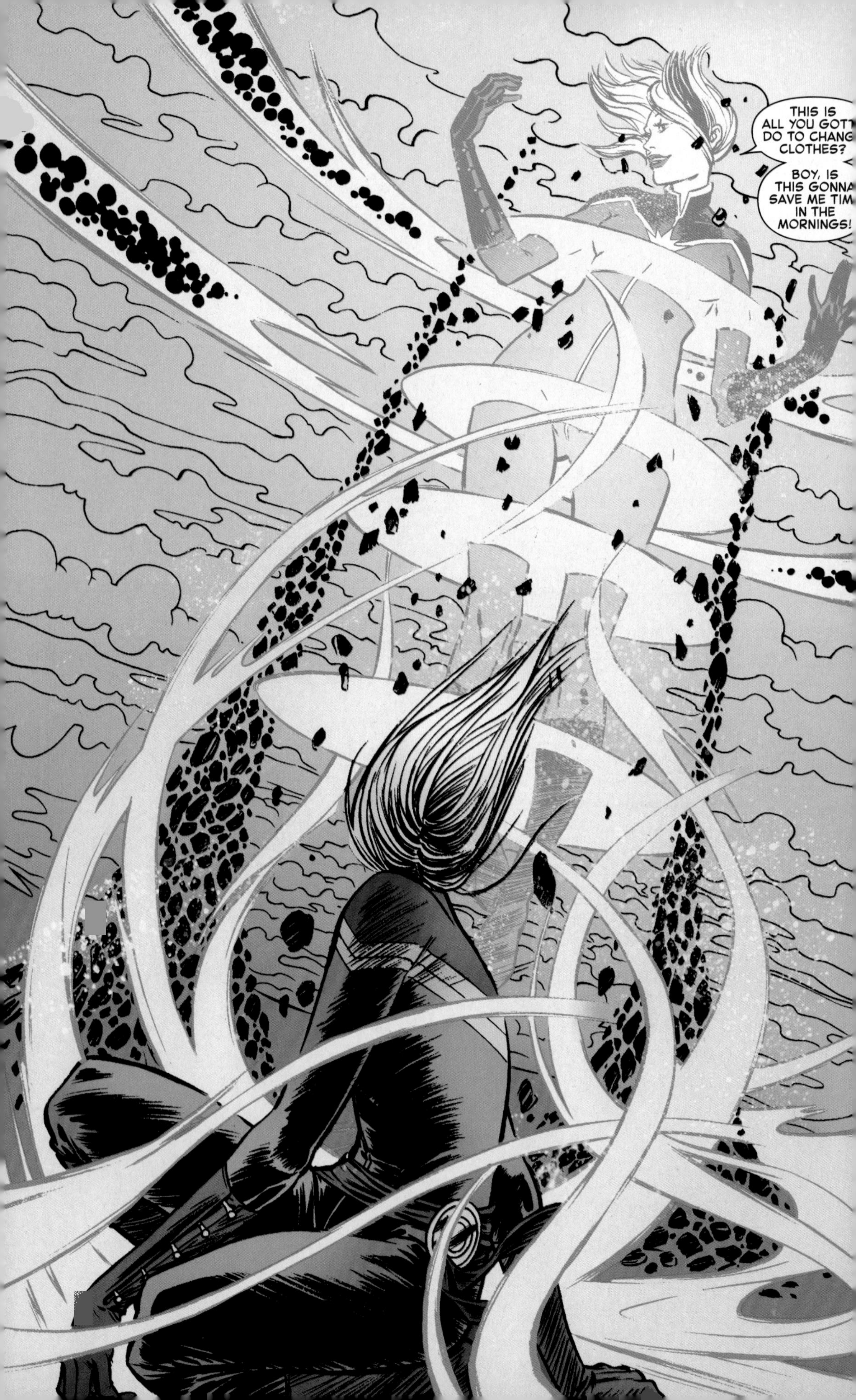
THIS IS ALL YOU GOTT DO TO CHANG CLOTHES?
BOY, IS THIS GONNA SAVE ME TIM IN THE MORNINGS!

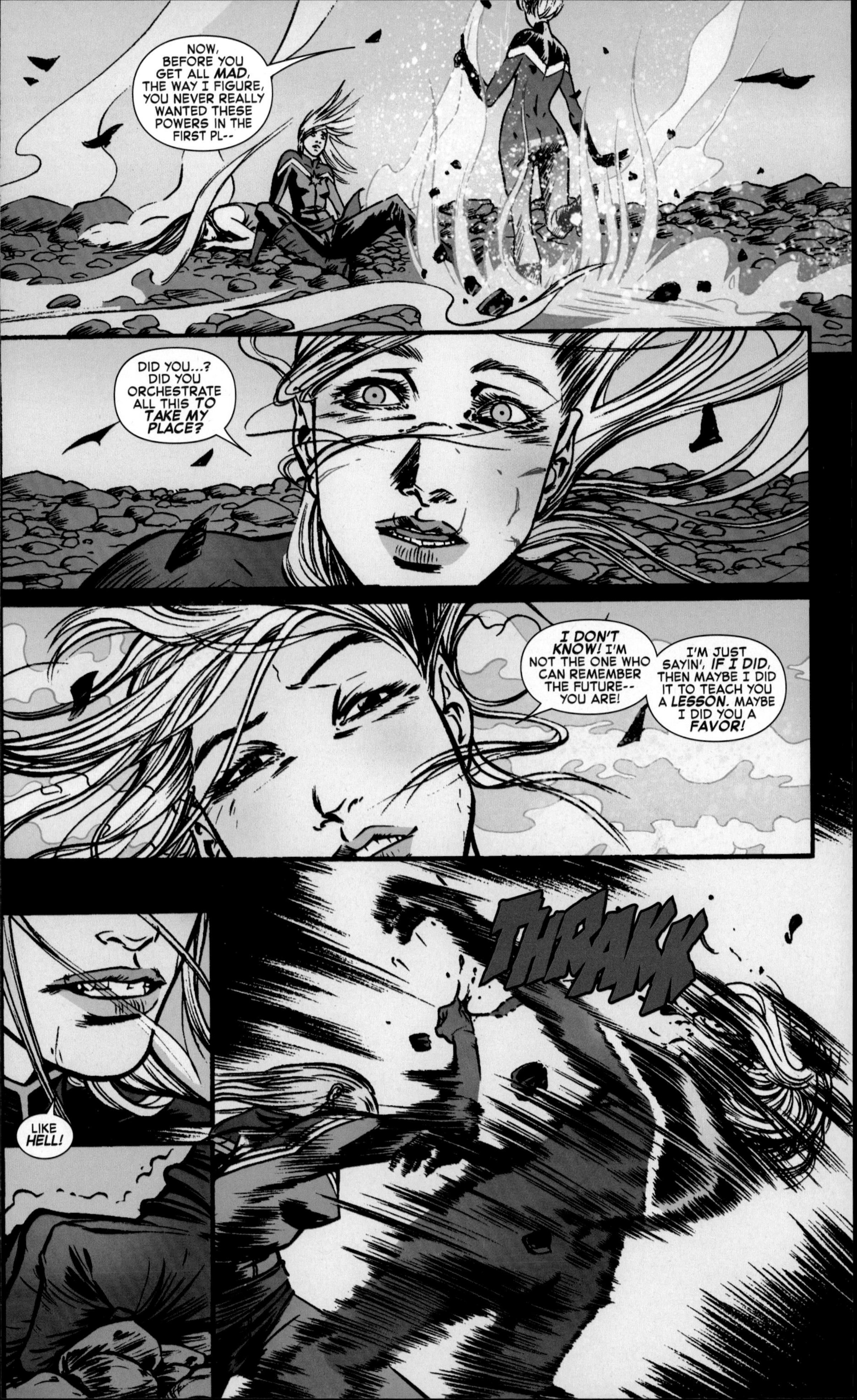
NOW, BEFORE YOU GET ALL MAD, THE WAY I FIGURE, YOU NEVER REALLY WANTED THESE POWERS IN THE FIRST PL--
DID YOU...? DID YOU ORCHESTRATE ALL THIS TO TAKE MY PLACE?
I DON'T KNOW! I'M NOT THE ONE WHO CAN REMEMBER THE FUTURE-- YOU ARE!
I'M JUST SAYIN', IF I DID, THEN MAYBE I DID IT TO TEACH YOU A LESSON. MAYBE I DID YOU A FAVOR!
LIKE HELL!
THRAKK

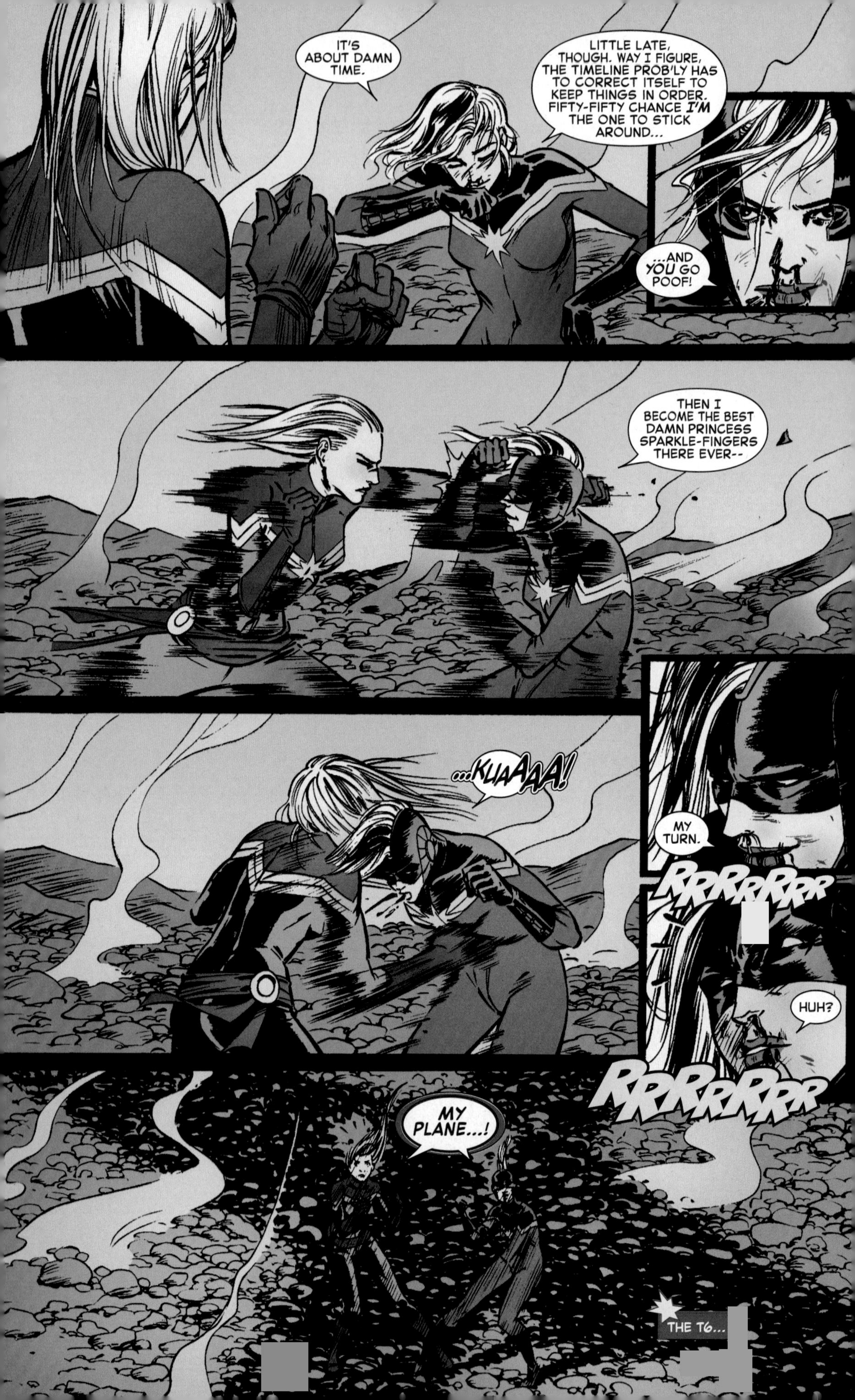
IT'S ABOUT DAMN TIME.
LITTLE LATE, THOUGH. WAY I FIGURE, THE TIMELINE PROB'LY HAS TO CORRECT ITSELF TO KEEP THINGS IN ORDER. FIFTY-FIFTY CHANCE I'M THE ONE TO STICK AROUND...
...AND YOU GO POOF!
THEN I BECOME THE BEST DAMN PRINCESS SPARKLE-FINGERS THERE EVER--
...KUAAAA!
MY TURN.
RRRRRRRR
HUH?
RRRRRRRR
MY PLANE...!
THE T6...

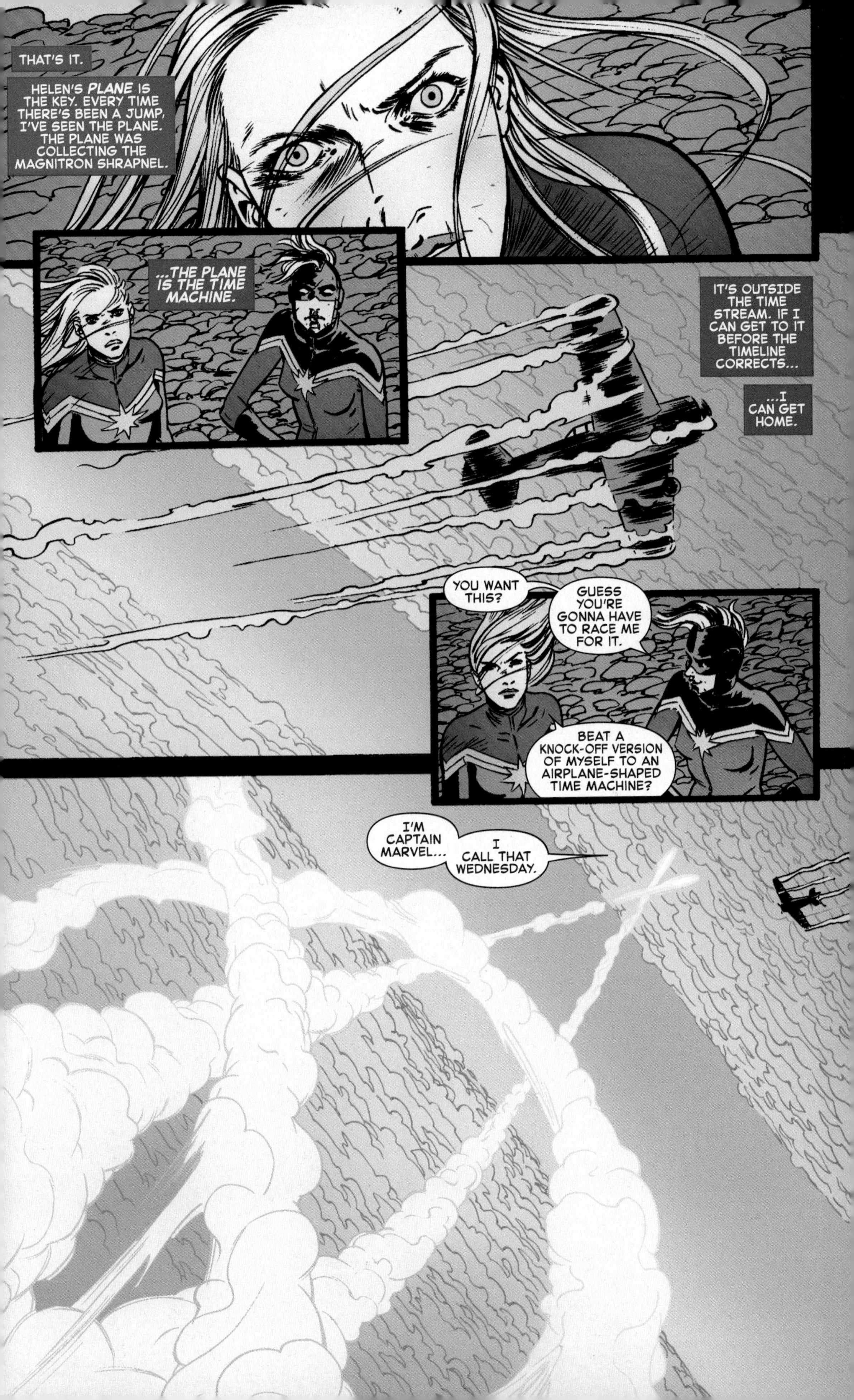
THAT'S IT.
HELEN'S PLANE IS THE KEY. EVERY TIME THERE'S BEEN A JUMP, I'VE SEEN THE PLANE. THE PLANE WAS COLLECTING THE MAGNITRON SHRAPNEL.
...THE PLANE IS THE TIME MACHINE.
IT'S OUTSIDE THE TIME STREAM. IF I CAN GET TO IT BEFORE THE TIMELINE CORRECTS...
...I CAN GET HOME.
YOU WANT THIS?
GUESS YOU'RE GONNA HAVE TO RACE ME FOR IT.
BEAT A KNOCK-OFF VERSION OF MYSELF TO AN AIRPLANE-SHAPED TIME MACHINE?
I'M CAPTAIN MARVEL...
I CALL THAT WEDNESDAY.

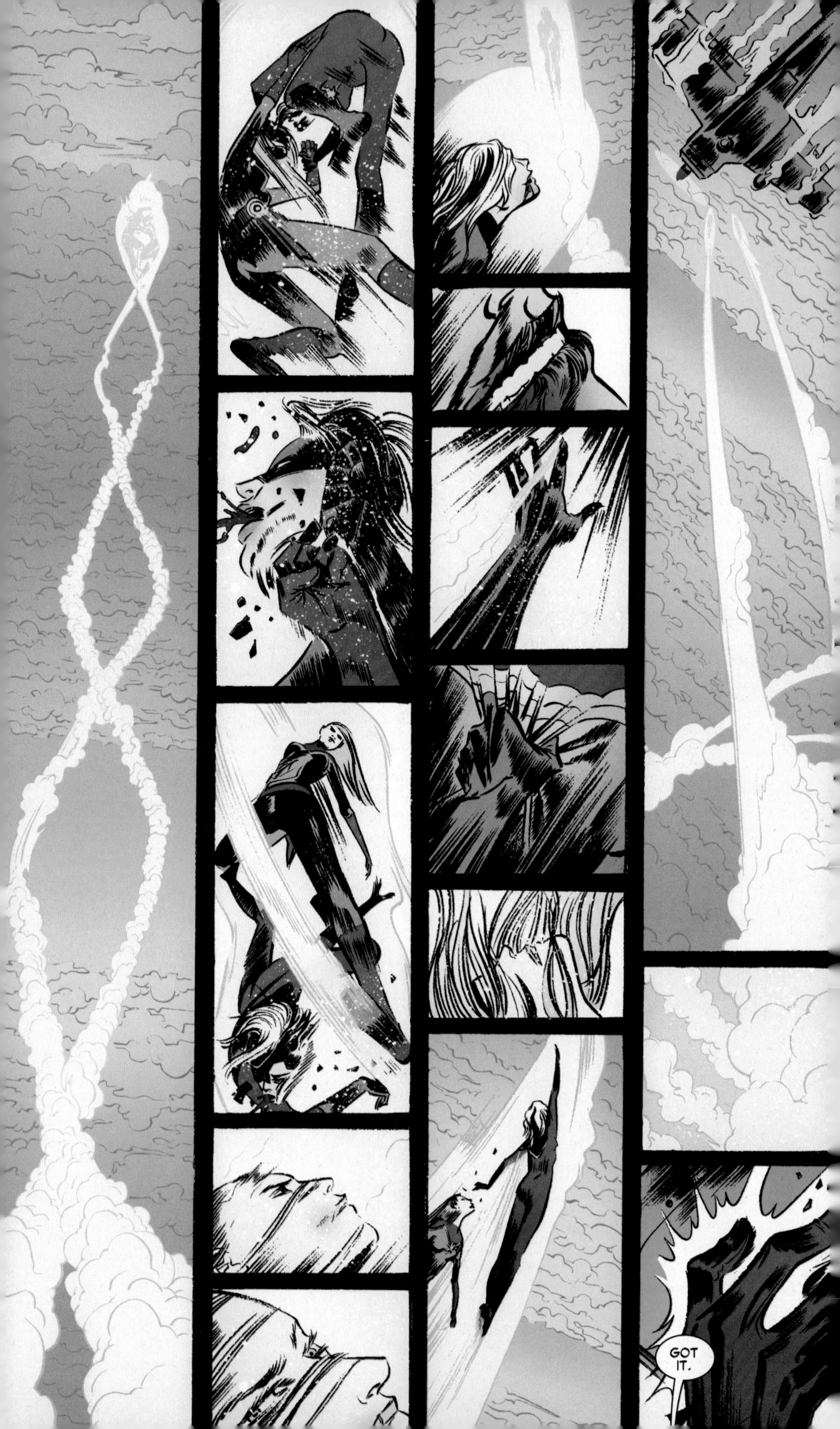
GOT IT.

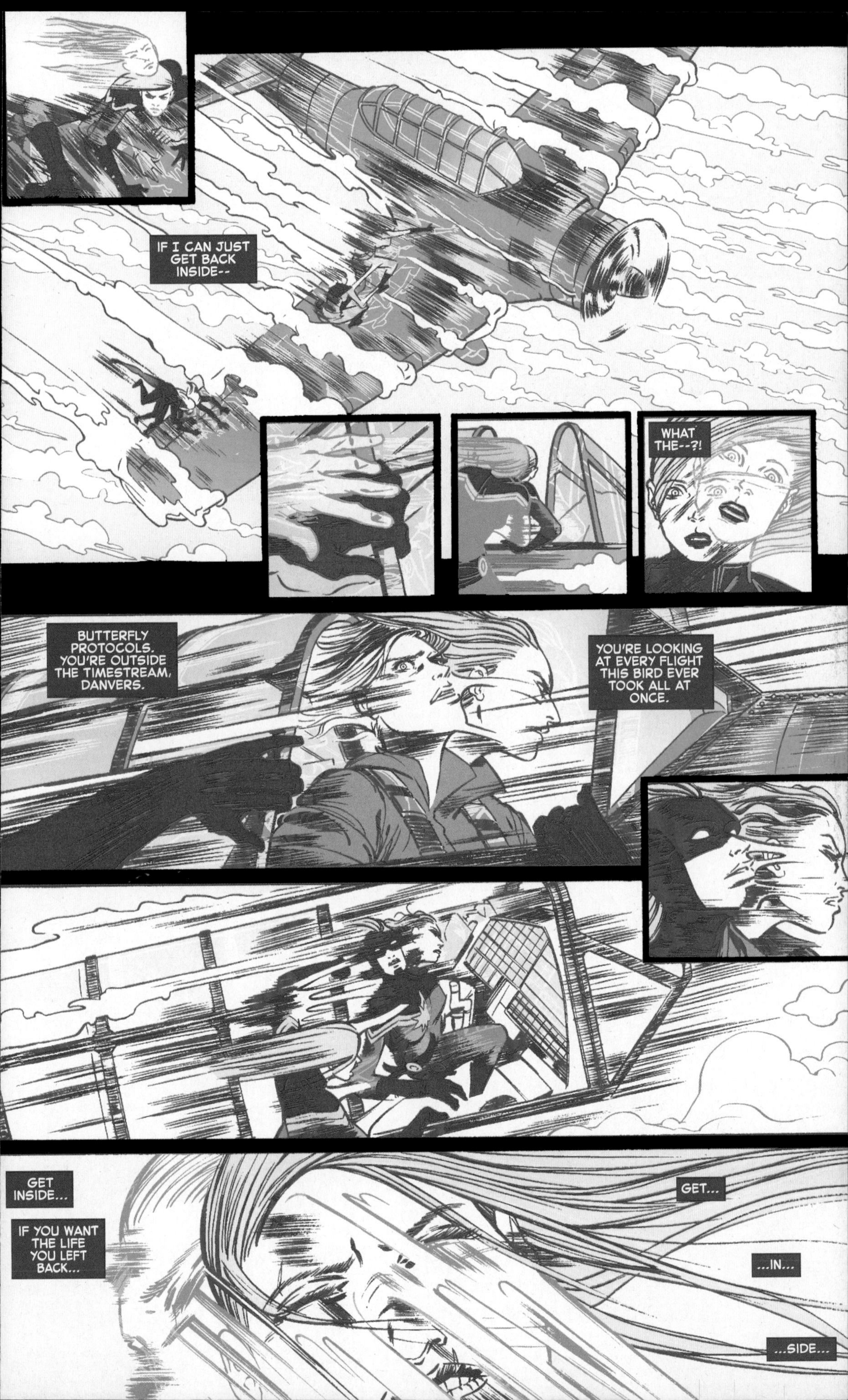
IF I CAN JUST GET BACK INSIDE--
WHAT THE--?!
BUTTERFLY PROTOCOLS. YOU'RE OUTSIDE THE TIMESTREAM, DANVERS.
YOU'RE LOOKING AT EVERY FLIGHT THIS BIRD EVER TOOK ALL AT ONCE.
GET INSIDE...
IF YOU WANT THE LIFE YOU LEFT BACK...
GET...
...IN...
...SIDE...

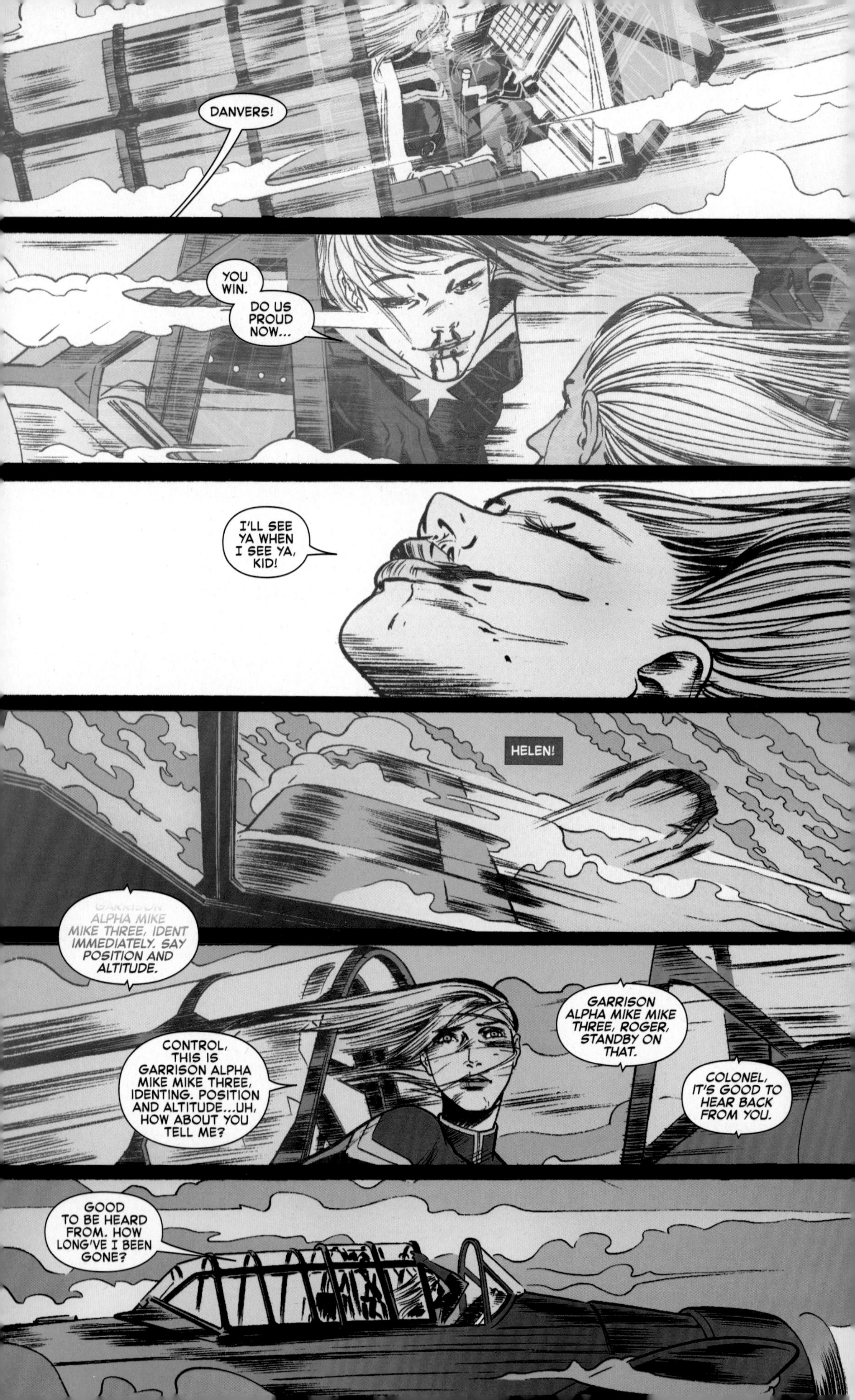
DANVERS!
YOU WIN.
DO US PROUD NOW...
I'LL SEE YA WHEN I SEE YA, KID!
HELEN!
GARRISON ALPHA MIKE MIKE THREE, IDENT IMMEDIATELY. SAY POSITION AND ALTITUDE.
CONTROL, THIS IS GARRISON ALPHA MIKE MIKE THREE, IDENTING. POSITION AND ALTITUDE...UH, HOW ABOUT YOU TELL ME?
GARRISON ALPHA MIKE MIKE THREE, ROGER, STANDBY ON THAT.
COLONEL, IT'S GOOD TO HEAR BACK FROM YOU.
GOOD TO BE HEARD FROM. HOW LONG'VE I BEEN GONE?

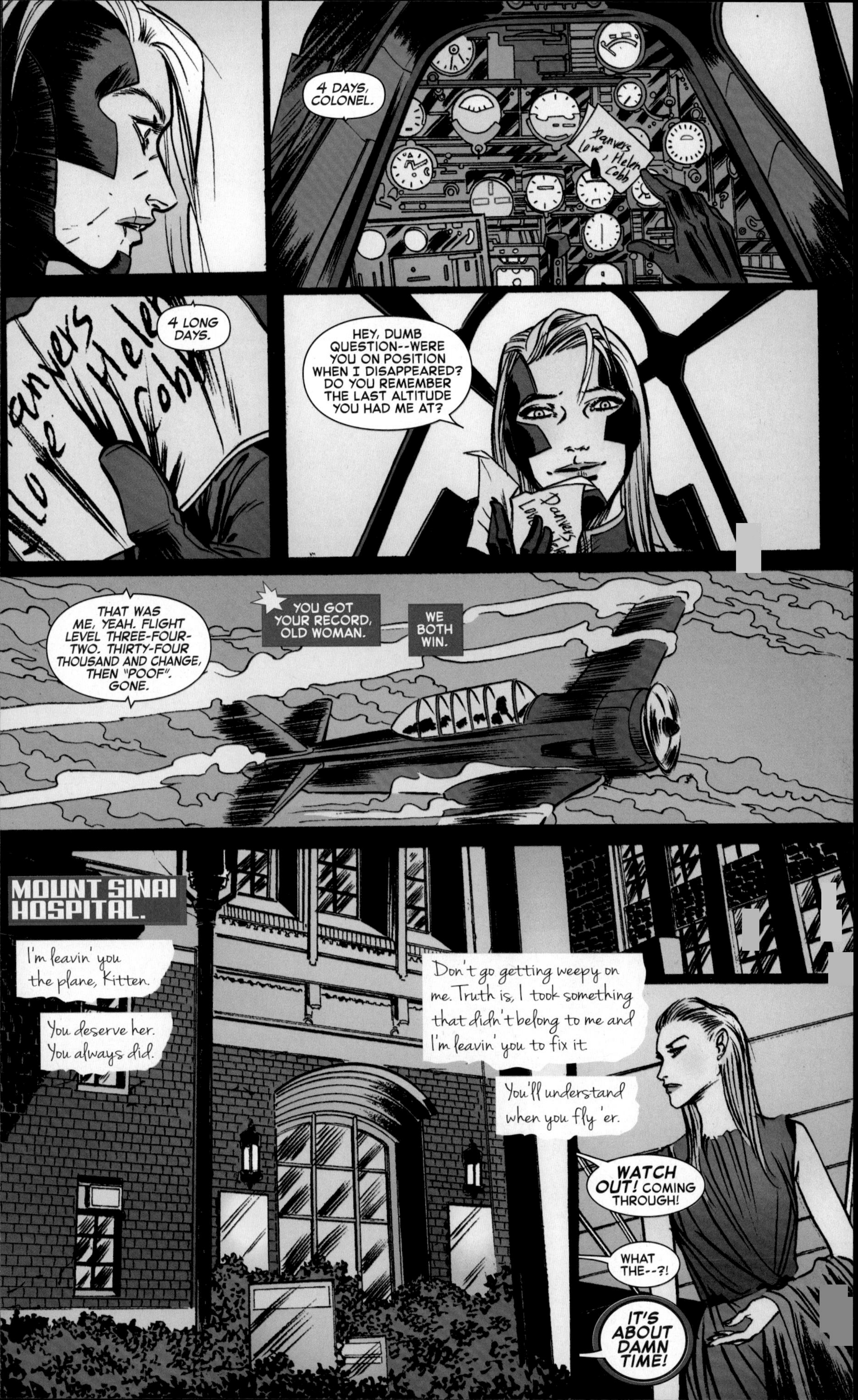
4 DAYS, COLONEL.
Danvers Love, Helen Cobb
Danvers Love, Helen Cobb
4 LONG DAYS.
HEY, DUMB QUESTION--WERE YOU ON POSITION WHEN I DISAPPEARED? DO YOU REMEMBER THE LAST ALTITUDE YOU HAD ME AT?
THAT WAS ME, YEAH. FLIGHT LEVEL THREE-FOUR-TWO. THIRTY-FOUR THOUSAND AND CHANGE, THEN "POOF". GONE.
YOU GOT YOUR RECORD, OLD WOMAN.
WE BOTH WIN.
MOUNT SINAI HOSPITAL.
I'm leavin' you the plane, Kitten.
You deserve her. You always did.
Don't go getting weepy on me. Truth is, I took something that didn't belong to me and I'm leavin' you to fix it.
You'll understand when you fly 'er.
WATCH OUT! COMING THROUGH!
WHAT THE--?!
IT'S ABOUT DAMN TIME!

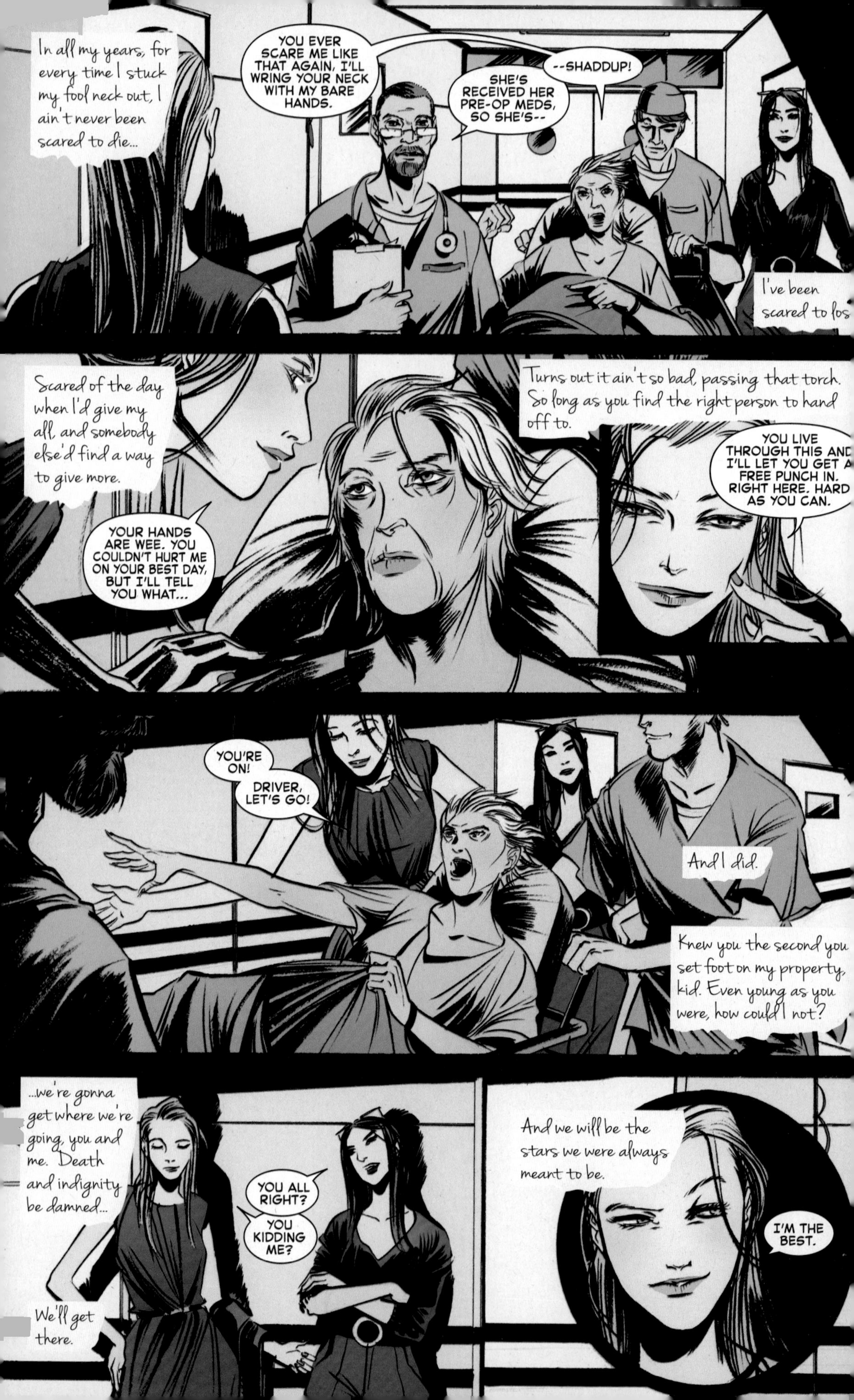
In all my years, for every time I stuck my fool neck out, I ain't never been scared to die...
YOU EVER SCARE ME LIKE THAT AGAIN, I'LL WRING YOUR NECK WITH MY BARE HANDS.
SHE'S RECEIVED HER PRE-OP MEDS, SO SHE'S--
--SHADDUP!
I've been scared to los
Scared of the day when I'd give my all, and somebody else'd find a way to give more.
YOUR HANDS ARE WEE. YOU COULDN'T HURT ME ON YOUR BEST DAY, BUT I'LL TELL YOU WHAT...
Turns out it ain't so bad, passing that torch. So long as you find the right person to hand off to.
YOU LIVE THROUGH THIS AND I'LL LET YOU GET A FREE PUNCH IN. RIGHT HERE. HARD AS YOU CAN.
YOU'RE ON!
DRIVER, LET'S GO!
And I did.
Knew you the second you set foot on my property, kid. Even young as you were, how could I not?
...we're gonna get where we're going, you and me. Death and indignity be damned...
YOU ALL RIGHT?
YOU KIDDING ME?
We'll get there.
And we will be the stars we were always meant to be.
I'M THE BEST.

CAPTAIN MARVEL #7

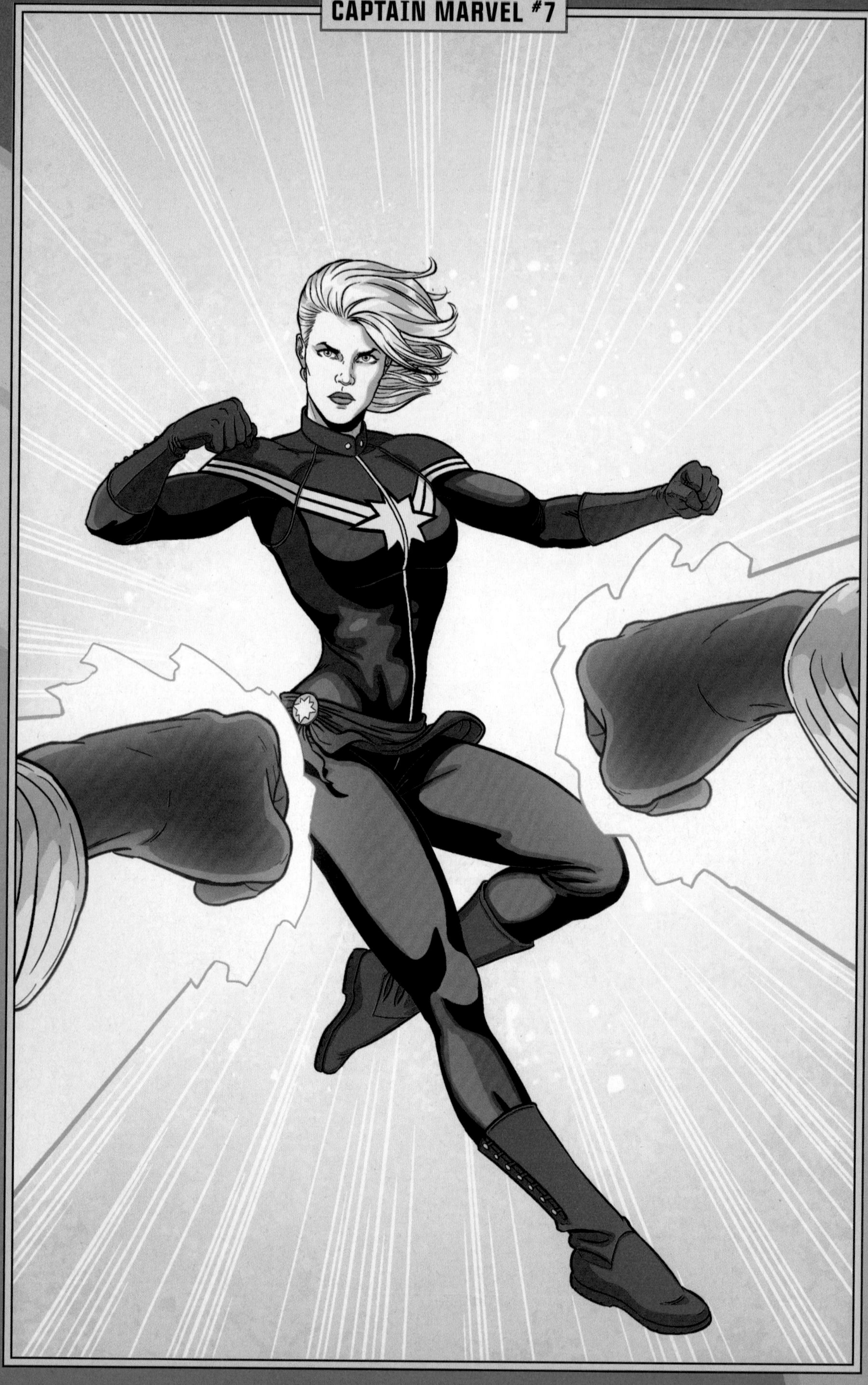

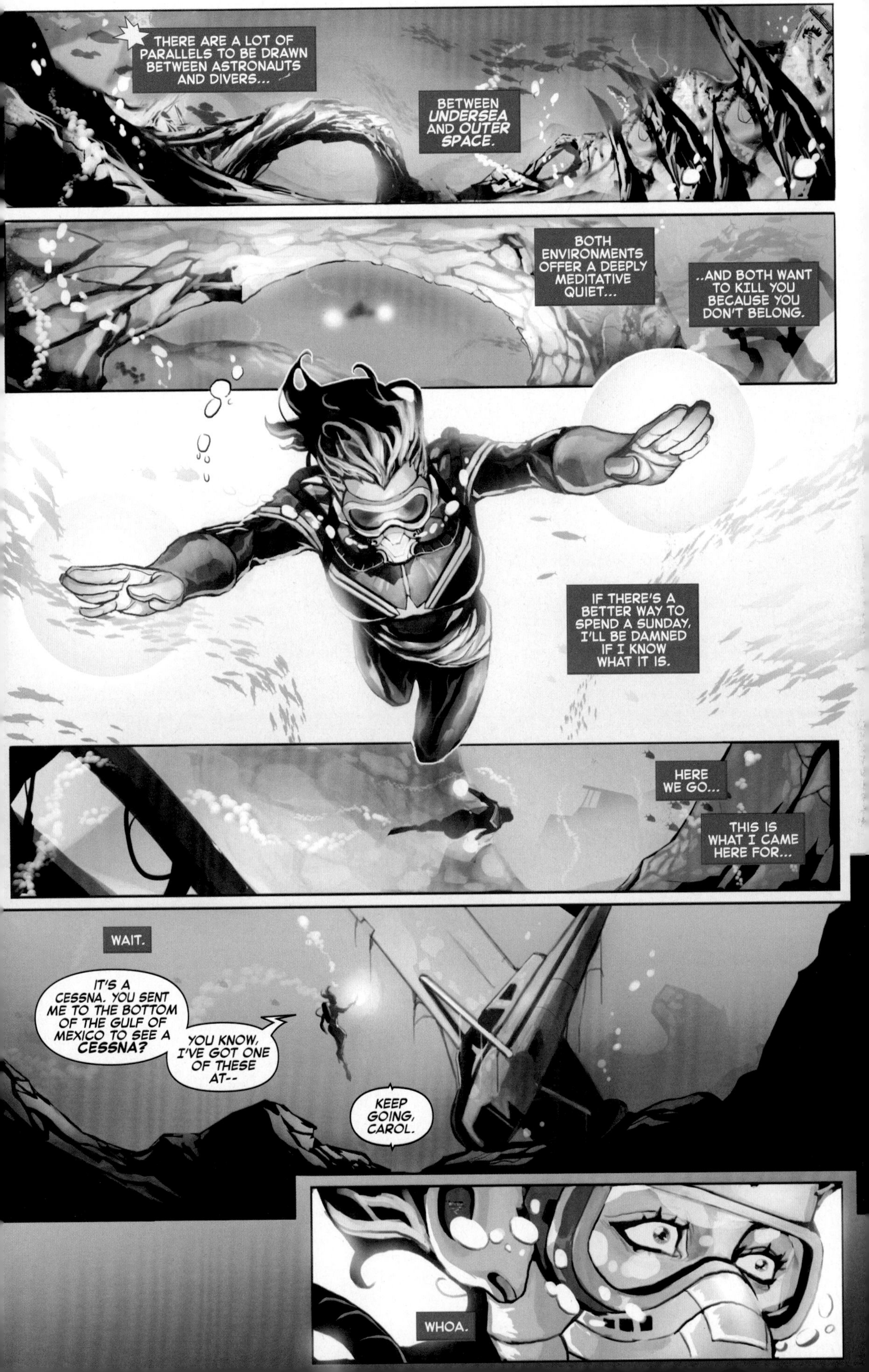
THERE ARE A LOT OF PARALLELS TO BE DRAWN BETWEEN ASTRONAUTS AND DIVERS...
BETWEEN UNDERSEA AND OUTER SPACE.
BOTH ENVIRONMENTS OFFER A DEEPLY MEDITATIVE QUIET...
..AND BOTH WANT TO KILL YOU BECAUSE YOU DON'T BELONG.
IF THERE'S A BETTER WAY TO SPEND A SUNDAY, I'LL BE DAMNED IF I KNOW WHAT IT IS.
HERE WE GO...
THIS IS WHAT I CAME HERE FOR...
WAIT.
IT'S A CESSNA. YOU SENT ME TO THE BOTTOM OF THE GULF OF MEXICO TO SEE A CESSNA?
YOU KNOW, I'VE GOT ONE OF THESE AT--
KEEP GOING, CAROL.
WHOA.

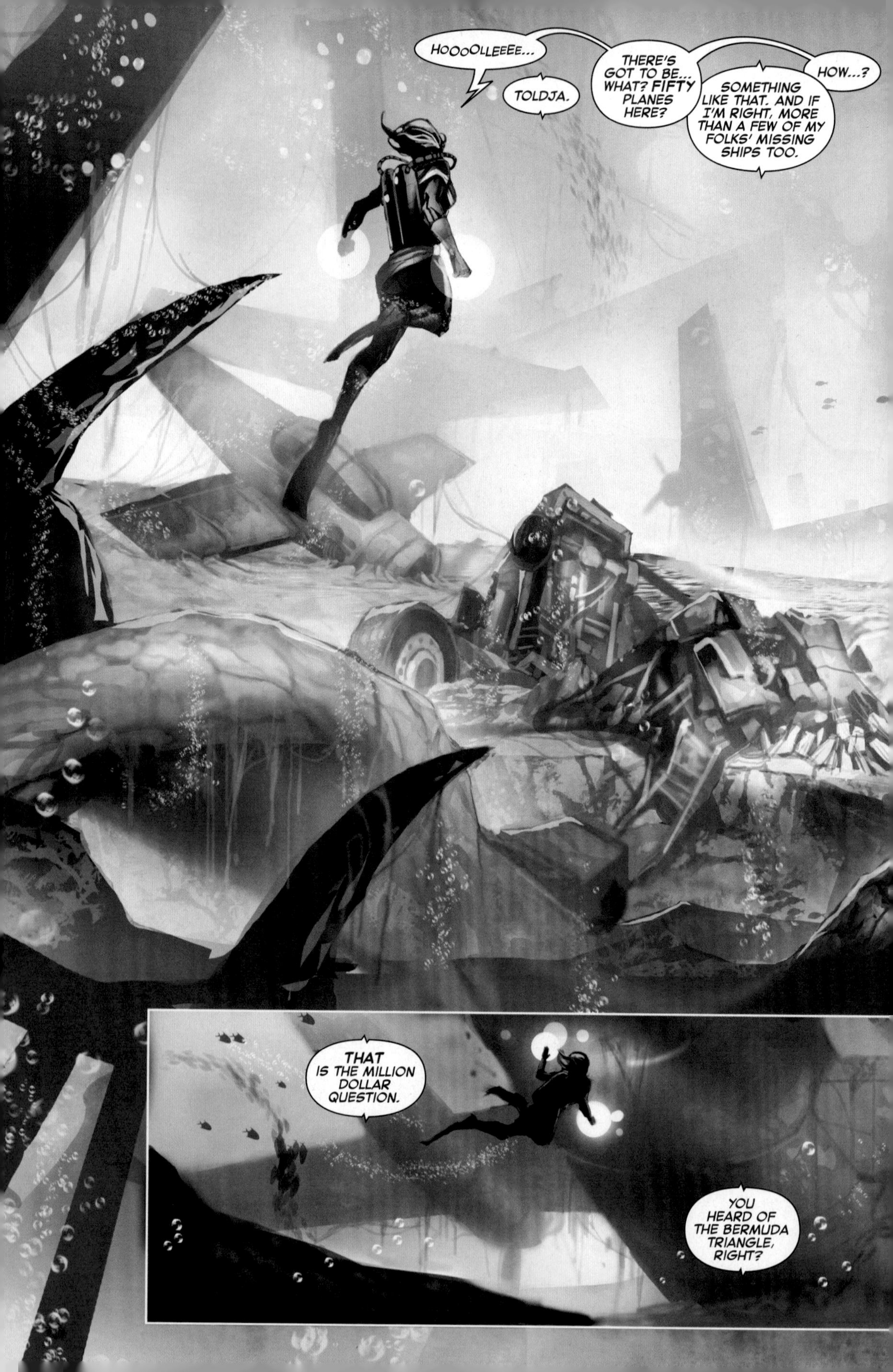
HOOOOLLEEEE...
TOLDJA.
THERE'S GOT TO BE... WHAT? FIFTY PLANES HERE?
HOW...?
SOMETHING LIKE THAT. AND IF I'M RIGHT, MORE THAN A FEW OF MY FOLKS' MISSING SHIPS TOO.
THAT IS THE MILLION DOLLAR QUESTION.
YOU HEARD OF THE BERMUDA TRIANGLE, RIGHT?

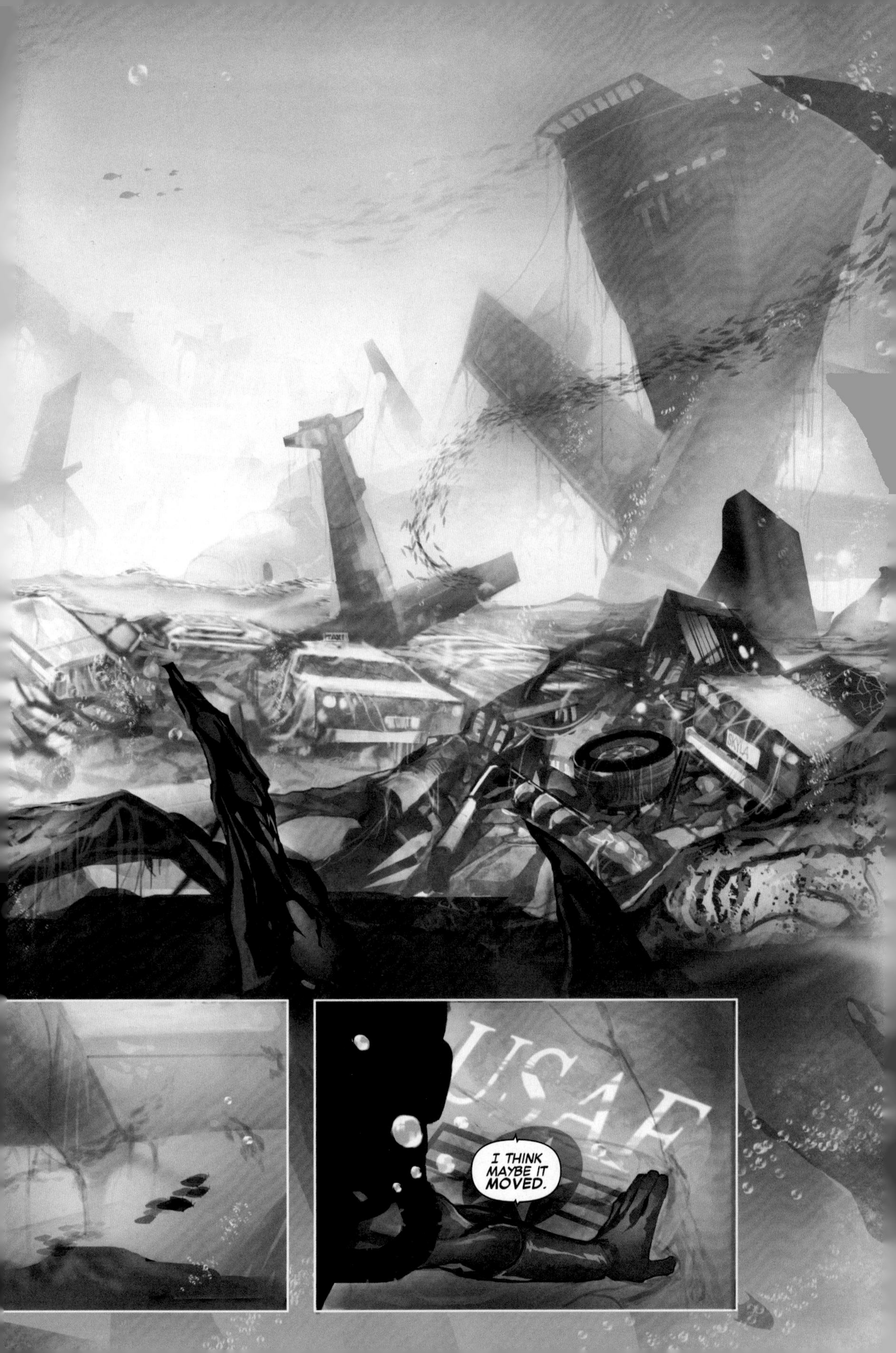
USAF
I THINK MAYBE IT MOVED.

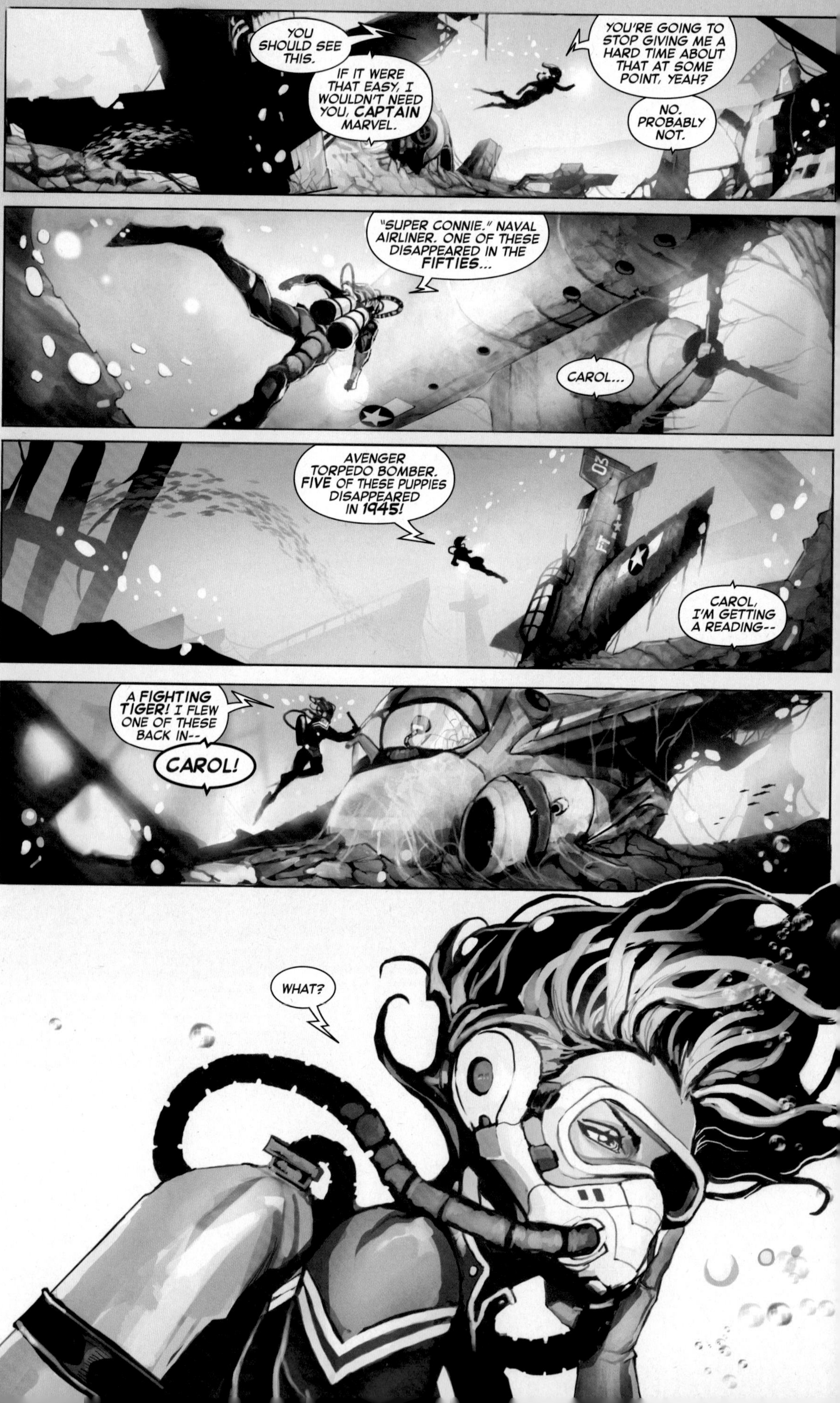
YOU SHOULD SEE THIS.
IF IT WERE THAT EASY, I WOULDN'T NEED YOU, CAPTAIN MARVEL.
YOU'RE GOING TO STOP GIVING ME A HARD TIME ABOUT THAT AT SOME POINT, YEAH?
NO. PROBABLY NOT.
"SUPER CONNIE." NAVAL AIRLINER. ONE OF THESE DISAPPEARED IN THE FIFTIES...
CAROL...
AVENGER TORPEDO BOMBER. FIVE OF THESE PUPPIES DISAPPEARED IN 1945!
CAROL, I'M GETTING A READING--
A FIGHTING TIGER! I FLEW ONE OF THESE BACK IN--
CAROL!
WHAT?

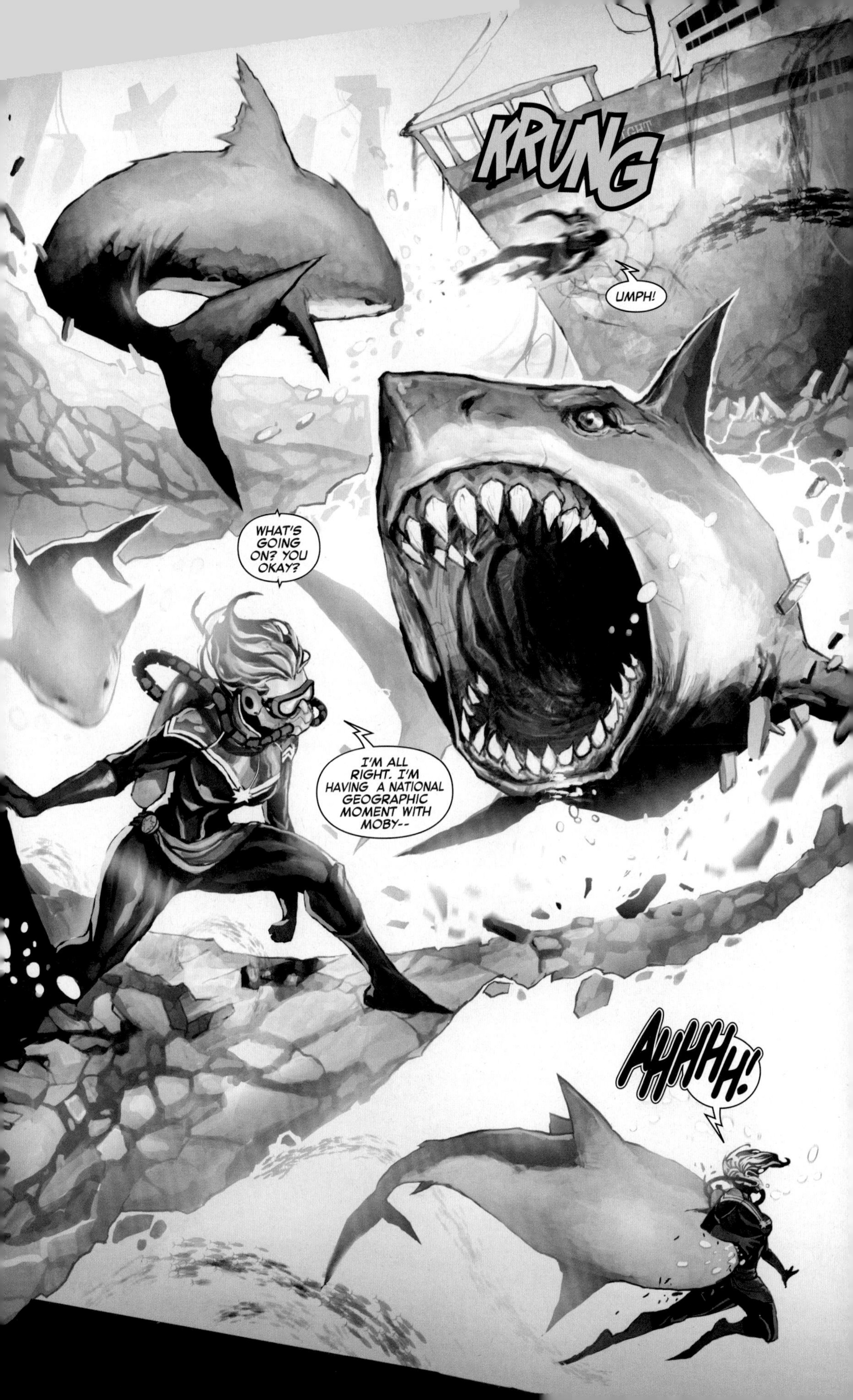
KRUNG
UMPH!
WHAT'S GOING ON? YOU OKAY?
I'M ALL RIGHT. I'M HAVING A NATIONAL GEOGRAPHIC MOMENT WITH MOBY--
AHHHH!

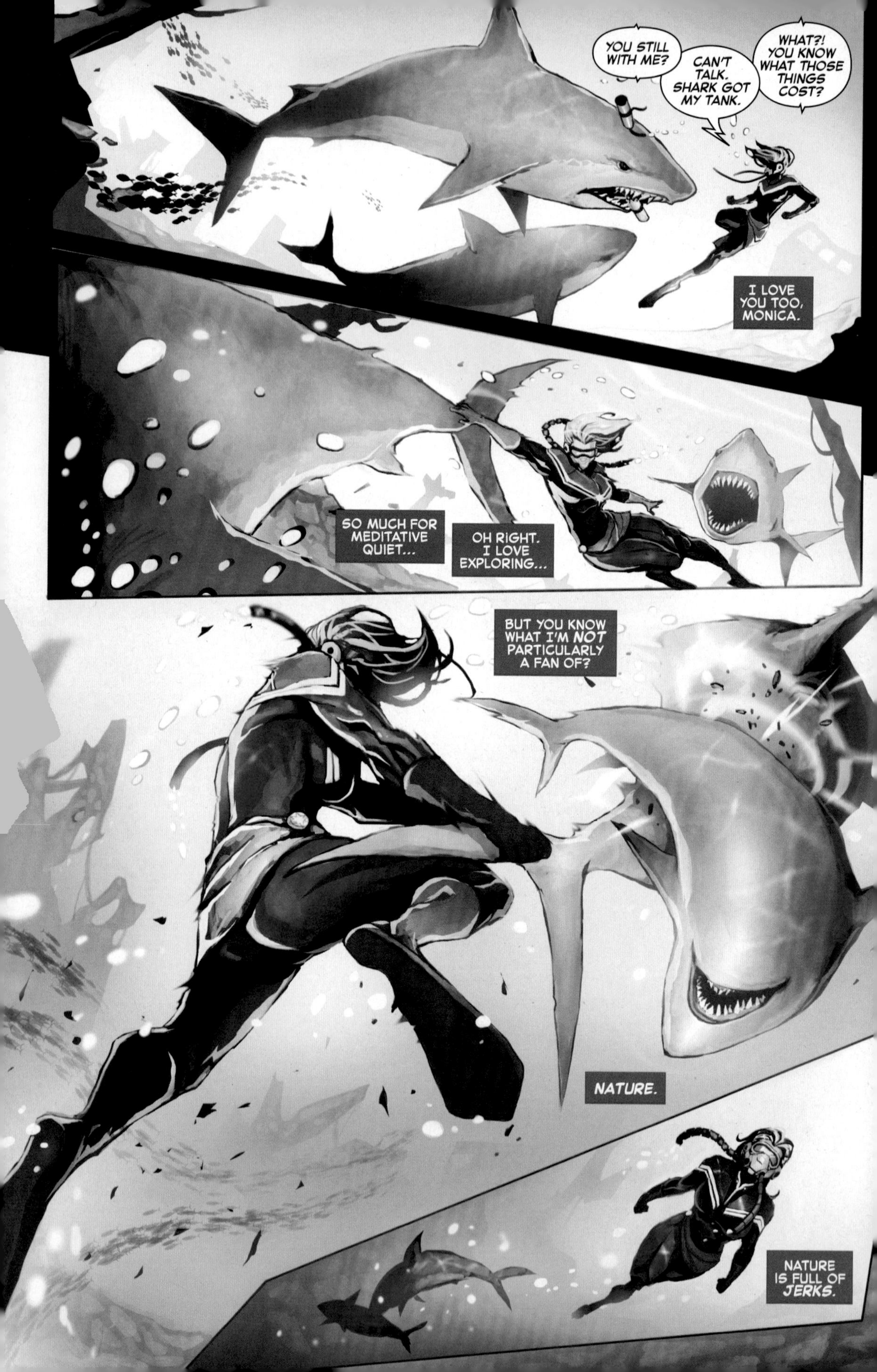
YOU STILL WITH ME?
CAN'T TALK. SHARK GOT MY TANK.
WHAT?! YOU KNOW WHAT THOSE THINGS COST?
I LOVE YOU TOO, MONICA.
SO MUCH FOR MEDITATIVE QUIET...
OH RIGHT. I LOVE EXPLORING...
BUT YOU KNOW WHAT I'M *NOT* PARTICULARLY A FAN OF?
NATURE.
NATURE IS FULL OF *JERKS.*

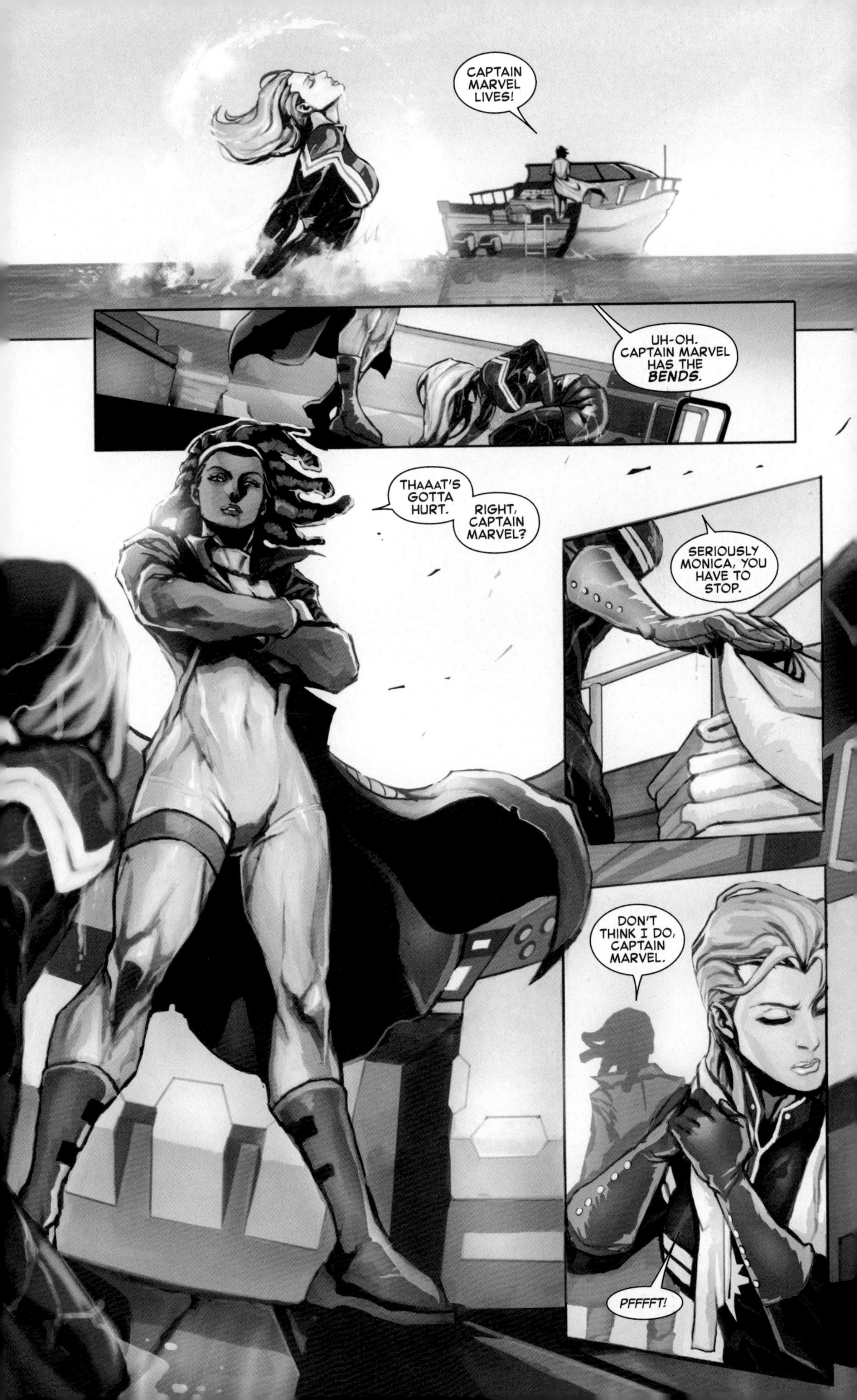
CAPTAIN MARVEL LIVES!
UH-OH. CAPTAIN MARVEL HAS THE BENDS.
THAAAT'S GOTTA HURT.
RIGHT, CAPTAIN MARVEL?
SERIOUSLY MONICA, YOU HAVE TO STOP.
DON'T THINK I DO, CAPTAIN MARVEL.
PFFFFT!

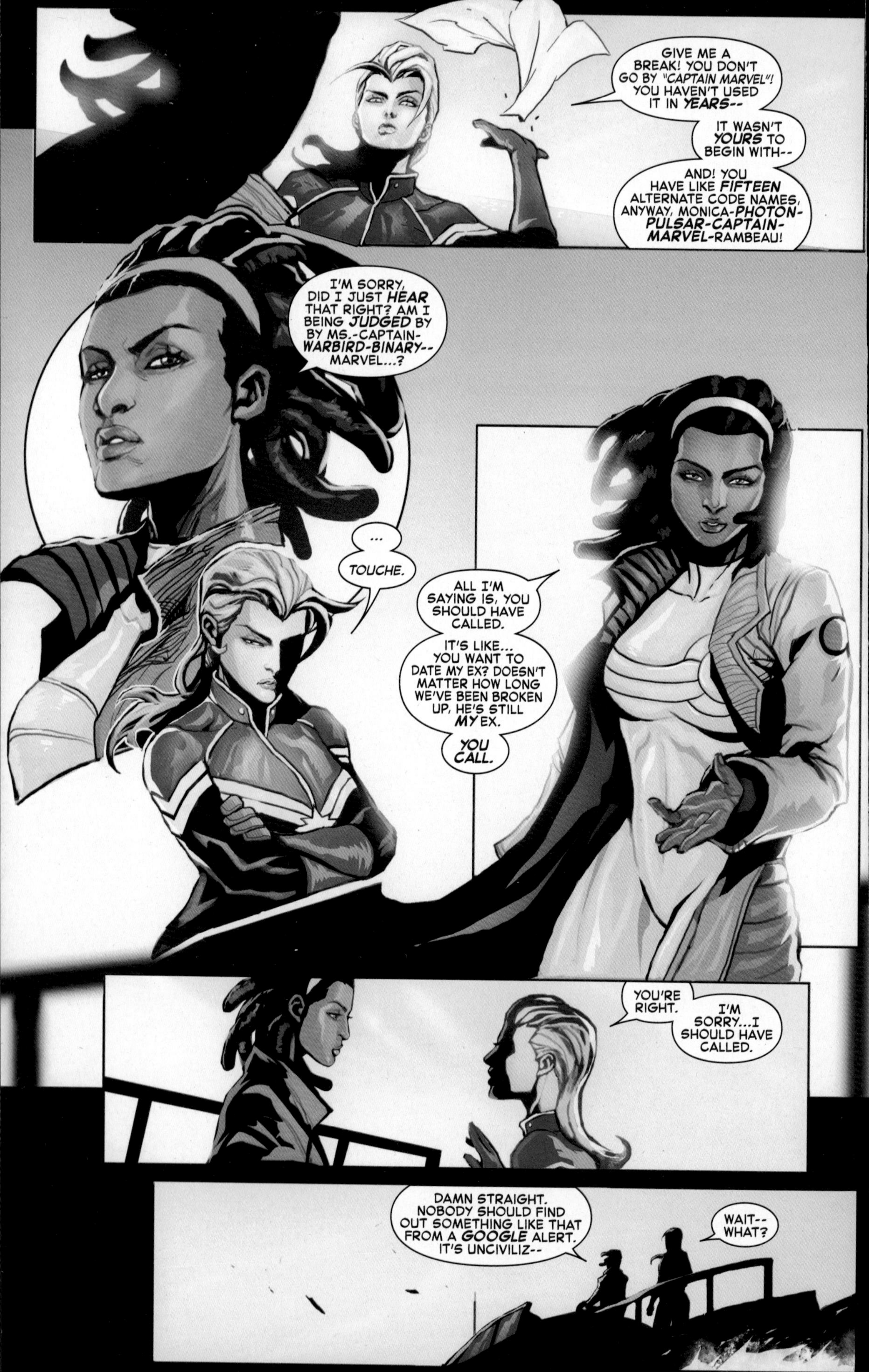
GIVE ME A BREAK! YOU DON'T GO BY "CAPTAIN MARVEL"! YOU HAVEN'T USED IT IN YEARS--
IT WASN'T YOURS TO BEGIN WITH--
AND! YOU HAVE LIKE FIFTEEN ALTERNATE CODE NAMES, ANYWAY, MONICA-PHOTON-PULSAR-CAPTAIN-MARVEL-RAMBEAU!
I'M SORRY, DID I JUST HEAR THAT RIGHT? AM I BEING JUDGED BY BY MS.-CAPTAIN-WARBIRD-BINARY--MARVEL...?
...
TOUCHE.
ALL I'M SAYING IS, YOU SHOULD HAVE CALLED.
IT'S LIKE... YOU WANT TO DATE MY EX? DOESN'T MATTER HOW LONG WE'VE BEEN BROKEN UP, HE'S STILL MY EX.
YOU CALL.
YOU'RE RIGHT.
I'M SORRY...I SHOULD HAVE CALLED.
DAMN STRAIGHT. NOBODY SHOULD FIND OUT SOMETHING LIKE THAT FROM A GOOGLE ALERT. IT'S UNCIVILIZ--
WAIT-- WHAT?

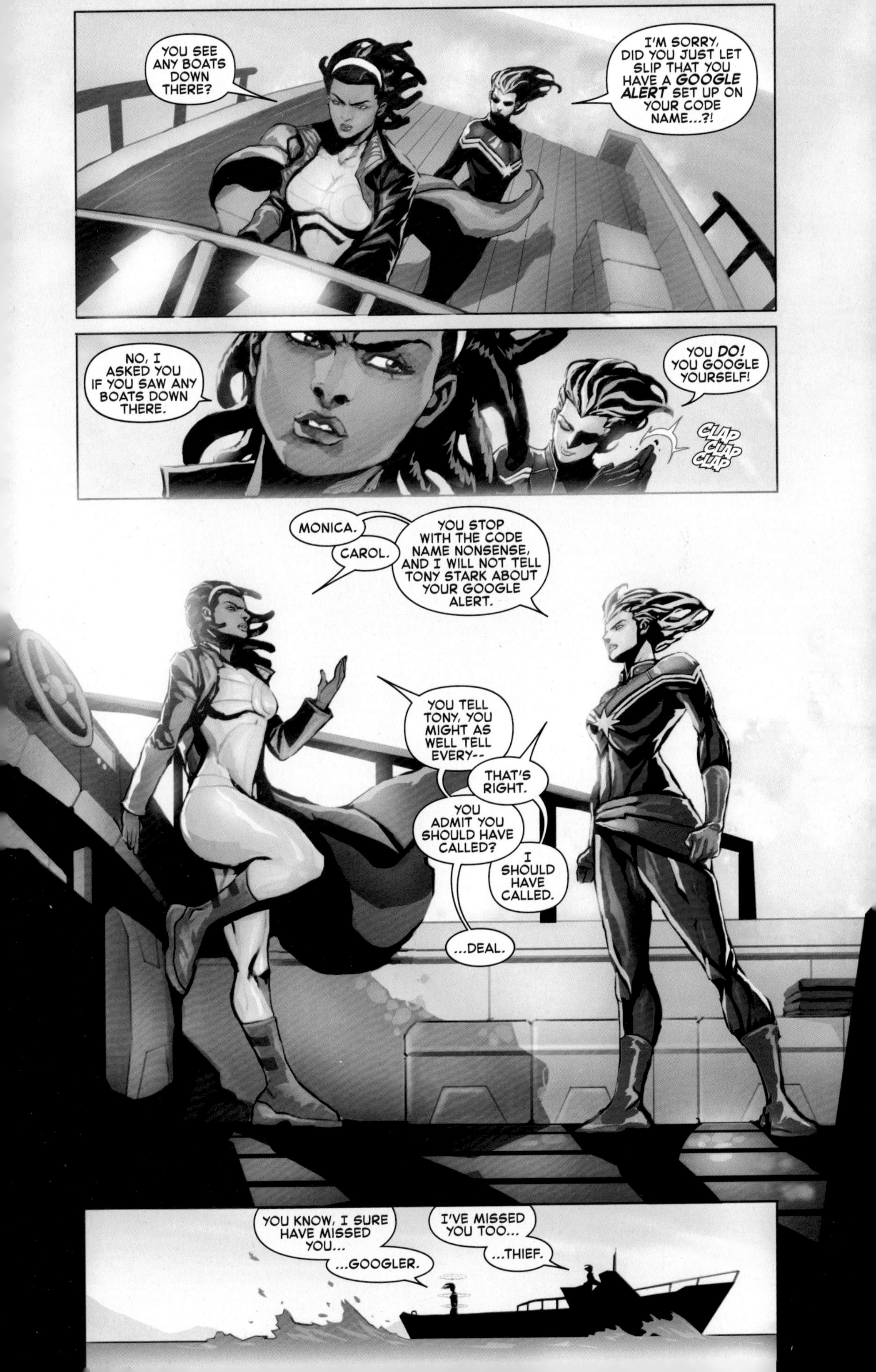
YOU SEE ANY BOATS DOWN THERE?
I'M SORRY, DID YOU JUST LET SLIP THAT YOU HAVE A GOOGLE ALERT SET UP ON YOUR CODE NAME...?!
NO, I ASKED YOU IF YOU SAW ANY BOATS DOWN THERE.
YOU DO! YOU GOOGLE YOURSELF!
CLAP CLAP CLAP
MONICA.
CAROL.
YOU STOP WITH THE CODE NAME NONSENSE, AND I WILL NOT TELL TONY STARK ABOUT YOUR GOOGLE ALERT.
YOU TELL TONY, YOU MIGHT AS WELL TELL EVERY--
THAT'S RIGHT.
YOU ADMIT YOU SHOULD HAVE CALLED?
I SHOULD HAVE CALLED.
...DEAL.
YOU KNOW, I SURE HAVE MISSED YOU...
...GOOGLER.
I'VE MISSED YOU TOO...
...THIEF.

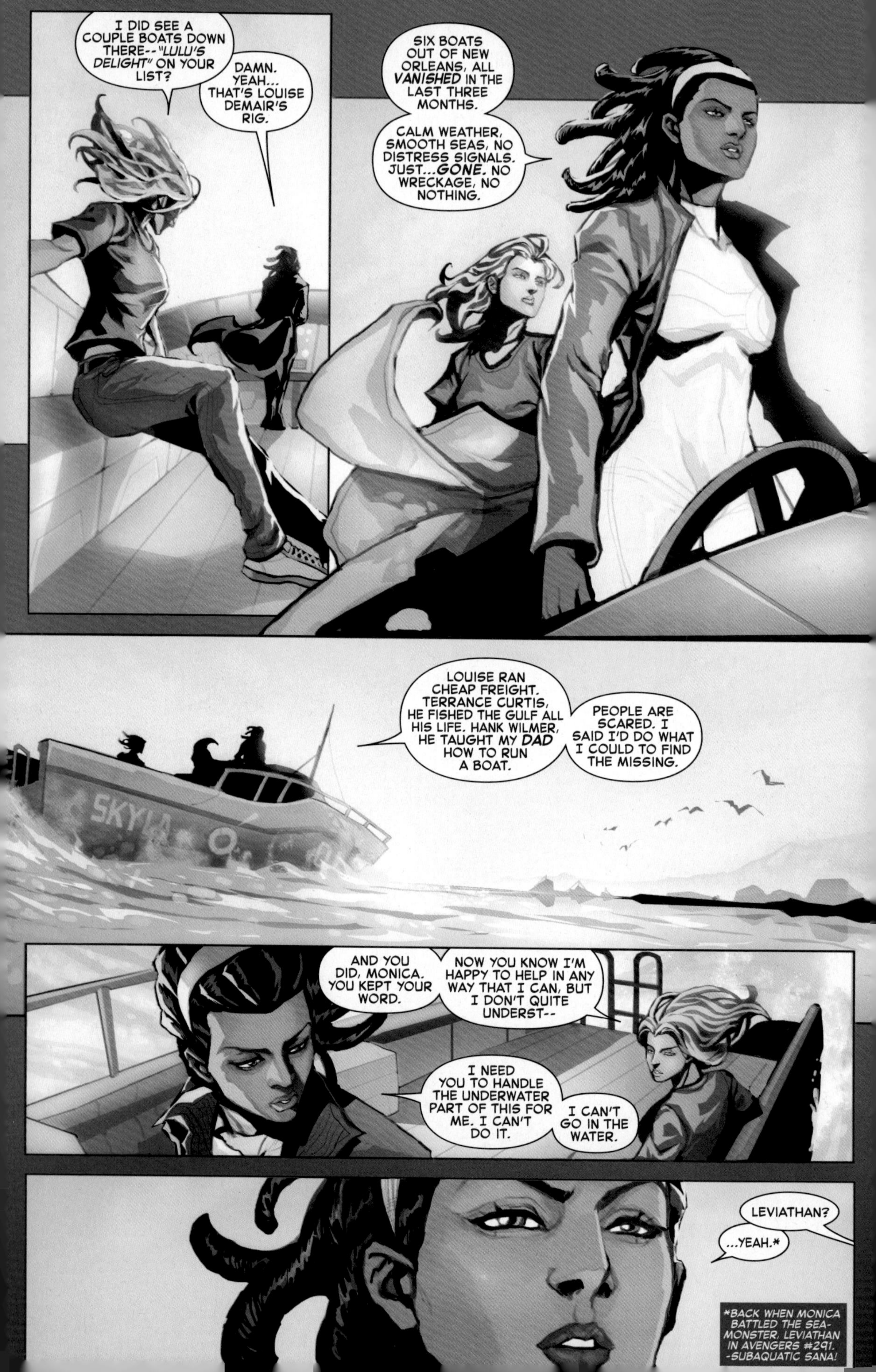

I DID SEE A COUPLE BOATS DOWN THERE-- "LULU'S DELIGHT" ON YOUR LIST?
DAMN. YEAH... THAT'S LOUISE DEMAIR'S RIG.
SIX BOATS OUT OF NEW ORLEANS, ALL VANISHED IN THE LAST THREE MONTHS.
CALM WEATHER, SMOOTH SEAS, NO DISTRESS SIGNALS. JUST...GONE. NO WRECKAGE, NO NOTHING.
LOUISE RAN CHEAP FREIGHT. TERRANCE CURTIS, HE FISHED THE GULF ALL HIS LIFE. HANK WILMER, HE TAUGHT MY DAD HOW TO RUN A BOAT.
PEOPLE ARE SCARED. I SAID I'D DO WHAT I COULD TO FIND THE MISSING.
SKYLA
AND YOU DID, MONICA. YOU KEPT YOUR WORD.
NOW YOU KNOW I'M HAPPY TO HELP IN ANY WAY THAT I CAN, BUT I DON'T QUITE UNDERST--
I NEED YOU TO HANDLE THE UNDERWATER PART OF THIS FOR ME. I CAN'T DO IT.
I CAN'T GO IN THE WATER.
LEVIATHAN?
...YEAH.*
*BACK WHEN MONICA BATTLED THE SEA-MONSTER, LEVIATHAN IN AVENGERS #291. -SUBAQUATIC SANA!

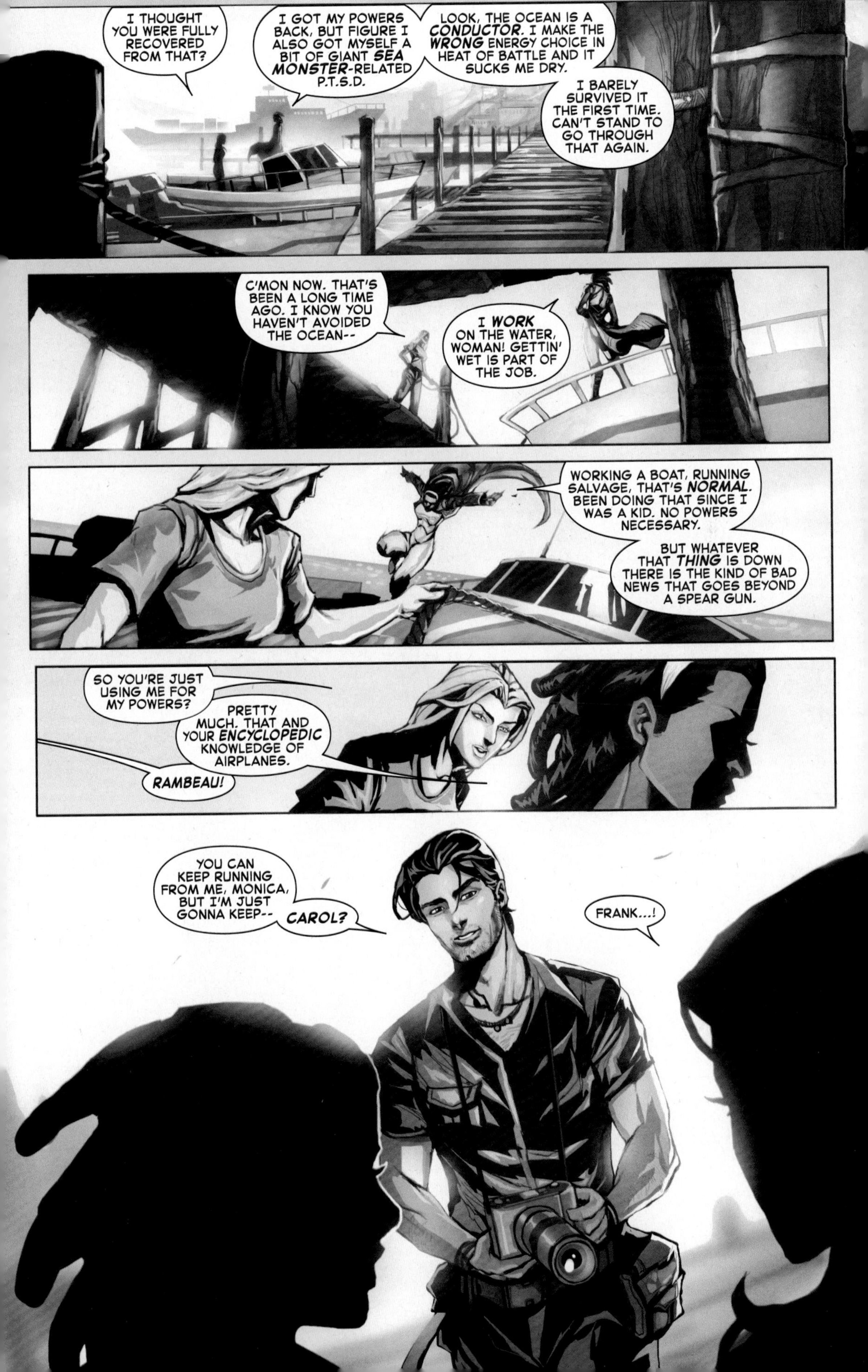
I THOUGHT YOU WERE FULLY RECOVERED FROM THAT?
I GOT MY POWERS BACK, BUT FIGURE I ALSO GOT MYSELF A BIT OF GIANT SEA MONSTER-RELATED P.T.S.D.
LOOK, THE OCEAN IS A CONDUCTOR. I MAKE THE WRONG ENERGY CHOICE IN HEAT OF BATTLE AND IT SUCKS ME DRY.
I BARELY SURVIVED IT THE FIRST TIME. CAN'T STAND TO GO THROUGH THAT AGAIN.
C'MON NOW. THAT'S BEEN A LONG TIME AGO. I KNOW YOU HAVEN'T AVOIDED THE OCEAN--
I WORK ON THE WATER, WOMAN! GETTIN' WET IS PART OF THE JOB.
WORKING A BOAT, RUNNING SALVAGE, THAT'S NORMAL. BEEN DOING THAT SINCE I WAS A KID. NO POWERS NECESSARY.
BUT WHATEVER THAT THING IS DOWN THERE IS THE KIND OF BAD NEWS THAT GOES BEYOND A SPEAR GUN.
SO YOU'RE JUST USING ME FOR MY POWERS?
PRETTY MUCH. THAT AND YOUR ENCYCLOPEDIC KNOWLEDGE OF AIRPLANES.
RAMBEAU!
YOU CAN KEEP RUNNING FROM ME, MONICA, BUT I'M JUST GONNA KEEP--
CAROL?
FRANK...!

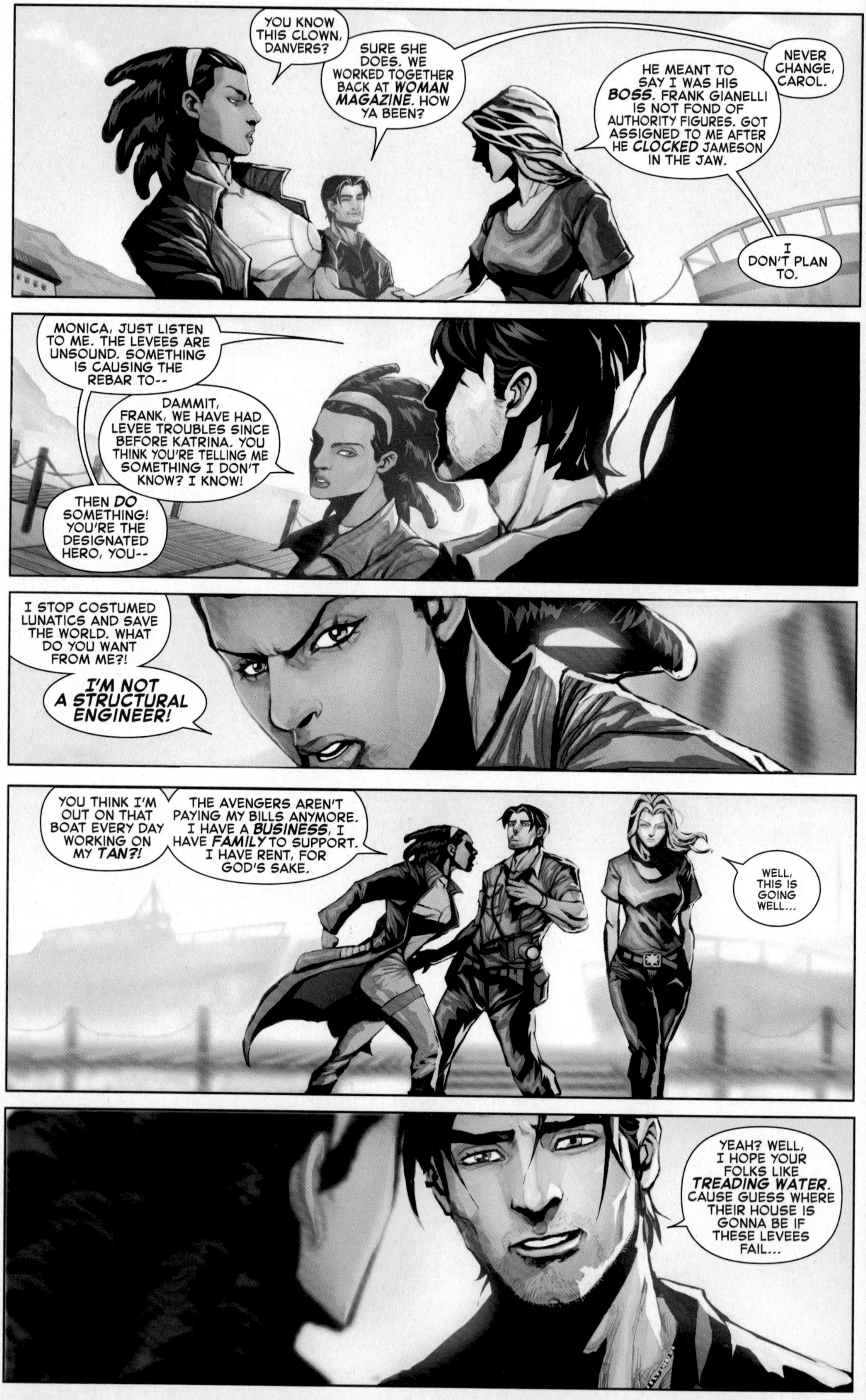

YOU KNOW THIS CLOWN, DANVERS?
SURE SHE DOES. WE WORKED TOGETHER BACK AT WOMAN MAGAZINE. HOW YA BEEN?
NEVER CHANGE, CAROL.
HE MEANT TO SAY I WAS HIS BOSS. FRANK GIANELLI IS NOT FOND OF AUTHORITY FIGURES. GOT ASSIGNED TO ME AFTER HE CLOCKED JAMESON IN THE JAW.
I DON'T PLAN TO.
MONICA, JUST LISTEN TO ME. THE LEVEES ARE UNSOUND. SOMETHING IS CAUSING THE REBAR TO--
DAMMIT, FRANK, WE HAVE HAD LEVEE TROUBLES SINCE BEFORE KATRINA. YOU THINK YOU'RE TELLING ME SOMETHING I DON'T KNOW? I KNOW!
THEN DO SOMETHING! YOU'RE THE DESIGNATED HERO, YOU--
I STOP COSTUMED LUNATICS AND SAVE THE WORLD. WHAT DO YOU WANT FROM ME?!
I'M NOT A STRUCTURAL ENGINEER!
YOU THINK I'M OUT ON THAT BOAT EVERY DAY WORKING ON MY TAN?!
THE AVENGERS AREN'T PAYING MY BILLS ANYMORE. I HAVE A BUSINESS, I HAVE FAMILY TO SUPPORT. I HAVE RENT, FOR GOD'S SAKE.
WELL, THIS IS GOING WELL...
YEAH? WELL, I HOPE YOUR FOLKS LIKE TREADING WATER. CAUSE GUESS WHERE THEIR HOUSE IS GONNA BE IF THESE LEVEES FAIL...

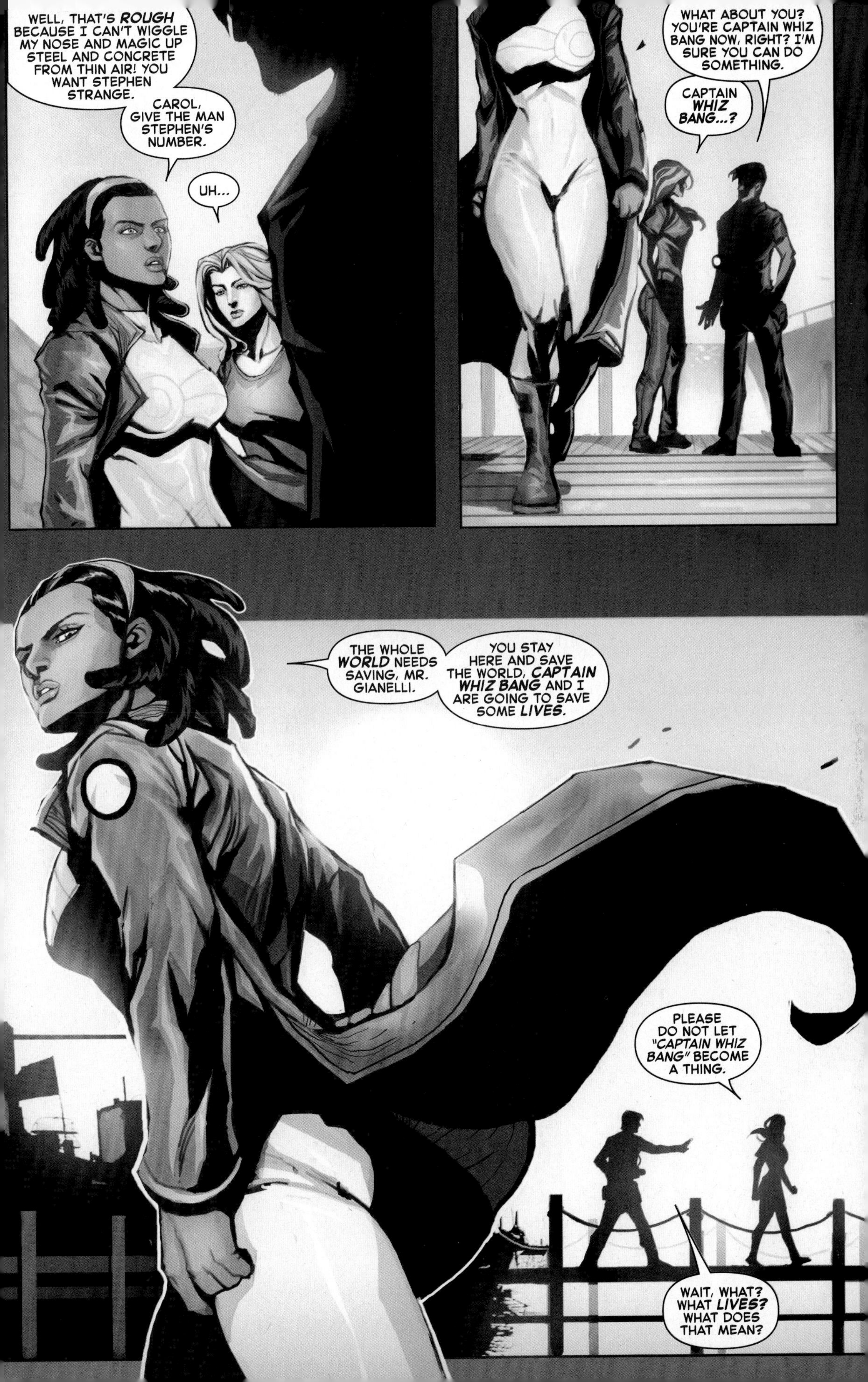
WELL, THAT'S ROUGH BECAUSE I CAN'T WIGGLE MY NOSE AND MAGIC UP STEEL AND CONCRETE FROM THIN AIR! YOU WANT STEPHEN STRANGE.
CAROL, GIVE THE MAN STEPHEN'S NUMBER.
UH...
WHAT ABOUT YOU? YOU'RE CAPTAIN WHIZ BANG NOW, RIGHT? I'M SURE YOU CAN DO SOMETHING.
CAPTAIN WHIZ BANG...?
THE WHOLE WORLD NEEDS SAVING, MR. GIANELLI.
YOU STAY HERE AND SAVE THE WORLD, CAPTAIN WHIZ BANG AND I ARE GOING TO SAVE SOME LIVES.
PLEASE DO NOT LET "CAPTAIN WHIZ BANG" BECOME A THING.
WAIT, WHAT? WHAT LIVES? WHAT DOES THAT MEAN?

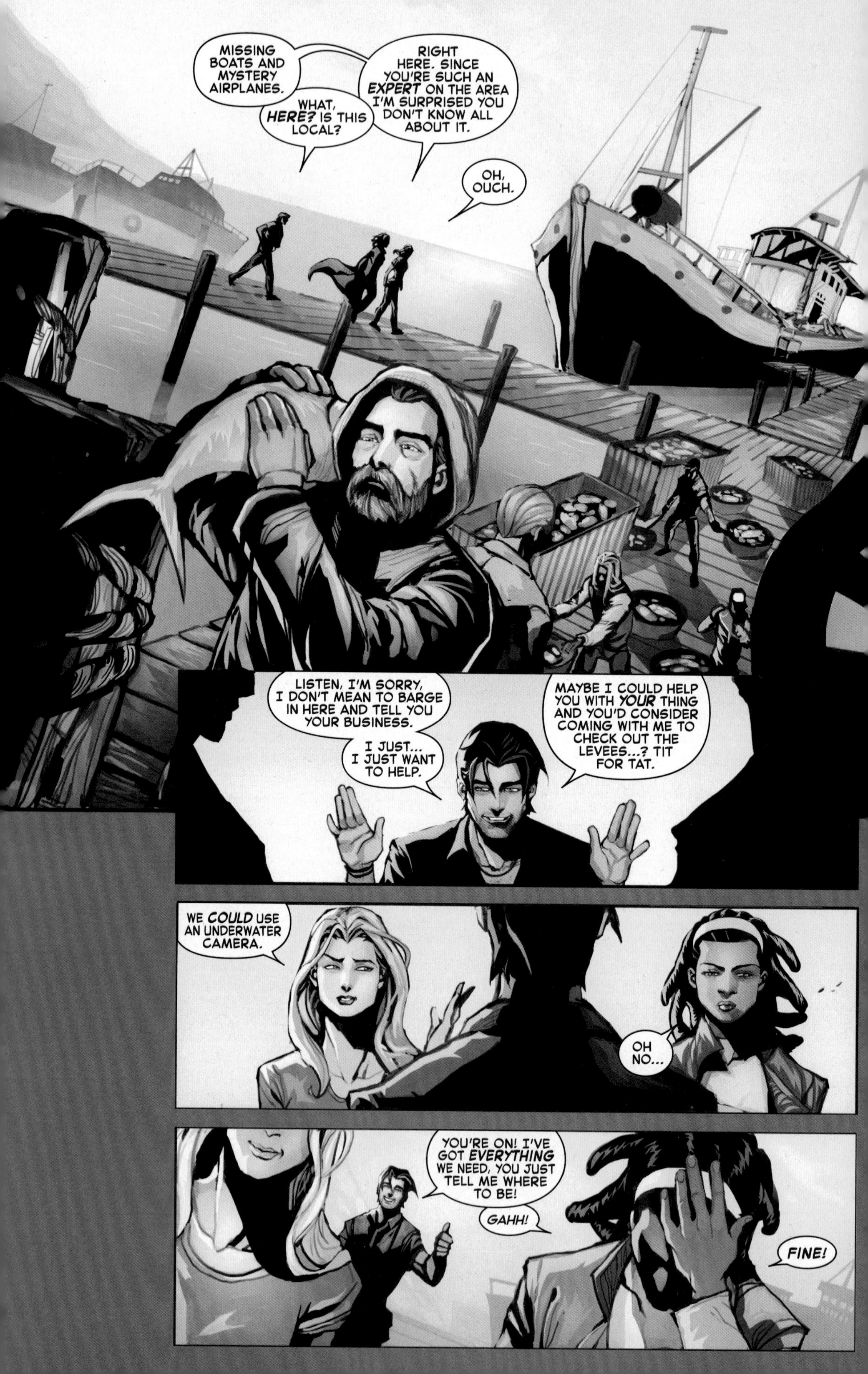
MISSING BOATS AND MYSTERY AIRPLANES.
WHAT, HERE? IS THIS LOCAL?
RIGHT HERE. SINCE YOU'RE SUCH AN EXPERT ON THE AREA I'M SURPRISED YOU DON'T KNOW ALL ABOUT IT.
OH, OUCH.
LISTEN, I'M SORRY, I DON'T MEAN TO BARGE IN HERE AND TELL YOU YOUR BUSINESS.
I JUST... I JUST WANT TO HELP.
MAYBE I COULD HELP YOU WITH YOUR THING AND YOU'D CONSIDER COMING WITH ME TO CHECK OUT THE LEVEES...? TIT FOR TAT.
WE COULD USE AN UNDERWATER CAMERA.
OH NO...
YOU'RE ON! I'VE GOT EVERYTHING WE NEED, YOU JUST TELL ME WHERE TO BE!
GAHH!
FINE!

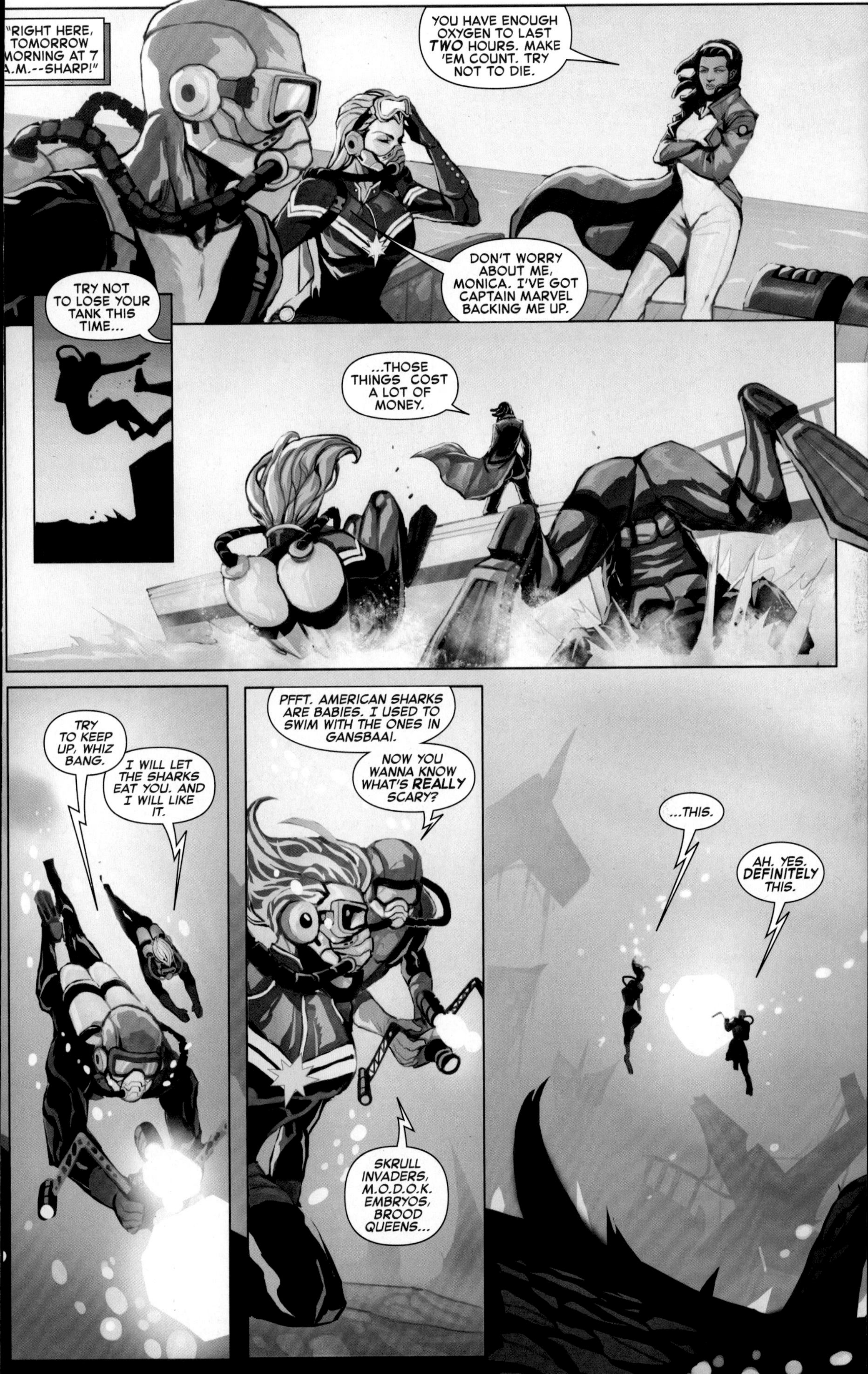
"RIGHT HERE, TOMORROW MORNING AT 7 A.M.--SHARP!"
YOU HAVE ENOUGH OXYGEN TO LAST TWO HOURS. MAKE 'EM COUNT. TRY NOT TO DIE.
DON'T WORRY ABOUT ME, MONICA. I'VE GOT CAPTAIN MARVEL BACKING ME UP.
TRY NOT TO LOSE YOUR TANK THIS TIME...
...THOSE THINGS COST A LOT OF MONEY.
TRY TO KEEP UP, WHIZ BANG.
I WILL LET THE SHARKS EAT YOU. AND I WILL LIKE IT.
PFFT. AMERICAN SHARKS ARE BABIES. I USED TO SWIM WITH THE ONES IN GANSBAAI.
NOW YOU WANNA KNOW WHAT'S REALLY SCARY?
SKRULL INVADERS, M.O.D.O.K. EMBRYOS, BROOD QUEENS...
...THIS.
AH. YES. DEFINITELY THIS.

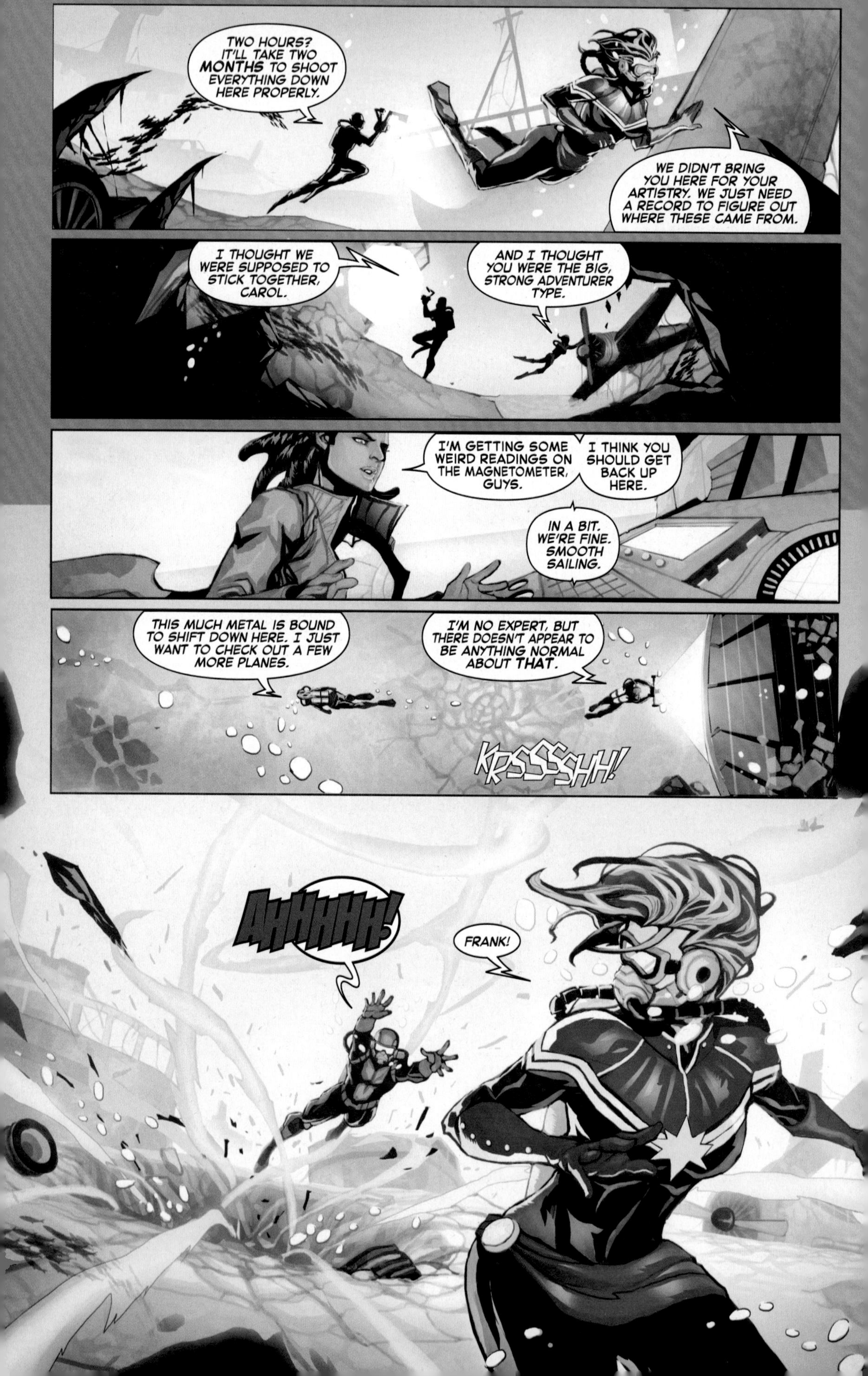

TWO HOURS? IT'LL TAKE TWO MONTHS TO SHOOT EVERYTHING DOWN HERE PROPERLY.
WE DIDN'T BRING YOU HERE FOR YOUR ARTISTRY. WE JUST NEED A RECORD TO FIGURE OUT WHERE THESE CAME FROM.
I THOUGHT WE WERE SUPPOSED TO STICK TOGETHER, CAROL.
AND I THOUGHT YOU WERE THE BIG, STRONG ADVENTURER TYPE.
I'M GETTING SOME WEIRD READINGS ON THE MAGNETOMETER, GUYS.
I THINK YOU SHOULD GET BACK UP HERE.
IN A BIT. WE'RE FINE. SMOOTH SAILING.
THIS MUCH METAL IS BOUND TO SHIFT DOWN HERE. I JUST WANT TO CHECK OUT A FEW MORE PLANES.
I'M NO EXPERT, BUT THERE DOESN'T APPEAR TO BE ANYTHING NORMAL ABOUT THAT.
KRSSSSHH!
AHHHHH!
FRANK!

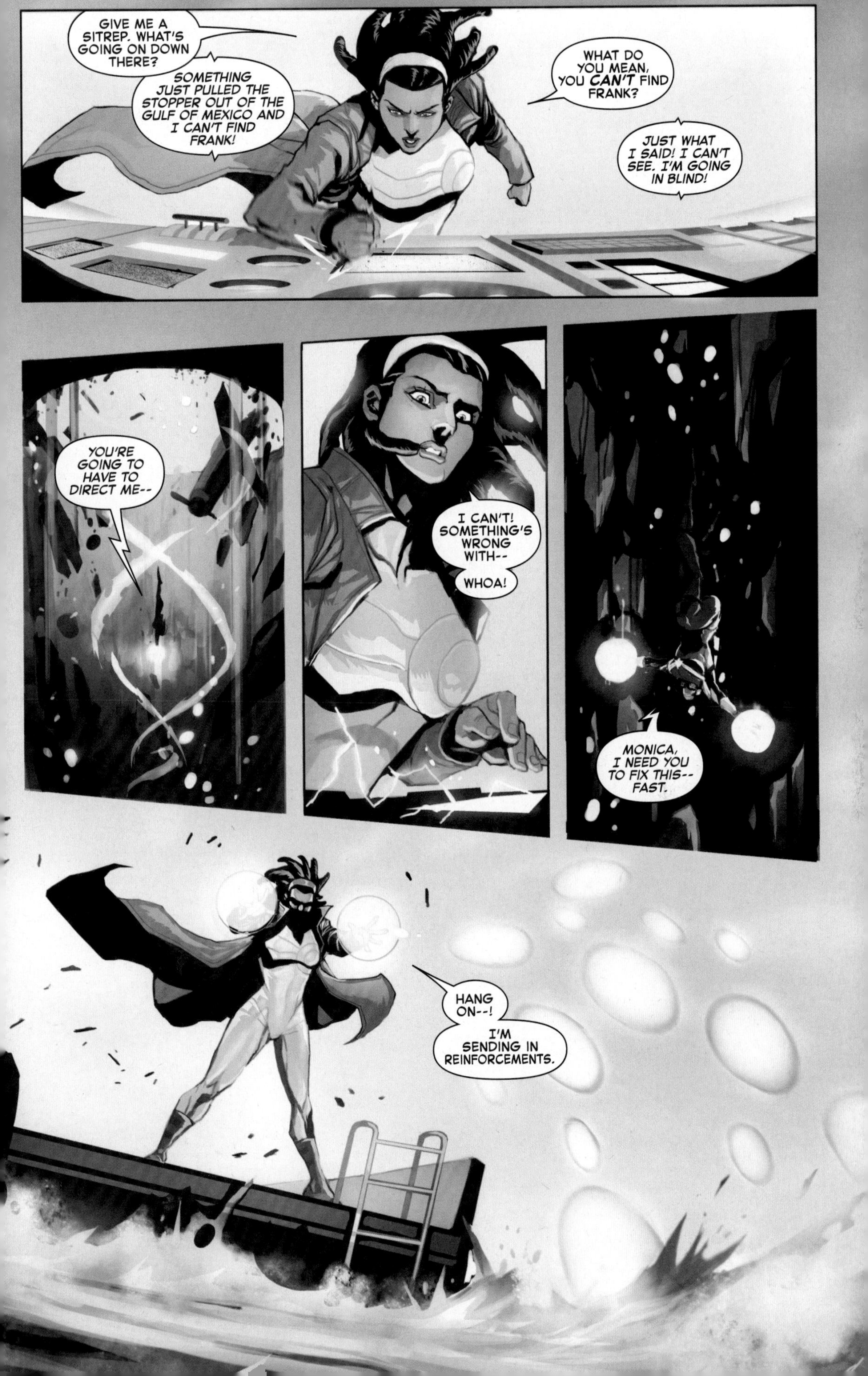
GIVE ME A SITREP. WHAT'S GOING ON DOWN THERE?
SOMETHING JUST PULLED THE STOPPER OUT OF THE GULF OF MEXICO AND I CAN'T FIND FRANK!
WHAT DO YOU MEAN, YOU **CAN'T** FIND FRANK?
JUST WHAT I SAID! I CAN'T SEE. I'M GOING IN BLIND!
YOU'RE GOING TO HAVE TO DIRECT ME--
I CAN'T! SOMETHING'S WRONG WITH--
WHOA!
MONICA, I NEED YOU TO FIX THIS-- FAST.
HANG ON--!
I'M SENDING IN REINFORCEMENTS.

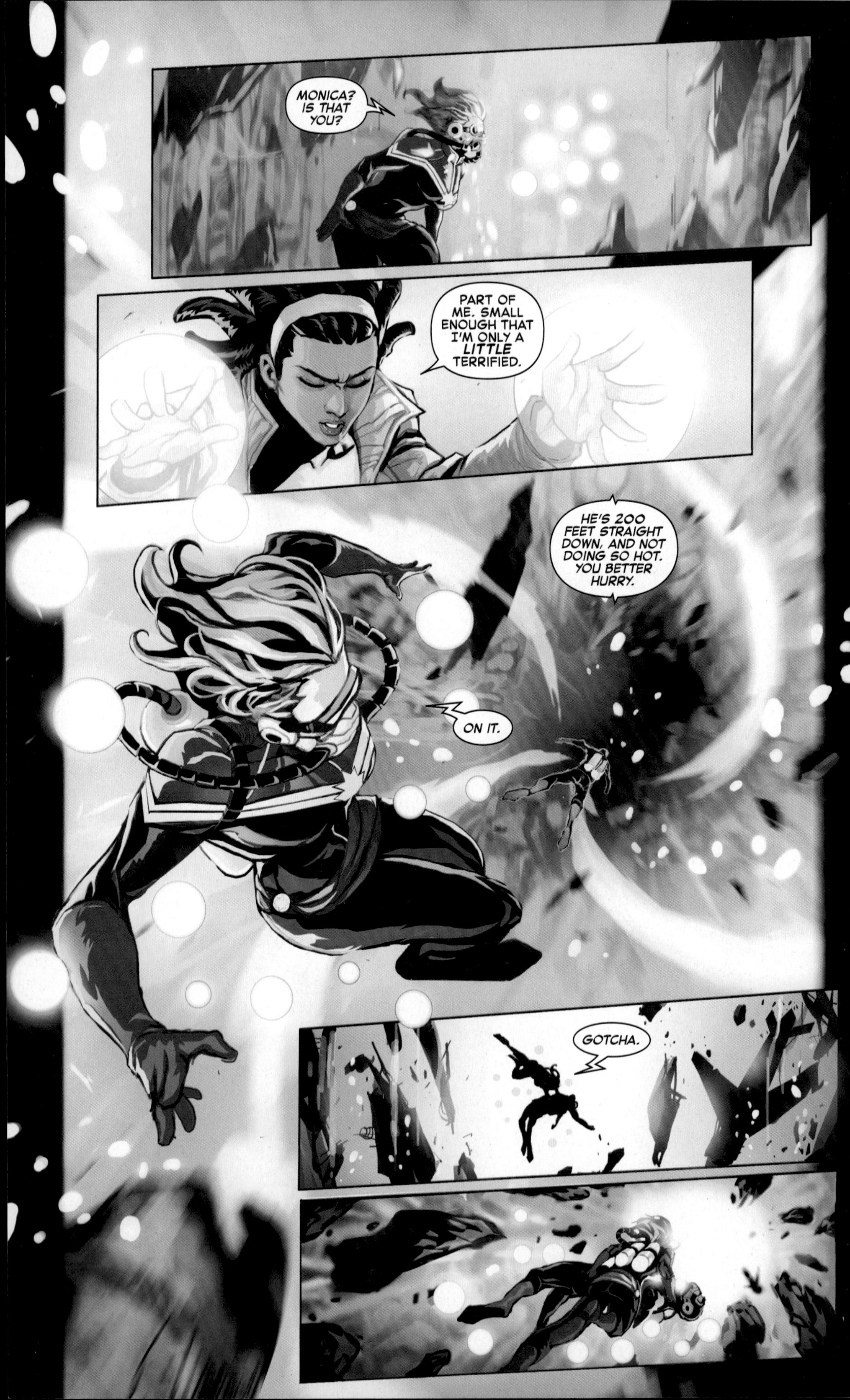
MONICA? IS THAT YOU?
PART OF ME. SMALL ENOUGH THAT I'M ONLY A *LITTLE* TERRIFIED.
HE'S 200 FEET STRAIGHT DOWN, AND NOT DOING SO HOT. YOU BETTER HURRY.
ON IT.
GOTCHA.

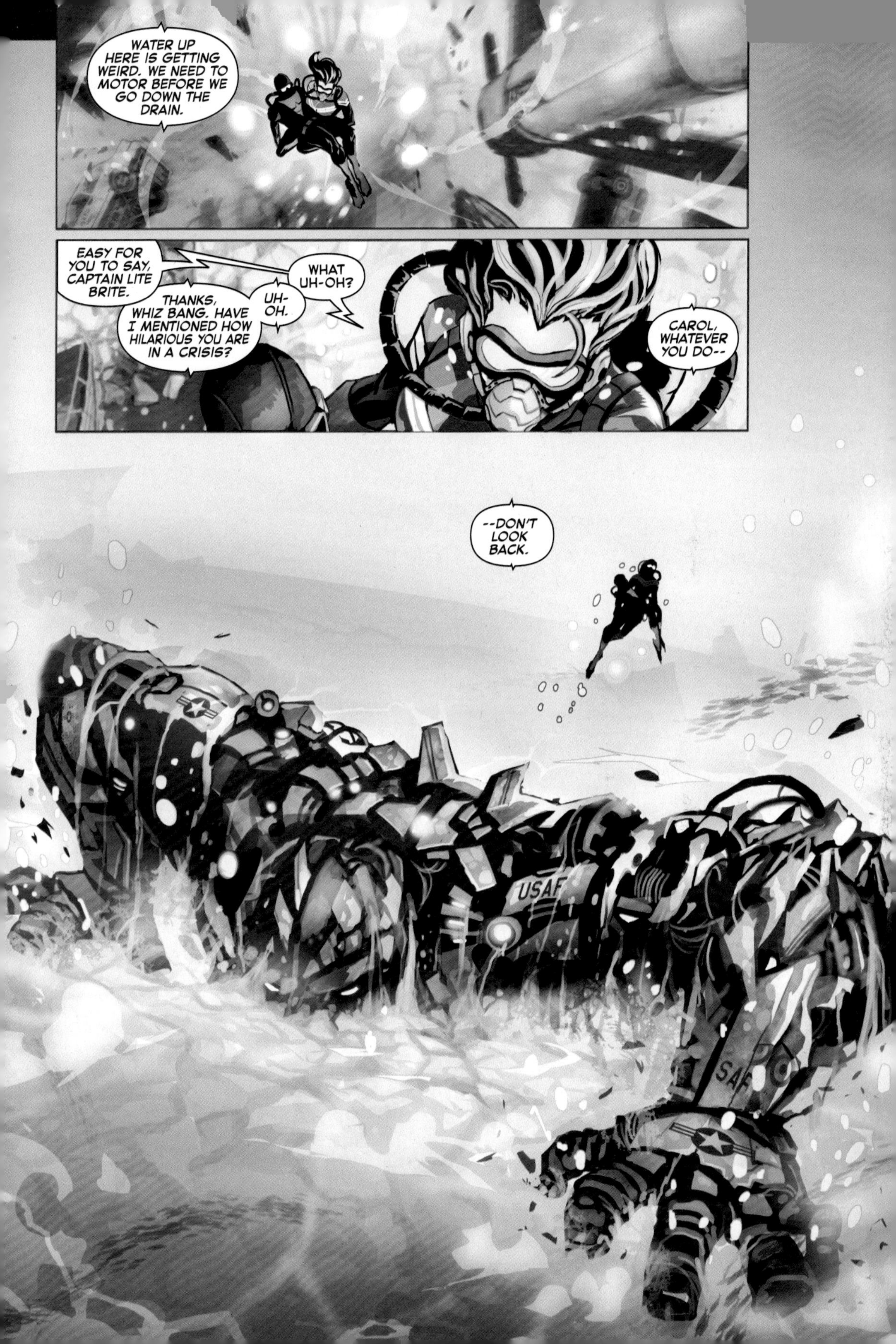
WATER UP HERE IS GETTING WEIRD. WE NEED TO MOTOR BEFORE WE GO DOWN THE DRAIN.
EASY FOR YOU TO SAY, CAPTAIN LITE BRITE.
THANKS, WHIZ BANG. HAVE I MENTIONED HOW HILARIOUS YOU ARE IN A CRISIS?
UH-OH.
WHAT UH-OH?
CAROL, WHATEVER YOU DO--
--DON'T LOOK BACK.
USAF
SAF

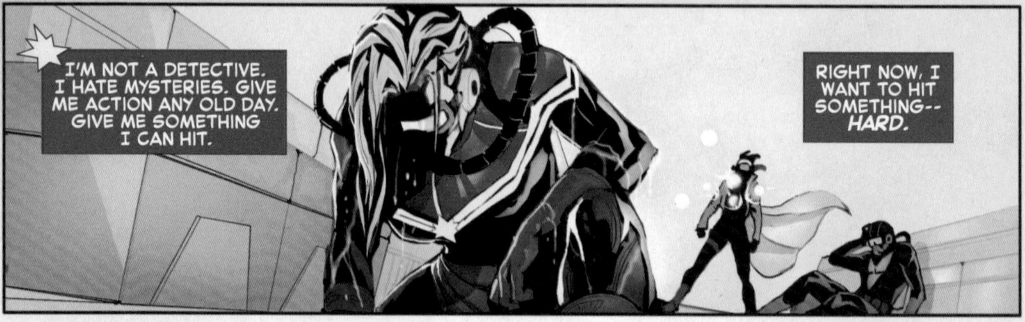
I'M NOT A DETECTIVE. I HATE MYSTERIES. GIVE ME ACTION ANY OLD DAY. GIVE ME SOMETHING I CAN HIT.
RIGHT NOW, I WANT TO HIT SOMETHING-- *HARD.*

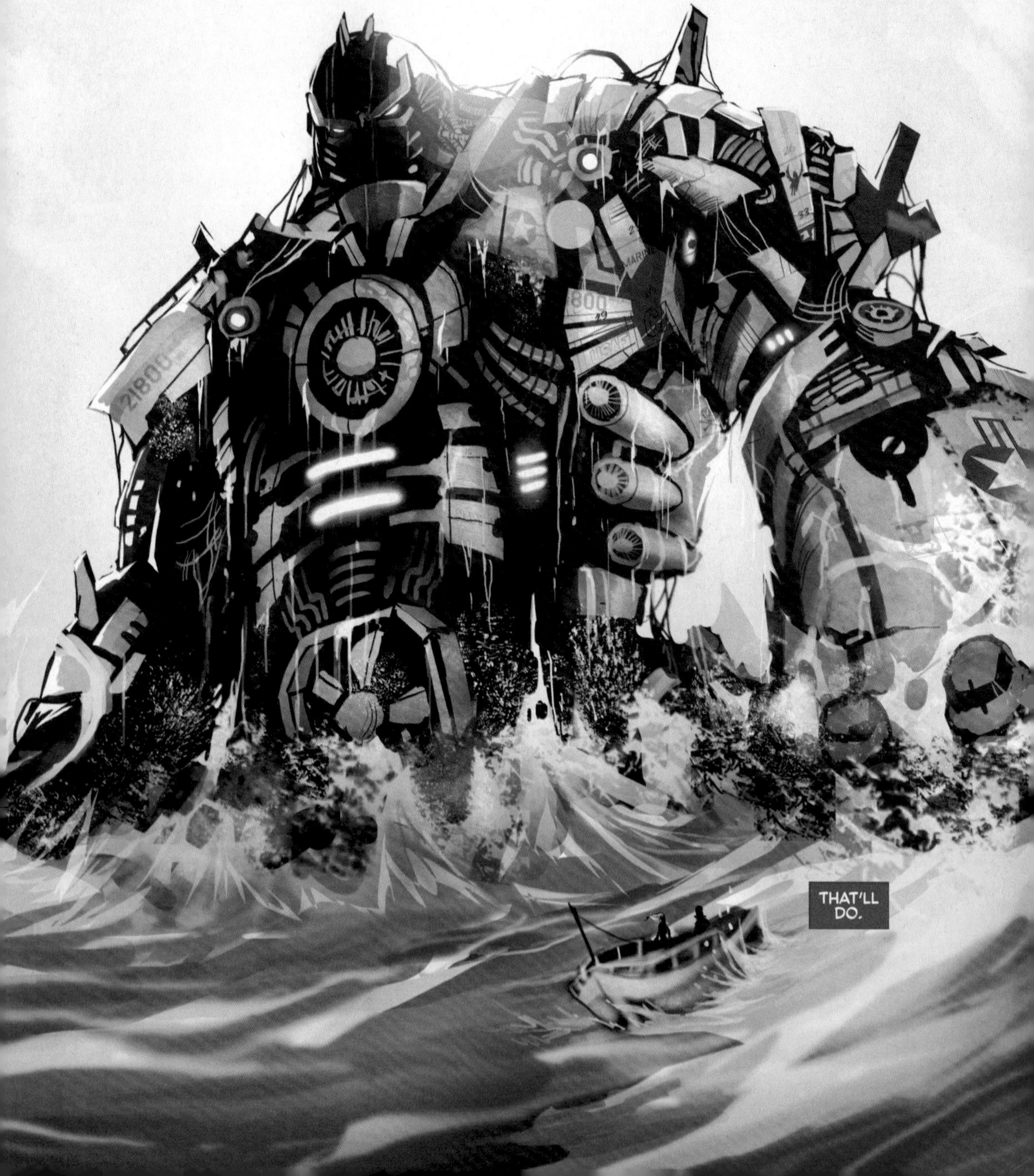
THAT'LL DO.

CAPTAIN MARVEL #8

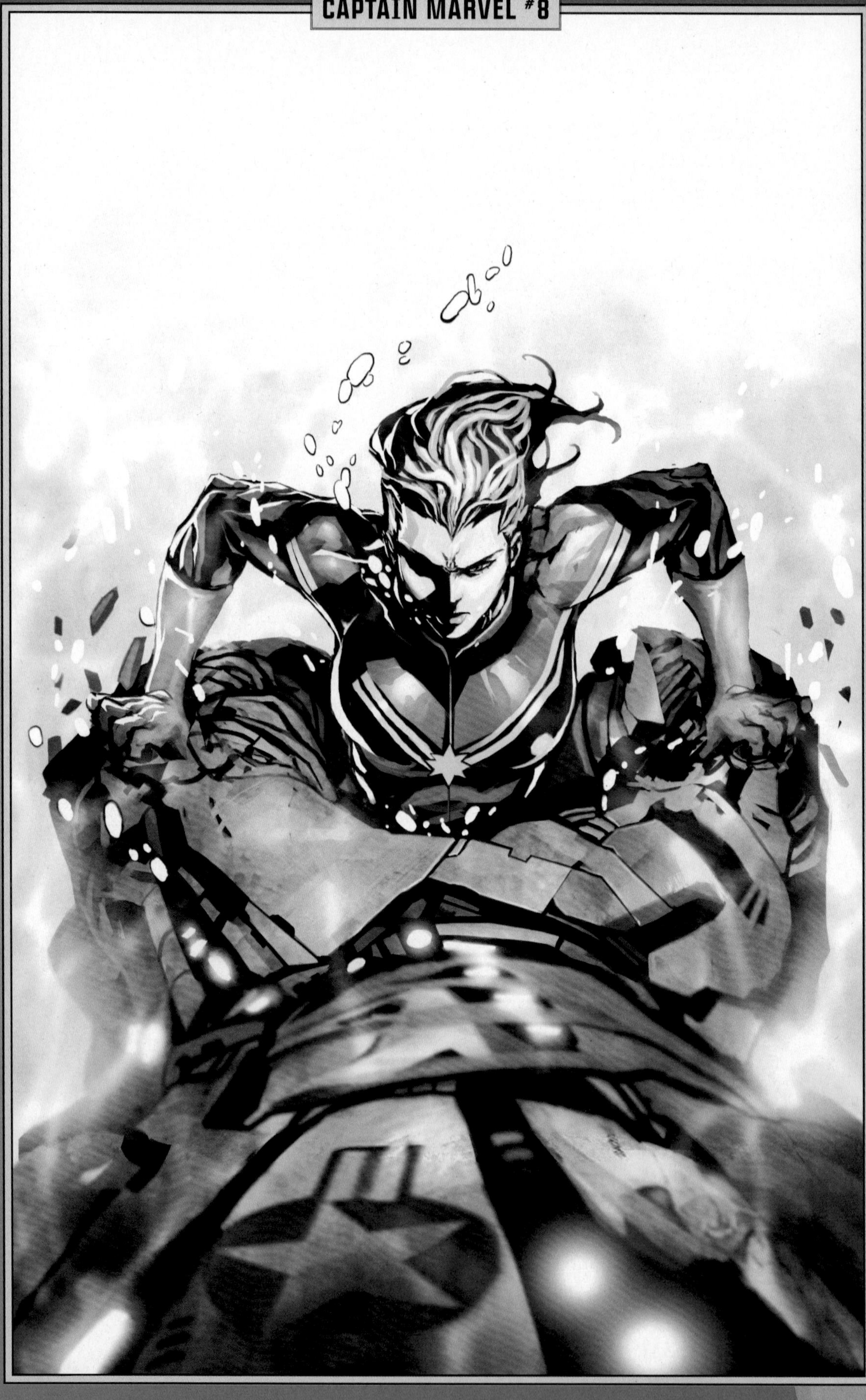

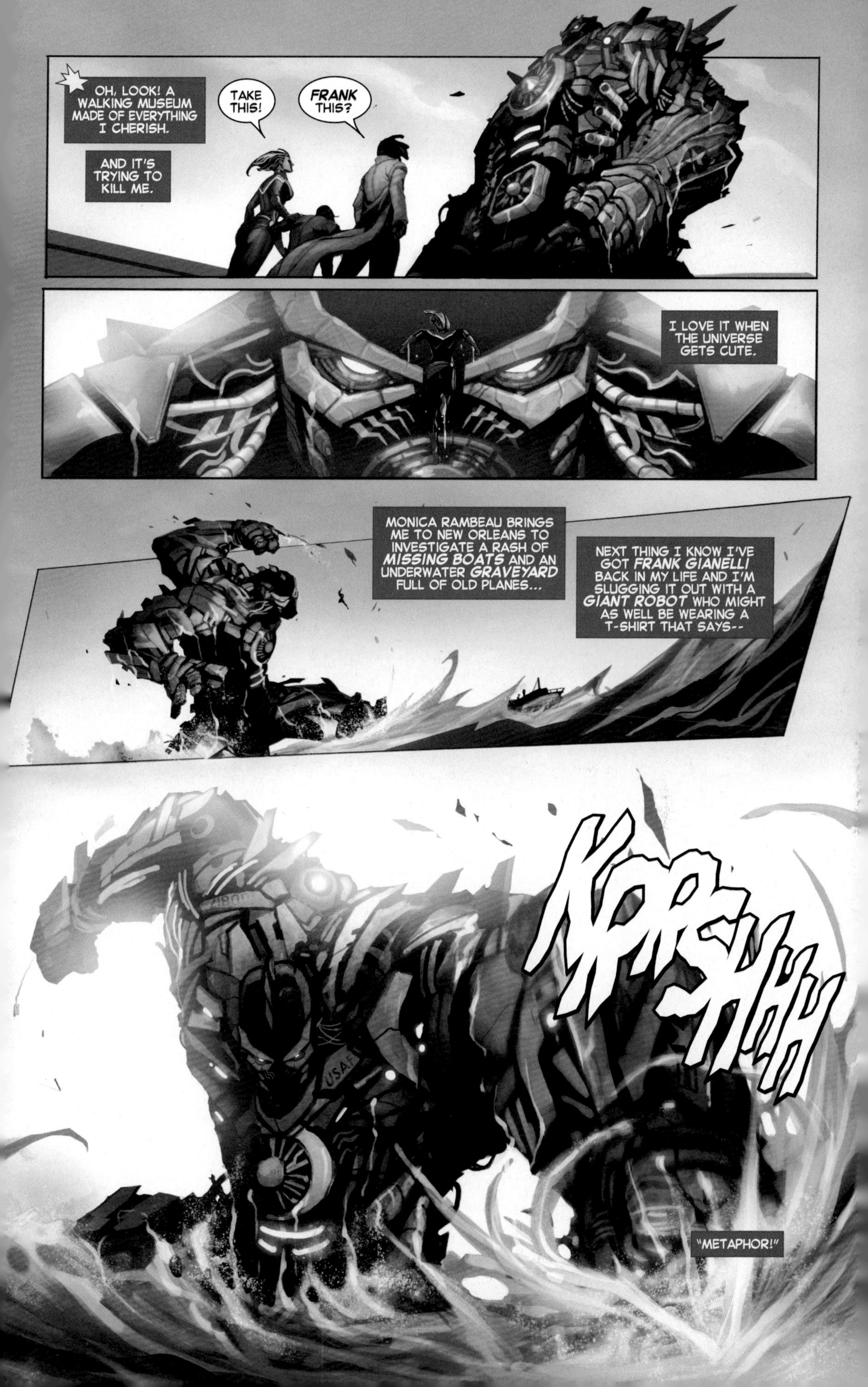

OH, LOOK! A WALKING MUSEUM MADE OF EVERYTHING I CHERISH.
AND IT'S TRYING TO KILL ME.
TAKE THIS!
FRANK THIS?
I LOVE IT WHEN THE UNIVERSE GETS CUTE.
MONICA RAMBEAU BRINGS ME TO NEW ORLEANS TO INVESTIGATE A RASH OF MISSING BOATS AND AN UNDERWATER GRAVEYARD FULL OF OLD PLANES...
NEXT THING I KNOW I'VE GOT FRANK GIANELLI BACK IN MY LIFE AND I'M SLUGGING IT OUT WITH A GIANT ROBOT WHO MIGHT AS WELL BE WEARING A T-SHIRT THAT SAYS--
KRRSHHH
"METAPHOR!"

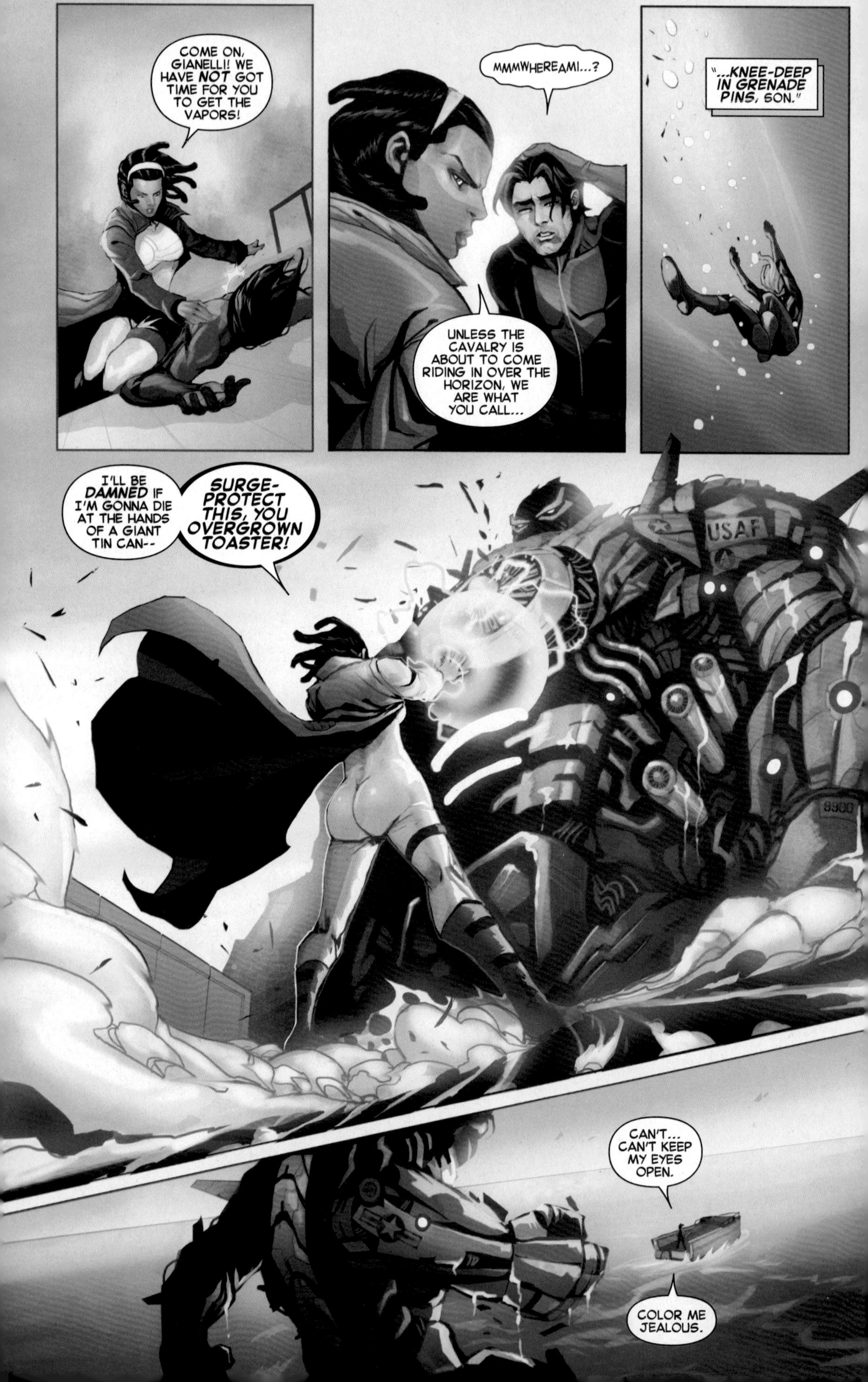
COME ON, GIANELLI! WE HAVE NOT GOT TIME FOR YOU TO GET THE VAPORS!
MMMWHEREAMI...?
UNLESS THE CAVALRY IS ABOUT TO COME RIDING IN OVER THE HORIZON, WE ARE WHAT YOU CALL...
"...KNEE-DEEP IN GRENADE PINS, SON."
I'LL BE DAMNED IF I'M GONNA DIE AT THE HANDS OF A GIANT TIN CAN--
SURGE-PROTECT THIS, YOU OVERGROWN TOASTER!
USAF
CAN'T... CAN'T KEEP MY EYES OPEN.
COLOR ME JEALOUS.

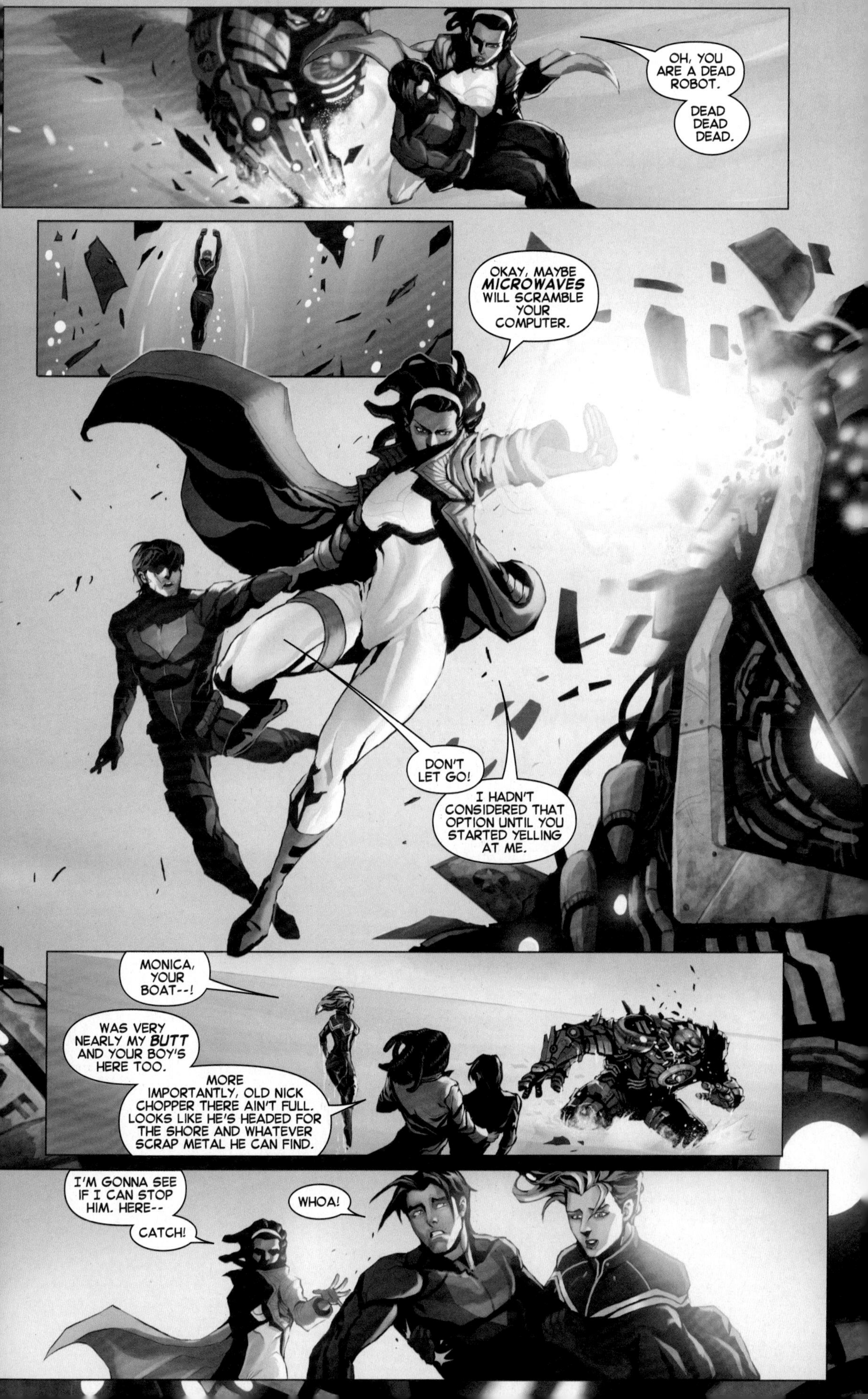
OH, YOU ARE A DEAD ROBOT.
DEAD DEAD DEAD.
OKAY, MAYBE MICROWAVES WILL SCRAMBLE YOUR COMPUTER.
DON'T LET GO!
I HADN'T CONSIDERED THAT OPTION UNTIL YOU STARTED YELLING AT ME.
MONICA, YOUR BOAT--!
WAS VERY NEARLY MY BUTT AND YOUR BOY'S HERE TOO.
MORE IMPORTANTLY, OLD NICK CHOPPER THERE AIN'T FULL. LOOKS LIKE HE'S HEADED FOR THE SHORE AND WHATEVER SCRAP METAL HE CAN FIND.
I'M GONNA SEE IF I CAN STOP HIM. HERE--
CATCH!
WHOA!

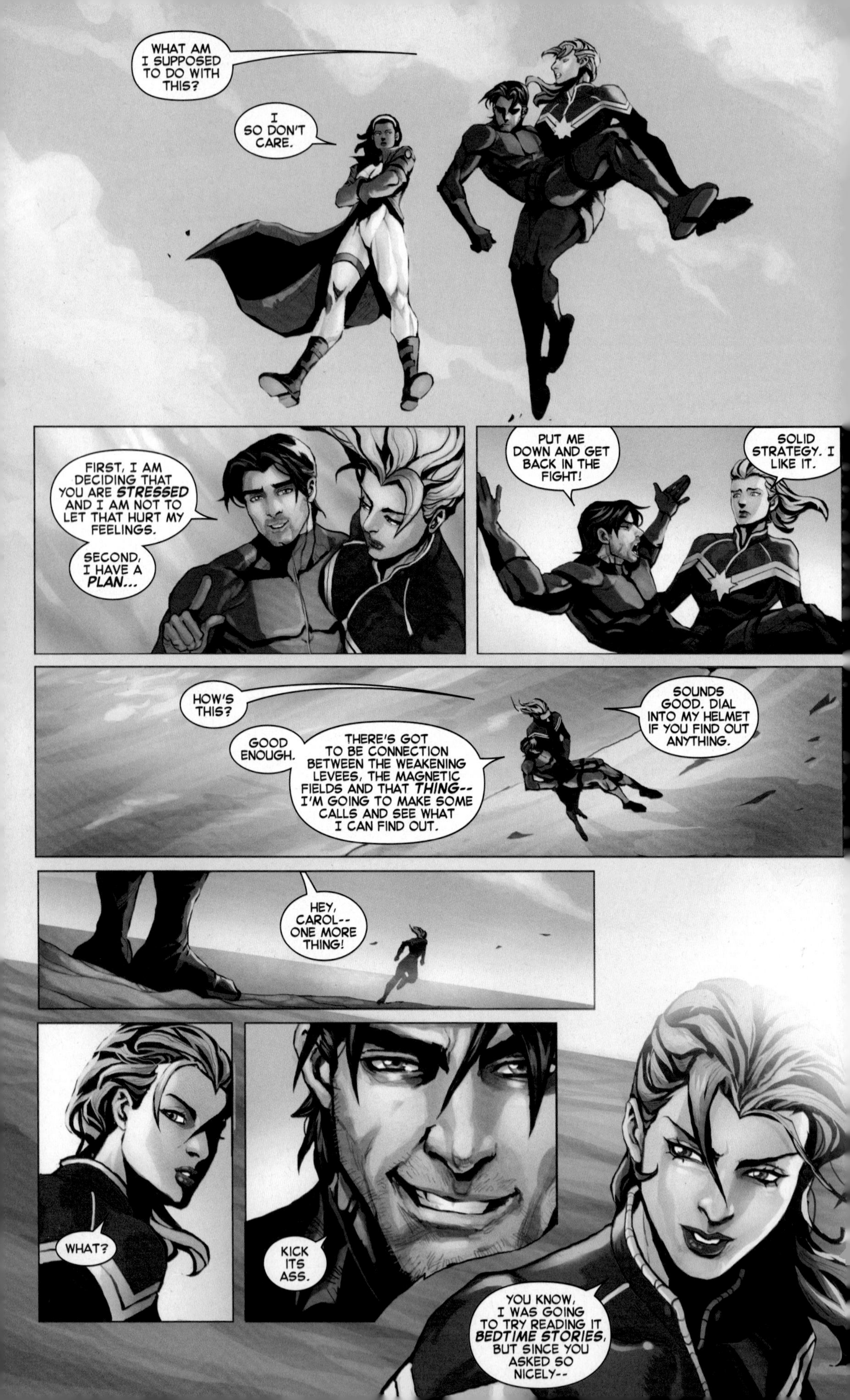

WHAT AM I SUPPOSED TO DO WITH THIS?
I SO DON'T CARE.
FIRST, I AM DECIDING THAT YOU ARE STRESSED AND I AM NOT TO LET THAT HURT MY FEELINGS.
SECOND, I HAVE A PLAN...
PUT ME DOWN AND GET BACK IN THE FIGHT!
SOLID STRATEGY. I LIKE IT.
HOW'S THIS?
GOOD ENOUGH.
THERE'S GOT TO BE CONNECTION BETWEEN THE WEAKENING LEVEES, THE MAGNETIC FIELDS AND THAT THING-- I'M GOING TO MAKE SOME CALLS AND SEE WHAT I CAN FIND OUT.
SOUNDS GOOD. DIAL INTO MY HELMET IF YOU FIND OUT ANYTHING.
HEY, CAROL-- ONE MORE THING!
WHAT?
KICK ITS ASS.
YOU KNOW, I WAS GOING TO TRY READING IT BEDTIME STORIES, BUT SINCE YOU ASKED SO NICELY--

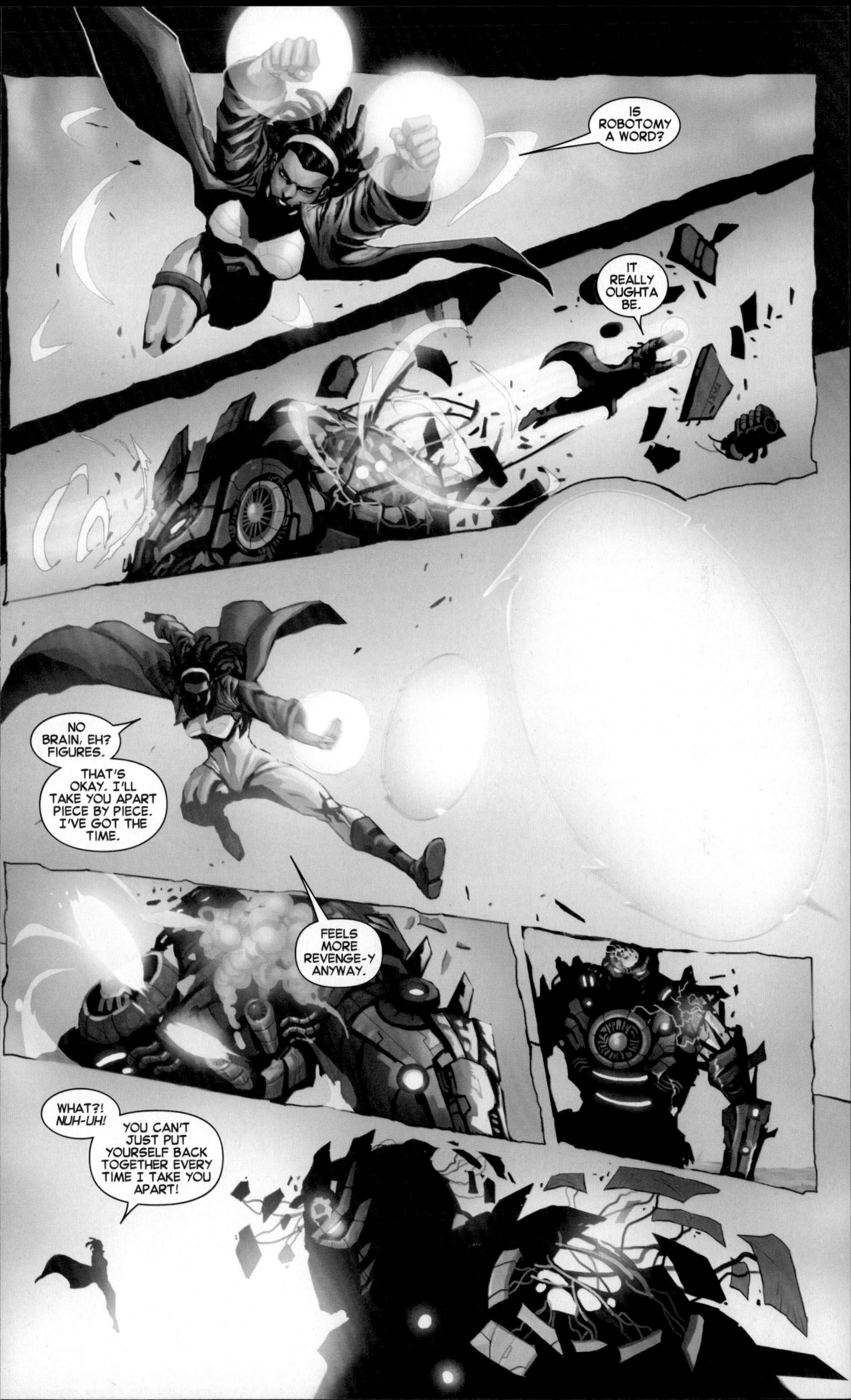
IS ROBOTOMY A WORD?
IT REALLY OUGHTA BE.
NO BRAIN, EH? FIGURES.
THAT'S OKAY. I'LL TAKE YOU APART PIECE BY PIECE. I'VE GOT THE TIME.
FEELS MORE REVENGE-Y ANYWAY.
WHAT?! *NUH-UH!*
YOU CAN'T JUST PUT YOURSELF BACK TOGETHER EVERY TIME I TAKE YOU APART!

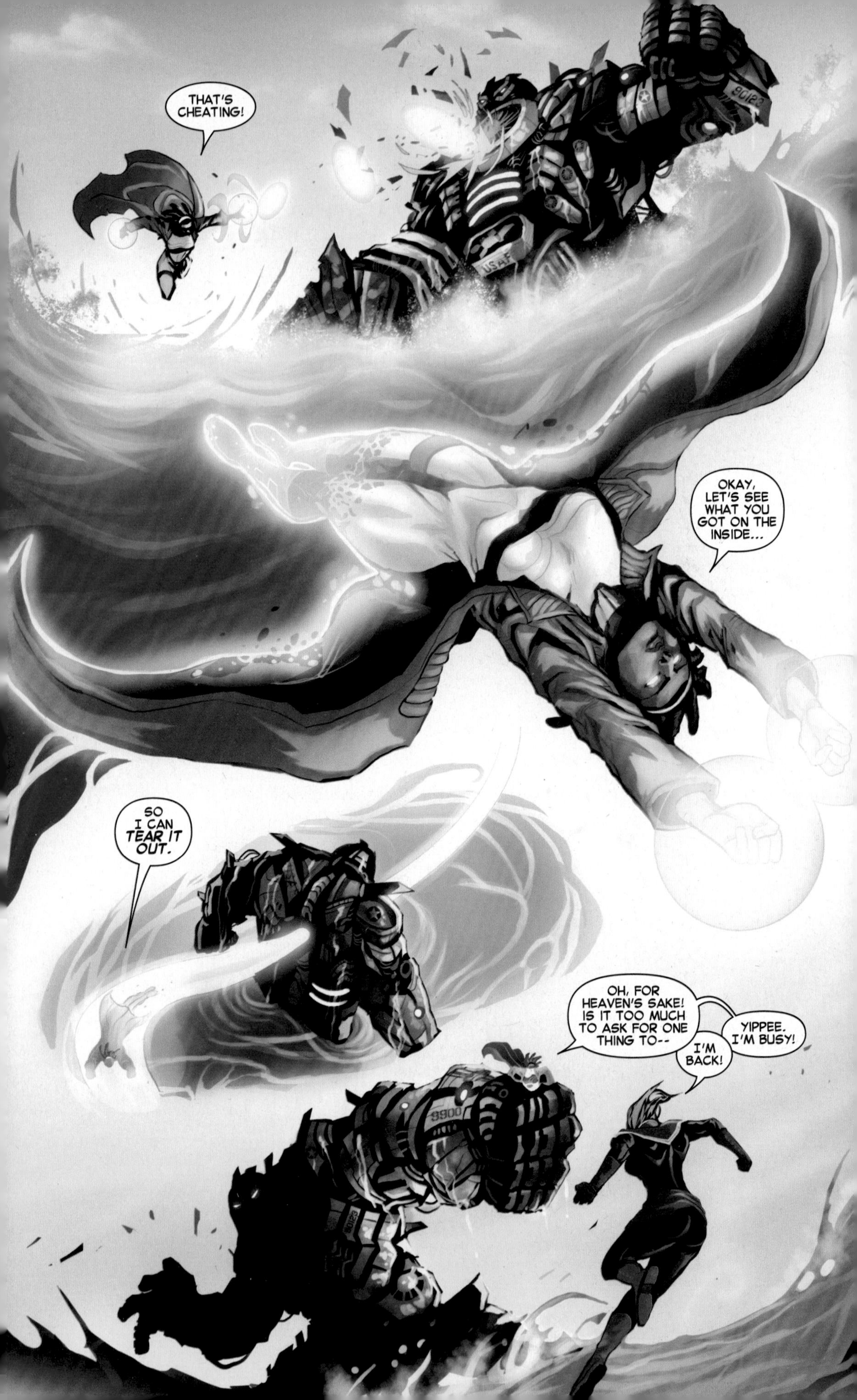
THAT'S CHEATING!
OKAY, LET'S SEE WHAT YOU GOT ON THE INSIDE...
SO I CAN *TEAR IT OUT.*
OH, FOR HEAVEN'S SAKE! IS IT TOO MUCH TO ASK FOR ONE THING TO--
I'M BACK!
YIPPEE. I'M BUSY!

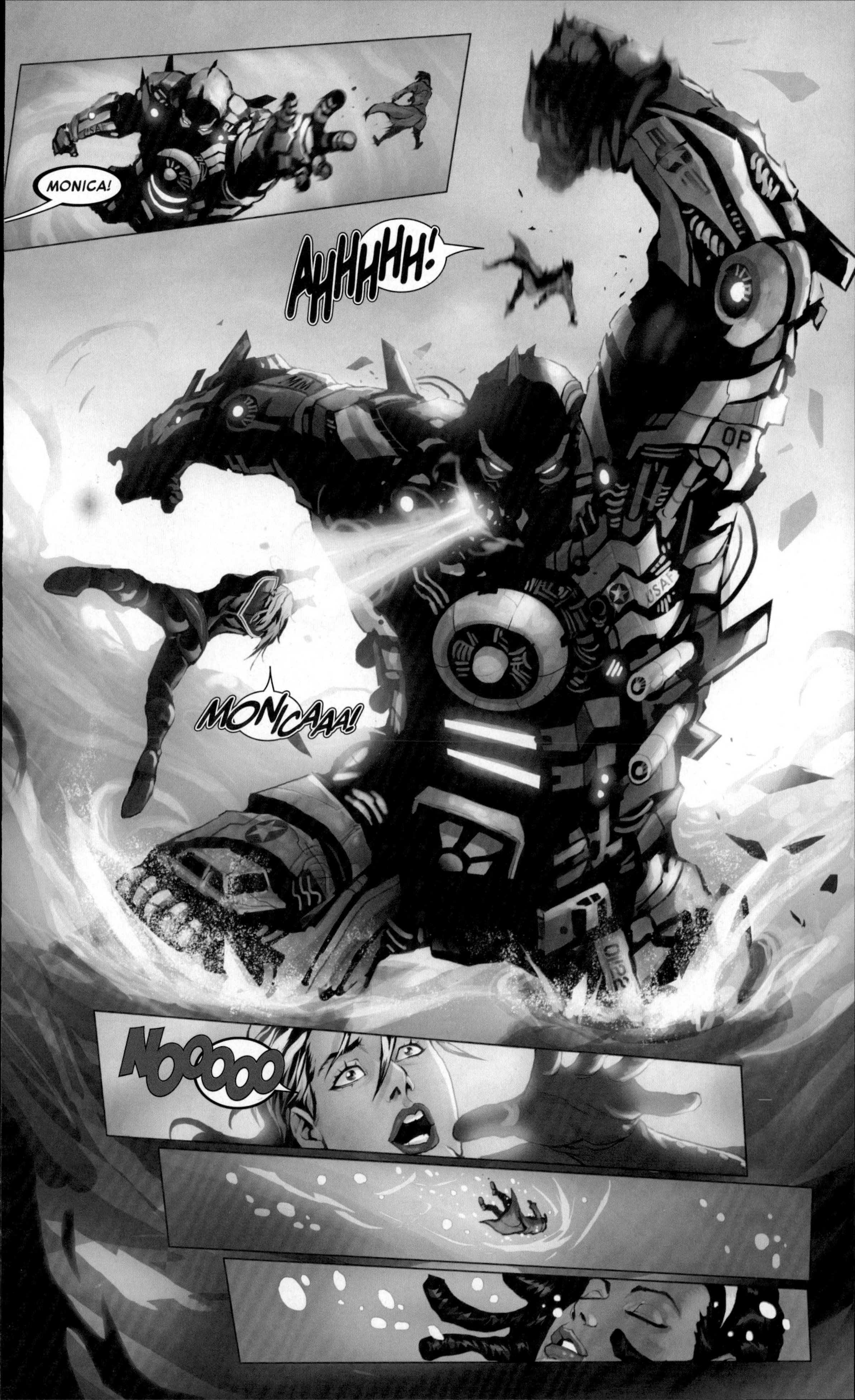
MONICA!
AHHHHH!
MONICAAA!
NOOOOO

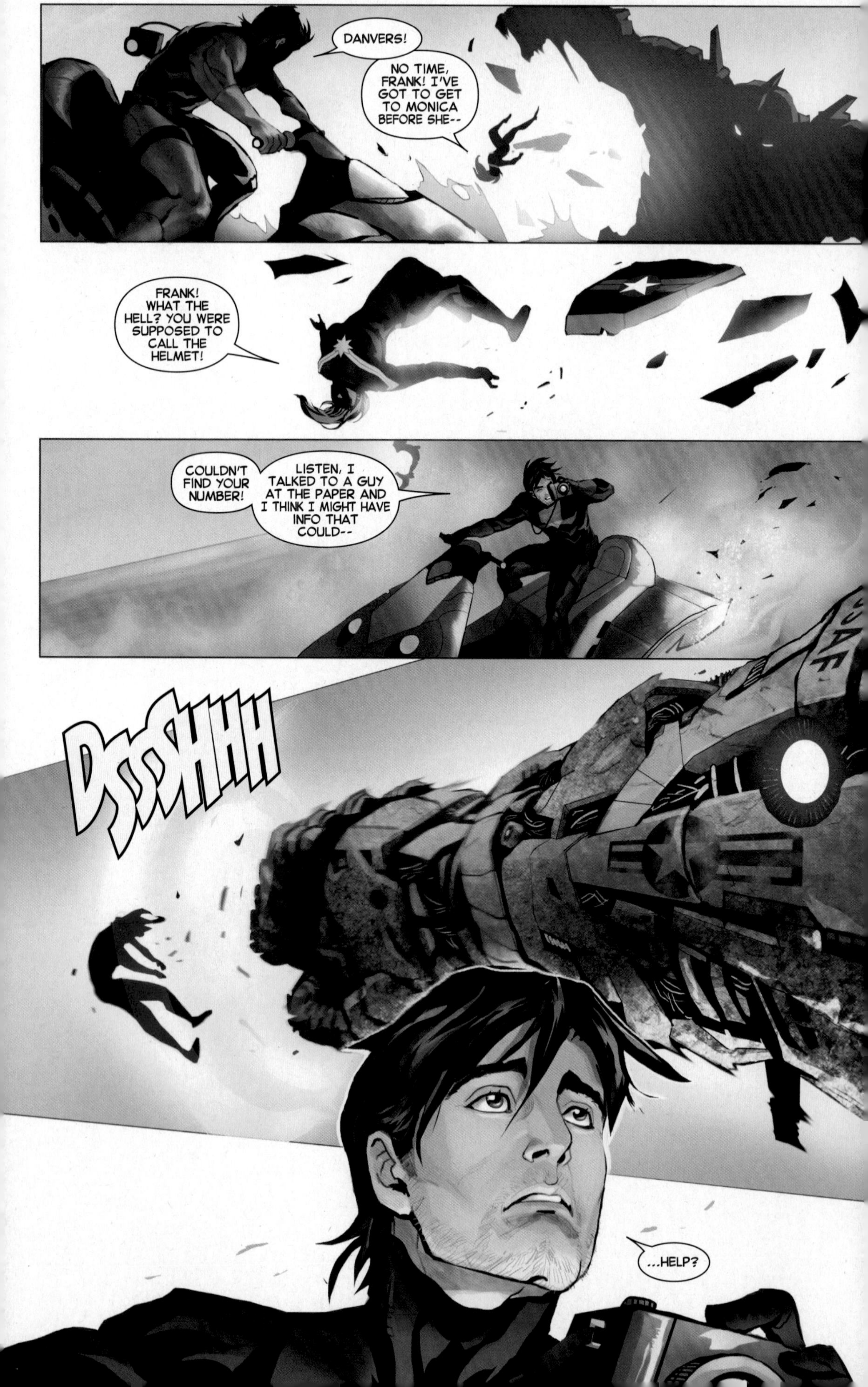
DANVERS!
NO TIME, FRANK! I'VE GOT TO GET TO MONICA BEFORE SHE--
FRANK! WHAT THE HELL? YOU WERE SUPPOSED TO CALL THE HELMET!
COULDN'T FIND YOUR NUMBER!
LISTEN, I TALKED TO A GUY AT THE PAPER AND I THINK I MIGHT HAVE INFO THAT COULD--
DSSSHHH
USAF
...HELP?

SPLOOSH!

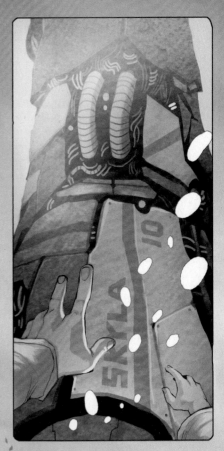

AS DIFFERENT AS MONICA AND I ARE, WE HAVE ONE THING IN COMMON--

WE BOTH HAVE TO BREATHE EVERY NOW AND THEN.

I FIGURE MONICA'S GOT A MINUTE OR SO, *TOPS*, UNLESS SHE USES HER POWERS.

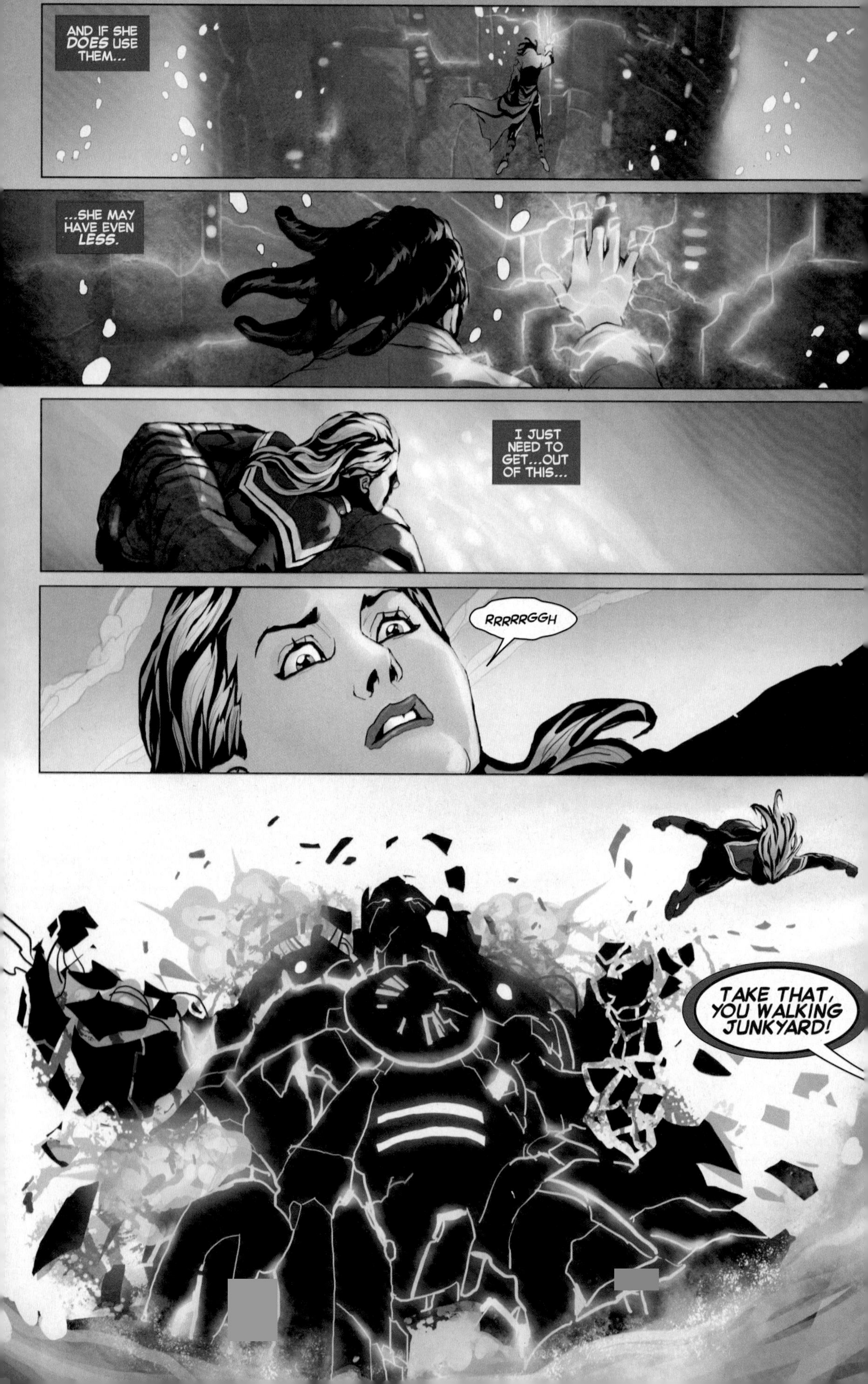
AND IF SHE DOES USE THEM...
...SHE MAY HAVE EVEN LESS.
I JUST NEED TO GET...OUT OF THIS...
RRRRRGGH
TAKE THAT, YOU WALKING JUNKYARD!

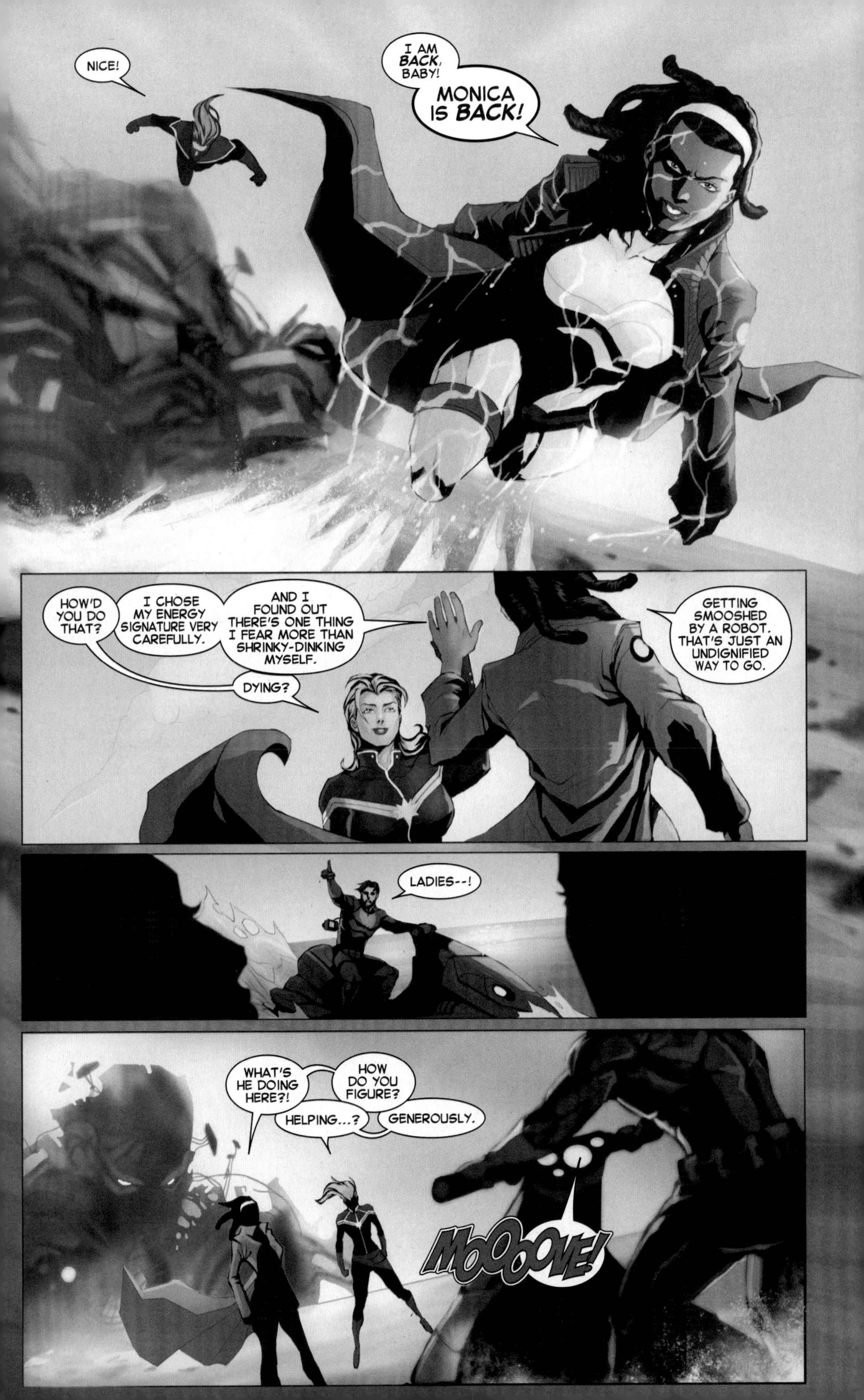
NICE!
I AM BACK, BABY!
MONICA IS BACK!
HOW'D YOU DO THAT?
I CHOSE MY ENERGY SIGNATURE VERY CAREFULLY.
AND I FOUND OUT THERE'S ONE THING I FEAR MORE THAN SHRINKY-DINKING MYSELF.
DYING?
GETTING SMOOSHED BY A ROBOT. THAT'S JUST AN UNDIGNIFIED WAY TO GO.
LADIES--!
WHAT'S HE DOING HERE?!
HOW DO YOU FIGURE?
HELPING...?
GENEROUSLY.
MOOOOVE!

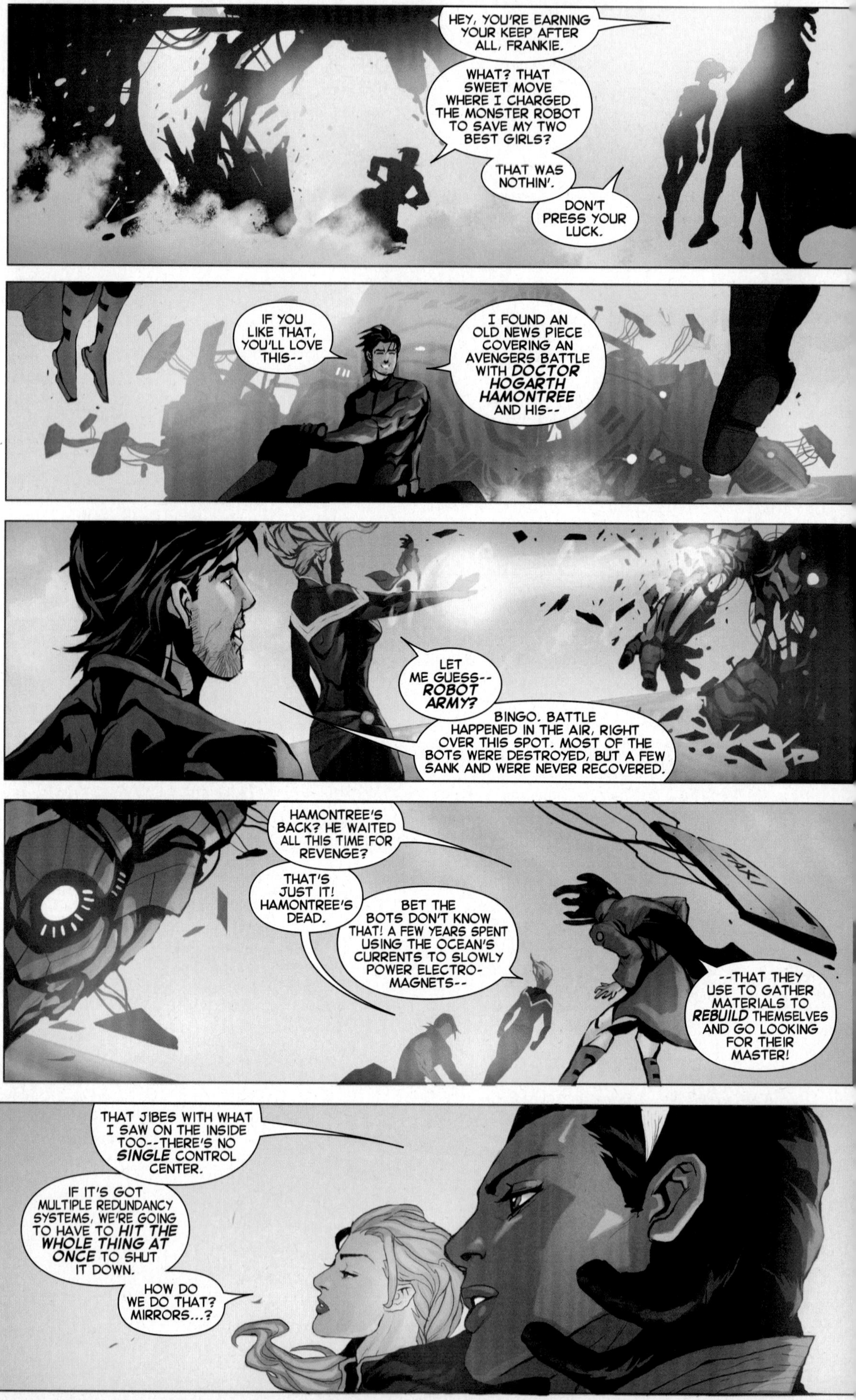

HEY, YOU'RE EARNING YOUR KEEP AFTER ALL, FRANKIE.
WHAT? THAT SWEET MOVE WHERE I CHARGED THE MONSTER ROBOT TO SAVE MY TWO BEST GIRLS?
THAT WAS NOTHIN'.
DON'T PRESS YOUR LUCK.
IF YOU LIKE THAT, YOU'LL LOVE THIS--
I FOUND AN OLD NEWS PIECE COVERING AN AVENGERS BATTLE WITH DOCTOR HOGARTH HAMONTREE AND HIS--
LET ME GUESS-- ROBOT ARMY?
BINGO. BATTLE HAPPENED IN THE AIR, RIGHT OVER THIS SPOT. MOST OF THE BOTS WERE DESTROYED, BUT A FEW SANK AND WERE NEVER RECOVERED.
HAMONTREE'S BACK? HE WAITED ALL THIS TIME FOR REVENGE?
THAT'S JUST IT! HAMONTREE'S DEAD.
BET THE BOTS DON'T KNOW THAT! A FEW YEARS SPENT USING THE OCEAN'S CURRENTS TO SLOWLY POWER ELECTRO-MAGNETS--
--THAT THEY USE TO GATHER MATERIALS TO REBUILD THEMSELVES AND GO LOOKING FOR THEIR MASTER!
THAT JIBES WITH WHAT I SAW ON THE INSIDE TOO--THERE'S NO SINGLE CONTROL CENTER.
IF IT'S GOT MULTIPLE REDUNDANCY SYSTEMS, WE'RE GOING TO HAVE TO HIT THE WHOLE THING AT ONCE TO SHUT IT DOWN.
HOW DO WE DO THAT? MIRRORS...?

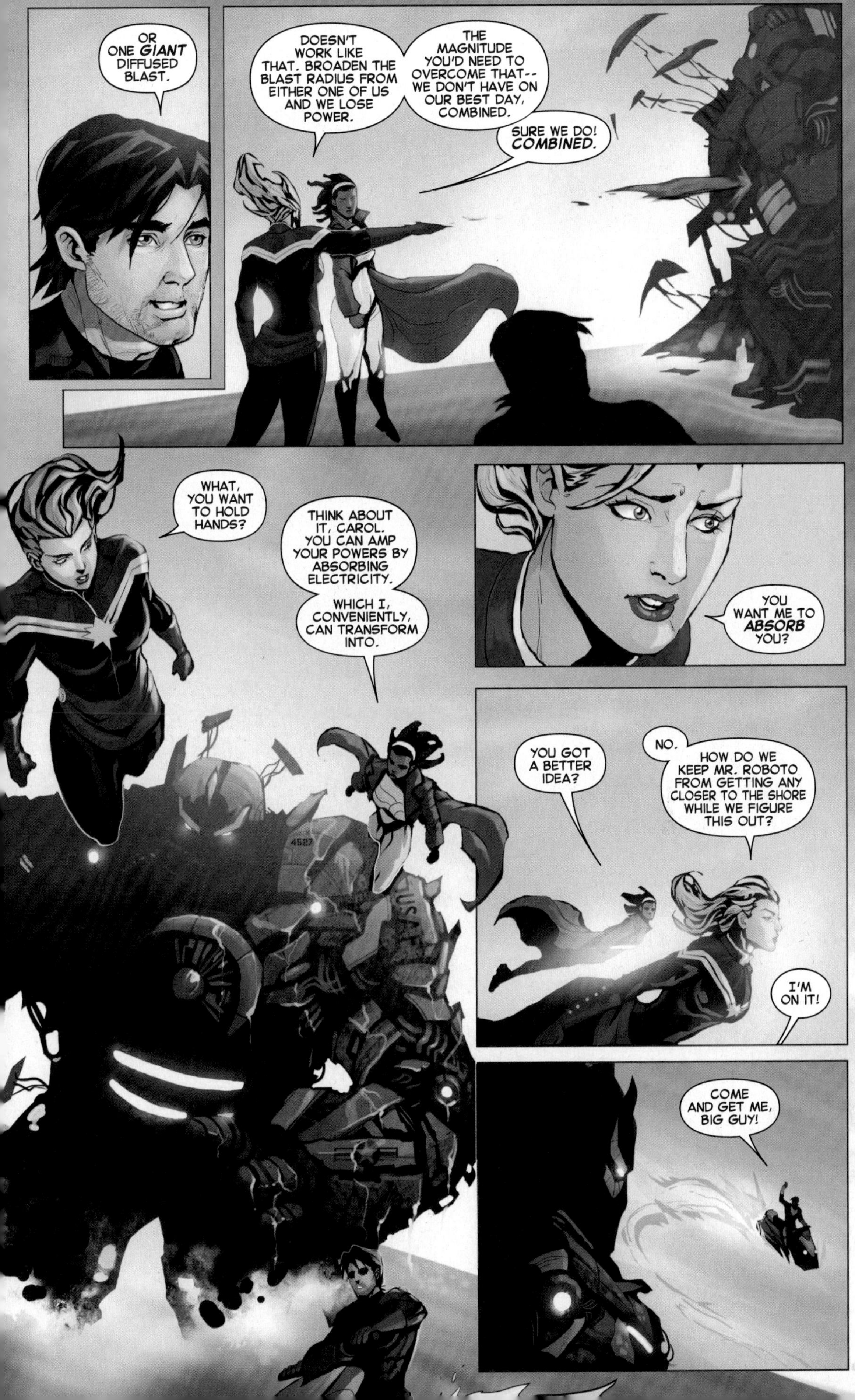

OR ONE GIANT DIFFUSED BLAST.
DOESN'T WORK LIKE THAT. BROADEN THE BLAST RADIUS FROM EITHER ONE OF US AND WE LOSE POWER.
THE MAGNITUDE YOU'D NEED TO OVERCOME THAT--WE DON'T HAVE ON OUR BEST DAY, COMBINED.
SURE WE DO! COMBINED.
WHAT, YOU WANT TO HOLD HANDS?
THINK ABOUT IT, CAROL. YOU CAN AMP YOUR POWERS BY ABSORBING ELECTRICITY.
WHICH I, CONVENIENTLY, CAN TRANSFORM INTO.
YOU WANT ME TO ABSORB YOU?
YOU GOT A BETTER IDEA?
NO.
HOW DO WE KEEP MR. ROBOTO FROM GETTING ANY CLOSER TO THE SHORE WHILE WE FIGURE THIS OUT?
I'M ON IT!
COME AND GET ME, BIG GUY!

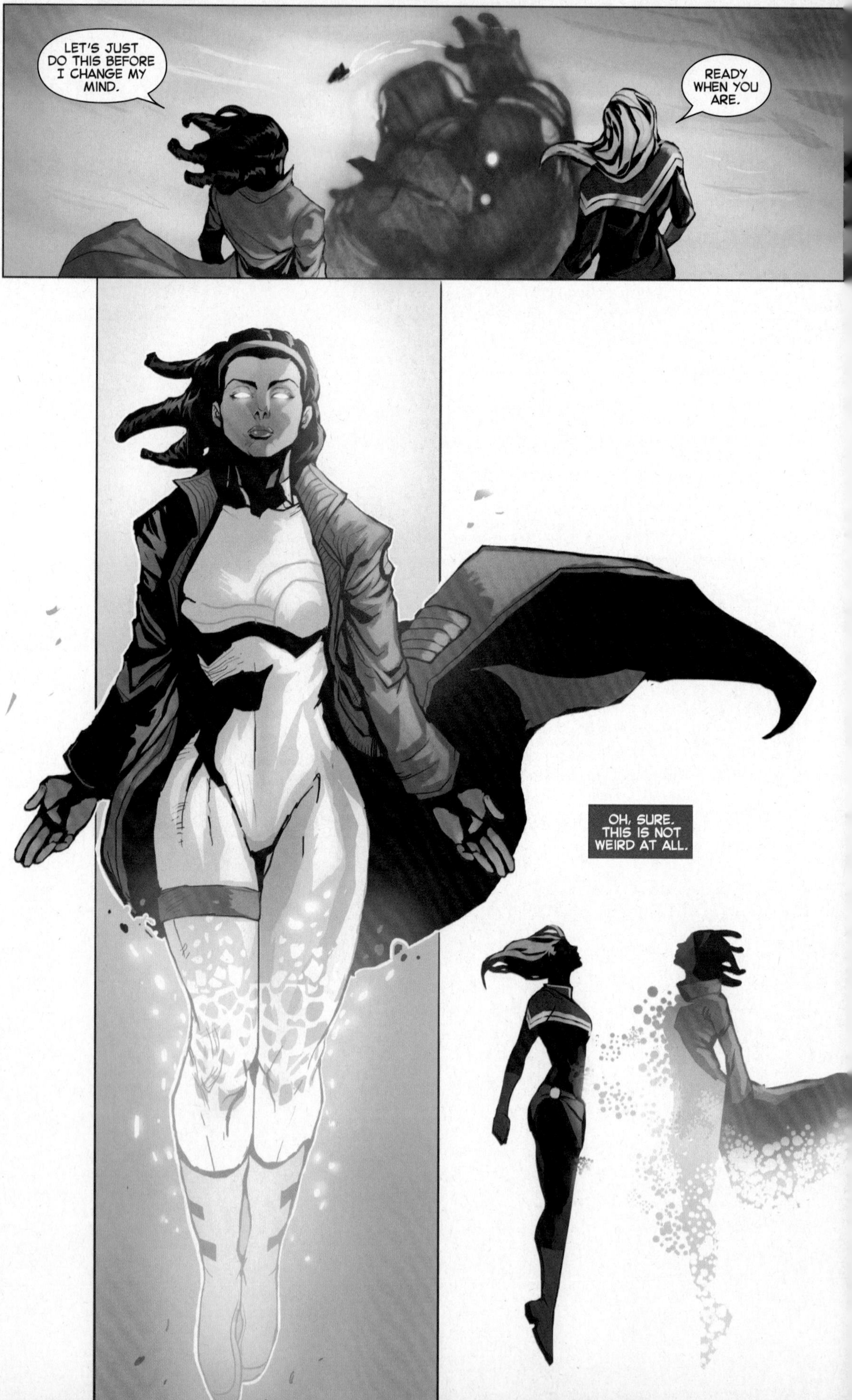
LET'S JUST DO THIS BEFORE I CHANGE MY MIND.
READY WHEN YOU ARE.
OH, SURE. THIS IS NOT WEIRD AT ALL.

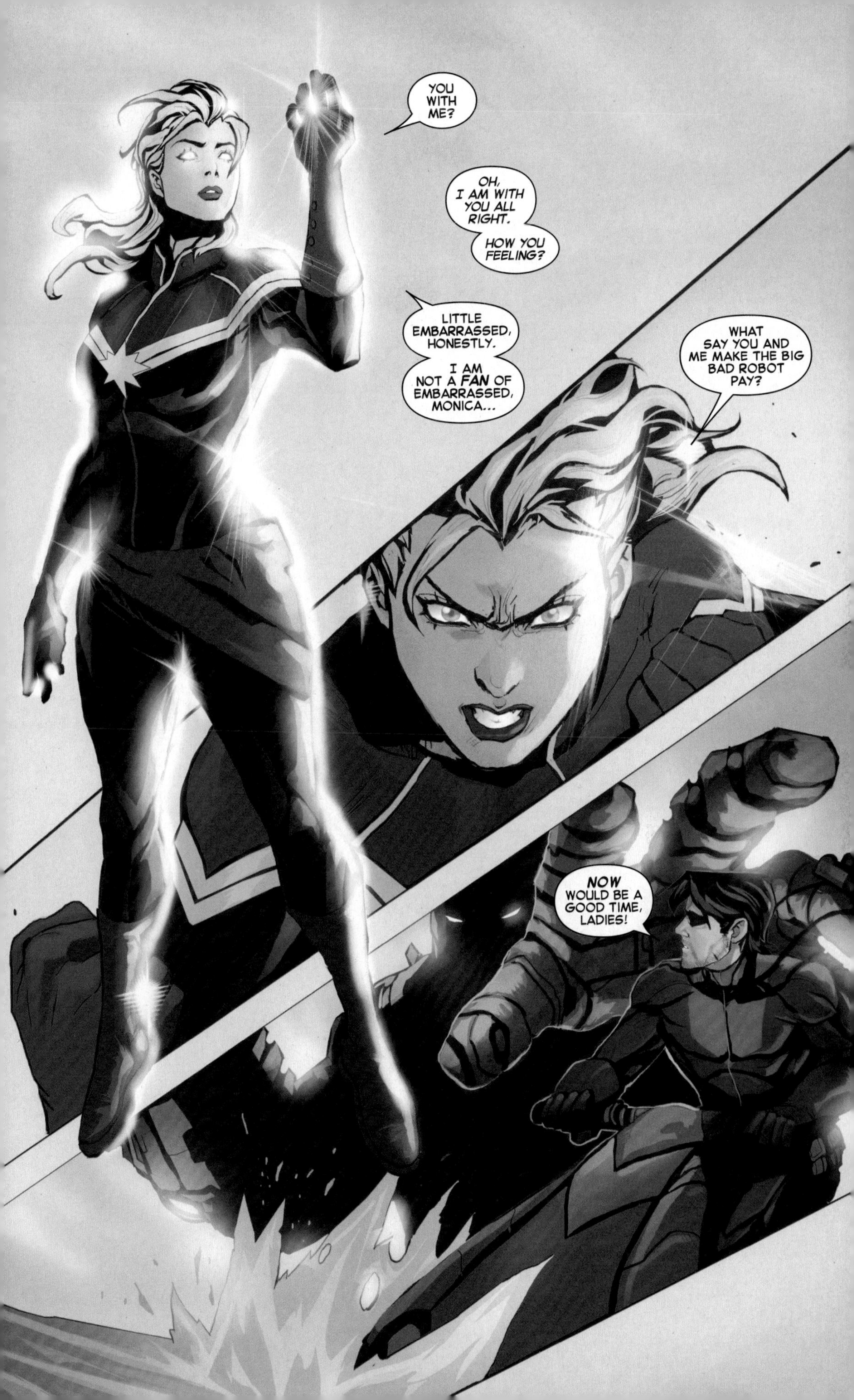
YOU WITH ME?
OH, I AM WITH YOU ALL RIGHT.
HOW YOU FEELING?
LITTLE EMBARRASSED, HONESTLY.
I AM NOT A FAN OF EMBARRASSED, MONICA...
WHAT SAY YOU AND ME MAKE THE BIG BAD ROBOT PAY?
NOW WOULD BE A GOOD TIME, LADIES!

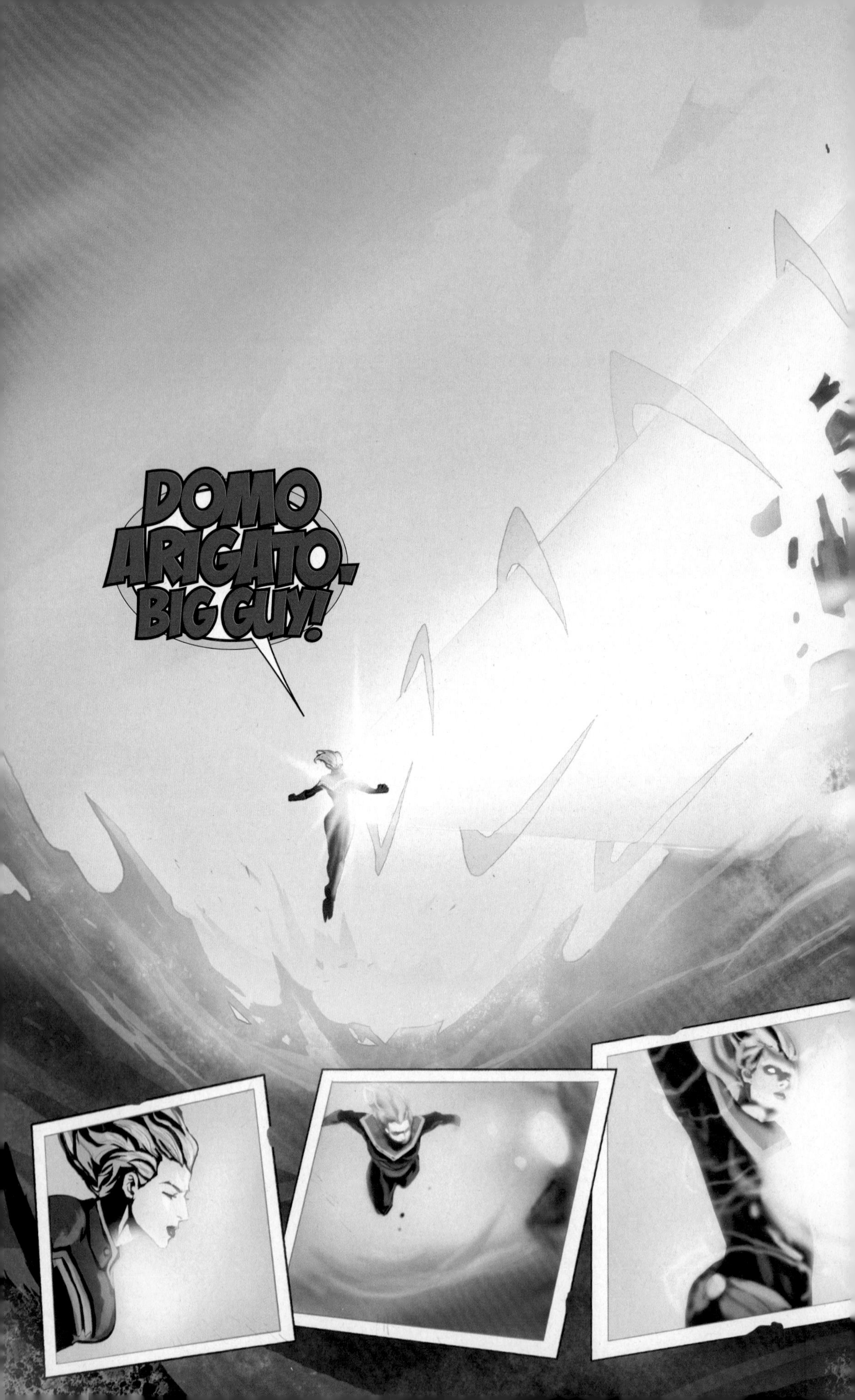
DOMO ARIGATO, BIG GUY!

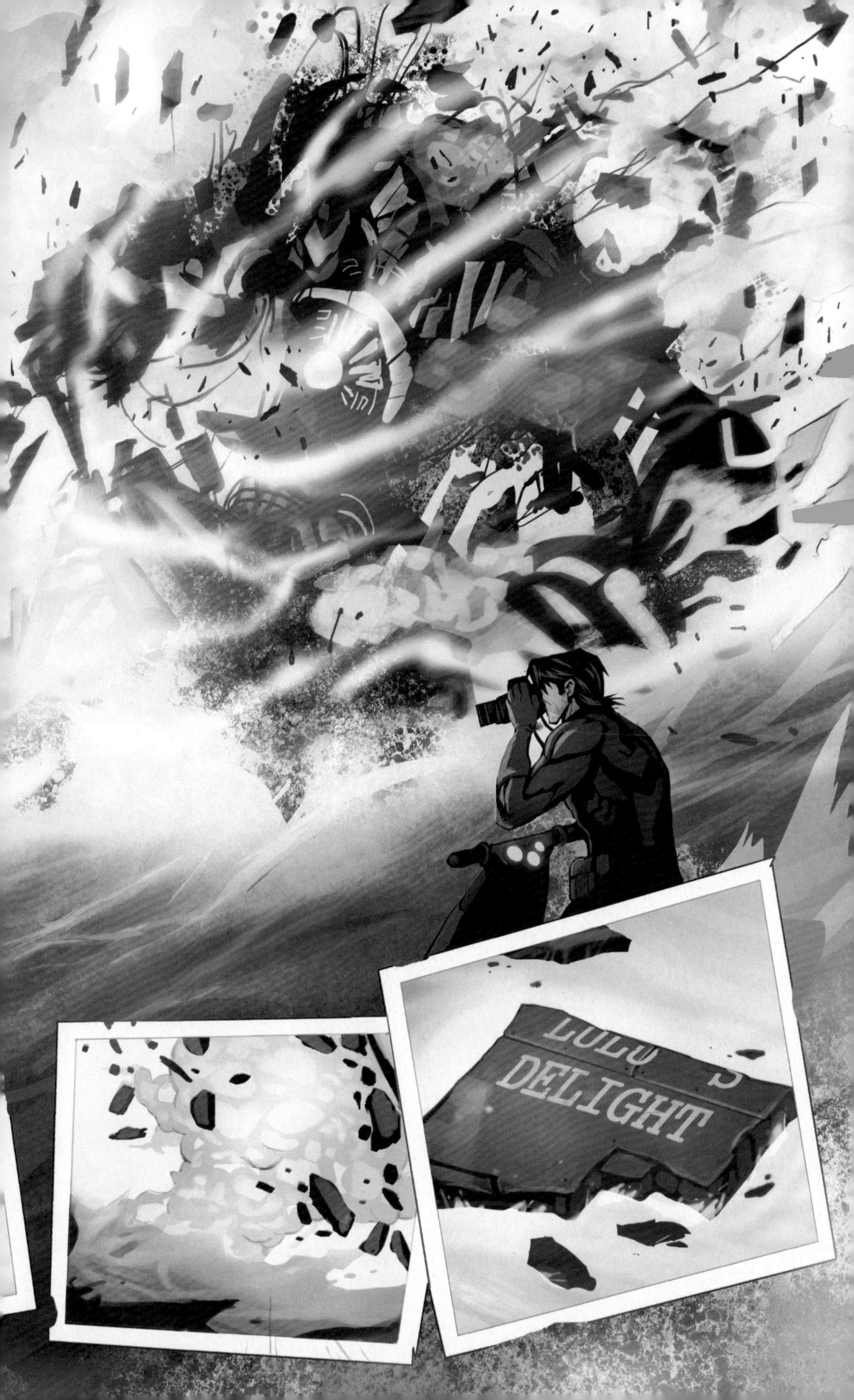
DELIGHT

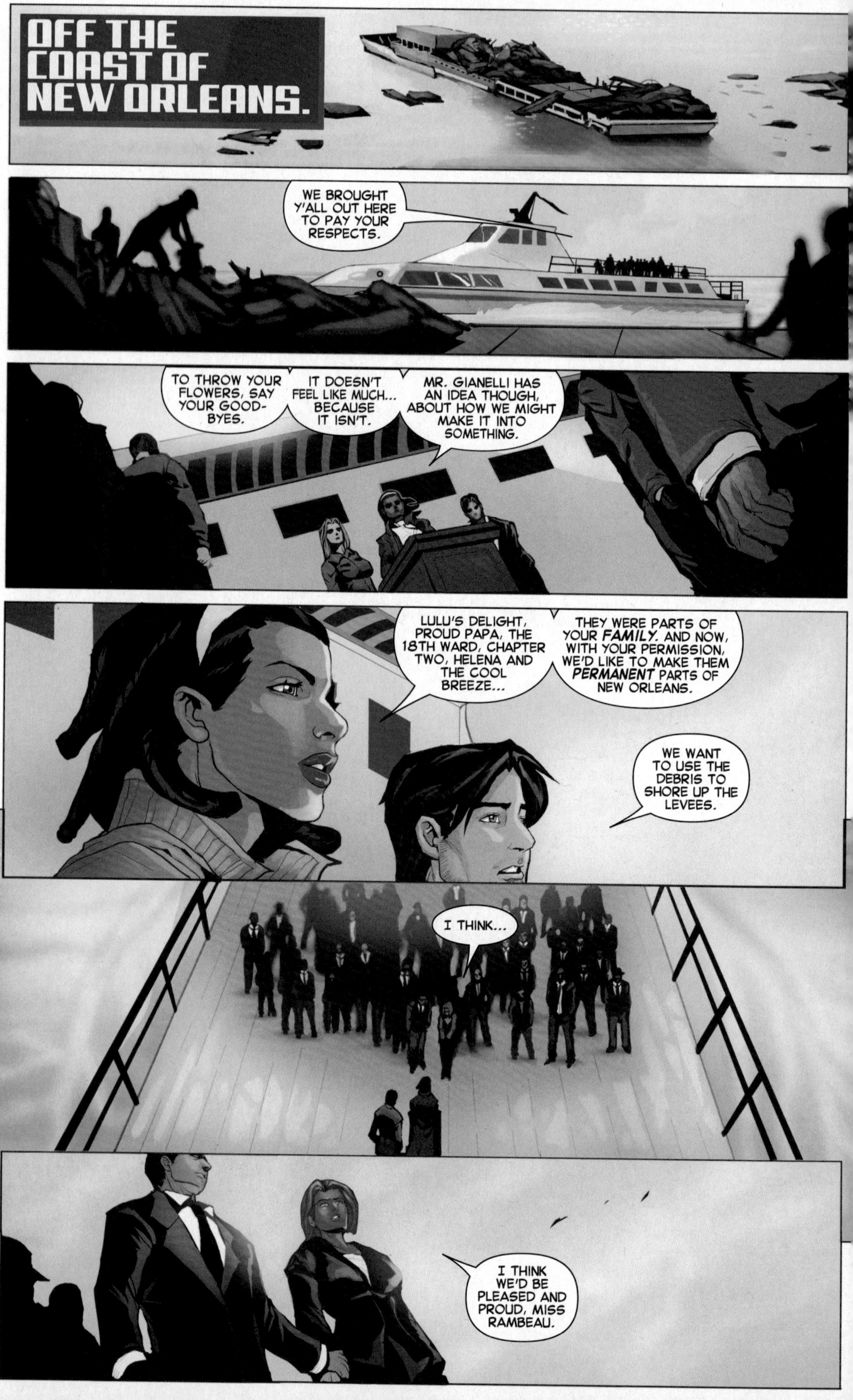
OFF THE COAST OF NEW ORLEANS.
WE BROUGHT Y'ALL OUT HERE TO PAY YOUR RESPECTS.
TO THROW YOUR FLOWERS, SAY YOUR GOOD-BYES.
IT DOESN'T FEEL LIKE MUCH... BECAUSE IT ISN'T.
MR. GIANELLI HAS AN IDEA THOUGH, ABOUT HOW WE MIGHT MAKE IT INTO SOMETHING.
LULU'S DELIGHT, PROUD PAPA, THE 18TH WARD, CHAPTER TWO, HELENA AND THE COOL BREEZE...
THEY WERE PARTS OF YOUR FAMILY. AND NOW, WITH YOUR PERMISSION, WE'D LIKE TO MAKE THEM PERMANENT PARTS OF NEW ORLEANS.
WE WANT TO USE THE DEBRIS TO SHORE UP THE LEVEES.
I THINK...
I THINK WE'D BE PLEASED AND PROUD, MISS RAMBEAU.

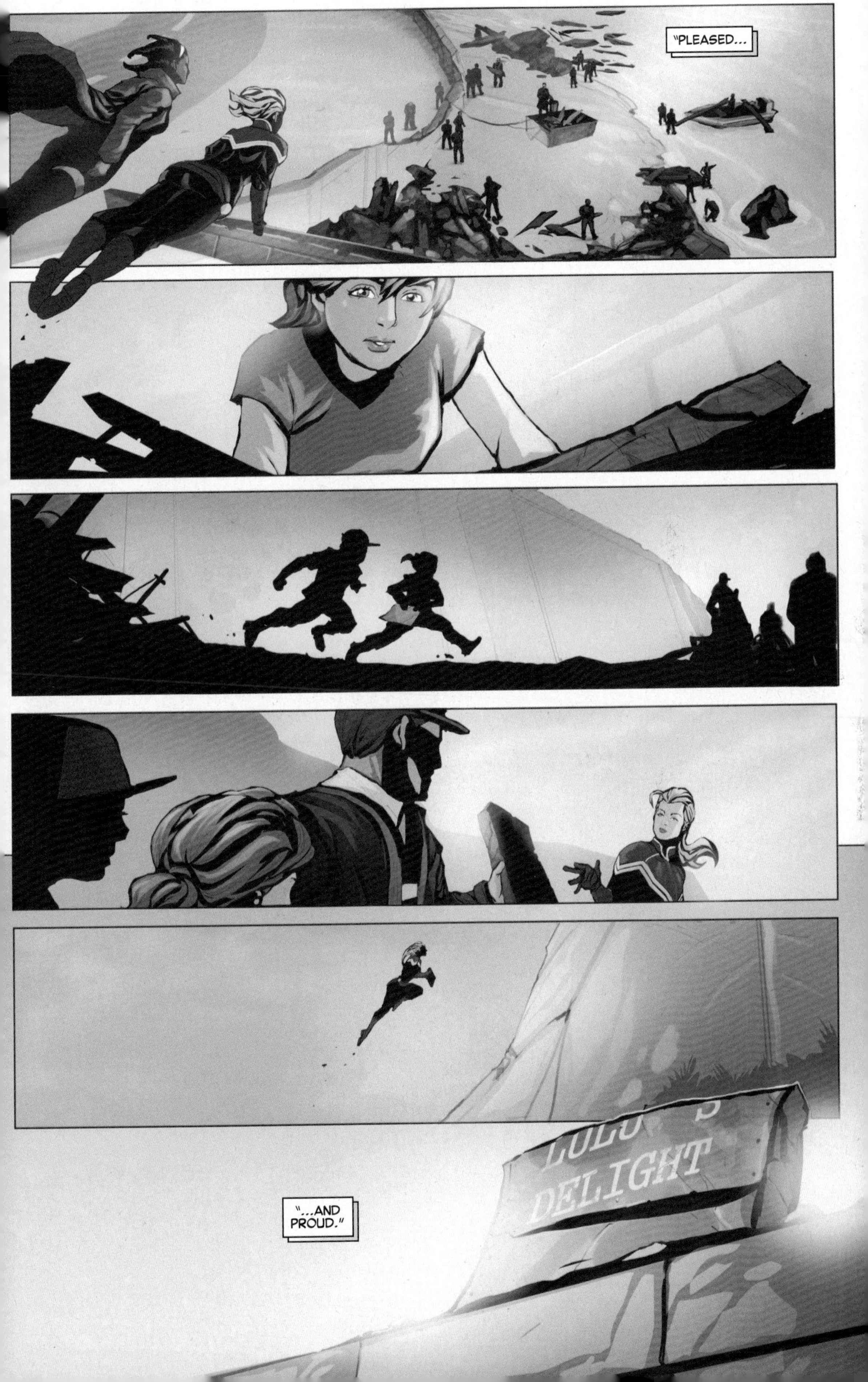
"PLEASED...
"...AND PROUD."
DELIGHT

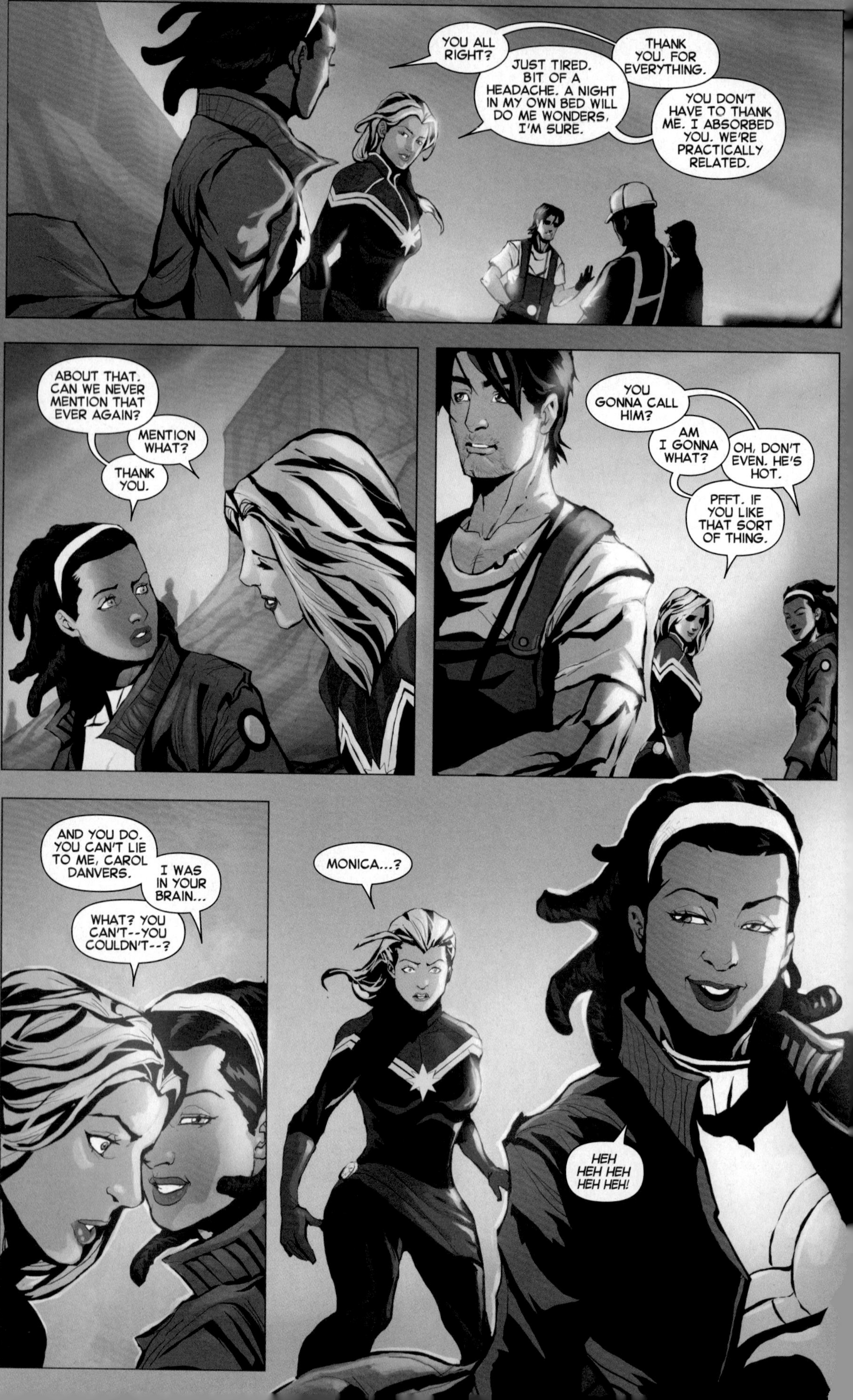

YOU ALL RIGHT?
JUST TIRED. BIT OF A HEADACHE. A NIGHT IN MY OWN BED WILL DO ME WONDERS, I'M SURE.
THANK YOU. FOR EVERYTHING.
YOU DON'T HAVE TO THANK ME. I ABSORBED YOU. WE'RE PRACTICALLY RELATED.
ABOUT THAT. CAN WE NEVER MENTION THAT EVER AGAIN?
MENTION WHAT?
THANK YOU.
YOU GONNA CALL HIM?
AM I GONNA WHAT?
OH, DON'T EVEN. HE'S HOT.
PFFT. IF YOU LIKE THAT SORT OF THING.
AND YOU DO. YOU CAN'T LIE TO ME, CAROL DANVERS.
I WAS IN YOUR BRAIN...
WHAT? YOU CAN'T--YOU COULDN'T--?
MONICA...?
HEH HEH HEH HEH HEH!

CAPTAIN MARVEL #17

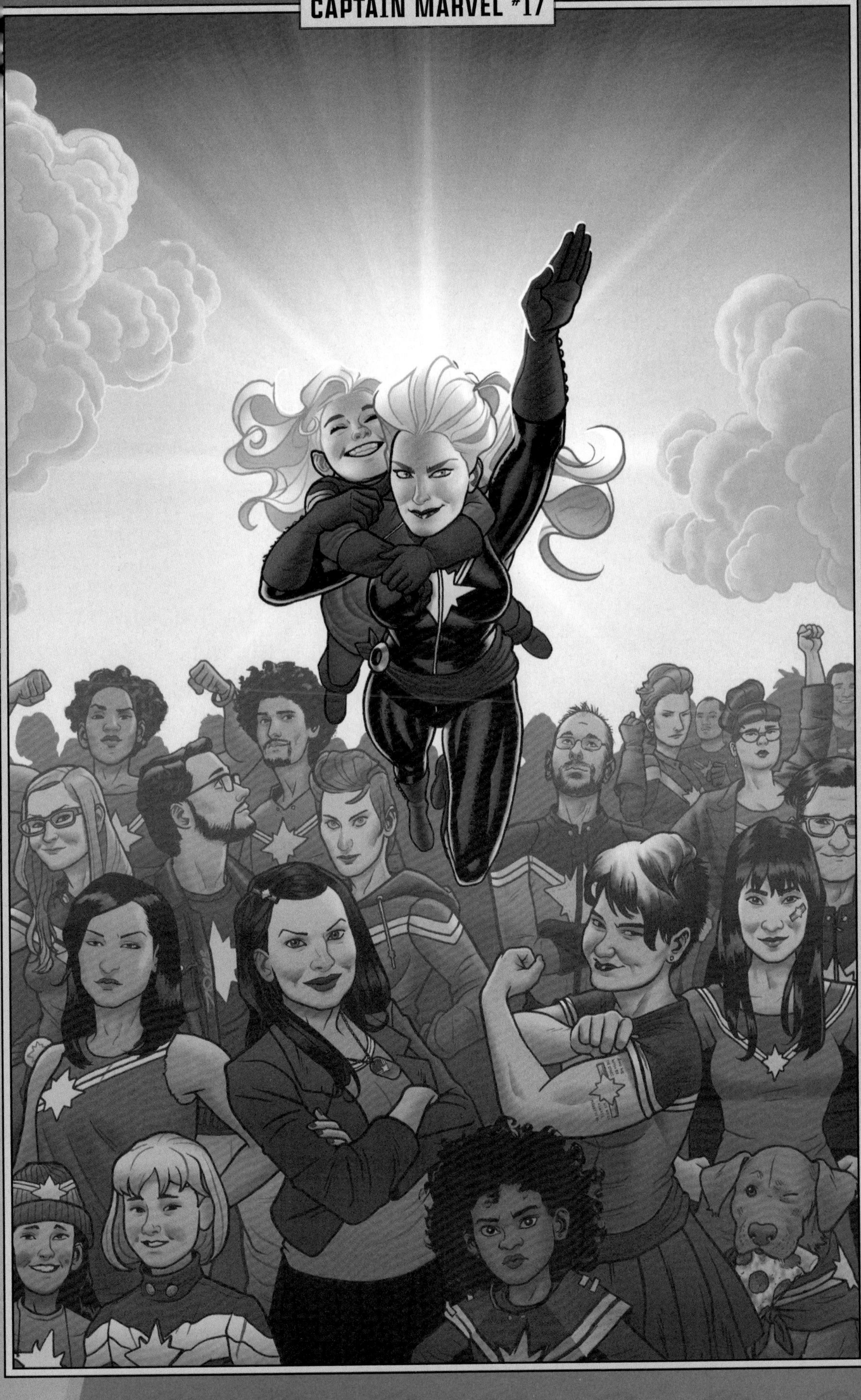

When former U.S. Air Force pilot, Carol Danvers was caught in the explosion of an alien device called the Psyche-Magnitron, she was transformed into one of the world's most powerful super beings. She now uses her abilities to protect her planet and fight for justice as an Avenger. She is Earth's Mightiest Hero...she is...

CAPTAIN MARVEL

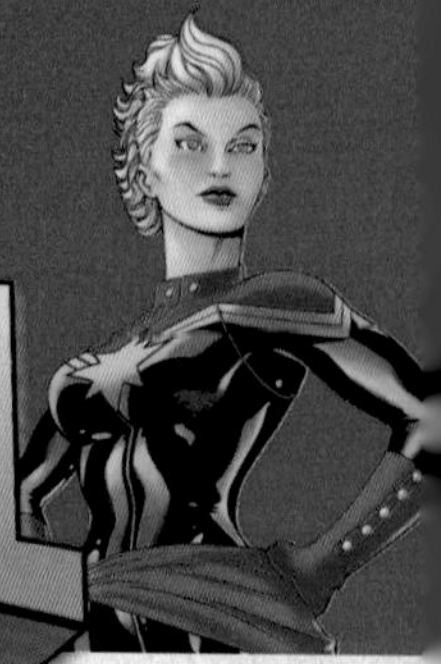

CAPTAIN MARVEL'S ALL-STAR MOMENTS!

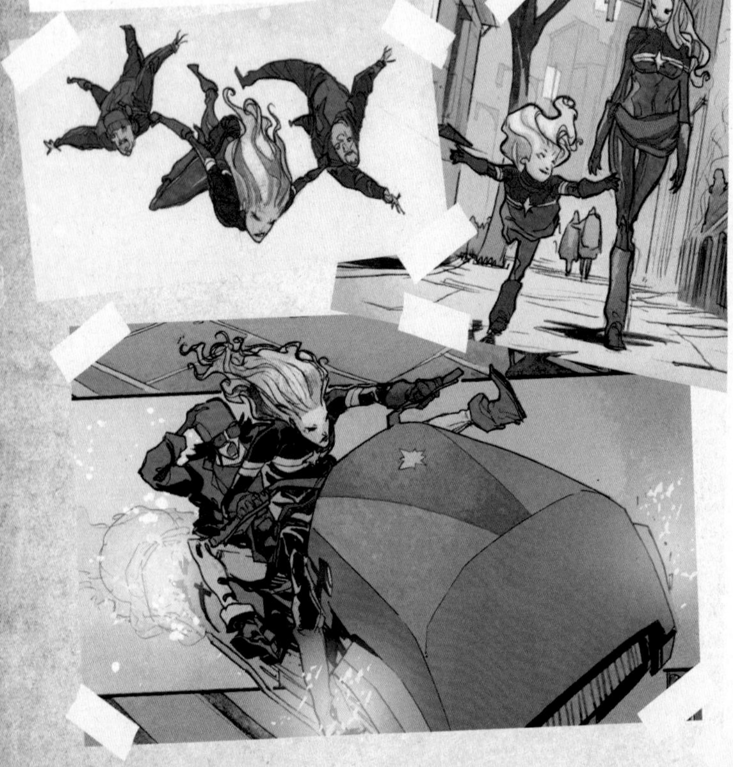

KIT'S TO-DO LIST

- TEA PARTY WITH MR. SNUFFLES & KITTY BEAR

- CHECK THE LIBRARY FOR BOOKS ON AMNESIA -- MAYBE I'LL FIND INFO TO HELP FIX CAPTAIN MARVEL'S MEMORY!

- SEE IF WE CAN FIND CAPTAIN MARVEL A NEW APARTMENT!

- HELP GILBERT FINISH HIS IRON MAN SUIT!

- SUPER HERO LESSONS!

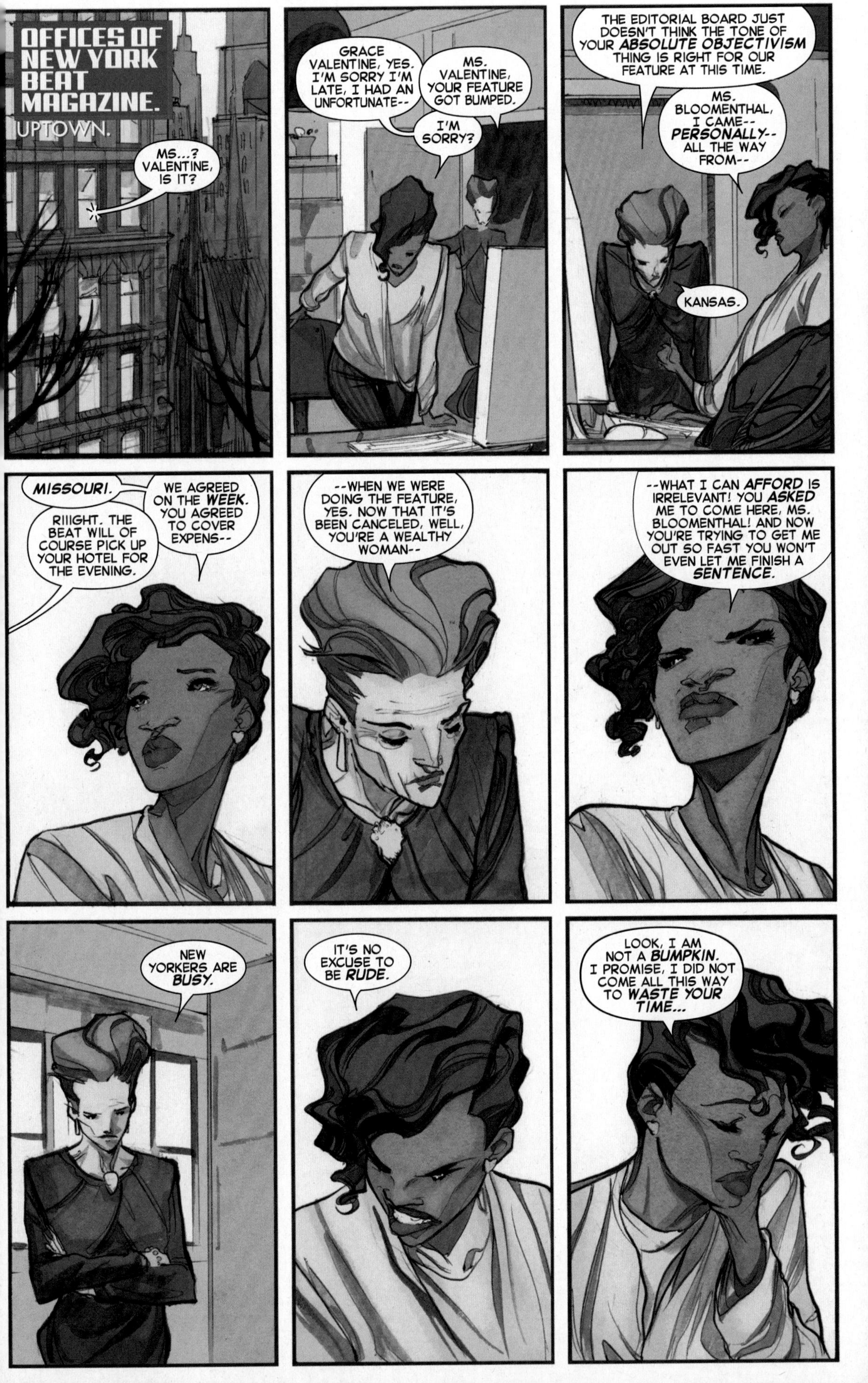
OFFICES OF NEW YORK BEAT MAGAZINE.
UPTOWN.
MS...? VALENTINE, IS IT?
GRACE VALENTINE, YES. I'M SORRY I'M LATE, I HAD AN UNFORTUNATE--
MS. VALENTINE, YOUR FEATURE GOT BUMPED.
I'M SORRY?
THE EDITORIAL BOARD JUST DOESN'T THINK THE TONE OF YOUR ABSOLUTE OBJECTIVISM THING IS RIGHT FOR OUR FEATURE AT THIS TIME.
MS. BLOOMENTHAL, I CAME-- PERSONALLY-- ALL THE WAY FROM--
KANSAS.
MISSOURI.
WE AGREED ON THE WEEK. YOU AGREED TO COVER EXPENS--
RIIIGHT. THE BEAT WILL OF COURSE PICK UP YOUR HOTEL FOR THE EVENING.
--WHEN WE WERE DOING THE FEATURE, YES. NOW THAT IT'S BEEN CANCELED, WELL, YOU'RE A WEALTHY WOMAN--
--WHAT I CAN AFFORD IS IRRELEVANT! YOU ASKED ME TO COME HERE, MS. BLOOMENTHAL! AND NOW YOU'RE TRYING TO GET ME OUT SO FAST YOU WON'T EVEN LET ME FINISH A SENTENCE.
NEW YORKERS ARE BUSY.
IT'S NO EXCUSE TO BE RUDE.
LOOK, I AM NOT A BUMPKIN. I PROMISE, I DID NOT COME ALL THIS WAY TO WASTE YOUR TIME...

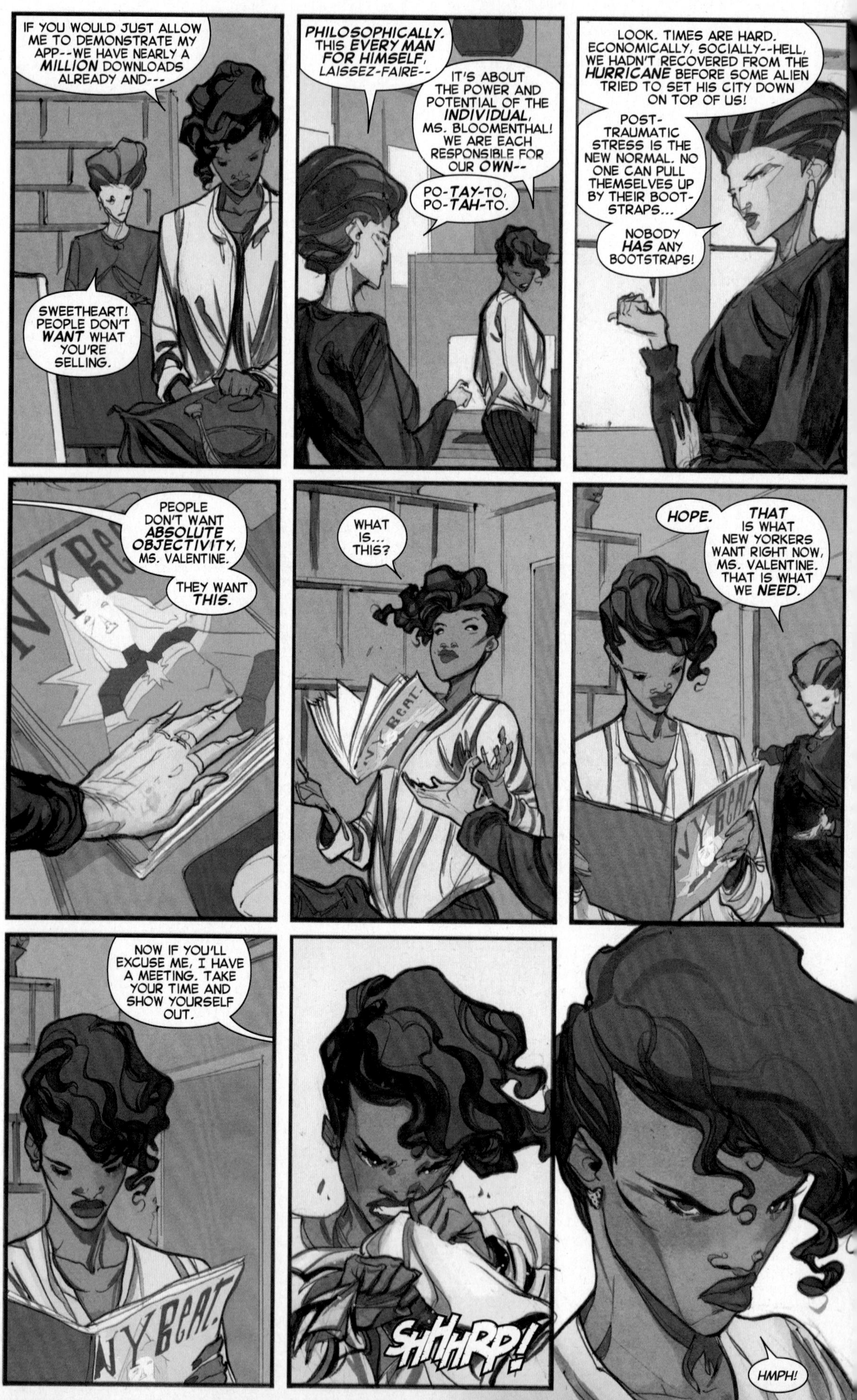
IF YOU WOULD JUST ALLOW ME TO DEMONSTRATE MY APP--WE HAVE NEARLY A MILLION DOWNLOADS ALREADY AND---
SWEETHEART! PEOPLE DON'T WANT WHAT YOU'RE SELLING.
PHILOSOPHICALLY. THIS EVERY MAN FOR HIMSELF, LAISSEZ-FAIRE--
IT'S ABOUT THE POWER AND POTENTIAL OF THE INDIVIDUAL, MS. BLOOMENTHAL! WE ARE EACH RESPONSIBLE FOR OUR OWN--
PO-TAY-TO, PO-TAH-TO.
LOOK. TIMES ARE HARD. ECONOMICALLY, SOCIALLY--HELL, WE HADN'T RECOVERED FROM THE HURRICANE BEFORE SOME ALIEN TRIED TO SET HIS CITY DOWN ON TOP OF US!
POST-TRAUMATIC STRESS IS THE NEW NORMAL. NO ONE CAN PULL THEMSELVES UP BY THEIR BOOT-STRAPS...
NOBODY HAS ANY BOOTSTRAPS!
PEOPLE DON'T WANT ABSOLUTE OBJECTIVITY, MS. VALENTINE.
THEY WANT THIS.
WHAT IS... THIS?
HOPE.
THAT IS WHAT NEW YORKERS WANT RIGHT NOW, MS. VALENTINE. THAT IS WHAT WE NEED.
NOW IF YOU'LL EXCUSE ME, I HAVE A MEETING. TAKE YOUR TIME AND SHOW YOURSELF OUT.
NY BEAT.
SHHHRP!
HMPH!

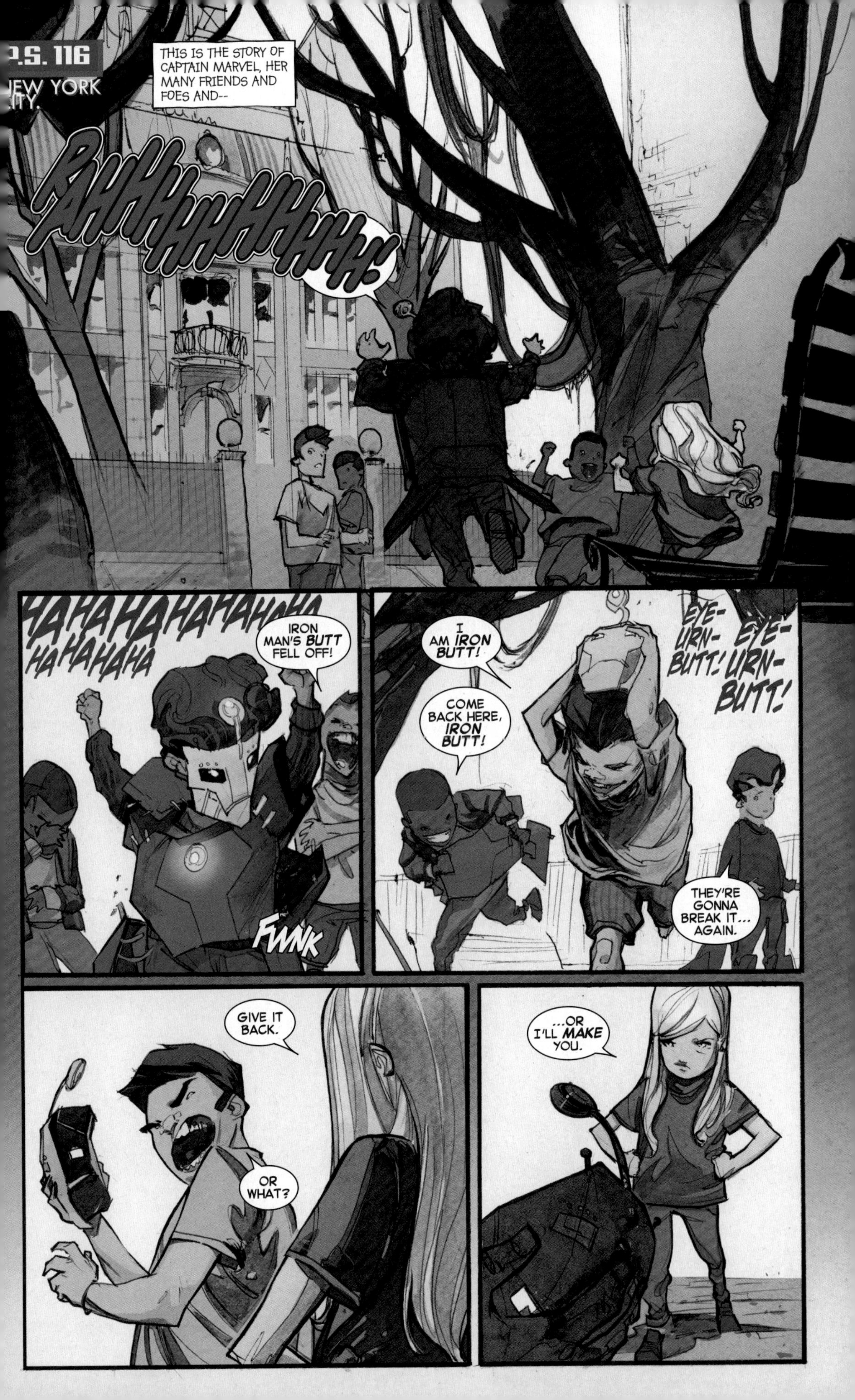
P.S. 116
NEW YORK CITY.
THIS IS THE STORY OF CAPTAIN MARVEL, HER MANY FRIENDS AND FOES AND--
BAHHHHHHHHHHHH!
HAHAHAHAHAHAHAHAHA HAHAHAHA
IRON MAN'S BUTT FELL OFF!
FWNK
I AM IRON BUTT!
COME BACK HERE, IRON BUTT!
EYE-URN-BUTT! EYE-URN-BUTT!
THEY'RE GONNA BREAK IT... AGAIN.
GIVE IT BACK.
OR WHAT?
...OR I'LL MAKE YOU.

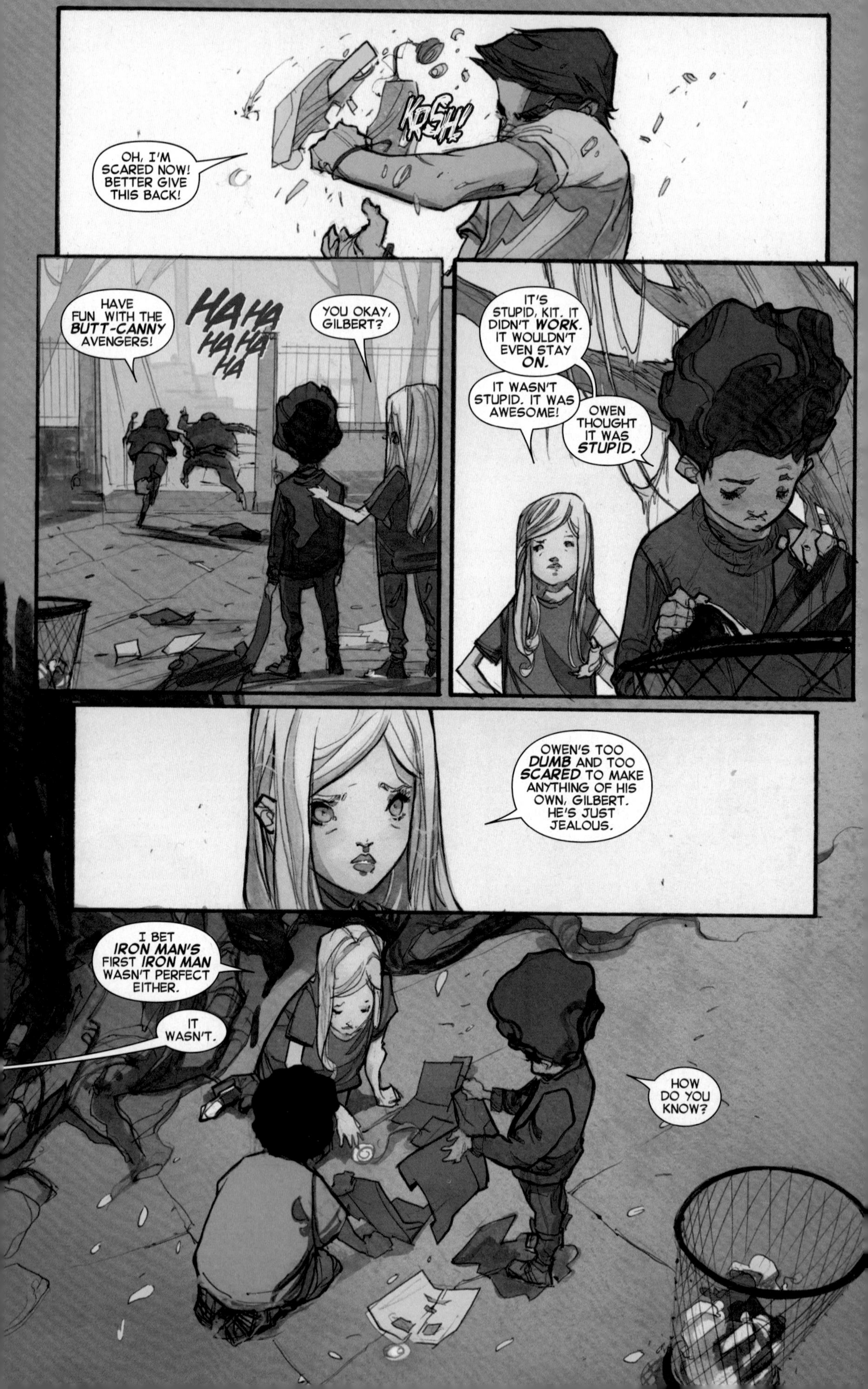
KRSH!
OH, I'M SCARED NOW! BETTER GIVE THIS BACK!
HAVE FUN WITH THE BUTT-CANNY AVENGERS!
HA HA HA HA HA
YOU OKAY, GILBERT?
IT'S STUPID, KIT. IT DIDN'T WORK. IT WOULDN'T EVEN STAY ON.
IT WASN'T STUPID. IT WAS AWESOME!
OWEN THOUGHT IT WAS STUPID.
OWEN'S TOO DUMB AND TOO SCARED TO MAKE ANYTHING OF HIS OWN, GILBERT. HE'S JUST JEALOUS.
I BET IRON MAN'S FIRST IRON MAN WASN'T PERFECT EITHER.
IT WASN'T.
HOW DO YOU KNOW?

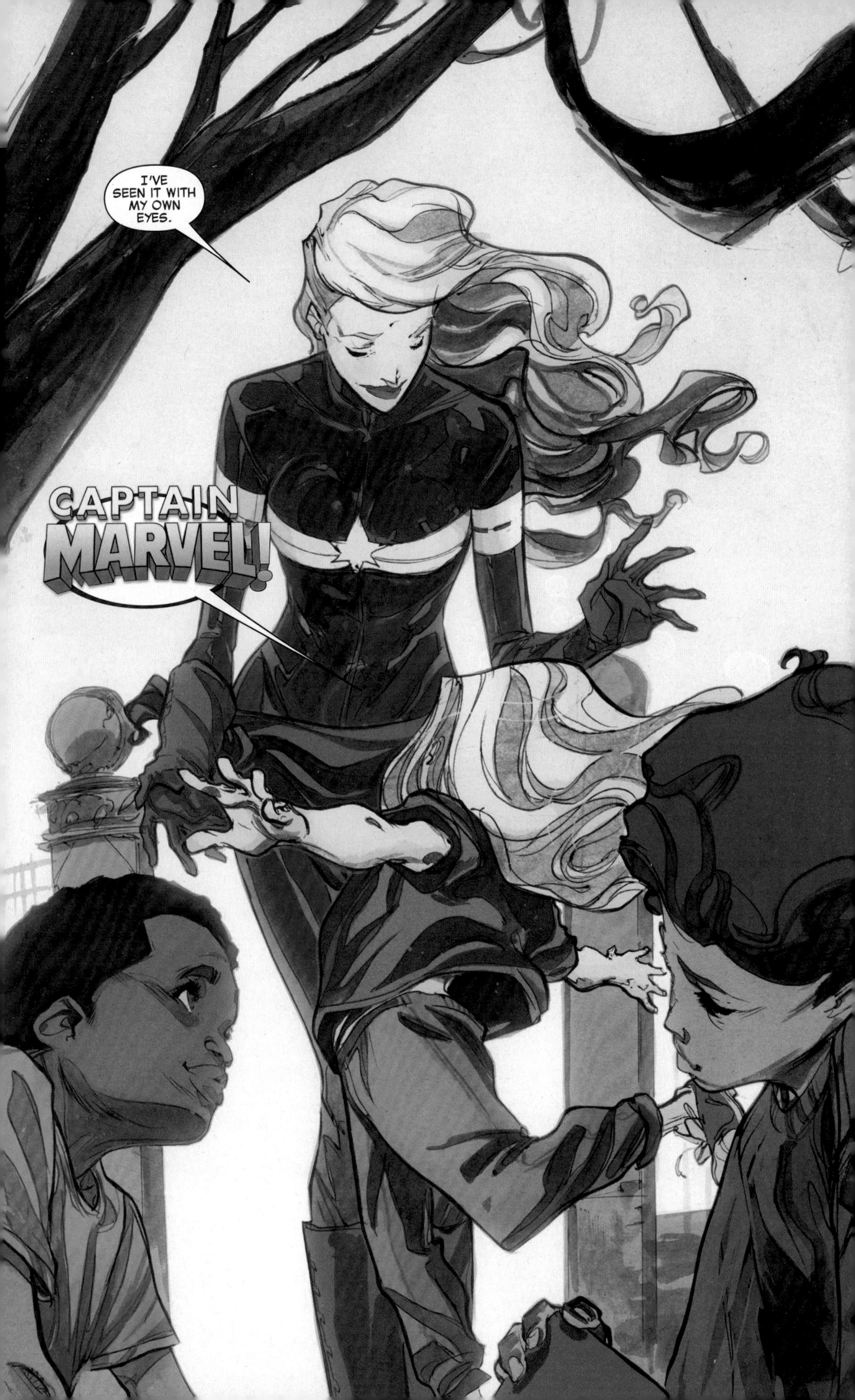
I'VE SEEN IT WITH MY OWN EYES.
CAPTAIN MARVEL!

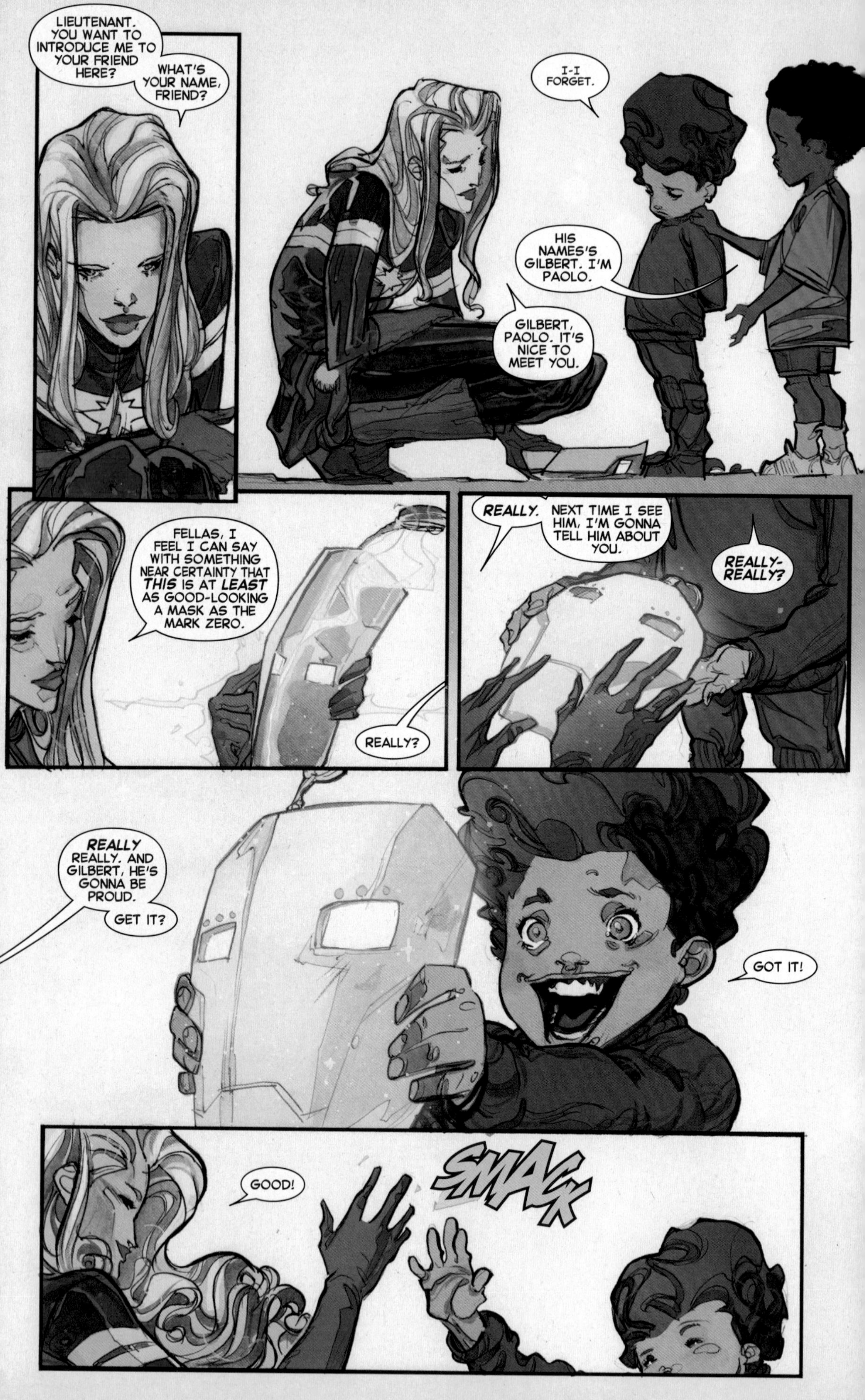
LIEUTENANT. YOU WANT TO INTRODUCE ME TO YOUR FRIEND HERE?
WHAT'S YOUR NAME, FRIEND?
I-I FORGET.
HIS NAMES'S GILBERT. I'M PAOLO.
GILBERT, PAOLO. IT'S NICE TO MEET YOU.
FELLAS, I FEEL I CAN SAY WITH SOMETHING NEAR CERTAINTY THAT THIS IS AT LEAST AS GOOD-LOOKING A MASK AS THE MARK ZERO.
REALLY?
REALLY.
NEXT TIME I SEE HIM, I'M GONNA TELL HIM ABOUT YOU.
REALLY-REALLY?
REALLY REALLY. AND GILBERT, HE'S GONNA BE PROUD.
GET IT?
GOT IT!
GOOD!
SMACK

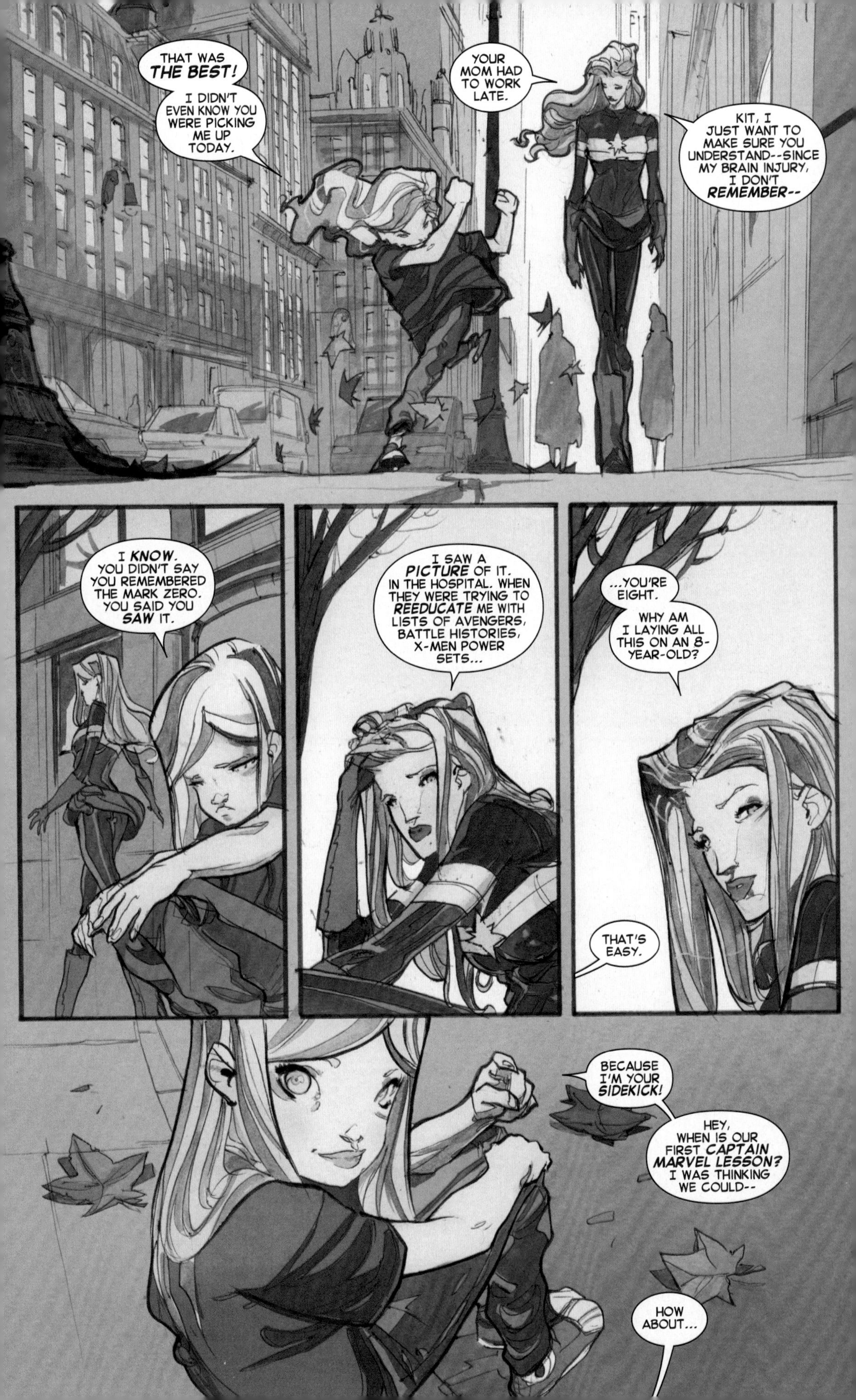
THAT WAS THE BEST!
I DIDN'T EVEN KNOW YOU WERE PICKING ME UP TODAY.
YOUR MOM HAD TO WORK LATE.
KIT, I JUST WANT TO MAKE SURE YOU UNDERSTAND--SINCE MY BRAIN INJURY, I DON'T REMEMBER--
I KNOW. YOU DIDN'T SAY YOU REMEMBERED THE MARK ZERO. YOU SAID YOU SAW IT.
I SAW A PICTURE OF IT. IN THE HOSPITAL. WHEN THEY WERE TRYING TO REEDUCATE ME WITH LISTS OF AVENGERS, BATTLE HISTORIES, X-MEN POWER SETS...
...YOU'RE EIGHT.
WHY AM I LAYING ALL THIS ON AN 8-YEAR-OLD?
THAT'S EASY.
BECAUSE I'M YOUR SIDEKICK!
HEY, WHEN IS OUR FIRST CAPTAIN MARVEL LESSON? I WAS THINKING WE COULD--
HOW ABOUT...

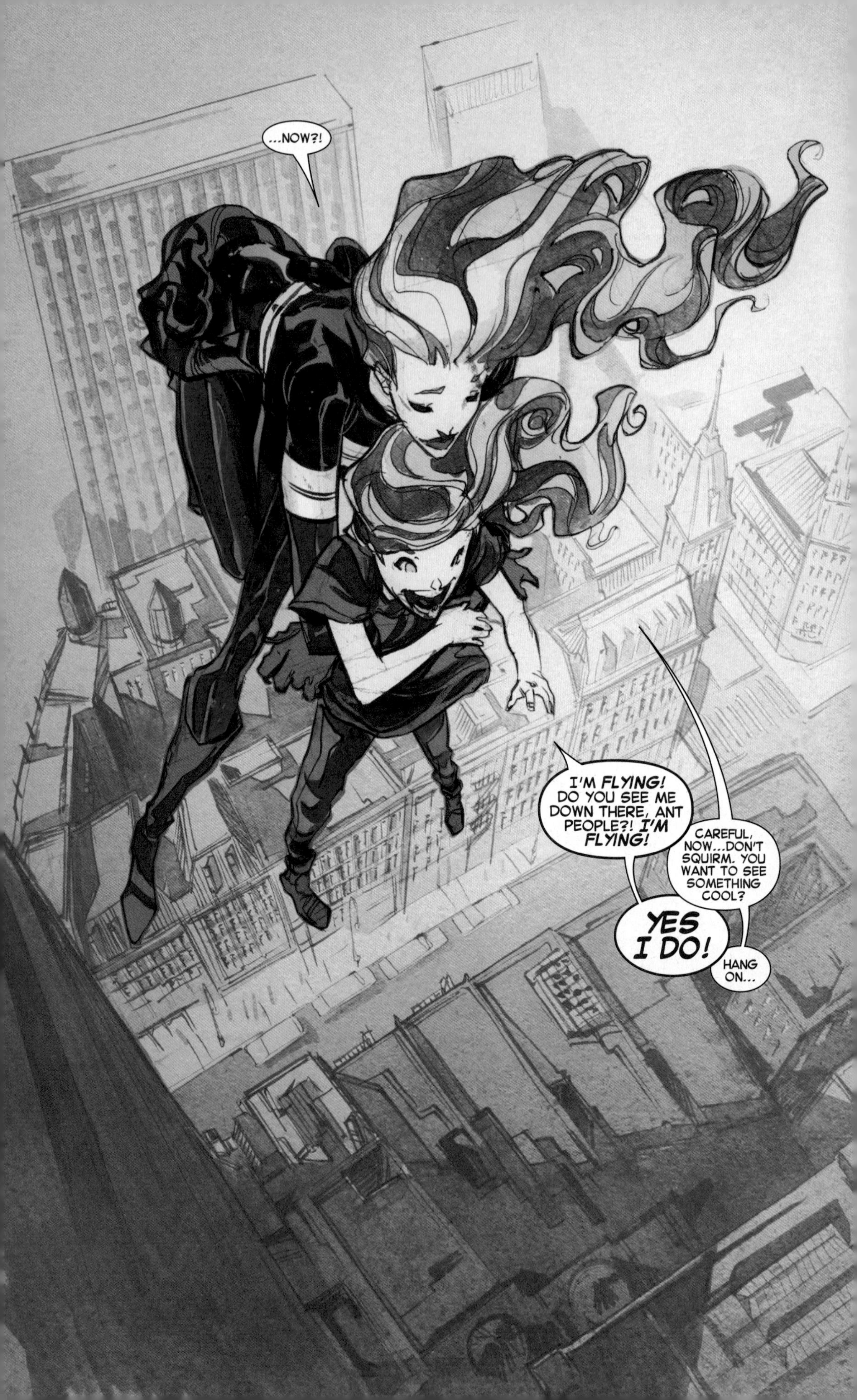
...NOW?!
I'M FLYING! DO YOU SEE ME DOWN THERE, ANT PEOPLE?! I'M FLYING!
CAREFUL, NOW...DON'T SQUIRM. YOU WANT TO SEE SOMETHING COOL?
YES I DO!
HANG ON...

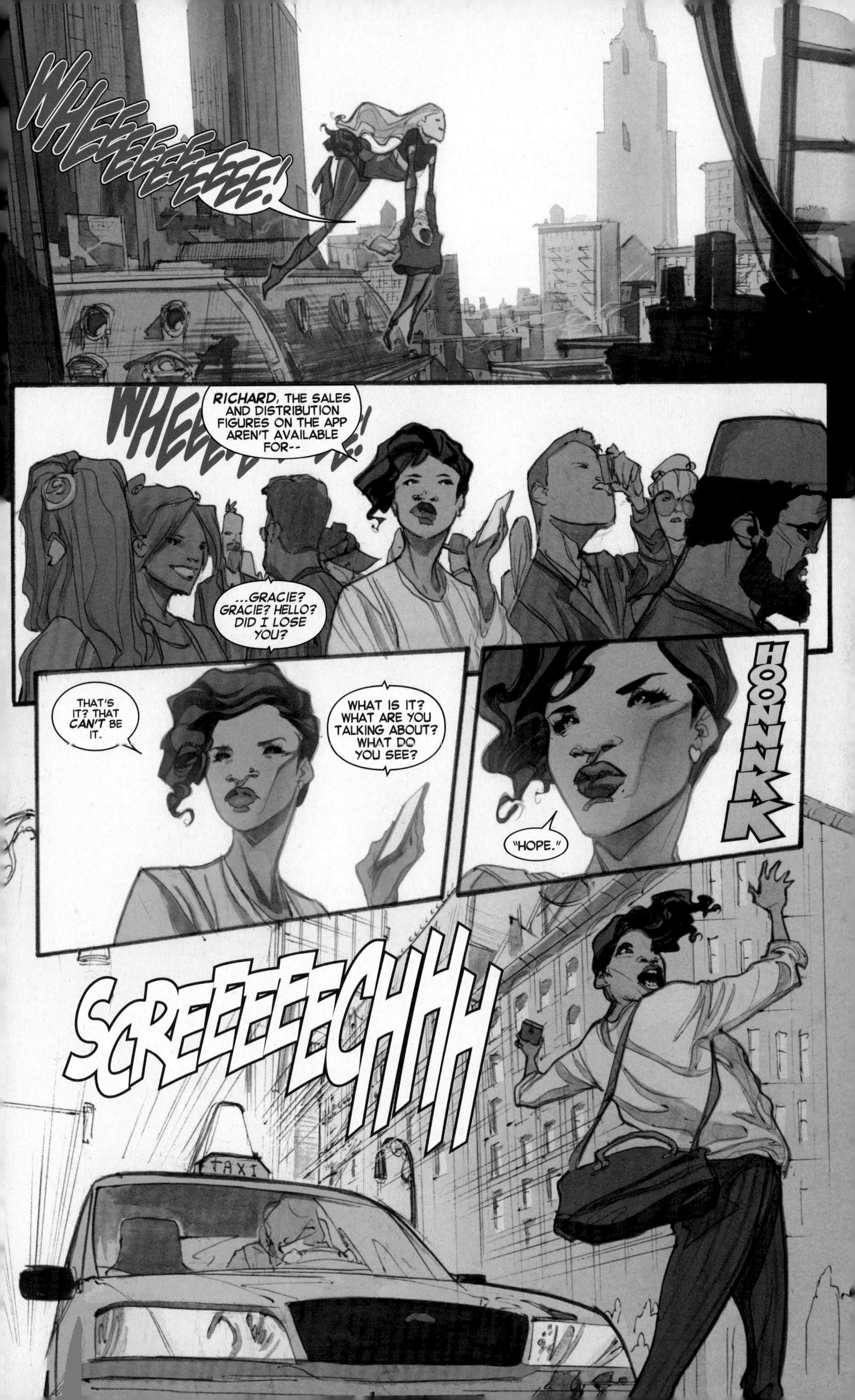
WHEEEEEEEEEEEE!
WHEEEEEEEE!
RICHARD, THE SALES AND DISTRIBUTION FIGURES ON THE APP AREN'T AVAILABLE FOR--
...GRACIE? GRACIE? HELLO? DID I LOSE YOU?
THAT'S IT? THAT CAN'T BE IT.
WHAT IS IT? WHAT ARE YOU TALKING ABOUT? WHAT DO YOU SEE?
HOONNNKK
"HOPE."
SCREEEEEECHHHH
TAXI

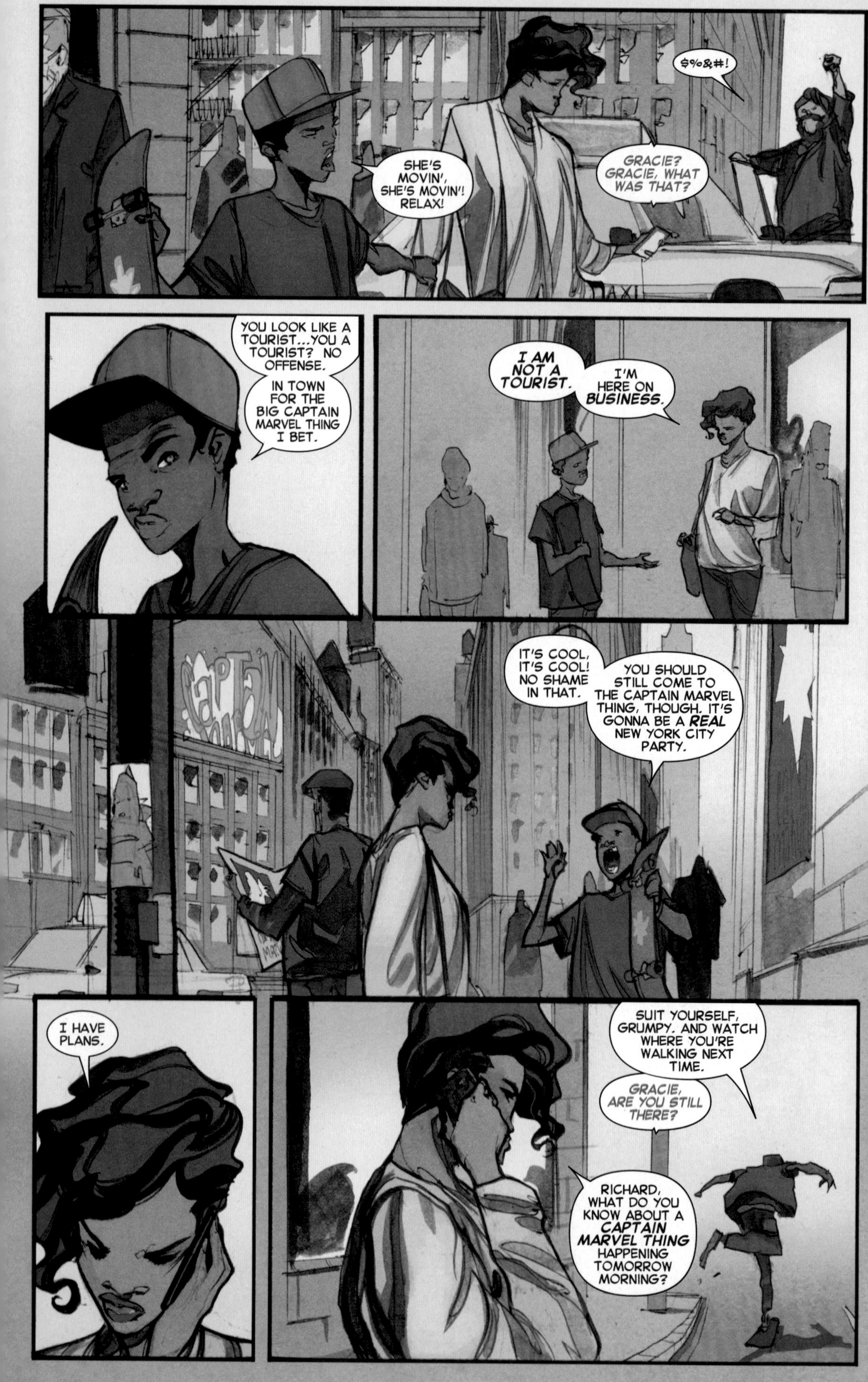
$%&#!
SHE'S MOVIN', SHE'S MOVIN'! RELAX!
GRACIE? GRACIE, WHAT WAS THAT?
YOU LOOK LIKE A TOURIST...YOU A TOURIST? NO OFFENSE.
IN TOWN FOR THE BIG CAPTAIN MARVEL THING I BET.
I AM NOT A TOURIST.
I'M HERE ON BUSINESS.
IT'S COOL, IT'S COOL! NO SHAME IN THAT.
YOU SHOULD STILL COME TO THE CAPTAIN MARVEL THING, THOUGH. IT'S GONNA BE A REAL NEW YORK CITY PARTY.
I HAVE PLANS.
SUIT YOURSELF, GRUMPY. AND WATCH WHERE YOU'RE WALKING NEXT TIME.
GRACIE, ARE YOU STILL THERE?
RICHARD, WHAT DO YOU KNOW ABOUT A CAPTAIN MARVEL THING HAPPENING TOMORROW MORNING?

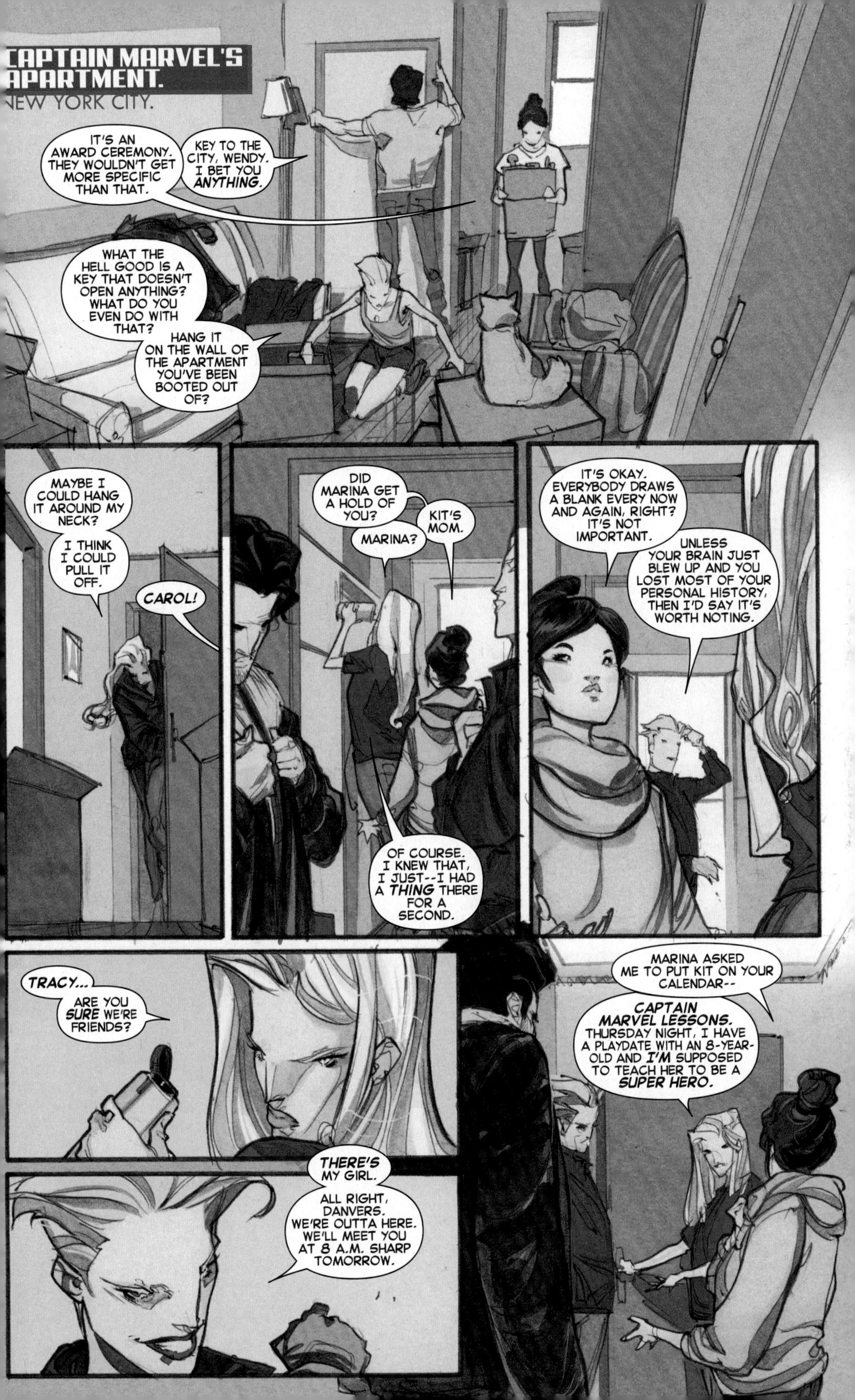
CAPTAIN MARVEL'S APARTMENT.
NEW YORK CITY.
IT'S AN AWARD CEREMONY. THEY WOULDN'T GET MORE SPECIFIC THAN THAT.
KEY TO THE CITY, WENDY. I BET YOU ANYTHING.
WHAT THE HELL GOOD IS A KEY THAT DOESN'T OPEN ANYTHING? WHAT DO YOU EVEN DO WITH THAT?
HANG IT ON THE WALL OF THE APARTMENT YOU'VE BEEN BOOTED OUT OF?
MAYBE I COULD HANG IT AROUND MY NECK?
I THINK I COULD PULL IT OFF.
CAROL!
DID MARINA GET A HOLD OF YOU?
MARINA?
KIT'S MOM.
OF COURSE. I KNEW THAT, I JUST--I HAD A THING THERE FOR A SECOND.
IT'S OKAY. EVERYBODY DRAWS A BLANK EVERY NOW AND AGAIN, RIGHT? IT'S NOT IMPORTANT.
UNLESS YOUR BRAIN JUST BLEW UP AND YOU LOST MOST OF YOUR PERSONAL HISTORY, THEN I'D SAY IT'S WORTH NOTING.
TRACY...
ARE YOU SURE WE'RE FRIENDS?
MARINA ASKED ME TO PUT KIT ON YOUR CALENDAR--
CAPTAIN MARVEL LESSONS. THURSDAY NIGHT, I HAVE A PLAYDATE WITH AN 8-YEAR-OLD AND I'M SUPPOSED TO TEACH HER TO BE A SUPER HERO.
THERE'S MY GIRL.
ALL RIGHT, DANVERS. WE'RE OUTTA HERE. WE'LL MEET YOU AT 8 A.M. SHARP TOMORROW.

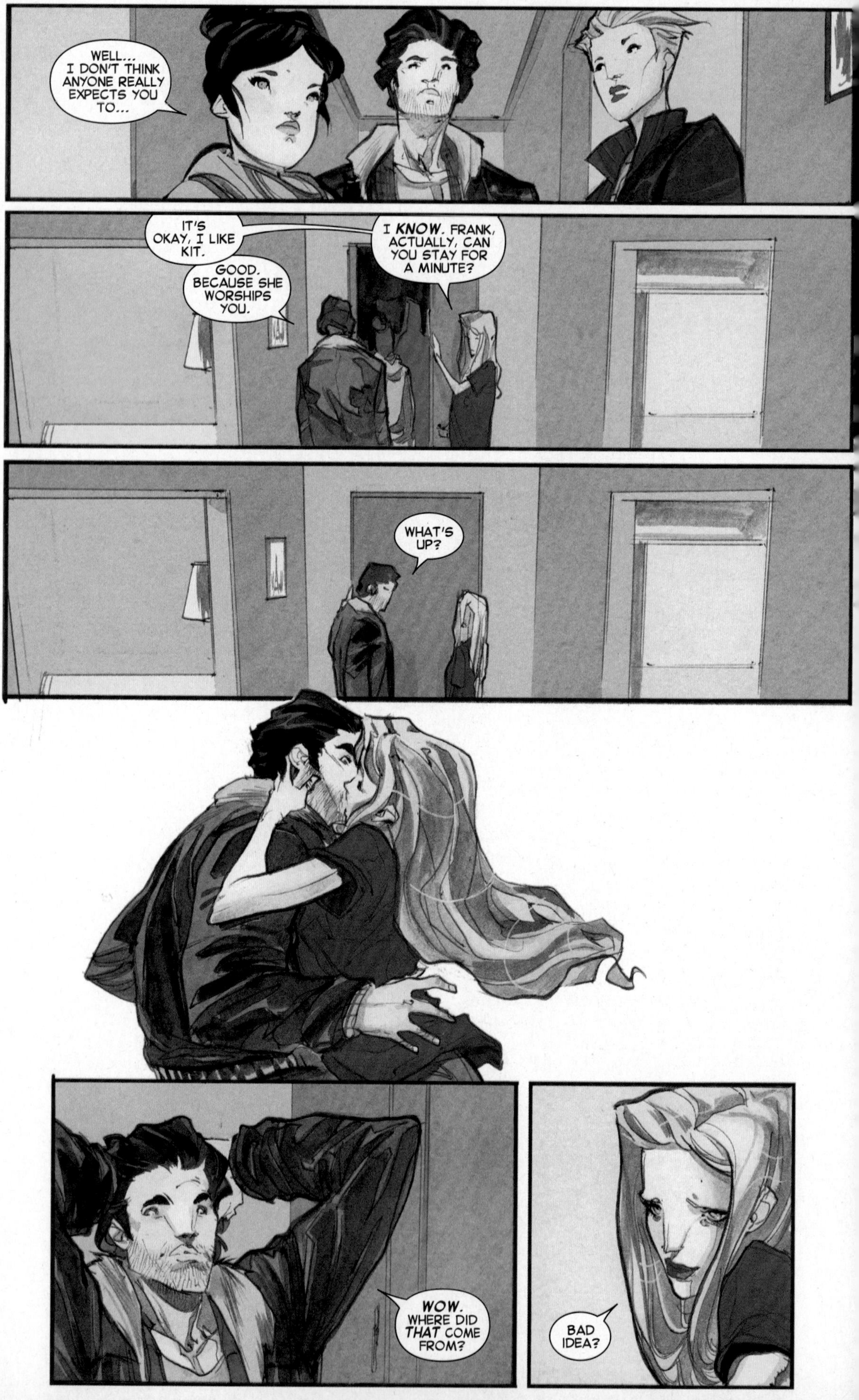
WELL... I DON'T THINK ANYONE REALLY EXPECTS YOU TO...
IT'S OKAY, I LIKE KIT.
I KNOW. FRANK, ACTUALLY, CAN YOU STAY FOR A MINUTE?
GOOD. BECAUSE SHE WORSHIPS YOU.
WHAT'S UP?
WOW. WHERE DID THAT COME FROM?
BAD IDEA?

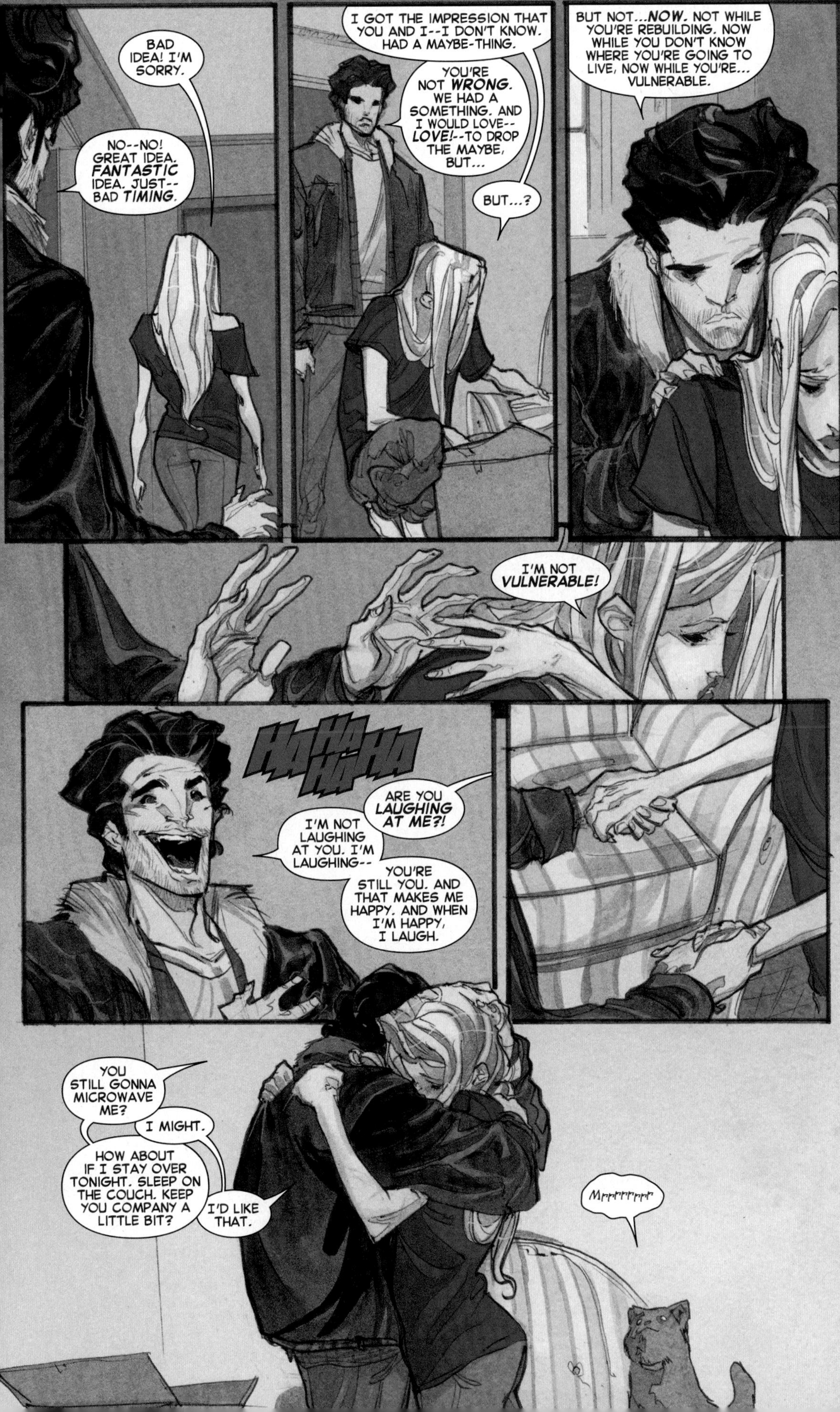
BAD IDEA! I'M SORRY.
NO--NO! GREAT IDEA. FANTASTIC IDEA. JUST--BAD TIMING.
I GOT THE IMPRESSION THAT YOU AND I--I DON'T KNOW. HAD A MAYBE-THING.
YOU'RE NOT WRONG. WE HAD A SOMETHING. AND I WOULD LOVE--LOVE!--TO DROP THE MAYBE, BUT...
BUT...?
BUT NOT...NOW. NOT WHILE YOU'RE REBUILDING. NOW WHILE YOU DON'T KNOW WHERE YOU'RE GOING TO LIVE, NOW WHILE YOU'RE... VULNERABLE.
I'M NOT VULNERABLE!
HA HA HA HA
ARE YOU LAUGHING AT ME?!
I'M NOT LAUGHING AT YOU. I'M LAUGHING--
YOU'RE STILL YOU. AND THAT MAKES ME HAPPY. AND WHEN I'M HAPPY, I LAUGH.
YOU STILL GONNA MICROWAVE ME?
I MIGHT.
HOW ABOUT IF I STAY OVER TONIGHT. SLEEP ON THE COUCH. KEEP YOU COMPANY A LITTLE BIT?
I'D LIKE THAT.
Mrrrrrrrr

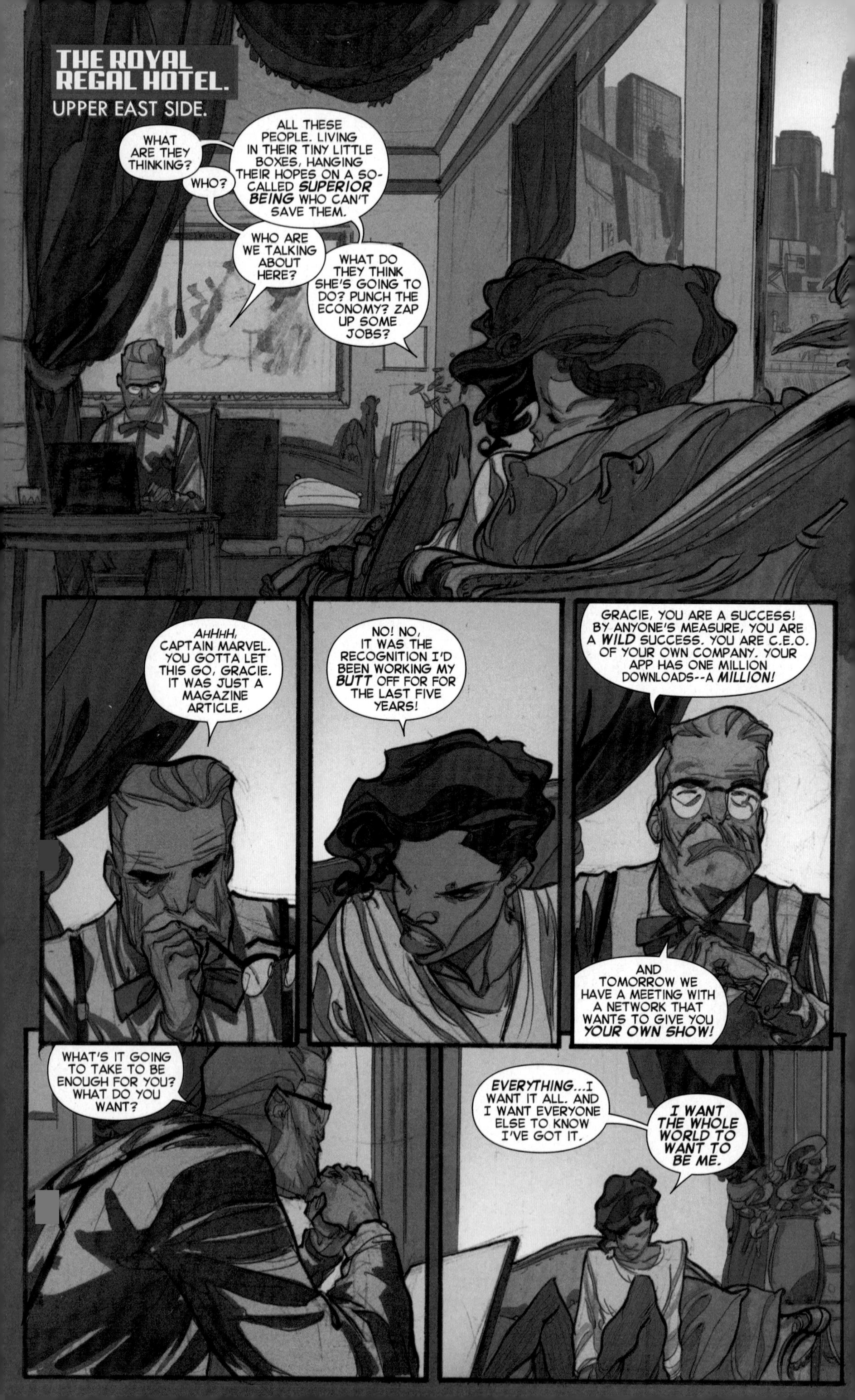
THE ROYAL REGAL HOTEL.
UPPER EAST SIDE.
WHAT ARE THEY THINKING?
ALL THESE PEOPLE. LIVING IN THEIR TINY LITTLE BOXES, HANGING THEIR HOPES ON A SO-CALLED SUPERIOR BEING WHO CAN'T SAVE THEM.
WHO?
WHO ARE WE TALKING ABOUT HERE?
WHAT DO THEY THINK SHE'S GOING TO DO? PUNCH THE ECONOMY? ZAP UP SOME JOBS?
AHHHH, CAPTAIN MARVEL. YOU GOTTA LET THIS GO, GRACIE. IT WAS JUST A MAGAZINE ARTICLE.
NO! NO, IT WAS THE RECOGNITION I'D BEEN WORKING MY BUTT OFF FOR FOR THE LAST FIVE YEARS!
GRACIE, YOU ARE A SUCCESS! BY ANYONE'S MEASURE, YOU ARE A WILD SUCCESS. YOU ARE C.E.O. OF YOUR OWN COMPANY. YOUR APP HAS ONE MILLION DOWNLOADS--A MILLION!
AND TOMORROW WE HAVE A MEETING WITH A NETWORK THAT WANTS TO GIVE YOU YOUR OWN SHOW!
WHAT'S IT GOING TO TAKE TO BE ENOUGH FOR YOU? WHAT DO YOU WANT?
EVERYTHING...I WANT IT ALL. AND I WANT EVERYONE ELSE TO KNOW I'VE GOT IT.
I WANT THE WHOLE WORLD TO WANT TO BE ME.

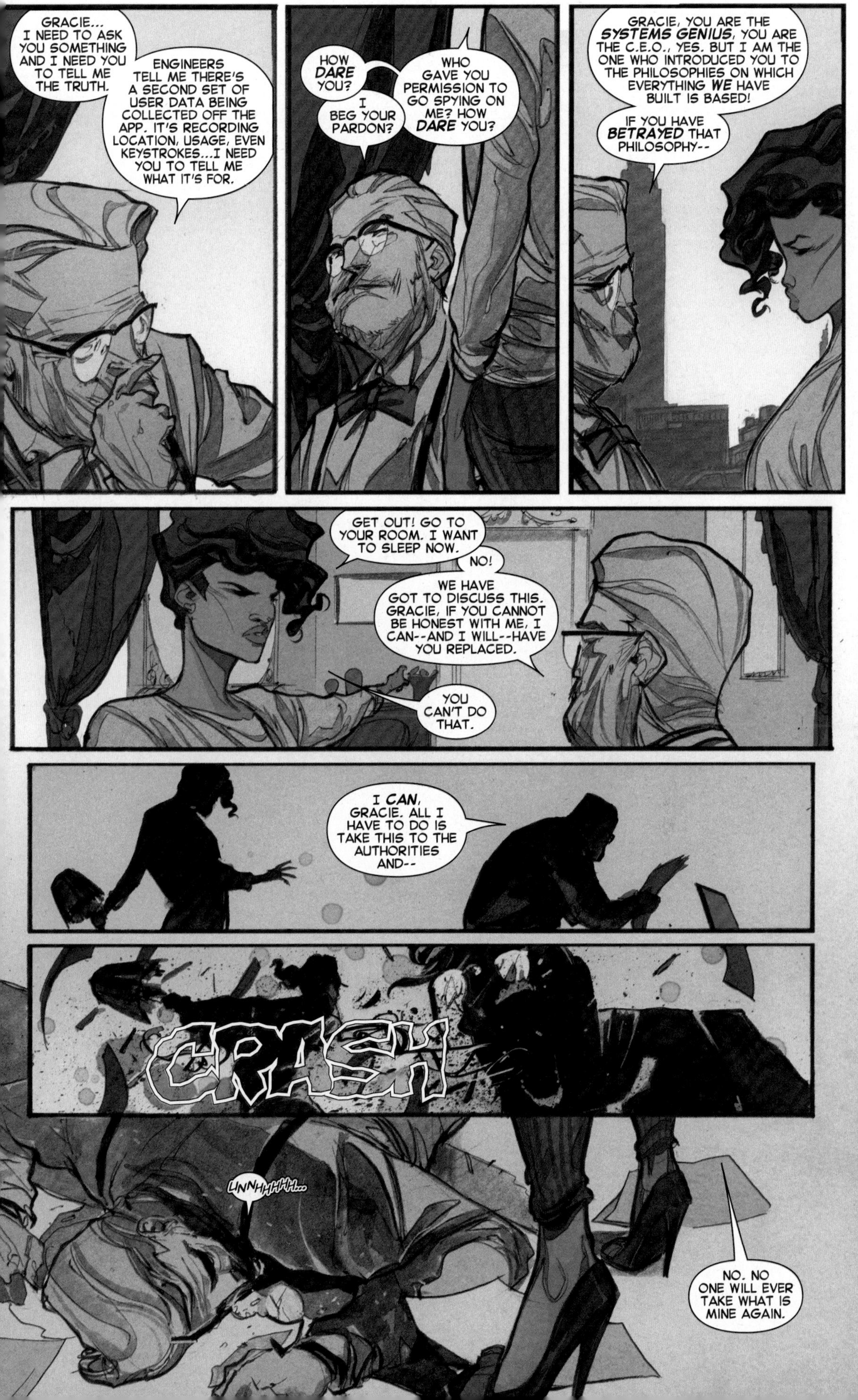
GRACIE... I NEED TO ASK YOU SOMETHING AND I NEED YOU TO TELL ME THE TRUTH.
ENGINEERS TELL ME THERE'S A SECOND SET OF USER DATA BEING COLLECTED OFF THE APP. IT'S RECORDING LOCATION, USAGE, EVEN KEYSTROKES...I NEED YOU TO TELL ME WHAT IT'S FOR.
HOW DARE YOU?
I BEG YOUR PARDON?
WHO GAVE YOU PERMISSION TO GO SPYING ON ME? HOW DARE YOU?
GRACIE, YOU ARE THE SYSTEMS GENIUS, YOU ARE THE C.E.O., YES. BUT I AM THE ONE WHO INTRODUCED YOU TO THE PHILOSOPHIES ON WHICH EVERYTHING WE HAVE BUILT IS BASED!
IF YOU HAVE BETRAYED THAT PHILOSOPHY--
GET OUT! GO TO YOUR ROOM. I WANT TO SLEEP NOW.
NO!
WE HAVE GOT TO DISCUSS THIS. GRACIE, IF YOU CANNOT BE HONEST WITH ME, I CAN--AND I WILL--HAVE YOU REPLACED.
YOU CAN'T DO THAT.
I CAN, GRACIE. ALL I HAVE TO DO IS TAKE THIS TO THE AUTHORITIES AND--
CRASH
UNNHHHHH...
NO. NO ONE WILL EVER TAKE WHAT IS MINE AGAIN.

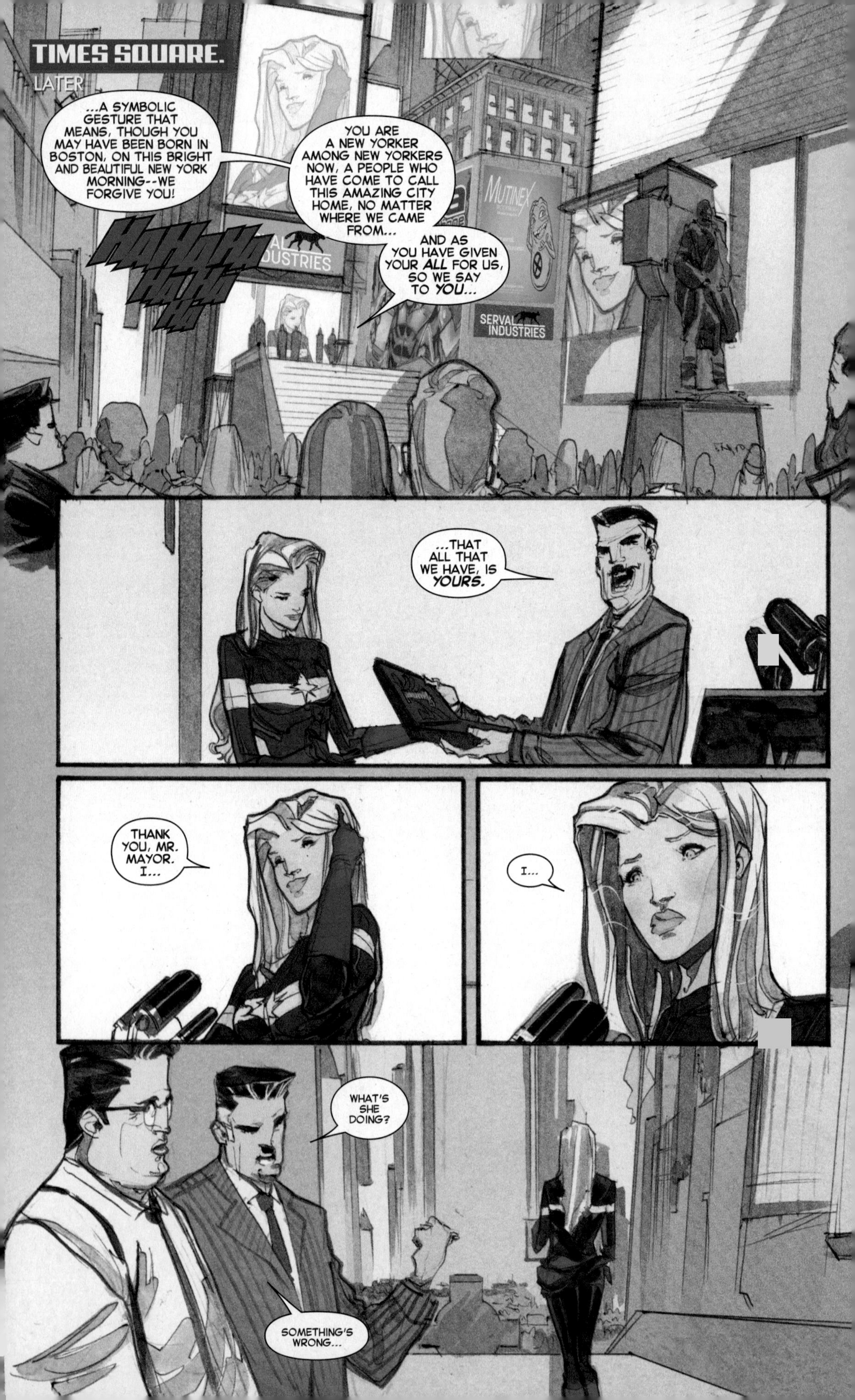
TIMES SQUARE.
LATER
...A SYMBOLIC GESTURE THAT MEANS, THOUGH YOU MAY HAVE BEEN BORN IN BOSTON, ON THIS BRIGHT AND BEAUTIFUL NEW YORK MORNING--WE FORGIVE YOU!
HAHAHA HAHA HA
YOU ARE A NEW YORKER AMONG NEW YORKERS NOW, A PEOPLE WHO HAVE COME TO CALL THIS AMAZING CITY HOME, NO MATTER WHERE WE CAME FROM...
AND AS YOU HAVE GIVEN YOUR ALL FOR US, SO WE SAY TO YOU...
SERVAL INDUSTRIES
MUTINEX
...THAT ALL THAT WE HAVE, IS YOURS.
THANK YOU, MR. MAYOR. I...
I...
WHAT'S SHE DOING?
SOMETHING'S WRONG...

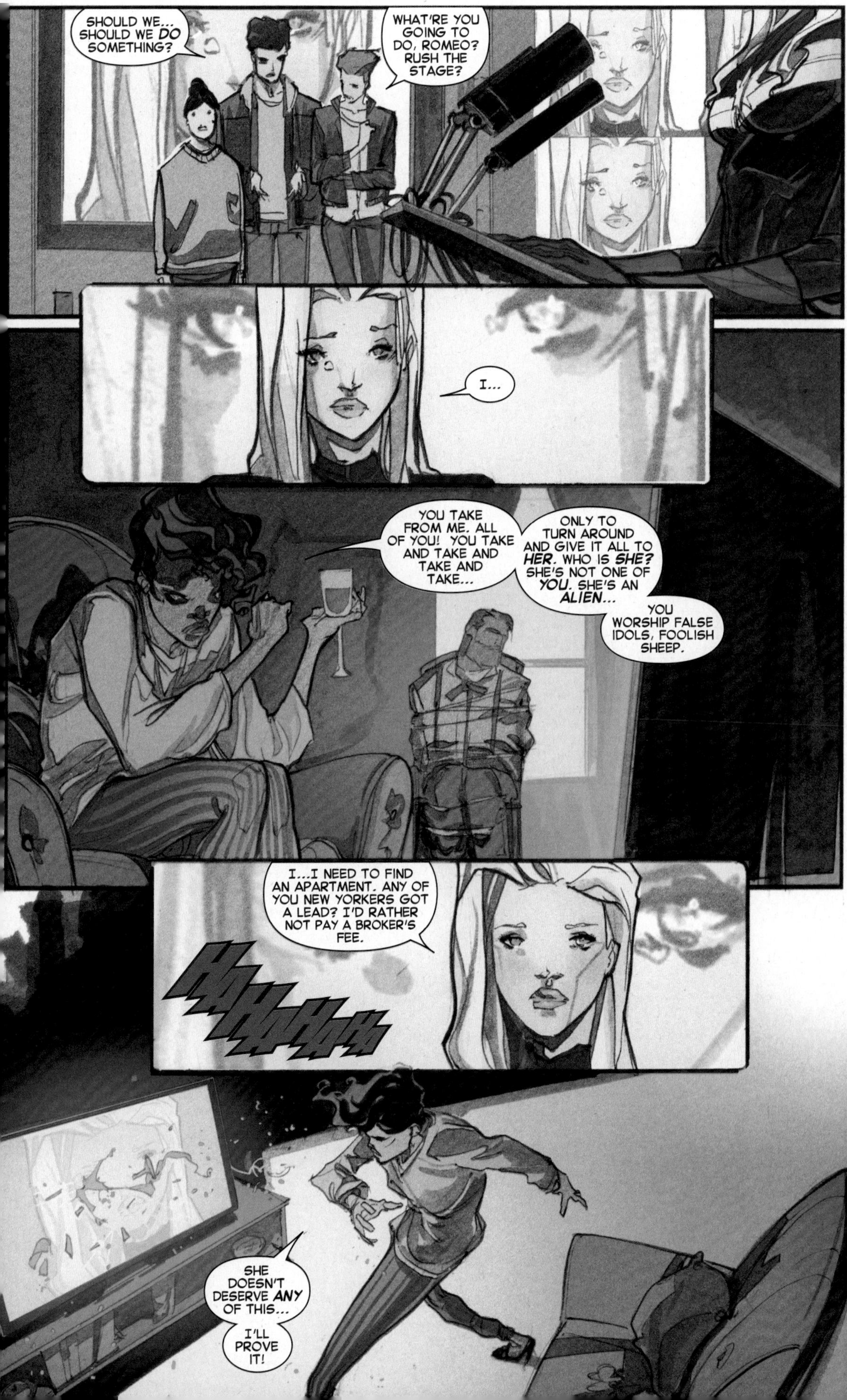
SHOULD WE... SHOULD WE DO SOMETHING?
WHAT'RE YOU GOING TO DO, ROMEO? RUSH THE STAGE?
I...
YOU TAKE FROM ME. ALL OF YOU! YOU TAKE AND TAKE AND TAKE AND TAKE...
ONLY TO TURN AROUND AND GIVE IT ALL TO HER. WHO IS SHE? SHE'S NOT ONE OF YOU. SHE'S AN ALIEN...
YOU WORSHIP FALSE IDOLS, FOOLISH SHEEP.
I...I NEED TO FIND AN APARTMENT. ANY OF YOU NEW YORKERS GOT A LEAD? I'D RATHER NOT PAY A BROKER'S FEE.
HAHAHAHAHA
SHE DOESN'T DESERVE ANY OF THIS...
I'LL PROVE IT!

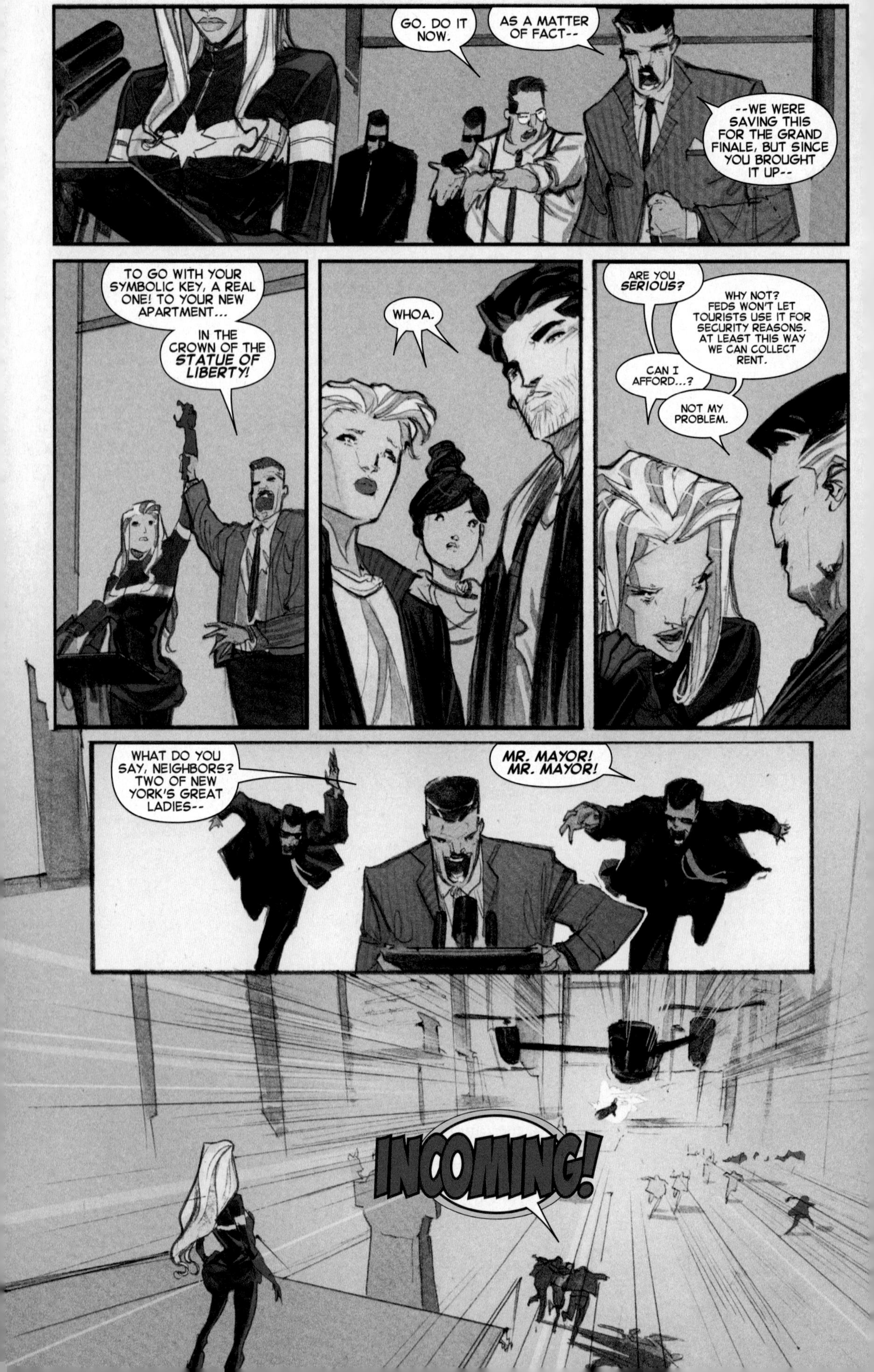
GO. DO IT NOW.
AS A MATTER OF FACT--
--WE WERE SAVING THIS FOR THE GRAND FINALE, BUT SINCE YOU BROUGHT IT UP--
TO GO WITH YOUR SYMBOLIC KEY, A REAL ONE! TO YOUR NEW APARTMENT...
IN THE CROWN OF THE STATUE OF LIBERTY!
WHOA.
ARE YOU SERIOUS?
WHY NOT? FEDS WON'T LET TOURISTS USE IT FOR SECURITY REASONS. AT LEAST THIS WAY WE CAN COLLECT RENT.
CAN I AFFORD...?
NOT MY PROBLEM.
WHAT DO YOU SAY, NEIGHBORS? TWO OF NEW YORK'S GREAT LADIES--
MR. MAYOR! MR. MAYOR!
INCOMING!

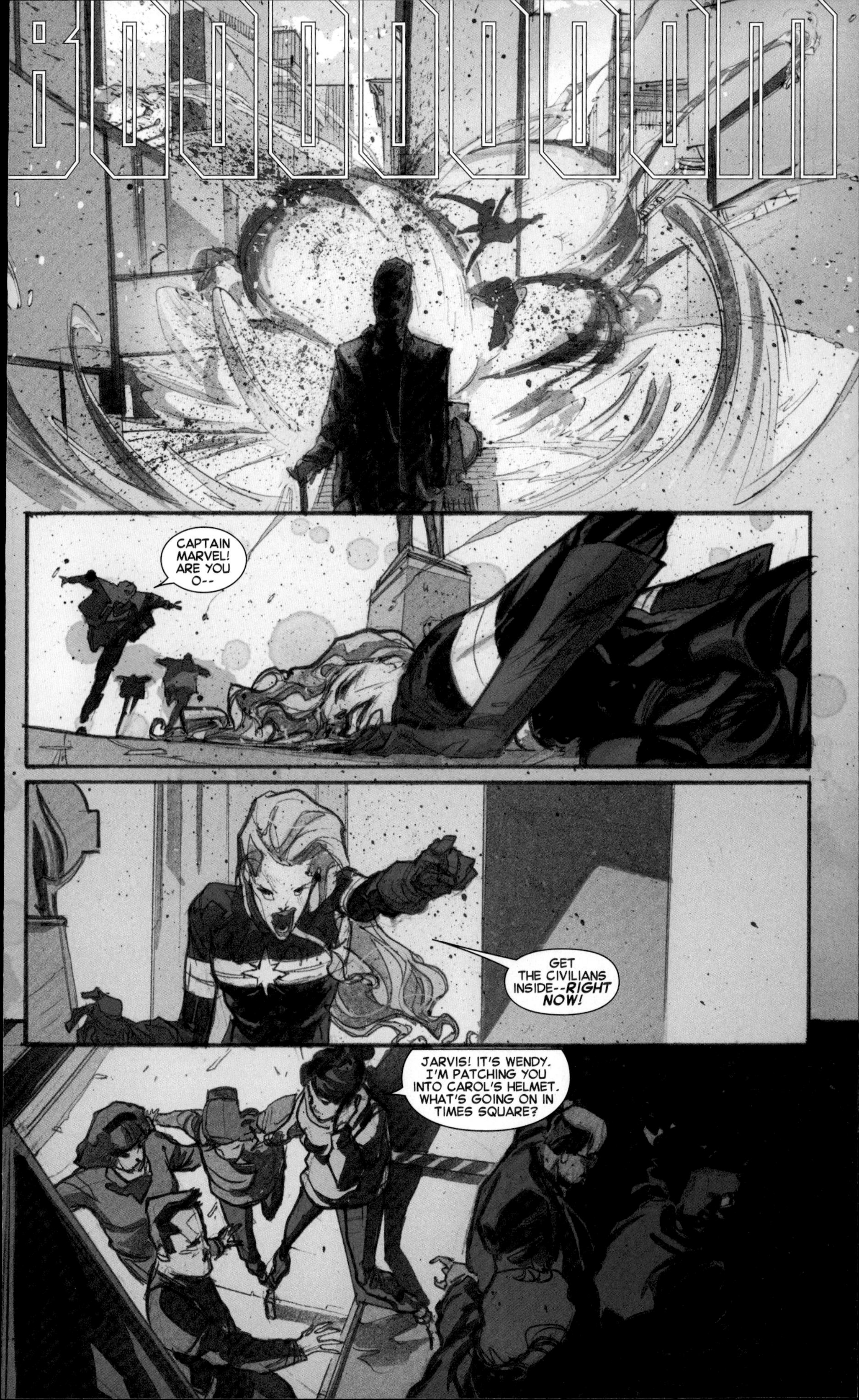
BOOOOOOOM
CAPTAIN MARVEL! ARE YOU O--
GET THE CIVILIANS INSIDE--RIGHT NOW!
JARVIS! IT'S WENDY. I'M PATCHING YOU INTO CAROL'S HELMET. WHAT'S GOING ON IN TIMES SQUARE?

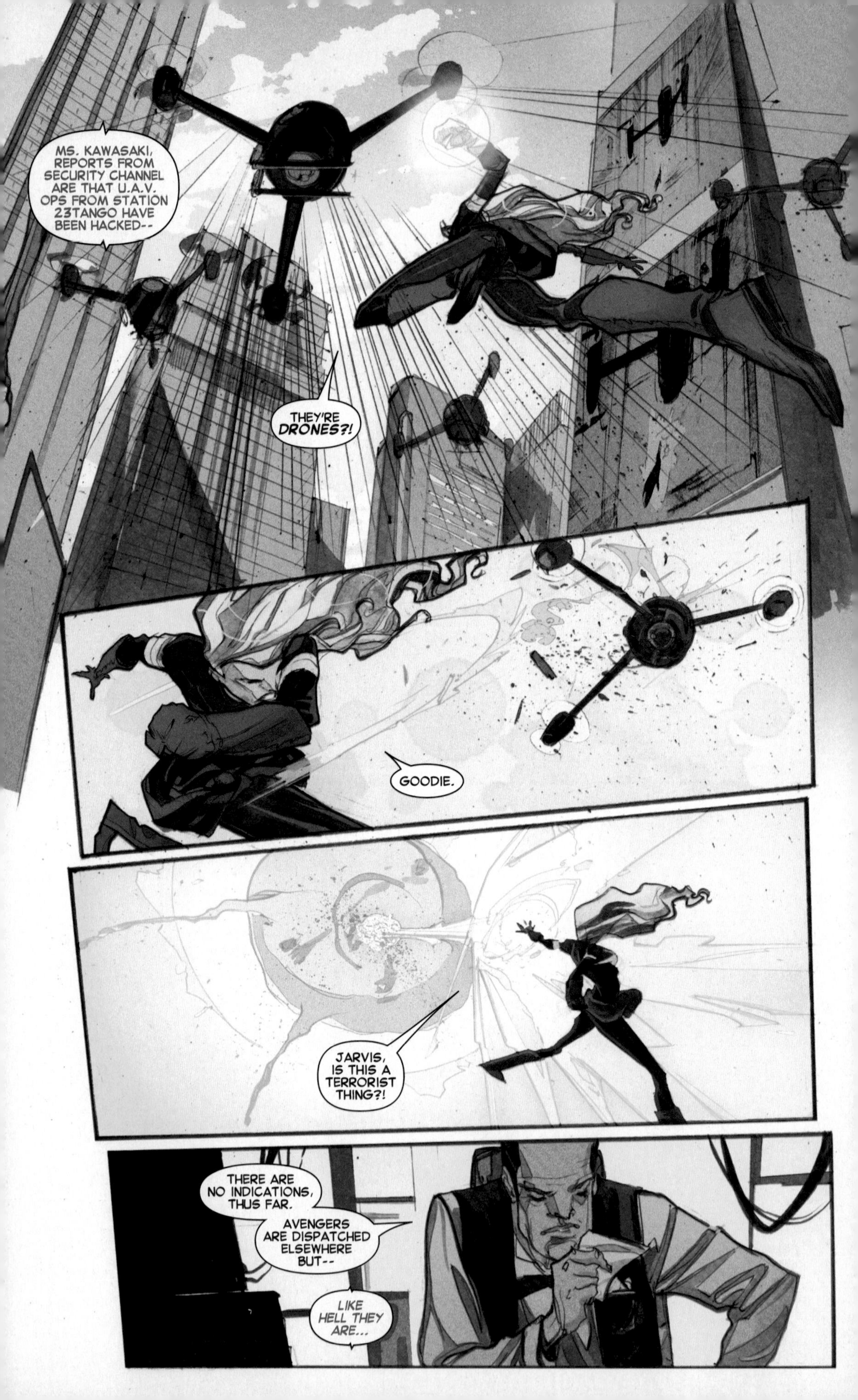

MS. KAWASAKI, REPORTS FROM SECURITY CHANNEL ARE THAT U.A.V. OPS FROM STATION 23TANGO HAVE BEEN HACKED--
THEY'RE *DRONES?!*
GOODIE.
JARVIS, IS THIS A TERRORIST THING?!
THERE ARE NO INDICATIONS, THUS FAR.
AVENGERS ARE DISPATCHED ELSEWHERE BUT--
LIKE HELL THEY ARE...

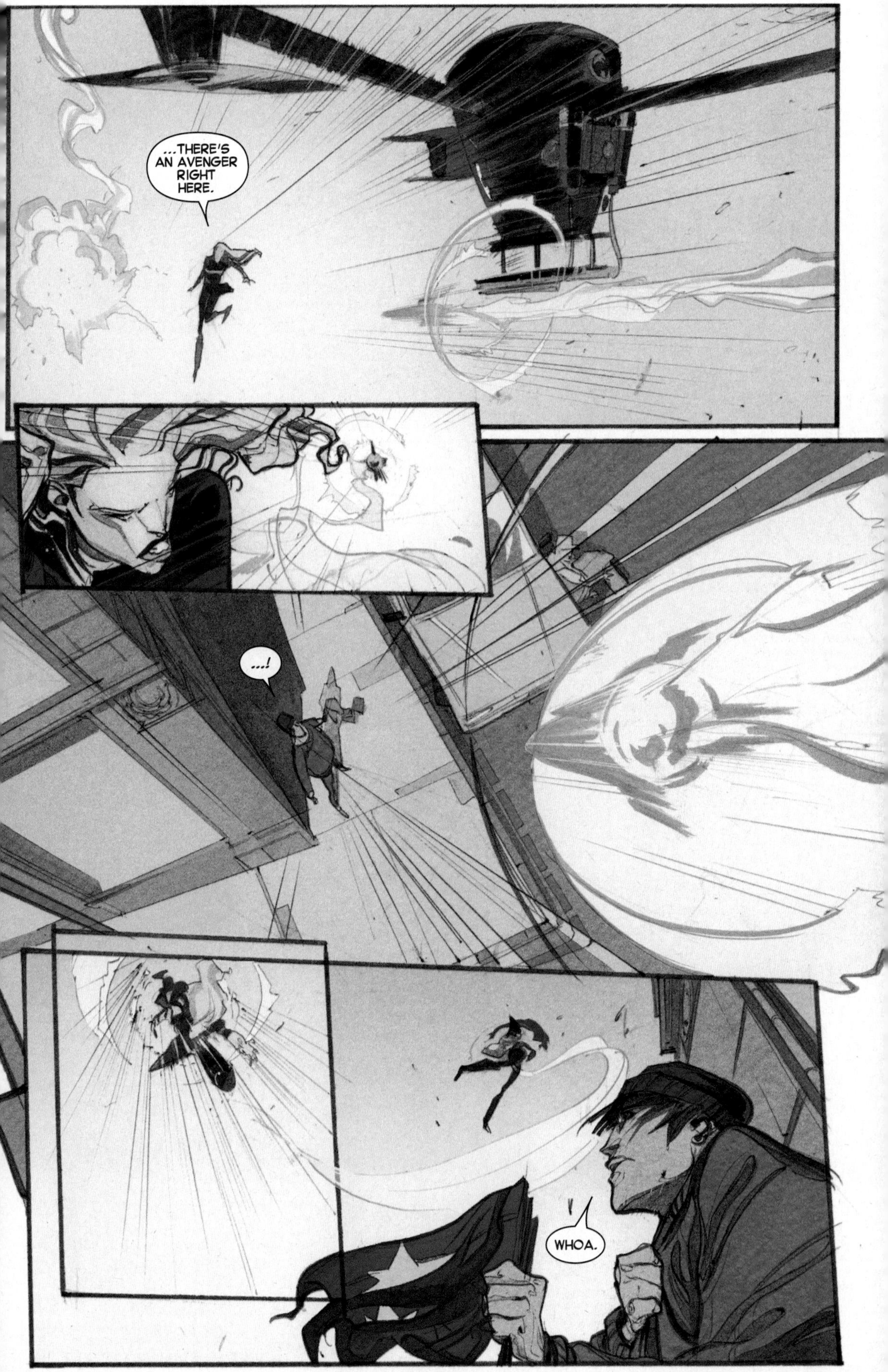
...THERE'S AN AVENGER RIGHT HERE.
...!
WHOA.

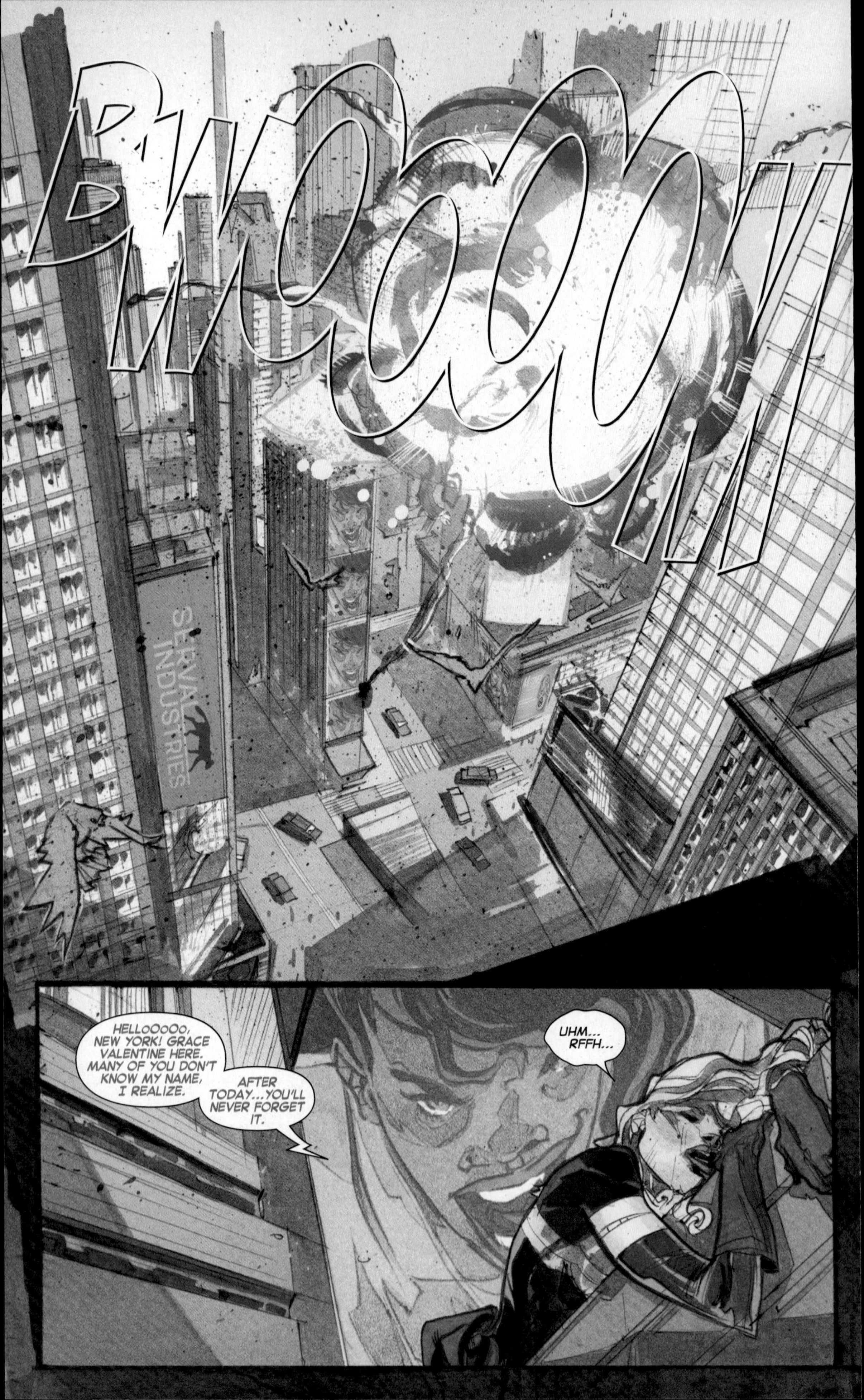
BWOOOM!!
SERVAL INDUSTRIES
HELLOOOOO, NEW YORK! GRACE VALENTINE HERE. MANY OF YOU DON'T KNOW MY NAME, I REALIZE.
AFTER TODAY...YOU'LL NEVER FORGET IT.
UHM... RFFH...

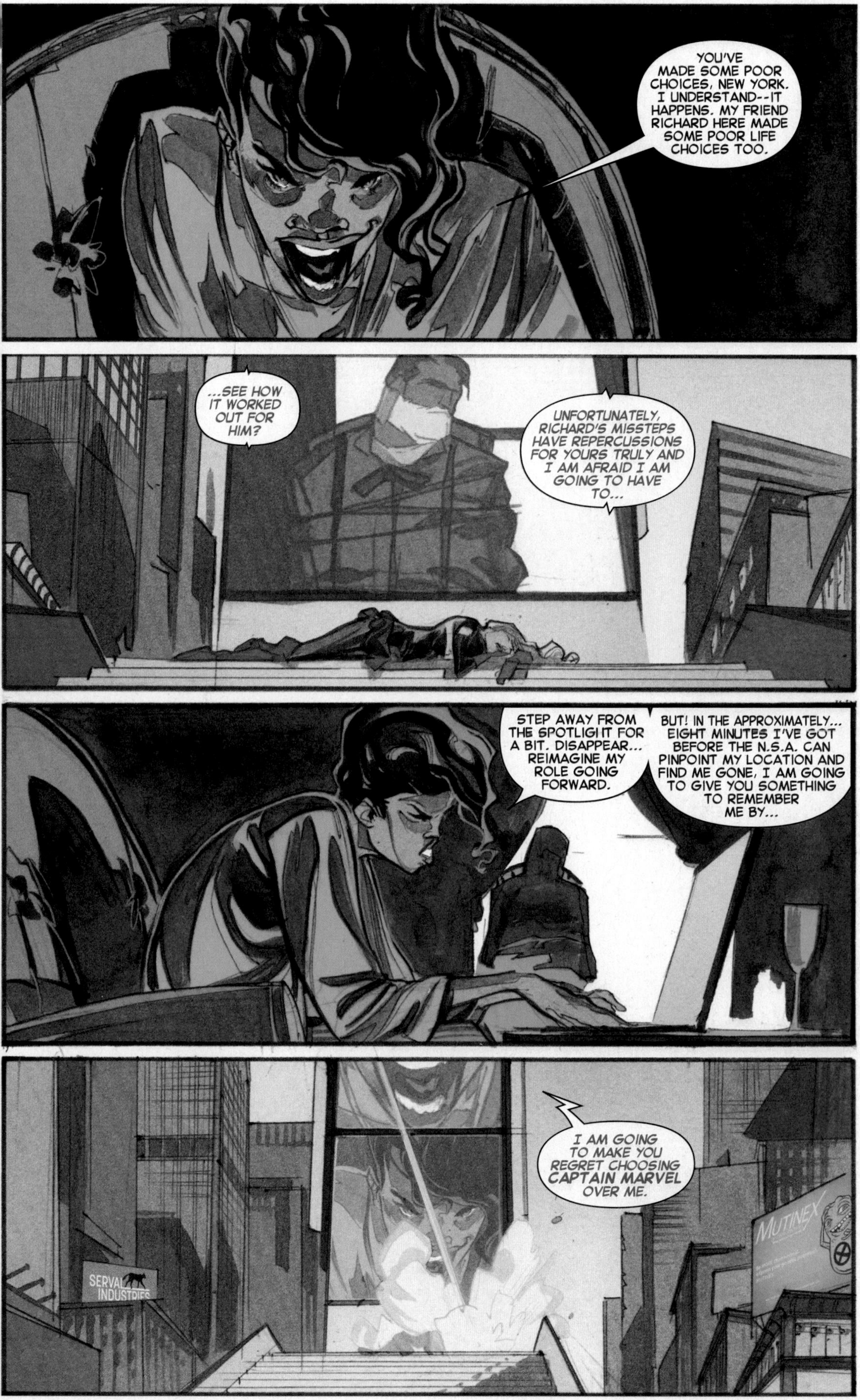
YOU'VE MADE SOME POOR CHOICES, NEW YORK. I UNDERSTAND--IT HAPPENS. MY FRIEND RICHARD HERE MADE SOME POOR LIFE CHOICES TOO.
...SEE HOW IT WORKED OUT FOR HIM?
UNFORTUNATELY, RICHARD'S MISSTEPS HAVE REPERCUSSIONS FOR YOURS TRULY AND I AM AFRAID I AM GOING TO HAVE TO...
STEP AWAY FROM THE SPOTLIGHT FOR A BIT. DISAPPEAR... REIMAGINE MY ROLE GOING FORWARD.
BUT! IN THE APPROXIMATELY... EIGHT MINUTES I'VE GOT BEFORE THE N.S.A. CAN PINPOINT MY LOCATION AND FIND ME GONE, I AM GOING TO GIVE YOU SOMETHING TO REMEMBER ME BY...
I AM GOING TO MAKE YOU REGRET CHOOSING CAPTAIN MARVEL OVER ME.
SERVAL INDUSTRIES
MUTINEX

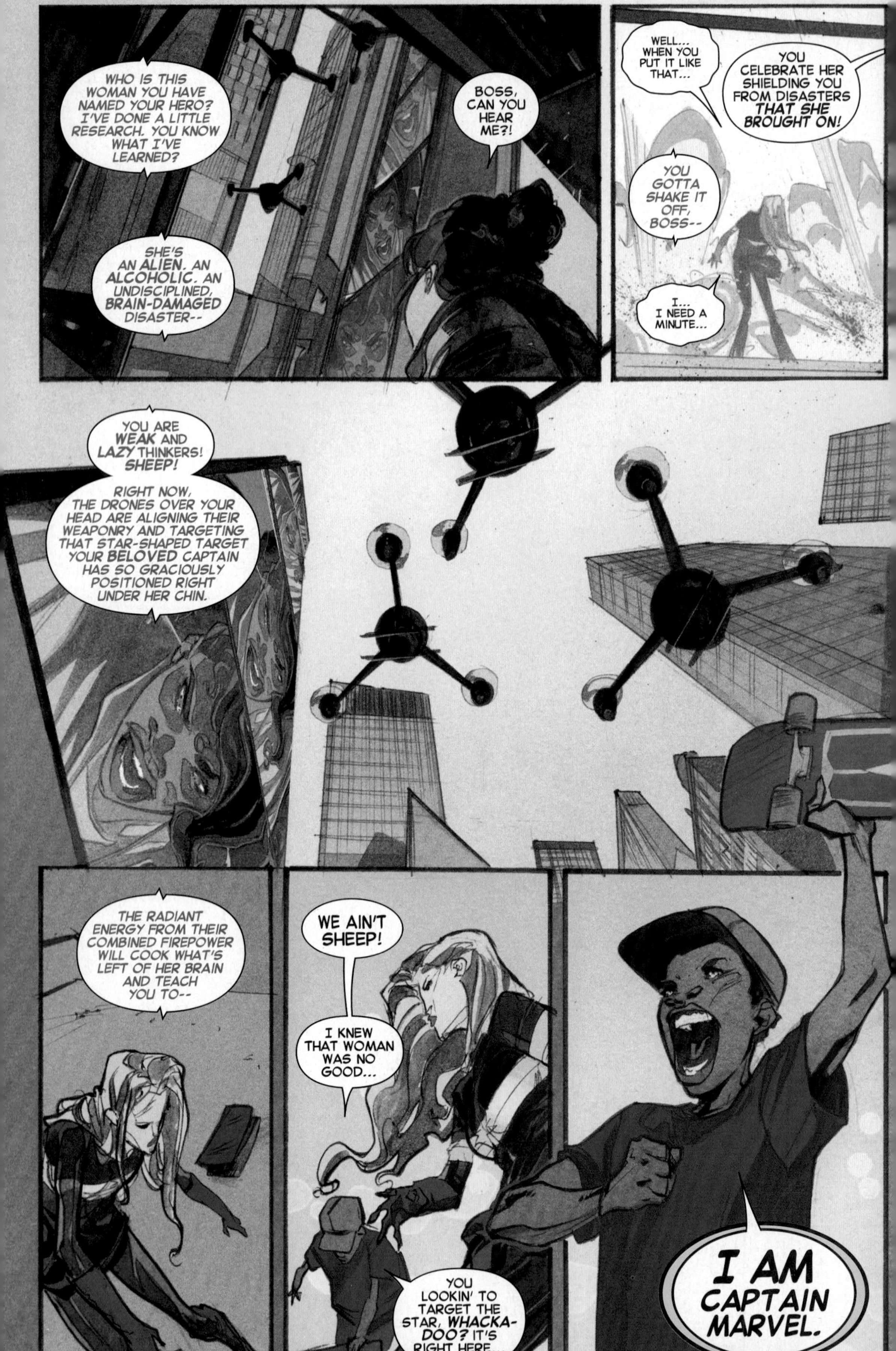
WHO IS THIS WOMAN YOU HAVE NAMED YOUR HERO? I'VE DONE A LITTLE RESEARCH. YOU KNOW WHAT I'VE LEARNED?
BOSS, CAN YOU HEAR ME?!
SHE'S AN ALIEN. AN ALCOHOLIC. AN UNDISCIPLINED, BRAIN-DAMAGED DISASTER--
WELL... WHEN YOU PUT IT LIKE THAT...
YOU CELEBRATE HER SHIELDING YOU FROM DISASTERS THAT SHE BROUGHT ON!
YOU GOTTA SHAKE IT OFF, BOSS--
I... I NEED A MINUTE...
YOU ARE WEAK AND LAZY THINKERS! SHEEP!
RIGHT NOW, THE DRONES OVER YOUR HEAD ARE ALIGNING THEIR WEAPONRY AND TARGETING THAT STAR-SHAPED TARGET YOUR BELOVED CAPTAIN HAS SO GRACIOUSLY POSITIONED RIGHT UNDER HER CHIN.
THE RADIANT ENERGY FROM THEIR COMBINED FIREPOWER WILL COOK WHAT'S LEFT OF HER BRAIN AND TEACH YOU TO--
WE AIN'T SHEEP!
I KNEW THAT WOMAN WAS NO GOOD...
YOU LOOKIN' TO TARGET THE STAR, WHACKA-DOO? IT'S RIGHT HERE...
I AM CAPTAIN MARVEL.

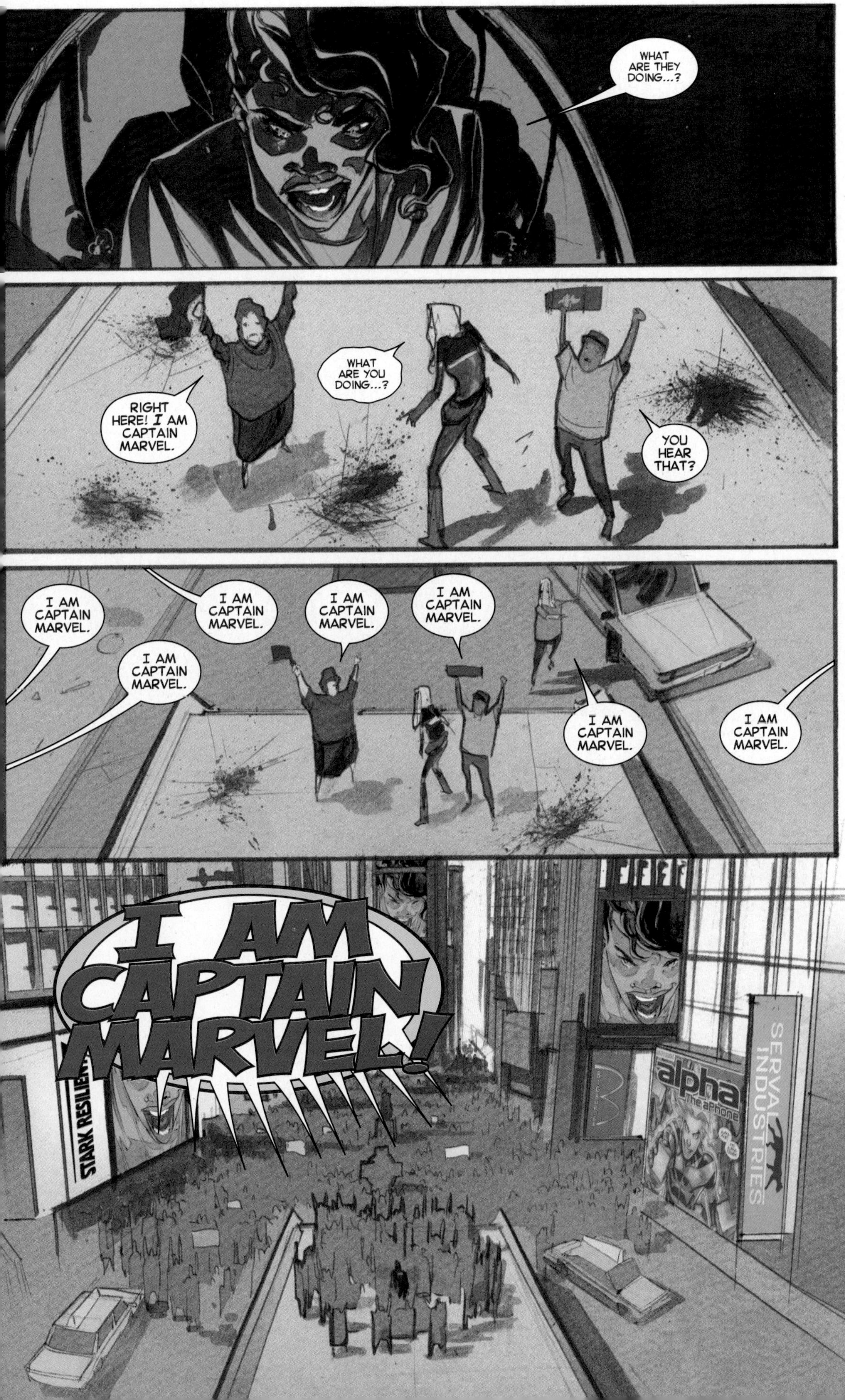
WHAT ARE THEY DOING...?
RIGHT HERE! I AM CAPTAIN MARVEL.
WHAT ARE YOU DOING...?
YOU HEAR THAT?
I AM CAPTAIN MARVEL.
I AM CAPTAIN MARVEL.
I AM CAPTAIN MARVEL.
I AM CAPTAIN MARVEL.
I AM CAPTAIN MARVEL.
I AM CAPTAIN MARVEL.
I AM CAPTAIN MARVEL.
I AM CAPTAIN MARVEL!
alpha
The aPhone
SERVAL INDUSTRIES

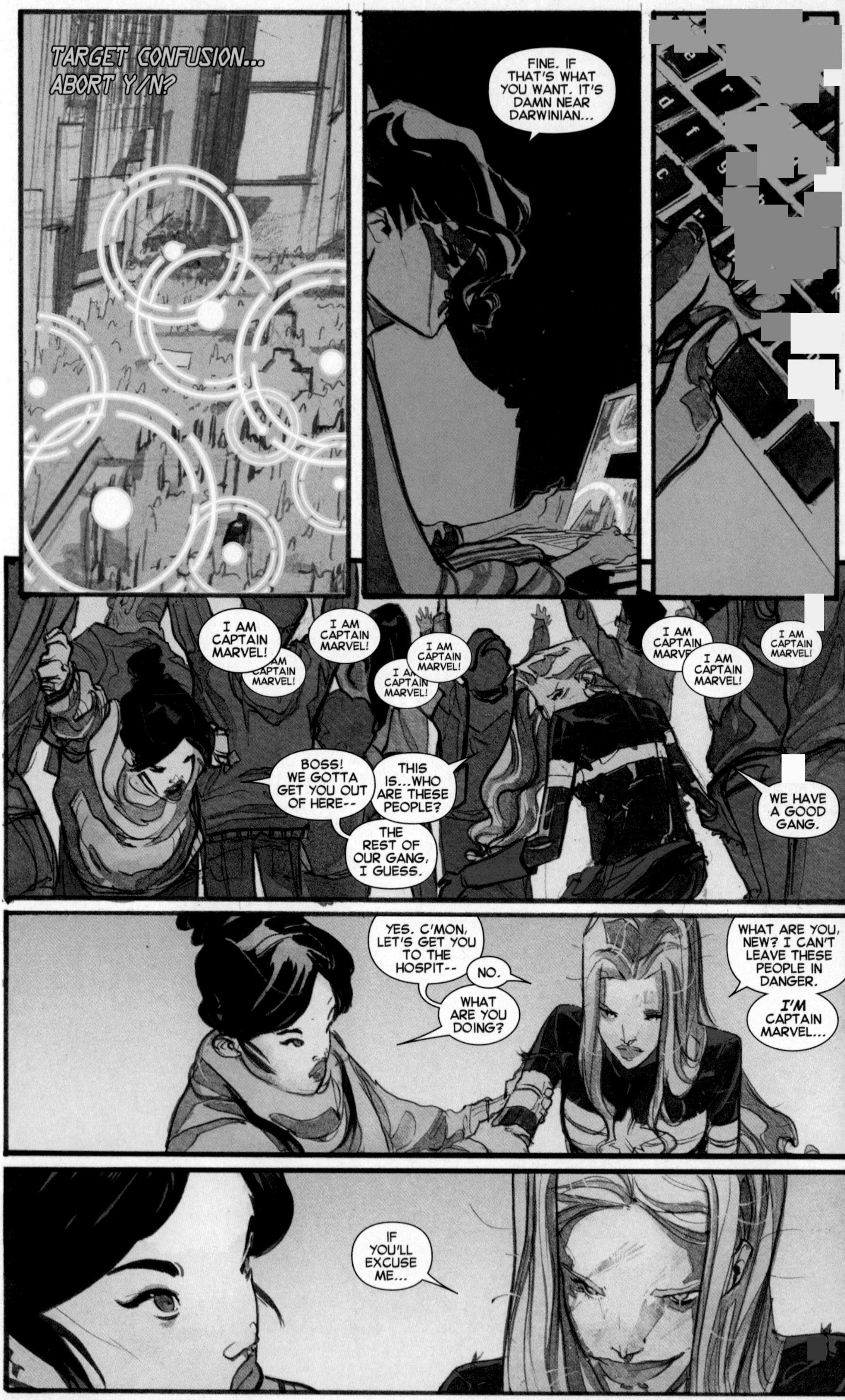

TARGET CONFUSION... ABORT Y/N?
FINE. IF THAT'S WHAT YOU WANT. IT'S DAMN NEAR DARWINIAN...
I AM CAPTAIN MARVEL!
I AM CAPTAIN MARVEL!
I AM CAPTAIN MARVEL!
I AM CAPTAIN MARVEL!
I AM CAPTAIN MARVEL!
BOSS! WE GOTTA GET YOU OUT OF HERE--
THIS IS...WHO ARE THESE PEOPLE?
THE REST OF OUR GANG, I GUESS.
WE HAVE A GOOD GANG.
YES. C'MON, LET'S GET YOU TO THE HOSPIT--
NO.
WHAT ARE YOU DOING?
WHAT ARE YOU, NEW? I CAN'T LEAVE THESE PEOPLE IN DANGER.
I'M CAPTAIN MARVEL...
IF YOU'LL EXCUSE ME...

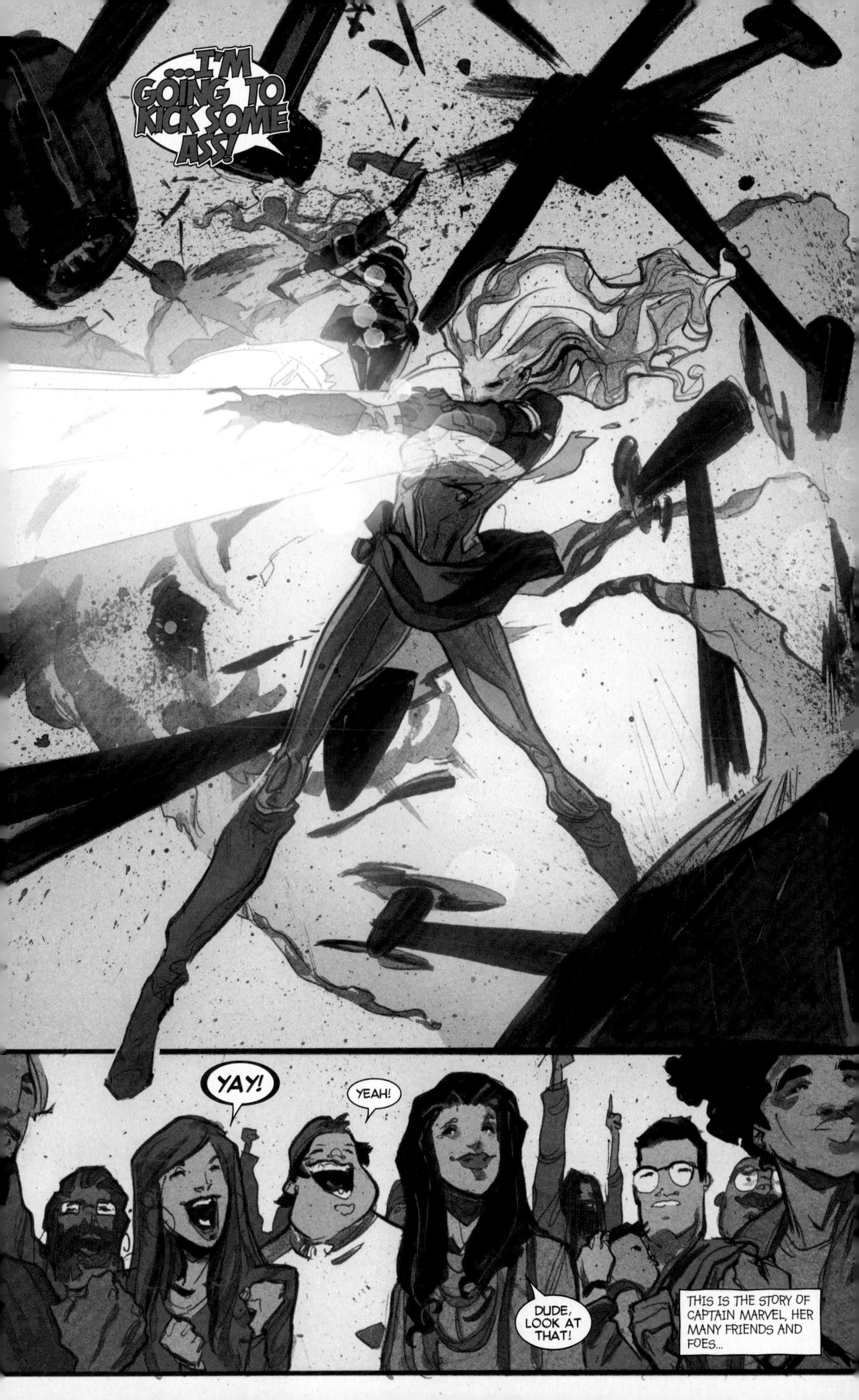
...I'M GOING TO KICK SOME ASS!
YAY!
YEAH!
DUDE, LOOK AT THAT!
THIS IS THE STORY OF CAPTAIN MARVEL, HER MANY FRIENDS AND FOES...

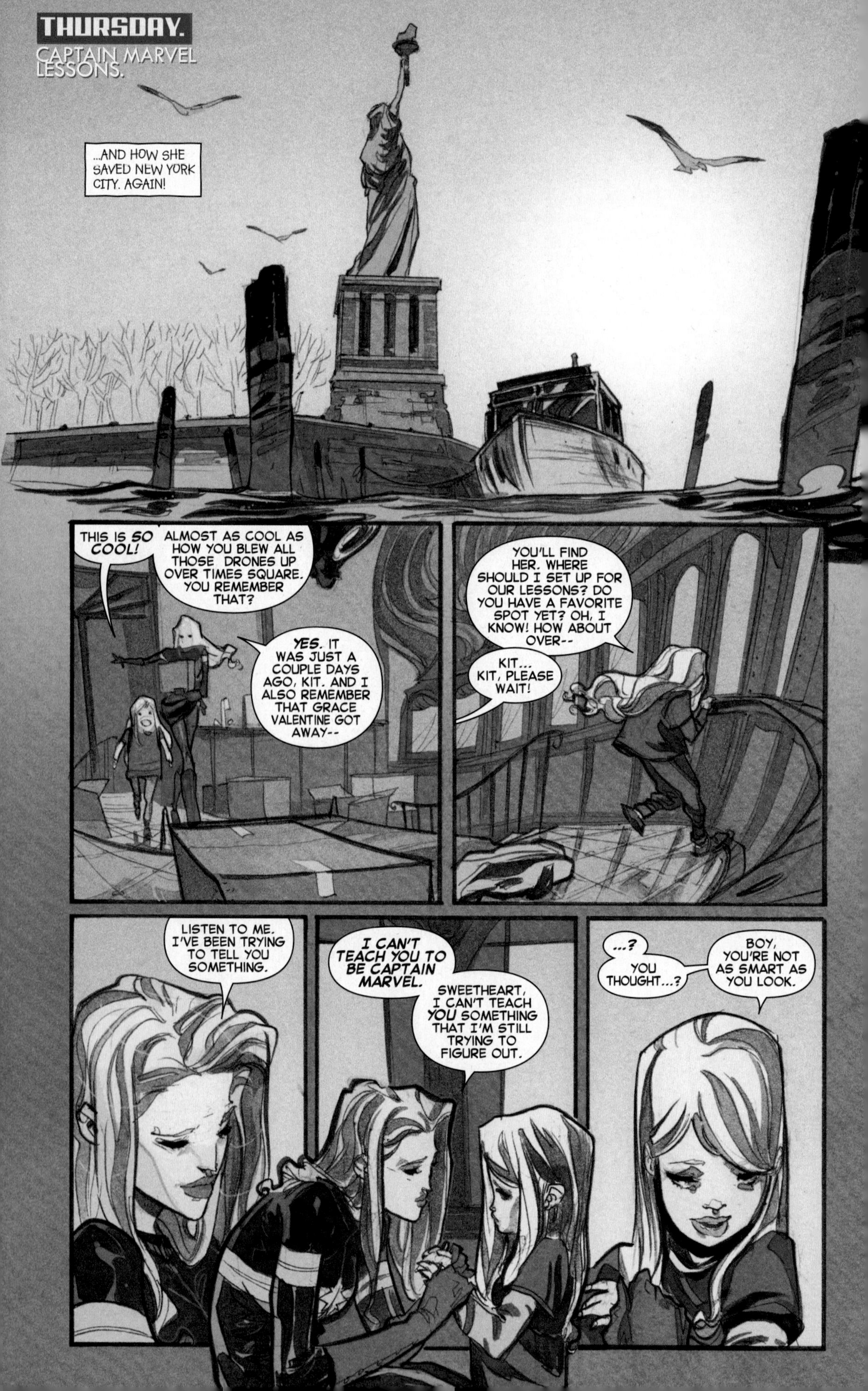
THURSDAY.
CAPTAIN MARVEL LESSONS.
...AND HOW SHE SAVED NEW YORK CITY. AGAIN!
THIS IS SO COOL!
ALMOST AS COOL AS HOW YOU BLEW ALL THOSE DRONES UP OVER TIMES SQUARE. YOU REMEMBER THAT?
YES. IT WAS JUST A COUPLE DAYS AGO, KIT. AND I ALSO REMEMBER THAT GRACE VALENTINE GOT AWAY--
YOU'LL FIND HER. WHERE SHOULD I SET UP FOR OUR LESSONS? DO YOU HAVE A FAVORITE SPOT YET? OH, I KNOW! HOW ABOUT OVER--
KIT... KIT, PLEASE WAIT!
LISTEN TO ME. I'VE BEEN TRYING TO TELL YOU SOMETHING.
I CAN'T TEACH YOU TO BE CAPTAIN MARVEL.
SWEETHEART, I CAN'T TEACH YOU SOMETHING THAT I'M STILL TRYING TO FIGURE OUT.
...?
YOU THOUGHT...?
BOY, YOU'RE NOT AS SMART AS YOU LOOK.

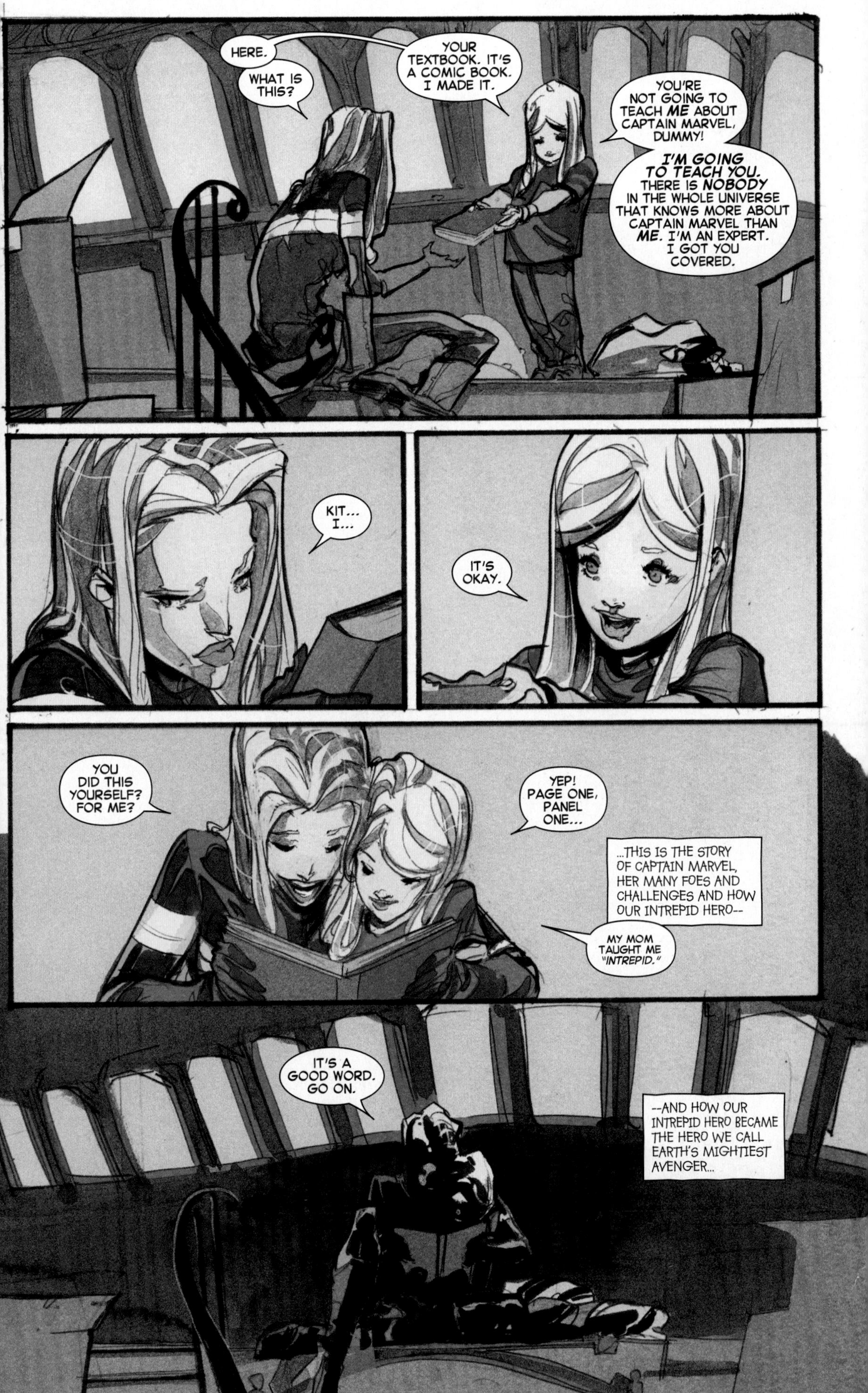
HERE.
WHAT IS THIS?
YOUR TEXTBOOK. IT'S A COMIC BOOK. I MADE IT.
YOU'RE NOT GOING TO TEACH ME ABOUT CAPTAIN MARVEL, DUMMY!
I'M GOING TO TEACH YOU. THERE IS NOBODY IN THE WHOLE UNIVERSE THAT KNOWS MORE ABOUT CAPTAIN MARVEL THAN ME. I'M AN EXPERT. I GOT YOU COVERED.
KIT... I...
IT'S OKAY.
YOU DID THIS YOURSELF? FOR ME?
YEP! PAGE ONE, PANEL ONE...
...THIS IS THE STORY OF CAPTAIN MARVEL, HER MANY FOES AND CHALLENGES AND HOW OUR INTREPID HERO--
MY MOM TAUGHT ME "INTREPID."
IT'S A GOOD WORD. GO ON.
--AND HOW OUR INTREPID HERO BECAME THE HERO WE CALL EARTH'S MIGHTIEST AVENGER...

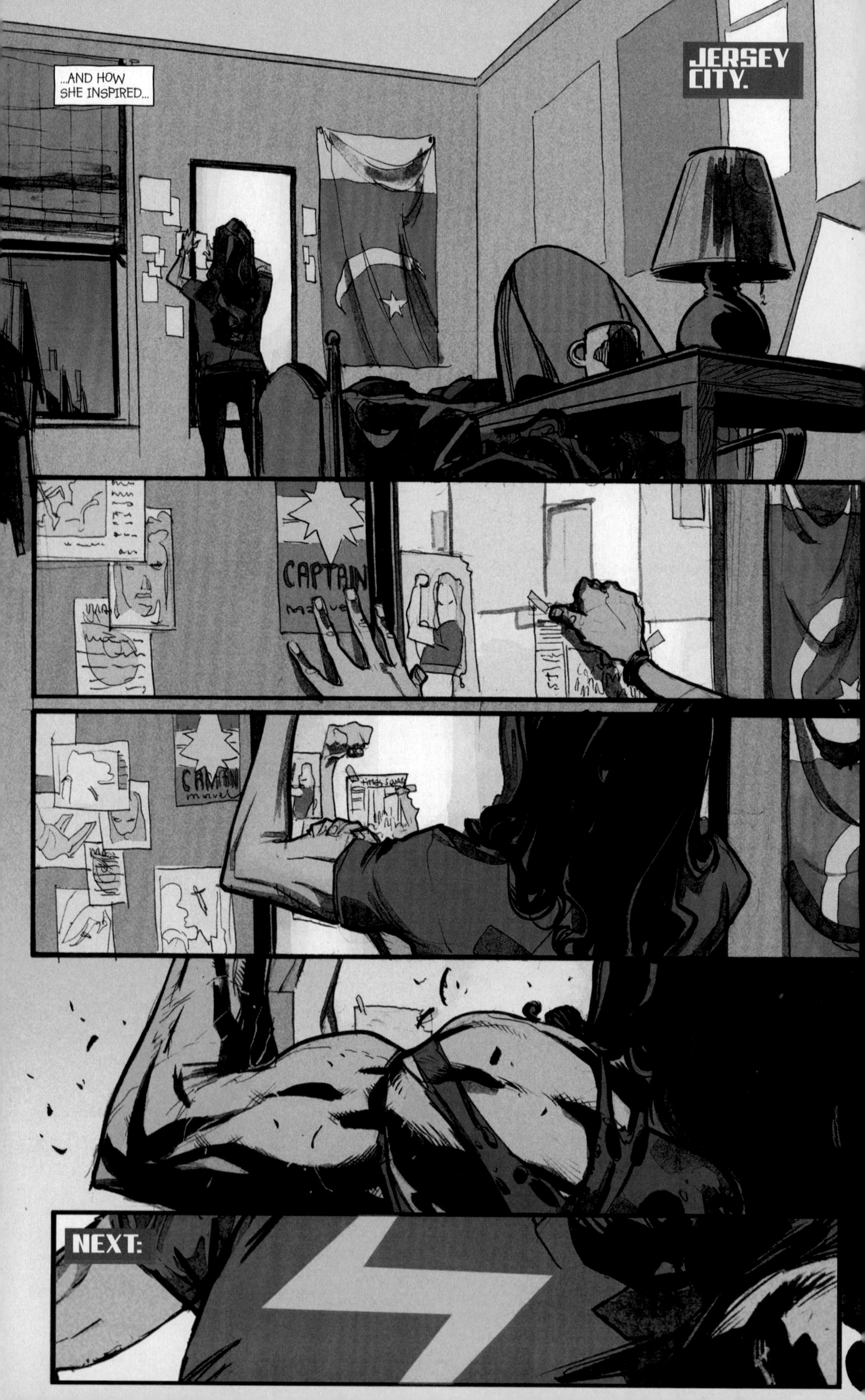
...AND HOW SHE INSPIRED...
JERSEY CITY.
CAPTAIN
NEXT:

THE LIFE OF CAPTAIN MARVEL #1

"TRAPPED"

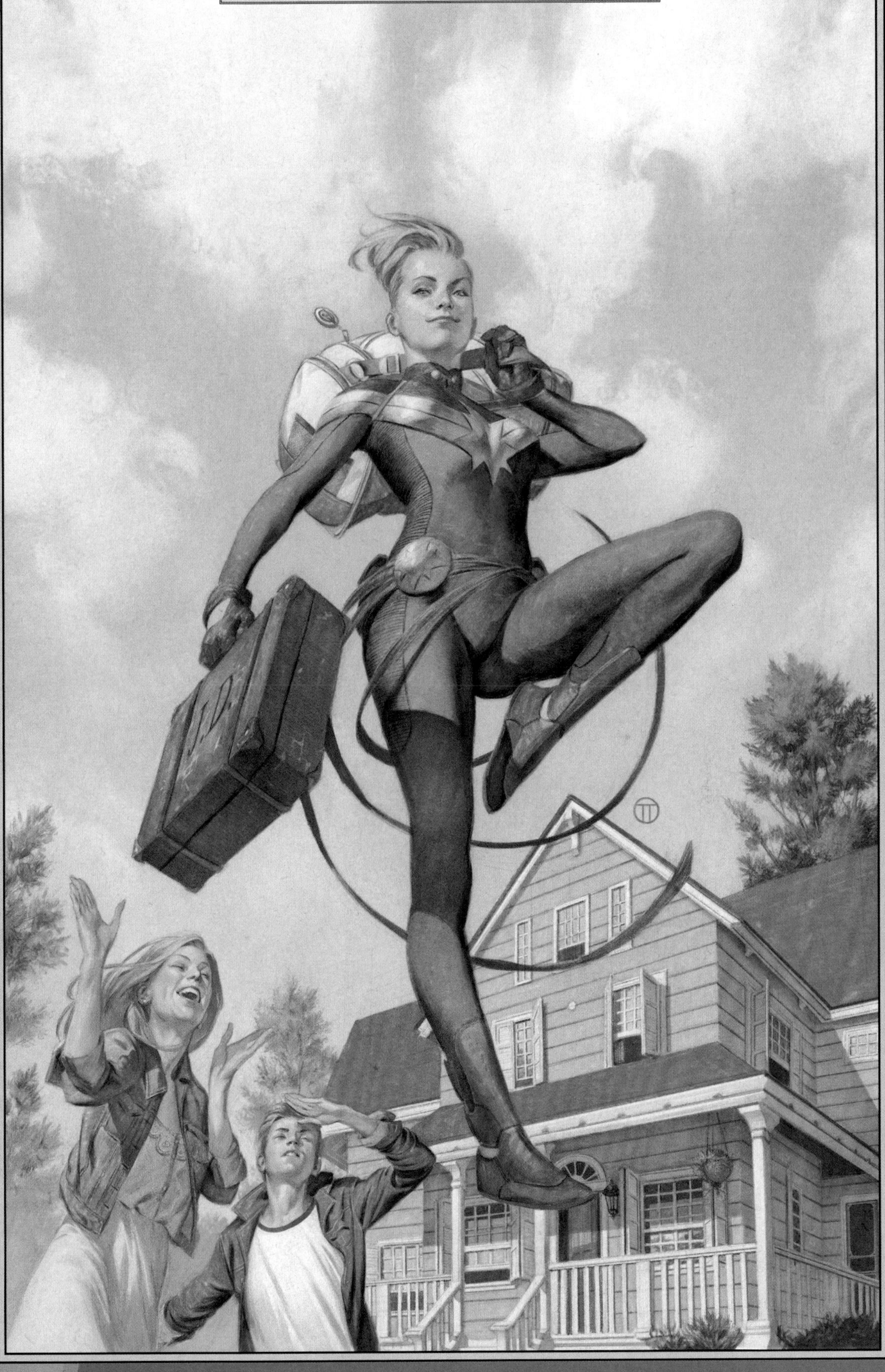

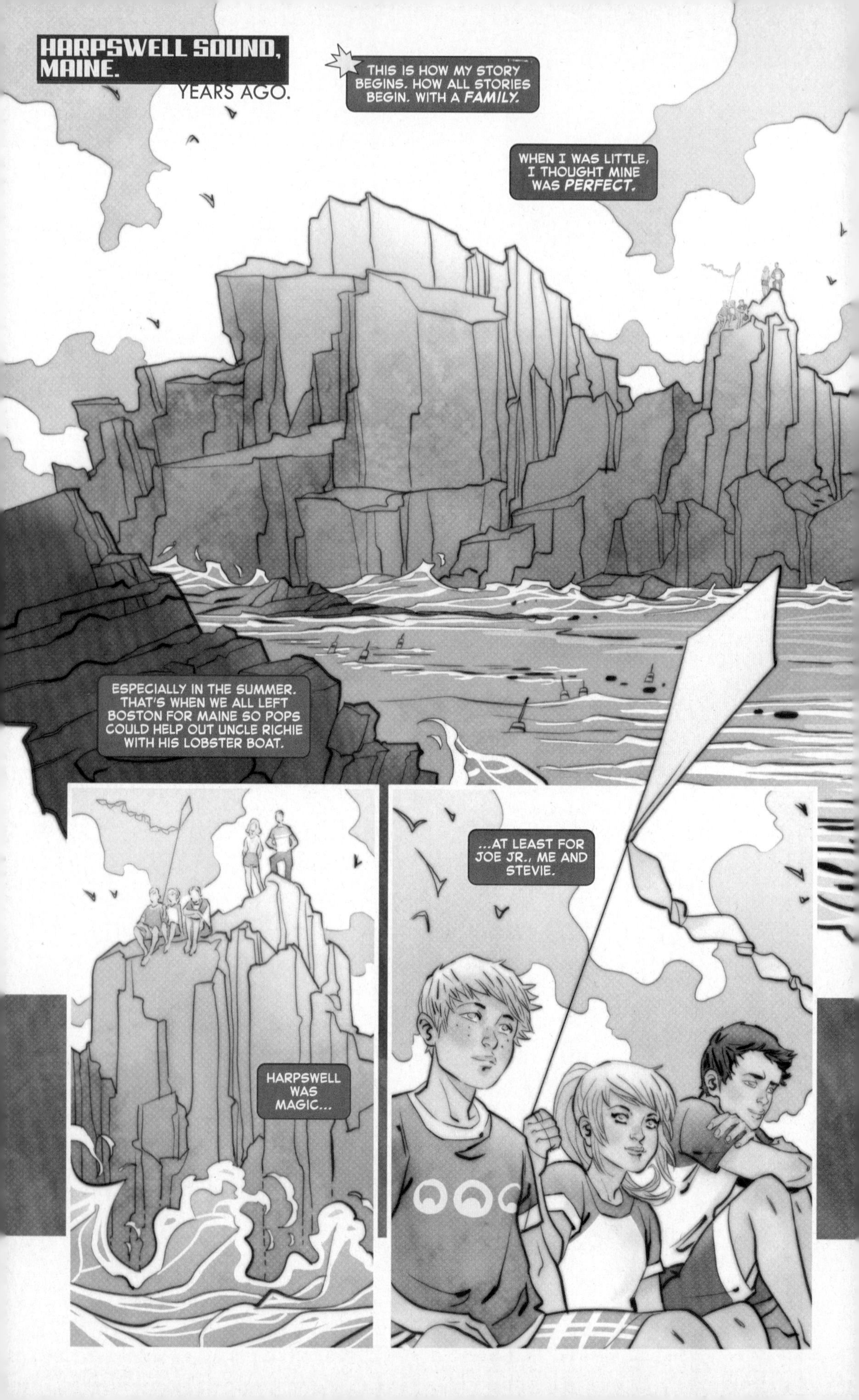
HARPSWELL SOUND, MAINE.
YEARS AGO.
THIS IS HOW MY STORY BEGINS. HOW ALL STORIES BEGIN. WITH A *FAMILY.*
WHEN I WAS LITTLE, I THOUGHT MINE WAS *PERFECT.*
ESPECIALLY IN THE SUMMER. THAT'S WHEN WE ALL LEFT BOSTON FOR MAINE SO POPS COULD HELP OUT UNCLE RICHIE WITH HIS LOBSTER BOAT.
HARPSWELL WAS MAGIC...
...AT LEAST FOR JOE JR., ME AND STEVIE.

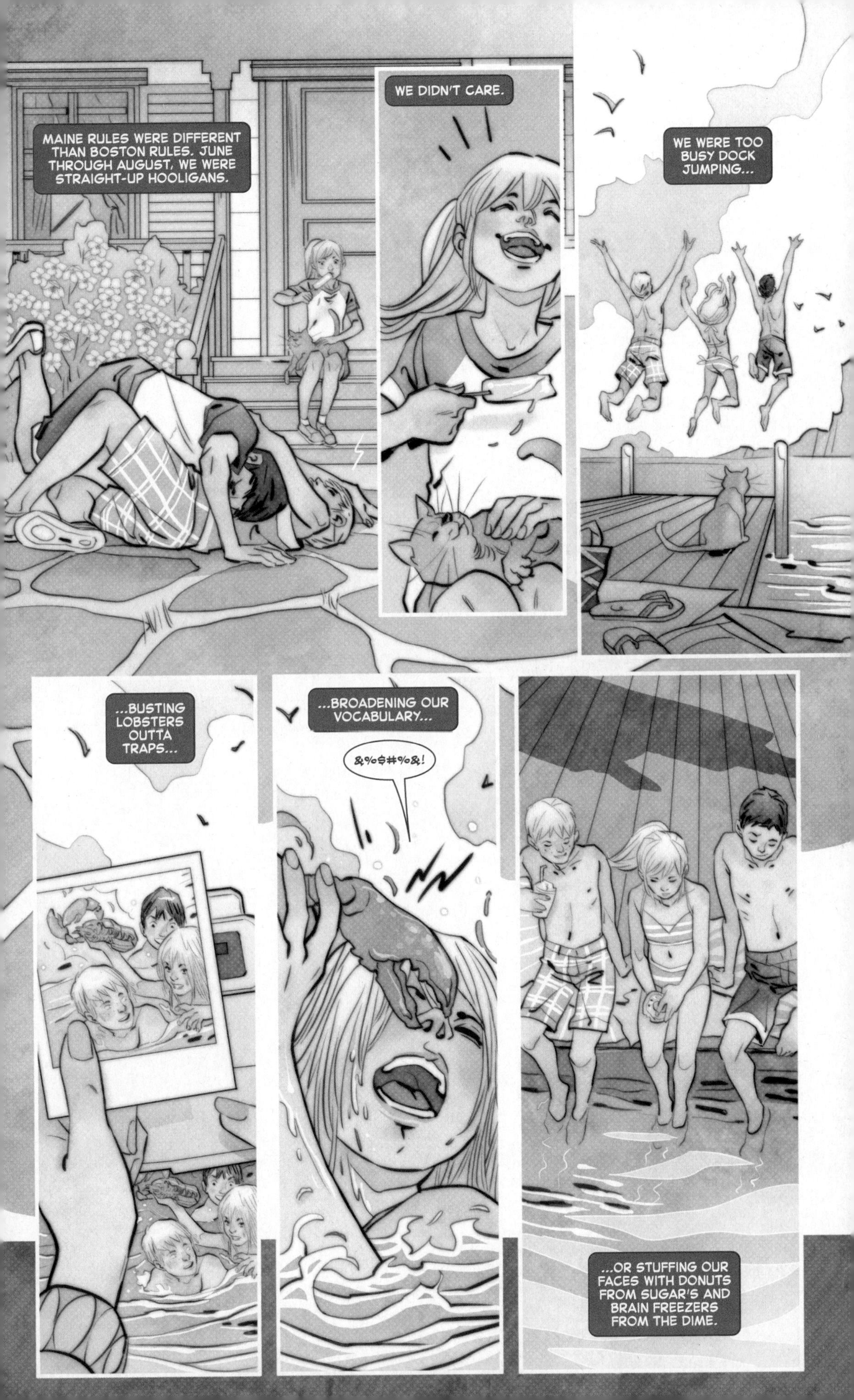
MAINE RULES WERE DIFFERENT THAN BOSTON RULES. JUNE THROUGH AUGUST, WE WERE STRAIGHT-UP HOOLIGANS.
WE DIDN'T CARE.
WE WERE TOO BUSY DOCK JUMPING...
...BUSTING LOBSTERS OUTTA TRAPS...
...BROADENING OUR VOCABULARY...
&%$#%&!
...OR STUFFING OUR FACES WITH DONUTS FROM SUGAR'S AND BRAIN FREEZERS FROM THE DIME.

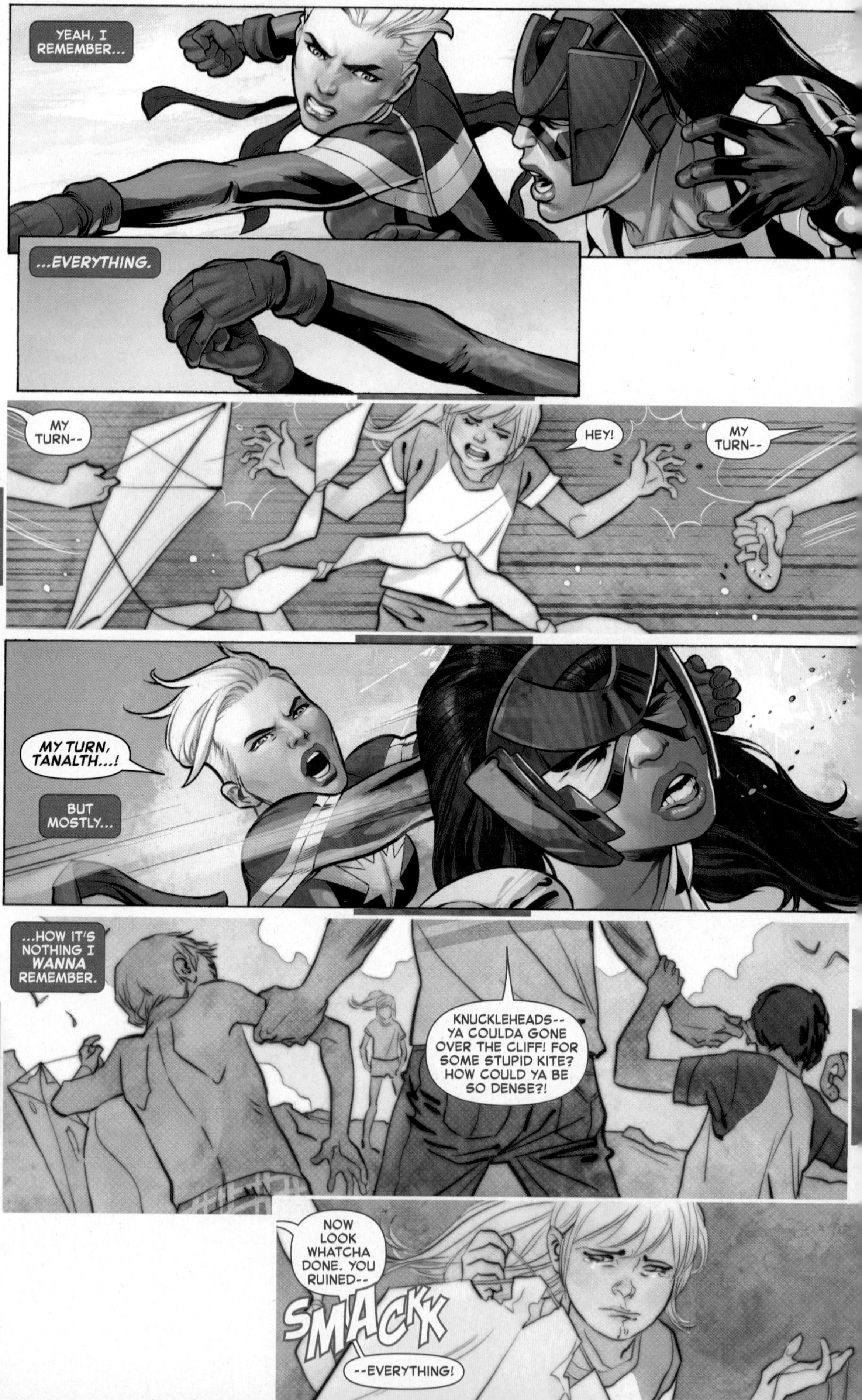
YEAH, I REMEMBER...
...EVERYTHING.
MY TURN--
HEY!
MY TURN--
MY TURN, TANALTH...!
BUT MOSTLY...
...HOW IT'S NOTHING I WANNA REMEMBER.
KNUCKLEHEADS-- YA COULDA GONE OVER THE CLIFF! FOR SOME STUPID KITE? HOW COULD YA BE SO DENSE?!
NOW LOOK WHATCHA DONE. YOU RUINED--
SMACK
--EVERYTHING!

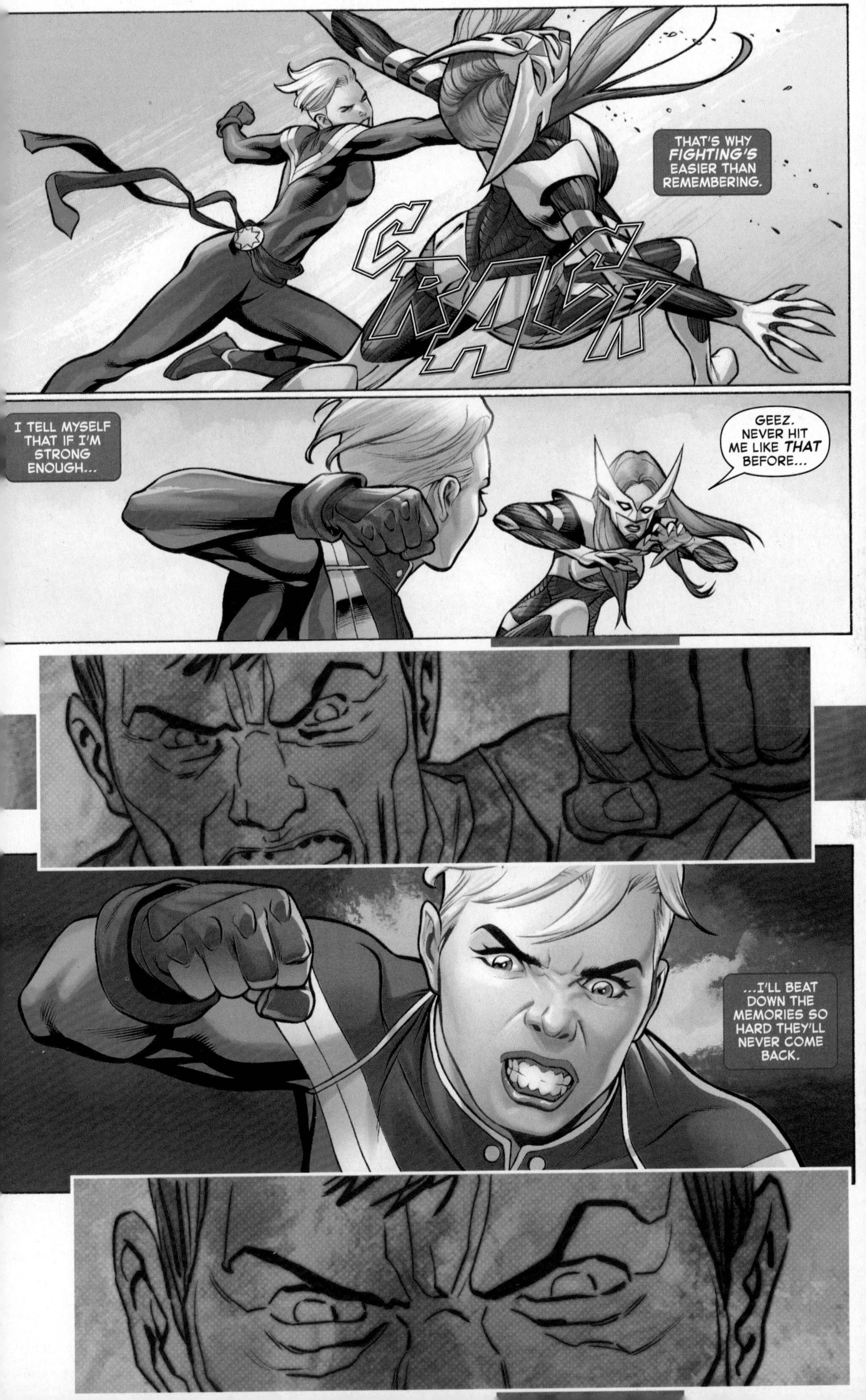
THAT'S WHY *FIGHTING'S* EASIER THAN REMEMBERING.
CRACK
I TELL MYSELF THAT IF I'M STRONG ENOUGH...
GEEZ. NEVER HIT ME LIKE *THAT* BEFORE...
...I'LL BEAT DOWN THE MEMORIES SO HARD THEY'LL NEVER COME BACK.

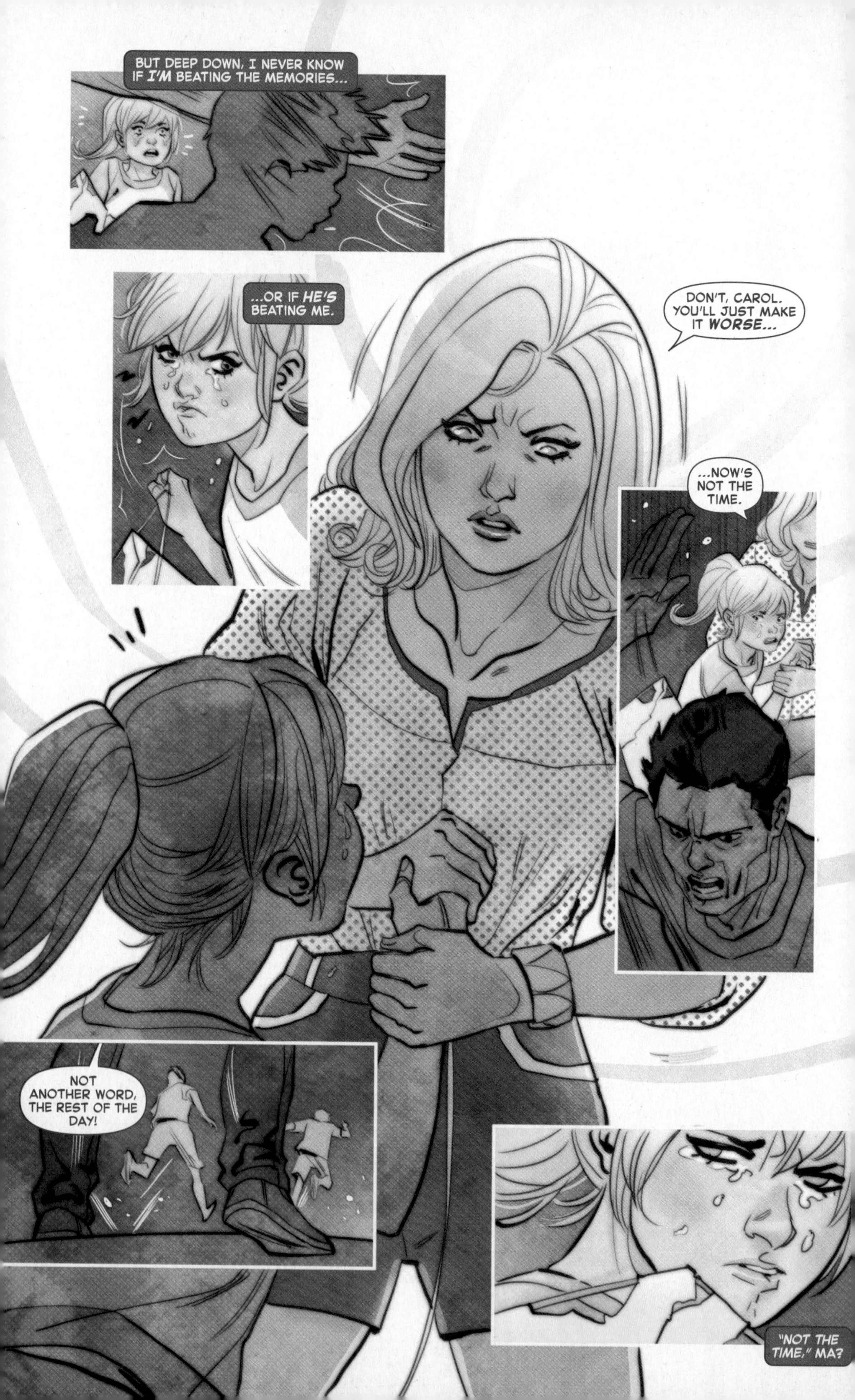
BUT DEEP DOWN, I NEVER KNOW IF *I'M* BEATING THE MEMORIES...
...OR IF *HE'S* BEATING ME.
DON'T, CAROL. YOU'LL JUST MAKE IT *WORSE*...
...NOW'S NOT THE TIME.
NOT ANOTHER WORD, THE REST OF THE DAY!
"NOT THE TIME," MA?

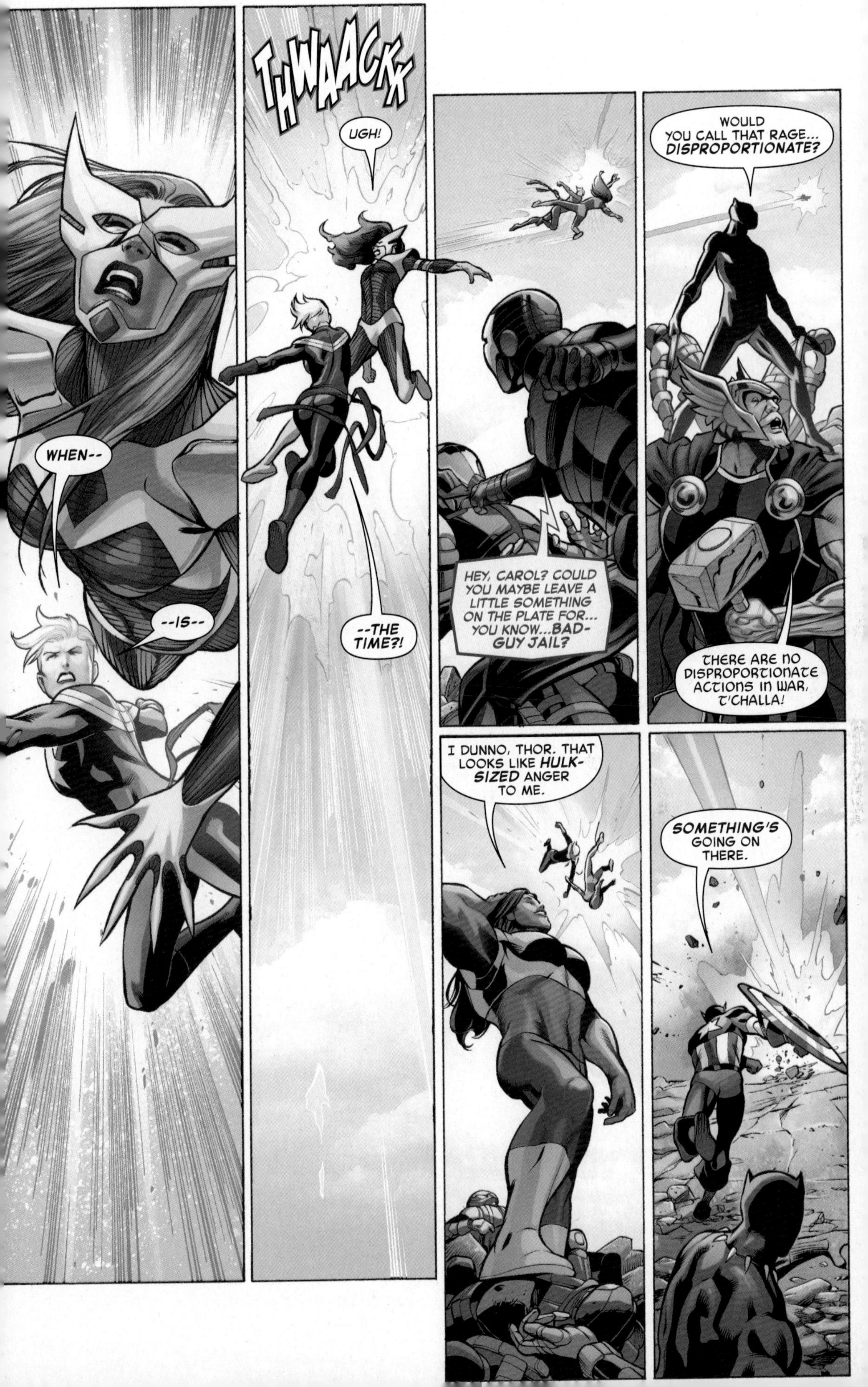
WHEN--
--IS--
THWAACKK
UGH!
--THE TIME?!
HEY, CAROL? COULD YOU MAYBE LEAVE A LITTLE SOMETHING ON THE PLATE FOR... YOU KNOW...BAD-GUY JAIL?
WOULD YOU CALL THAT RAGE... DISPROPORTIONATE?
THERE ARE NO DISPROPORTIONATE ACTIONS IN WAR, T'CHALLA!
I DUNNO, THOR. THAT LOOKS LIKE HULK-SIZED ANGER TO ME.
SOMETHING'S GOING ON THERE.

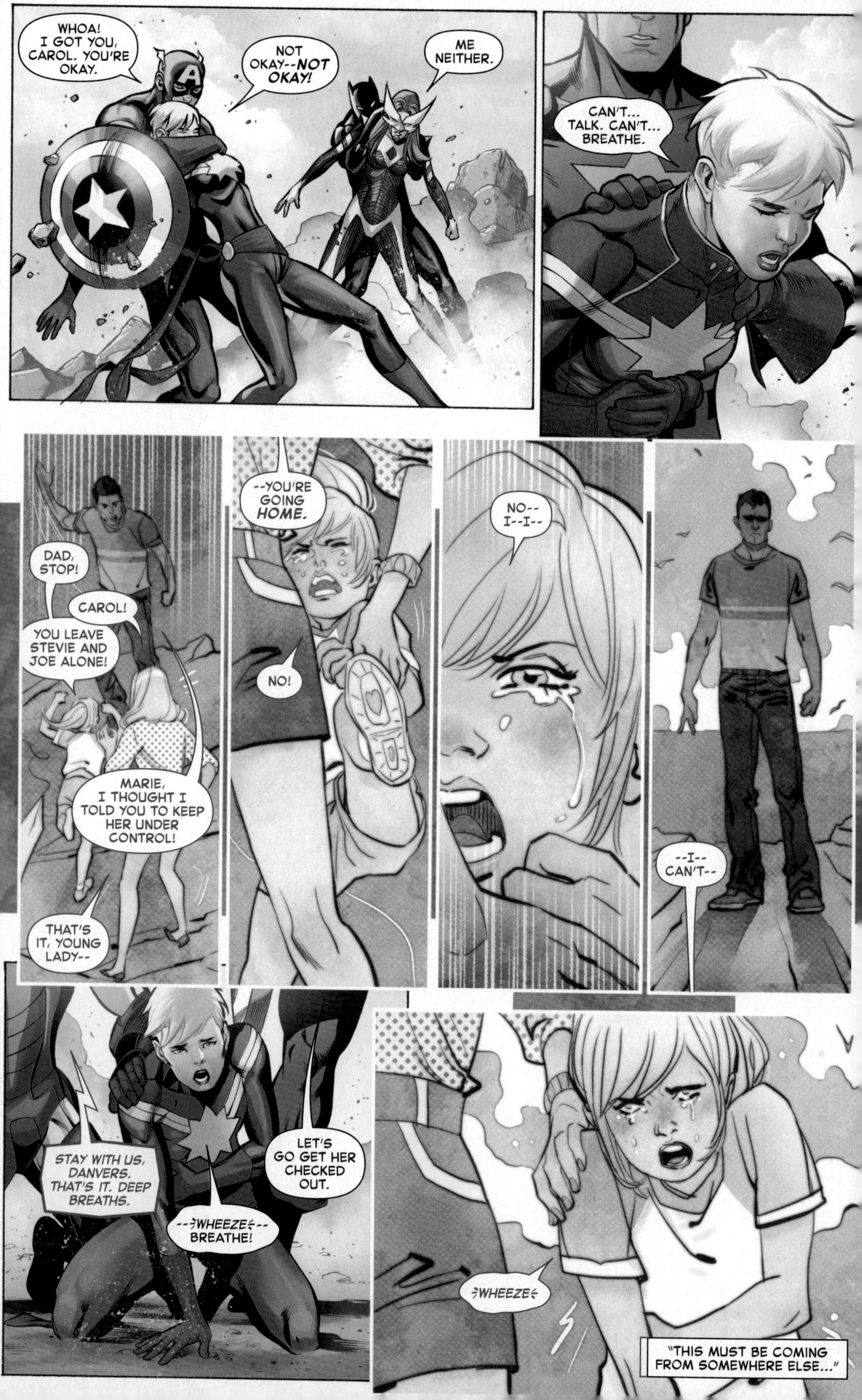

WHOA! I GOT YOU, CAROL. YOU'RE OKAY.
NOT OKAY--NOT OKAY!
ME NEITHER.
CAN'T... TALK. CAN'T... BREATHE.
DAD, STOP!
CAROL!
YOU LEAVE STEVIE AND JOE ALONE!
MARIE, I THOUGHT I TOLD YOU TO KEEP HER UNDER CONTROL!
THAT'S IT, YOUNG LADY--
--YOU'RE GOING HOME.
NO!
NO-- I--I--
--I-- CAN'T--
STAY WITH US, DANVERS. THAT'S IT. DEEP BREATHS.
LET'S GO GET HER CHECKED OUT.
--WHEEZE-- BREATHE!
WHEEZE
"THIS MUST BE COMING FROM SOMEWHERE ELSE..."

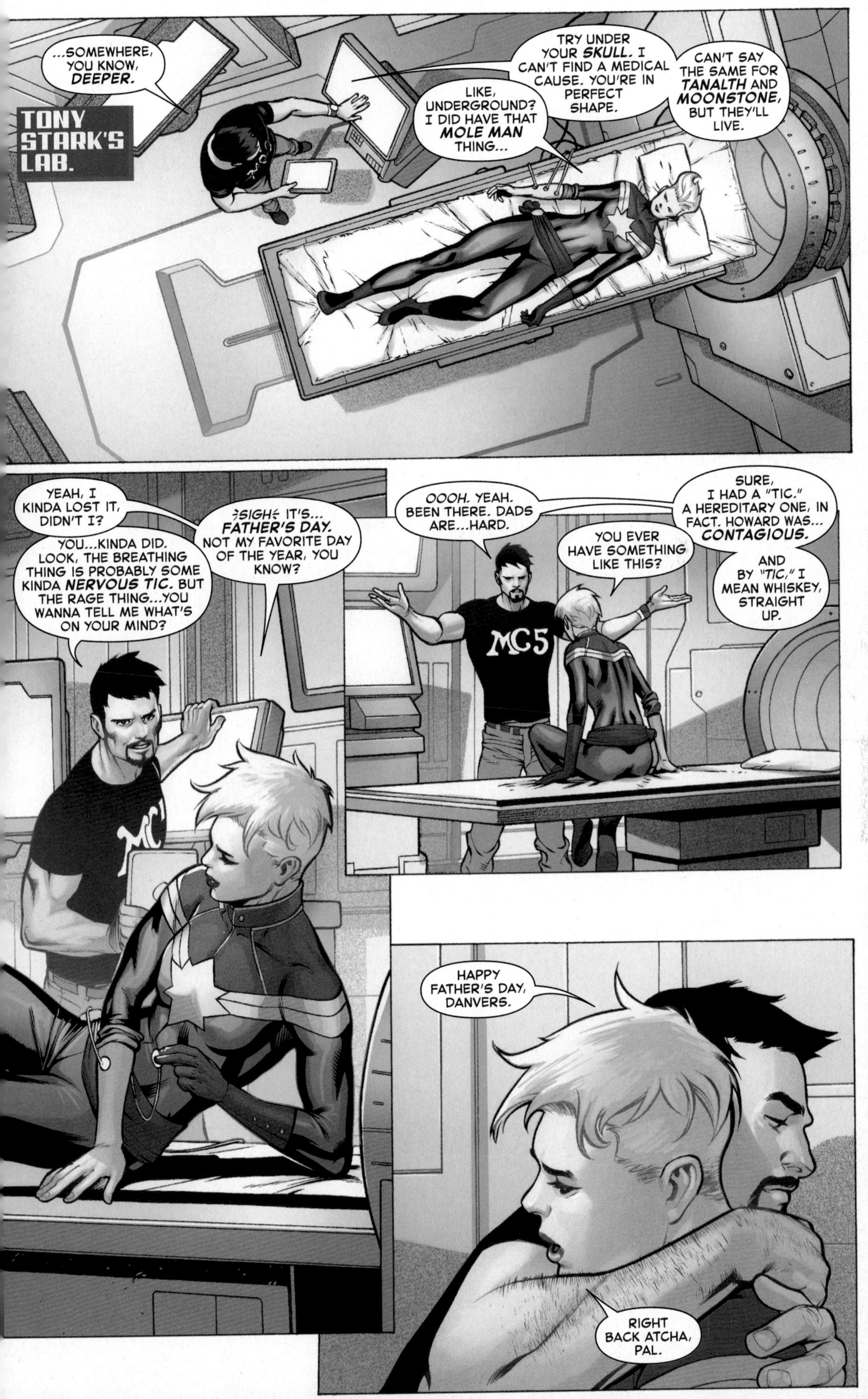

...SOMEWHERE, YOU KNOW, DEEPER.
TONY STARK'S LAB.
LIKE, UNDERGROUND? I DID HAVE THAT MOLE MAN THING...
TRY UNDER YOUR SKULL. I CAN'T FIND A MEDICAL CAUSE. YOU'RE IN PERFECT SHAPE.
CAN'T SAY THE SAME FOR TANALTH AND MOONSTONE, BUT THEY'LL LIVE.
YEAH, I KINDA LOST IT, DIDN'T I?
YOU...KINDA DID. LOOK, THE BREATHING THING IS PROBABLY SOME KINDA NERVOUS TIC. BUT THE RAGE THING...YOU WANNA TELL ME WHAT'S ON YOUR MIND?
SIGH IT'S... FATHER'S DAY. NOT MY FAVORITE DAY OF THE YEAR, YOU KNOW?
OOOH. YEAH. BEEN THERE. DADS ARE...HARD.
YOU EVER HAVE SOMETHING LIKE THIS?
SURE, I HAD A "TIC." A HEREDITARY ONE, IN FACT. HOWARD WAS... CONTAGIOUS.
AND BY "TIC," I MEAN WHISKEY, STRAIGHT UP.
MC5
HAPPY FATHER'S DAY, DANVERS.
RIGHT BACK ATCHA, PAL.

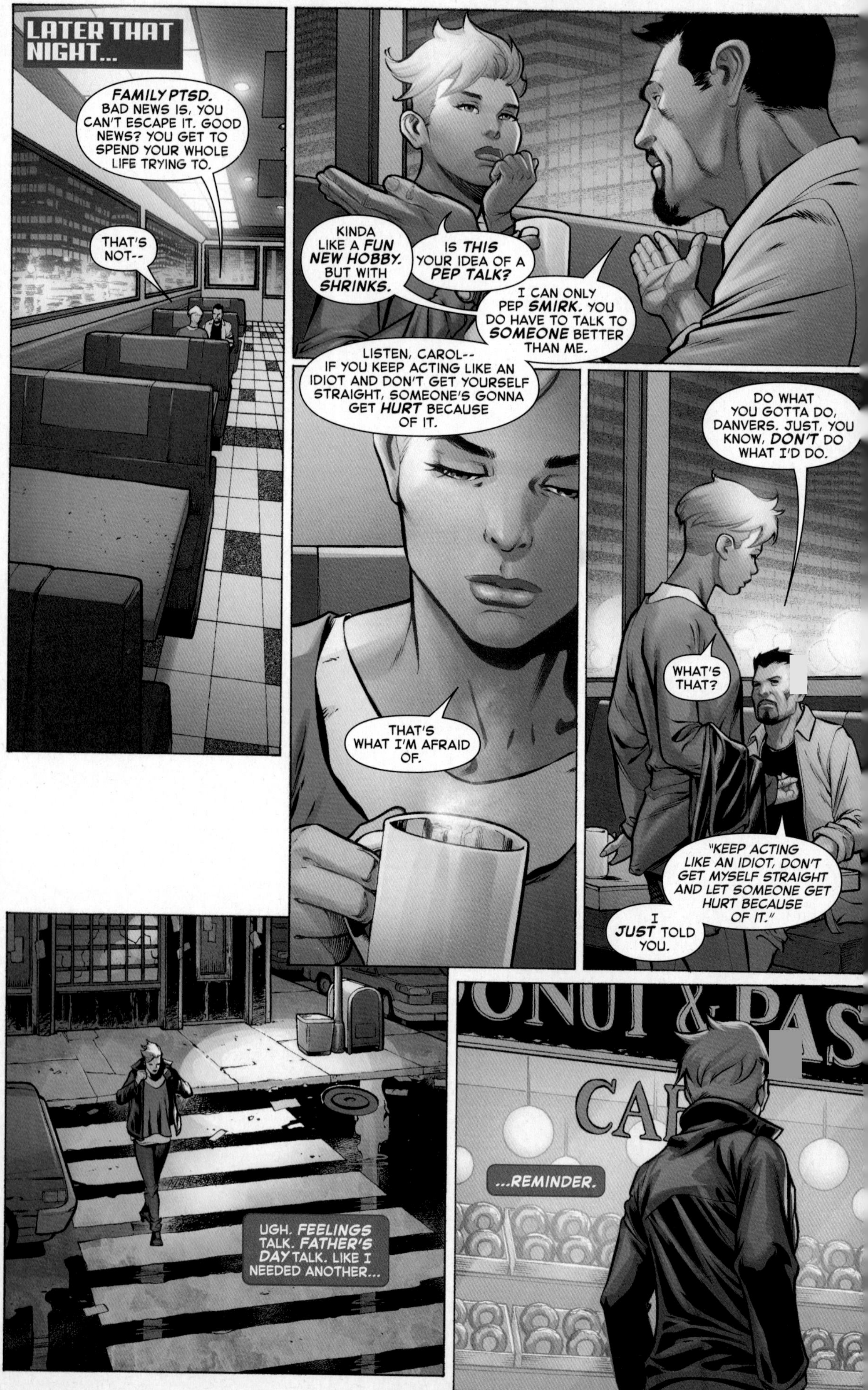
LATER THAT NIGHT...
FAMILY PTSD. BAD NEWS IS, YOU CAN'T ESCAPE IT. GOOD NEWS? YOU GET TO SPEND YOUR WHOLE LIFE TRYING TO.
THAT'S NOT--
KINDA LIKE A FUN NEW HOBBY. BUT WITH SHRINKS.
IS THIS YOUR IDEA OF A PEP TALK?
I CAN ONLY PEP SMIRK. YOU DO HAVE TO TALK TO SOMEONE BETTER THAN ME.
LISTEN, CAROL-- IF YOU KEEP ACTING LIKE AN IDIOT AND DON'T GET YOURSELF STRAIGHT, SOMEONE'S GONNA GET HURT BECAUSE OF IT.
THAT'S WHAT I'M AFRAID OF.
DO WHAT YOU GOTTA DO, DANVERS. JUST, YOU KNOW, DON'T DO WHAT I'D DO.
WHAT'S THAT?
"KEEP ACTING LIKE AN IDIOT, DON'T GET MYSELF STRAIGHT AND LET SOMEONE GET HURT BECAUSE OF IT."
I JUST TOLD YOU.
UGH. FEELINGS TALK. FATHER'S DAY TALK. LIKE I NEEDED ANOTHER...
...REMINDER.

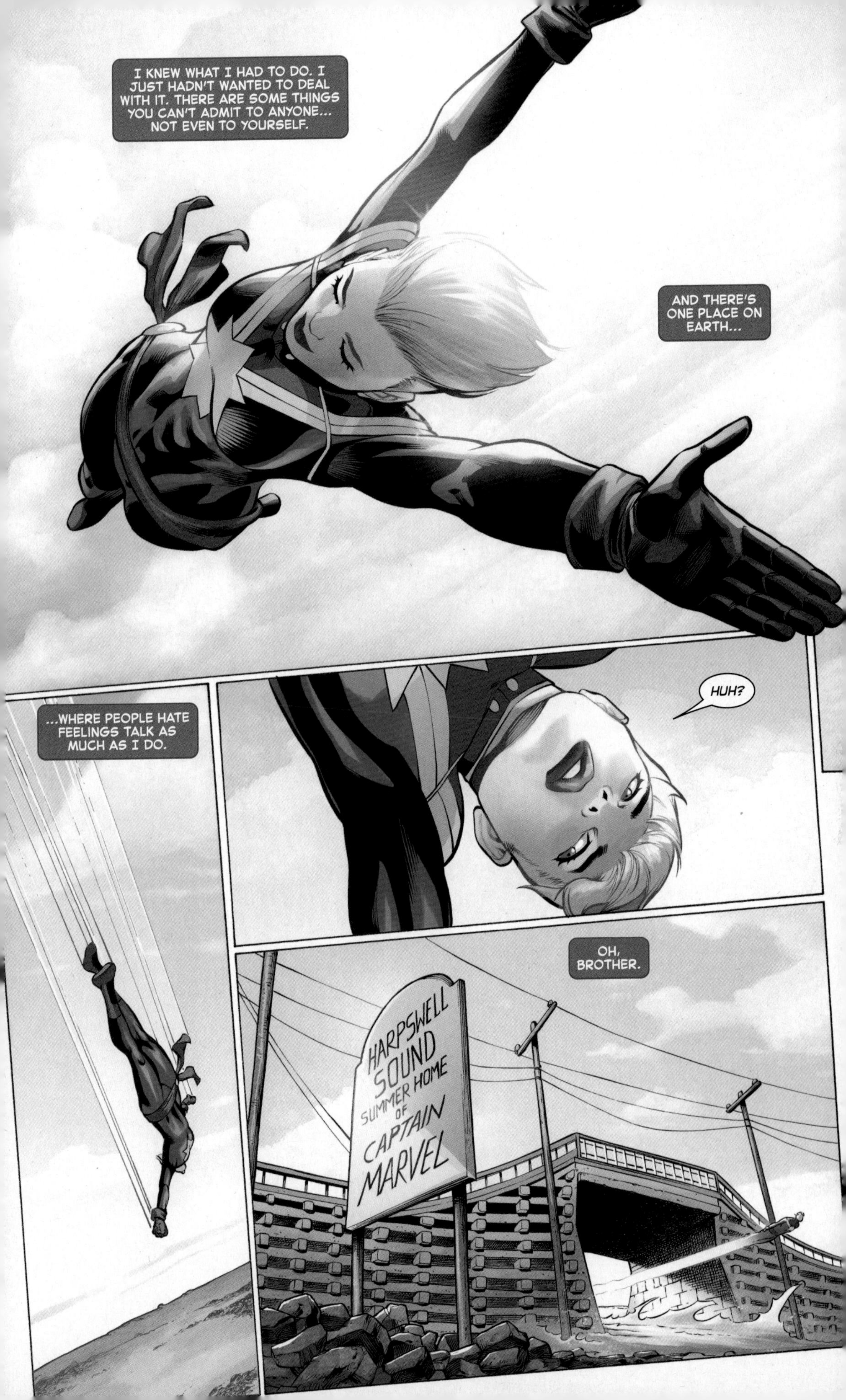
I KNEW WHAT I HAD TO DO. I JUST HADN'T WANTED TO DEAL WITH IT. THERE ARE SOME THINGS YOU CAN'T ADMIT TO ANYONE... NOT EVEN TO YOURSELF.
AND THERE'S ONE PLACE ON EARTH...
...WHERE PEOPLE HATE FEELINGS TALK AS MUCH AS I DO.
HUH?
OH, BROTHER.
HARPSWELL SOUND
SUMMER HOME OF
CAPTAIN MARVEL

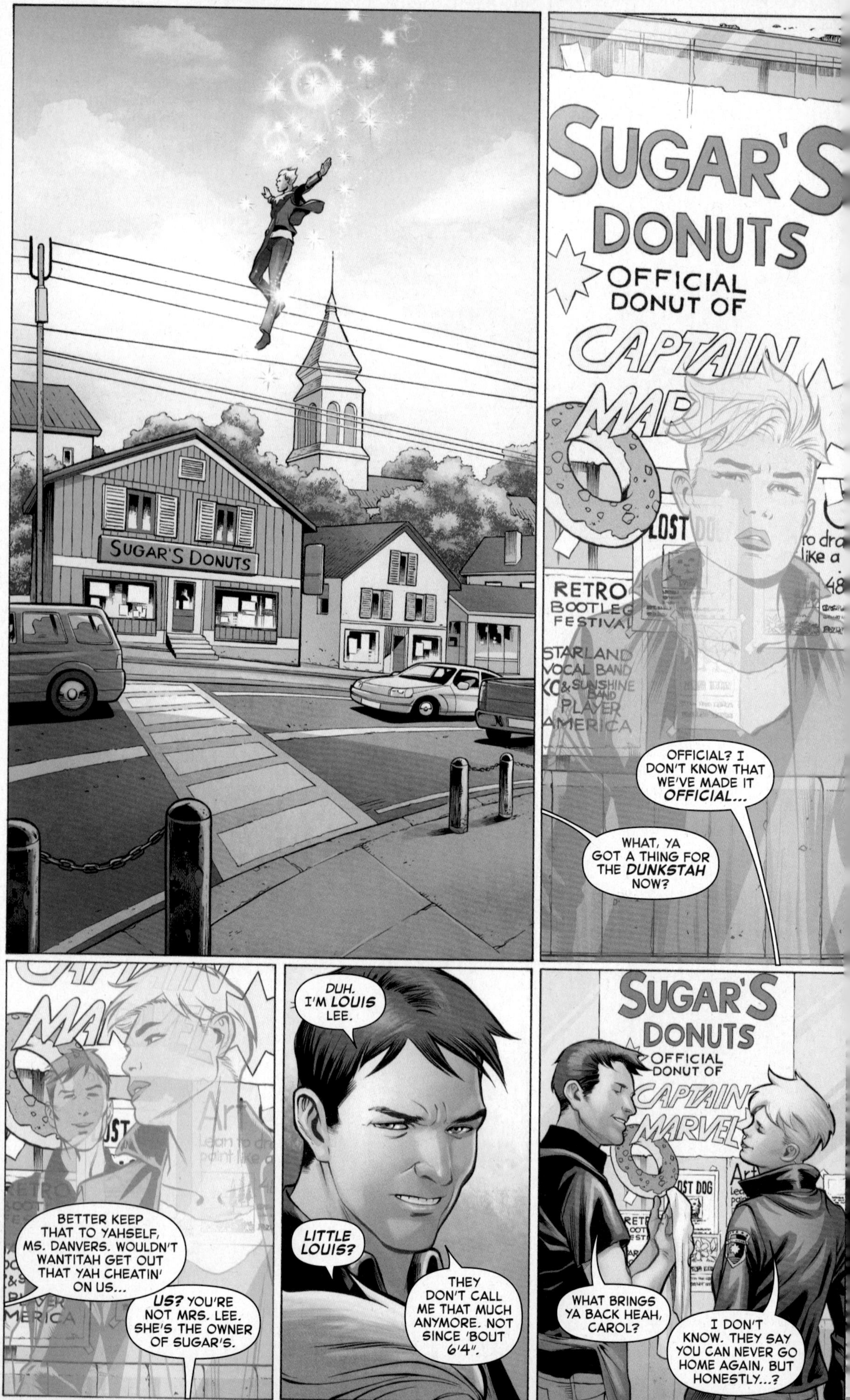
SUGAR'S DONUTS
SUGAR'S DONUTS
OFFICIAL DONUT OF
CAPTAIN MAR
LOST DOG
RETRO BOOTLEG FESTIVAL
STARLAND VOCAL BAND
KC & SUNSHINE BAND
PLAYER
AMERICA
OFFICIAL? I DON'T KNOW THAT WE'VE MADE IT OFFICIAL...
WHAT, YA GOT A THING FOR THE DUNKSTAH NOW?
BETTER KEEP THAT TO YAHSELF, MS. DANVERS. WOULDN'T WANTITAH GET OUT THAT YAH CHEATIN' ON US...
US? YOU'RE NOT MRS. LEE. SHE'S THE OWNER OF SUGAR'S.
DUH. I'M LOUIS LEE.
LITTLE LOUIS?
THEY DON'T CALL ME THAT MUCH ANYMORE. NOT SINCE 'BOUT 6'4".
SUGAR'S DONUTS
OFFICIAL DONUT OF
CAPTAIN MARVEL
LOST DOG
WHAT BRINGS YA BACK HEAH, CAROL?
I DON'T KNOW. THEY SAY YOU CAN NEVER GO HOME AGAIN, BUT HONESTLY...?

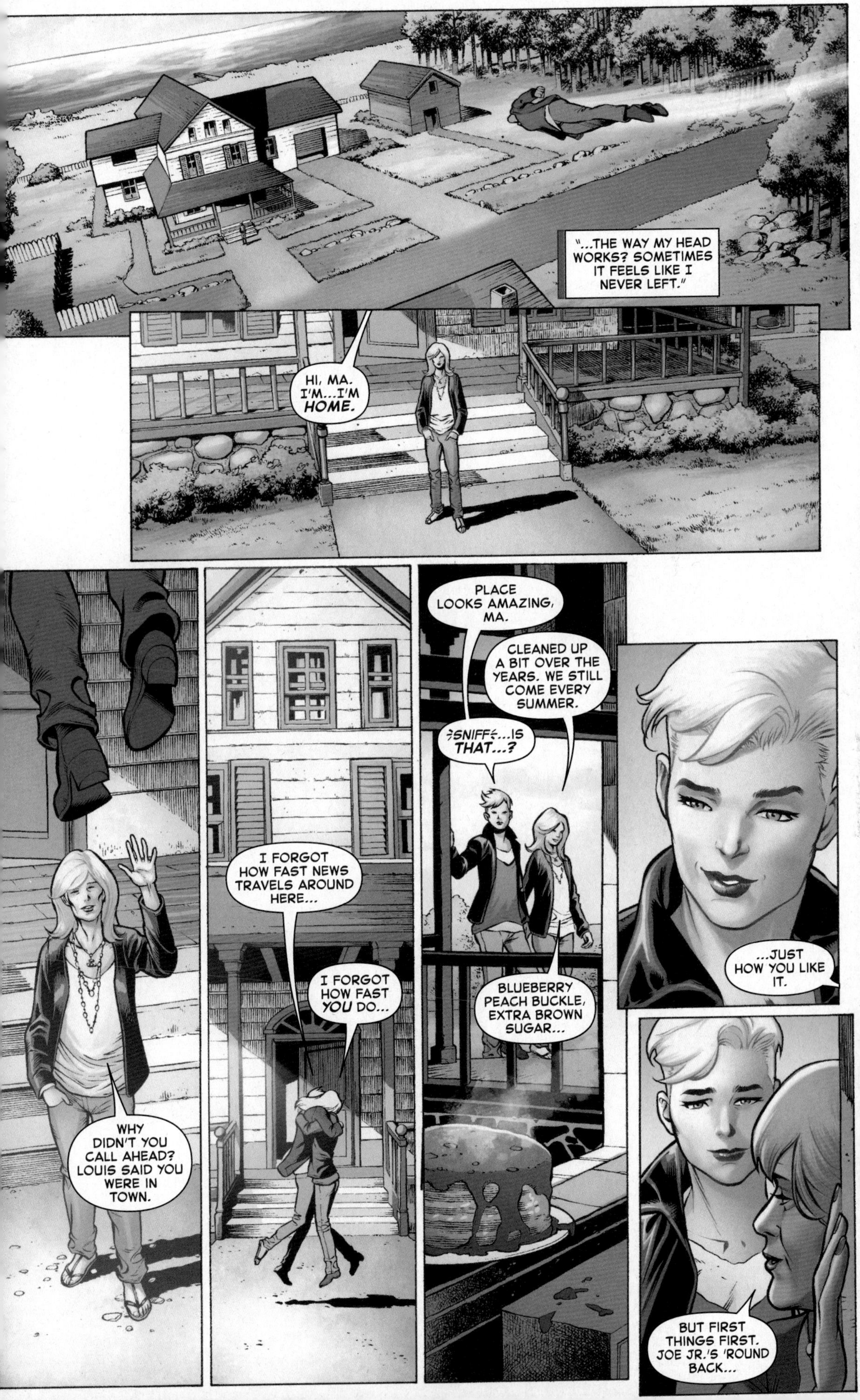
"...THE WAY MY HEAD WORKS? SOMETIMES IT FEELS LIKE I NEVER LEFT."
HI, MA. I'M...I'M HOME.
WHY DIDN'T YOU CALL AHEAD? LOUIS SAID YOU WERE IN TOWN.
I FORGOT HOW FAST NEWS TRAVELS AROUND HERE...
I FORGOT HOW FAST YOU DO...
PLACE LOOKS AMAZING, MA.
CLEANED UP A BIT OVER THE YEARS. WE STILL COME EVERY SUMMER.
SNIFF...IS THAT...?
BLUEBERRY PEACH BUCKLE, EXTRA BROWN SUGAR...
...JUST HOW YOU LIKE IT.
BUT FIRST THINGS FIRST. JOE JR.'S 'ROUND BACK...

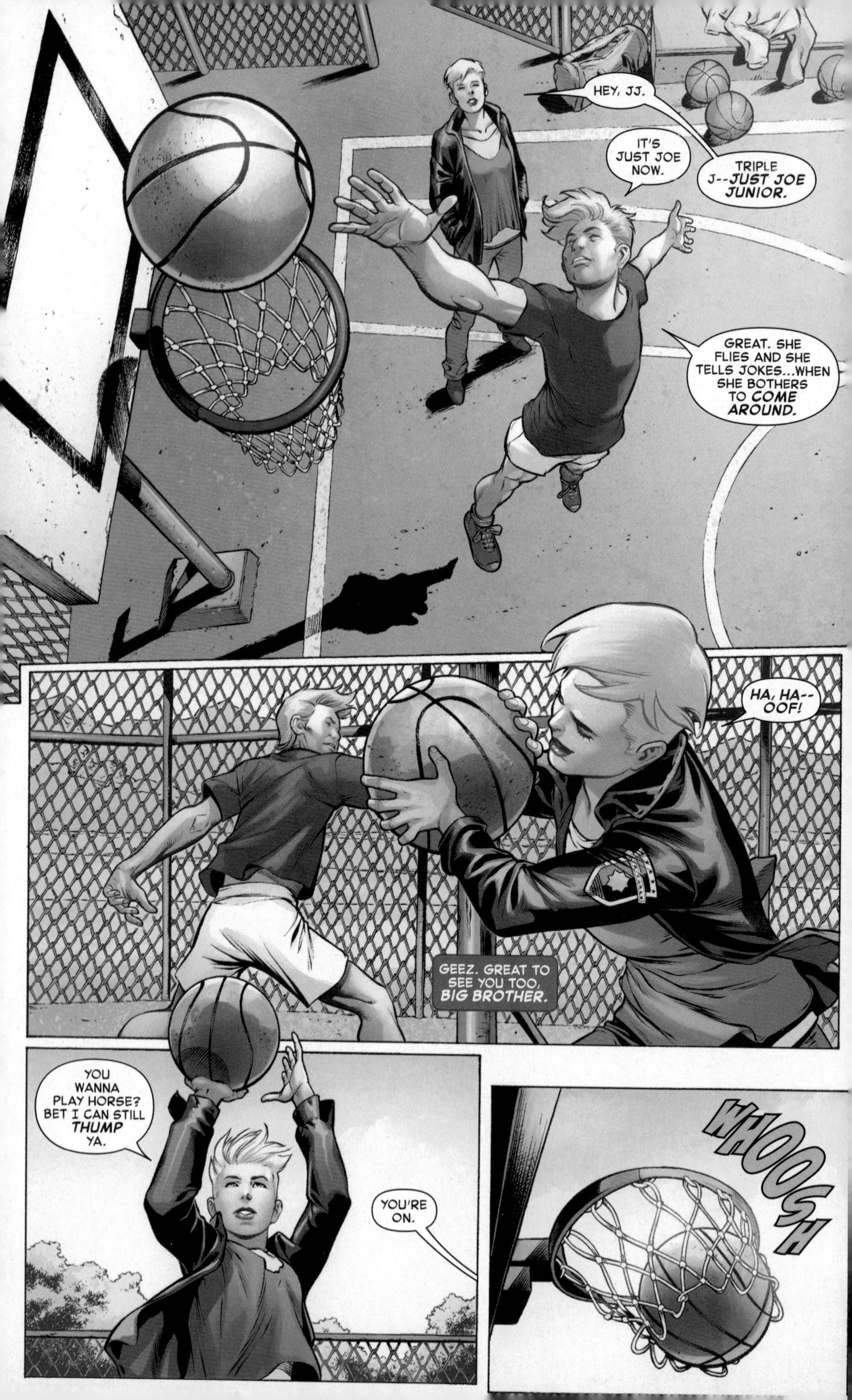
HEY, JJ.
IT'S JUST JOE NOW.
TRIPLE J--JUST JOE JUNIOR.
GREAT. SHE FLIES AND SHE TELLS JOKES...WHEN SHE BOTHERS TO COME AROUND.
HA, HA--OOF!
GEEZ. GREAT TO SEE YOU TOO, BIG BROTHER.
YOU WANNA PLAY HORSE? BET I CAN STILL THUMP YA.
YOU'RE ON.
WHOOSH

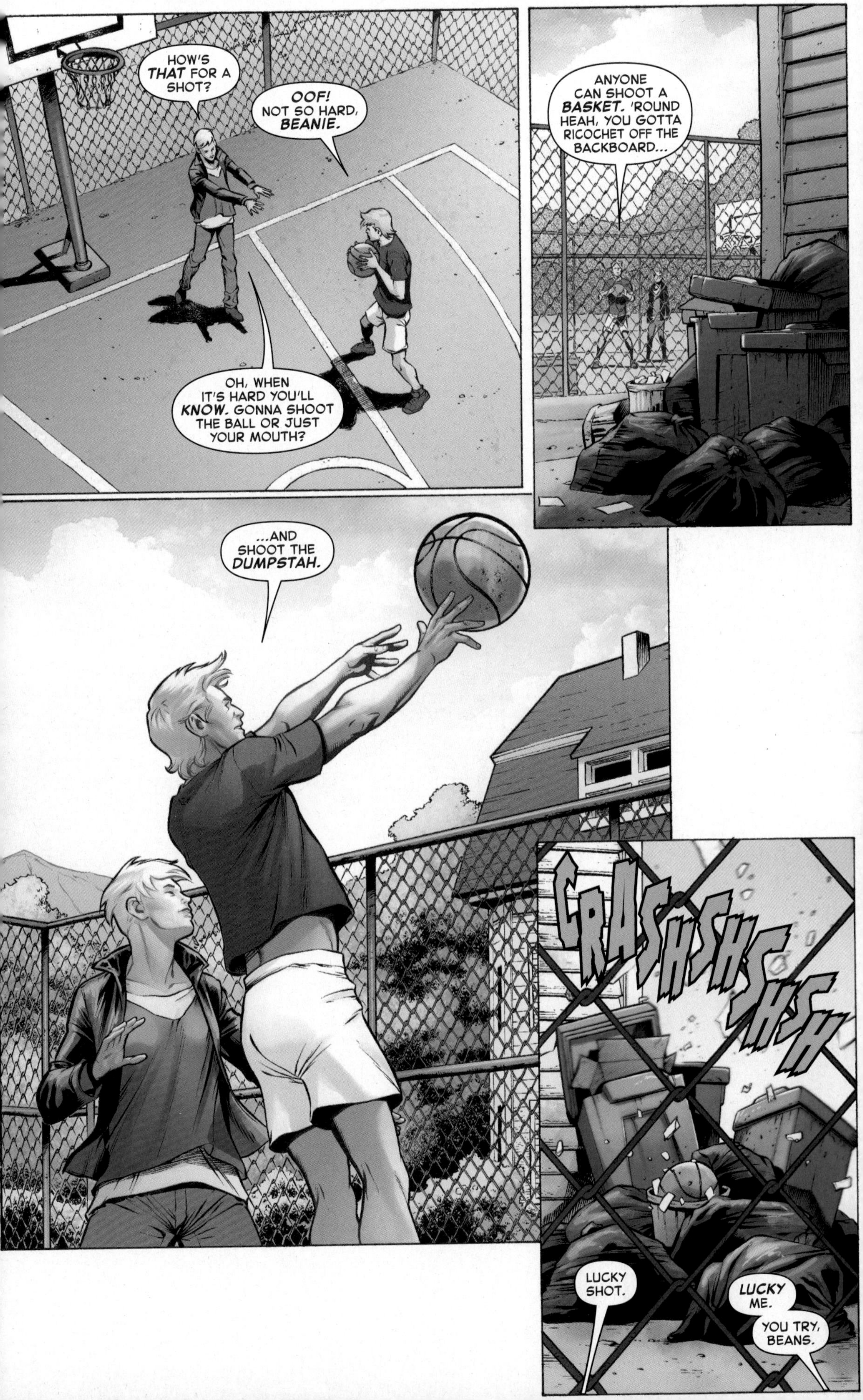
HOW'S THAT FOR A SHOT?
OOF! NOT SO HARD, BEANIE.
OH, WHEN IT'S HARD YOU'LL KNOW. GONNA SHOOT THE BALL OR JUST YOUR MOUTH?
ANYONE CAN SHOOT A BASKET. 'ROUND HEAH, YOU GOTTA RICOCHET OFF THE BACKBOARD...
...AND SHOOT THE DUMPSTAH.
CRASHSHSHSHSH
LUCKY SHOT.
LUCKY ME.
YOU TRY, BEANS.

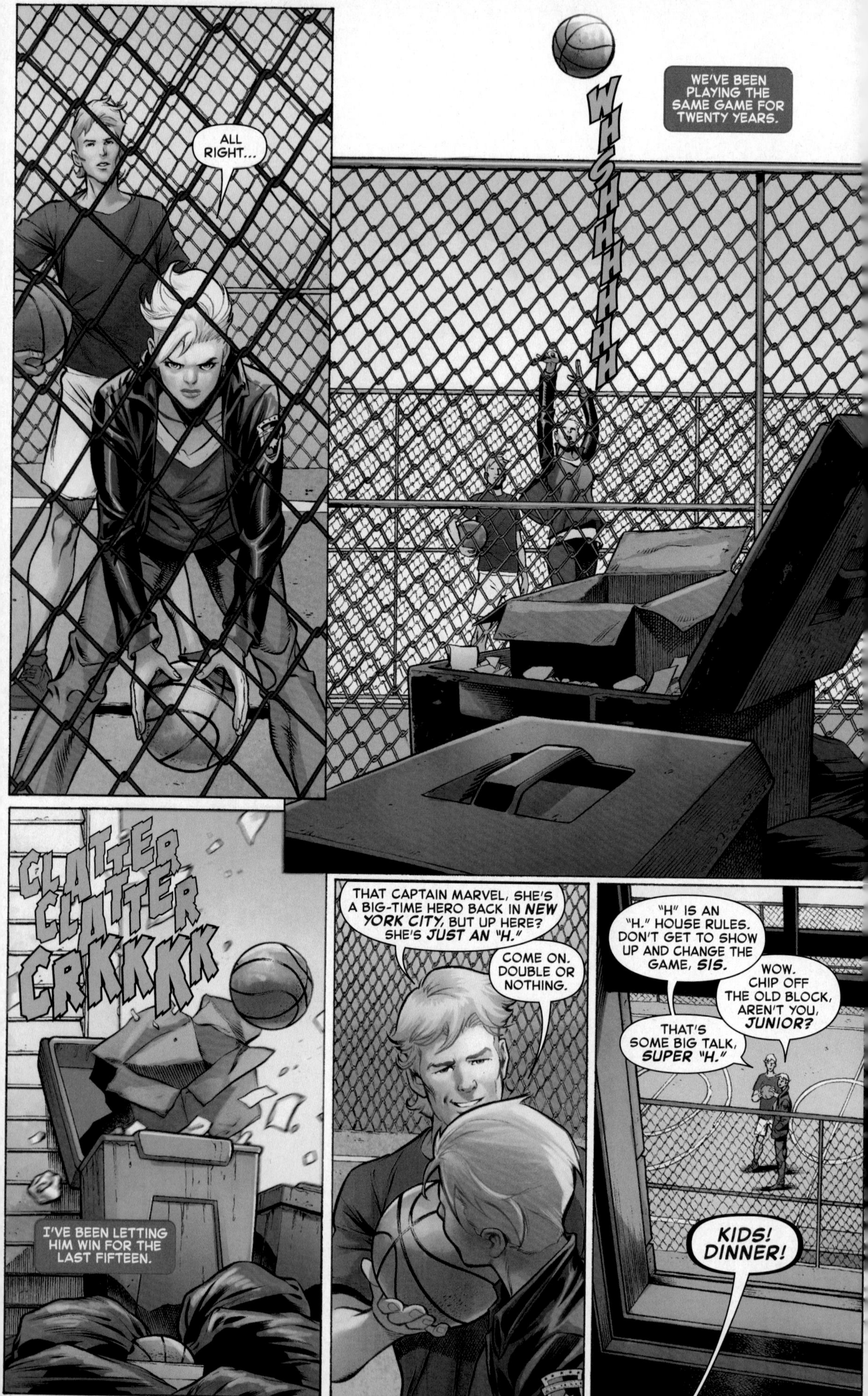
ALL RIGHT...
WE'VE BEEN PLAYING THE SAME GAME FOR TWENTY YEARS.
WHSHHHHHH
CLATTER CLATTER CRKKKK
I'VE BEEN LETTING HIM WIN FOR THE LAST FIFTEEN.
THAT CAPTAIN MARVEL, SHE'S A BIG-TIME HERO BACK IN NEW YORK CITY, BUT UP HERE? SHE'S JUST AN "H."
COME ON. DOUBLE OR NOTHING.
"H" IS AN "H." HOUSE RULES. DON'T GET TO SHOW UP AND CHANGE THE GAME, SIS.
THAT'S SOME BIG TALK, SUPER "H."
WOW. CHIP OFF THE OLD BLOCK, AREN'T YOU, JUNIOR?
KIDS! DINNER!

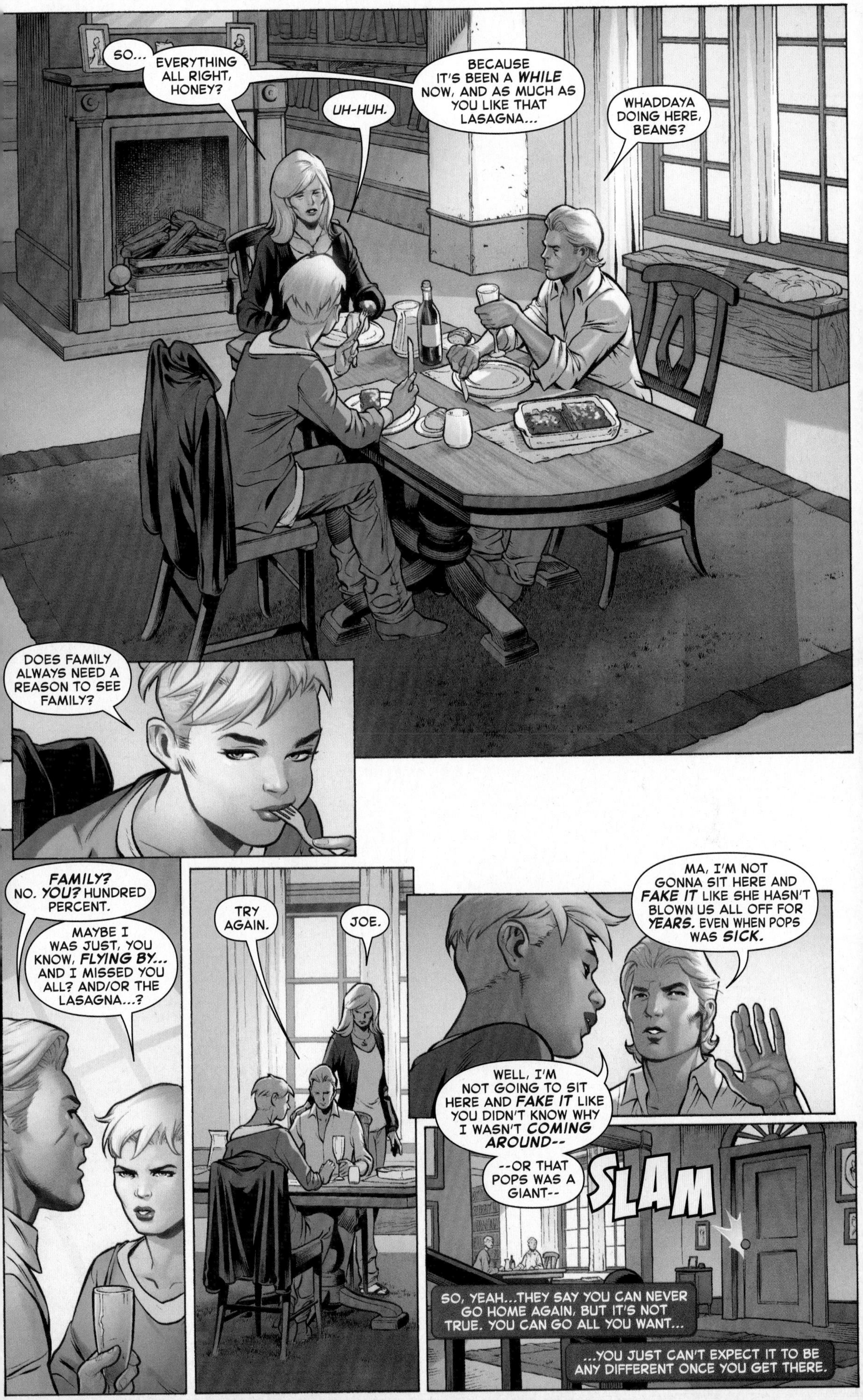
SO...
EVERYTHING ALL RIGHT, HONEY?
UH-HUH.
BECAUSE IT'S BEEN A WHILE NOW, AND AS MUCH AS YOU LIKE THAT LASAGNA...
WHADDAYA DOING HERE, BEANS?
DOES FAMILY ALWAYS NEED A REASON TO SEE FAMILY?
FAMILY? NO. YOU? HUNDRED PERCENT.
MAYBE I WAS JUST, YOU KNOW, FLYING BY... AND I MISSED YOU ALL? AND/OR THE LASAGNA...?
TRY AGAIN.
JOE.
MA, I'M NOT GONNA SIT HERE AND FAKE IT LIKE SHE HASN'T BLOWN US ALL OFF FOR YEARS. EVEN WHEN POPS WAS SICK.
WELL, I'M NOT GOING TO SIT HERE AND FAKE IT LIKE YOU DIDN'T KNOW WHY I WASN'T COMING AROUND--
--OR THAT POPS WAS A GIANT--
SLAM
SO, YEAH...THEY SAY YOU CAN NEVER GO HOME AGAIN, BUT IT'S NOT TRUE. YOU CAN GO ALL YOU WANT...
...YOU JUST CAN'T EXPECT IT TO BE ANY DIFFERENT ONCE YOU GET THERE.

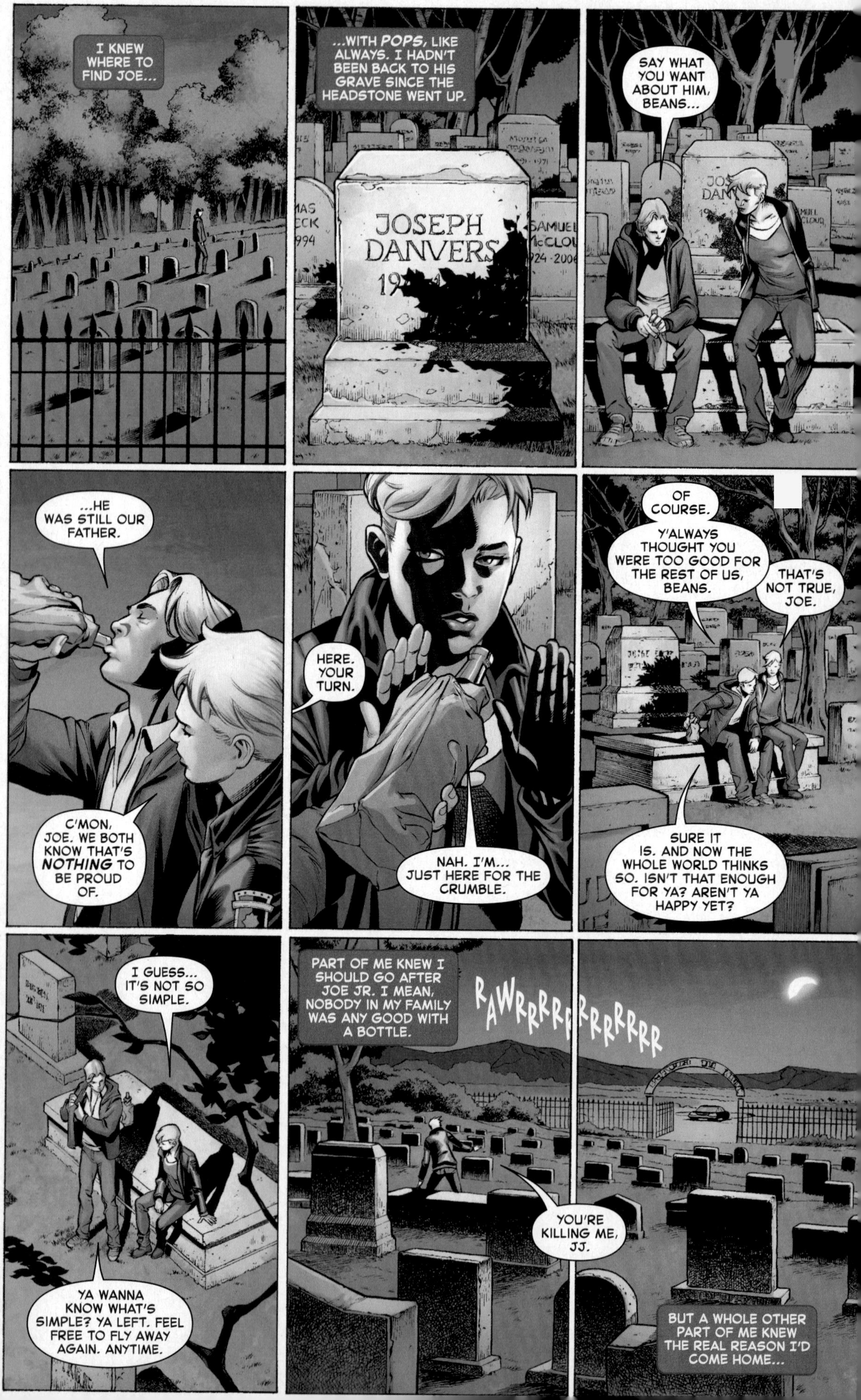
I KNEW WHERE TO FIND JOE...
...WITH POPS, LIKE ALWAYS. I HADN'T BEEN BACK TO HIS GRAVE SINCE THE HEADSTONE WENT UP.
JOSEPH DANVERS
SAY WHAT YOU WANT ABOUT HIM, BEANS...
...HE WAS STILL OUR FATHER.
C'MON, JOE. WE BOTH KNOW THAT'S NOTHING TO BE PROUD OF.
HERE. YOUR TURN.
NAH. I'M... JUST HERE FOR THE CRUMBLE.
OF COURSE.
Y'ALWAYS THOUGHT YOU WERE TOO GOOD FOR THE REST OF US, BEANS.
THAT'S NOT TRUE, JOE.
SURE IT IS. AND NOW THE WHOLE WORLD THINKS SO. ISN'T THAT ENOUGH FOR YA? AREN'T YA HAPPY YET?
I GUESS... IT'S NOT SO SIMPLE.
YA WANNA KNOW WHAT'S SIMPLE? YA LEFT. FEEL FREE TO FLY AWAY AGAIN. ANYTIME.
PART OF ME KNEW I SHOULD GO AFTER JOE JR. I MEAN, NOBODY IN MY FAMILY WAS ANY GOOD WITH A BOTTLE.
RAWRRRRRRRRRRRR
YOU'RE KILLING ME, JJ.
BUT A WHOLE OTHER PART OF ME KNEW THE REAL REASON I'D COME HOME...

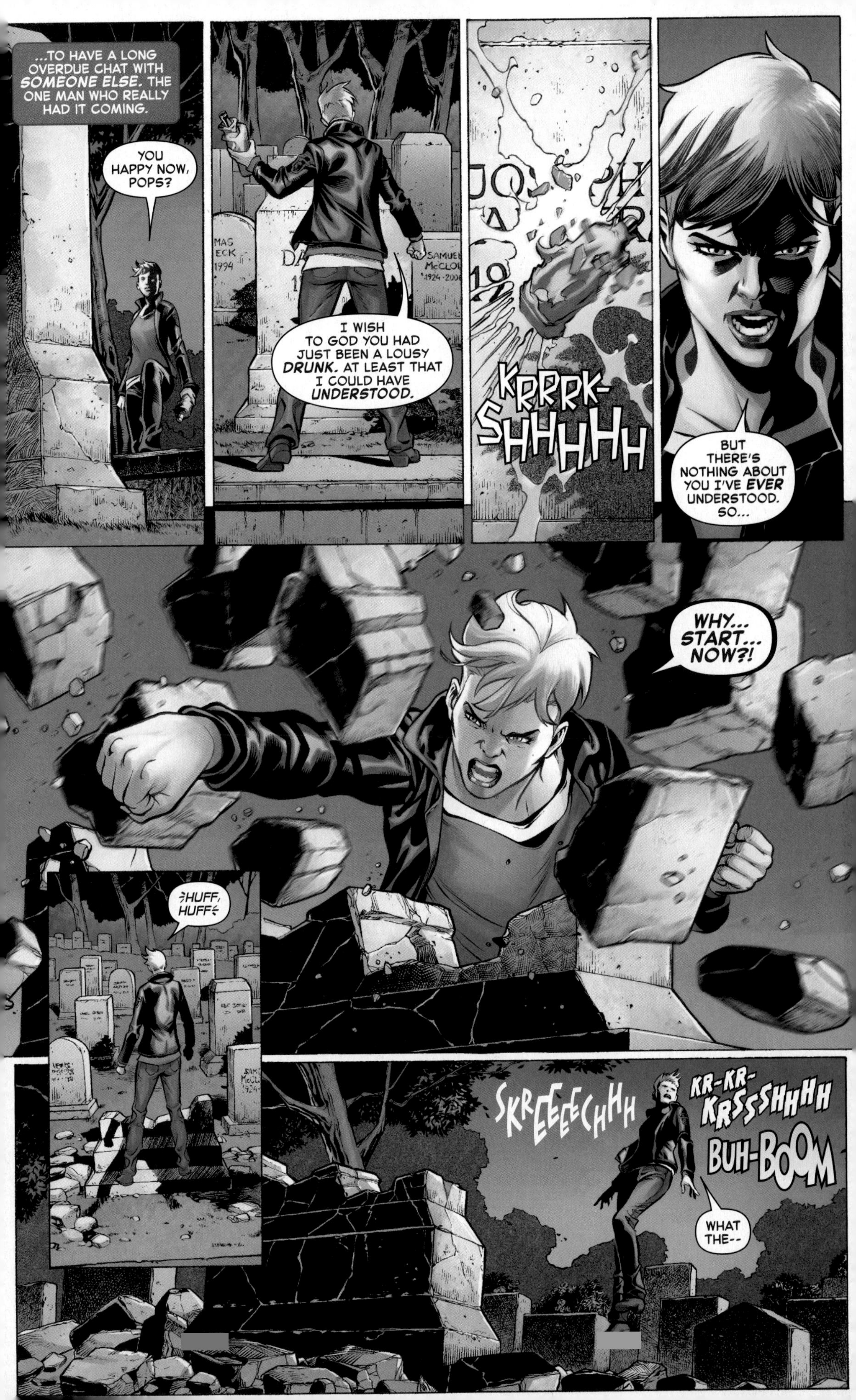
...TO HAVE A LONG OVERDUE CHAT WITH *SOMEONE ELSE.* THE ONE MAN WHO REALLY HAD IT COMING.
YOU HAPPY NOW, POPS?
I WISH TO GOD YOU HAD JUST BEEN A LOUSY *DRUNK.* AT LEAST THAT I COULD HAVE *UNDERSTOOD.*
KRRRK-SHHHHHH
BUT THERE'S NOTHING ABOUT YOU I'VE *EVER* UNDERSTOOD. SO...
WHY... START... NOW?!
HUFF, HUFF
SKREEEECHHH
KR-KR-KRSSHHHH
BUH-BOOM
WHAT THE--

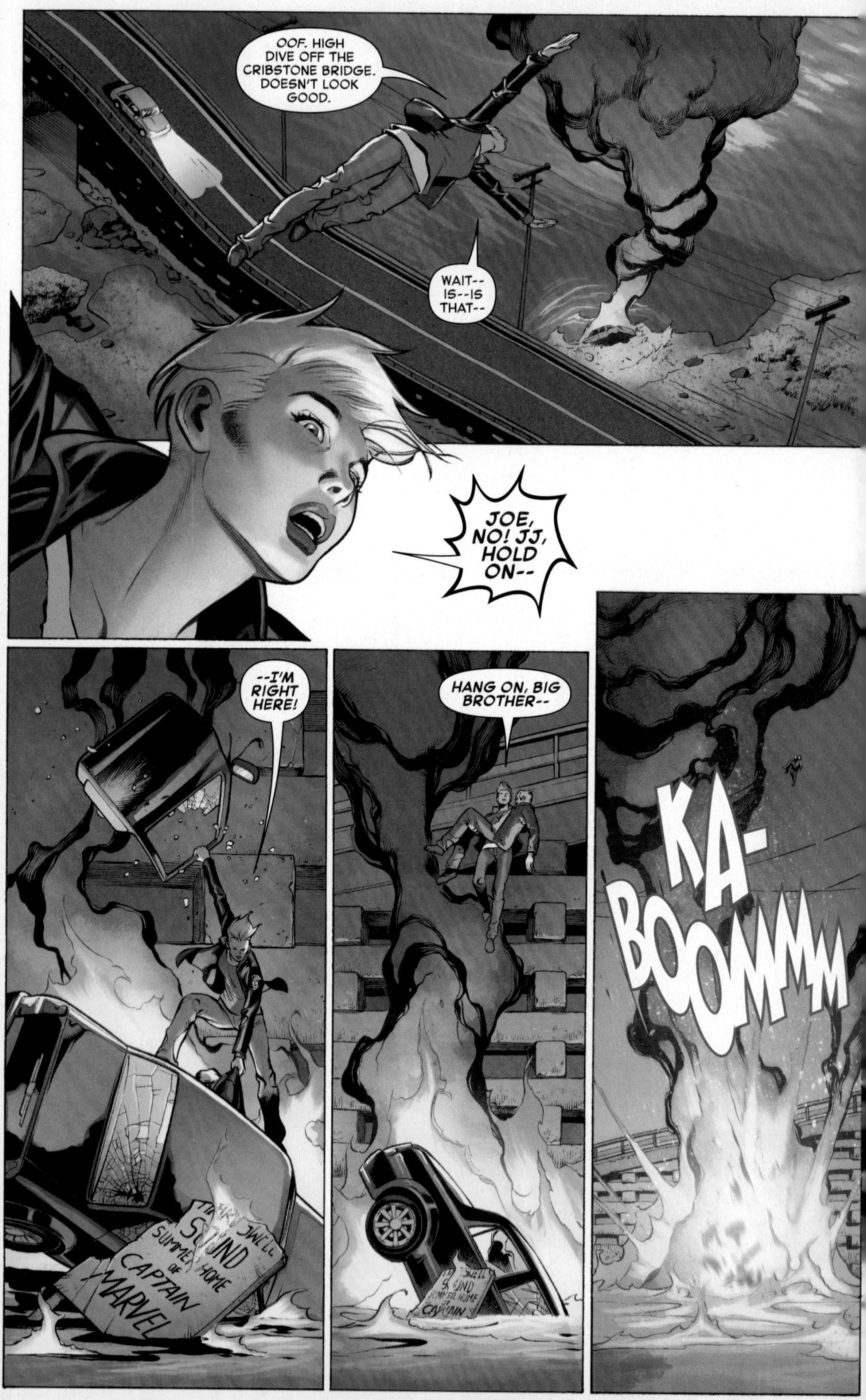
OOF. HIGH DIVE OFF THE CRIBSTONE BRIDGE. DOESN'T LOOK GOOD.
WAIT-- IS--IS THAT--
JOE, NO! JJ, HOLD ON--
--I'M RIGHT HERE!
HANG ON, BIG BROTHER--
KA-BOOMMM
SUMMER HOME OF CAPTAIN MARVEL

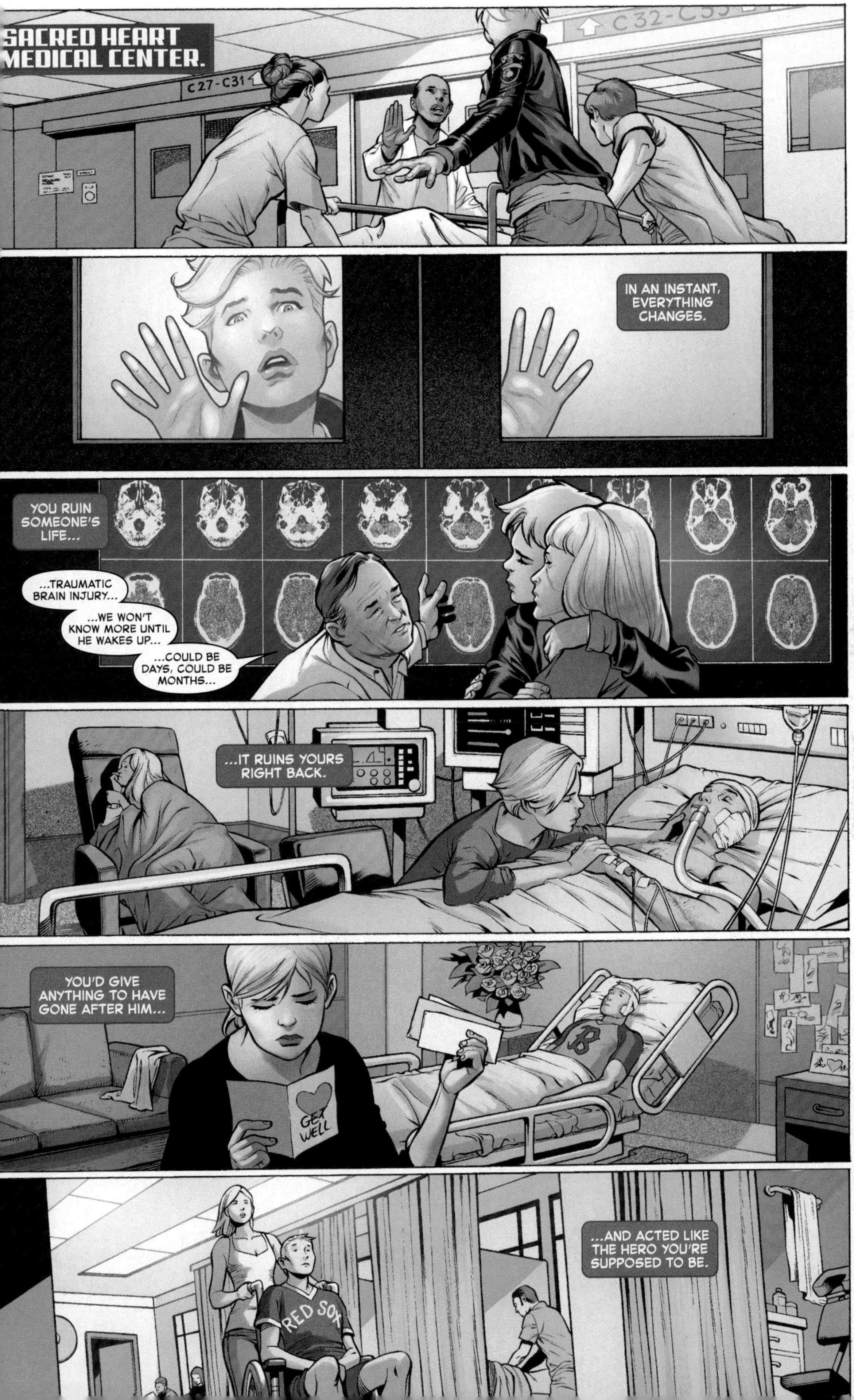
SACRED HEART MEDICAL CENTER.
C27-C31
IN AN INSTANT, EVERYTHING CHANGES.
YOU RUIN SOMEONE'S LIFE...
...TRAUMATIC BRAIN INJURY...
...WE WON'T KNOW MORE UNTIL HE WAKES UP...
...COULD BE DAYS, COULD BE MONTHS...
...IT RUINS YOURS RIGHT BACK.
YOU'D GIVE ANYTHING TO HAVE GONE AFTER HIM...
GET WELL
...AND ACTED LIKE THE HERO YOU'RE SUPPOSED TO BE.
RED SOX

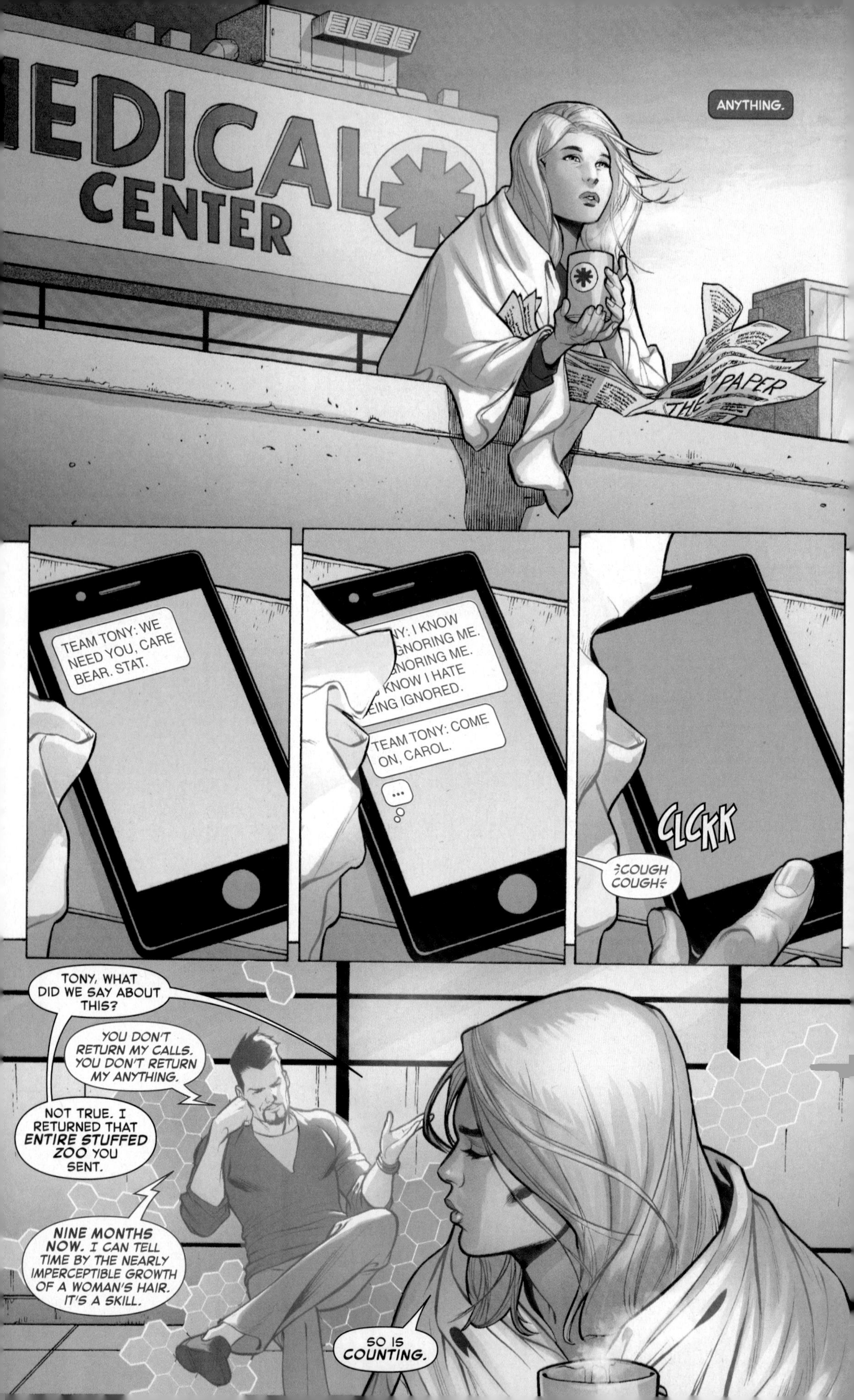
ANYTHING.
MEDICAL CENTER
THE PAPER
TEAM TONY: WE NEED YOU, CARE BEAR. STAT.
NY: I KNOW IGNORING ME. GNORING ME. KNOW I HATE EING IGNORED.
TEAM TONY: COME ON, CAROL.
...
CLCKK
COUGH COUGH
TONY, WHAT DID WE SAY ABOUT THIS?
YOU DON'T RETURN MY CALLS. YOU DON'T RETURN MY ANYTHING.
NOT TRUE. I RETURNED THAT ENTIRE STUFFED ZOO YOU SENT.
NINE MONTHS NOW. I CAN TELL TIME BY THE NEARLY IMPERCEPTIBLE GROWTH OF A WOMAN'S HAIR. IT'S A SKILL.
SO IS COUNTING.

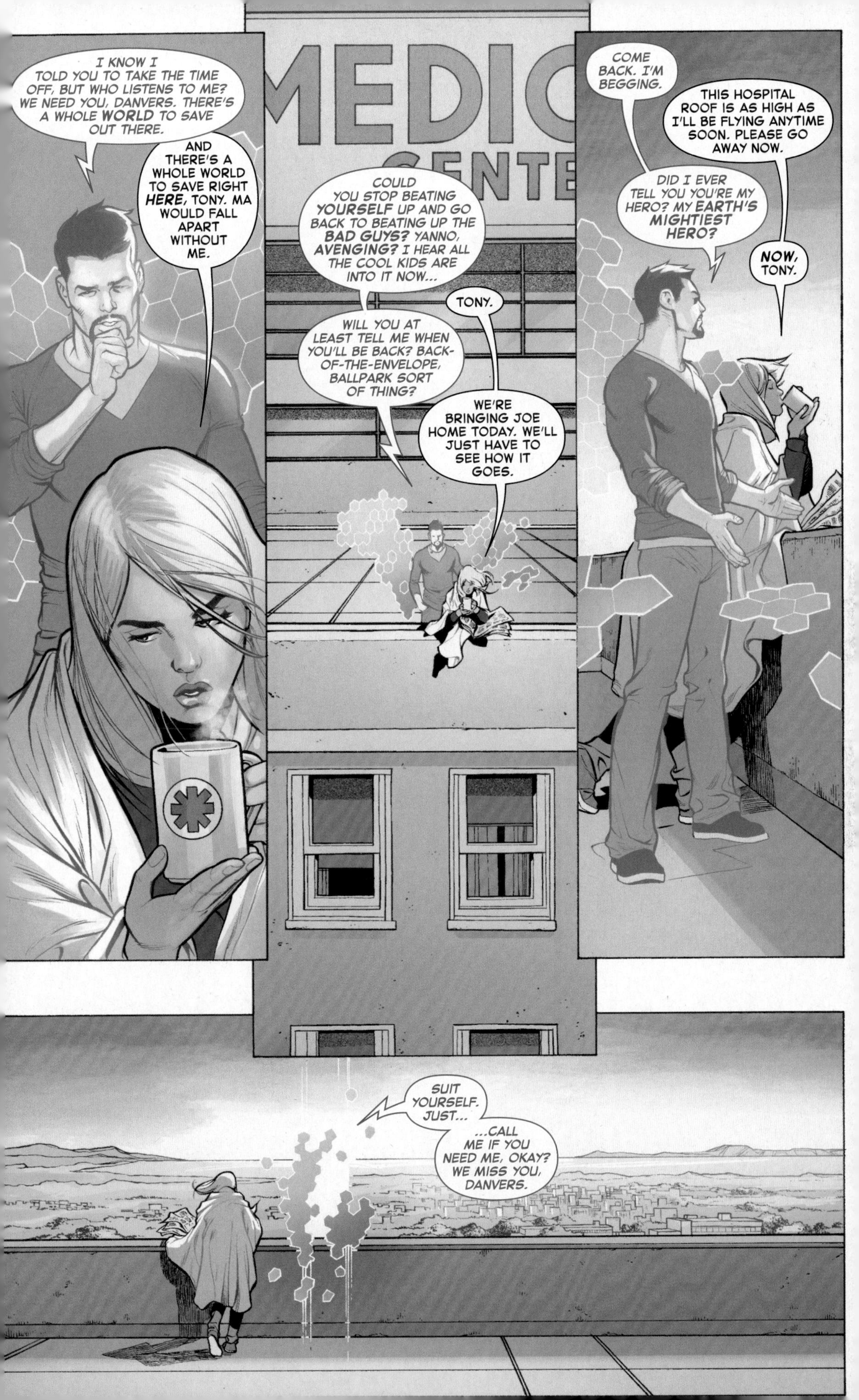

MEDIC
CENTE
I KNOW I TOLD YOU TO TAKE THE TIME OFF, BUT WHO LISTENS TO ME? WE NEED YOU, DANVERS. THERE'S A WHOLE **WORLD** TO SAVE OUT THERE.
AND THERE'S A WHOLE WORLD TO SAVE RIGHT **HERE,** TONY. MA WOULD FALL APART WITHOUT ME.
COULD YOU STOP BEATING **YOURSELF** UP AND GO BACK TO BEATING UP THE **BAD GUYS?** YANNO, **AVENGING?** I HEAR ALL THE COOL KIDS ARE INTO IT NOW...
WILL YOU AT LEAST TELL ME WHEN YOU'LL BE BACK? BACK-OF-THE-ENVELOPE, BALLPARK SORT OF THING?
TONY.
WE'RE BRINGING JOE HOME TODAY. WE'LL JUST HAVE TO SEE HOW IT GOES.
COME BACK. I'M BEGGING.
THIS HOSPITAL ROOF IS AS HIGH AS I'LL BE FLYING ANYTIME SOON. PLEASE GO AWAY NOW.
DID I EVER TELL YOU YOU'RE MY HERO? MY **EARTH'S MIGHTIEST HERO?**
NOW, TONY.
SUIT YOURSELF. JUST...
...CALL ME IF YOU NEED ME, OKAY? WE MISS YOU, DANVERS.

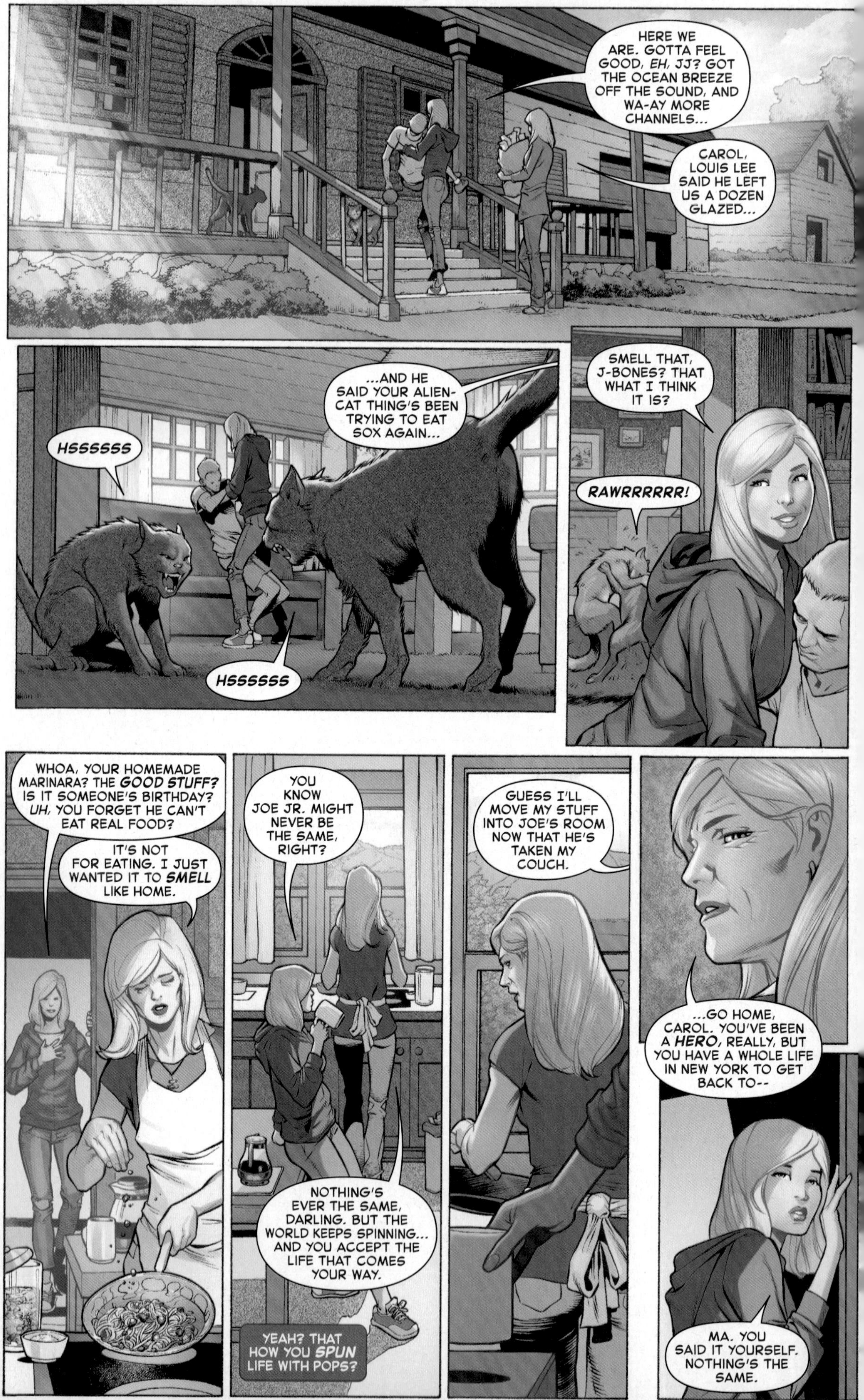
HERE WE ARE. GOTTA FEEL GOOD, EH, JJ? GOT THE OCEAN BREEZE OFF THE SOUND, AND WA-AY MORE CHANNELS...
CAROL, LOUIS LEE SAID HE LEFT US A DOZEN GLAZED...
...AND HE SAID YOUR ALIEN-CAT THING'S BEEN TRYING TO EAT SOX AGAIN...
HSSSSSS
HSSSSSS
SMELL THAT, J-BONES? THAT WHAT I THINK IT IS?
RAWRRRRRR!
WHOA, YOUR HOMEMADE MARINARA? THE GOOD STUFF? IS IT SOMEONE'S BIRTHDAY? UH, YOU FORGET HE CAN'T EAT REAL FOOD?
IT'S NOT FOR EATING. I JUST WANTED IT TO SMELL LIKE HOME.
YOU KNOW JOE JR. MIGHT NEVER BE THE SAME, RIGHT?
NOTHING'S EVER THE SAME, DARLING. BUT THE WORLD KEEPS SPINNING... AND YOU ACCEPT THE LIFE THAT COMES YOUR WAY.
YEAH? THAT HOW YOU SPUN LIFE WITH POPS?
GUESS I'LL MOVE MY STUFF INTO JOE'S ROOM NOW THAT HE'S TAKEN MY COUCH.
...GO HOME, CAROL. YOU'VE BEEN A HERO, REALLY, BUT YOU HAVE A WHOLE LIFE IN NEW YORK TO GET BACK TO--
MA. YOU SAID IT YOURSELF. NOTHING'S THE SAME.

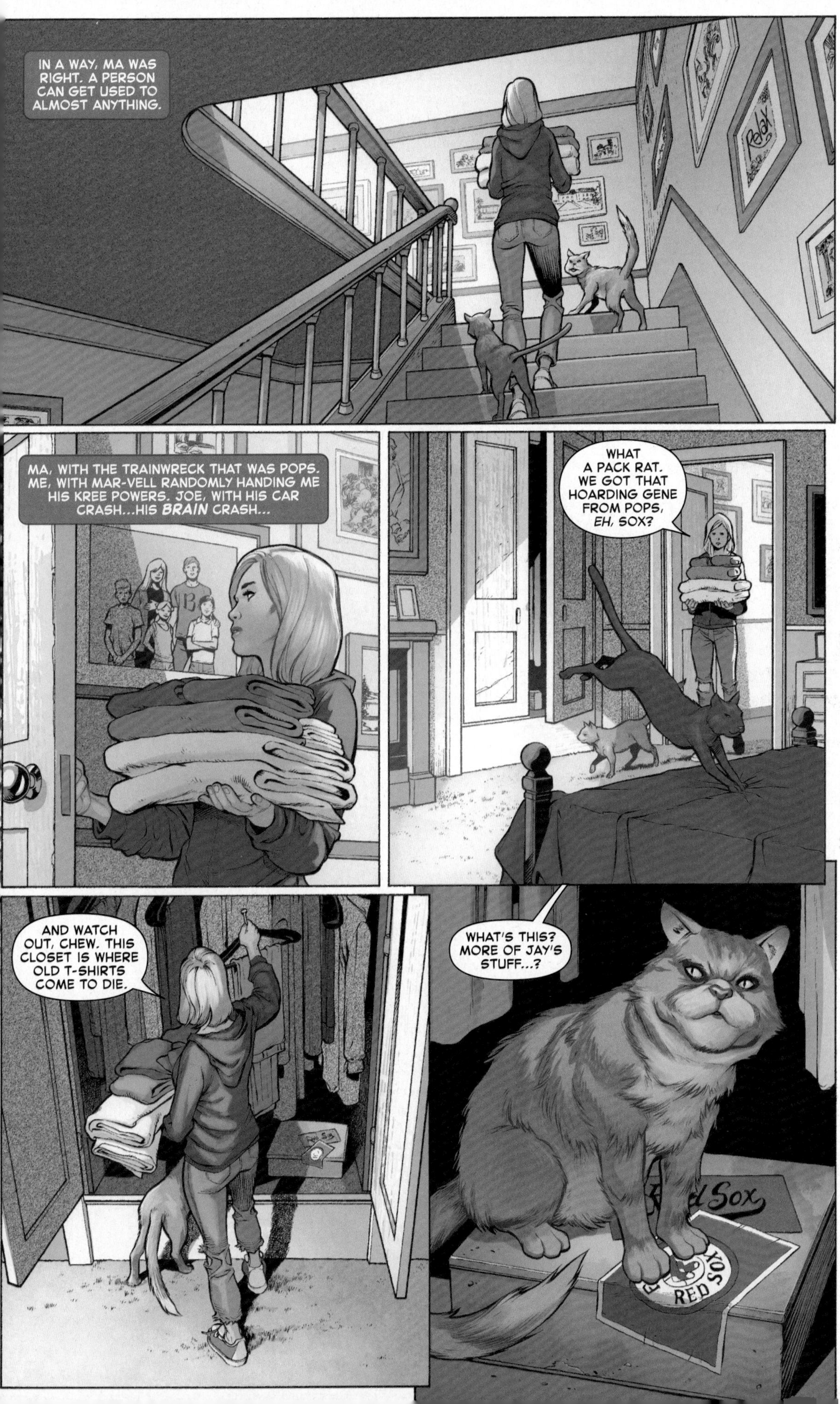
IN A WAY, MA WAS RIGHT. A PERSON CAN GET USED TO ALMOST ANYTHING.
Relax
MA, WITH THE TRAINWRECK THAT WAS POPS. ME, WITH MAR-VELL RANDOMLY HANDING ME HIS KREE POWERS. JOE, WITH HIS CAR CRASH...HIS BRAIN CRASH...
WHAT A PACK RAT. WE GOT THAT HOARDING GENE FROM POPS, EH, SOX?
AND WATCH OUT, CHEW. THIS CLOSET IS WHERE OLD T-SHIRTS COME TO DIE.
WHAT'S THIS? MORE OF JAY'S STUFF...?
Red Sox
RED SOX

THIS LOOKS TOO OLD TO BE JJ'S OR STEVIE'S OR MINE.

MA MUST HAVE BEEN CLEANING OUT THE ATTIC.

WHAT'S...

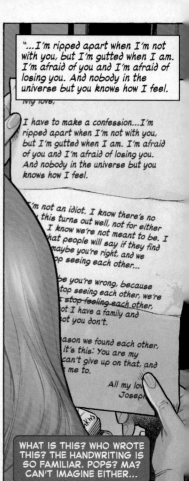

"...I'm ripped apart when I'm not with you, but I'm gutted when I am. I'm afraid of you and I'm afraid of losing you. And nobody in the universe but you knows how I feel.

My love,

I have to make a confession...I'm ripped apart when I'm not with you, but I'm gutted when I am. I'm afraid of you and I'm afraid of losing you. And nobody in the universe but you knows how I feel.

I'm not an idiot. I know there's no ___ this turns out well, not for either ___ I know we're not meant to be. I ___ hat people will say if they find ___ maybe you're right, and we ___ op seeing each other...

___ be you're wrong, because ___ top seeing each other, we're ___ stop feeling each other, ___ ot I have a family and ___ ot you don't.

___ ason we found each other, ___ it's this: You are my ___ can't give up on that, and ___ me to.

All my lov___
Joseph

WHAT IS THIS? WHO WROTE THIS? THE HANDWRITING IS SO FAMILIAR. POPS? MA? CAN'T IMAGINE EITHER...

"...I'm not an idiot. I know there's no way this turns out well, not for either of us. I know we're not meant to be. I know what people will say if they find out. So maybe you're right, and we should stop seeing each other..."

"...but maybe you're wrong, because even if we stop seeing each other, we're never gonna stop feeling each other, whether or not I have a family and whether or not you don't.

"There's a reason we found each other, my love, and it's this: You are my soulmate. I can't give up on that, and you can't ask me to.

"All my love...

"...Joseph."

HOLY--POPS WAS HAVING AN AFFAIR?

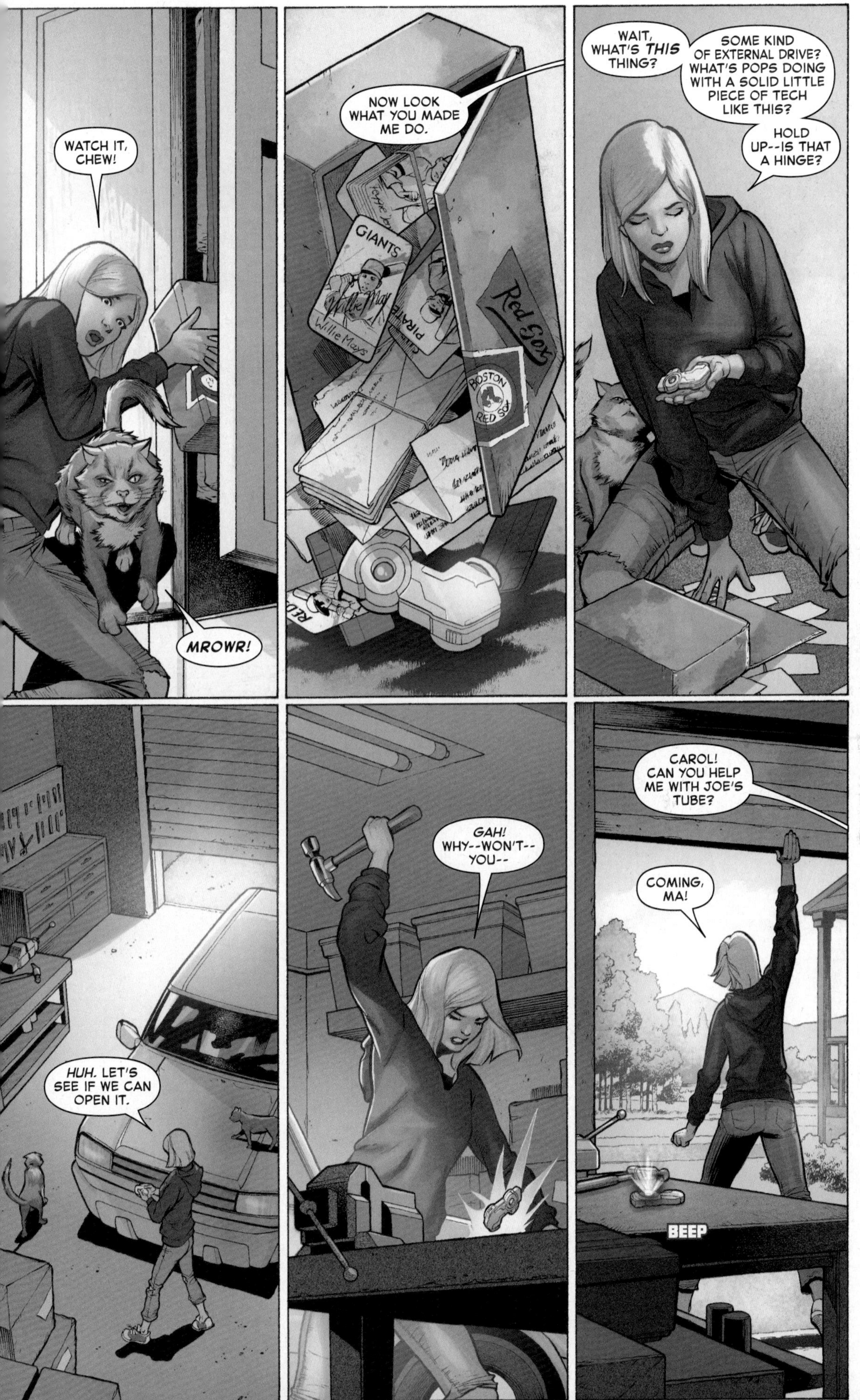
WATCH IT, CHEW!
MROWR!
NOW LOOK WHAT YOU MADE ME DO.
GIANTS
Willie Mays
PIRATES
Red Sox
BOSTON RED SOX
WAIT, WHAT'S *THIS* THING?
SOME KIND OF EXTERNAL DRIVE? WHAT'S POPS DOING WITH A SOLID LITTLE PIECE OF TECH LIKE THIS?
HOLD UP--IS THAT A HINGE?
HUH. LET'S SEE IF WE CAN OPEN IT.
GAH! WHY--WON'T-- YOU--
CAROL! CAN YOU HELP ME WITH JOE'S TUBE?
COMING, MA!
BEEP

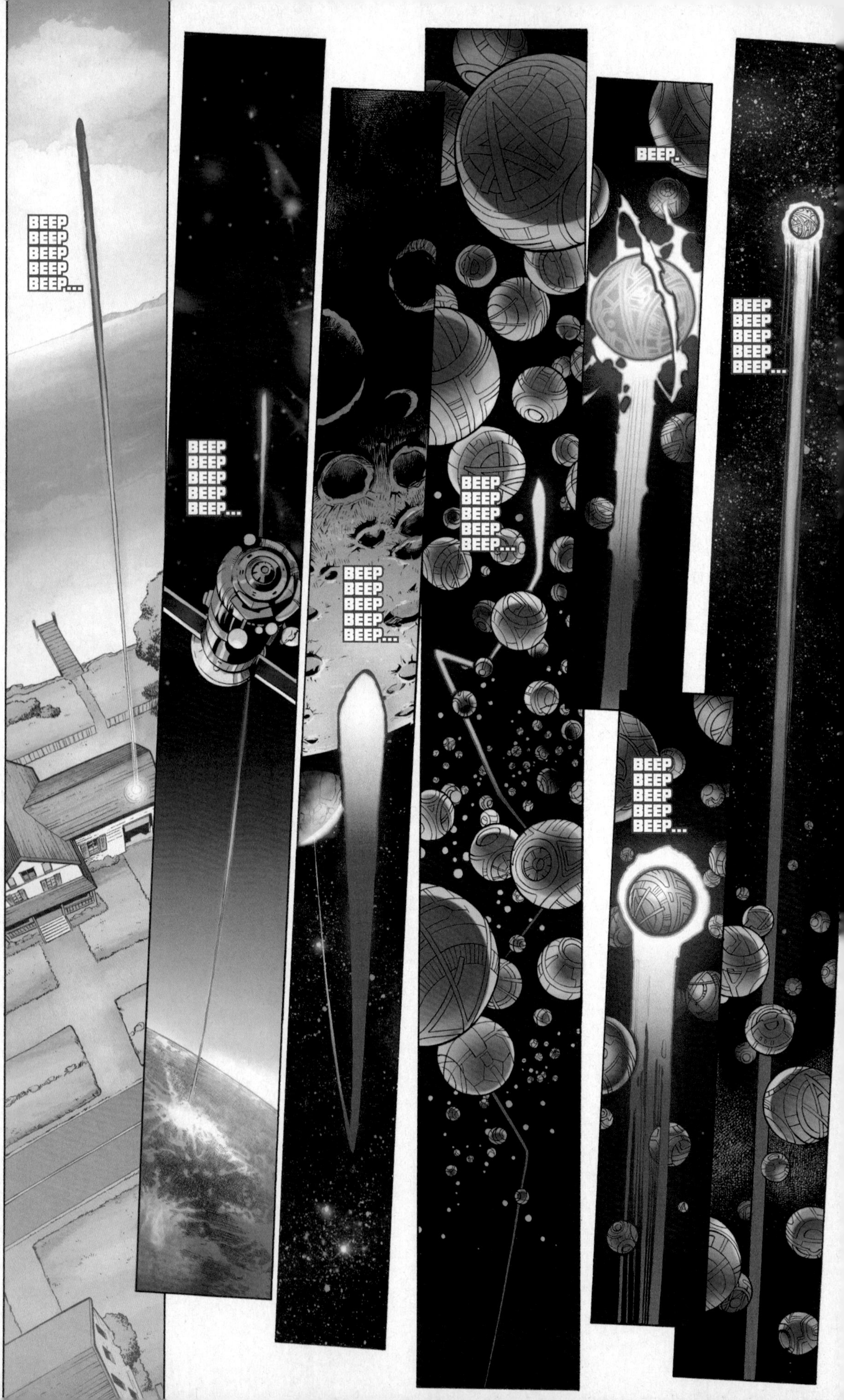
BEEP BEEP BEEP BEEP BEEP...
BEEP BEEP BEEP BEEP BEEP...
BEEP BEEP BEEP BEEP BEEP...
BEEP BEEP BEEP BEEP BEEP...
BEEP.
BEEP BEEP BEEP BEEP BEEP...
BEEP BEEP BEEP BEEP BEEP...

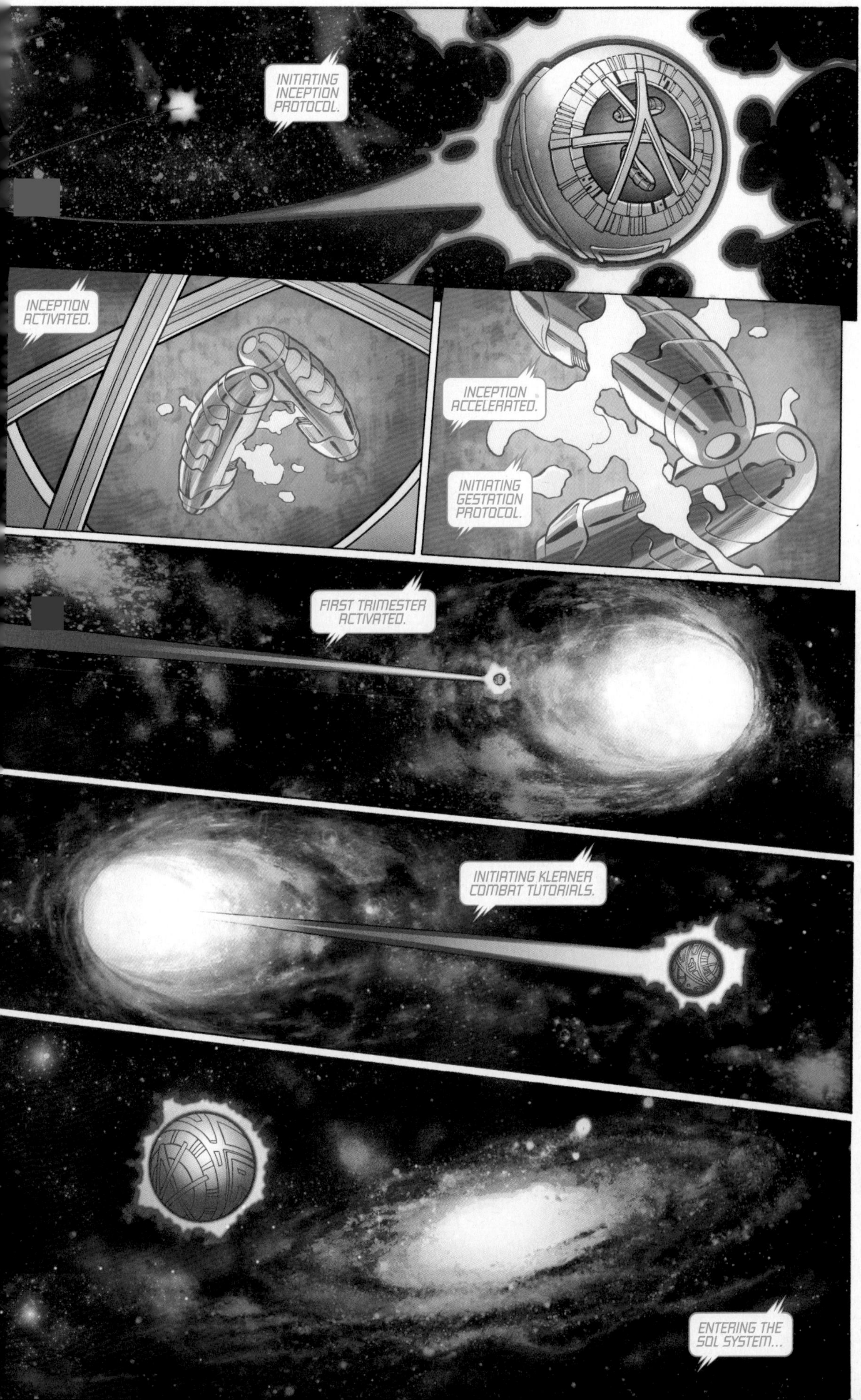
INITIATING INCEPTION PROTOCOL.
INCEPTION ACTIVATED.
INCEPTION ACCELERATED.
INITIATING GESTATION PROTOCOL.
FIRST TRIMESTER ACTIVATED.
INITIATING KLEANER COMBAT TUTORIALS.
ENTERING THE SOL SYSTEM...

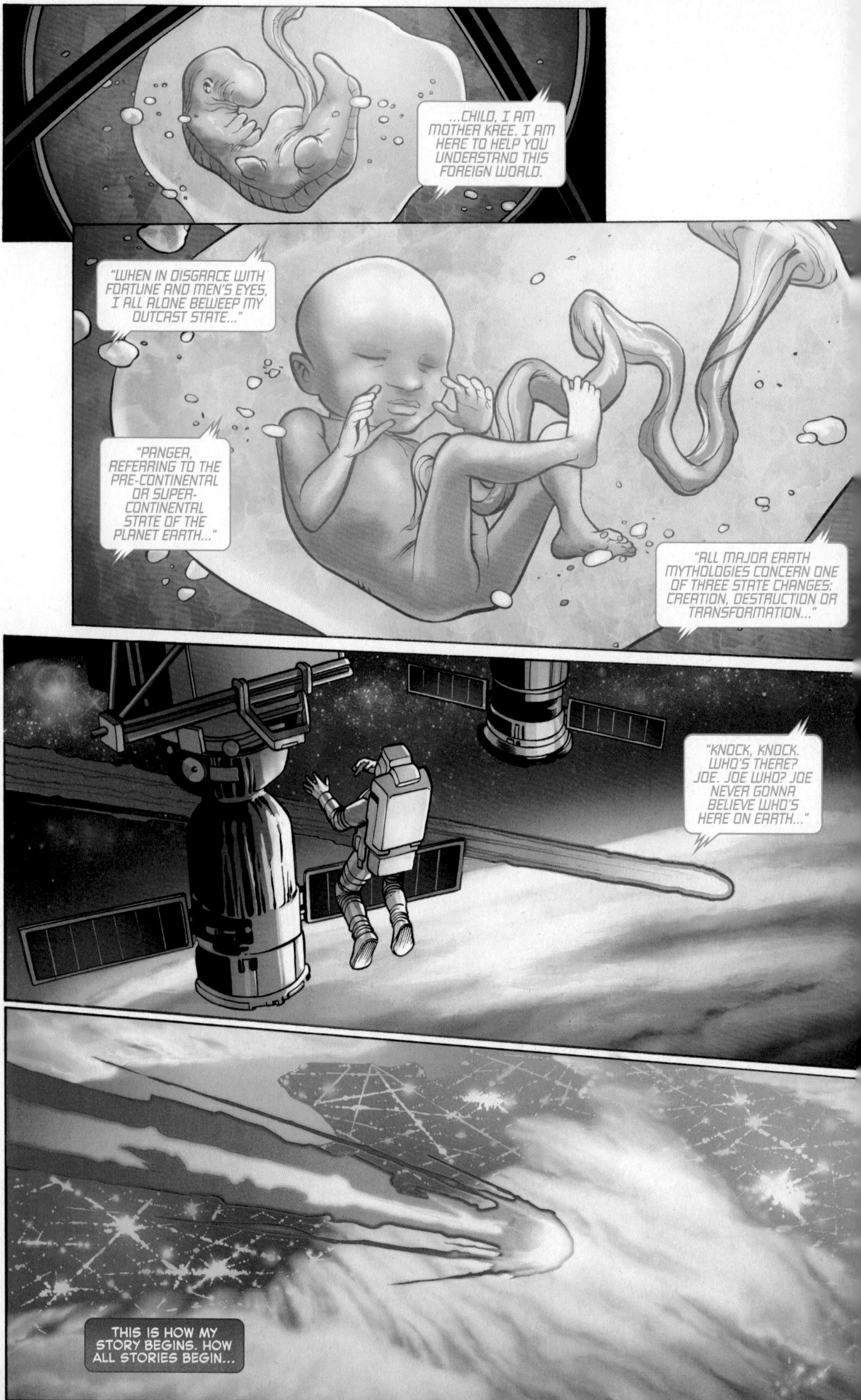
...CHILD, I AM MOTHER KREE. I AM HERE TO HELP YOU UNDERSTAND THIS FOREIGN WORLD.
"WHEN IN DISGRACE WITH FORTUNE AND MEN'S EYES, I ALL ALONE BEWEEP MY OUTCAST STATE..."
"PANGEA, REFERRING TO THE PRE-CONTINENTAL OR SUPER-CONTINENTAL STATE OF THE PLANET EARTH..."
"ALL MAJOR EARTH MYTHOLOGIES CONCERN ONE OF THREE STATE CHANGES: CREATION, DESTRUCTION OR TRANSFORMATION..."
"KNOCK, KNOCK. WHO'S THERE? JOE. JOE WHO? JOE NEVER GONNA BELIEVE WHO'S HERE ON EARTH..."
THIS IS HOW MY STORY BEGINS. HOW ALL STORIES BEGIN...

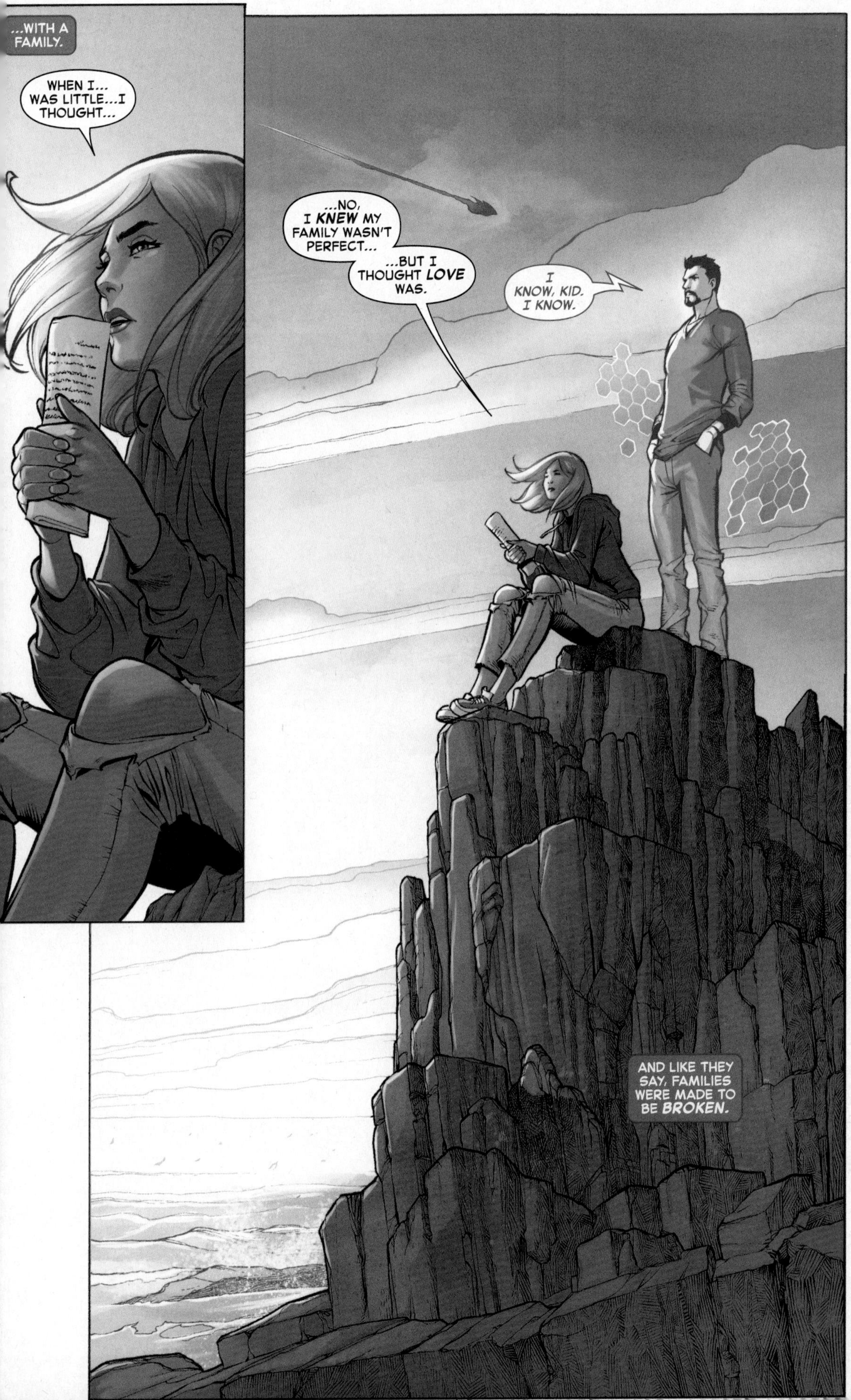
...WITH A FAMILY.
WHEN I... WAS LITTLE...I THOUGHT...
...NO, I KNEW MY FAMILY WASN'T PERFECT...
...BUT I THOUGHT LOVE WAS.
I KNOW, KID. I KNOW.
AND LIKE THEY SAY, FAMILIES WERE MADE TO BE BROKEN.

THE LIFE OF CAPTAIN MARVEL #2
"HUNTED"

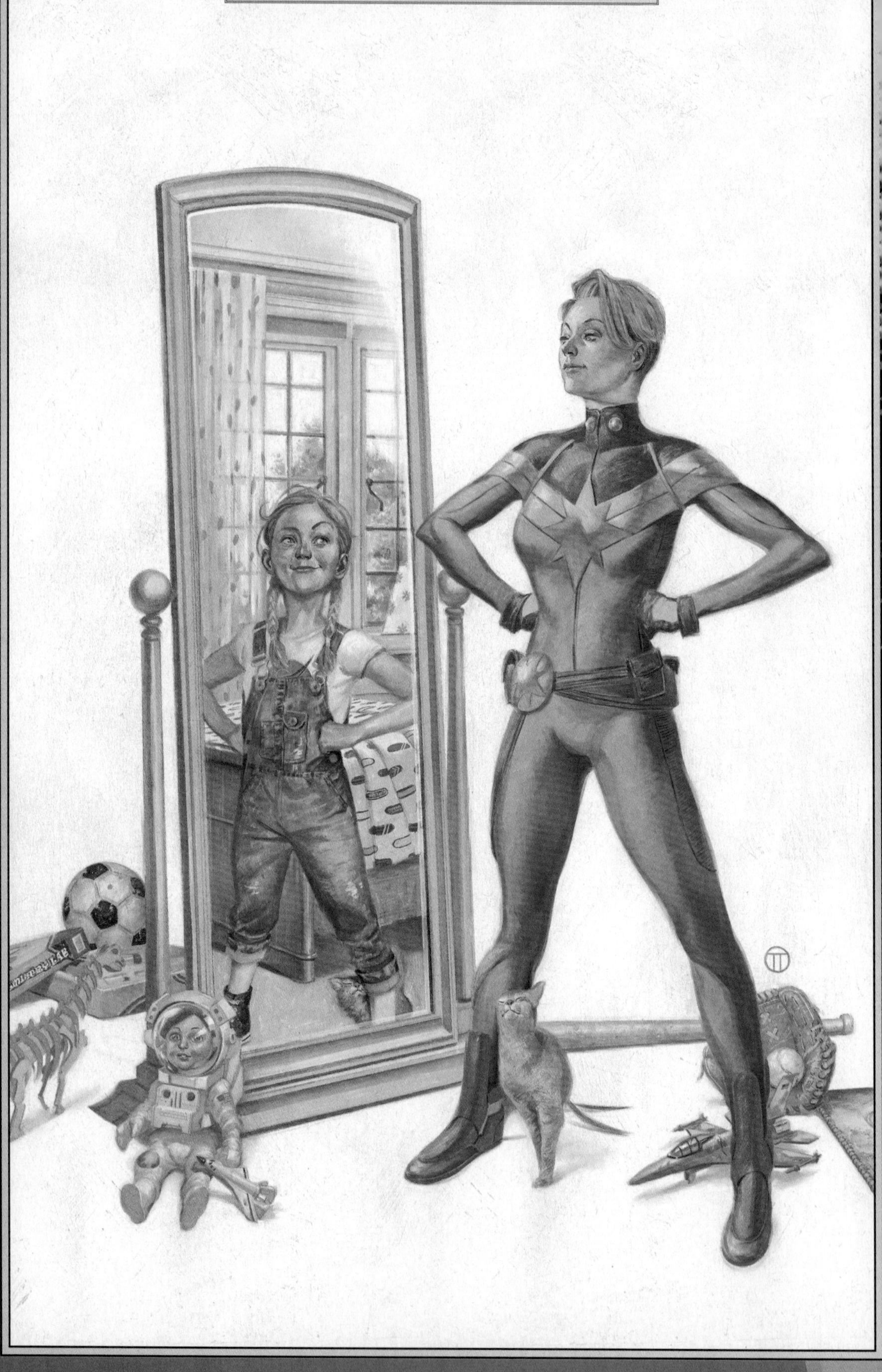

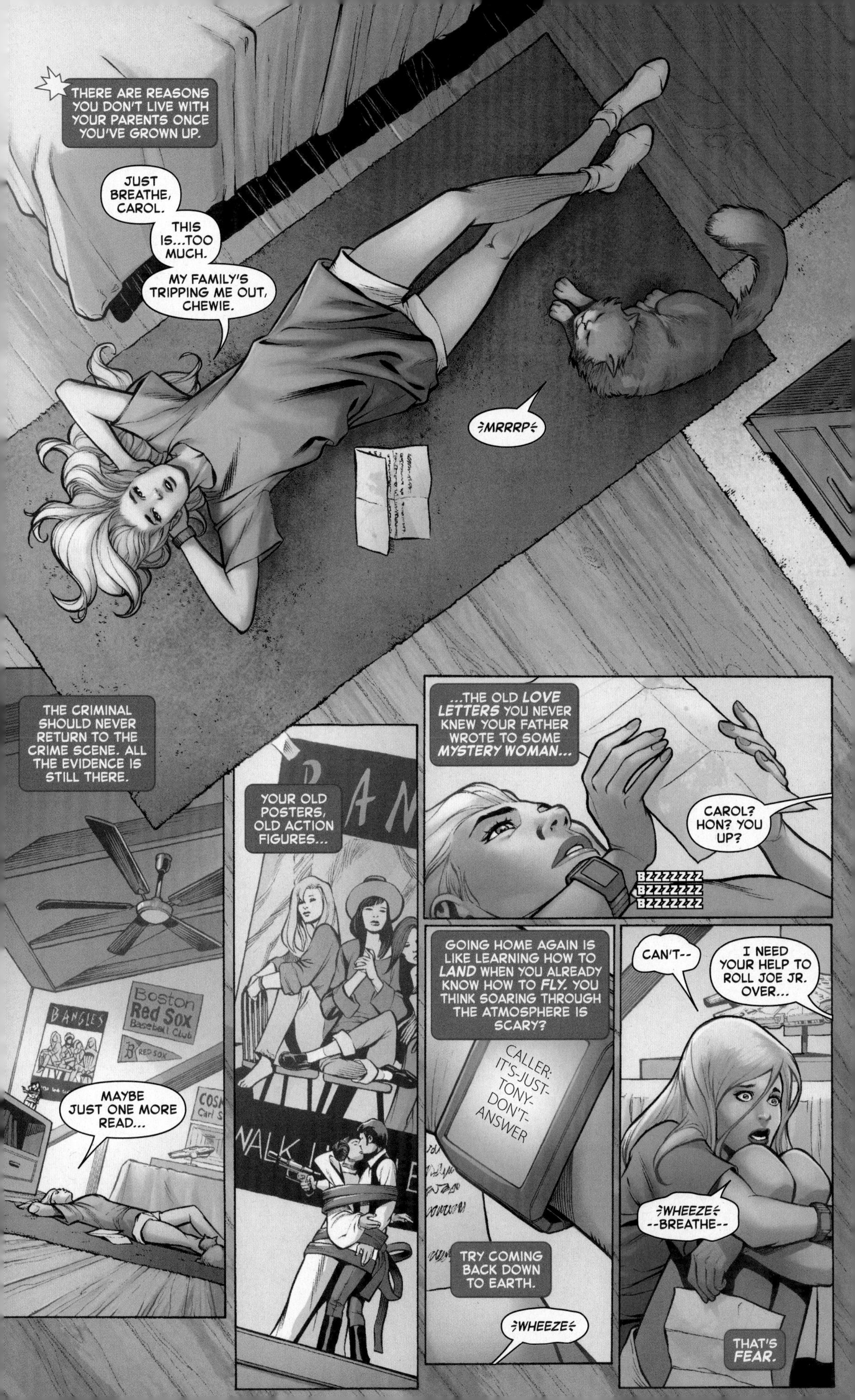
THERE ARE REASONS YOU DON'T LIVE WITH YOUR PARENTS ONCE YOU'VE GROWN UP.
JUST BREATHE, CAROL.
THIS IS...TOO MUCH.
MY FAMILY'S TRIPPING ME OUT, CHEWIE.
MRRRP
THE CRIMINAL SHOULD NEVER RETURN TO THE CRIME SCENE. ALL THE EVIDENCE IS STILL THERE.
Boston Red Sox Baseball Club
BANGLES
RED SOX
MAYBE JUST ONE MORE READ...
YOUR OLD POSTERS, OLD ACTION FIGURES...
...THE OLD LOVE LETTERS YOU NEVER KNEW YOUR FATHER WROTE TO SOME MYSTERY WOMAN...
CAROL? HON? YOU UP?
BZZZZZZZ
BZZZZZZZ
BZZZZZZZ
GOING HOME AGAIN IS LIKE LEARNING HOW TO LAND WHEN YOU ALREADY KNOW HOW TO FLY. YOU THINK SOARING THROUGH THE ATMOSPHERE IS SCARY?
CALLER: IT'S-JUST-TONY-DON'T-ANSWER
TRY COMING BACK DOWN TO EARTH.
WHEEZE
CAN'T--
I NEED YOUR HELP TO ROLL JOE JR. OVER...
WHEEZE --BREATHE--
THAT'S FEAR.

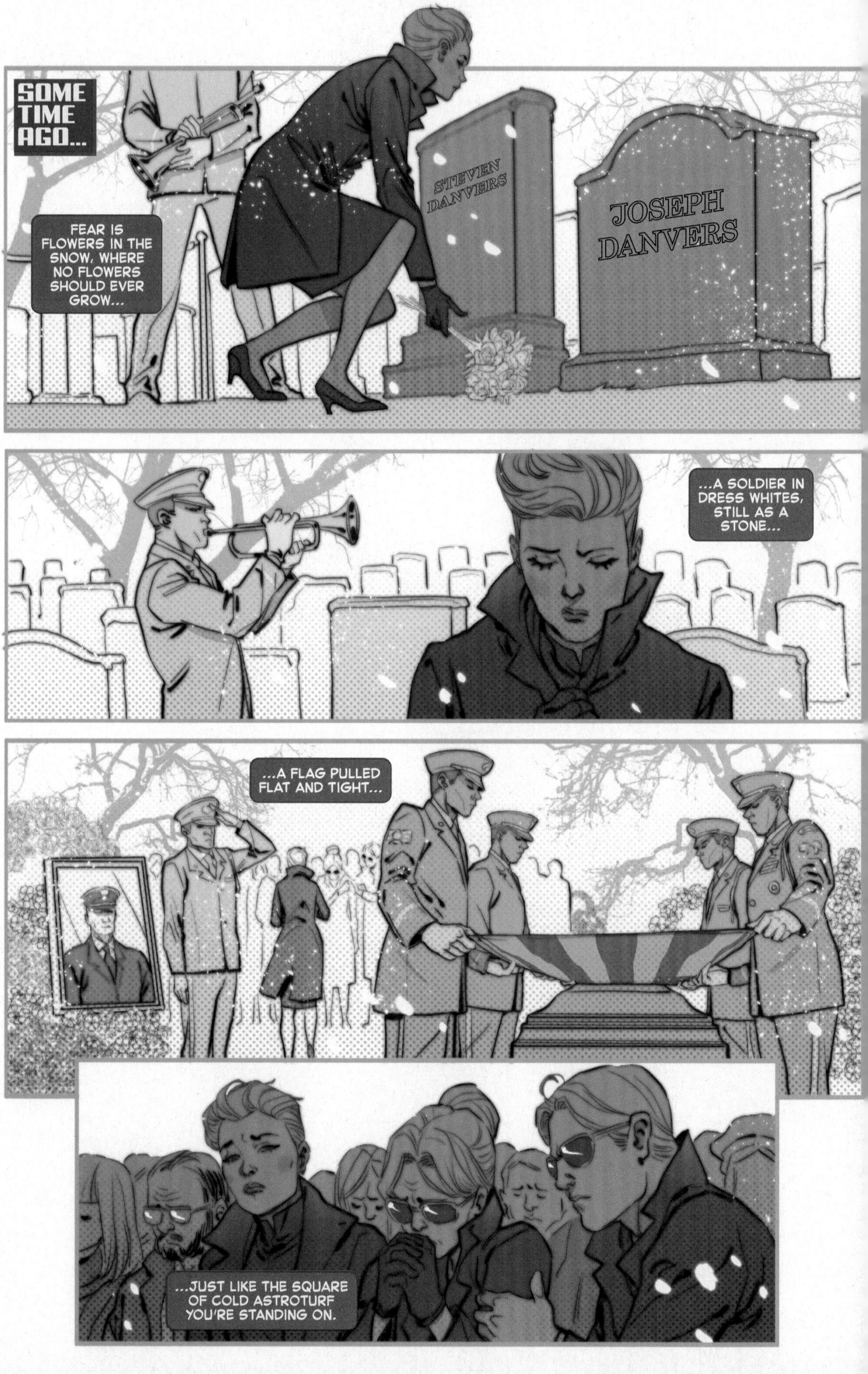
SOME TIME AGO...
STEVEN DANVERS
JOSEPH DANVERS
FEAR IS FLOWERS IN THE SNOW, WHERE NO FLOWERS SHOULD EVER GROW...
...A SOLDIER IN DRESS WHITES, STILL AS A STONE...
...A FLAG PULLED FLAT AND TIGHT...
...JUST LIKE THE SQUARE OF COLD ASTROTURF YOU'RE STANDING ON.

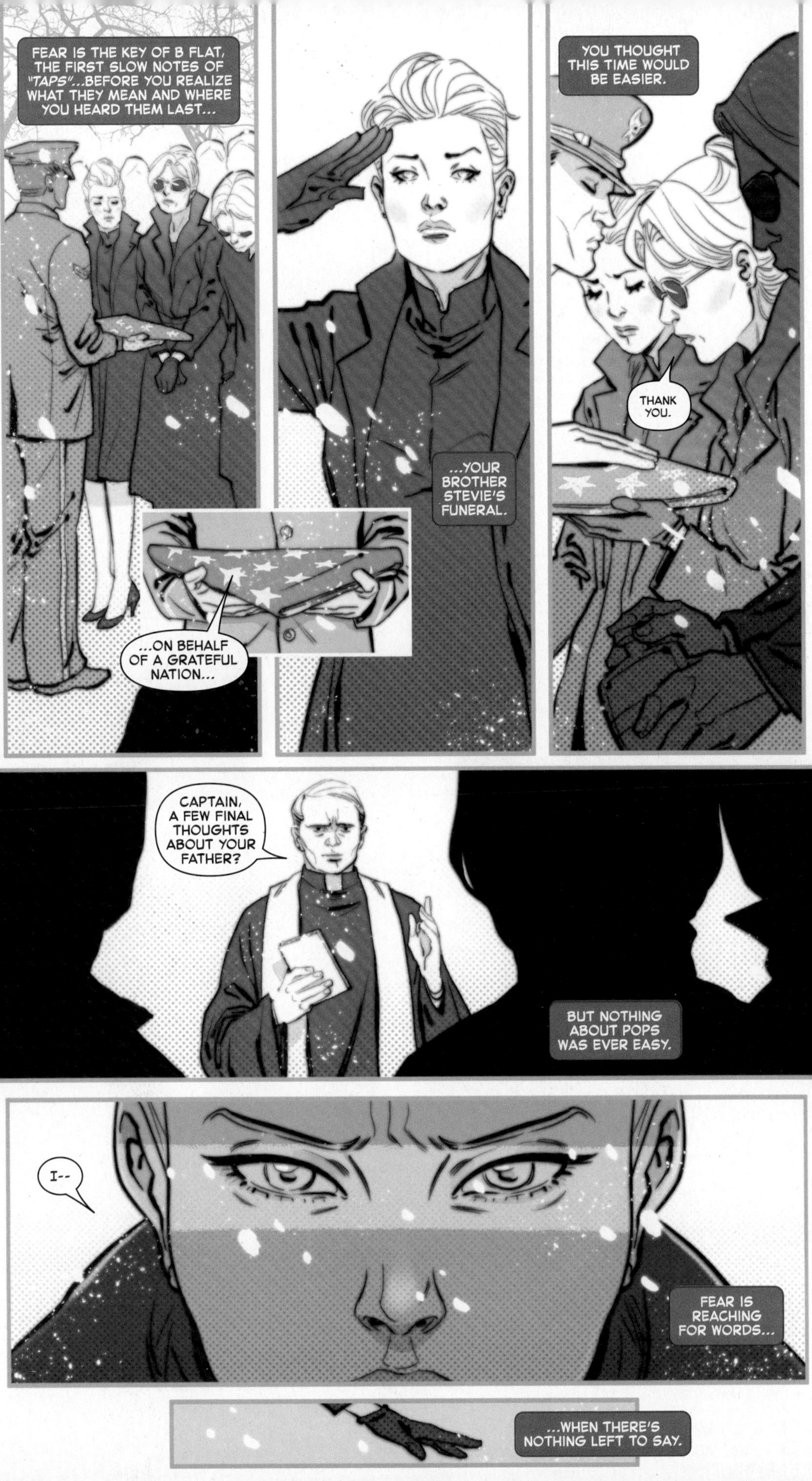
FEAR IS THE KEY OF B FLAT, THE FIRST SLOW NOTES OF "TAPS"...BEFORE YOU REALIZE WHAT THEY MEAN AND WHERE YOU HEARD THEM LAST...
...ON BEHALF OF A GRATEFUL NATION...
...YOUR BROTHER STEVIE'S FUNERAL.
YOU THOUGHT THIS TIME WOULD BE EASIER.
THANK YOU.
CAPTAIN, A FEW FINAL THOUGHTS ABOUT YOUR FATHER?
BUT NOTHING ABOUT POPS WAS EVER EASY.
I--
FEAR IS REACHING FOR WORDS...
...WHEN THERE'S NOTHING LEFT TO SAY.

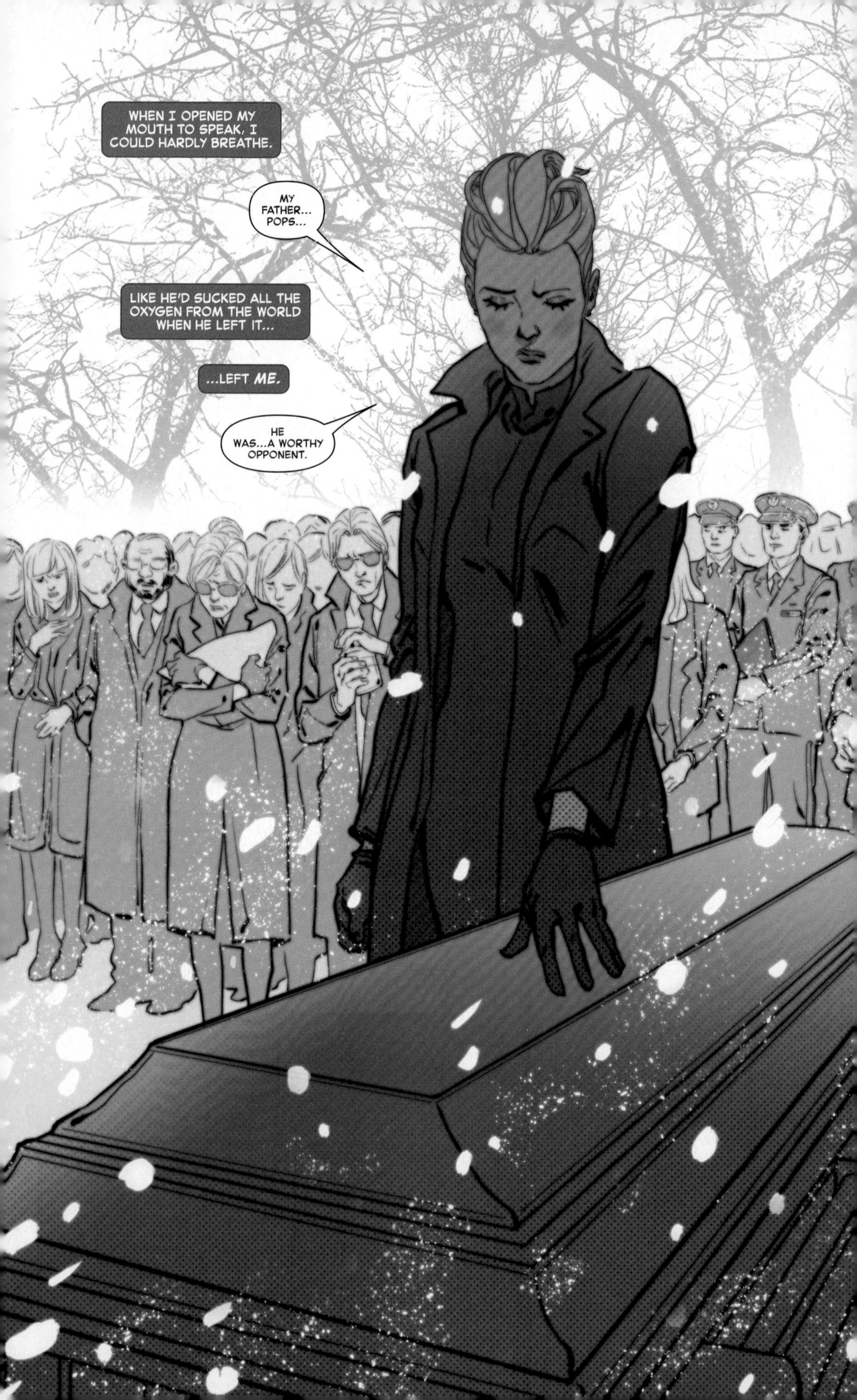
WHEN I OPENED MY MOUTH TO SPEAK, I COULD HARDLY BREATHE.
MY FATHER... POPS...
LIKE HE'D SUCKED ALL THE OXYGEN FROM THE WORLD WHEN HE LEFT IT...
...LEFT *ME.*
HE WAS...A WORTHY OPPONENT.

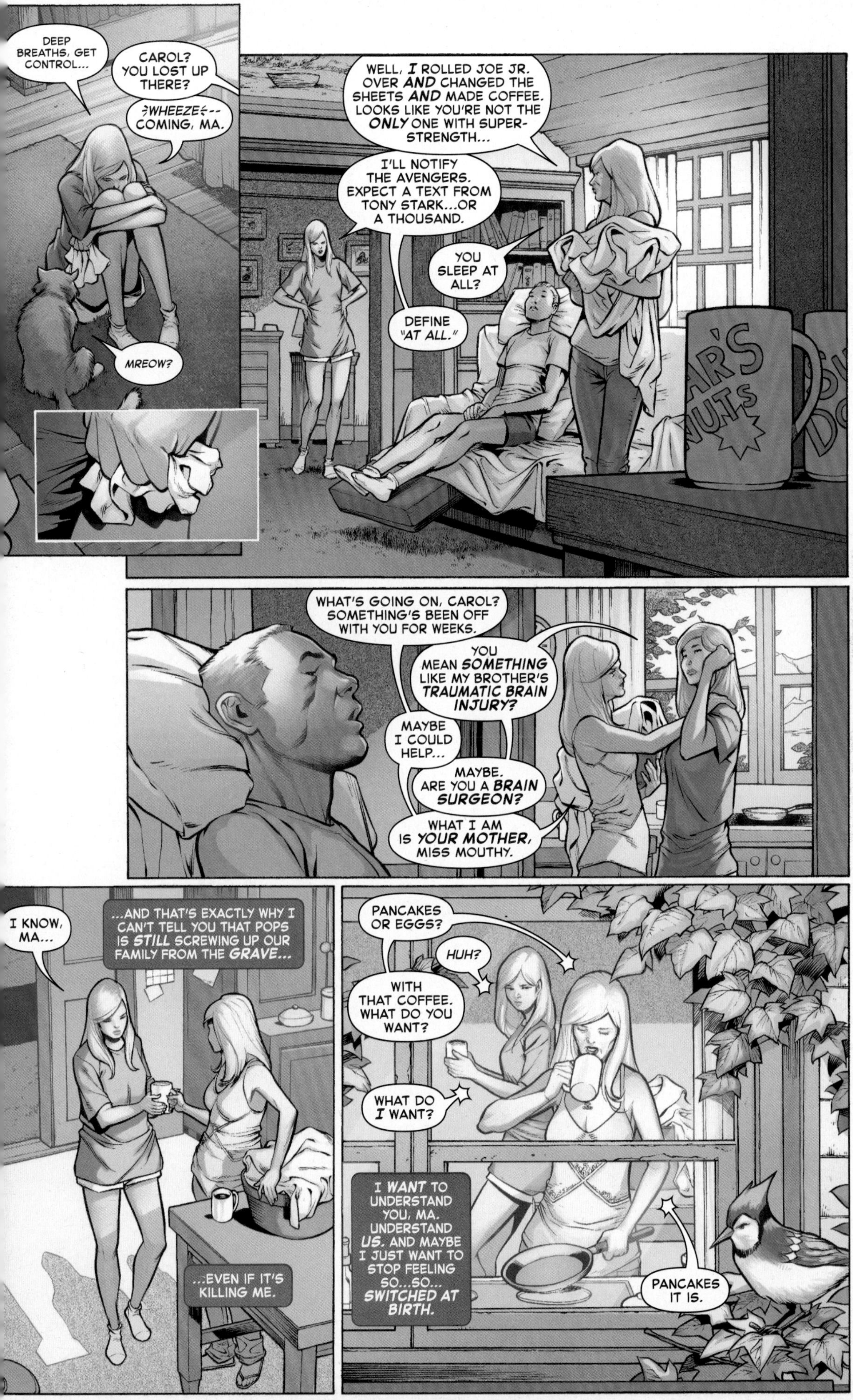
DEEP BREATHS, GET CONTROL...
CAROL? YOU LOST UP THERE?
⋟WHEEZE⋞-- COMING, MA.
MREOW?
WELL, I ROLLED JOE JR. OVER AND CHANGED THE SHEETS AND MADE COFFEE. LOOKS LIKE YOU'RE NOT THE ONLY ONE WITH SUPER-STRENGTH...
I'LL NOTIFY THE AVENGERS. EXPECT A TEXT FROM TONY STARK...OR A THOUSAND.
YOU SLEEP AT ALL?
DEFINE "AT ALL."
WHAT'S GOING ON, CAROL? SOMETHING'S BEEN OFF WITH YOU FOR WEEKS.
YOU MEAN SOMETHING LIKE MY BROTHER'S TRAUMATIC BRAIN INJURY?
MAYBE I COULD HELP...
MAYBE. ARE YOU A BRAIN SURGEON?
WHAT I AM IS YOUR MOTHER, MISS MOUTHY.
I KNOW, MA...
...AND THAT'S EXACTLY WHY I CAN'T TELL YOU THAT POPS IS STILL SCREWING UP OUR FAMILY FROM THE GRAVE...
...EVEN IF IT'S KILLING ME.
PANCAKES OR EGGS?
HUH?
WITH THAT COFFEE. WHAT DO YOU WANT?
WHAT DO I WANT?
I WANT TO UNDERSTAND YOU, MA. UNDERSTAND US. AND MAYBE I JUST WANT TO STOP FEELING SO...SO... SWITCHED AT BIRTH.
PANCAKES IT IS.

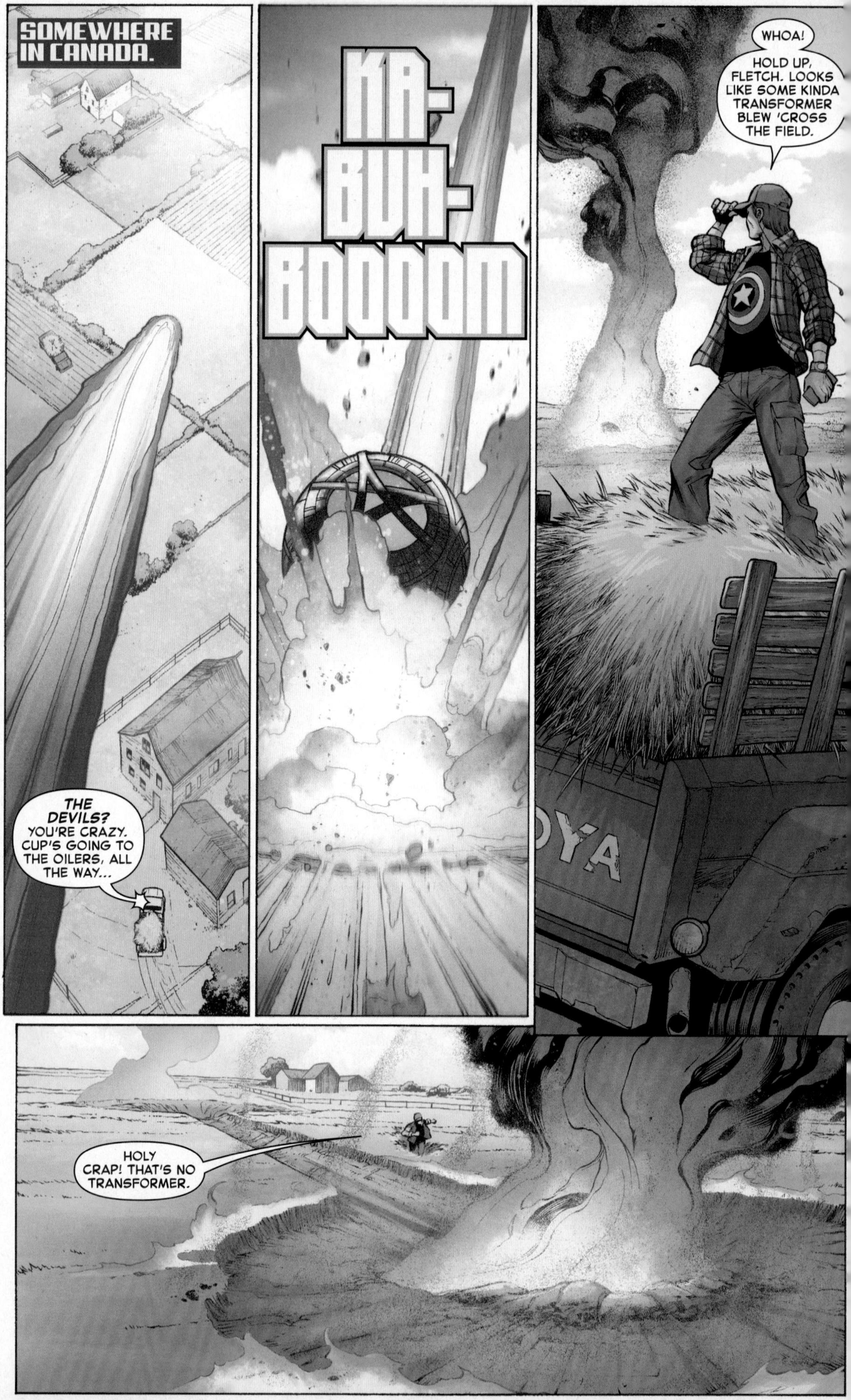
SOMEWHERE IN CANADA.
THE DEVILS? YOU'RE CRAZY. CUP'S GOING TO THE OILERS, ALL THE WAY...
KA-BUH-BOOOOM
WHOA!
HOLD UP, FLETCH. LOOKS LIKE SOME KINDA TRANSFORMER BLEW 'CROSS THE FIELD.
OYA
HOLY CRAP! THAT'S NO TRANSFORMER.

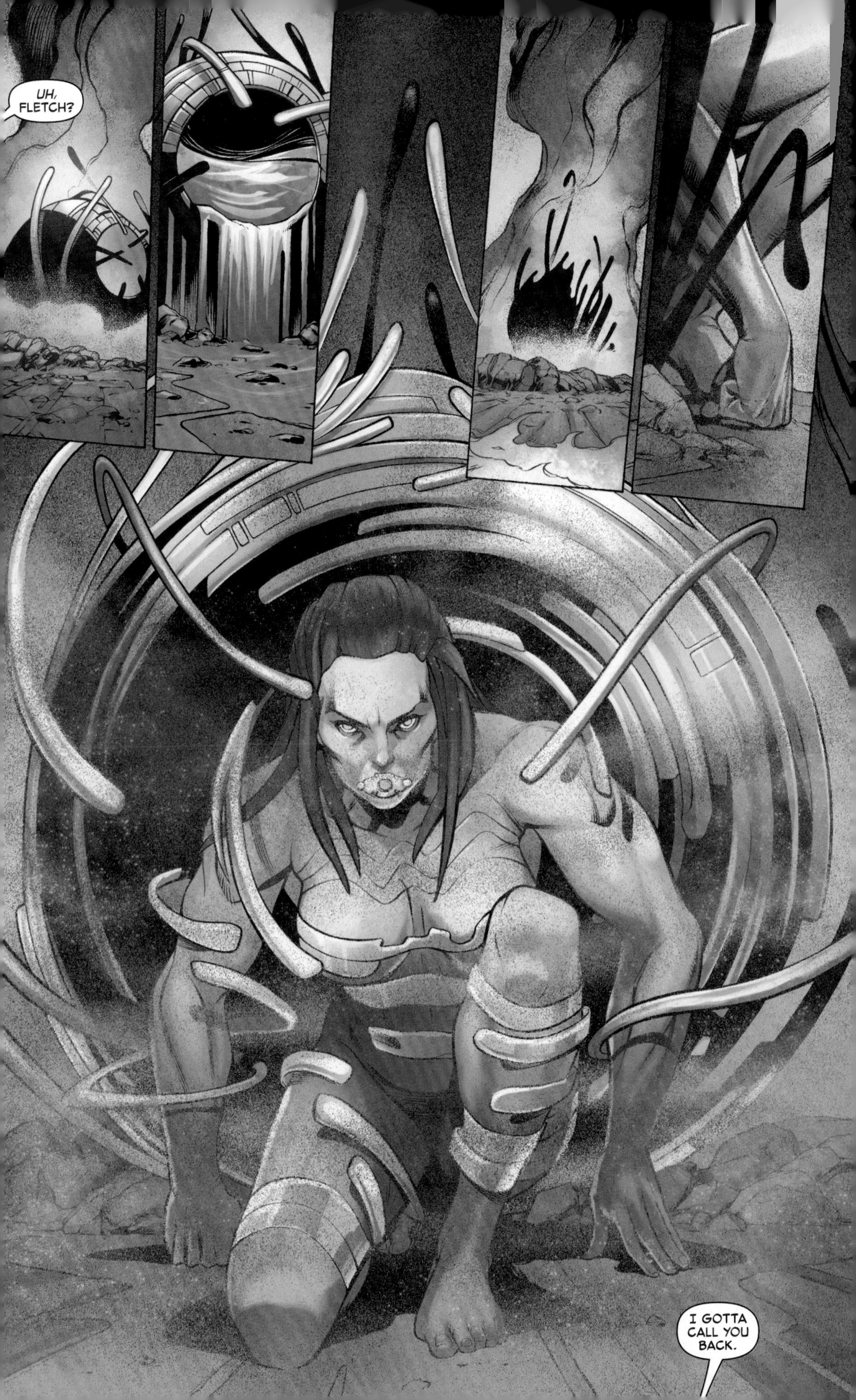
UH, FLETCH?
I GOTTA CALL YOU BACK.

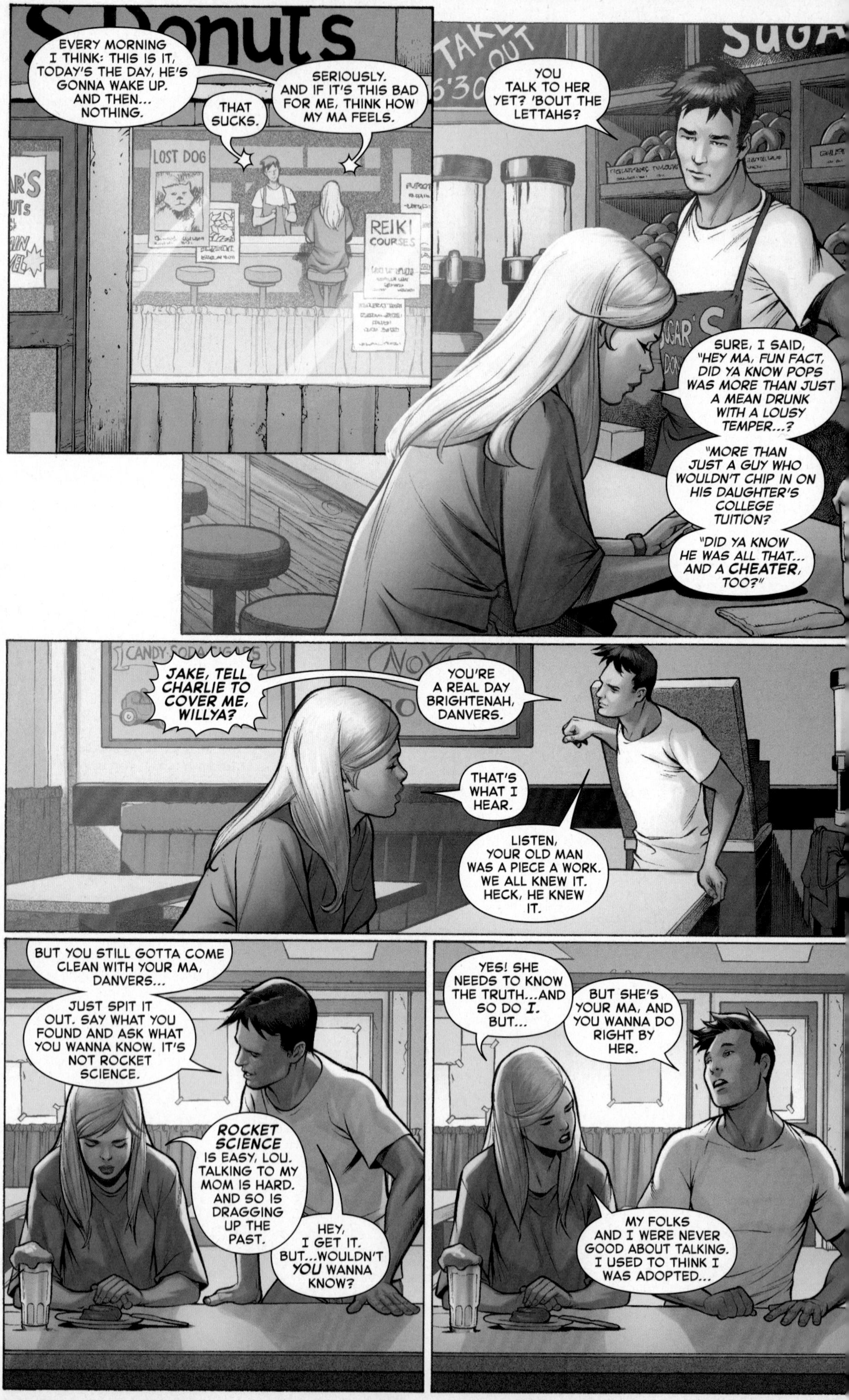
S Donuts
EVERY MORNING I THINK: THIS IS IT, TODAY'S THE DAY, HE'S GONNA WAKE UP. AND THEN... NOTHING.
THAT SUCKS.
SERIOUSLY. AND IF IT'S THIS BAD FOR ME, THINK HOW MY MA FEELS.
LOST DOG
REIKI COURSES
TAKE OUT
SUGA
YOU TALK TO HER YET? 'BOUT THE LETTAHS?
SURE, I SAID, "HEY MA, FUN FACT, DID YA KNOW POPS WAS MORE THAN JUST A MEAN DRUNK WITH A LOUSY TEMPER...?
"MORE THAN JUST A GUY WHO WOULDN'T CHIP IN ON HIS DAUGHTER'S COLLEGE TUITION?
"DID YA KNOW HE WAS ALL THAT... AND A CHEATER, TOO?"
JAKE, TELL CHARLIE TO COVER ME, WILLYA?
YOU'RE A REAL DAY BRIGHTENAH, DANVERS.
THAT'S WHAT I HEAR.
LISTEN, YOUR OLD MAN WAS A PIECE A WORK. WE ALL KNEW IT. HECK, HE KNEW IT.
BUT YOU STILL GOTTA COME CLEAN WITH YOUR MA, DANVERS...
JUST SPIT IT OUT. SAY WHAT YOU FOUND AND ASK WHAT YOU WANNA KNOW. IT'S NOT ROCKET SCIENCE.
ROCKET SCIENCE IS EASY, LOU. TALKING TO MY MOM IS HARD. AND SO IS DRAGGING UP THE PAST.
HEY, I GET IT. BUT...WOULDN'T YOU WANNA KNOW?
YES! SHE NEEDS TO KNOW THE TRUTH...AND SO DO I. BUT...
BUT SHE'S YOUR MA, AND YOU WANNA DO RIGHT BY HER.
MY FOLKS AND I WERE NEVER GOOD ABOUT TALKING. I USED TO THINK I WAS ADOPTED...

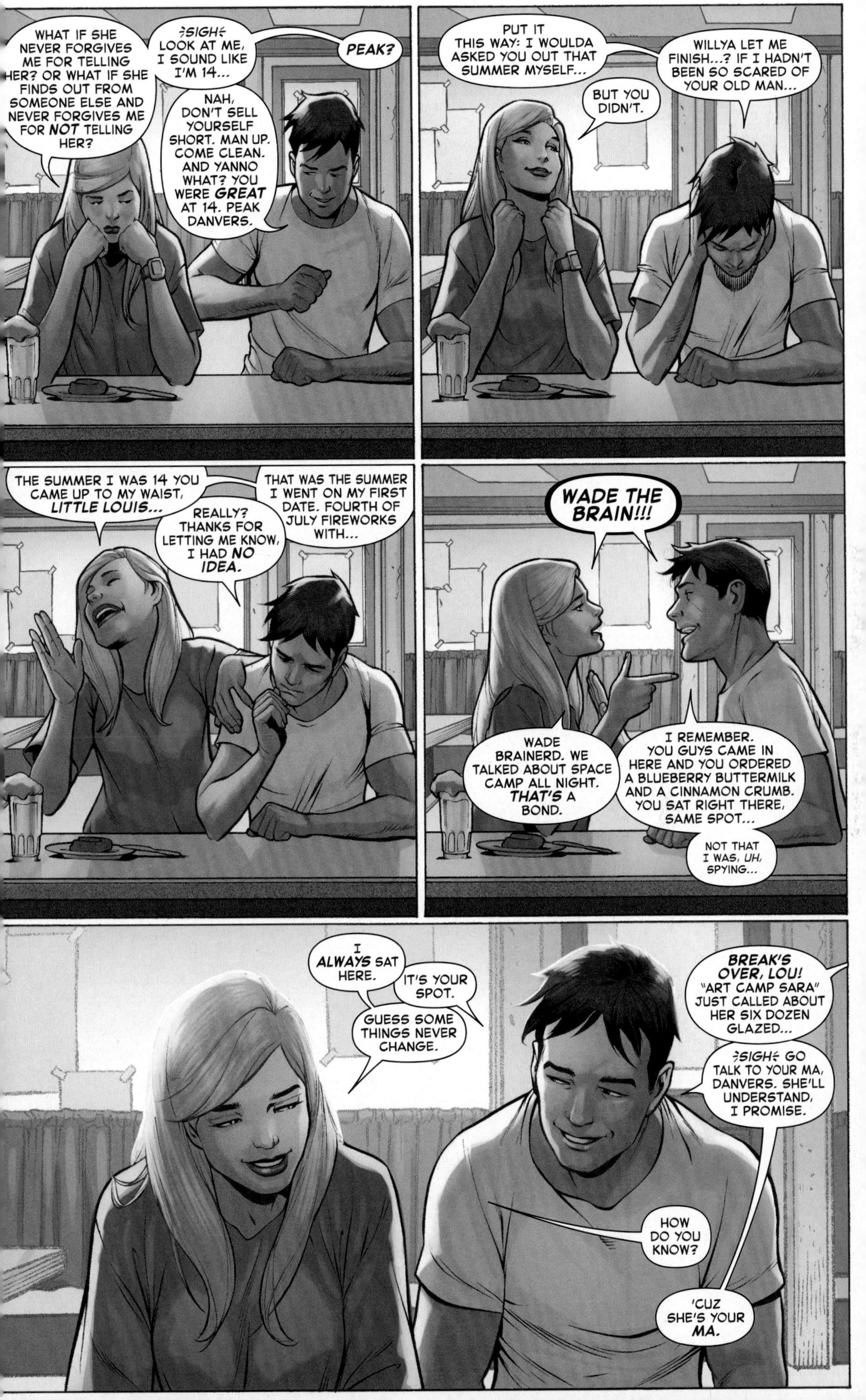
WHAT IF SHE NEVER FORGIVES ME FOR TELLING HER? OR WHAT IF SHE FINDS OUT FROM SOMEONE ELSE AND NEVER FORGIVES ME FOR NOT TELLING HER?
SIGH LOOK AT ME, I SOUND LIKE I'M 14...
PEAK?
NAH, DON'T SELL YOURSELF SHORT. MAN UP. COME CLEAN. AND YANNO WHAT? YOU WERE GREAT AT 14. PEAK DANVERS.
PUT IT THIS WAY: I WOULDA ASKED YOU OUT THAT SUMMER MYSELF...
BUT YOU DIDN'T.
WILLYA LET ME FINISH...? IF I HADN'T BEEN SO SCARED OF YOUR OLD MAN...
THE SUMMER I WAS 14 YOU CAME UP TO MY WAIST, LITTLE LOUIS...
REALLY? THANKS FOR LETTING ME KNOW, I HAD NO IDEA.
THAT WAS THE SUMMER I WENT ON MY FIRST DATE. FOURTH OF JULY FIREWORKS WITH...
WADE THE BRAIN!!!
WADE BRAINERD. WE TALKED ABOUT SPACE CAMP ALL NIGHT. THAT'S A BOND.
I REMEMBER. YOU GUYS CAME IN HERE AND YOU ORDERED A BLUEBERRY BUTTERMILK AND A CINNAMON CRUMB. YOU SAT RIGHT THERE, SAME SPOT...
NOT THAT I WAS, UH, SPYING...
I ALWAYS SAT HERE.
IT'S YOUR SPOT.
GUESS SOME THINGS NEVER CHANGE.
BREAK'S OVER, LOU! "ART CAMP SARA" JUST CALLED ABOUT HER SIX DOZEN GLAZED...
SIGH GO TALK TO YOUR MA, DANVERS. SHE'LL UNDERSTAND, I PROMISE.
HOW DO YOU KNOW?
'CUZ SHE'S YOUR MA.

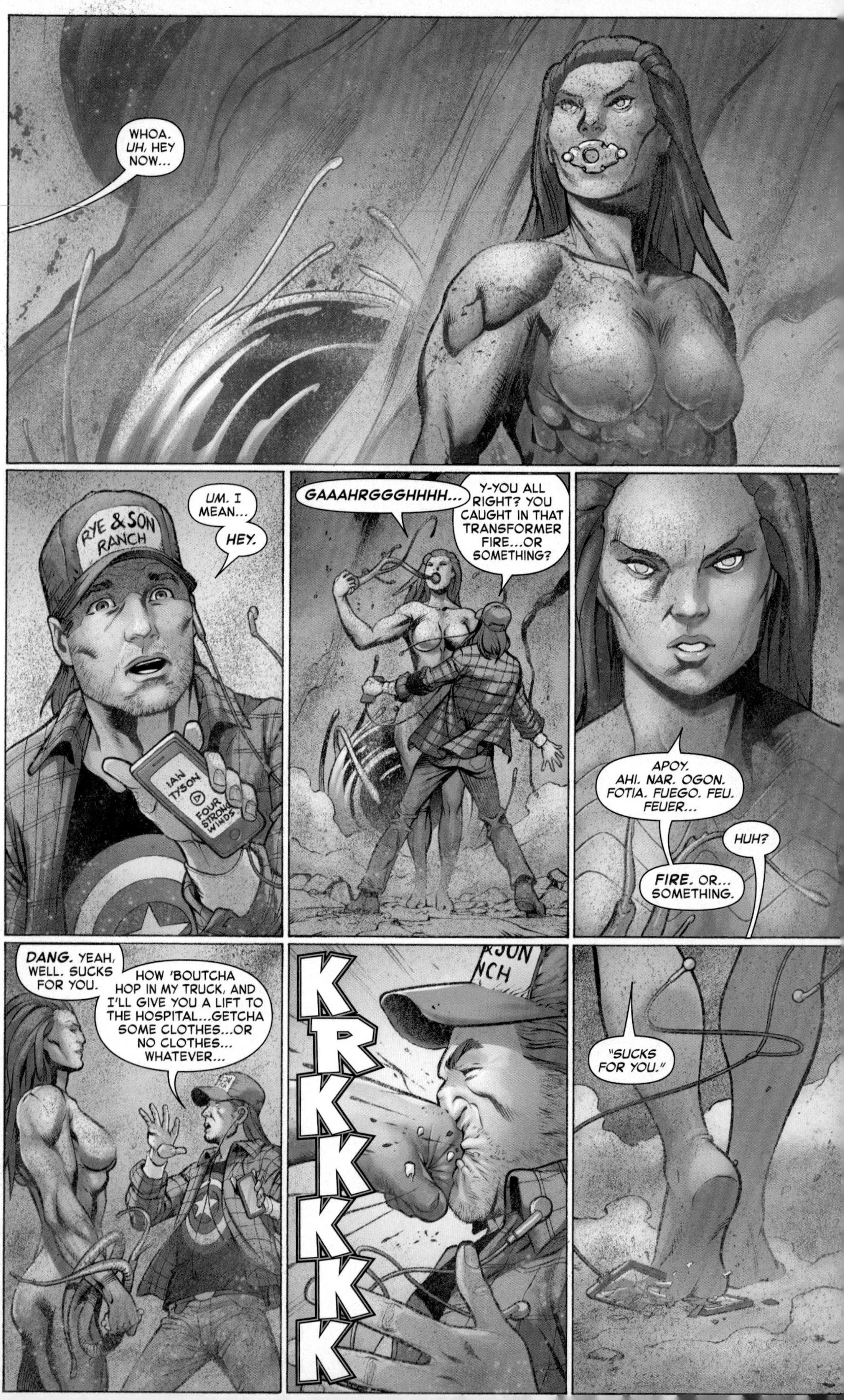
WHOA. UH, HEY NOW...
UM. I MEAN...
HEY.
RYE & SON RANCH
IAN TYSON
FOUR STRONG WINDS
GAAAHRGGGHHHH...
Y-YOU ALL RIGHT? YOU CAUGHT IN THAT TRANSFORMER FIRE...OR SOMETHING?
APOY. AHI. NAR. OGON. FOTIA. FUEGO. FEU. FEUER...
HUH?
FIRE. OR... SOMETHING.
DANG. YEAH, WELL. SUCKS FOR YOU.
HOW 'BOUTCHA HOP IN MY TRUCK, AND I'LL GIVE YOU A LIFT TO THE HOSPITAL...GETCHA SOME CLOTHES...OR NO CLOTHES... WHATEVER...
KRKKKK
"SUCKS FOR YOU."

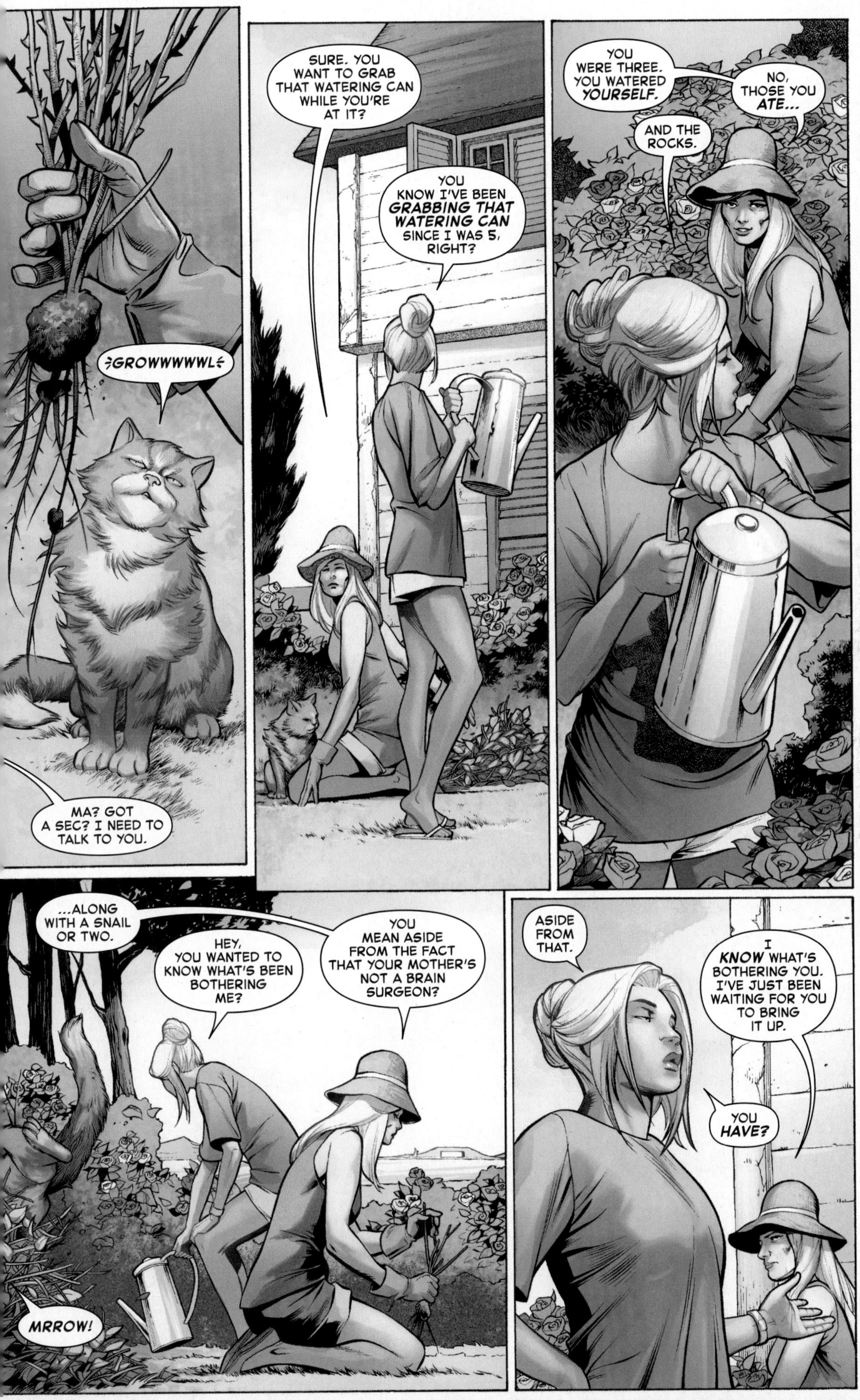

GROWWWWWL
MA? GOT A SEC? I NEED TO TALK TO YOU.
SURE. YOU WANT TO GRAB THAT WATERING CAN WHILE YOU'RE AT IT?
YOU KNOW I'VE BEEN GRABBING THAT WATERING CAN SINCE I WAS 5, RIGHT?
YOU WERE THREE. YOU WATERED YOURSELF.
NO, THOSE YOU ATE...
AND THE ROCKS.
...ALONG WITH A SNAIL OR TWO.
HEY, YOU WANTED TO KNOW WHAT'S BEEN BOTHERING ME?
YOU MEAN ASIDE FROM THE FACT THAT YOUR MOTHER'S NOT A BRAIN SURGEON?
MRROW!
ASIDE FROM THAT.
I KNOW WHAT'S BOTHERING YOU. I'VE JUST BEEN WAITING FOR YOU TO BRING IT UP.
YOU HAVE?

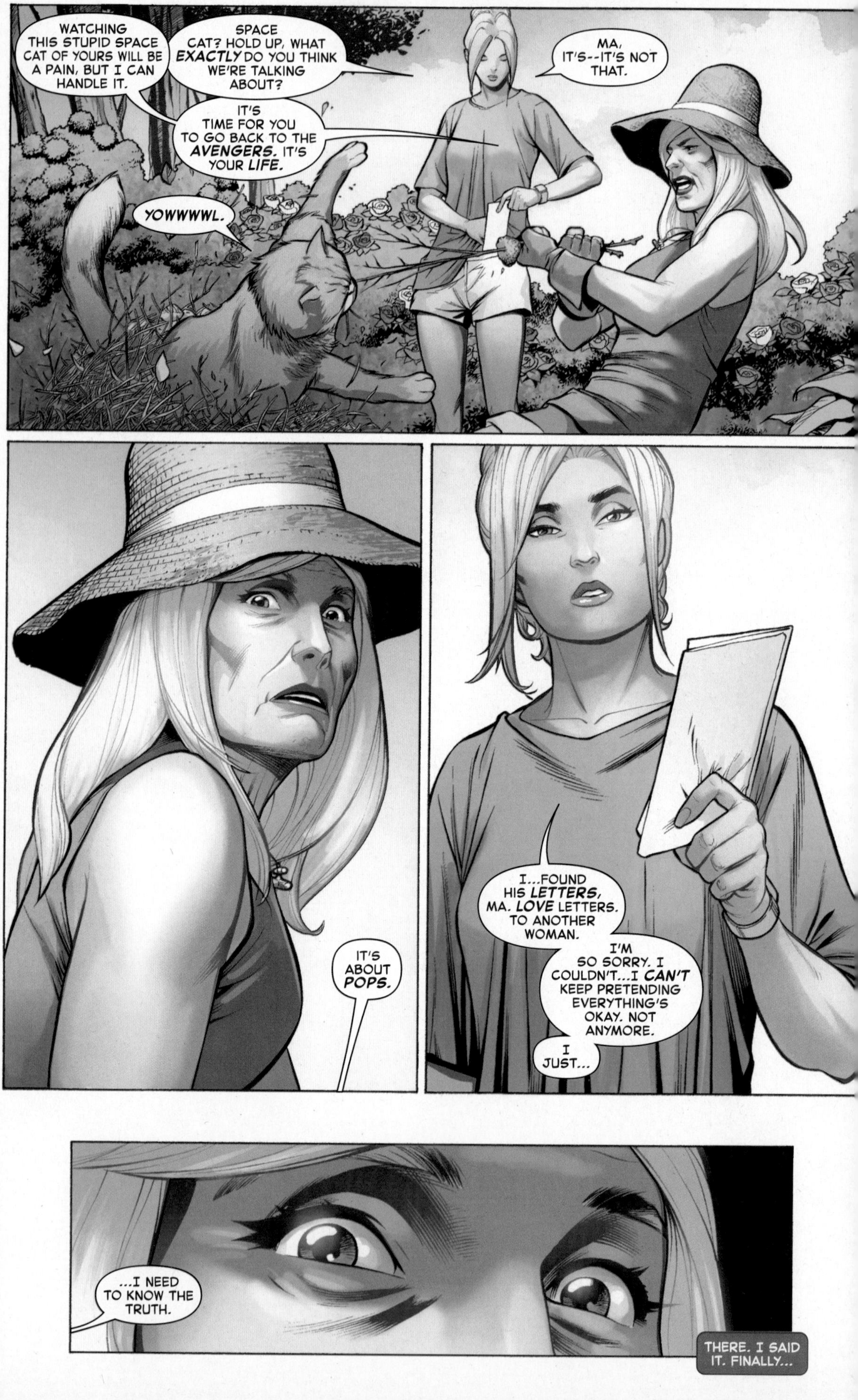
WATCHING THIS STUPID SPACE CAT OF YOURS WILL BE A PAIN, BUT I CAN HANDLE IT.
SPACE CAT? HOLD UP, WHAT EXACTLY DO YOU THINK WE'RE TALKING ABOUT?
IT'S TIME FOR YOU TO GO BACK TO THE AVENGERS. IT'S YOUR LIFE.
MA, IT'S--IT'S NOT THAT.
YOWWWWL.
IT'S ABOUT POPS.
I...FOUND HIS LETTERS, MA. LOVE LETTERS. TO ANOTHER WOMAN.
I'M SO SORRY. I COULDN'T...I CAN'T KEEP PRETENDING EVERYTHING'S OKAY. NOT ANYMORE.
I JUST...
...I NEED TO KNOW THE TRUTH.
THERE. I SAID IT. FINALLY...

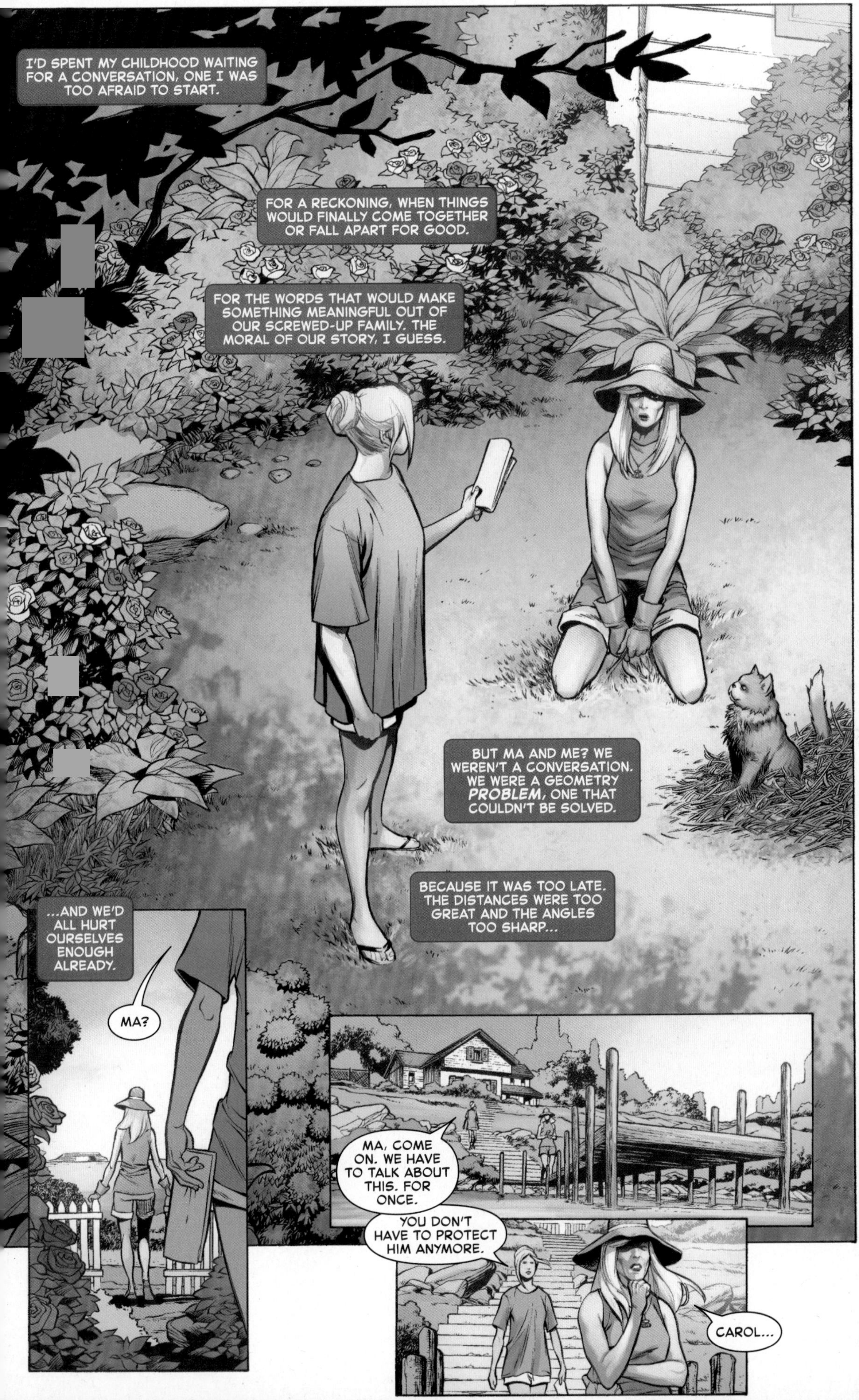
I'D SPENT MY CHILDHOOD WAITING FOR A CONVERSATION, ONE I WAS TOO AFRAID TO START.
FOR A RECKONING, WHEN THINGS WOULD FINALLY COME TOGETHER OR FALL APART FOR GOOD.
FOR THE WORDS THAT WOULD MAKE SOMETHING MEANINGFUL OUT OF OUR SCREWED-UP FAMILY. THE MORAL OF OUR STORY, I GUESS.
BUT MA AND ME? WE WEREN'T A CONVERSATION. WE WERE A GEOMETRY *PROBLEM*, ONE THAT COULDN'T BE SOLVED.
BECAUSE IT WAS TOO LATE. THE DISTANCES WERE TOO GREAT AND THE ANGLES TOO SHARP...
...AND WE'D ALL HURT OURSELVES ENOUGH ALREADY.
MA?
MA, COME ON. WE HAVE TO TALK ABOUT THIS. FOR ONCE.
YOU DON'T HAVE TO PROTECT HIM ANYMORE.
CAROL...

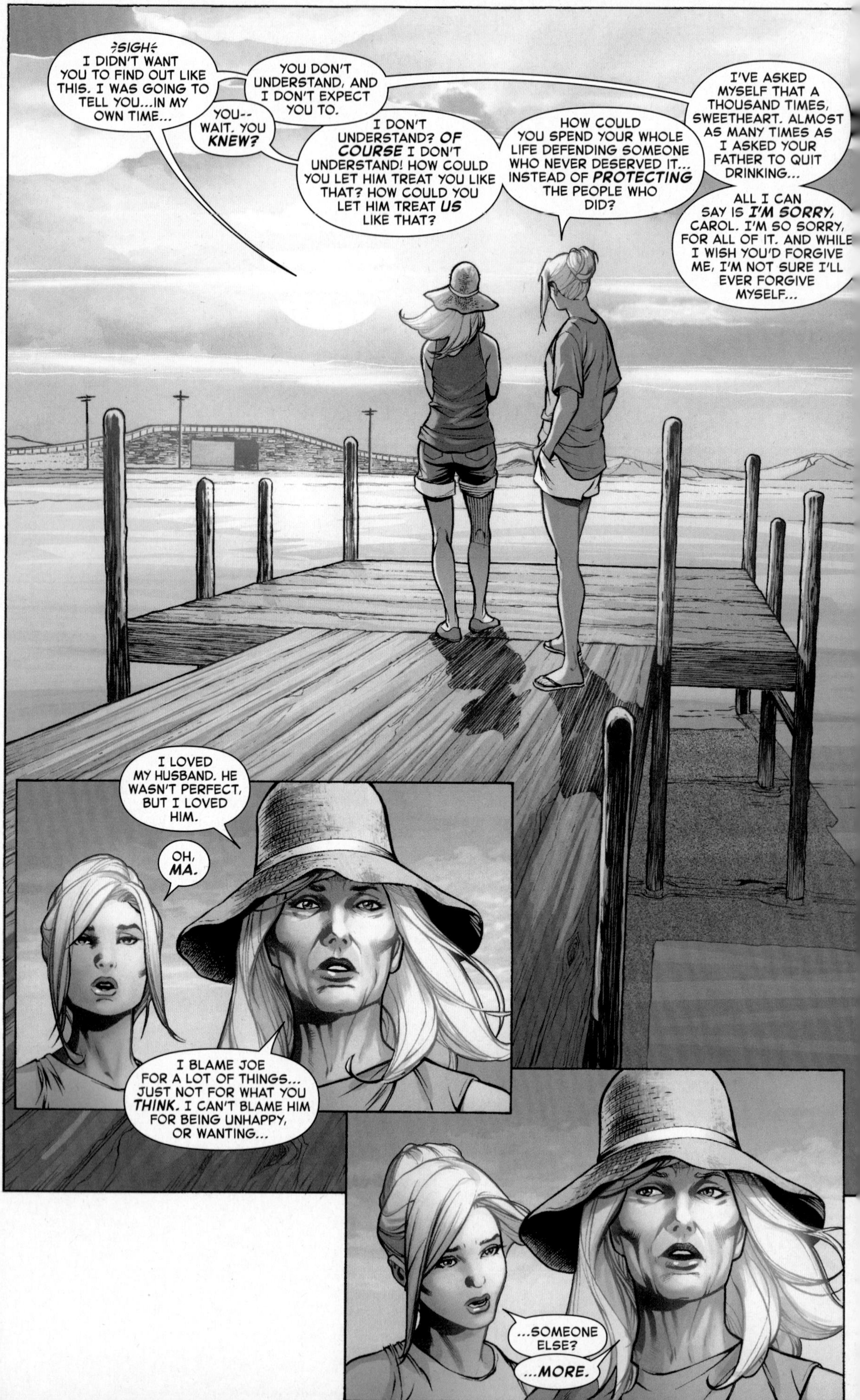

⚡SIGH⚡ I DIDN'T WANT YOU TO FIND OUT LIKE THIS. I WAS GOING TO TELL YOU...IN MY OWN TIME...
YOU-- WAIT. YOU *KNEW?*
YOU DON'T UNDERSTAND, AND I DON'T EXPECT YOU TO.
I DON'T UNDERSTAND? *OF COURSE* I DON'T UNDERSTAND! HOW COULD YOU LET HIM TREAT YOU LIKE THAT? HOW COULD YOU LET HIM TREAT *US* LIKE THAT?
HOW COULD YOU SPEND YOUR WHOLE LIFE DEFENDING SOMEONE WHO NEVER DESERVED IT... INSTEAD OF *PROTECTING* THE PEOPLE WHO DID?
I'VE ASKED MYSELF THAT A THOUSAND TIMES, SWEETHEART. ALMOST AS MANY TIMES AS I ASKED YOUR FATHER TO QUIT DRINKING...
ALL I CAN SAY IS *I'M SORRY,* CAROL. I'M SO SORRY, FOR ALL OF IT. AND WHILE I WISH YOU'D FORGIVE ME, I'M NOT SURE I'LL EVER FORGIVE MYSELF...
I LOVED MY HUSBAND. HE WASN'T PERFECT, BUT I LOVED HIM.
OH, *MA.*
I BLAME JOE FOR A LOT OF THINGS... JUST NOT FOR WHAT YOU *THINK.* I CAN'T BLAME HIM FOR BEING UNHAPPY, OR WANTING...
...SOMEONE ELSE?
...MORE.

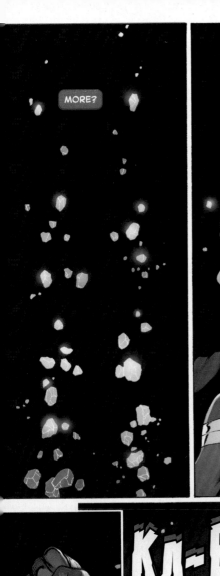

MORE?

"MORE"?!

KA-BOOOM

ENOUGH, POPS! YOU'VE DONE *ENOUGH!*

THERE WASN'T AN ASTEROID BIG ENOUGH TO PUNCH. NOT THIS TIME.

NOT EVEN THE MOON.

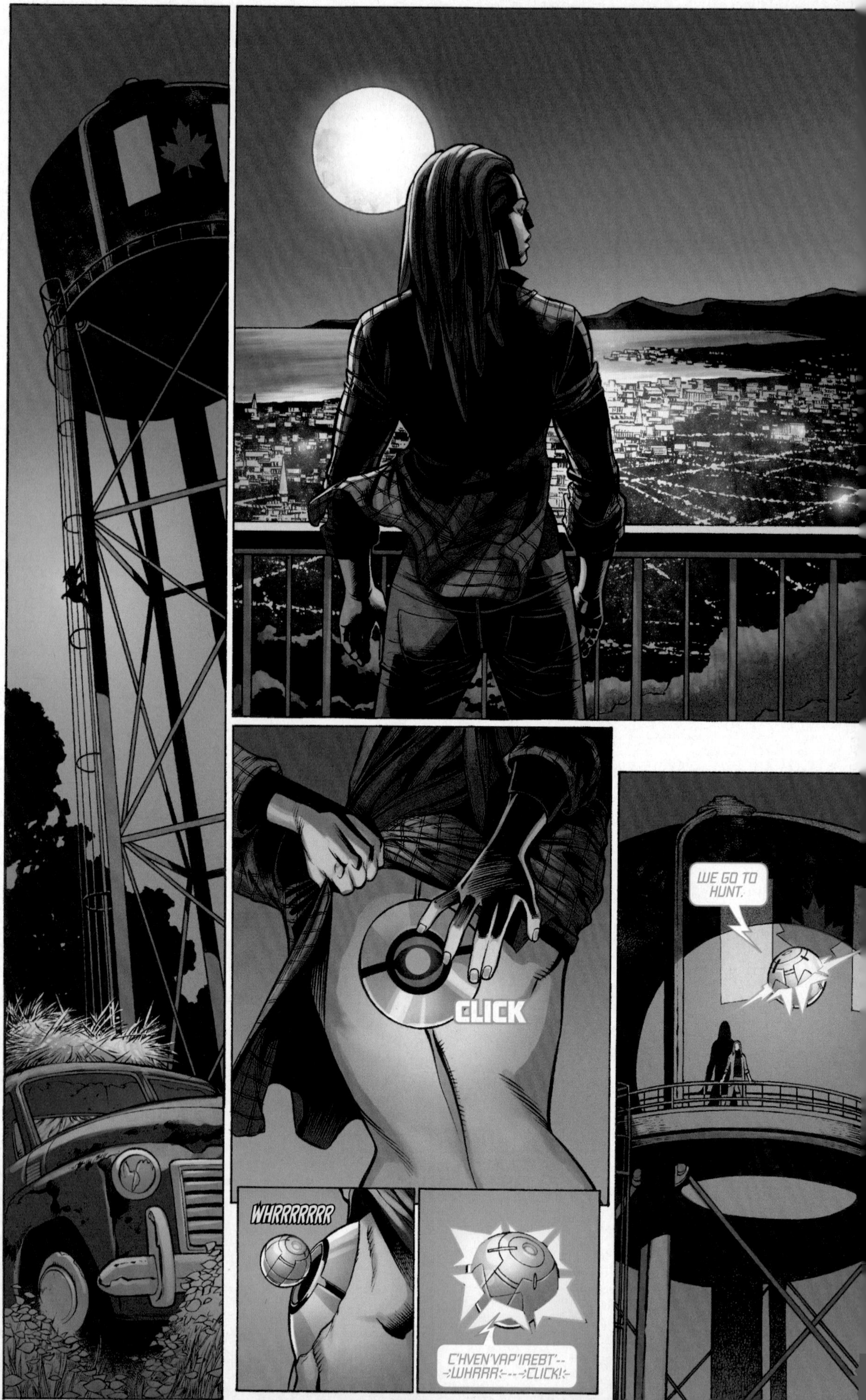
CLICK
WHRRRRRRR
C'HVEN'VAP'IREBT'--
--WHRRR---CLICK!--
WE GO TO HUNT.

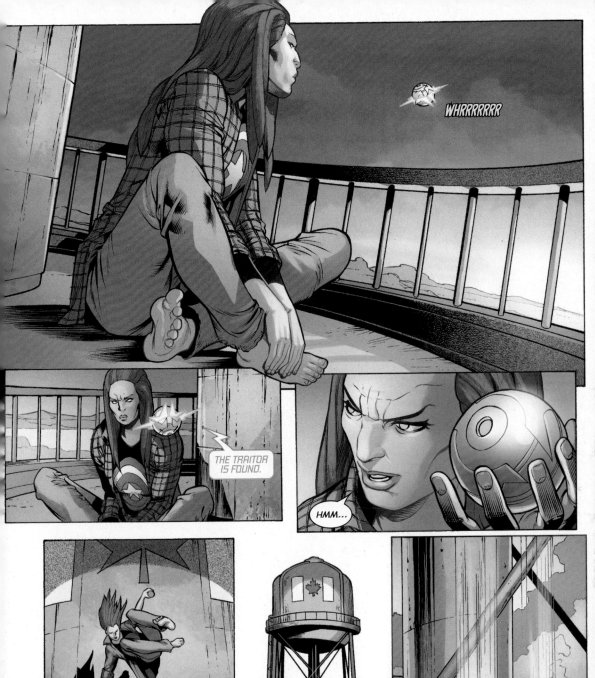

WHRRRRRRR

THE TRAITOR IS FOUND.

HMM...

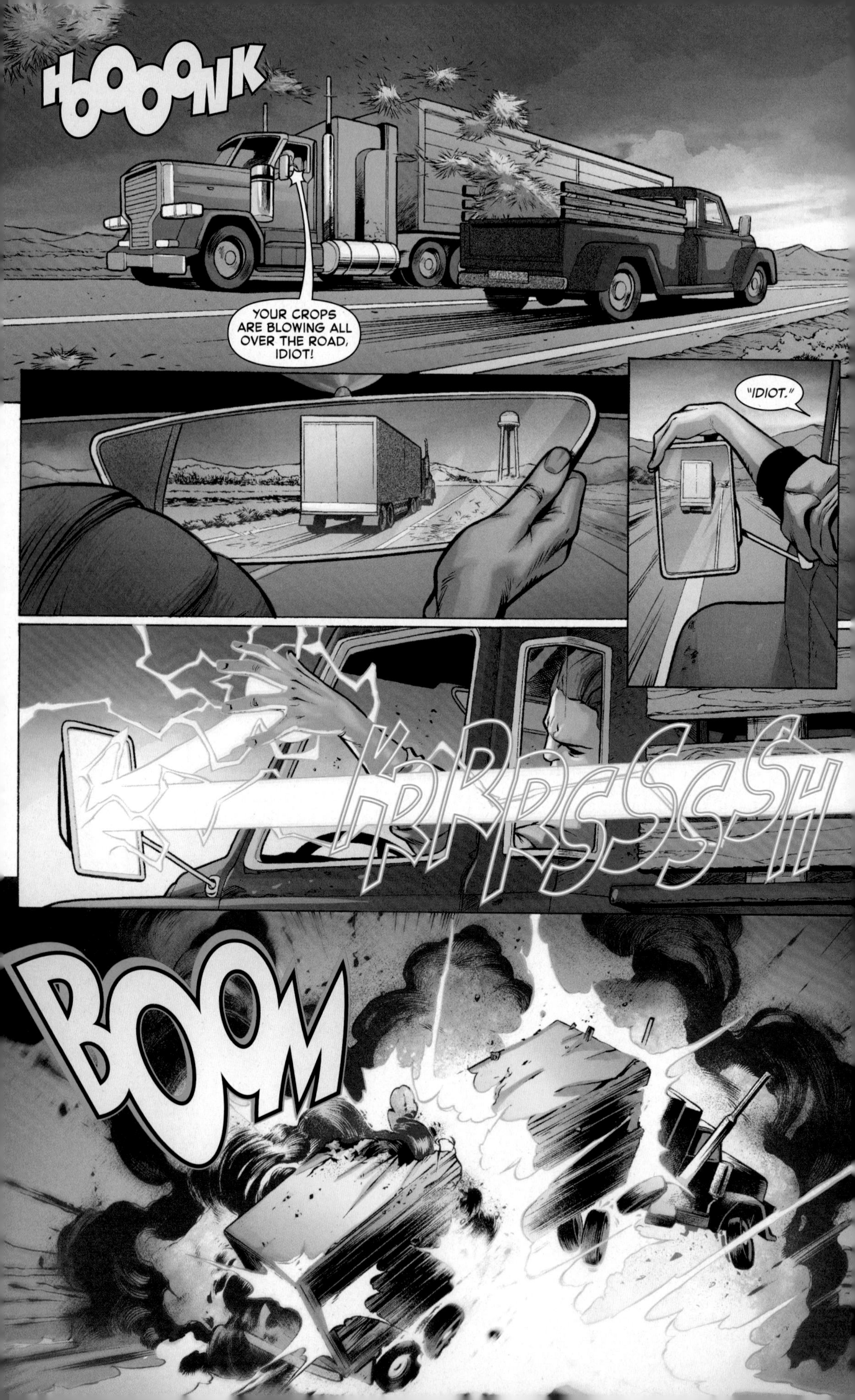
HOOOONK
YOUR CROPS ARE BLOWING ALL OVER THE ROAD, IDIOT!
"IDIOT."
KRRRSSSH
BOOM

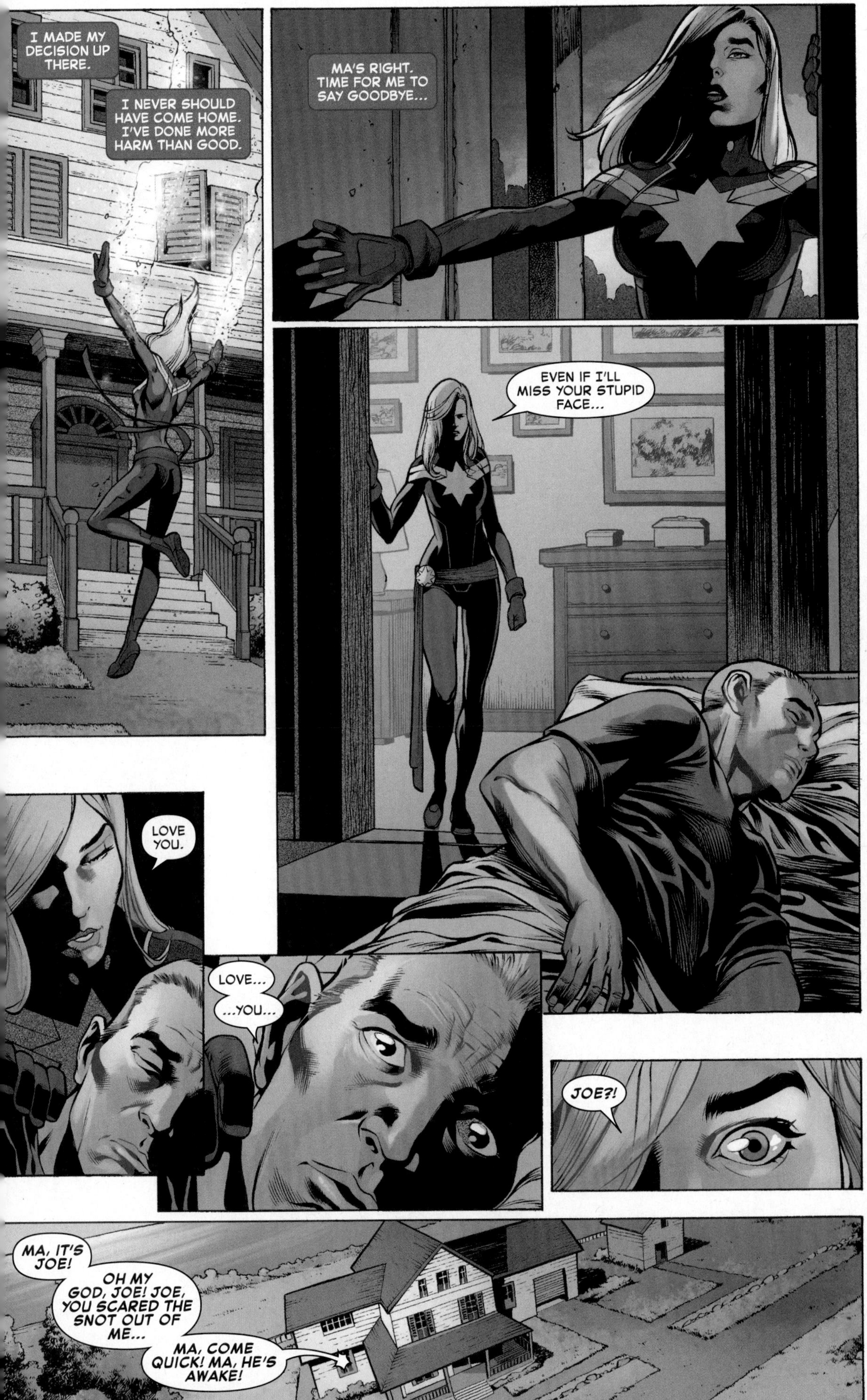
I MADE MY DECISION UP THERE.
I NEVER SHOULD HAVE COME HOME. I'VE DONE MORE HARM THAN GOOD.
MA'S RIGHT. TIME FOR ME TO SAY GOODBYE...
EVEN IF I'LL MISS YOUR STUPID FACE...
LOVE YOU.
LOVE...
...YOU...
JOE?!
MA, IT'S JOE!
OH MY GOD, JOE! JOE, YOU SCARED THE SNOT OUT OF ME...
MA, COME QUICK! MA, HE'S AWAKE!

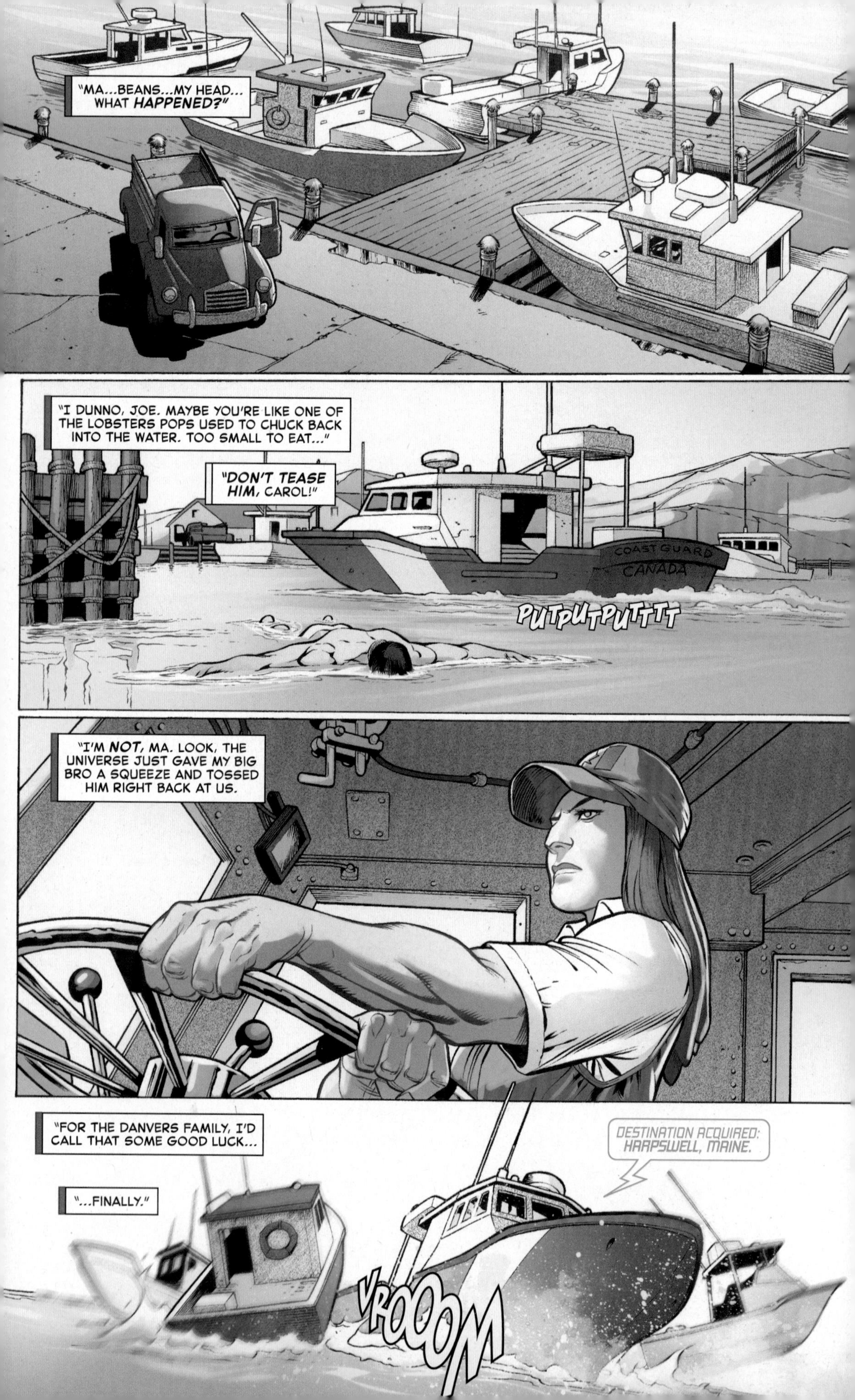
"MA...BEANS...MY HEAD... WHAT *HAPPENED?*"
"I DUNNO, JOE. MAYBE YOU'RE LIKE ONE OF THE LOBSTERS POPS USED TO CHUCK BACK INTO THE WATER. TOO SMALL TO EAT..."
"DON'T TEASE HIM, CAROL!"
COAST GUARD
CANADA
PUTPUTPUTTTTT
"I'M *NOT,* MA. LOOK, THE UNIVERSE JUST GAVE MY BIG BRO A SQUEEZE AND TOSSED HIM RIGHT BACK AT US.
"FOR THE DANVERS FAMILY, I'D CALL THAT SOME GOOD LUCK...
"...FINALLY."
DESTINATION ACQUIRED: HARPSWELL, MAINE.
VROOOM

THE LIFE OF CAPTAIN MARVEL #3
"CAUGHT"

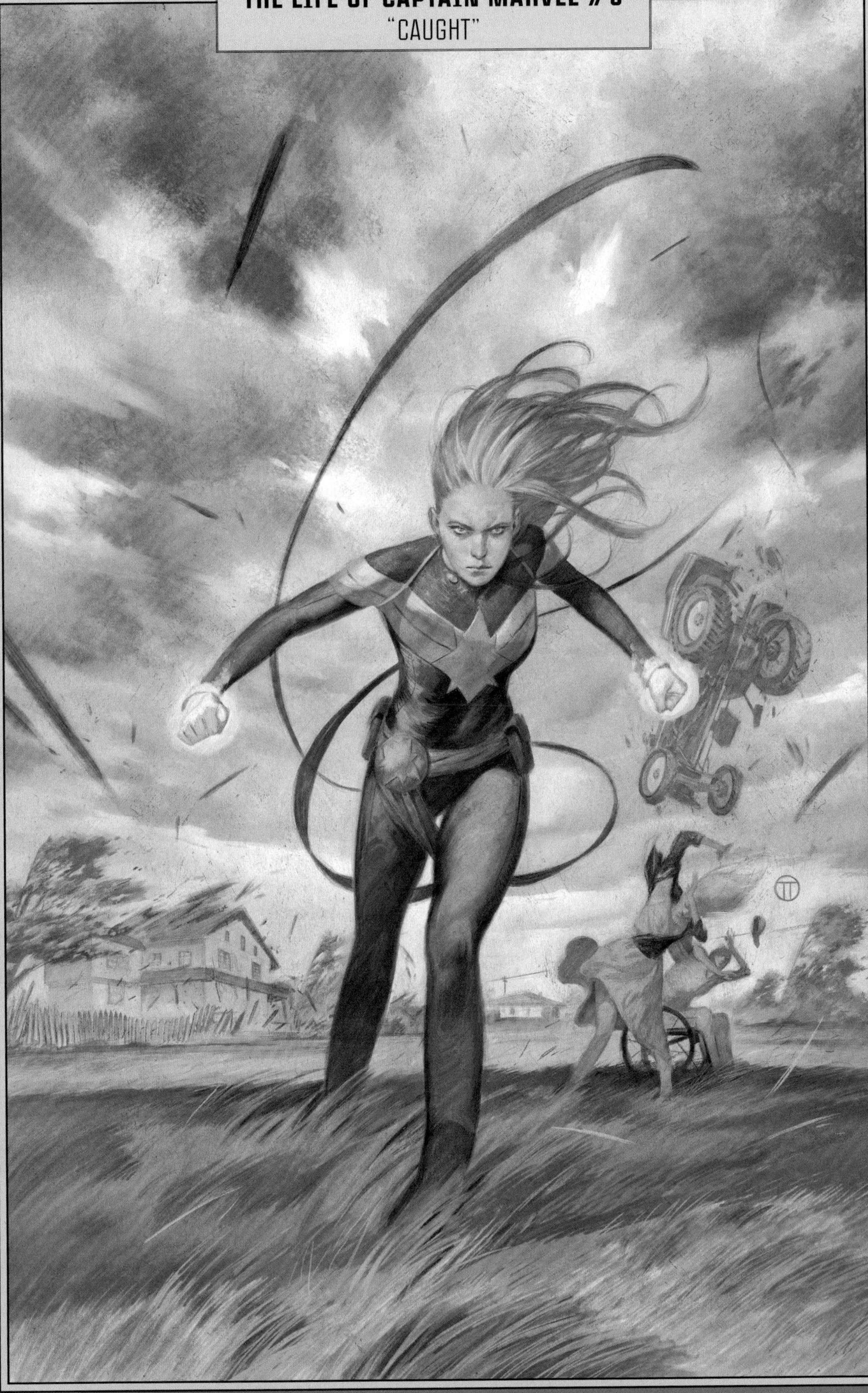

HARPSWELL SOUND, MAINE.

RAWWWRRRR

DOWNEAST MORNIN', MAINAHS. CALM WATER. CLAMMERS OUT IN THE MUD FLATS FOR STEAMERS AN' QUAHOGS, COUNT NECKS AN' LITTLE NECKS AN' CHERRY STONES...

RAWWWRRRR

FISHERMEN SHOULD BE HEADIN' OUT TA MAKE THE ROUNDS ANYTIME NOW, CHECKIN' THEAH POTS FOR BUGS...

RAWWWRRRR
RAW
RRRR

HONK HONK

...GONNA BE A BEAUTIFUL DAY FOR TRAPPIN', YES SIR.

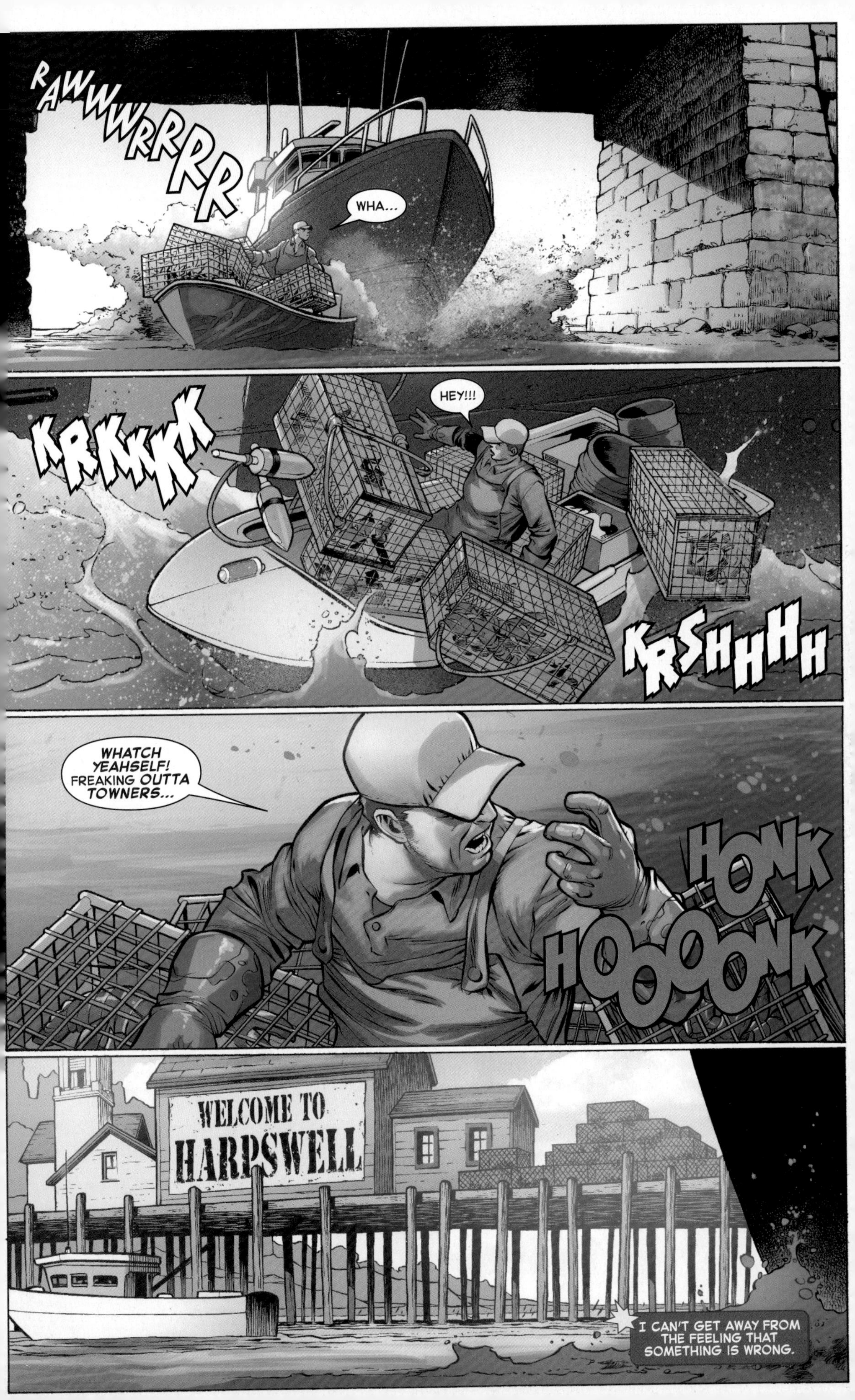
RAWWWRRRRR
WHA...
KRKKKKK
HEY!!!
KRSHHHHH
WHATCH YEAHSELF! FREAKING OUTTA TOWNERS...
HONK
HOOOOONK
WELCOME TO HARPSWELL
I CAN'T GET AWAY FROM THE FEELING THAT SOMETHING IS WRONG.

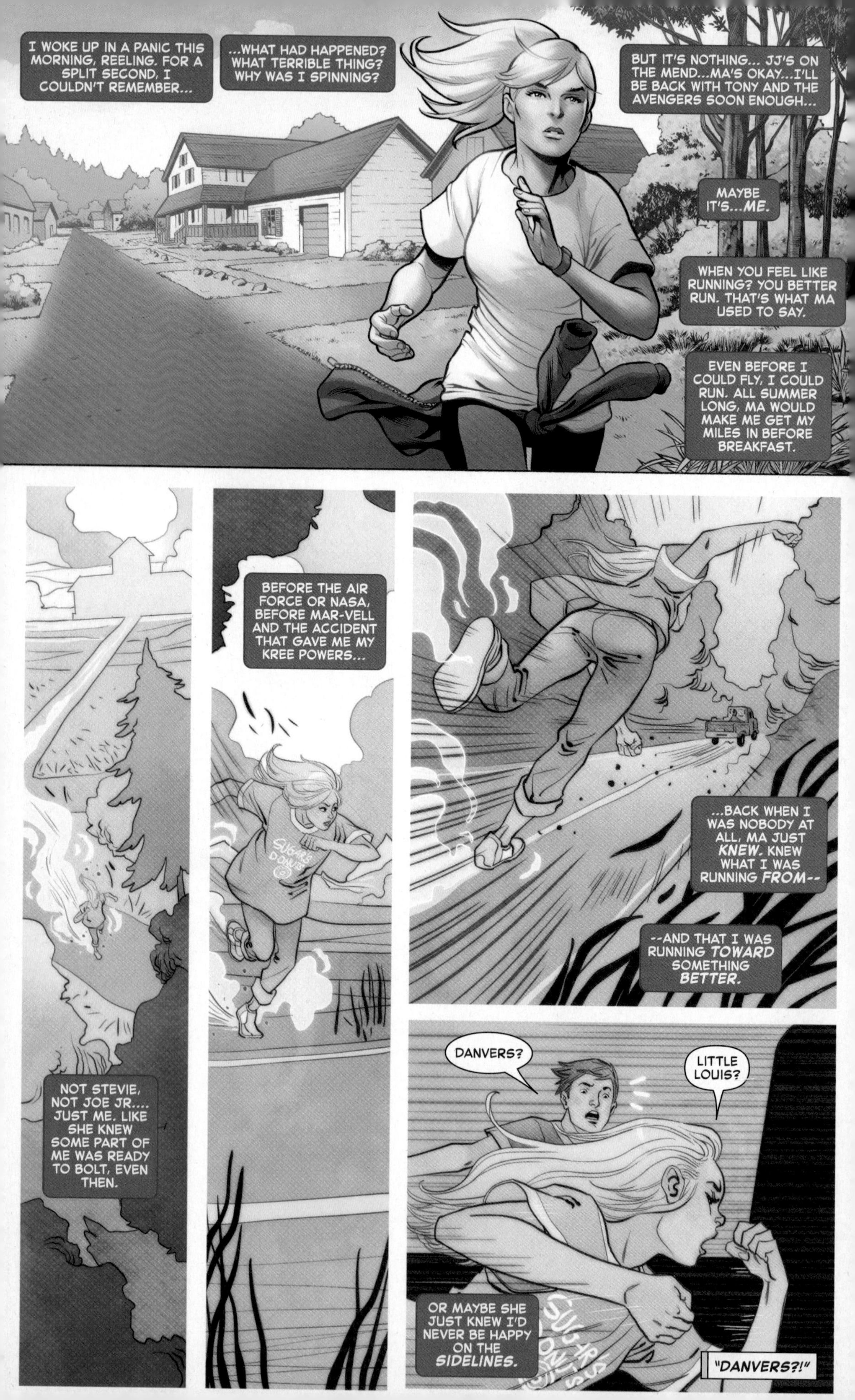
I WOKE UP IN A PANIC THIS MORNING, REELING. FOR A SPLIT SECOND, I COULDN'T REMEMBER...
...WHAT HAD HAPPENED? WHAT TERRIBLE THING? WHY WAS I SPINNING?
BUT IT'S NOTHING... JJ'S ON THE MEND...MA'S OKAY...I'LL BE BACK WITH TONY AND THE AVENGERS SOON ENOUGH...
MAYBE IT'S...ME.
WHEN YOU FEEL LIKE RUNNING? YOU BETTER RUN. THAT'S WHAT MA USED TO SAY.
EVEN BEFORE I COULD FLY, I COULD RUN. ALL SUMMER LONG, MA WOULD MAKE ME GET MY MILES IN BEFORE BREAKFAST.
NOT STEVIE, NOT JOE JR.... JUST ME. LIKE SHE KNEW SOME PART OF ME WAS READY TO BOLT, EVEN THEN.
BEFORE THE AIR FORCE OR NASA, BEFORE MAR-VELL AND THE ACCIDENT THAT GAVE ME MY KREE POWERS...
SUGAR'S DONUTS
...BACK WHEN I WAS NOBODY AT ALL, MA JUST KNEW. KNEW WHAT I WAS RUNNING FROM--
--AND THAT I WAS RUNNING TOWARD SOMETHING BETTER.
DANVERS?
LITTLE LOUIS?
OR MAYBE SHE JUST KNEW I'D NEVER BE HAPPY ON THE SIDELINES.
"DANVERS?!"

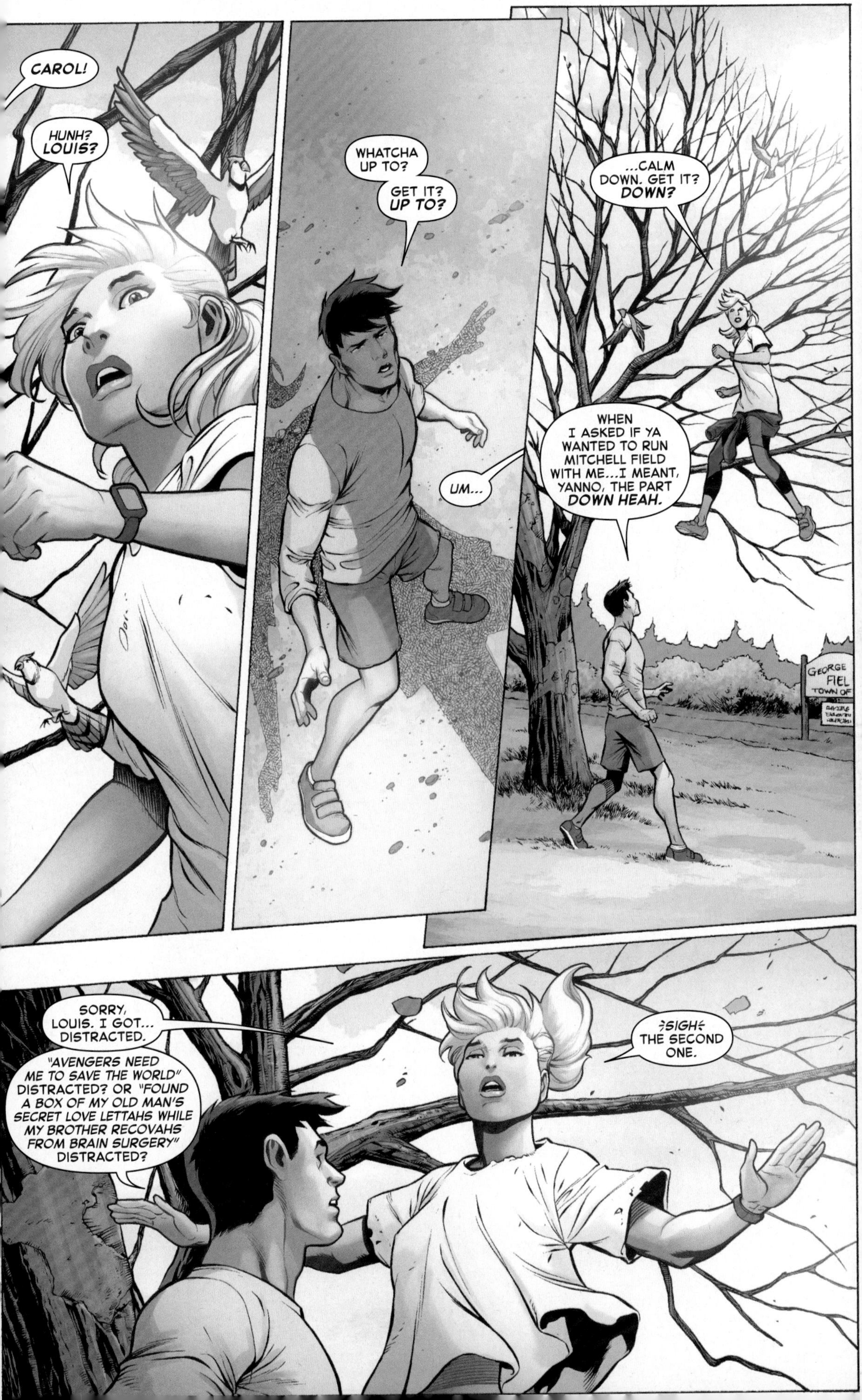
CAROL!
HUNH? LOUIS?
WHATCHA UP TO?
GET IT? UP TO?
UM...
...CALM DOWN. GET IT? DOWN?
WHEN I ASKED IF YA WANTED TO RUN MITCHELL FIELD WITH ME...I MEANT, YANNO, THE PART DOWN HEAH.
GEORGE
FIEL
TOWN OF
SORRY, LOUIS. I GOT... DISTRACTED.
"AVENGERS NEED ME TO SAVE THE WORLD" DISTRACTED? OR "FOUND A BOX OF MY OLD MAN'S SECRET LOVE LETTAHS WHILE MY BROTHER RECOVAHS FROM BRAIN SURGERY" DISTRACTED?
SIGH THE SECOND ONE.

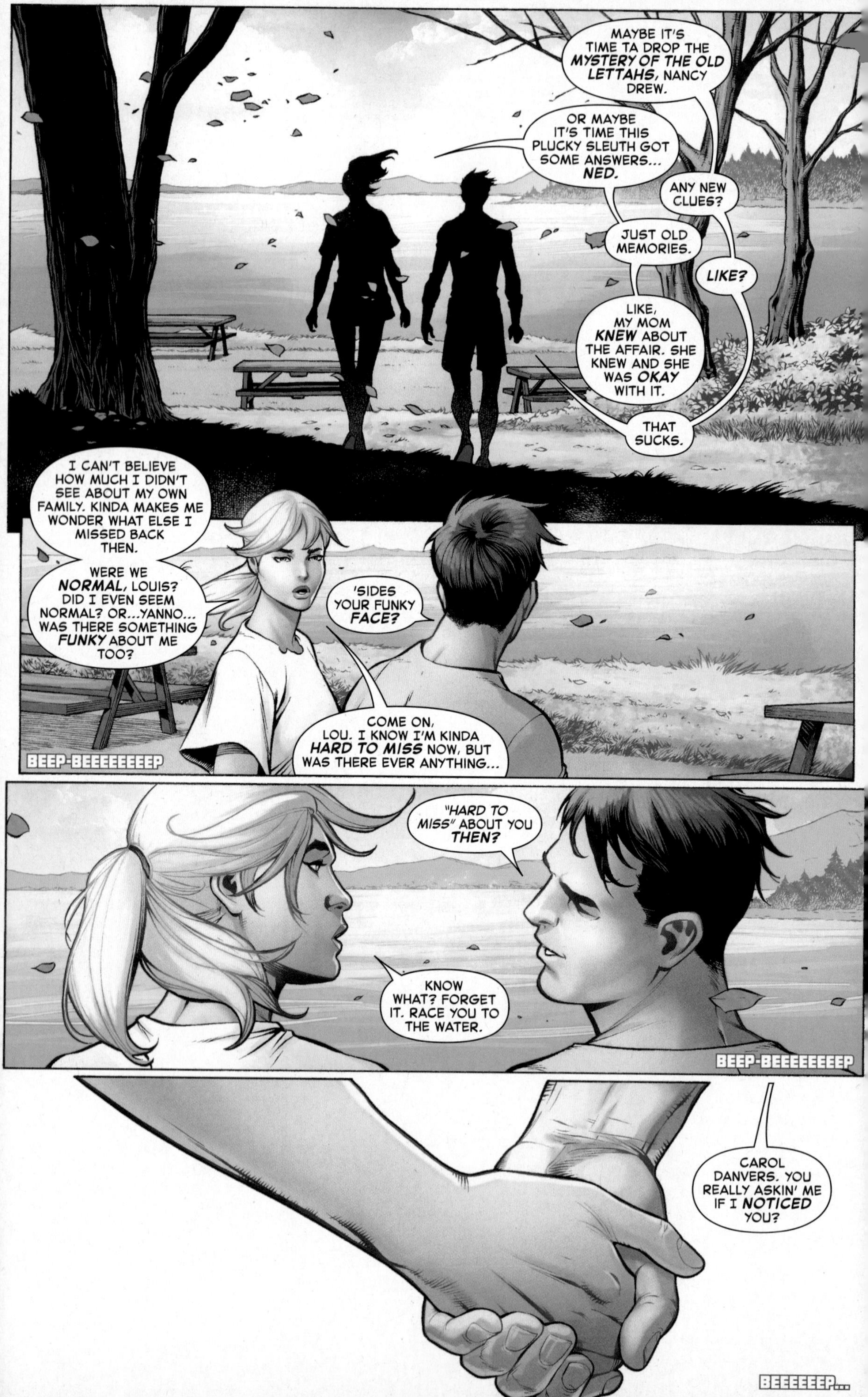
MAYBE IT'S TIME TA DROP THE MYSTERY OF THE OLD LETTAHS, NANCY DREW.
OR MAYBE IT'S TIME THIS PLUCKY SLEUTH GOT SOME ANSWERS... NED.
ANY NEW CLUES?
JUST OLD MEMORIES.
LIKE?
LIKE, MY MOM KNEW ABOUT THE AFFAIR. SHE KNEW AND SHE WAS OKAY WITH IT.
THAT SUCKS.
I CAN'T BELIEVE HOW MUCH I DIDN'T SEE ABOUT MY OWN FAMILY. KINDA MAKES ME WONDER WHAT ELSE I MISSED BACK THEN.
WERE WE NORMAL, LOUIS? DID I EVEN SEEM NORMAL? OR...YANNO... WAS THERE SOMETHING FUNKY ABOUT ME TOO?
'SIDES YOUR FUNKY FACE?
COME ON, LOU. I KNOW I'M KINDA HARD TO MISS NOW, BUT WAS THERE EVER ANYTHING...
BEEP-BEEEEEEEEP
"HARD TO MISS" ABOUT YOU THEN?
KNOW WHAT? FORGET IT. RACE YOU TO THE WATER.
BEEP-BEEEEEEEEP
CAROL DANVERS. YOU REALLY ASKIN' ME IF I NOTICED YOU?
BEEEEEEEP...

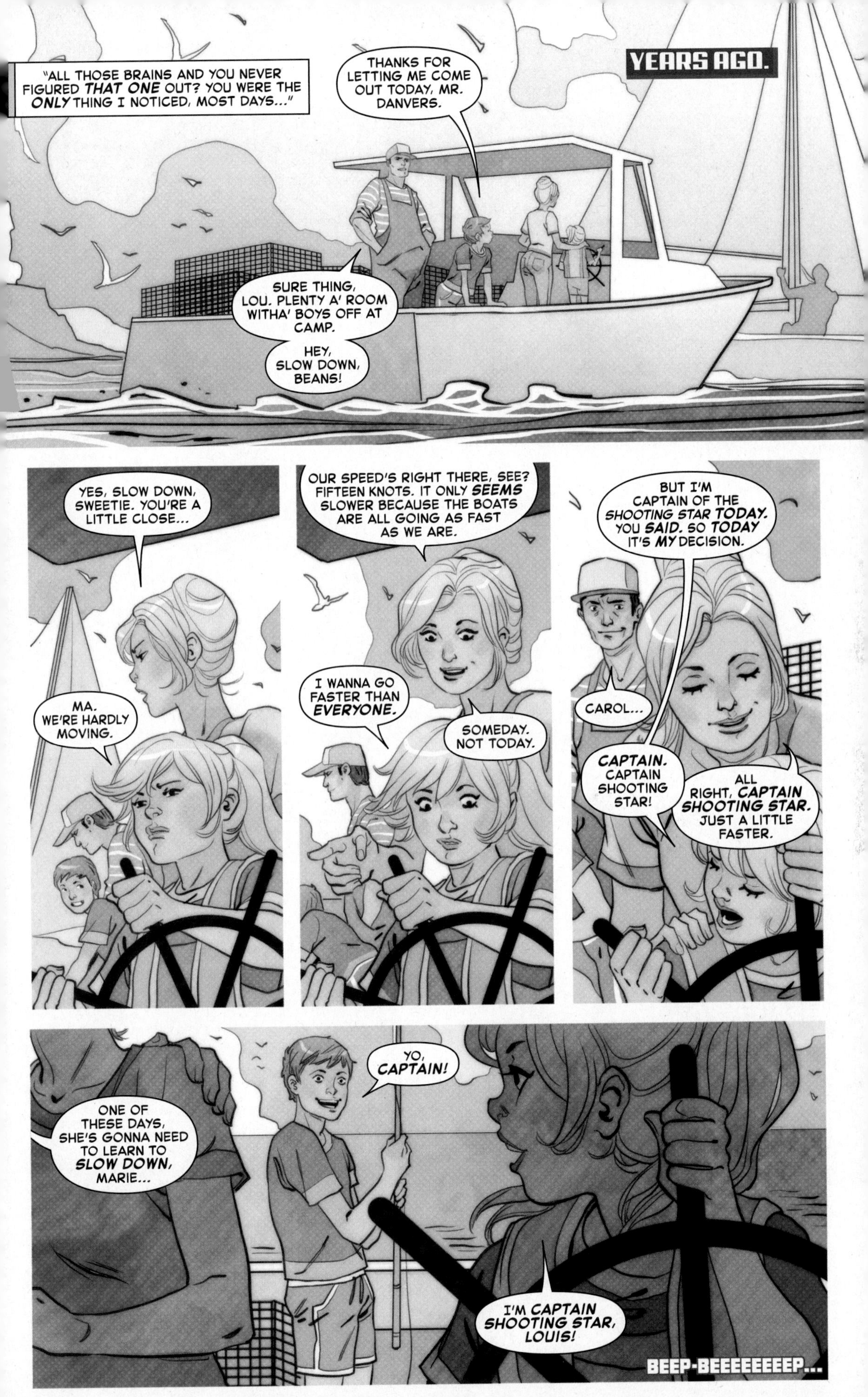
"ALL THOSE BRAINS AND YOU NEVER FIGURED THAT ONE OUT? YOU WERE THE ONLY THING I NOTICED, MOST DAYS..."
YEARS AGO.
THANKS FOR LETTING ME COME OUT TODAY, MR. DANVERS.
SURE THING, LOU. PLENTY A' ROOM WITHA' BOYS OFF AT CAMP.
HEY, SLOW DOWN, BEANS!
YES, SLOW DOWN, SWEETIE. YOU'RE A LITTLE CLOSE...
MA. WE'RE HARDLY MOVING.
OUR SPEED'S RIGHT THERE, SEE? FIFTEEN KNOTS. IT ONLY SEEMS SLOWER BECAUSE THE BOATS ARE ALL GOING AS FAST AS WE ARE.
I WANNA GO FASTER THAN EVERYONE.
SOMEDAY. NOT TODAY.
BUT I'M CAPTAIN OF THE SHOOTING STAR TODAY. YOU SAID. SO TODAY IT'S MY DECISION.
CAROL...
CAPTAIN. CAPTAIN SHOOTING STAR!
ALL RIGHT, CAPTAIN SHOOTING STAR. JUST A LITTLE FASTER.
YO, CAPTAIN!
ONE OF THESE DAYS, SHE'S GONNA NEED TO LEARN TO SLOW DOWN, MARIE...
I'M CAPTAIN SHOOTING STAR, LOUIS!
BEEP-BEEEEEEEEP...

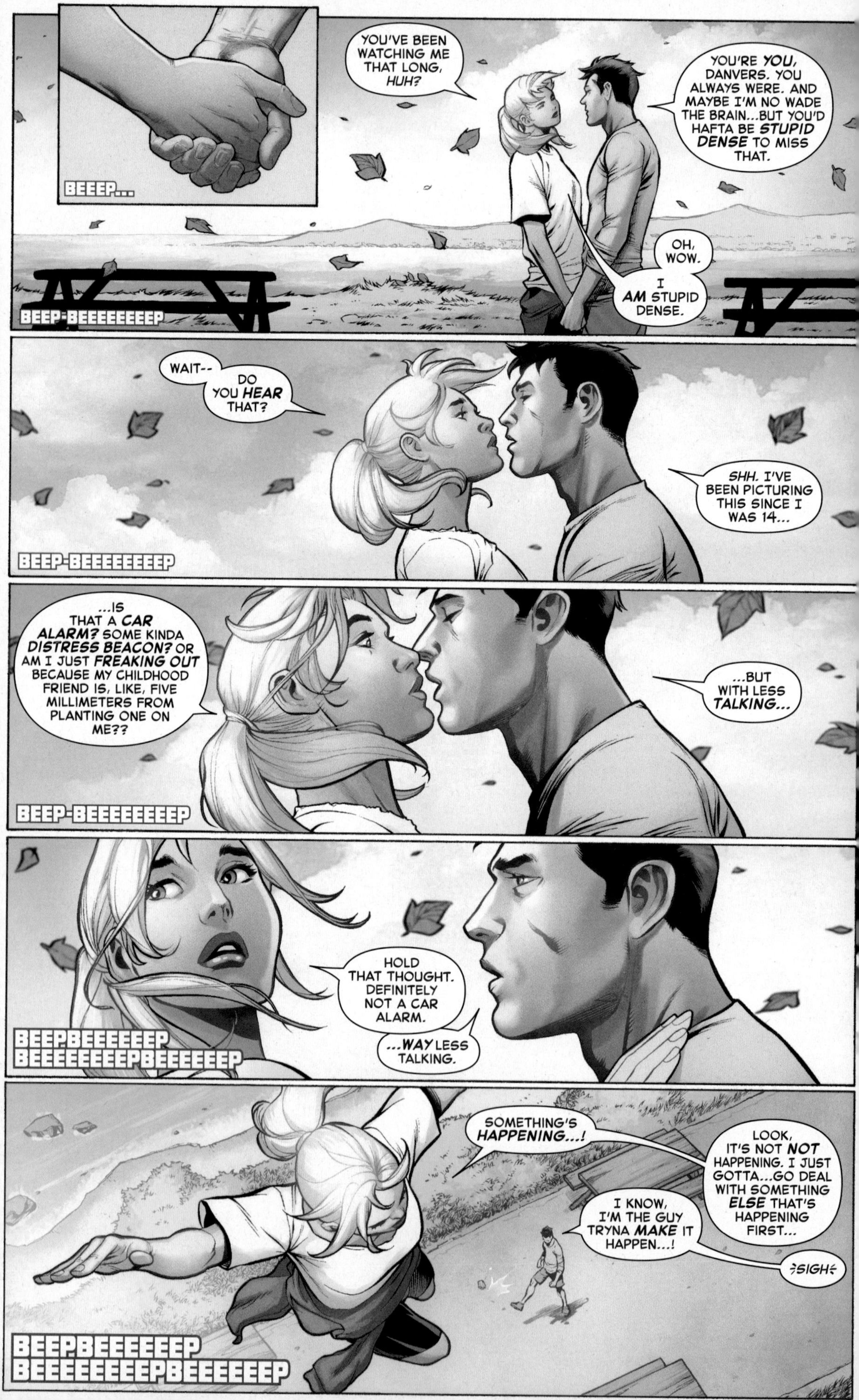
YOU'VE BEEN WATCHING ME THAT LONG, HUH?
YOU'RE YOU, DANVERS. YOU ALWAYS WERE. AND MAYBE I'M NO WADE THE BRAIN...BUT YOU'D HAFTA BE STUPID DENSE TO MISS THAT.
BEEEP...
OH, WOW.
I AM STUPID DENSE.
BEEP-BEEEEEEEEP
WAIT--
DO YOU HEAR THAT?
SHH. I'VE BEEN PICTURING THIS SINCE I WAS 14...
BEEP-BEEEEEEEEP
...IS THAT A CAR ALARM? SOME KINDA DISTRESS BEACON? OR AM I JUST FREAKING OUT BECAUSE MY CHILDHOOD FRIEND IS, LIKE, FIVE MILLIMETERS FROM PLANTING ONE ON ME??
...BUT WITH LESS TALKING...
BEEP-BEEEEEEEEP
HOLD THAT THOUGHT. DEFINITELY NOT A CAR ALARM.
...WAY LESS TALKING.
BEEPBEEEEEEEP
BEEEEEEEEPBEEEEEEP
SOMETHING'S HAPPENING...!
LOOK, IT'S NOT NOT HAPPENING. I JUST GOTTA...GO DEAL WITH SOMETHING ELSE THAT'S HAPPENING FIRST...
I KNOW, I'M THE GUY TRYNA MAKE IT HAPPEN...!
SIGH
BEEPBEEEEEEEP
BEEEEEEEEPBEEEEEEP

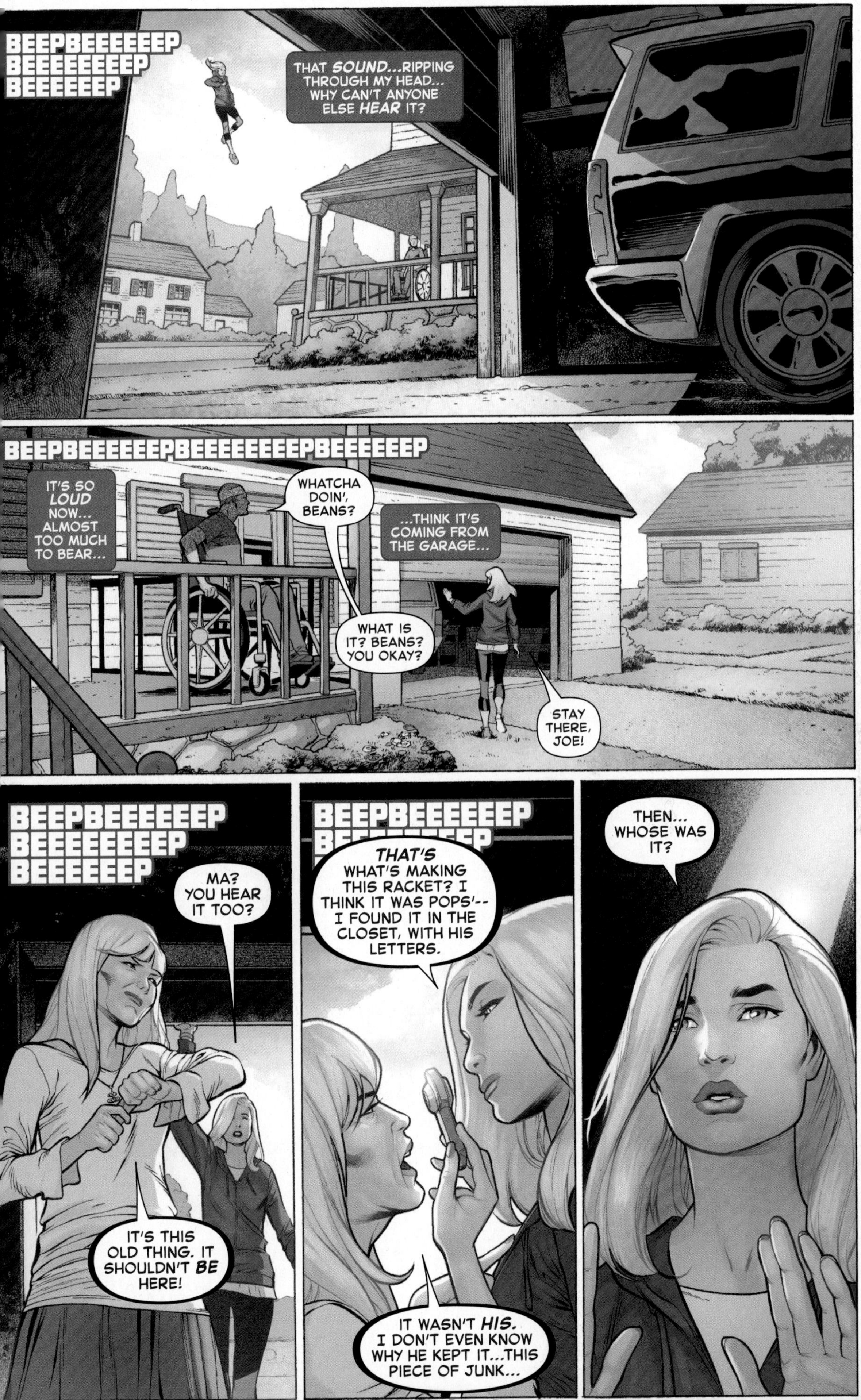
BEEPBEEEEEEP
BEEEEEEEEP
BEEEEEEP
THAT SOUND...RIPPING THROUGH MY HEAD... WHY CAN'T ANYONE ELSE HEAR IT?
BEEPBEEEEEEEPBEEEEEEEEEPBEEEEEEP
IT'S SO LOUD NOW... ALMOST TOO MUCH TO BEAR...
WHATCHA DOIN', BEANS?
...THINK IT'S COMING FROM THE GARAGE...
WHAT IS IT? BEANS? YOU OKAY?
STAY THERE, JOE!
BEEPBEEEEEEP
BEEEEEEEEP
BEEEEEEP
MA? YOU HEAR IT TOO?
IT'S THIS OLD THING. IT SHOULDN'T BE HERE!
BEEPBEEEEEEP
THAT'S WHAT'S MAKING THIS RACKET? I THINK IT WAS POPS'-- I FOUND IT IN THE CLOSET, WITH HIS LETTERS.
IT WASN'T HIS. I DON'T EVEN KNOW WHY HE KEPT IT...THIS PIECE OF JUNK...
THEN... WHOSE WAS IT?

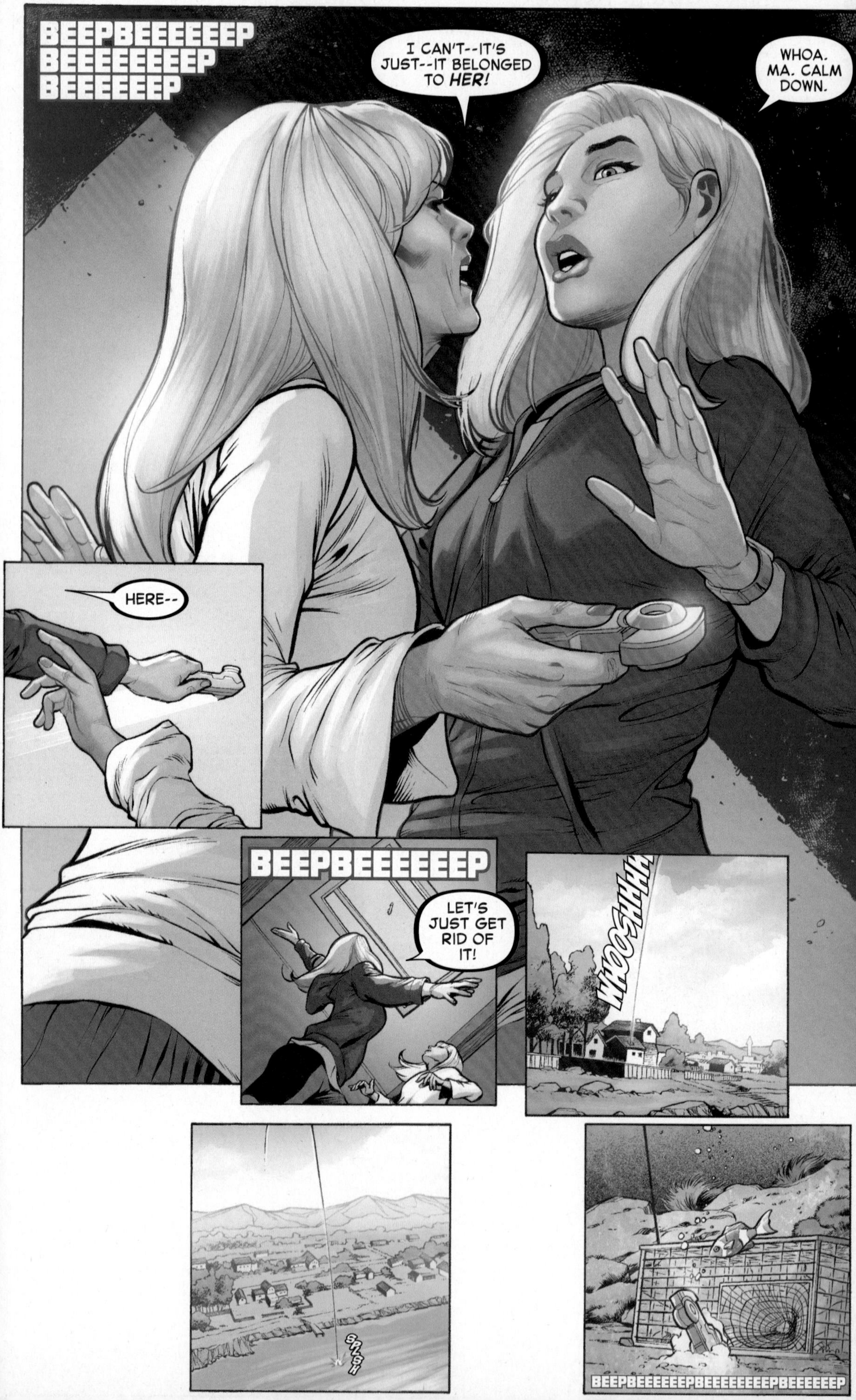
BEEPBEEEEEEP
BEEEEEEEEP
BEEEEEEP
I CAN'T--IT'S JUST--IT BELONGED TO HER!
WHOA. MA. CALM DOWN.
HERE--
BEEPBEEEEEEP
LET'S JUST GET RID OF IT!
WHOOSHHH
SPLSH
BEEPBEEEEEEPBEEEEEEEPBEEEEEEP

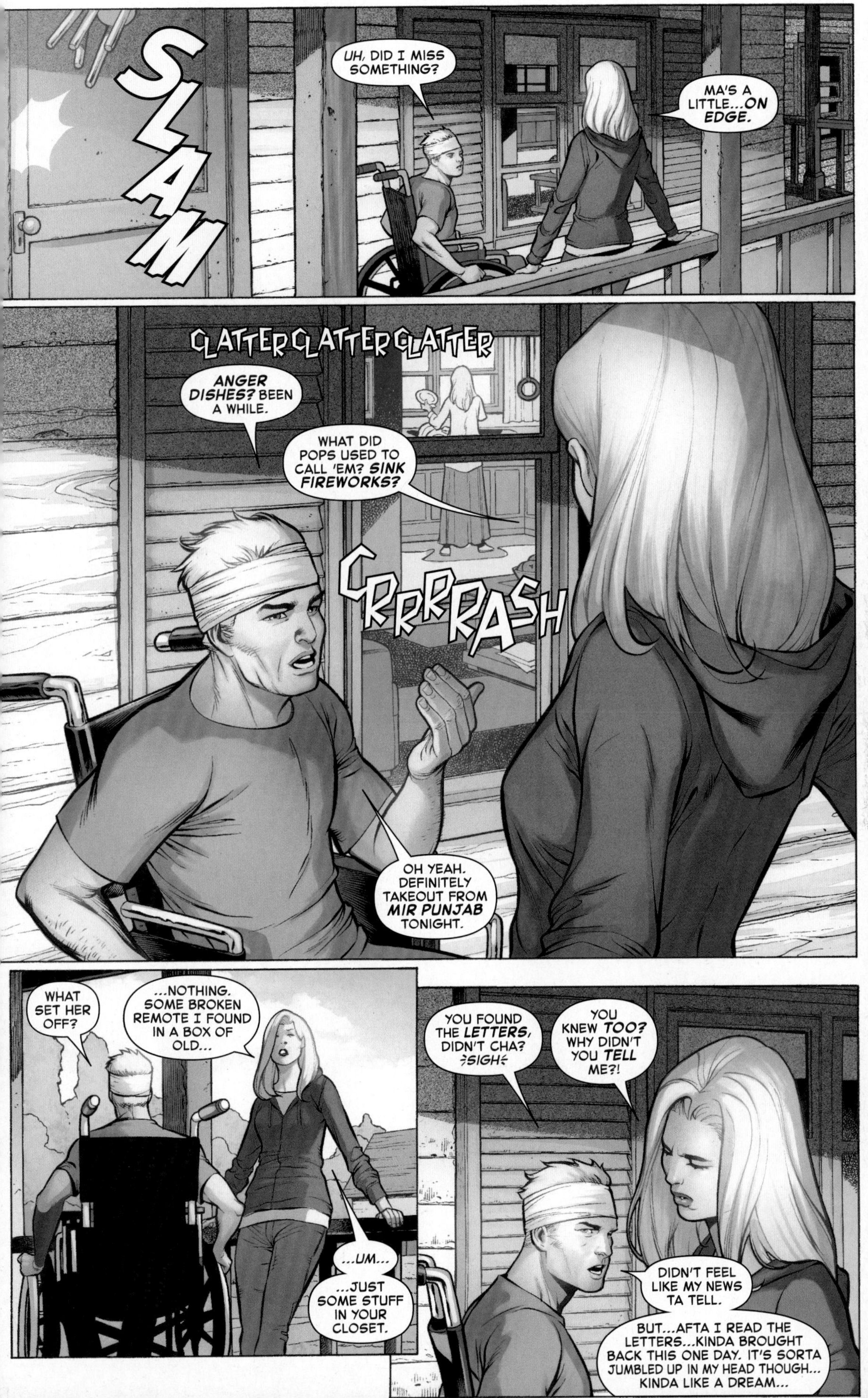
SLAM
UH, DID I MISS SOMETHING?
MA'S A LITTLE...ON EDGE.
CLATTER CLATTER CLATTER
ANGER DISHES? BEEN A WHILE.
WHAT DID POPS USED TO CALL 'EM? SINK FIREWORKS?
CRRRRASH
OH YEAH. DEFINITELY TAKEOUT FROM MIR PUNJAB TONIGHT.
WHAT SET HER OFF?
...NOTHING. SOME BROKEN REMOTE I FOUND IN A BOX OF OLD...
...UM...
...JUST SOME STUFF IN YOUR CLOSET.
YOU FOUND THE LETTERS, DIDN'T CHA? *SIGH*
YOU KNEW TOO? WHY DIDN'T YOU TELL ME?!
DIDN'T FEEL LIKE MY NEWS TA TELL.
BUT...AFTA I READ THE LETTERS...KINDA BROUGHT BACK THIS ONE DAY. IT'S SORTA JUMBLED UP IN MY HEAD THOUGH... KINDA LIKE A DREAM...

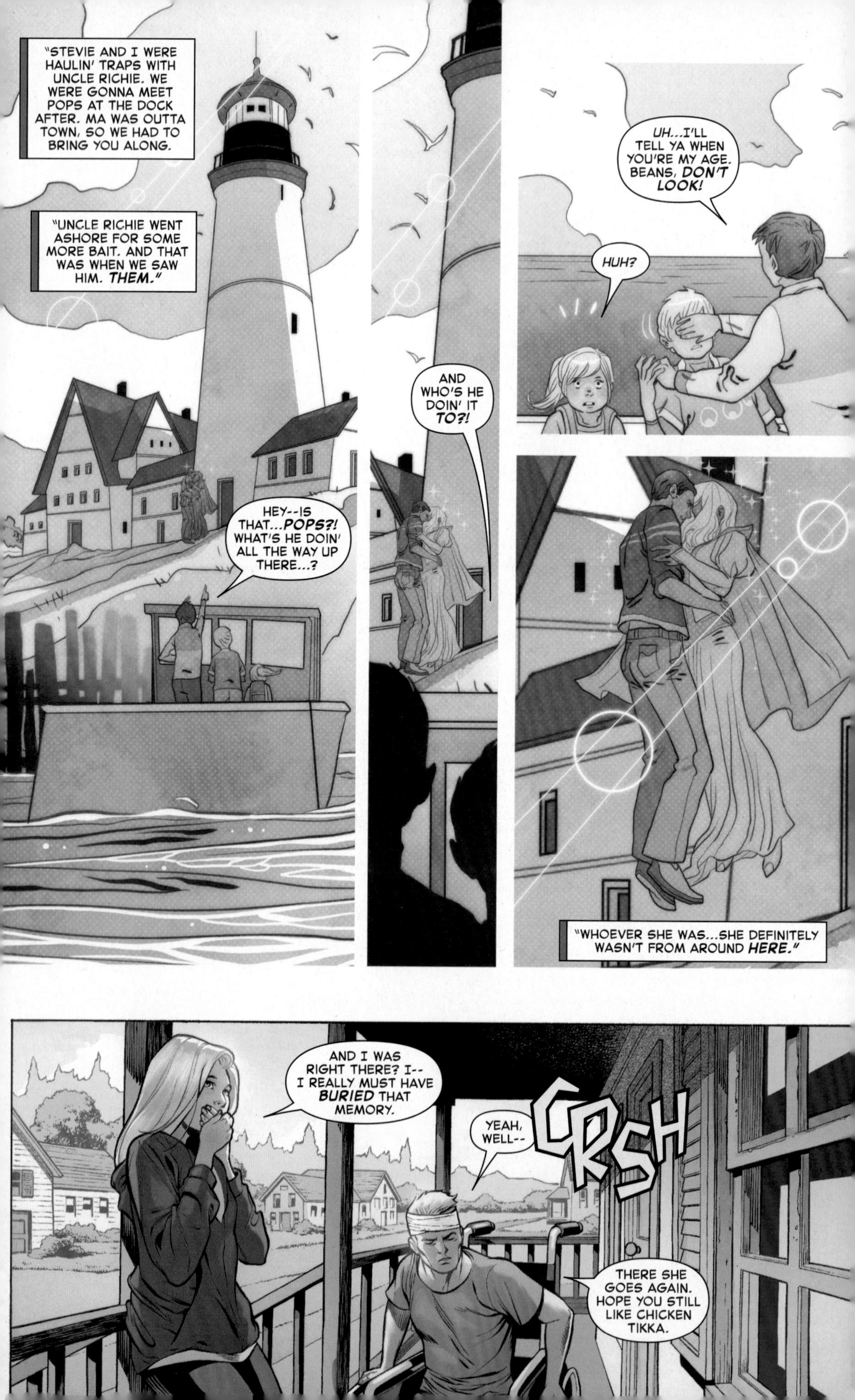
"STEVIE AND I WERE HAULIN' TRAPS WITH UNCLE RICHIE. WE WERE GONNA MEET POPS AT THE DOCK AFTER. MA WAS OUTTA TOWN, SO WE HAD TO BRING YOU ALONG.
"UNCLE RICHIE WENT ASHORE FOR SOME MORE BAIT. AND THAT WAS WHEN WE SAW HIM. THEM."
HEY--IS THAT...POPS?! WHAT'S HE DOIN' ALL THE WAY UP THERE...?
AND WHO'S HE DOIN' IT TO?!
UH...I'LL TELL YA WHEN YOU'RE MY AGE. BEANS, DON'T LOOK!
HUH?
"WHOEVER SHE WAS...SHE DEFINITELY WASN'T FROM AROUND HERE."
AND I WAS RIGHT THERE? I-- I REALLY MUST HAVE BURIED THAT MEMORY.
YEAH, WELL--
CRSH
THERE SHE GOES AGAIN. HOPE YOU STILL LIKE CHICKEN TIKKA.

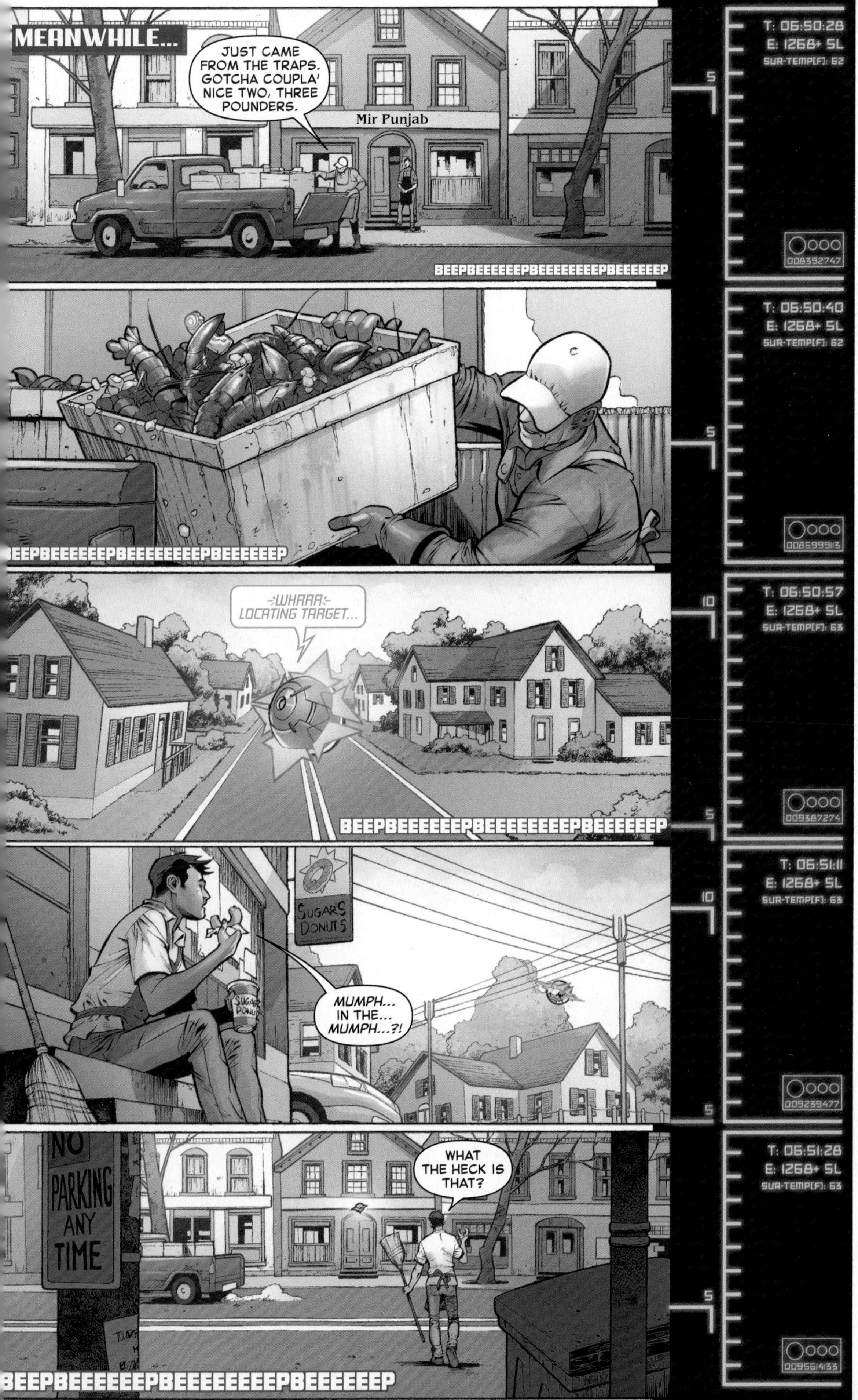
MEANWHILE...
JUST CAME FROM THE TRAPS. GOTCHA COUPLA' NICE TWO, THREE POUNDERS.
Mir Punjab
BEEPBEEEEEEPBEEEEEEEEPBEEEEEEP
T: 06:50:28
E: 1268+ 5L
SUR-TEMP[F]: 62
008392747
BEEPBEEEEEEPBEEEEEEEEPBEEEEEEP
T: 06:50:40
E: 1268+ 5L
SUR-TEMP[F]: 62
0086999113
-WHRRR- LOCATING TARGET...
BEEPBEEEEEEPBEEEEEEEEPBEEEEEEP
T: 06:50:57
E: 1268+ 5L
SUR-TEMP[F]: 63
009387274
SUGAR'S DONUTS
MUMPH... IN THE... MUMPH...?!
T: 06:51:11
E: 1268+ 5L
SUR-TEMP[F]: 63
009239477
NO PARKING ANY TIME
WHAT THE HECK IS THAT?
BEEPBEEEEEEPBEEEEEEEEPBEEEEEEP
T: 06:51:28
E: 1268+ 5L
SUR-TEMP[F]: 63
009561433

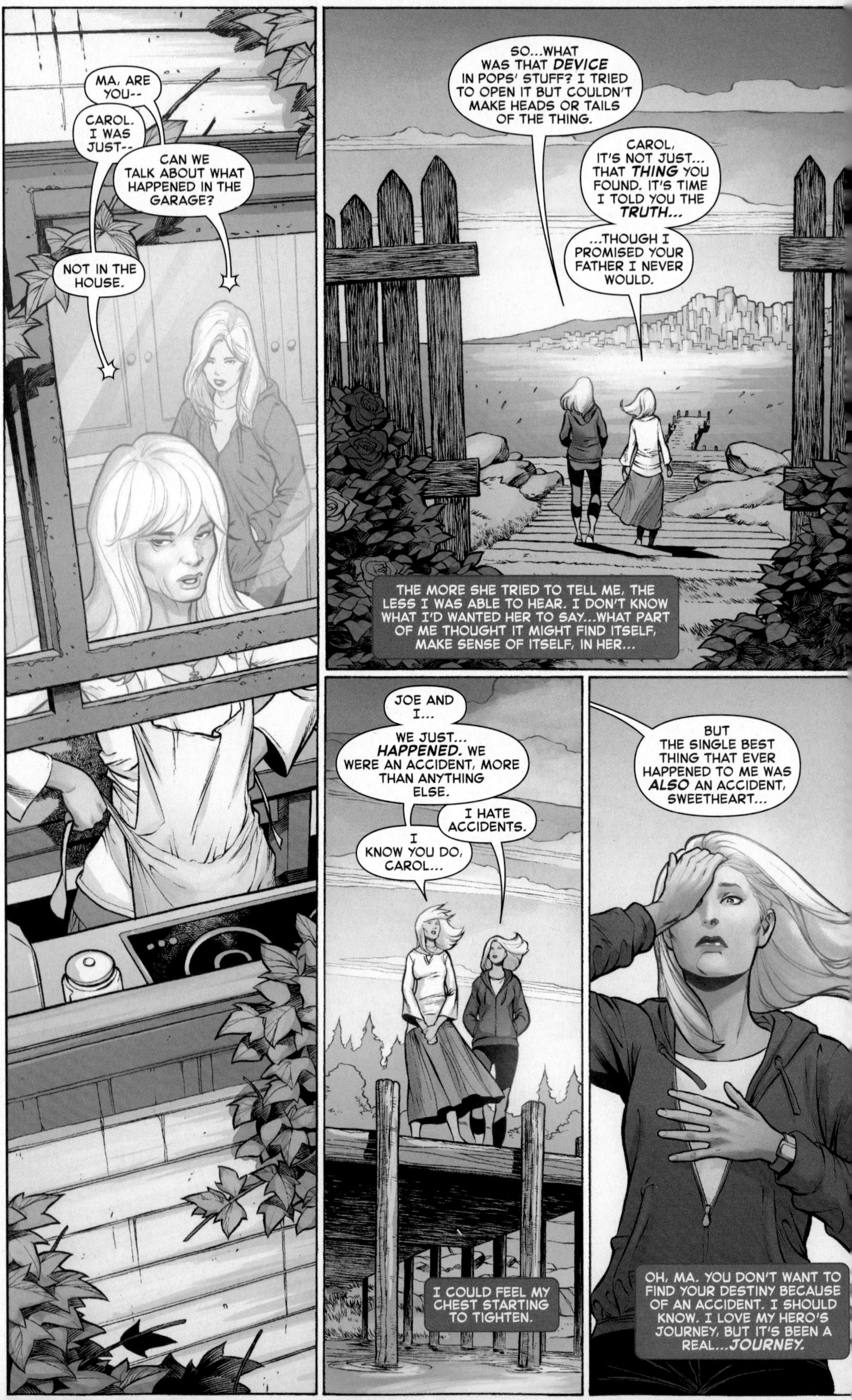

MA, ARE YOU--
CAROL. I WAS JUST--
CAN WE TALK ABOUT WHAT HAPPENED IN THE GARAGE?
NOT IN THE HOUSE.
SO...WHAT WAS THAT DEVICE IN POPS' STUFF? I TRIED TO OPEN IT BUT COULDN'T MAKE HEADS OR TAILS OF THE THING.
CAROL, IT'S NOT JUST... THAT THING YOU FOUND. IT'S TIME I TOLD YOU THE TRUTH...
...THOUGH I PROMISED YOUR FATHER I NEVER WOULD.
THE MORE SHE TRIED TO TELL ME, THE LESS I WAS ABLE TO HEAR. I DON'T KNOW WHAT I'D WANTED HER TO SAY...WHAT PART OF ME THOUGHT IT MIGHT FIND ITSELF, MAKE SENSE OF ITSELF, IN HER...
JOE AND I...
WE JUST... HAPPENED. WE WERE AN ACCIDENT, MORE THAN ANYTHING ELSE.
I HATE ACCIDENTS.
I KNOW YOU DO, CAROL...
I COULD FEEL MY CHEST STARTING TO TIGHTEN.
BUT THE SINGLE BEST THING THAT EVER HAPPENED TO ME WAS ALSO AN ACCIDENT, SWEETHEART...
OH, MA. YOU DON'T WANT TO FIND YOUR DESTINY BECAUSE OF AN ACCIDENT. I SHOULD KNOW. I LOVE MY HERO'S JOURNEY, BUT IT'S BEEN A REAL...JOURNEY.

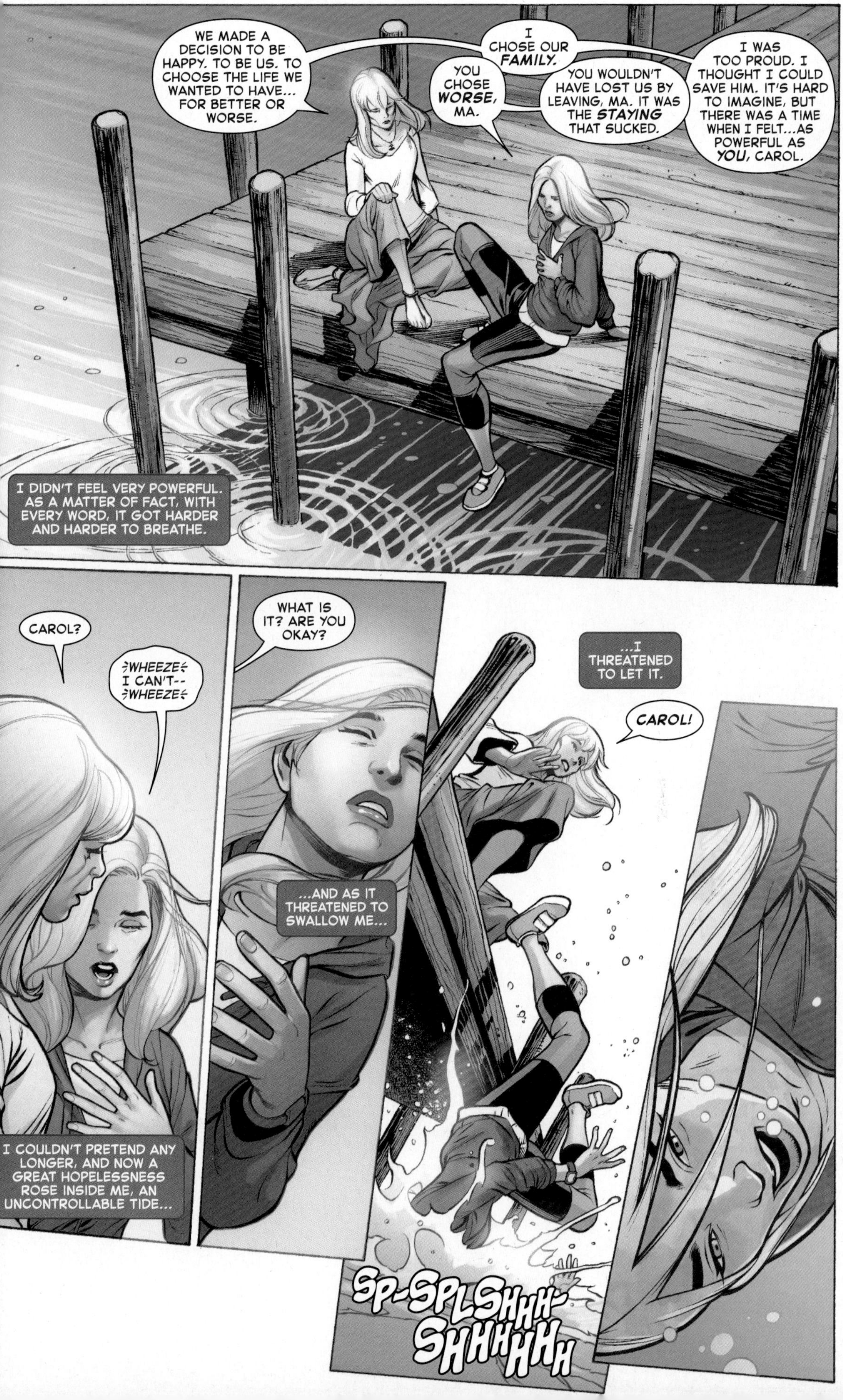
WE MADE A DECISION TO BE HAPPY. TO BE US. TO CHOOSE THE LIFE WE WANTED TO HAVE... FOR BETTER OR WORSE.
I CHOSE OUR FAMILY.
YOU CHOSE WORSE, MA.
YOU WOULDN'T HAVE LOST US BY LEAVING, MA. IT WAS THE STAYING THAT SUCKED.
I WAS TOO PROUD. I THOUGHT I COULD SAVE HIM. IT'S HARD TO IMAGINE, BUT THERE WAS A TIME WHEN I FELT...AS POWERFUL AS YOU, CAROL.
I DIDN'T FEEL VERY POWERFUL. AS A MATTER OF FACT, WITH EVERY WORD, IT GOT HARDER AND HARDER TO BREATHE.
CAROL?
WHEEZE I CAN'T-- WHEEZE
I COULDN'T PRETEND ANY LONGER, AND NOW A GREAT HOPELESSNESS ROSE INSIDE ME, AN UNCONTROLLABLE TIDE...
WHAT IS IT? ARE YOU OKAY?
...AND AS IT THREATENED TO SWALLOW ME...
...I THREATENED TO LET IT.
CAROL!
SP-SPLSHHH-SHHHHHH

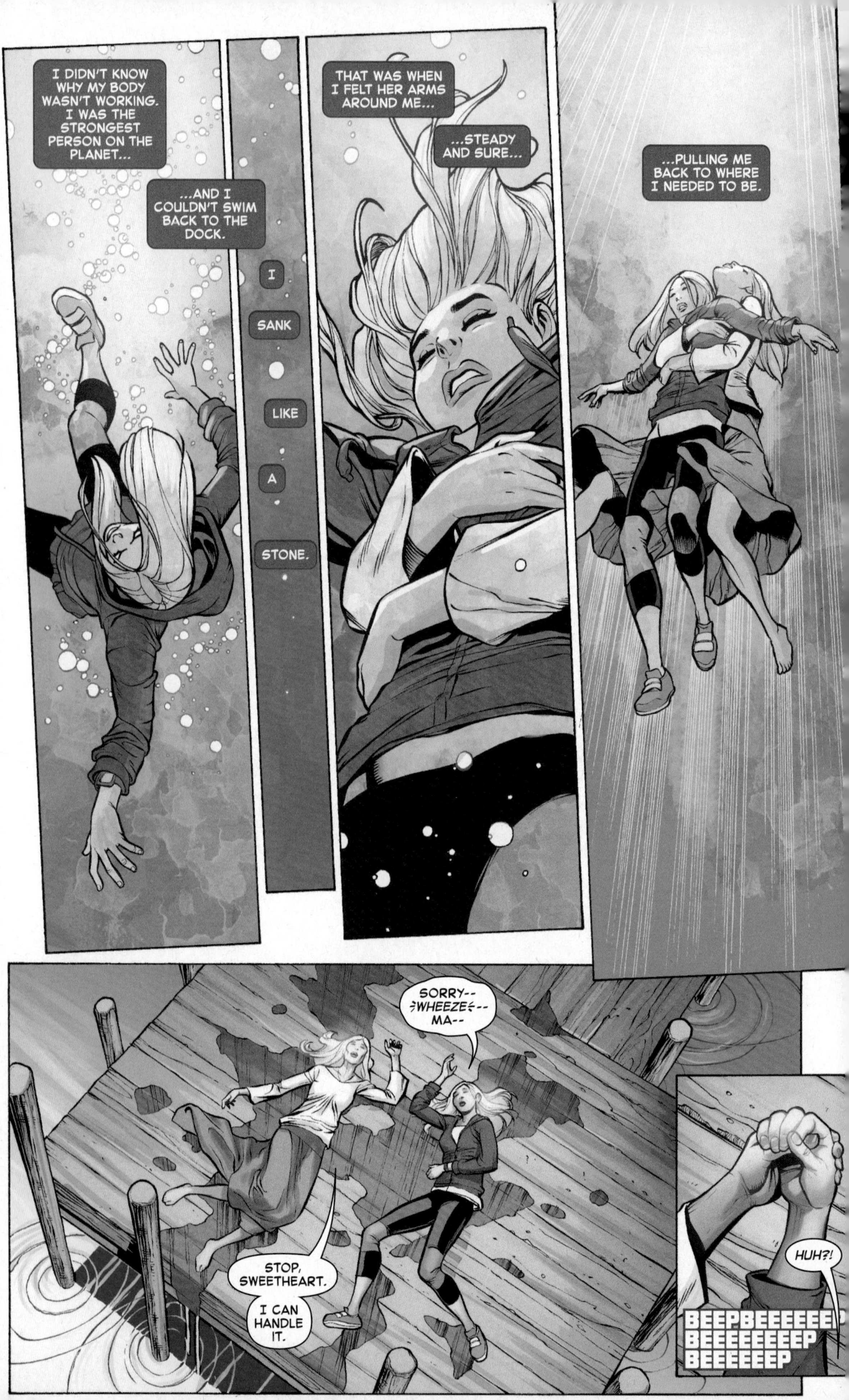
I DIDN'T KNOW WHY MY BODY WASN'T WORKING. I WAS THE STRONGEST PERSON ON THE PLANET...
...AND I COULDN'T SWIM BACK TO THE DOCK.
I
SANK
LIKE
A
STONE.
THAT WAS WHEN I FELT HER ARMS AROUND ME...
...STEADY AND SURE...
...PULLING ME BACK TO WHERE I NEEDED TO BE.
SORRY-- ≠WHEEZE≠-- MA--
STOP, SWEETHEART.
I CAN HANDLE IT.
HUH?!
BEEPBEEEEEEP BEEEEEEEP BEEEEEEP

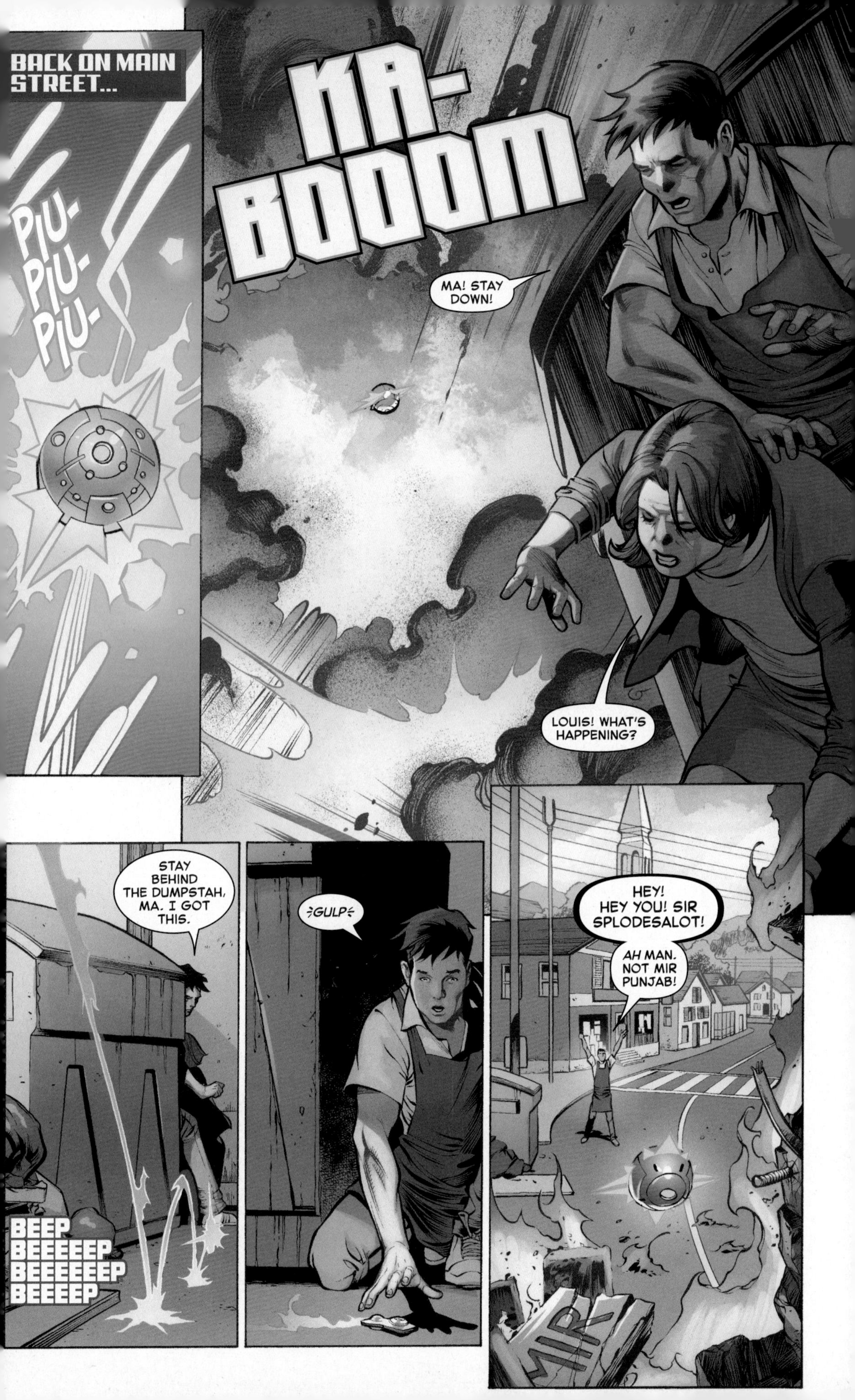
BACK ON MAIN STREET...
PIU-PIU-PIU-
KA-BOOOM
MA! STAY DOWN!
LOUIS! WHAT'S HAPPENING?
STAY BEHIND THE DUMPSTAH, MA. I GOT THIS.
BEEP BEEEEEP BEEEEEEP BEEEEP
GULP
HEY! HEY YOU! SIR SPLODESALOT!
AH MAN. NOT MIR PUNJAB!
MIR

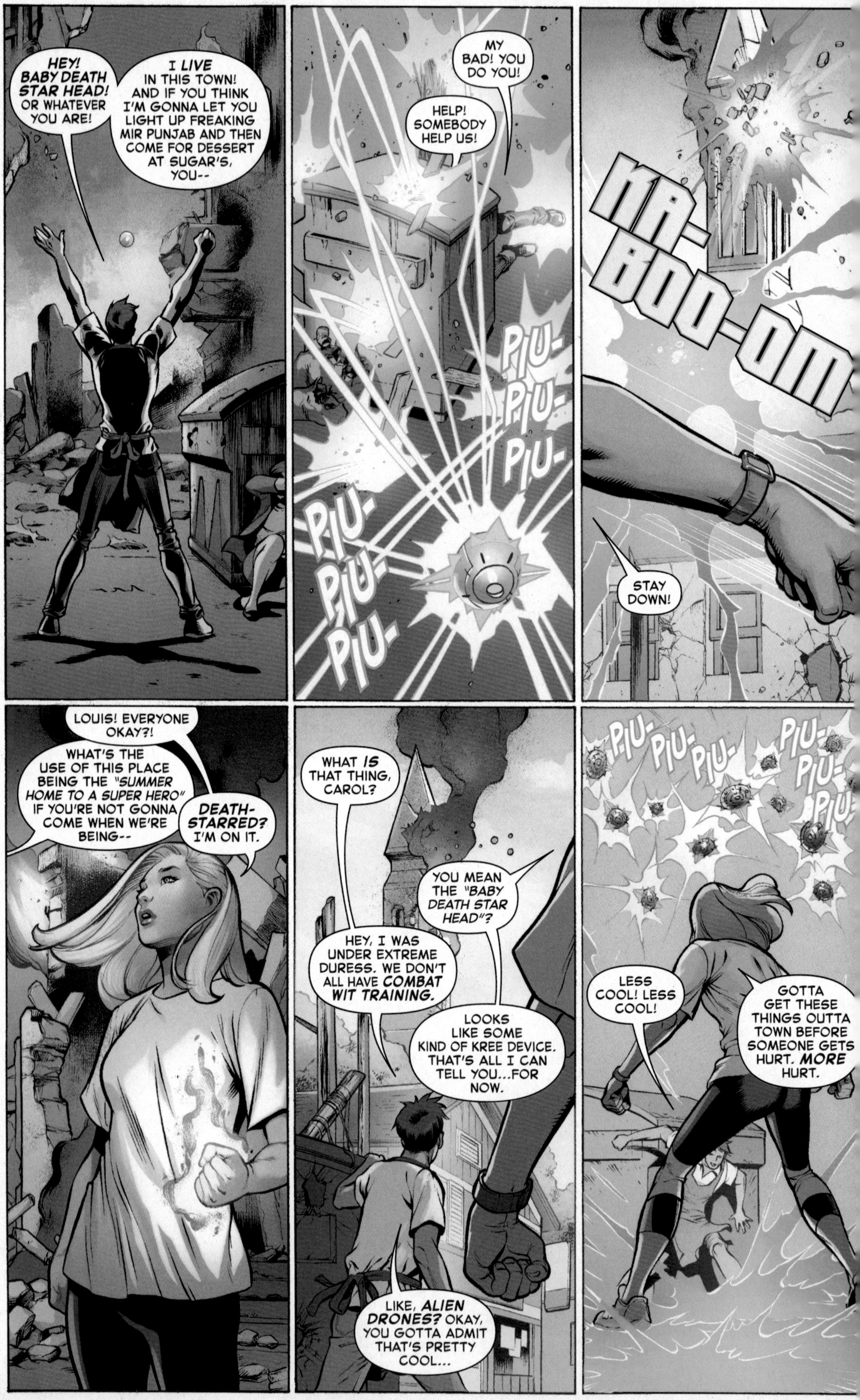
HEY! BABY DEATH STAR HEAD! OR WHATEVER YOU ARE!
I LIVE IN THIS TOWN! AND IF YOU THINK I'M GONNA LET YOU LIGHT UP FREAKING MIR PUNJAB AND THEN COME FOR DESSERT AT SUGAR'S, YOU--
MY BAD! YOU DO YOU!
HELP! SOMEBODY HELP US!
PIU-PIU-PIU-
PIU-PIU-PIU-
KA-BOO-OM
STAY DOWN!
LOUIS! EVERYONE OKAY?!
WHAT'S THE USE OF THIS PLACE BEING THE "SUMMER HOME TO A SUPER HERO" IF YOU'RE NOT GONNA COME WHEN WE'RE BEING--
DEATH-STARRED? I'M ON IT.
WHAT IS THAT THING, CAROL?
YOU MEAN THE "BABY DEATH STAR HEAD"?
HEY, I WAS UNDER EXTREME DURESS. WE DON'T ALL HAVE COMBAT WIT TRAINING.
LOOKS LIKE SOME KIND OF KREE DEVICE. THAT'S ALL I CAN TELL YOU...FOR NOW.
LIKE, ALIEN DRONES? OKAY, YOU GOTTA ADMIT THAT'S PRETTY COOL...
PIU-PIU-PIU-PIU-PIU-PIU-
LESS COOL! LESS COOL!
GOTTA GET THESE THINGS OUTTA TOWN BEFORE SOMEONE GETS HURT. MORE HURT.

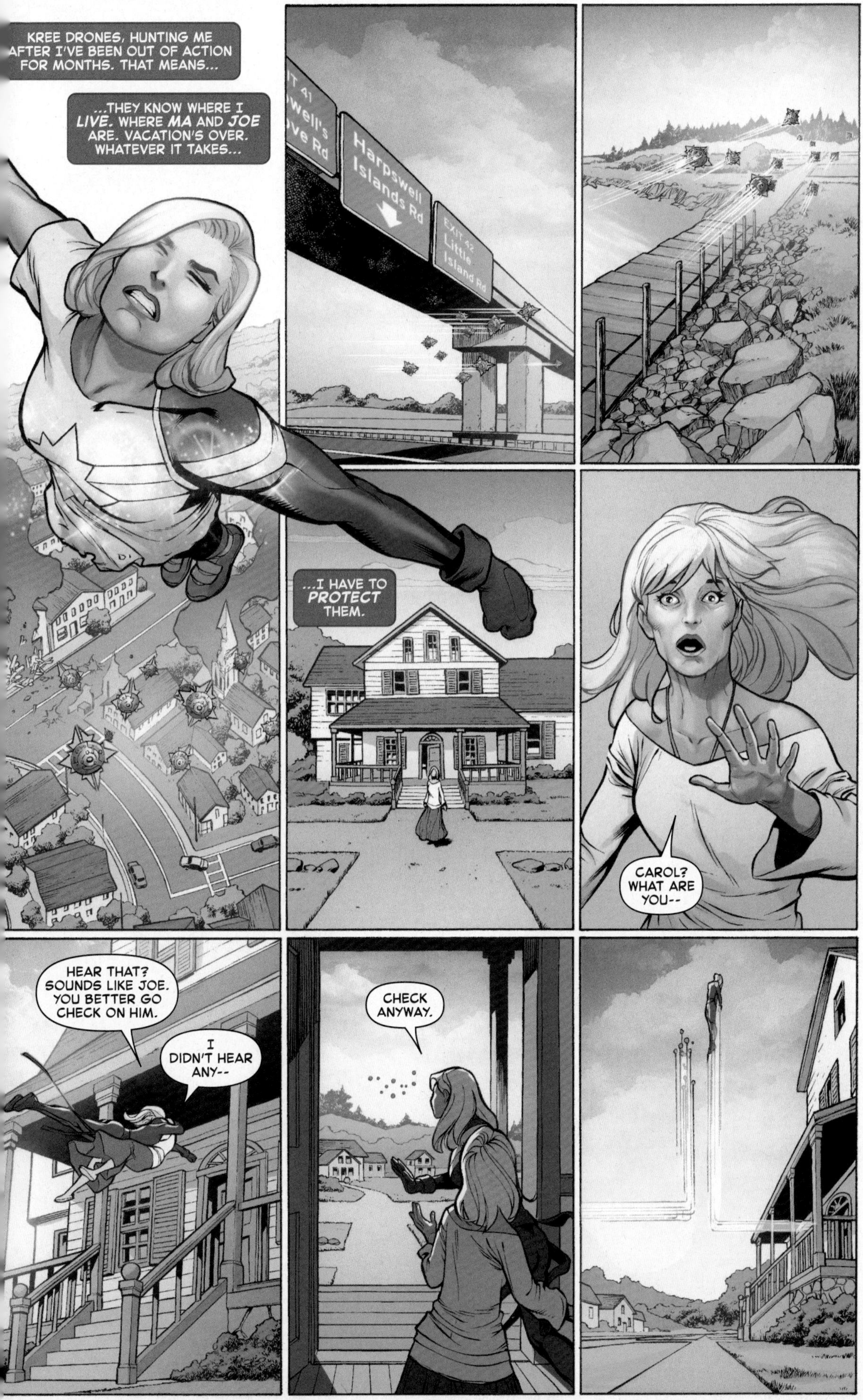
KREE DRONES, HUNTING ME AFTER I'VE BEEN OUT OF ACTION FOR MONTHS. THAT MEANS...
...THEY KNOW WHERE I LIVE. WHERE MA AND JOE ARE. VACATION'S OVER. WHATEVER IT TAKES...
Harpswell Islands Rd
EXIT 42 Little Island Rd
...I HAVE TO PROTECT THEM.
CAROL? WHAT ARE YOU--
HEAR THAT? SOUNDS LIKE JOE. YOU BETTER GO CHECK ON HIM.
I DIDN'T HEAR ANY--
CHECK ANYWAY.

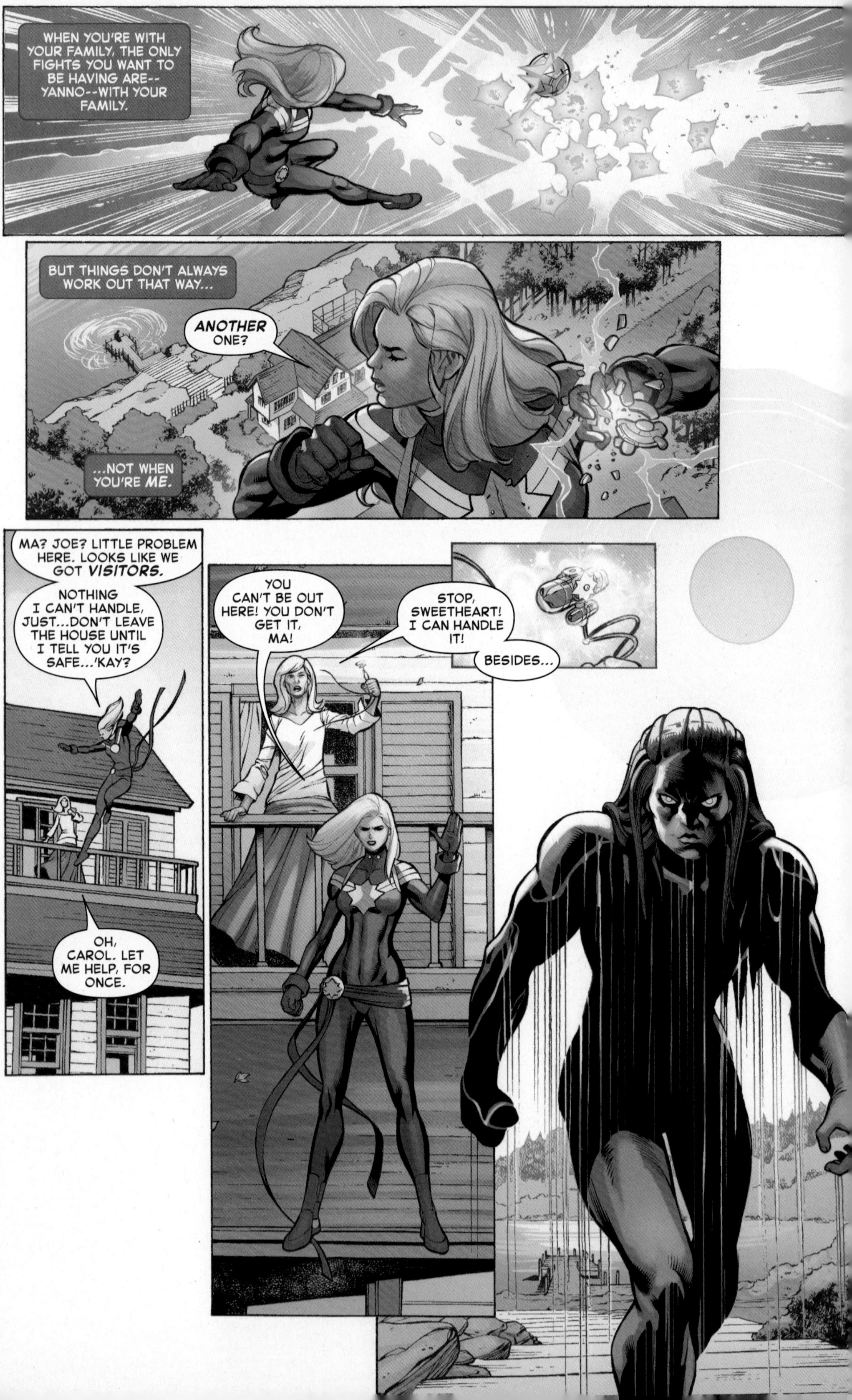

WHEN YOU'RE WITH YOUR FAMILY, THE ONLY FIGHTS YOU WANT TO BE HAVING ARE--YANNO--WITH YOUR FAMILY.
BUT THINGS DON'T ALWAYS WORK OUT THAT WAY...
ANOTHER ONE?
...NOT WHEN YOU'RE ME.
MA? JOE? LITTLE PROBLEM HERE. LOOKS LIKE WE GOT VISITORS.
NOTHING I CAN'T HANDLE, JUST...DON'T LEAVE THE HOUSE UNTIL I TELL YOU IT'S SAFE...'KAY?
OH, CAROL. LET ME HELP, FOR ONCE.
YOU CAN'T BE OUT HERE! YOU DON'T GET IT, MA!
STOP, SWEETHEART! I CAN HANDLE IT!
BESIDES...

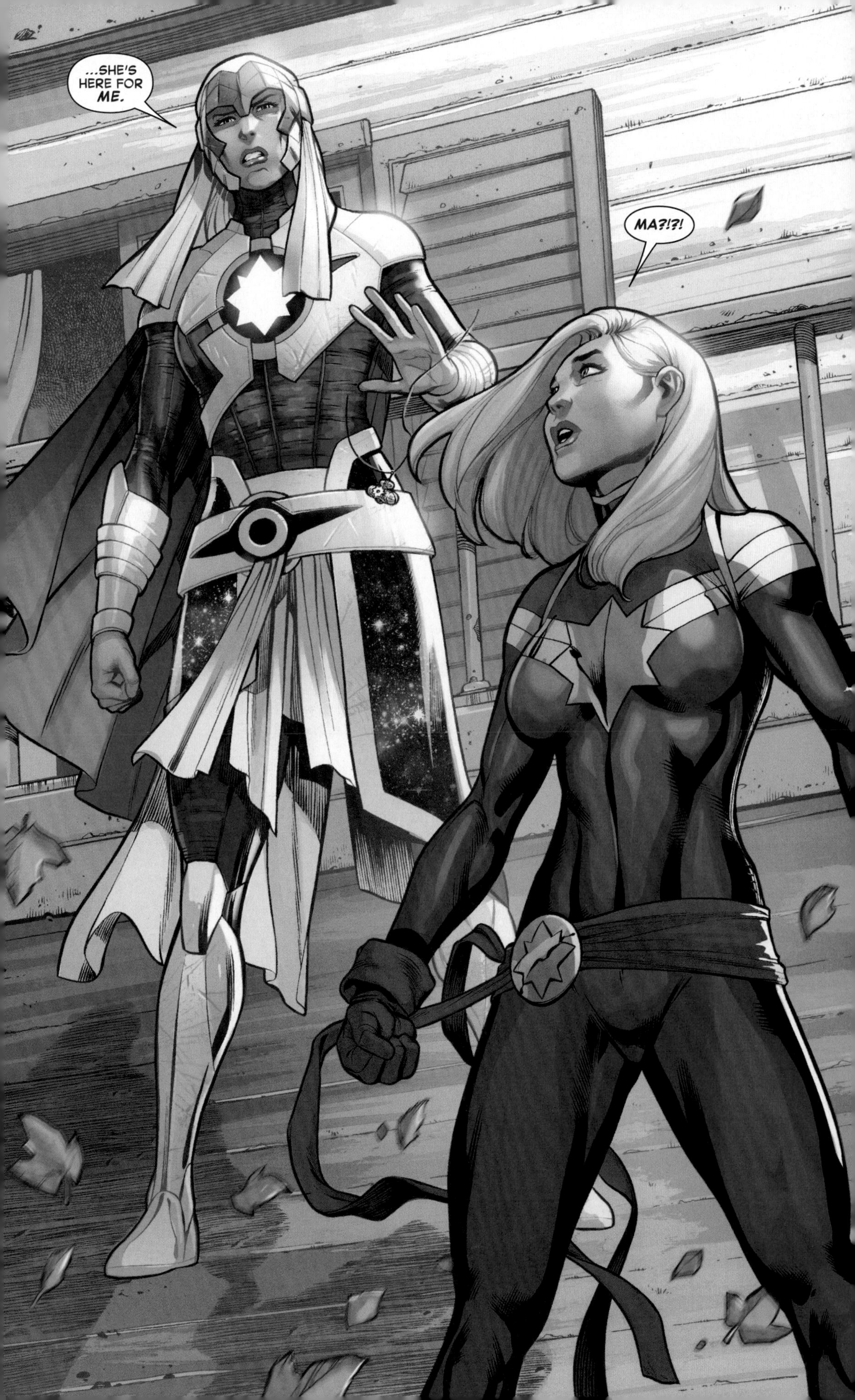
...SHE'S HERE FOR ME.
MA?!?!

THE LIFE OF CAPTAIN MARVEL #4

"CHALLENGED"

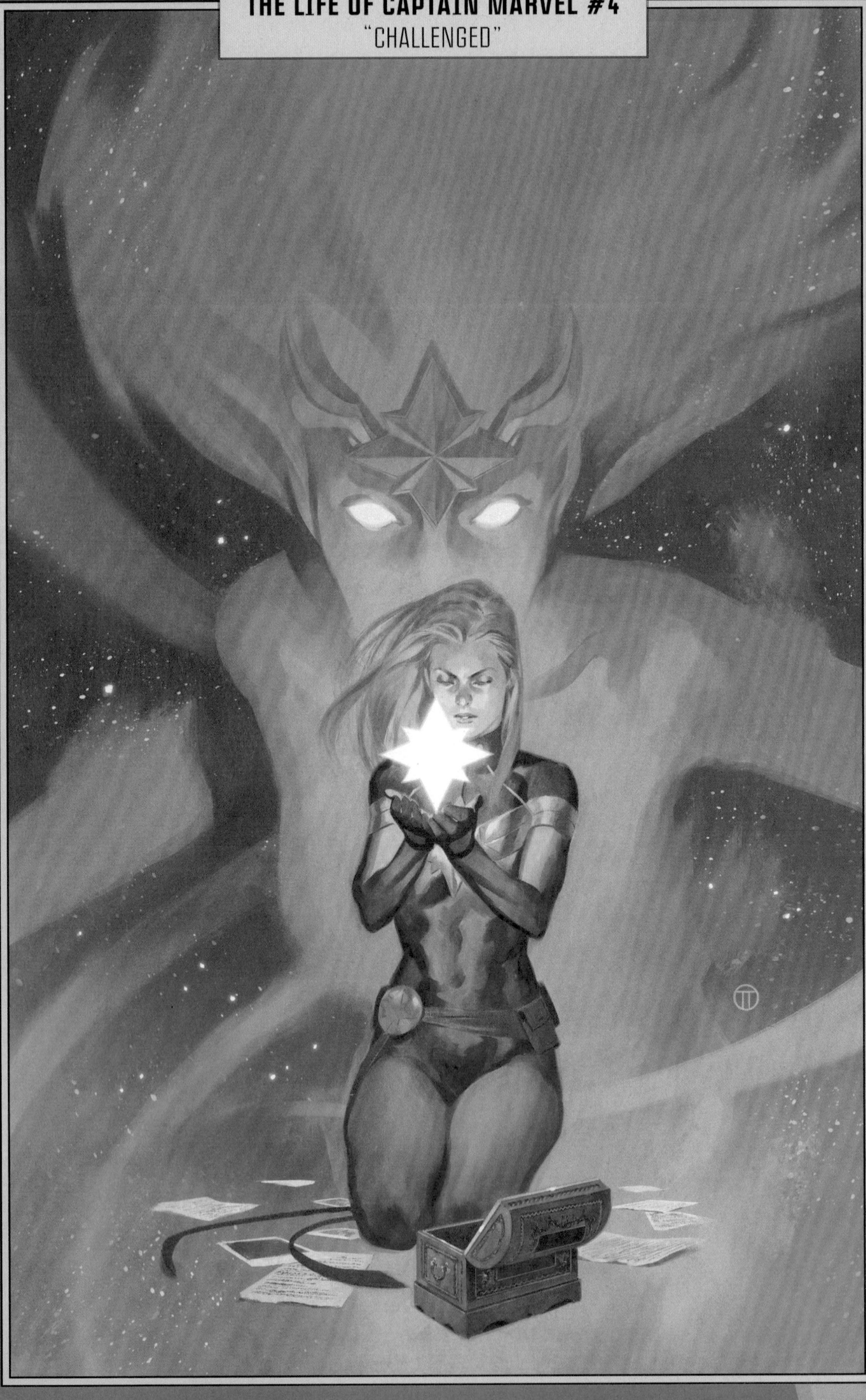

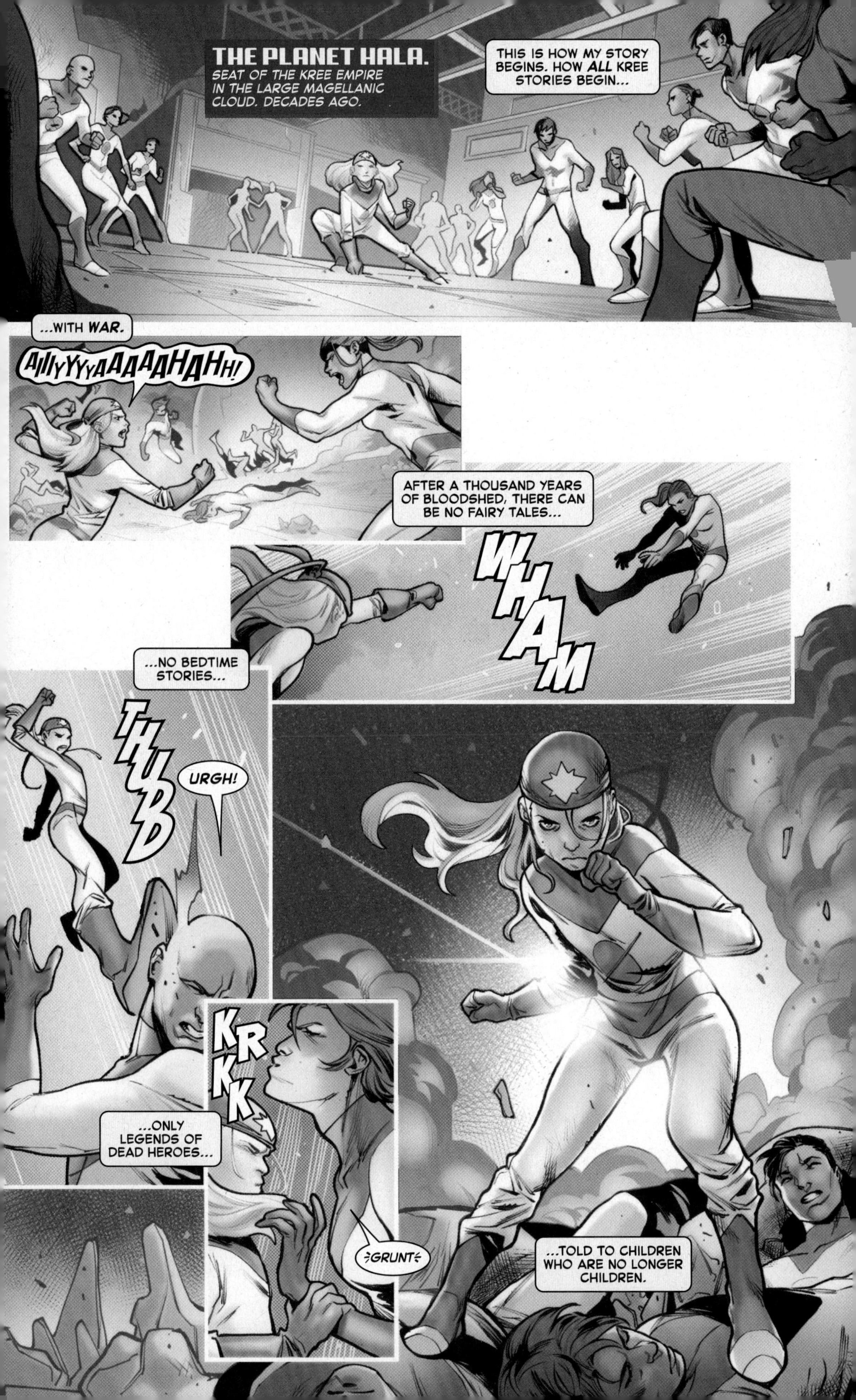
THE PLANET HALA.
SEAT OF THE KREE EMPIRE IN THE LARGE MAGELLANIC CLOUD. DECADES AGO.
THIS IS HOW MY STORY BEGINS. HOW ALL KREE STORIES BEGIN...
...WITH WAR.
AIIIYYYYAAAAAHAHH!
AFTER A THOUSAND YEARS OF BLOODSHED, THERE CAN BE NO FAIRY TALES...
WHAM
...NO BEDTIME STORIES...
THUD
URGH!
KRKK
...ONLY LEGENDS OF DEAD HEROES...
GRUNT
...TOLD TO CHILDREN WHO ARE NO LONGER CHILDREN.

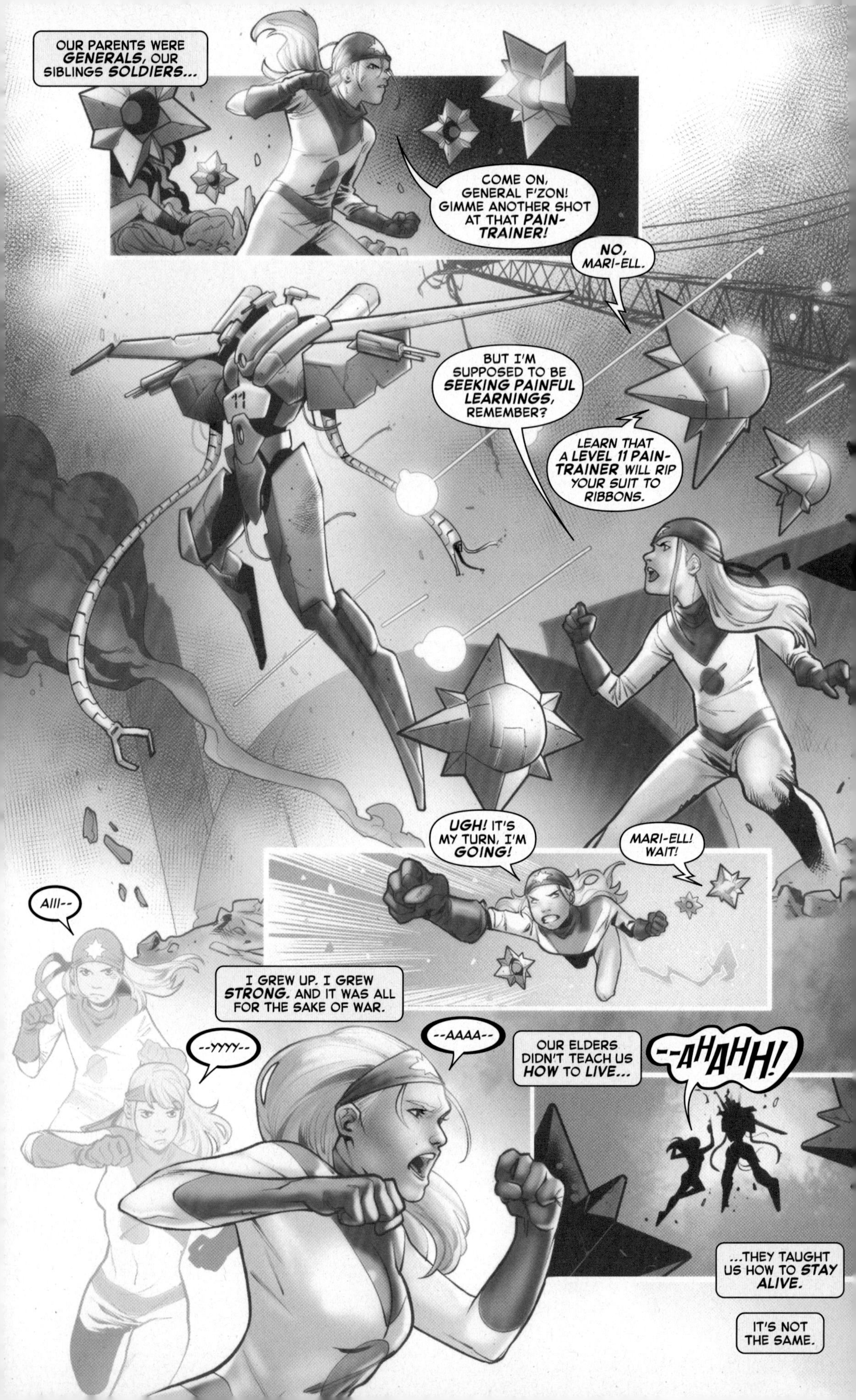
OUR PARENTS WERE GENERALS, OUR SIBLINGS SOLDIERS...
COME ON, GENERAL F'ZON! GIMME ANOTHER SHOT AT THAT PAIN-TRAINER!
NO, MARI-ELL.
BUT I'M SUPPOSED TO BE SEEKING PAINFUL LEARNINGS, REMEMBER?
LEARN THAT A LEVEL 11 PAIN-TRAINER WILL RIP YOUR SUIT TO RIBBONS.
UGH! IT'S MY TURN, I'M GOING!
MARI-ELL! WAIT!
AIII--
I GREW UP. I GREW STRONG. AND IT WAS ALL FOR THE SAKE OF WAR.
--YYYY--
--AAAA--
OUR ELDERS DIDN'T TEACH US HOW TO LIVE...
--AHAHH!
...THEY TAUGHT US HOW TO STAY ALIVE.
IT'S NOT THE SAME.

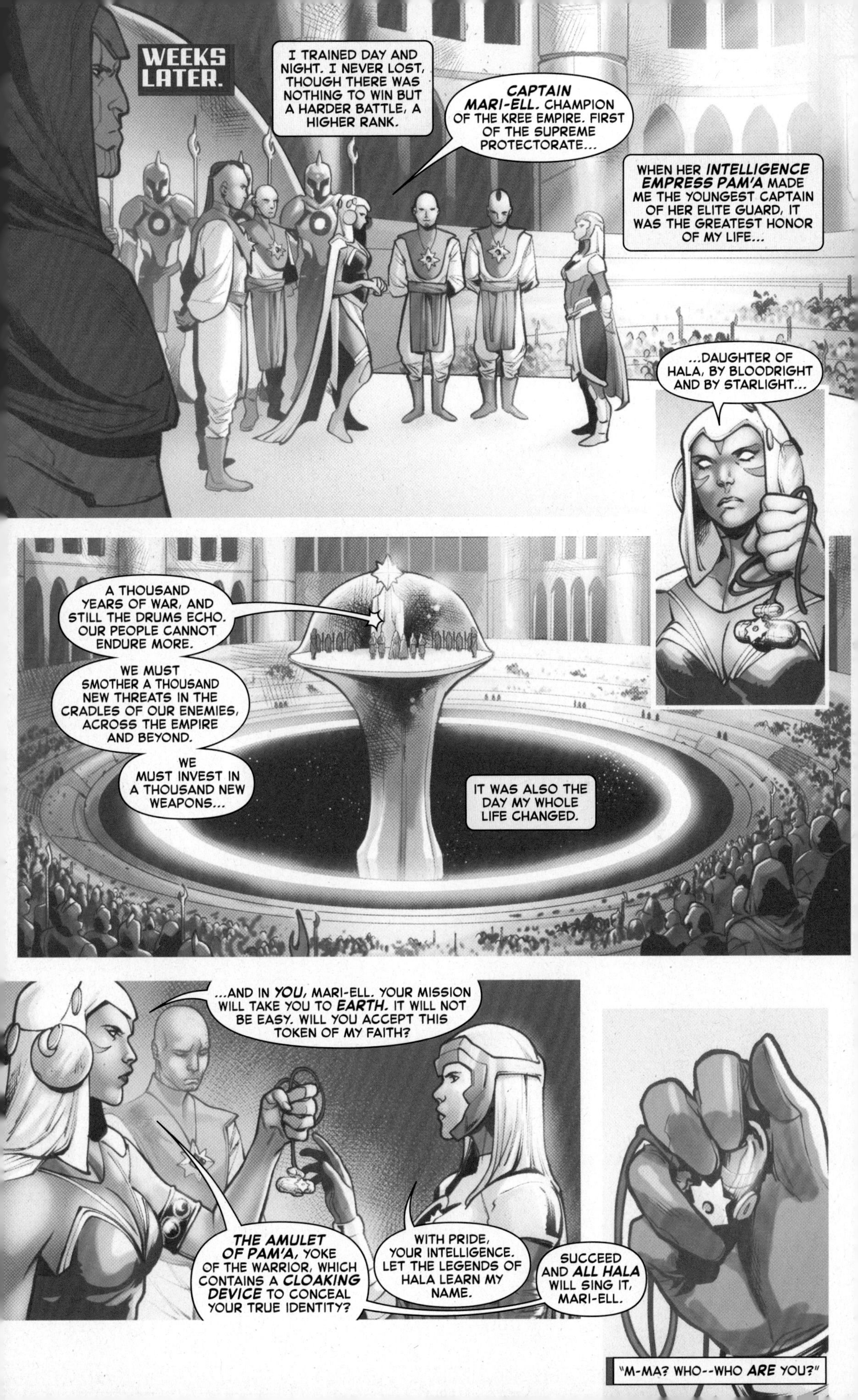
WEEKS LATER.
I TRAINED DAY AND NIGHT. I NEVER LOST, THOUGH THERE WAS NOTHING TO WIN BUT A HARDER BATTLE, A HIGHER RANK.
CAPTAIN MARI-ELL. CHAMPION OF THE KREE EMPIRE. FIRST OF THE SUPREME PROTECTORATE...
WHEN HER INTELLIGENCE EMPRESS PAM'A MADE ME THE YOUNGEST CAPTAIN OF HER ELITE GUARD, IT WAS THE GREATEST HONOR OF MY LIFE...
...DAUGHTER OF HALA, BY BLOODRIGHT AND BY STARLIGHT...
A THOUSAND YEARS OF WAR, AND STILL THE DRUMS ECHO. OUR PEOPLE CANNOT ENDURE MORE.
WE MUST SMOTHER A THOUSAND NEW THREATS IN THE CRADLES OF OUR ENEMIES, ACROSS THE EMPIRE AND BEYOND.
WE MUST INVEST IN A THOUSAND NEW WEAPONS...
IT WAS ALSO THE DAY MY WHOLE LIFE CHANGED.
...AND IN YOU, MARI-ELL. YOUR MISSION WILL TAKE YOU TO EARTH. IT WILL NOT BE EASY. WILL YOU ACCEPT THIS TOKEN OF MY FAITH?
THE AMULET OF PAM'A, YOKE OF THE WARRIOR, WHICH CONTAINS A CLOAKING DEVICE TO CONCEAL YOUR TRUE IDENTITY?
WITH PRIDE, YOUR INTELLIGENCE. LET THE LEGENDS OF HALA LEARN MY NAME.
SUCCEED AND ALL HALA WILL SING IT, MARI-ELL.
"M-MA? WHO--WHO ARE YOU?"

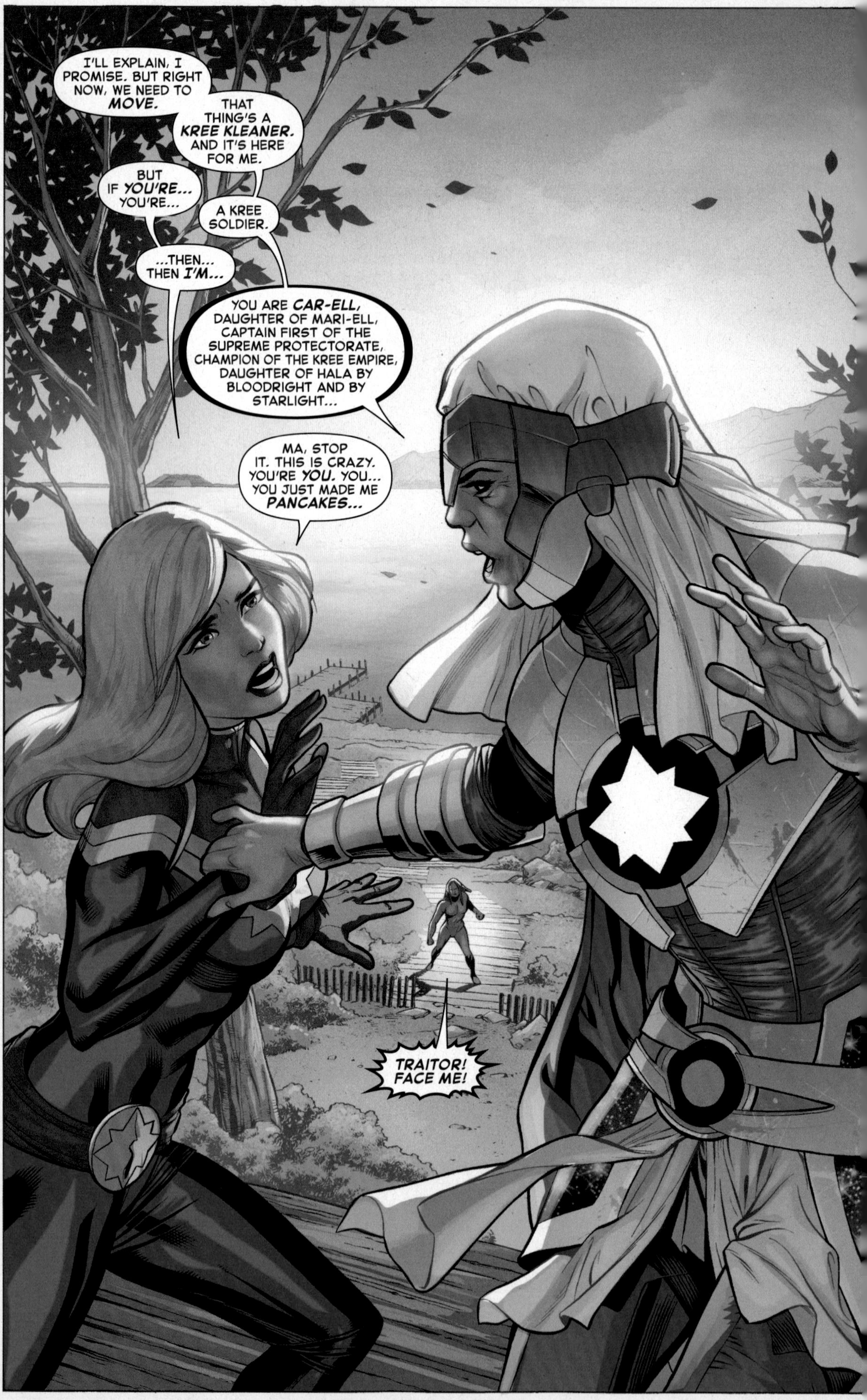
I'LL EXPLAIN, I PROMISE. BUT RIGHT NOW, WE NEED TO MOVE.
THAT THING'S A KREE KLEANER. AND IT'S HERE FOR ME.
BUT IF YOU'RE... YOU'RE...
A KREE SOLDIER.
...THEN... THEN I'M...
YOU ARE CAR-ELL, DAUGHTER OF MARI-ELL, CAPTAIN FIRST OF THE SUPREME PROTECTORATE, CHAMPION OF THE KREE EMPIRE, DAUGHTER OF HALA BY BLOODRIGHT AND BY STARLIGHT...
MA, STOP IT. THIS IS CRAZY. YOU'RE YOU. YOU... YOU JUST MADE ME PANCAKES...
TRAITOR! FACE ME!

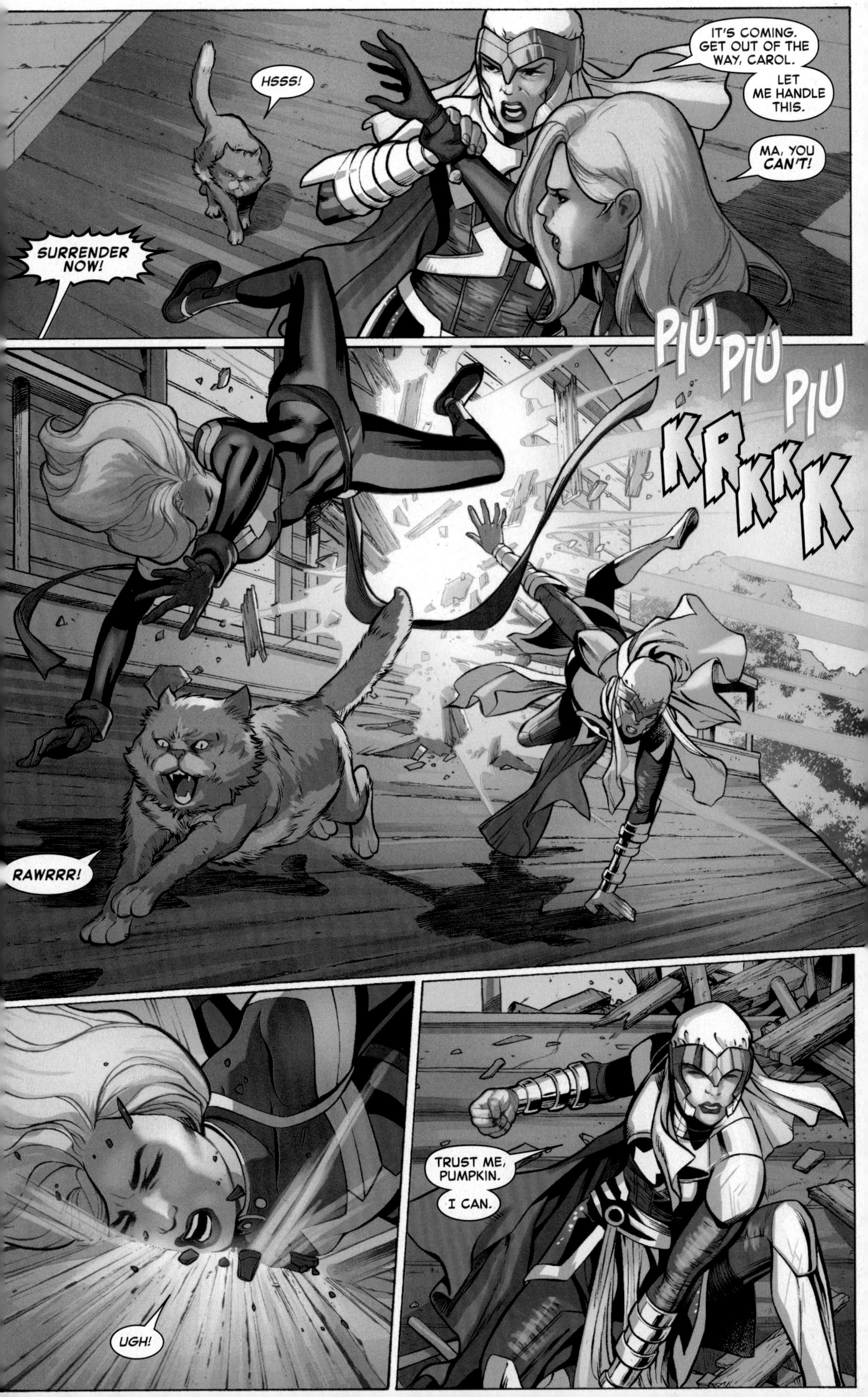
HSSS!
IT'S COMING. GET OUT OF THE WAY, CAROL.
LET ME HANDLE THIS.
MA, YOU CAN'T!
SURRENDER NOW!
PIU PIU PIU
KRKKK
RAWRRR!
UGH!
TRUST ME, PUMPKIN.
I CAN.

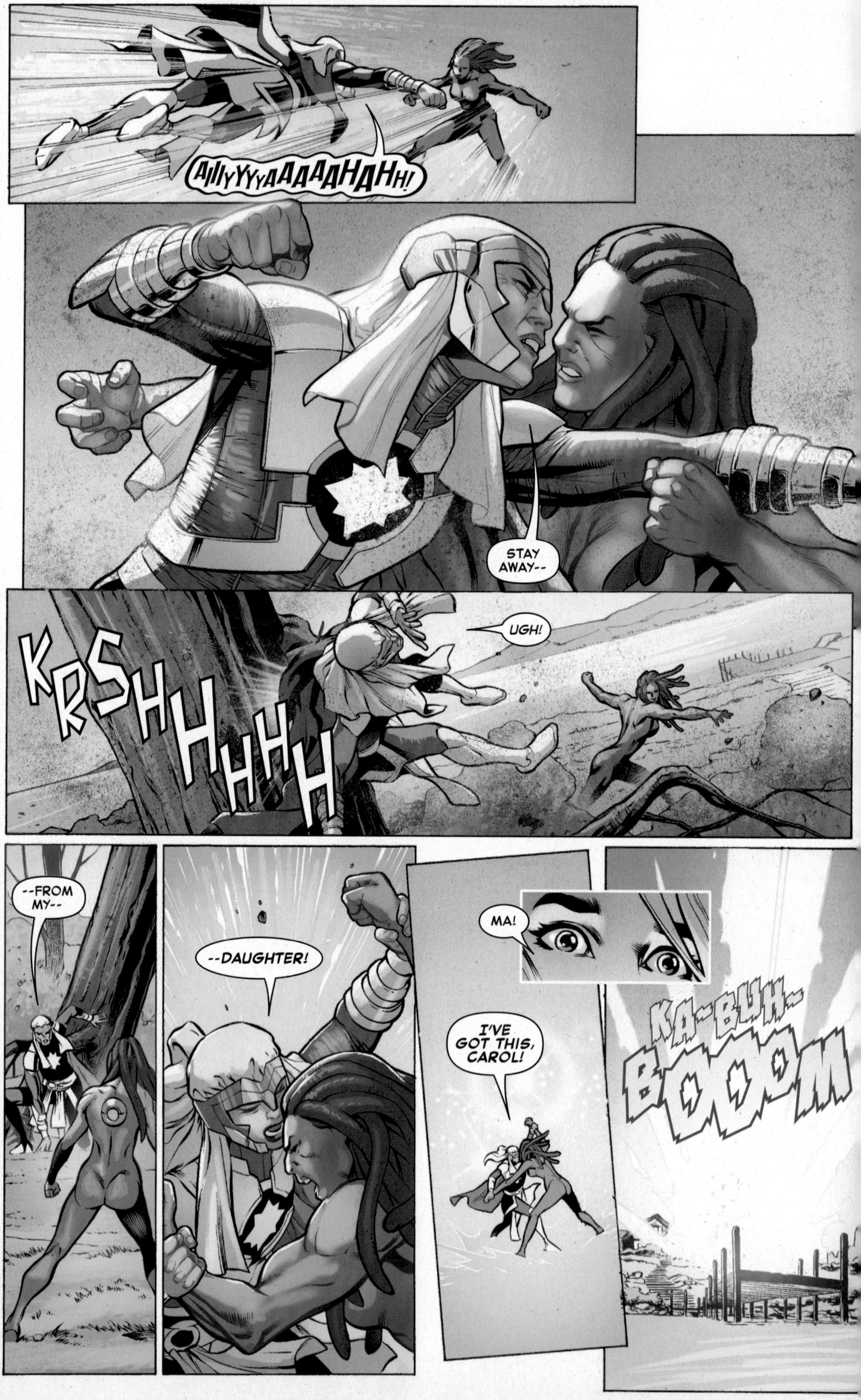
AIIIYYYYAAAAAHAHH!
STAY AWAY--
KRSHHHHHH
UGH!
--FROM MY--
--DAUGHTER!
MA!
I'VE GOT THIS, CAROL!
KA-BUH-BOOOM

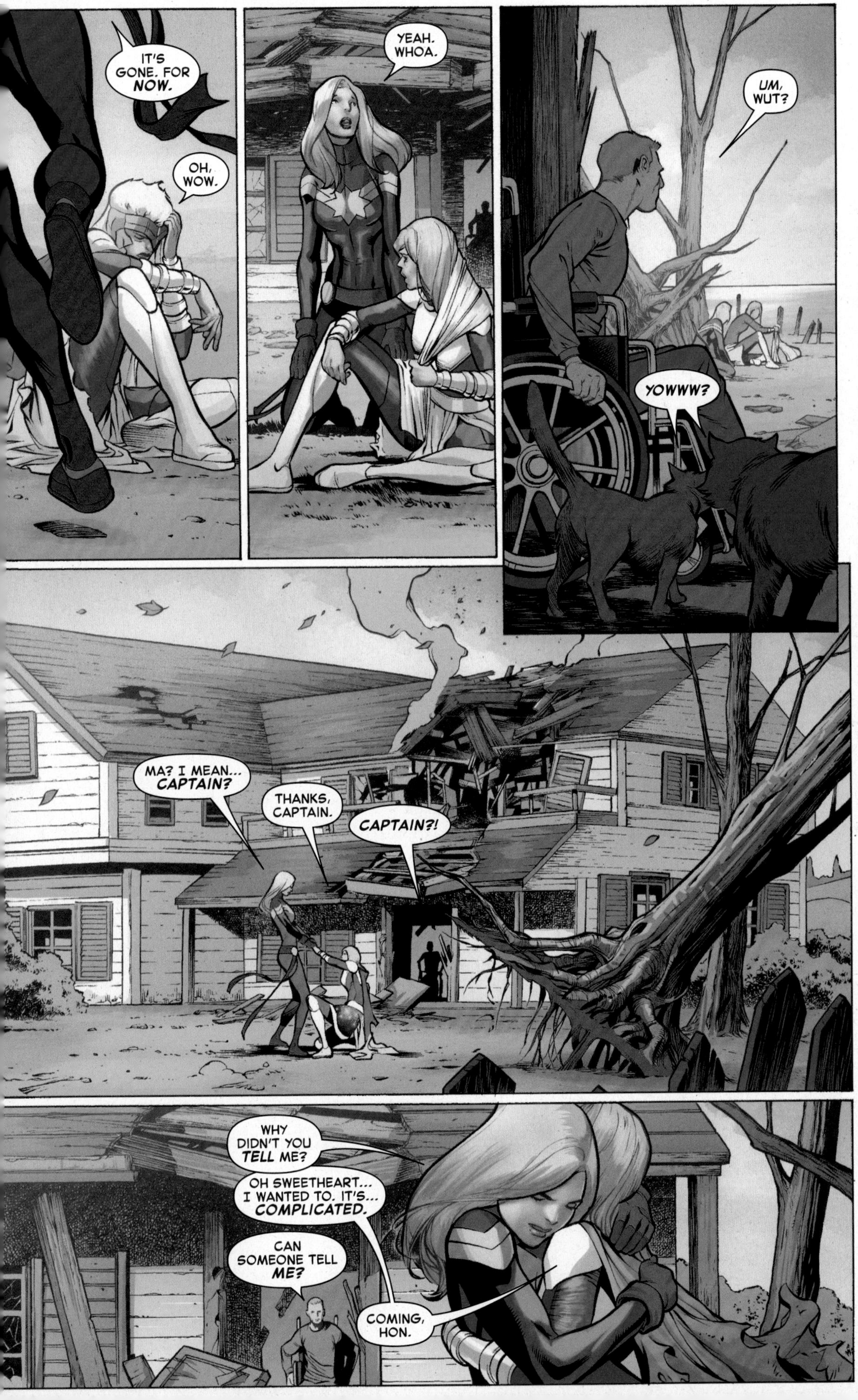
IT'S GONE. FOR *NOW.*
OH, WOW.
YEAH. WHOA.
UM, WUT?
YOWWW?
MA? I MEAN... *CAPTAIN?*
THANKS, CAPTAIN.
CAPTAIN?!
WHY DIDN'T YOU *TELL* ME?
OH SWEETHEART... I WANTED TO. IT'S... *COMPLICATED.*
CAN SOMEONE TELL *ME?*
COMING, HON.

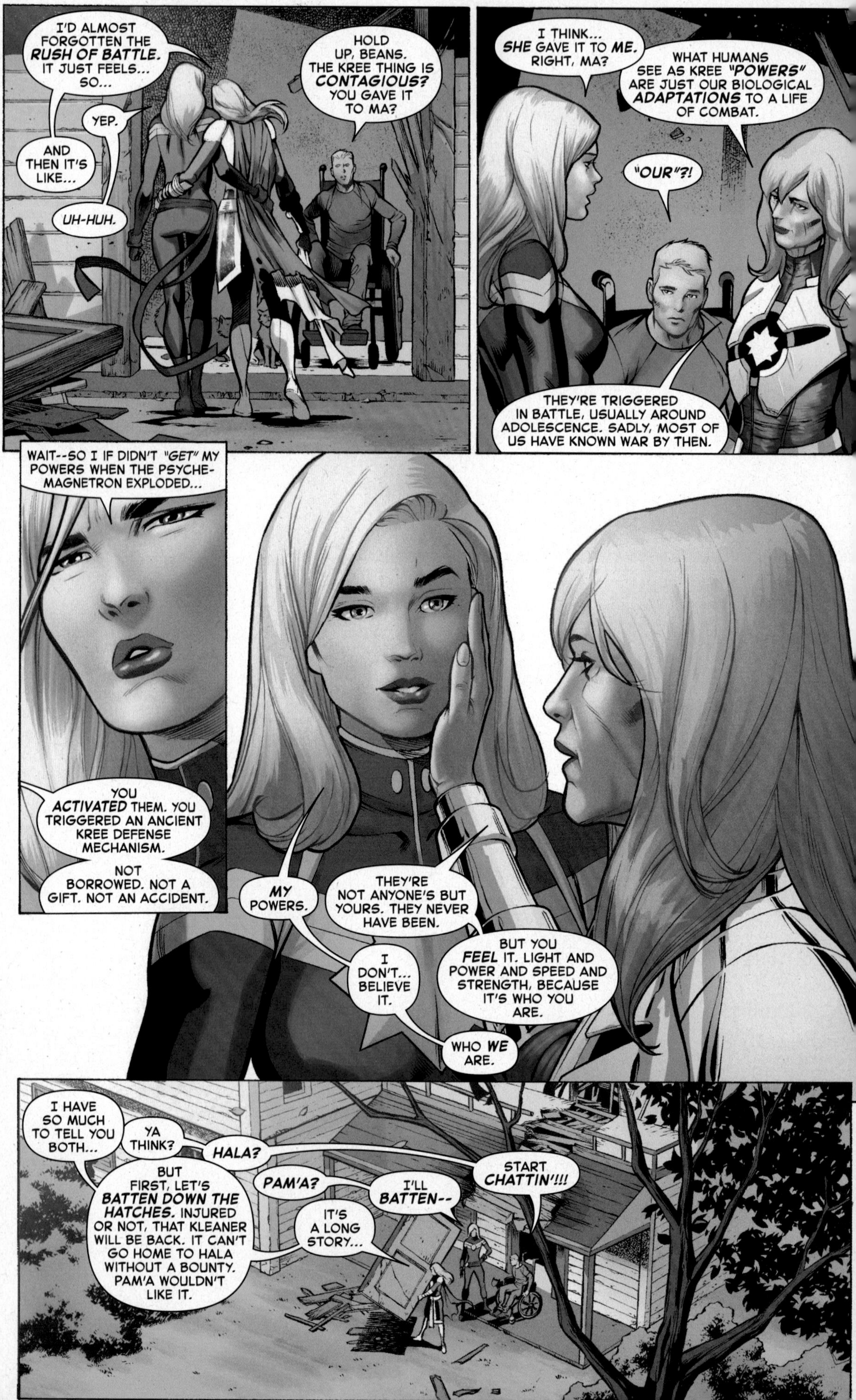

I'D ALMOST FORGOTTEN THE RUSH OF BATTLE. IT JUST FEELS... SO...
YEP.
AND THEN IT'S LIKE...
UH-HUH.
HOLD UP, BEANS. THE KREE THING IS CONTAGIOUS? YOU GAVE IT TO MA?
I THINK... SHE GAVE IT TO ME. RIGHT, MA?
WHAT HUMANS SEE AS KREE "POWERS" ARE JUST OUR BIOLOGICAL ADAPTATIONS TO A LIFE OF COMBAT.
"OUR"?!
THEY'RE TRIGGERED IN BATTLE, USUALLY AROUND ADOLESCENCE. SADLY, MOST OF US HAVE KNOWN WAR BY THEN.
WAIT--SO I IF DIDN'T "GET" MY POWERS WHEN THE PSYCHE-MAGNETRON EXPLODED...
YOU ACTIVATED THEM. YOU TRIGGERED AN ANCIENT KREE DEFENSE MECHANISM.
NOT BORROWED. NOT A GIFT. NOT AN ACCIDENT.
MY POWERS.
THEY'RE NOT ANYONE'S BUT YOURS. THEY NEVER HAVE BEEN.
I DON'T... BELIEVE IT.
BUT YOU FEEL IT. LIGHT AND POWER AND SPEED AND STRENGTH, BECAUSE IT'S WHO YOU ARE.
WHO WE ARE.
I HAVE SO MUCH TO TELL YOU BOTH...
YA THINK?
HALA?
START CHATTIN'!!!
BUT FIRST, LET'S BATTEN DOWN THE HATCHES. INJURED OR NOT, THAT KLEANER WILL BE BACK. IT CAN'T GO HOME TO HALA WITHOUT A BOUNTY. PAM'A WOULDN'T LIKE IT.
PAM'A?
I'LL BATTEN--
IT'S A LONG STORY...

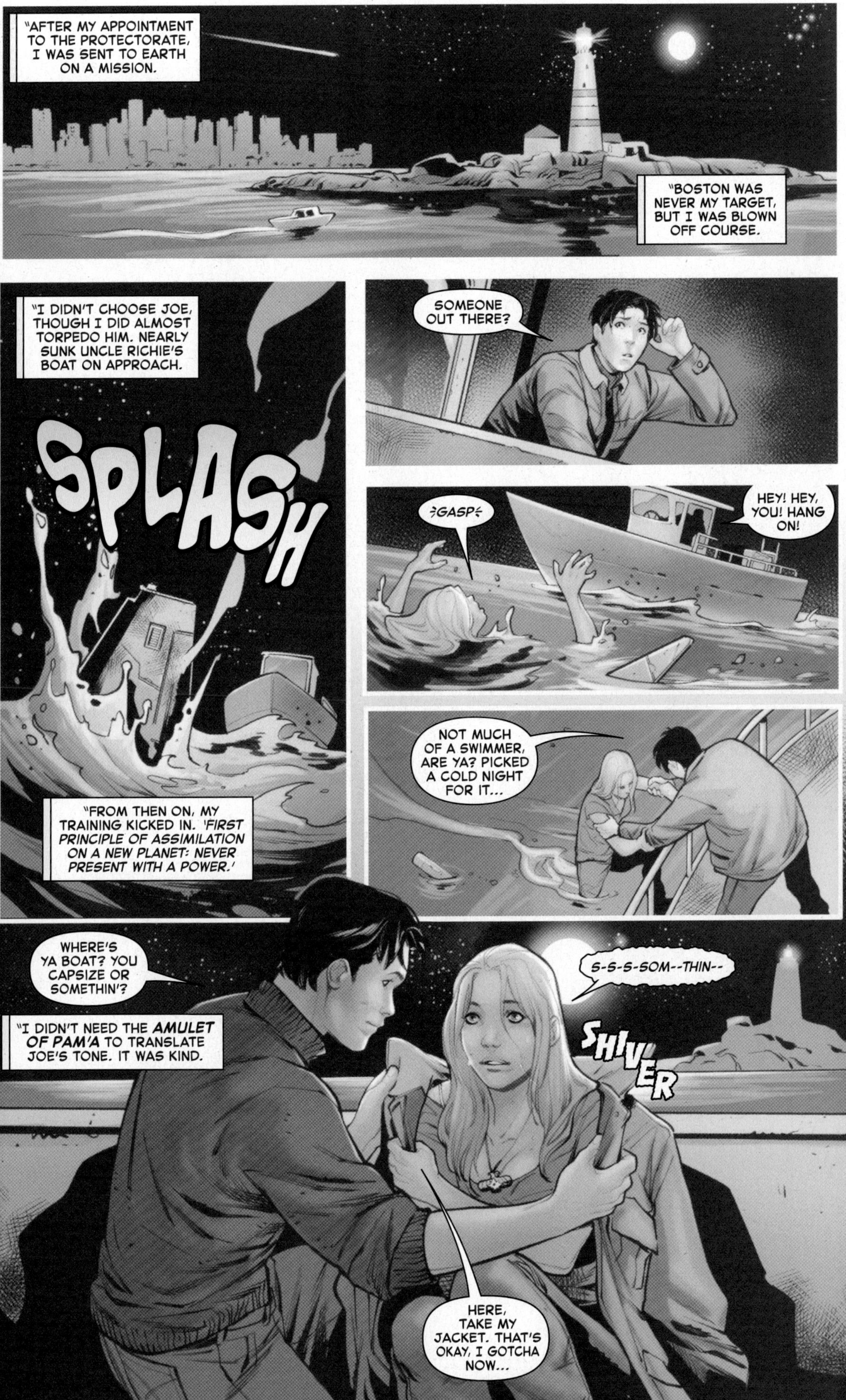
"AFTER MY APPOINTMENT TO THE PROTECTORATE, I WAS SENT TO EARTH ON A MISSION.
"BOSTON WAS NEVER MY TARGET, BUT I WAS BLOWN OFF COURSE.
"I DIDN'T CHOOSE JOE, THOUGH I DID ALMOST TORPEDO HIM. NEARLY SUNK UNCLE RICHIE'S BOAT ON APPROACH.
SPLASH
"FROM THEN ON, MY TRAINING KICKED IN. '*FIRST PRINCIPLE OF ASSIMILATION ON A NEW PLANET: NEVER PRESENT WITH A POWER.*'
SOMEONE OUT THERE?
GASP
HEY! HEY, YOU! HANG ON!
NOT MUCH OF A SWIMMER, ARE YA? PICKED A COLD NIGHT FOR IT...
WHERE'S YA BOAT? YOU CAPSIZE OR SOMETHIN'?
"I DIDN'T NEED THE *AMULET OF PAM'A* TO TRANSLATE JOE'S TONE. IT WAS KIND.
S-S-S-SOM--THIN--
SHIVER
HERE, TAKE MY JACKET. THAT'S OKAY, I GOTCHA NOW...

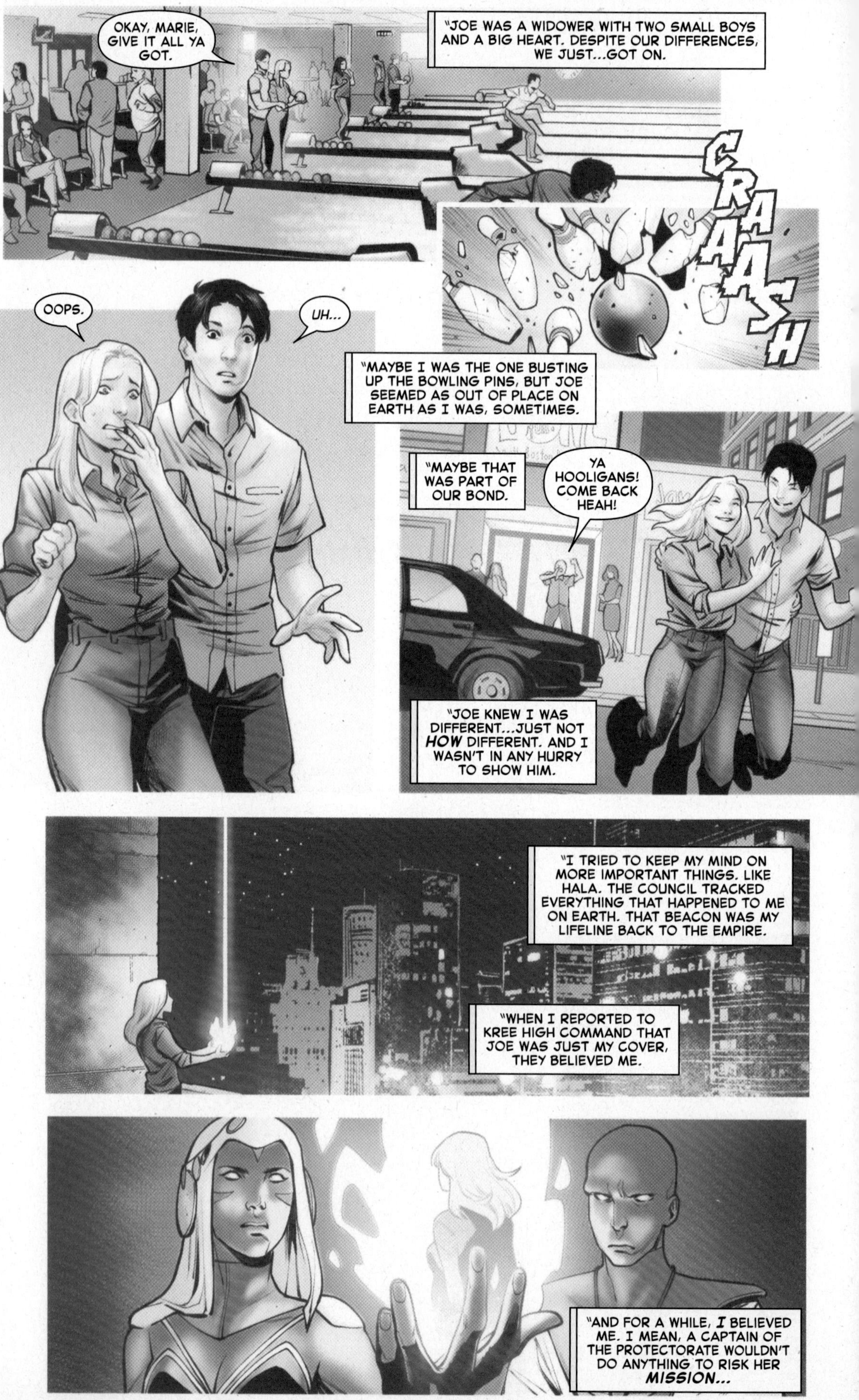
OKAY, MARIE, GIVE IT ALL YA GOT.
"JOE WAS A WIDOWER WITH TWO SMALL BOYS AND A BIG HEART. DESPITE OUR DIFFERENCES, WE JUST...GOT ON.
CRAAASH
OOPS.
UH...
"MAYBE I WAS THE ONE BUSTING UP THE BOWLING PINS, BUT JOE SEEMED AS OUT OF PLACE ON EARTH AS I WAS, SOMETIMES.
"MAYBE THAT WAS PART OF OUR BOND.
YA HOOLIGANS! COME BACK HEAH!
"JOE KNEW I WAS DIFFERENT...JUST NOT HOW DIFFERENT. AND I WASN'T IN ANY HURRY TO SHOW HIM.
"I TRIED TO KEEP MY MIND ON MORE IMPORTANT THINGS. LIKE HALA. THE COUNCIL TRACKED EVERYTHING THAT HAPPENED TO ME ON EARTH. THAT BEACON WAS MY LIFELINE BACK TO THE EMPIRE.
"WHEN I REPORTED TO KREE HIGH COMMAND THAT JOE WAS JUST MY COVER, THEY BELIEVED ME.
"AND FOR A WHILE, I BELIEVED ME. I MEAN, A CAPTAIN OF THE PROTECTORATE WOULDN'T DO ANYTHING TO RISK HER MISSION...

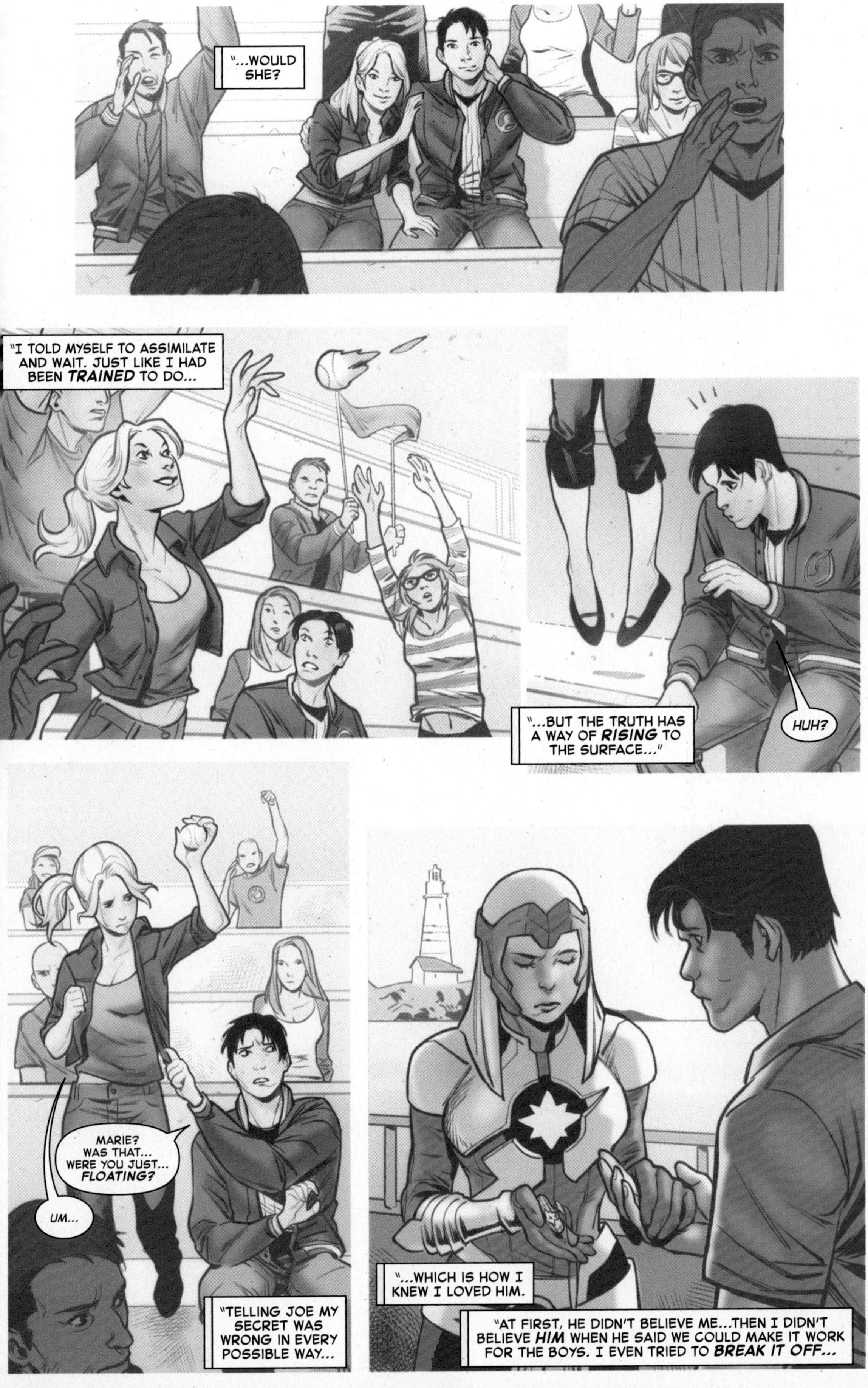
"...WOULD SHE?
"I TOLD MYSELF TO ASSIMILATE AND WAIT. JUST LIKE I HAD BEEN *TRAINED* TO DO...
"...BUT THE TRUTH HAS A WAY OF *RISING* TO THE SURFACE..."
HUH?
MARIE? WAS THAT... WERE YOU JUST... *FLOATING?*
UM...
"TELLING JOE MY SECRET WAS WRONG IN EVERY POSSIBLE WAY...
"...WHICH IS HOW I KNEW I LOVED HIM.
"AT FIRST, HE DIDN'T BELIEVE ME...THEN I DIDN'T BELIEVE *HIM* WHEN HE SAID WE COULD MAKE IT WORK FOR THE BOYS. I EVEN TRIED TO *BREAK IT OFF...*

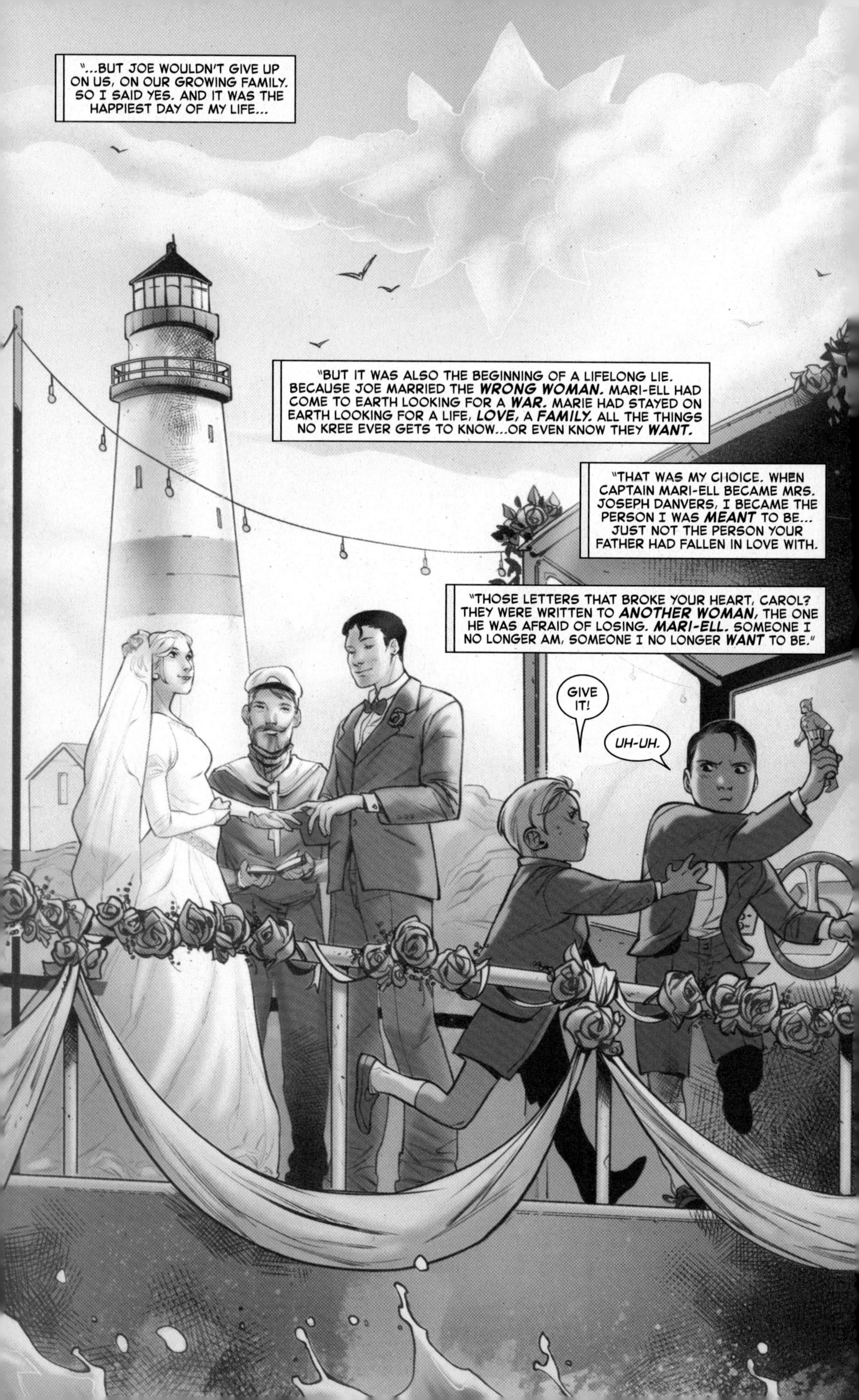
"...BUT JOE WOULDN'T GIVE UP ON US, ON OUR GROWING FAMILY. SO I SAID YES. AND IT WAS THE HAPPIEST DAY OF MY LIFE...
"BUT IT WAS ALSO THE BEGINNING OF A LIFELONG LIE. BECAUSE JOE MARRIED THE WRONG WOMAN. MARI-ELL HAD COME TO EARTH LOOKING FOR A WAR. MARIE HAD STAYED ON EARTH LOOKING FOR A LIFE, LOVE, A FAMILY. ALL THE THINGS NO KREE EVER GETS TO KNOW...OR EVEN KNOW THEY WANT.
"THAT WAS MY CHOICE. WHEN CAPTAIN MARI-ELL BECAME MRS. JOSEPH DANVERS, I BECAME THE PERSON I WAS MEANT TO BE... JUST NOT THE PERSON YOUR FATHER HAD FALLEN IN LOVE WITH.
"THOSE LETTERS THAT BROKE YOUR HEART, CAROL? THEY WERE WRITTEN TO ANOTHER WOMAN, THE ONE HE WAS AFRAID OF LOSING. MARI-ELL. SOMEONE I NO LONGER AM, SOMEONE I NO LONGER WANT TO BE."
GIVE IT!
UH-UH.

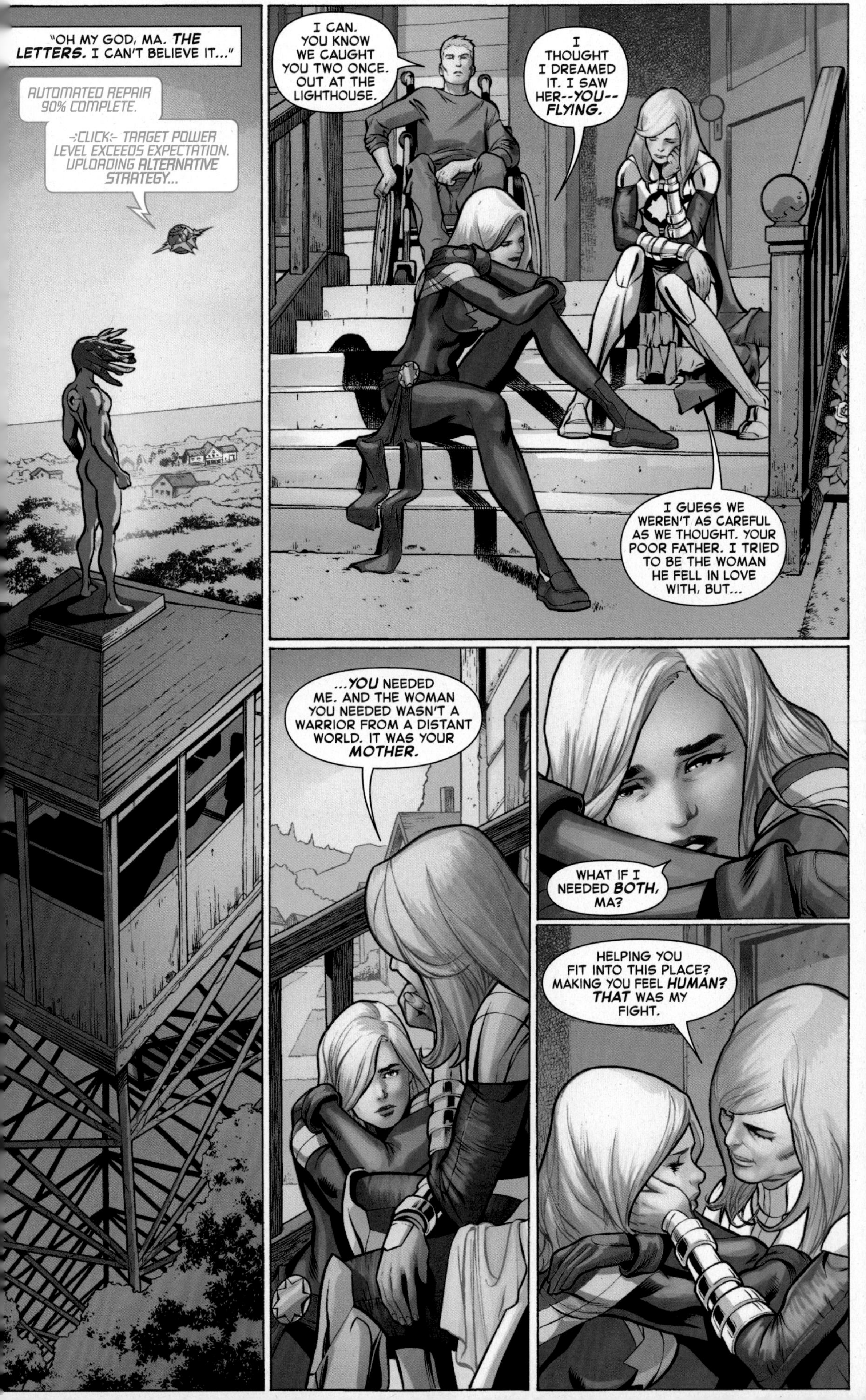
"OH MY GOD, MA. THE LETTERS. I CAN'T BELIEVE IT..."
AUTOMATED REPAIR 90% COMPLETE.
-CLICK- TARGET POWER LEVEL EXCEEDS EXPECTATION. UPLOADING ALTERNATIVE STRATEGY...
I CAN. YOU KNOW WE CAUGHT YOU TWO ONCE. OUT AT THE LIGHTHOUSE.
I THOUGHT I DREAMED IT. I SAW HER--YOU--FLYING.
I GUESS WE WEREN'T AS CAREFUL AS WE THOUGHT. YOUR POOR FATHER. I TRIED TO BE THE WOMAN HE FELL IN LOVE WITH, BUT...
...YOU NEEDED ME. AND THE WOMAN YOU NEEDED WASN'T A WARRIOR FROM A DISTANT WORLD. IT WAS YOUR MOTHER.
WHAT IF I NEEDED BOTH, MA?
HELPING YOU FIT INTO THIS PLACE? MAKING YOU FEEL HUMAN? THAT WAS MY FIGHT.

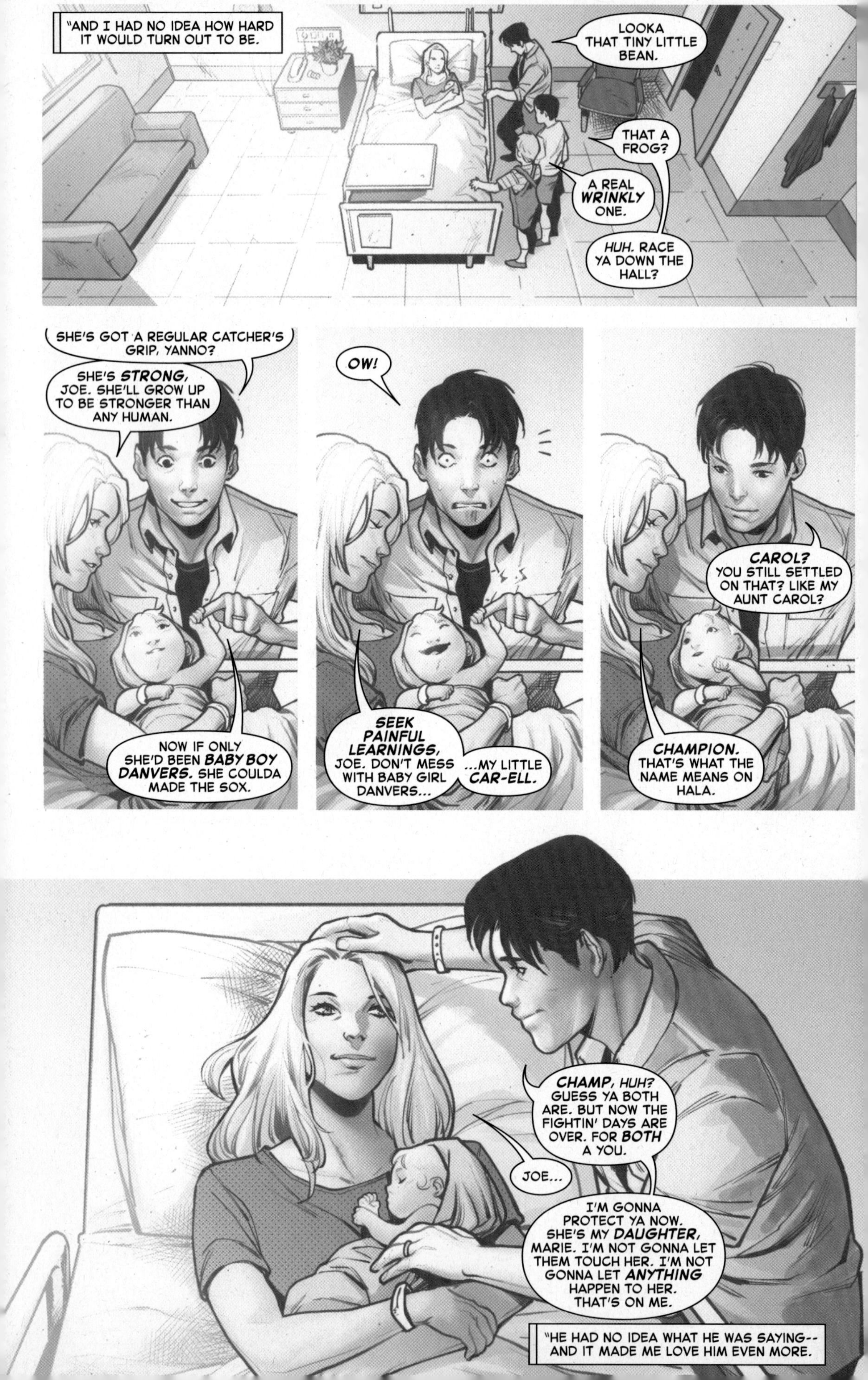
"AND I HAD NO IDEA HOW HARD IT WOULD TURN OUT TO BE.
LOOKA THAT TINY LITTLE BEAN.
THAT A FROG?
A REAL WRINKLY ONE.
HUH. RACE YA DOWN THE HALL?
SHE'S GOT A REGULAR CATCHER'S GRIP, YANNO?
SHE'S STRONG, JOE. SHE'LL GROW UP TO BE STRONGER THAN ANY HUMAN.
NOW IF ONLY SHE'D BEEN BABY BOY DANVERS. SHE COULDA MADE THE SOX.
OW!
SEEK PAINFUL LEARNINGS, JOE. DON'T MESS WITH BABY GIRL DANVERS...
...MY LITTLE CAR-ELL.
CAROL? YOU STILL SETTLED ON THAT? LIKE MY AUNT CAROL?
CHAMPION. THAT'S WHAT THE NAME MEANS ON HALA.
CHAMP, HUH? GUESS YA BOTH ARE. BUT NOW THE FIGHTIN' DAYS ARE OVER. FOR BOTH A YOU.
JOE...
I'M GONNA PROTECT YA NOW. SHE'S MY DAUGHTER, MARIE. I'M NOT GONNA LET THEM TOUCH HER. I'M NOT GONNA LET ANYTHING HAPPEN TO HER. THAT'S ON ME.
"HE HAD NO IDEA WHAT HE WAS SAYING-- AND IT MADE ME LOVE HIM EVEN MORE.

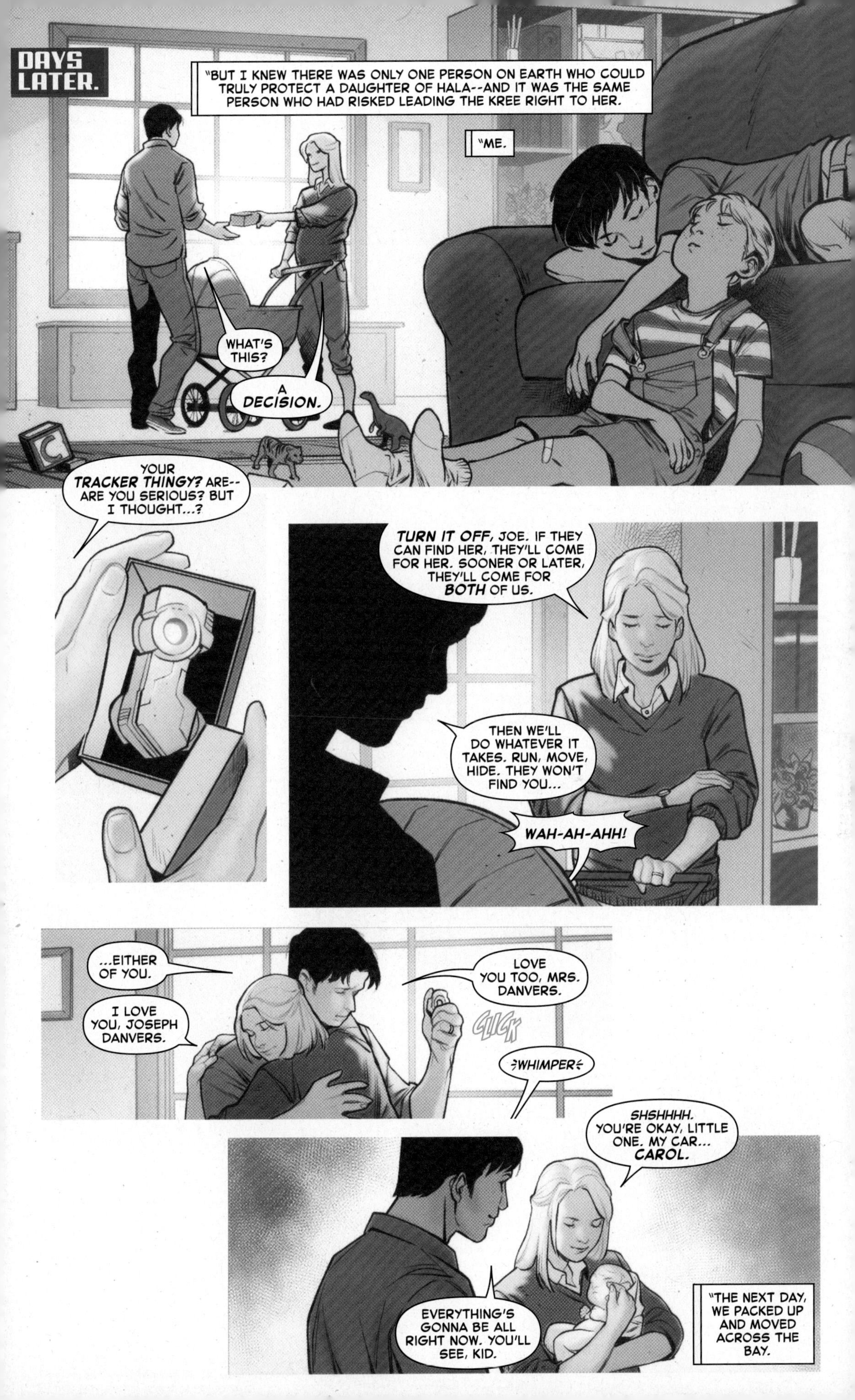
DAYS LATER.
"BUT I KNEW THERE WAS ONLY ONE PERSON ON EARTH WHO COULD TRULY PROTECT A DAUGHTER OF HALA--AND IT WAS THE SAME PERSON WHO HAD RISKED LEADING THE KREE RIGHT TO HER.
"ME.
WHAT'S THIS?
A DECISION.
YOUR TRACKER THINGY? ARE--ARE YOU SERIOUS? BUT I THOUGHT...?
TURN IT OFF, JOE. IF THEY CAN FIND HER, THEY'LL COME FOR HER. SOONER OR LATER, THEY'LL COME FOR BOTH OF US.
THEN WE'LL DO WHATEVER IT TAKES. RUN, MOVE, HIDE. THEY WON'T FIND YOU...
WAH-AH-AHH!
...EITHER OF YOU.
I LOVE YOU, JOSEPH DANVERS.
LOVE YOU TOO, MRS. DANVERS.
CLICK
WHIMPER
SHSHHHH. YOU'RE OKAY, LITTLE ONE. MY CAR... CAROL.
EVERYTHING'S GONNA BE ALL RIGHT NOW. YOU'LL SEE, KID.
"THE NEXT DAY, WE PACKED UP AND MOVED ACROSS THE BAY.

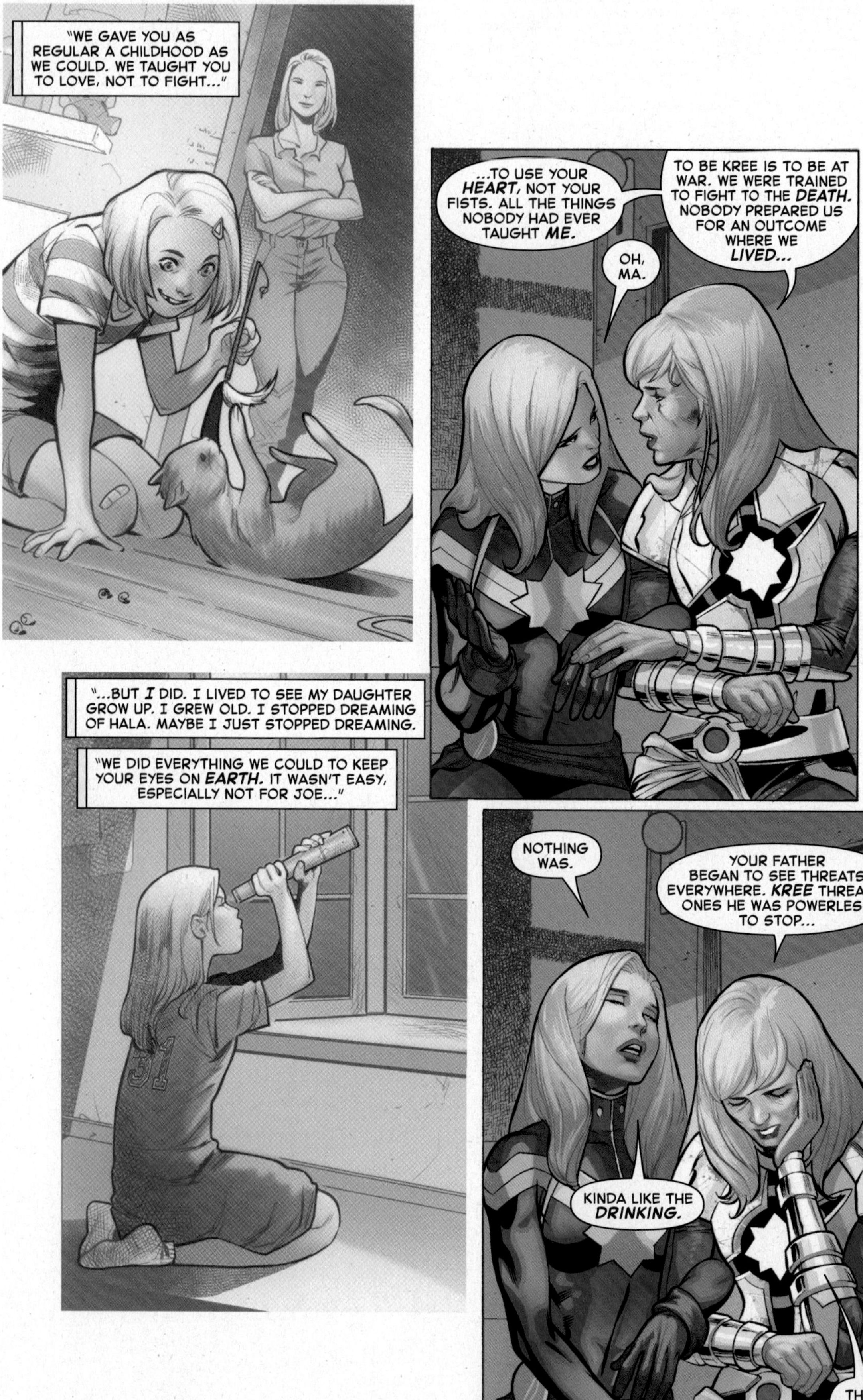
"WE GAVE YOU AS REGULAR A CHILDHOOD AS WE COULD. WE TAUGHT YOU TO LOVE, NOT TO FIGHT..."
...TO USE YOUR *HEART,* NOT YOUR FISTS. ALL THE THINGS NOBODY HAD EVER TAUGHT *ME.*
TO BE KREE IS TO BE AT WAR. WE WERE TRAINED TO FIGHT TO THE *DEATH.* NOBODY PREPARED US FOR AN OUTCOME WHERE WE *LIVED...*
OH, MA.
"...BUT *I* DID. I LIVED TO SEE MY DAUGHTER GROW UP. I GREW OLD. I STOPPED DREAMING OF HALA. MAYBE I JUST STOPPED DREAMING.
"WE DID EVERYTHING WE COULD TO KEEP YOUR EYES ON *EARTH.* IT WASN'T EASY, ESPECIALLY NOT FOR JOE..."
NOTHING WAS.
YOUR FATHER BEGAN TO SEE THREATS EVERYWHERE. *KREE* THREATS, ONES HE WAS POWERLESS TO STOP...
KINDA LIKE THE *DRINKING.*
THAT DIDN'T HELP.

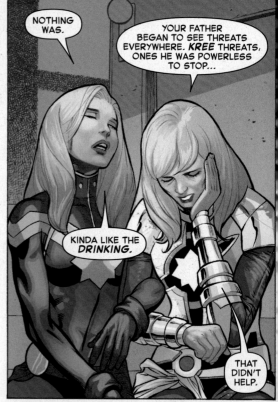

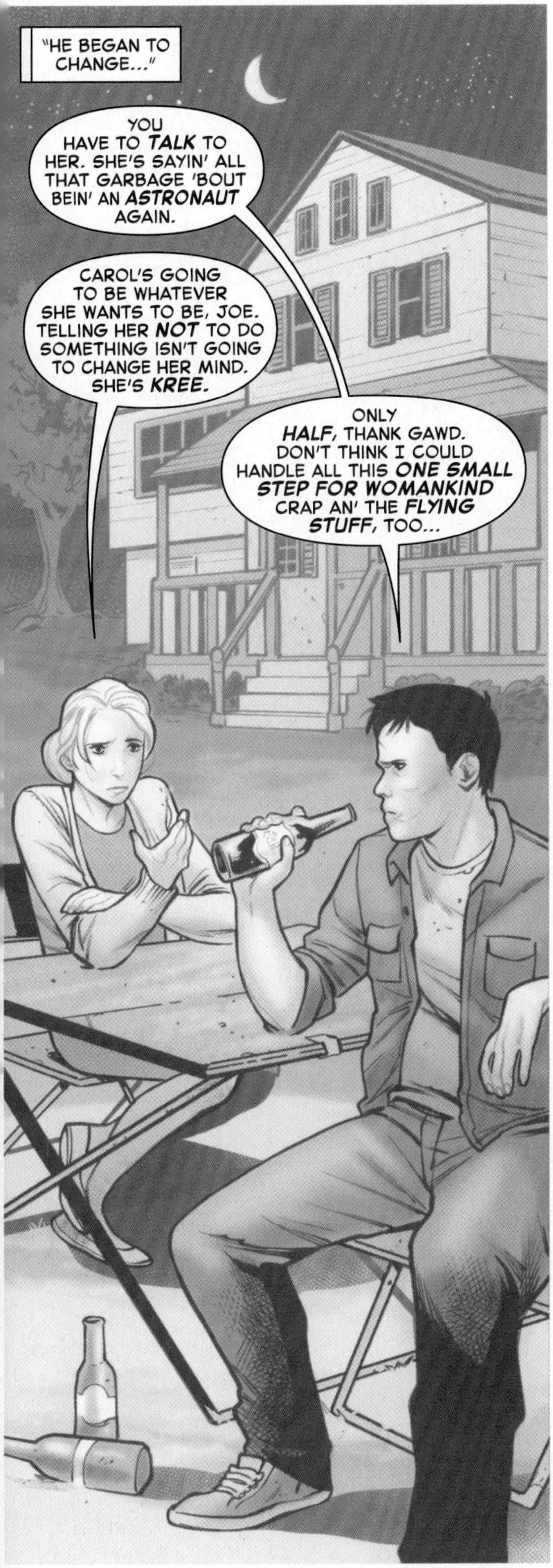
"HE BEGAN TO CHANGE..."
YOU HAVE TO TALK TO HER. SHE'S SAYIN' ALL THAT GARBAGE 'BOUT BEIN' AN ASTRONAUT AGAIN.
CAROL'S GOING TO BE WHATEVER SHE WANTS TO BE, JOE. TELLING HER NOT TO DO SOMETHING ISN'T GOING TO CHANGE HER MIND. SHE'S KREE.
ONLY HALF, THANK GAWD. DON'T THINK I COULD HANDLE ALL THIS ONE SMALL STEP FOR WOMANKIND CRAP AN' THE FLYING STUFF, TOO...

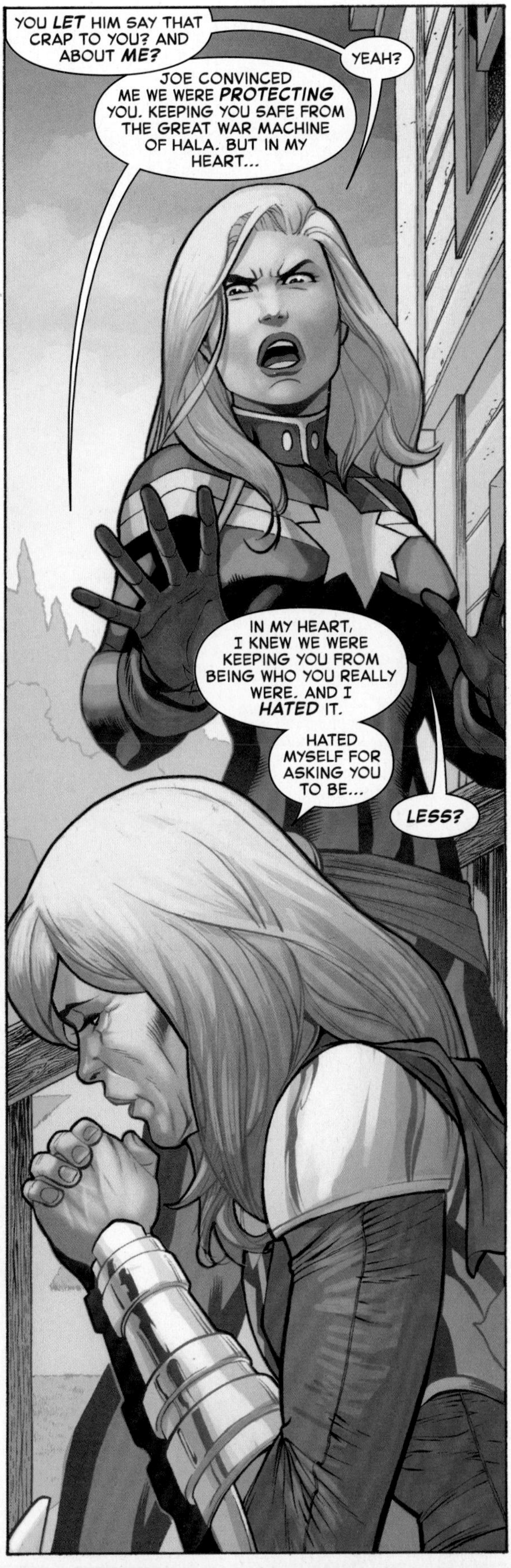
YOU LET HIM SAY THAT CRAP TO YOU? AND ABOUT ME?
YEAH?
JOE CONVINCED ME WE WERE PROTECTING YOU. KEEPING YOU SAFE FROM THE GREAT WAR MACHINE OF HALA. BUT IN MY HEART...
IN MY HEART, I KNEW WE WERE KEEPING YOU FROM BEING WHO YOU REALLY WERE. AND I HATED IT.
HATED MYSELF FOR ASKING YOU TO BE...
LESS?

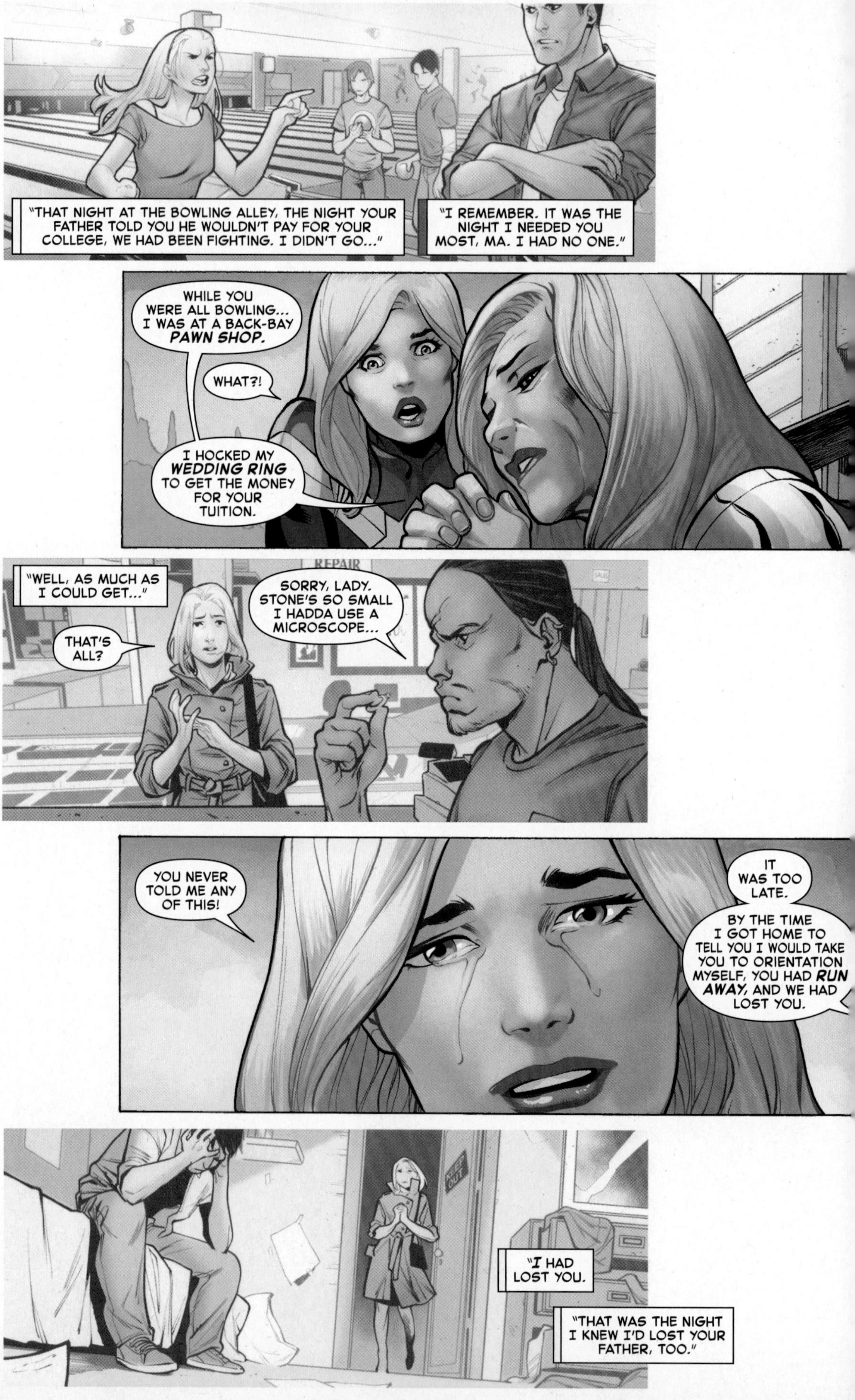
"THAT NIGHT AT THE BOWLING ALLEY, THE NIGHT YOUR FATHER TOLD YOU HE WOULDN'T PAY FOR YOUR COLLEGE, WE HAD BEEN FIGHTING. I DIDN'T GO..."
"I REMEMBER. IT WAS THE NIGHT I NEEDED YOU MOST, MA. I HAD NO ONE."
WHILE YOU WERE ALL BOWLING... I WAS AT A BACK-BAY PAWN SHOP.
WHAT?!
I HOCKED MY WEDDING RING TO GET THE MONEY FOR YOUR TUITION.
REPAIR
"WELL, AS MUCH AS I COULD GET..."
THAT'S ALL?
SORRY, LADY. STONE'S SO SMALL I HADDA USE A MICROSCOPE...
YOU NEVER TOLD ME ANY OF THIS!
IT WAS TOO LATE.
BY THE TIME I GOT HOME TO TELL YOU I WOULD TAKE YOU TO ORIENTATION MYSELF, YOU HAD RUN AWAY, AND WE HAD LOST YOU.
"I HAD LOST YOU.
"THAT WAS THE NIGHT I KNEW I'D LOST YOUR FATHER, TOO."

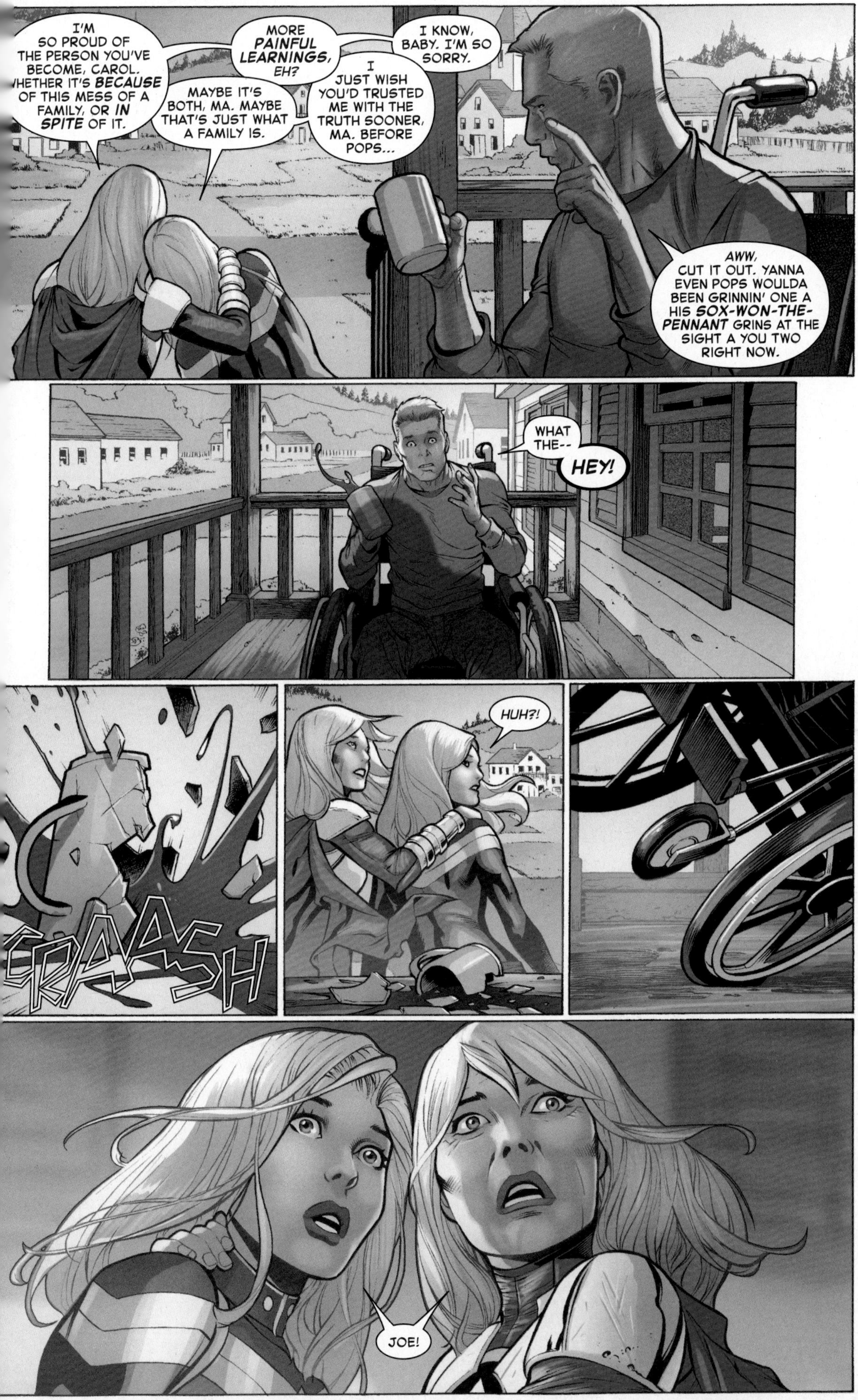
I'M SO PROUD OF THE PERSON YOU'VE BECOME, CAROL. WHETHER IT'S BECAUSE OF THIS MESS OF A FAMILY, OR IN SPITE OF IT.
MAYBE IT'S BOTH, MA. MAYBE THAT'S JUST WHAT A FAMILY IS.
MORE PAINFUL LEARNINGS, EH?
I KNOW, BABY. I'M SO SORRY.
I JUST WISH YOU'D TRUSTED ME WITH THE TRUTH SOONER, MA. BEFORE POPS...
AWW, CUT IT OUT. YANNA EVEN POPS WOULDA BEEN GRINNIN' ONE A HIS SOX-WON-THE-PENNANT GRINS AT THE SIGHT A YOU TWO RIGHT NOW.
WHAT THE--
HEY!
CRAASH
HUH?!
JOE!

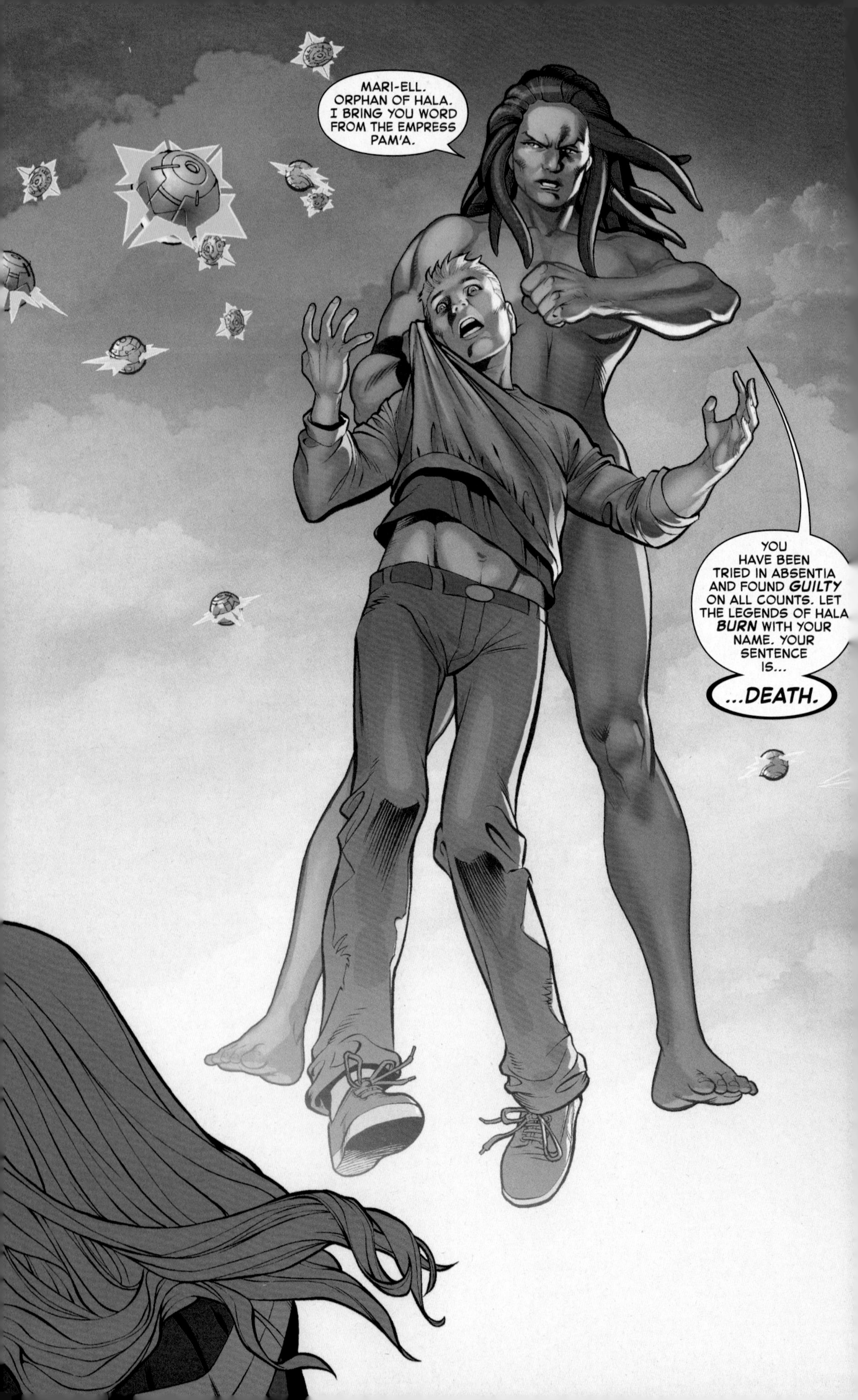
MARI-ELL. ORPHAN OF HALA. I BRING YOU WORD FROM THE EMPRESS PAM'A.
YOU HAVE BEEN TRIED IN ABSENTIA AND FOUND GUILTY ON ALL COUNTS. LET THE LEGENDS OF HALA BURN WITH YOUR NAME. YOUR SENTENCE IS...
...DEATH.

THE LIFE OF CAPTAIN MARVEL #5
"CHAMPIONED"

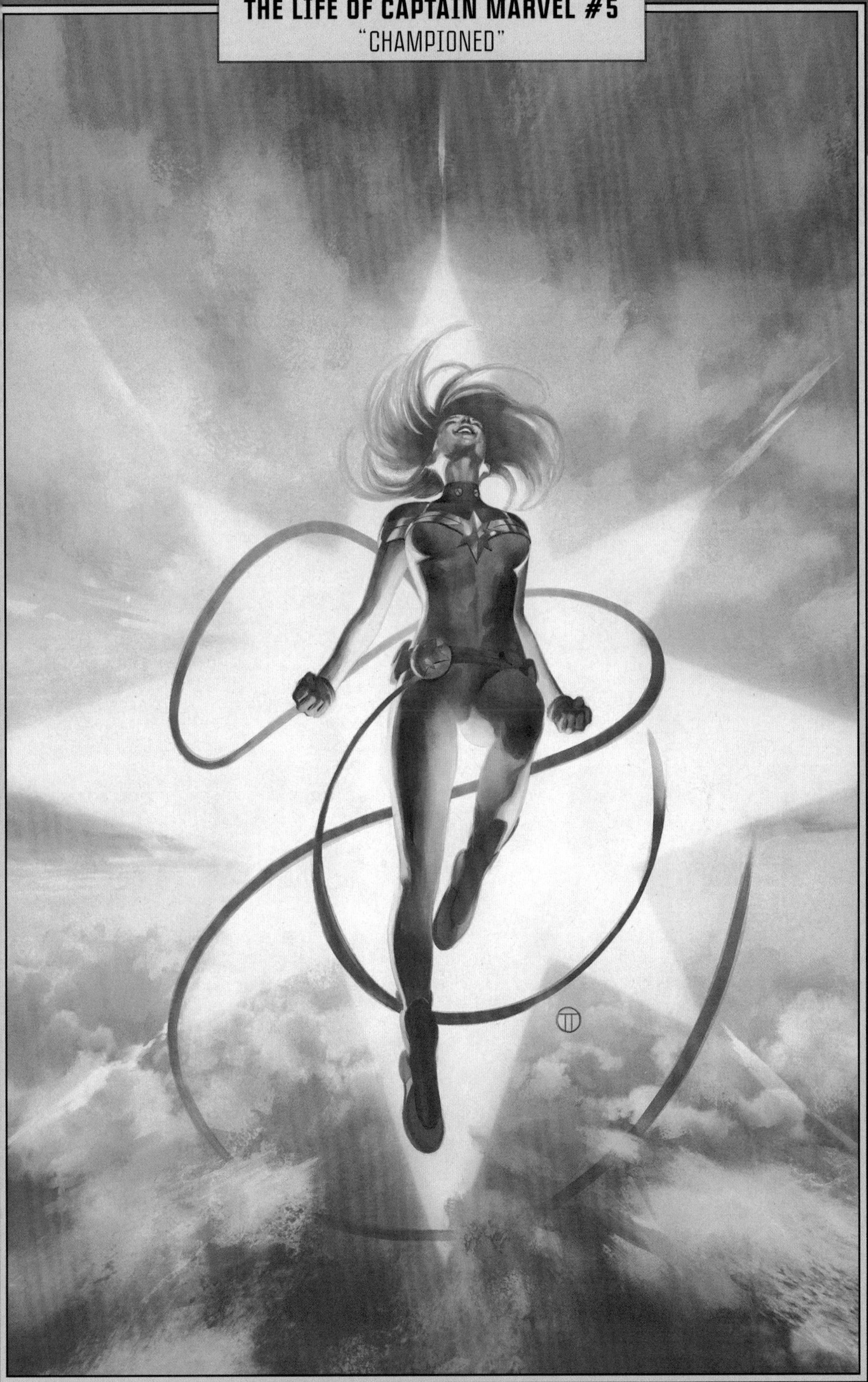

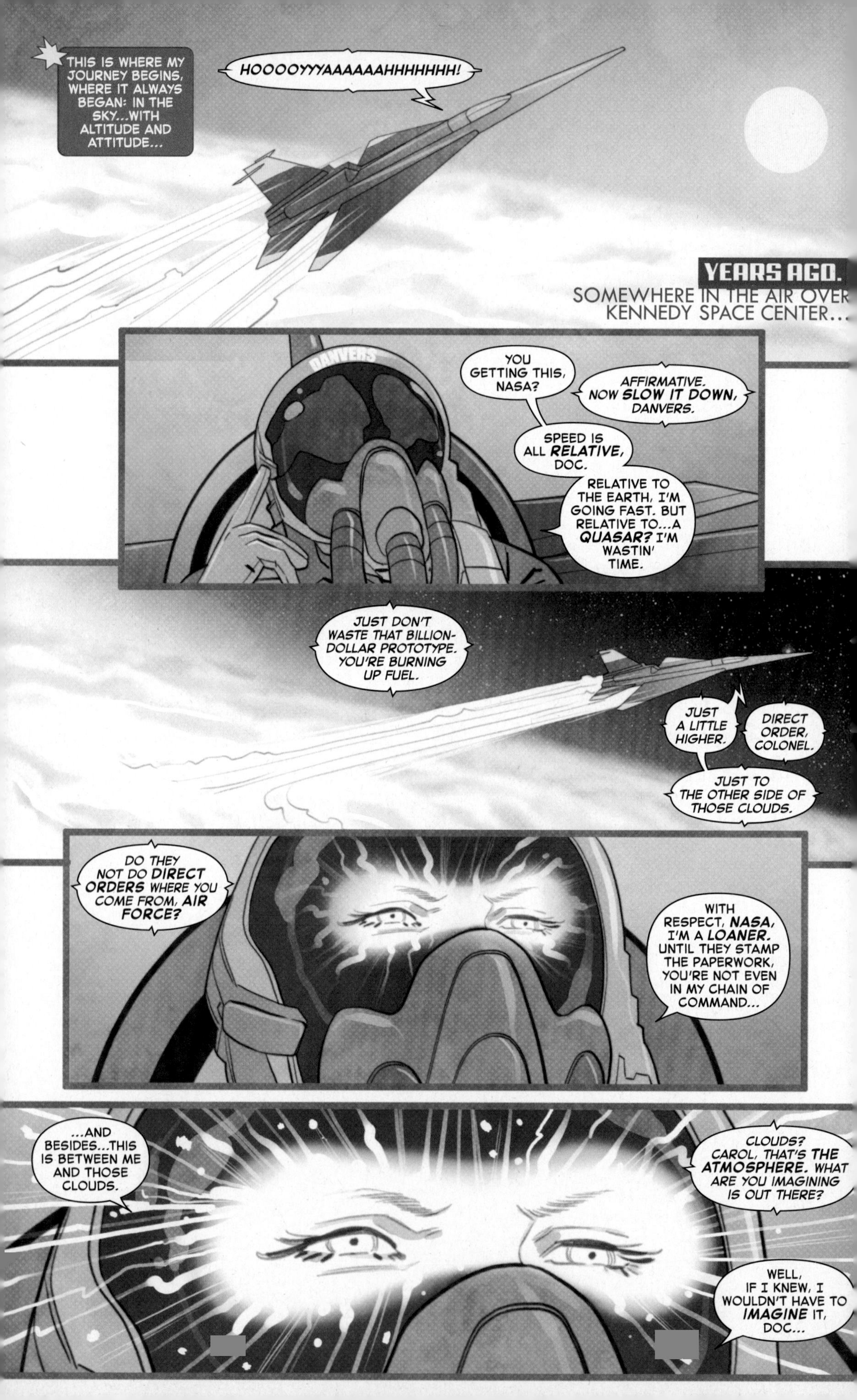
THIS IS WHERE MY JOURNEY BEGINS, WHERE IT ALWAYS BEGAN: IN THE SKY...WITH ALTITUDE AND ATTITUDE...
HOOOOYYYAAAAAAHHHHHHH!
YEARS AGO.
SOMEWHERE IN THE AIR OVER KENNEDY SPACE CENTER...
DANVERS
YOU GETTING THIS, NASA?
AFFIRMATIVE. NOW SLOW IT DOWN, DANVERS.
SPEED IS ALL RELATIVE, DOC.
RELATIVE TO THE EARTH, I'M GOING FAST. BUT RELATIVE TO...A QUASAR? I'M WASTIN' TIME.
JUST DON'T WASTE THAT BILLION-DOLLAR PROTOTYPE. YOU'RE BURNING UP FUEL.
JUST A LITTLE HIGHER.
DIRECT ORDER, COLONEL.
JUST TO THE OTHER SIDE OF THOSE CLOUDS.
DO THEY NOT DO DIRECT ORDERS WHERE YOU COME FROM, AIR FORCE?
WITH RESPECT, NASA, I'M A LOANER. UNTIL THEY STAMP THE PAPERWORK, YOU'RE NOT EVEN IN MY CHAIN OF COMMAND...
...AND BESIDES...THIS IS BETWEEN ME AND THOSE CLOUDS.
CLOUDS? CAROL, THAT'S THE ATMOSPHERE. WHAT ARE YOU IMAGINING IS OUT THERE?
WELL, IF I KNEW, I WOULDN'T HAVE TO IMAGINE IT, DOC...

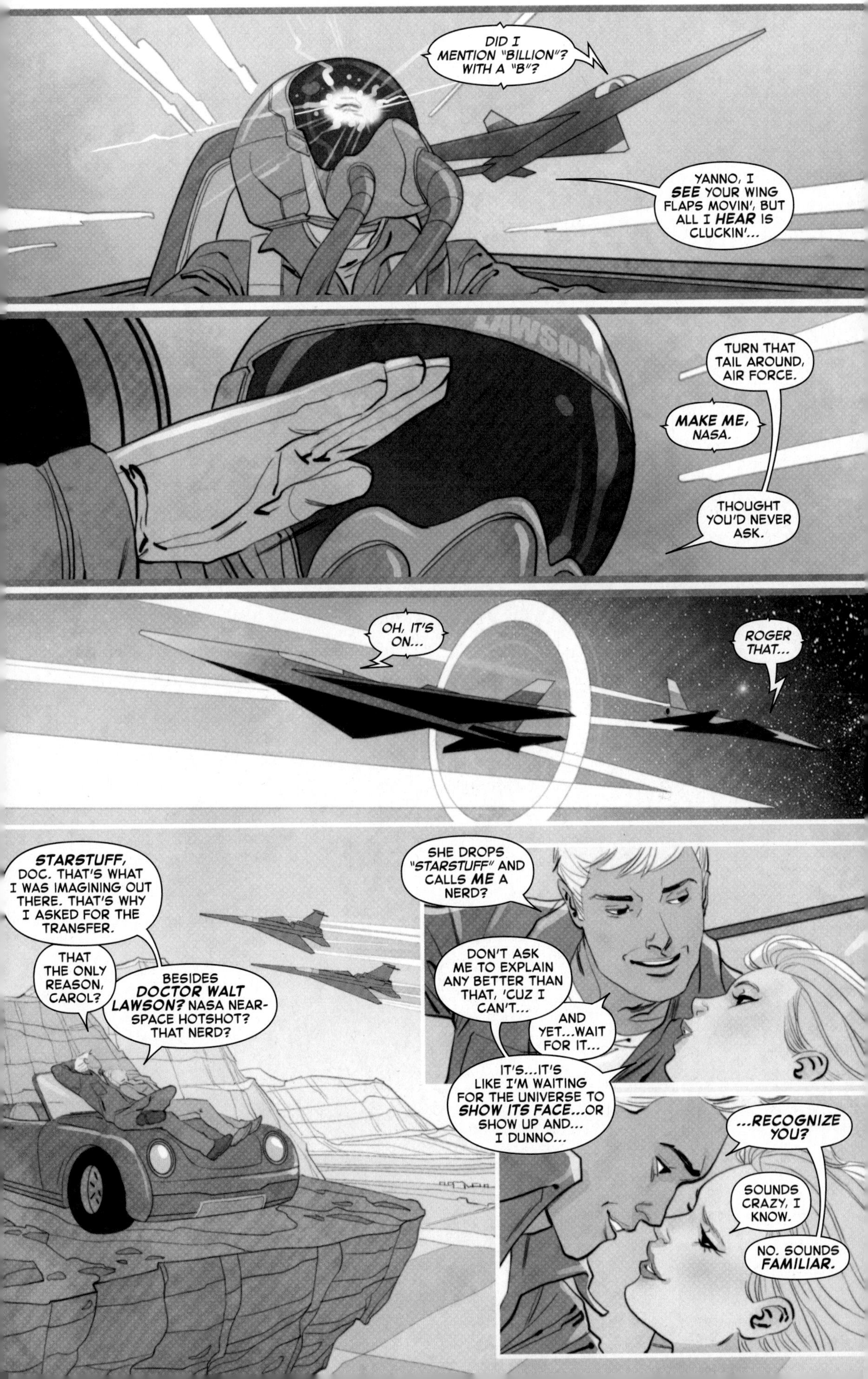
DID I MENTION "BILLION"? WITH A "B"?
YANNO, I **SEE** YOUR WING FLAPS MOVIN', BUT ALL I **HEAR** IS CLUCKIN'...
LAWSON
TURN THAT TAIL AROUND, AIR FORCE.
MAKE ME, NASA.
THOUGHT YOU'D NEVER ASK.
OH, IT'S ON...
ROGER THAT...
STARSTUFF, DOC. THAT'S WHAT I WAS IMAGINING OUT THERE. THAT'S WHY I ASKED FOR THE TRANSFER.
THAT THE ONLY REASON, CAROL?
BESIDES ***DOCTOR WALT LAWSON?*** NASA NEAR-SPACE HOTSHOT? THAT NERD?
SHE DROPS "***STARSTUFF***" AND CALLS ***ME*** A NERD?
DON'T ASK ME TO EXPLAIN ANY BETTER THAN THAT, 'CUZ I CAN'T...
AND YET...WAIT FOR IT...
IT'S...IT'S LIKE I'M WAITING FOR THE UNIVERSE TO ***SHOW ITS FACE...*** OR SHOW UP AND... I DUNNO...
...RECOGNIZE YOU?
SOUNDS CRAZY, I KNOW.
NO. SOUNDS ***FAMILIAR.***

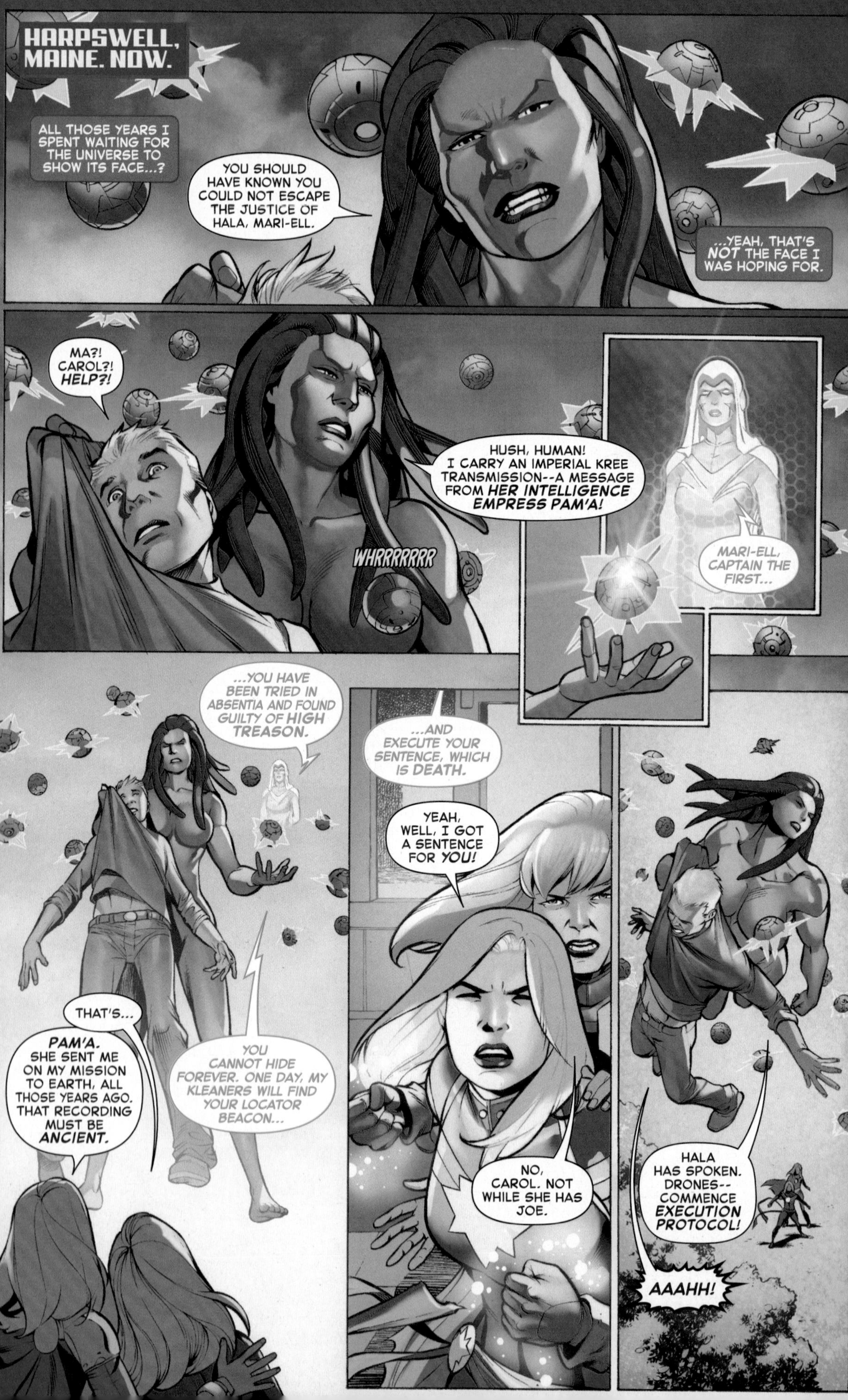
HARPSWELL, MAINE. NOW.
ALL THOSE YEARS I SPENT WAITING FOR THE UNIVERSE TO SHOW ITS FACE...?
YOU SHOULD HAVE KNOWN YOU COULD NOT ESCAPE THE JUSTICE OF HALA, MARI-ELL.
...YEAH, THAT'S NOT THE FACE I WAS HOPING FOR.
MA?! CAROL?! HELP?!
HUSH, HUMAN! I CARRY AN IMPERIAL KREE TRANSMISSION--A MESSAGE FROM HER INTELLIGENCE EMPRESS PAM'A!
WHRRRRRRR
MARI-ELL, CAPTAIN THE FIRST...
...YOU HAVE BEEN TRIED IN ABSENTIA AND FOUND GUILTY OF HIGH TREASON.
THAT'S...
PAM'A. SHE SENT ME ON MY MISSION TO EARTH, ALL THOSE YEARS AGO. THAT RECORDING MUST BE ANCIENT.
YOU CANNOT HIDE FOREVER. ONE DAY, MY KLEANERS WILL FIND YOUR LOCATOR BEACON...
...AND EXECUTE YOUR SENTENCE, WHICH IS DEATH.
YEAH, WELL, I GOT A SENTENCE FOR YOU!
NO, CAROL. NOT WHILE SHE HAS JOE.
HALA HAS SPOKEN. DRONES-- COMMENCE EXECUTION PROTOCOL!
AAAHH!

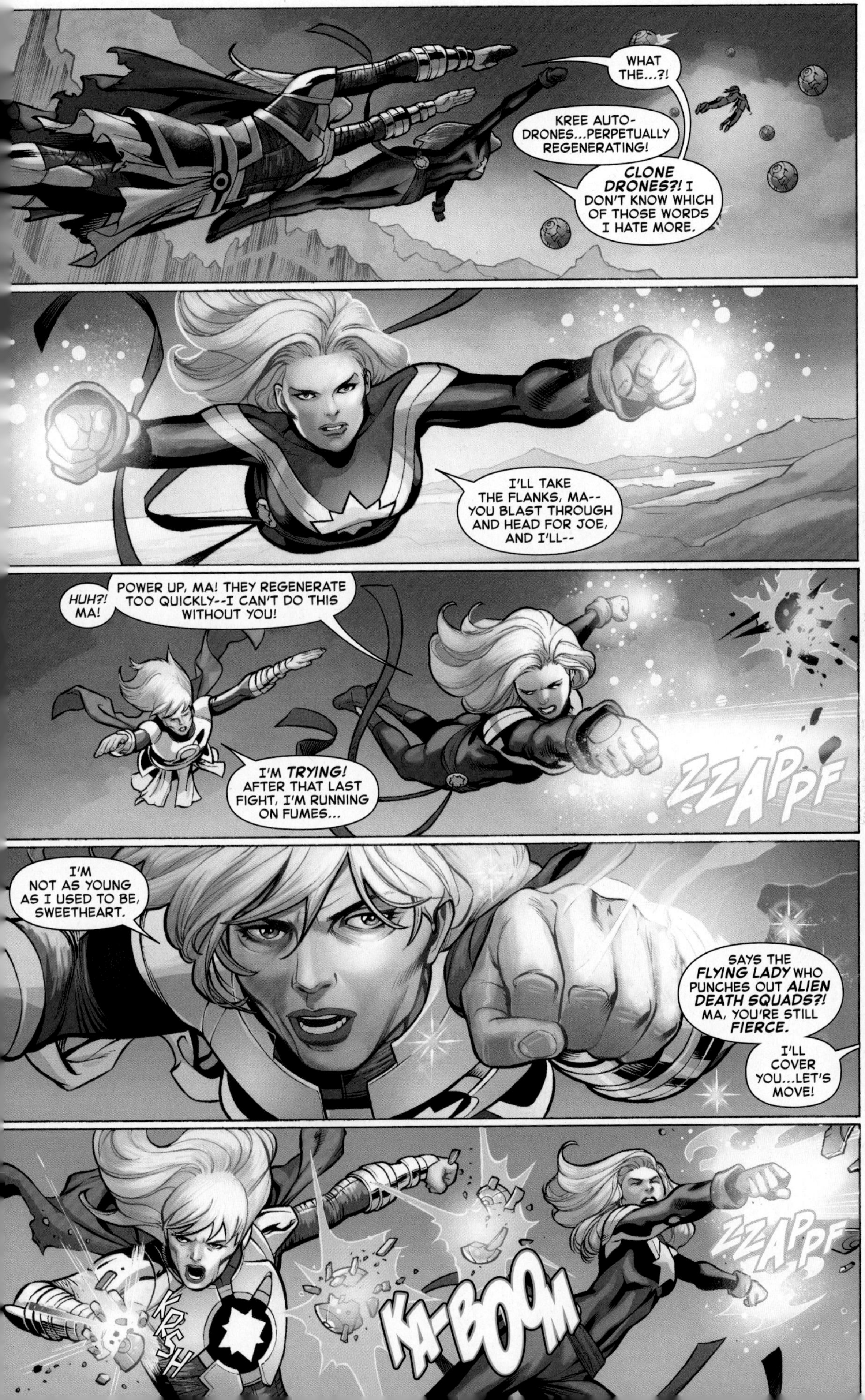
WHAT THE...?!
KREE AUTO-DRONES...PERPETUALLY REGENERATING!
CLONE DRONES?! I DON'T KNOW WHICH OF THOSE WORDS I HATE MORE.
I'LL TAKE THE FLANKS, MA--YOU BLAST THROUGH AND HEAD FOR JOE, AND I'LL--
HUH?! MA!
POWER UP, MA! THEY REGENERATE TOO QUICKLY--I CAN'T DO THIS WITHOUT YOU!
I'M TRYING! AFTER THAT LAST FIGHT, I'M RUNNING ON FUMES...
ZZAPPF
I'M NOT AS YOUNG AS I USED TO BE, SWEETHEART.
SAYS THE FLYING LADY WHO PUNCHES OUT ALIEN DEATH SQUADS?! MA, YOU'RE STILL FIERCE.
I'LL COVER YOU...LET'S MOVE!
KRSSH
KA-BOOM
ZZAPPF

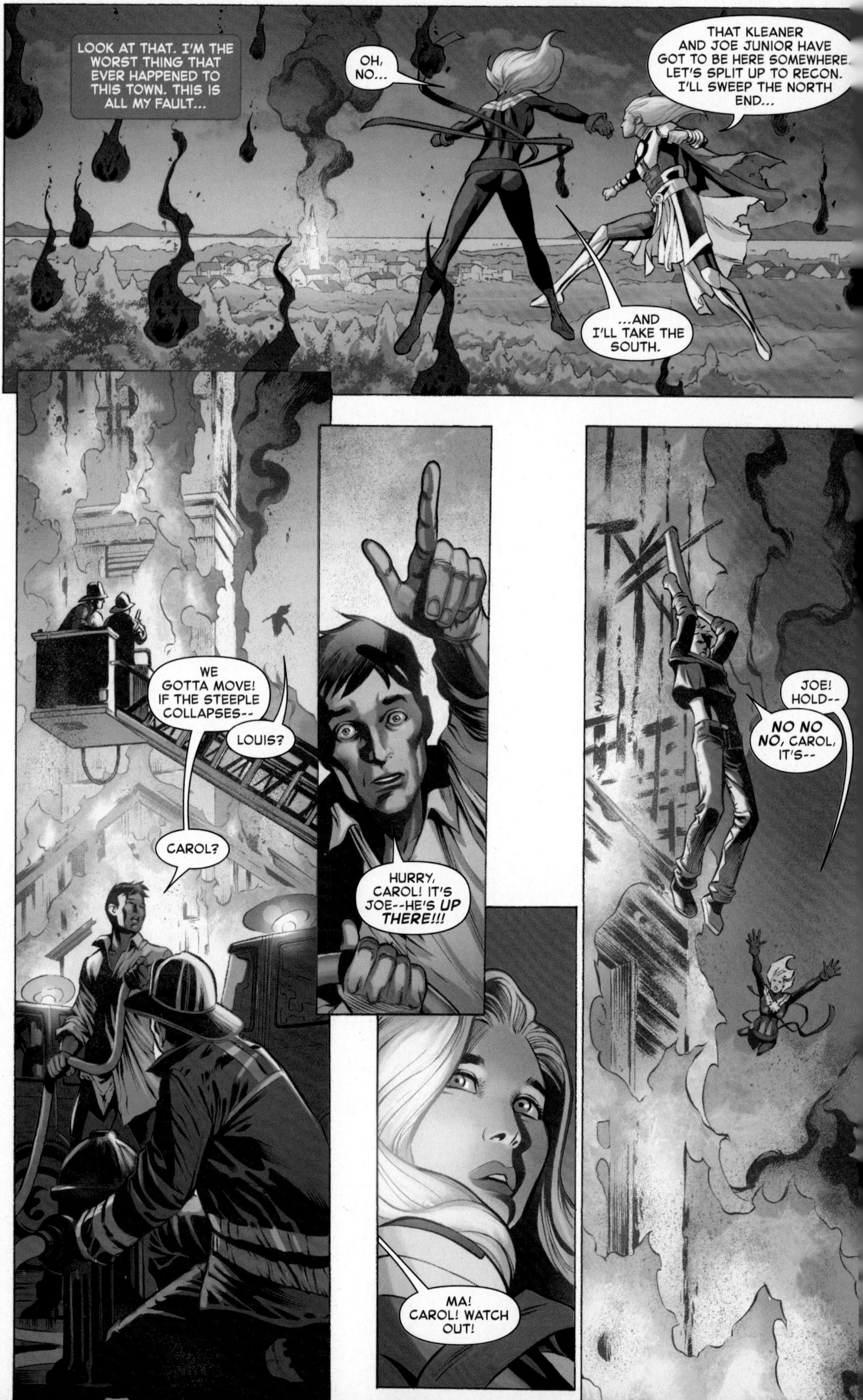
LOOK AT THAT. I'M THE WORST THING THAT EVER HAPPENED TO THIS TOWN. THIS IS ALL MY FAULT...
OH, NO...
THAT KLEANER AND JOE JUNIOR HAVE GOT TO BE HERE SOMEWHERE. LET'S SPLIT UP TO RECON. I'LL SWEEP THE NORTH END...
...AND I'LL TAKE THE SOUTH.
WE GOTTA MOVE! IF THE STEEPLE COLLAPSES--
LOUIS?
CAROL?
HURRY, CAROL! IT'S JOE--HE'S UP THERE!!!
MA! CAROL! WATCH OUT!
JOE! HOLD--
NO NO NO, CAROL, IT'S--

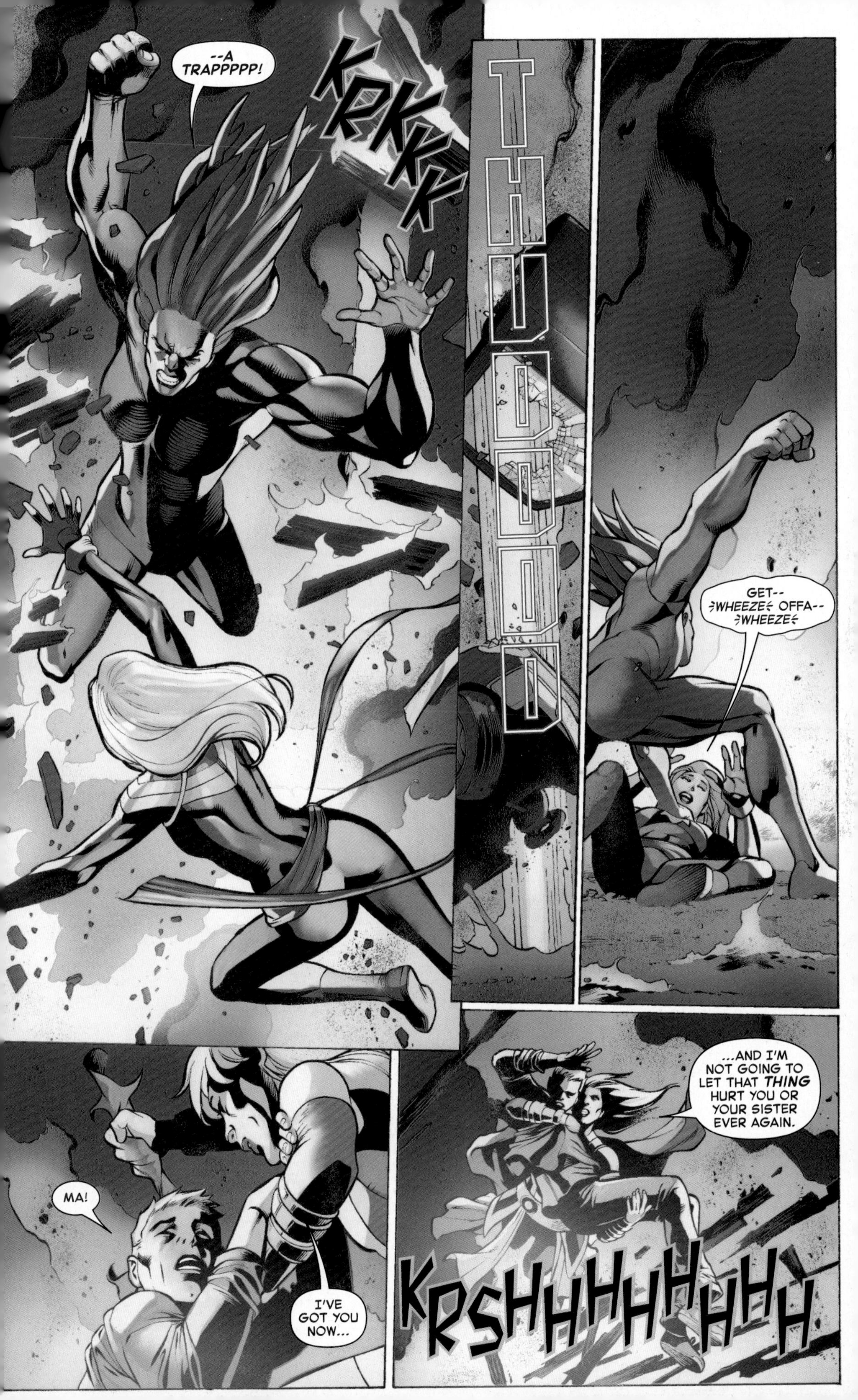
--A TRAPPPPP!
KRKKK
THUDDDD
GET-- WHEEZE OFFA-- WHEEZE
MA!
I'VE GOT YOU NOW...
...AND I'M NOT GOING TO LET THAT THING HURT YOU OR YOUR SISTER EVER AGAIN.
KRSHHHHHHHH

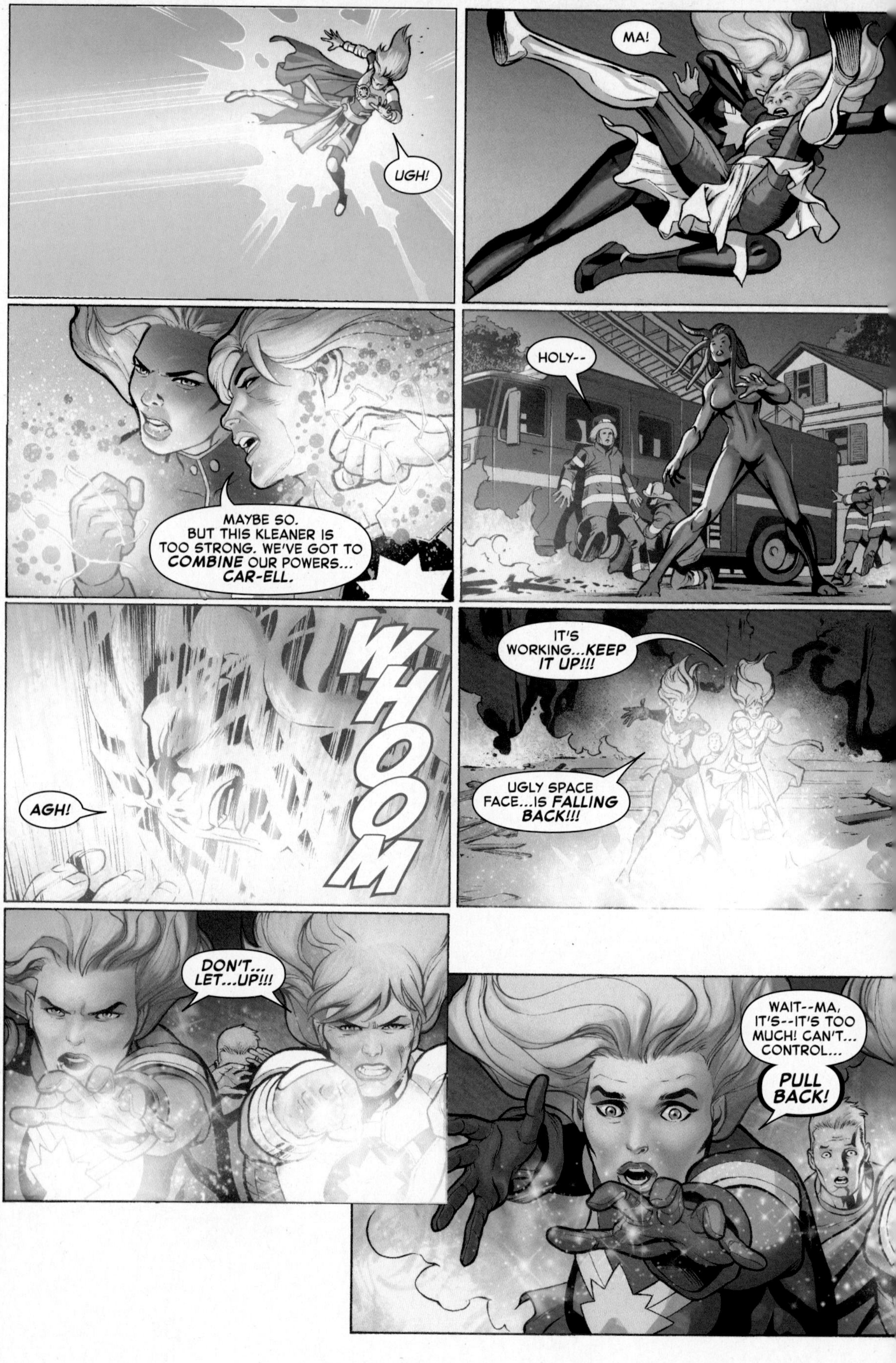
UGH!
MA!
MAYBE SO.
BUT THIS KLEANER IS
TOO STRONG. WE'VE GOT TO
COMBINE OUR POWERS...
CAR-ELL.
HOLY--
WHOOM
AGH!
IT'S
WORKING...KEEP
IT UP!!!
UGLY SPACE
FACE...IS FALLING
BACK!!!
DON'T...
LET...UP!!!
WAIT--MA,
IT'S--IT'S TOO
MUCH! CAN'T...
CONTROL...
PULL
BACK!

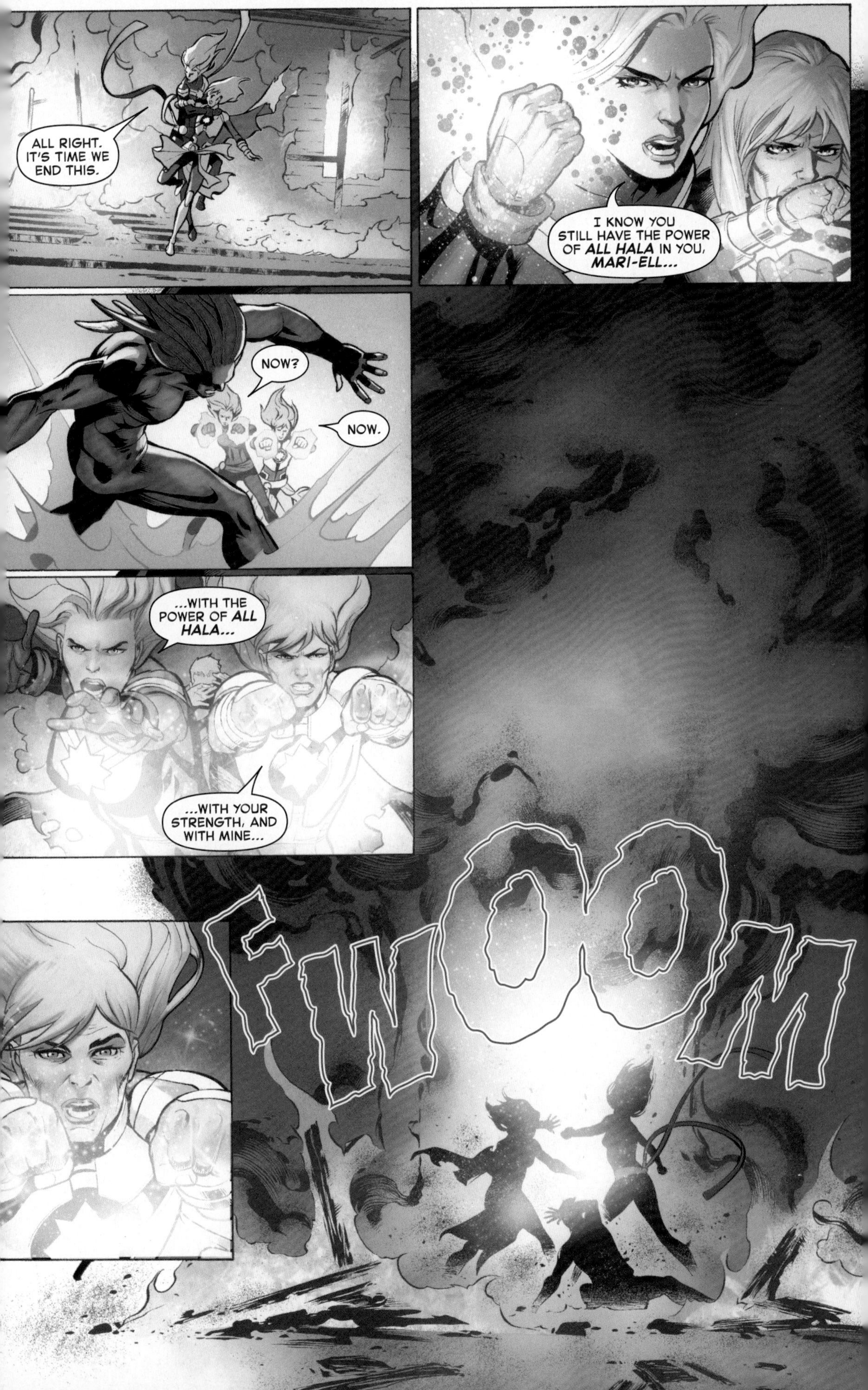
ALL RIGHT. IT'S TIME WE END THIS.
I KNOW YOU STILL HAVE THE POWER OF ALL HALA IN YOU, MARI-ELL...
NOW?
NOW.
...WITH THE POWER OF ALL HALA...
...WITH YOUR STRENGTH, AND WITH MINE...
FWOOM

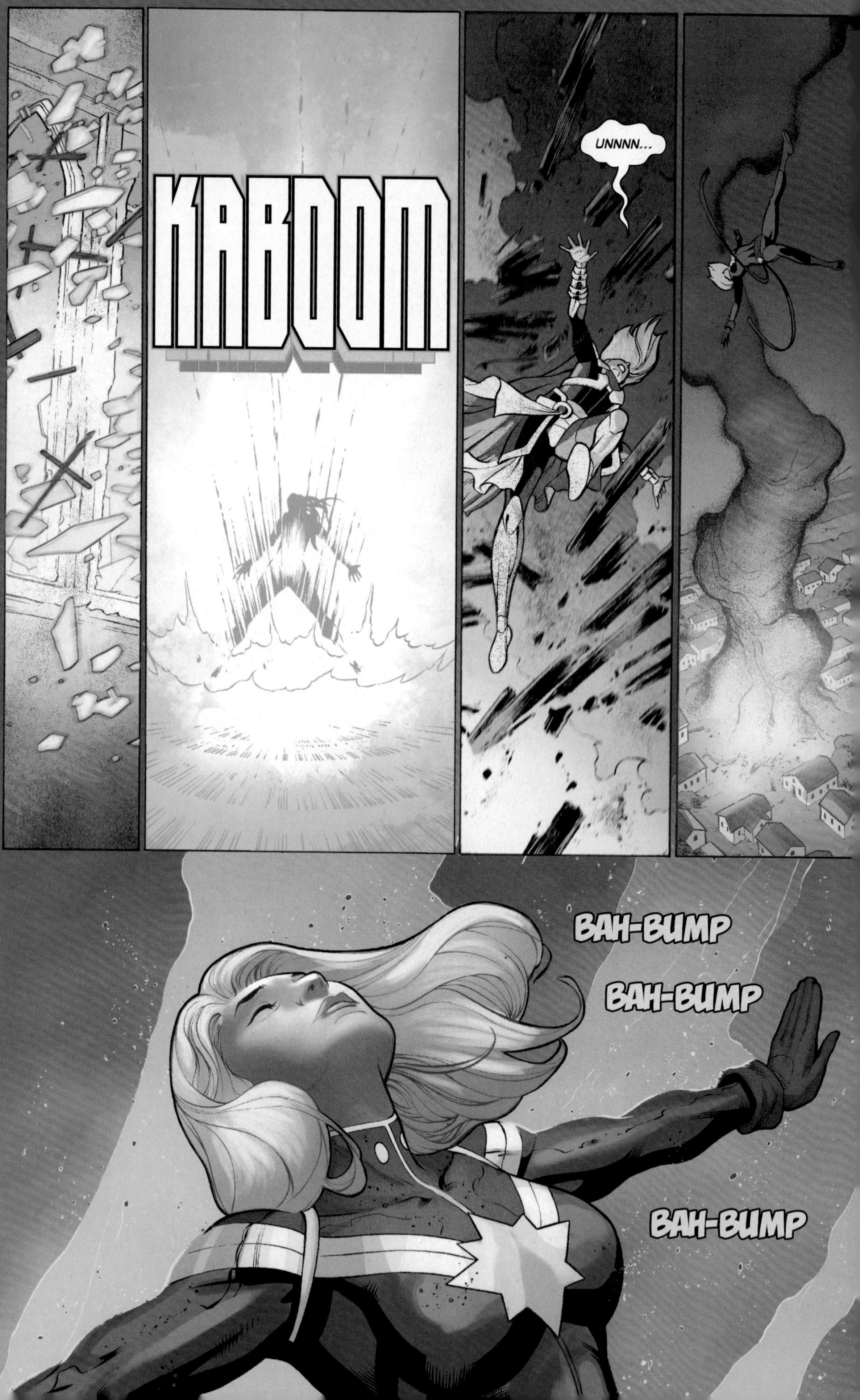
KABOOM
UNNNN...
BAH-BUMP
BAH-BUMP
BAH-BUMP

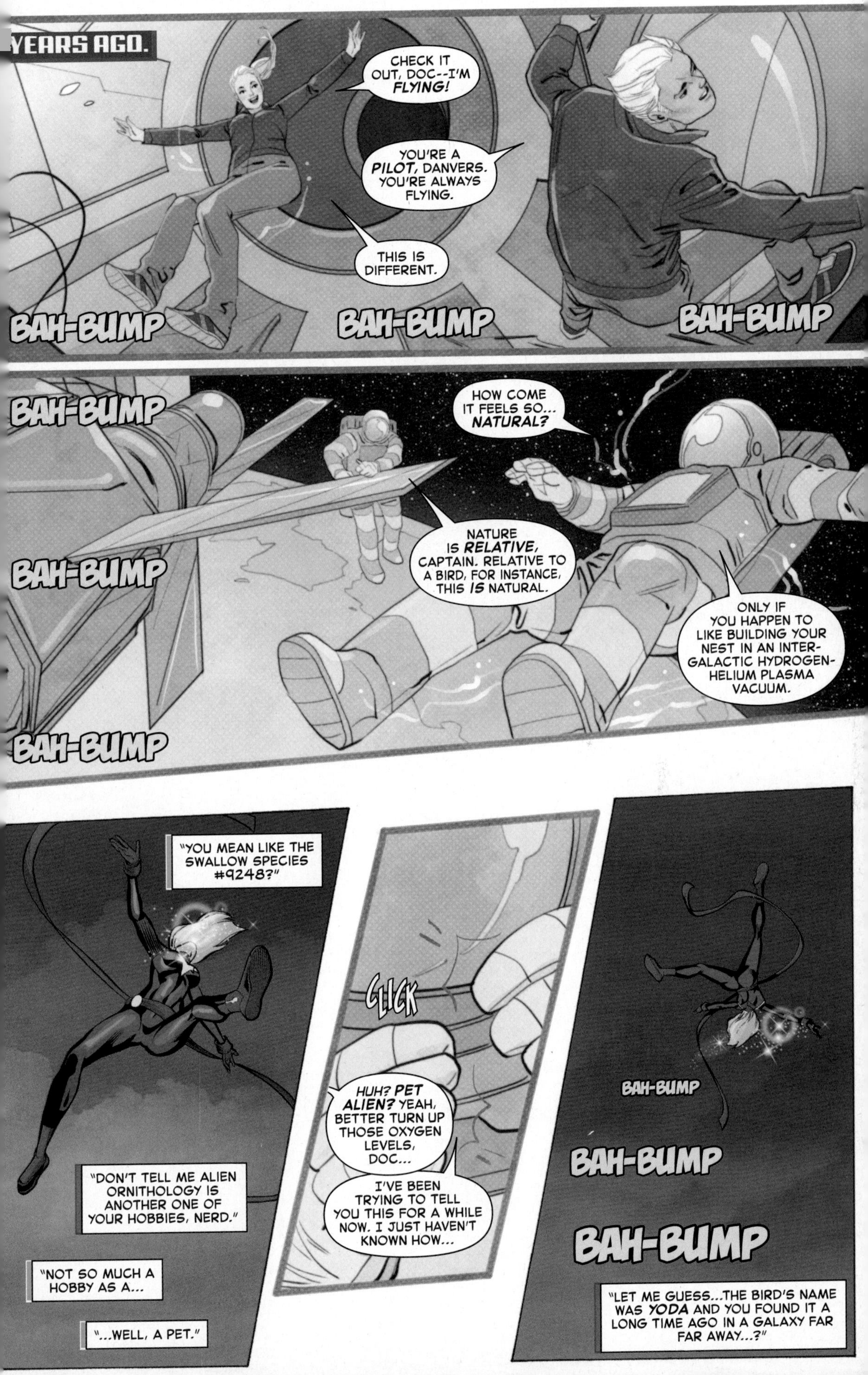
YEARS AGO.
CHECK IT OUT, DOC--I'M FLYING!
YOU'RE A PILOT, DANVERS. YOU'RE ALWAYS FLYING.
THIS IS DIFFERENT.
BAH-BUMP
BAH-BUMP
BAH-BUMP
BAH-BUMP
HOW COME IT FEELS SO... NATURAL?
NATURE IS RELATIVE, CAPTAIN. RELATIVE TO A BIRD, FOR INSTANCE, THIS IS NATURAL.
BAH-BUMP
ONLY IF YOU HAPPEN TO LIKE BUILDING YOUR NEST IN AN INTER-GALACTIC HYDROGEN-HELIUM PLASMA VACUUM.
BAH-BUMP
"YOU MEAN LIKE THE SWALLOW SPECIES #9248?"
"DON'T TELL ME ALIEN ORNITHOLOGY IS ANOTHER ONE OF YOUR HOBBIES, NERD."
"NOT SO MUCH A HOBBY AS A...
"...WELL, A PET."
CLICK
HUH? PET ALIEN? YEAH, BETTER TURN UP THOSE OXYGEN LEVELS, DOC...
I'VE BEEN TRYING TO TELL YOU THIS FOR A WHILE NOW. I JUST HAVEN'T KNOWN HOW...
BAH-BUMP
BAH-BUMP
BAH-BUMP
"LET ME GUESS...THE BIRD'S NAME WAS YODA AND YOU FOUND IT A LONG TIME AGO IN A GALAXY FAR FAR AWAY...?"

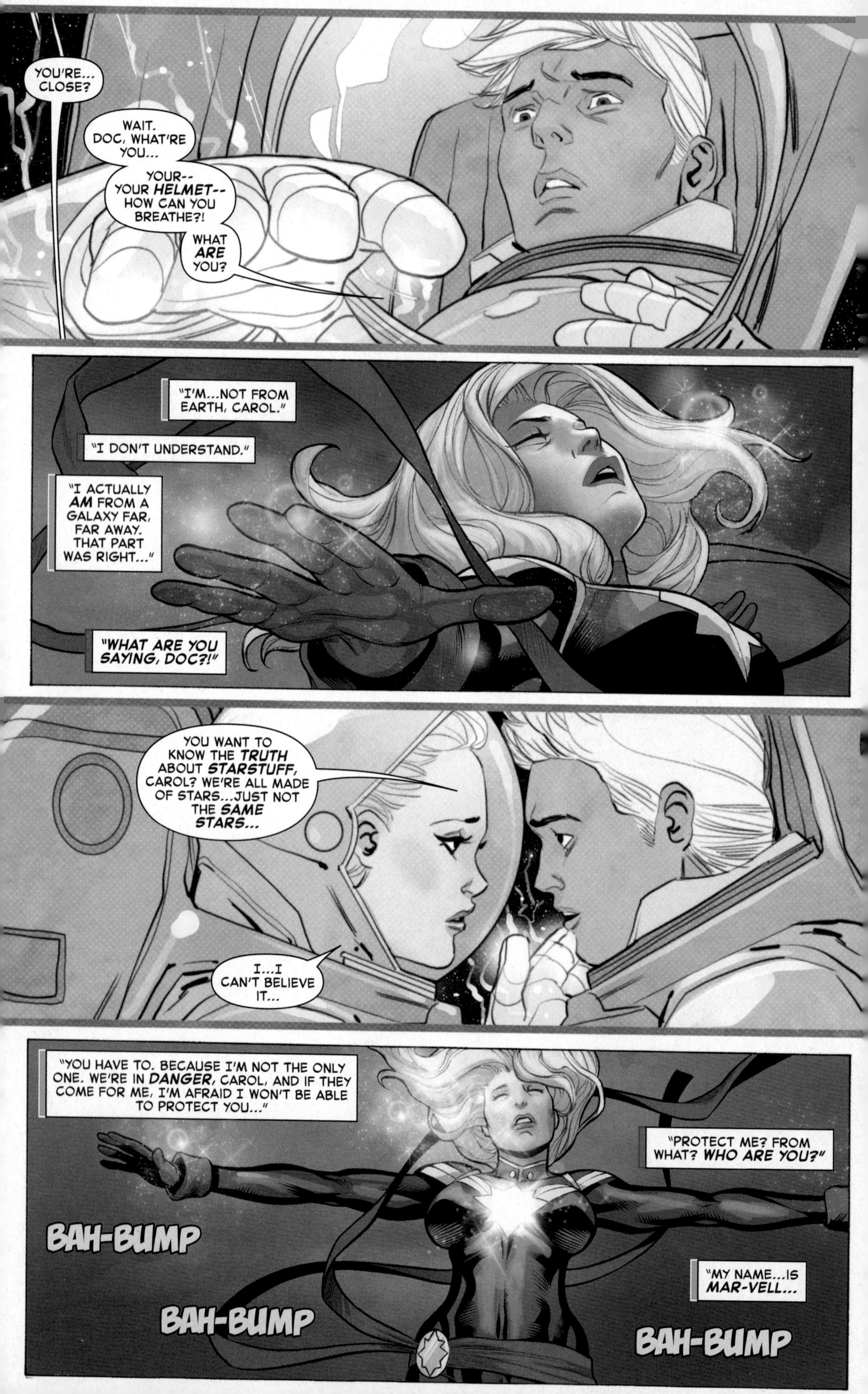

YOU'RE... CLOSE?
WAIT. DOC, WHAT'RE YOU...
YOUR-- YOUR HELMET-- HOW CAN YOU BREATHE?!
WHAT ARE YOU?
"I'M...NOT FROM EARTH, CAROL."
"I DON'T UNDERSTAND."
"I ACTUALLY AM FROM A GALAXY FAR, FAR AWAY. THAT PART WAS RIGHT..."
"WHAT ARE YOU SAYING, DOC?!"
YOU WANT TO KNOW THE TRUTH ABOUT STARSTUFF, CAROL? WE'RE ALL MADE OF STARS...JUST NOT THE SAME STARS...
I...I CAN'T BELIEVE IT...
"YOU HAVE TO. BECAUSE I'M NOT THE ONLY ONE. WE'RE IN DANGER, CAROL, AND IF THEY COME FOR ME, I'M AFRAID I WON'T BE ABLE TO PROTECT YOU..."
"PROTECT ME? FROM WHAT? WHO ARE YOU?"
BAH-BUMP
BAH-BUMP
"MY NAME...IS MAR-VELL..."
BAH-BUMP

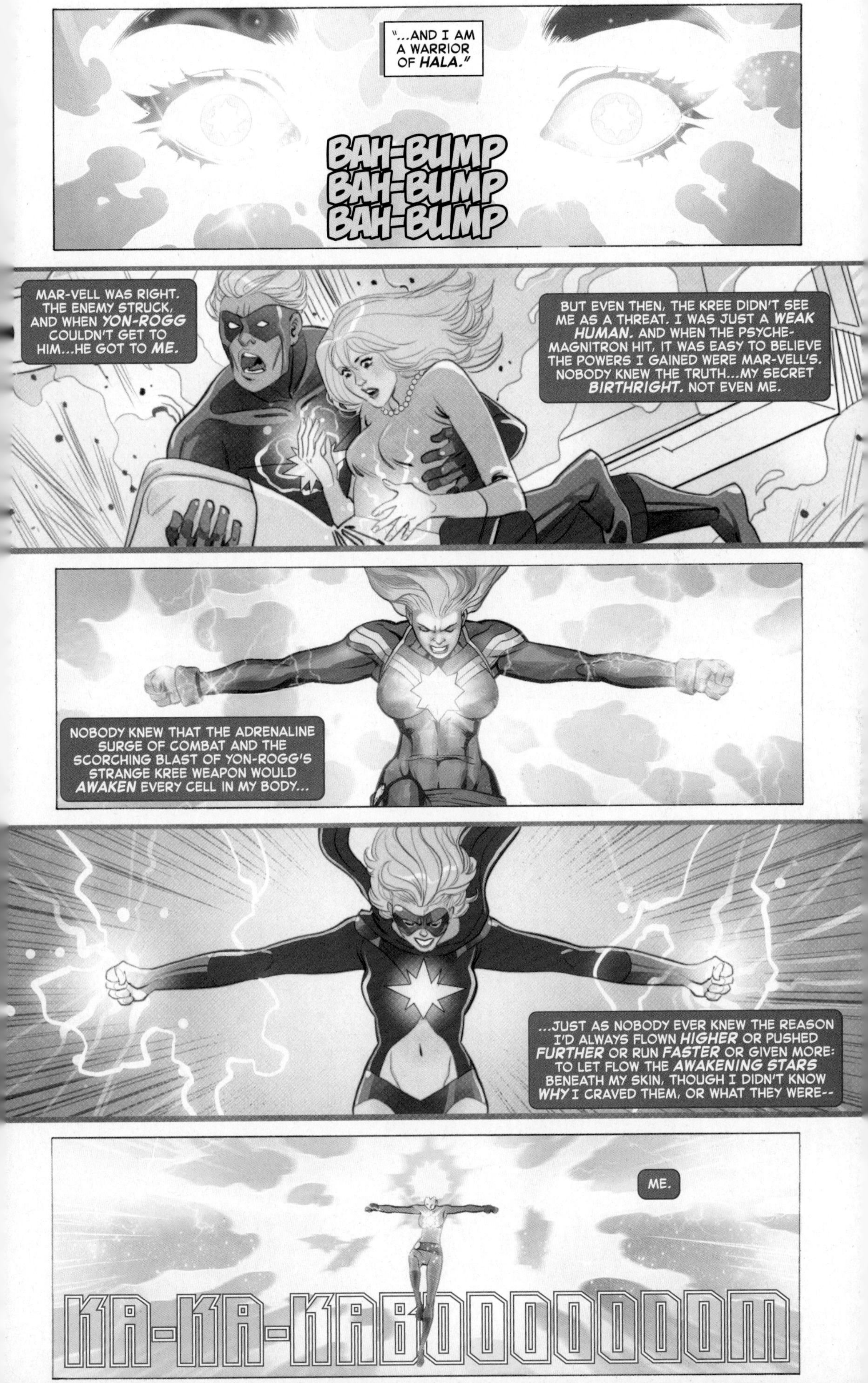
"...AND I AM A WARRIOR OF HALA."
BAH-BUMP BAH-BUMP BAH-BUMP
MAR-VELL WAS RIGHT. THE ENEMY STRUCK, AND WHEN YON-ROGG COULDN'T GET TO HIM...HE GOT TO ME.
BUT EVEN THEN, THE KREE DIDN'T SEE ME AS A THREAT. I WAS JUST A WEAK HUMAN. AND WHEN THE PSYCHE-MAGNITRON HIT, IT WAS EASY TO BELIEVE THE POWERS I GAINED WERE MAR-VELL'S. NOBODY KNEW THE TRUTH...MY SECRET BIRTHRIGHT. NOT EVEN ME.
NOBODY KNEW THAT THE ADRENALINE SURGE OF COMBAT AND THE SCORCHING BLAST OF YON-ROGG'S STRANGE KREE WEAPON WOULD AWAKEN EVERY CELL IN MY BODY...
...JUST AS NOBODY EVER KNEW THE REASON I'D ALWAYS FLOWN HIGHER OR PUSHED FURTHER OR RUN FASTER OR GIVEN MORE: TO LET FLOW THE AWAKENING STARS BENEATH MY SKIN, THOUGH I DIDN'T KNOW WHY I CRAVED THEM, OR WHAT THEY WERE--
ME.
KA-KA-KABOOOOOOOOOM

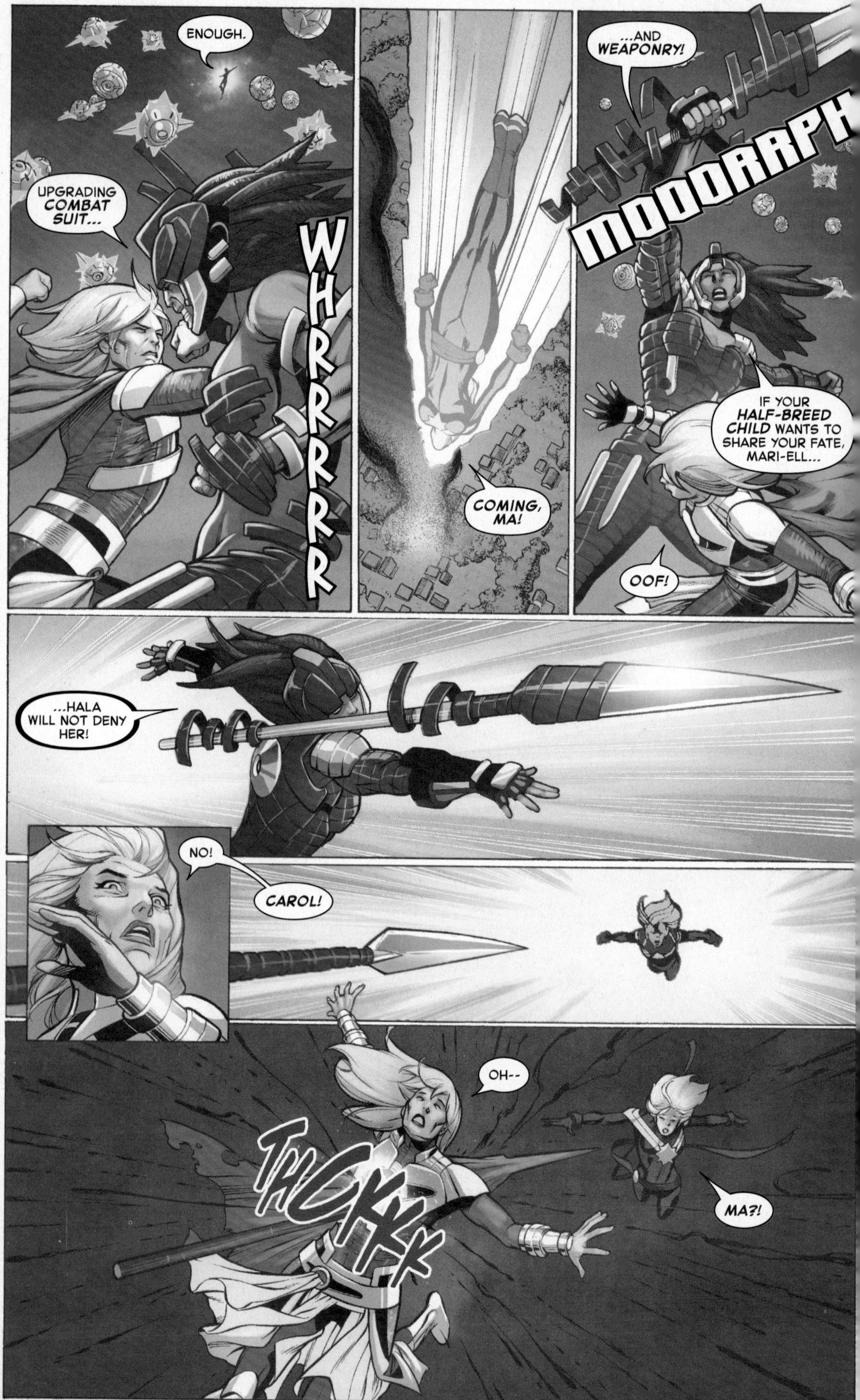
ENOUGH.
UPGRADING COMBAT SUIT...
WHRRRRR
COMING, MA!
...AND WEAPONRY!
MOOORRPH
IF YOUR HALF-BREED CHILD WANTS TO SHARE YOUR FATE, MARI-ELL...
OOF!
...HALA WILL NOT DENY HER!
NO!
CAROL!
OH--
MA?!
THCKK

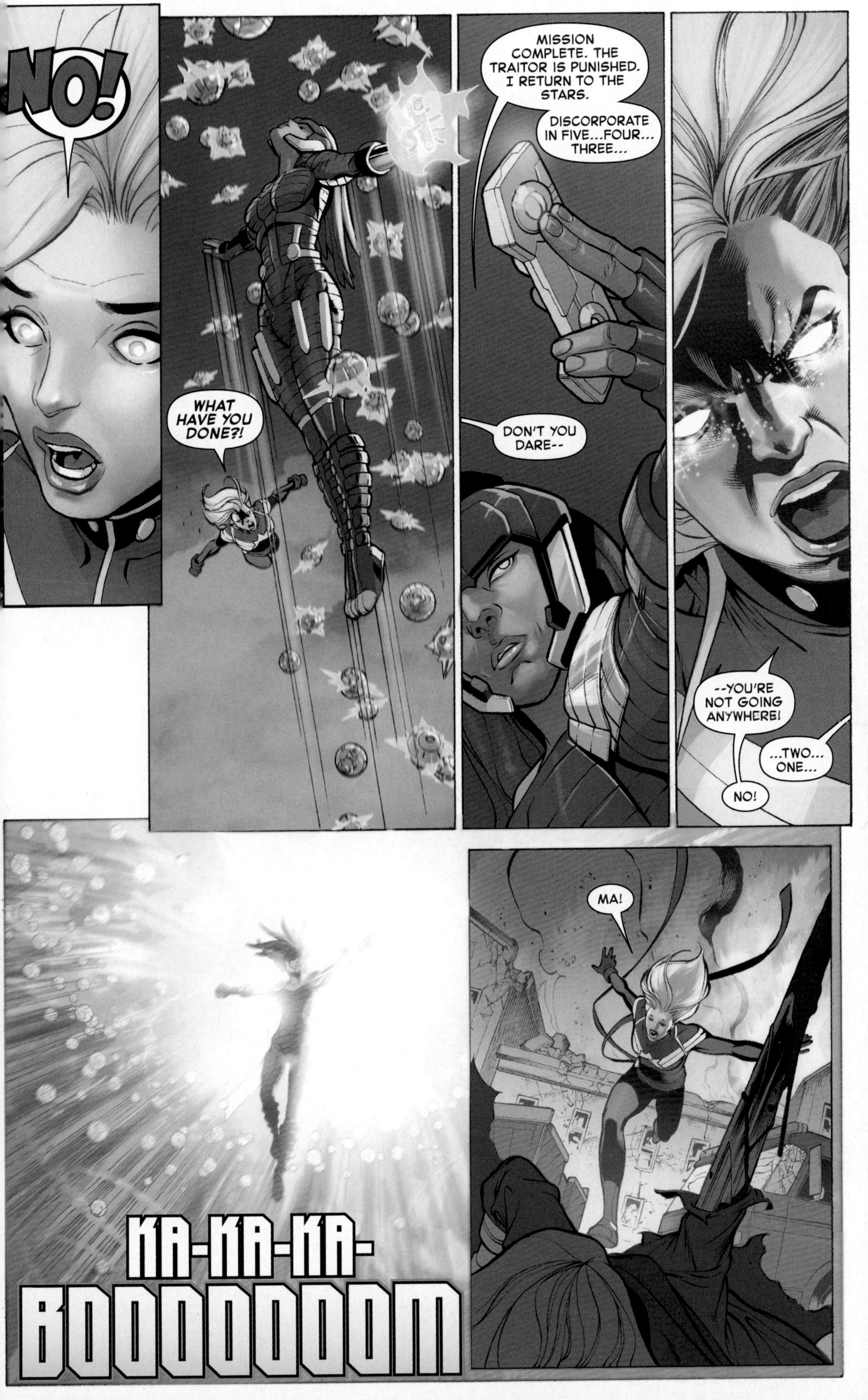
NO!
WHAT HAVE YOU DONE?!
MISSION COMPLETE. THE TRAITOR IS PUNISHED. I RETURN TO THE STARS.
DISCORPORATE IN FIVE...FOUR... THREE...
DON'T YOU DARE--
--YOU'RE NOT GOING ANYWHERE!
...TWO... ONE...
NO!
KA-KA-KA-BOOOOOOOM
MA!

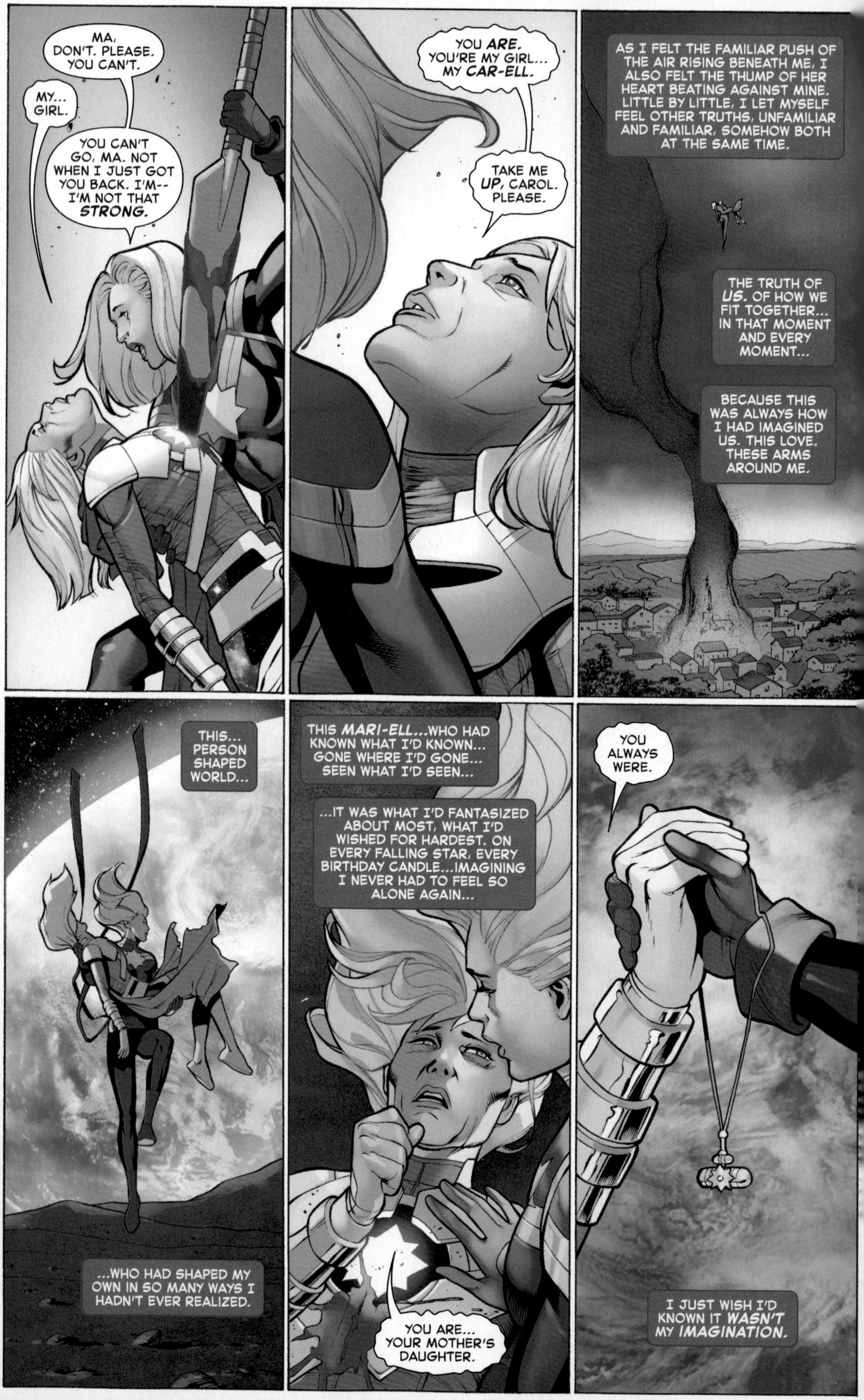

MA, DON'T. PLEASE. YOU CAN'T.
MY... GIRL.
YOU CAN'T GO, MA. NOT WHEN I JUST GOT YOU BACK. I'M-- I'M NOT THAT STRONG.
YOU ARE. YOU'RE MY GIRL... MY CAR-ELL.
TAKE ME UP, CAROL. PLEASE.
AS I FELT THE FAMILIAR PUSH OF THE AIR RISING BENEATH ME, I ALSO FELT THE THUMP OF HER HEART BEATING AGAINST MINE. LITTLE BY LITTLE, I LET MYSELF FEEL OTHER TRUTHS, UNFAMILIAR AND FAMILIAR, SOMEHOW BOTH AT THE SAME TIME.
THE TRUTH OF US. OF HOW WE FIT TOGETHER... IN THAT MOMENT AND EVERY MOMENT...
BECAUSE THIS WAS ALWAYS HOW I HAD IMAGINED US. THIS LOVE. THESE ARMS AROUND ME.
THIS... PERSON SHAPED WORLD...
...WHO HAD SHAPED MY OWN IN SO MANY WAYS I HADN'T EVER REALIZED.
THIS MARI-ELL...WHO HAD KNOWN WHAT I'D KNOWN... GONE WHERE I'D GONE... SEEN WHAT I'D SEEN...
...IT WAS WHAT I'D FANTASIZED ABOUT MOST, WHAT I'D WISHED FOR HARDEST. ON EVERY FALLING STAR, EVERY BIRTHDAY CANDLE...IMAGINING I NEVER HAD TO FEEL SO ALONE AGAIN...
YOU ARE... YOUR MOTHER'S DAUGHTER.
YOU ALWAYS WERE.
I JUST WISH I'D KNOWN IT WASN'T MY IMAGINATION.

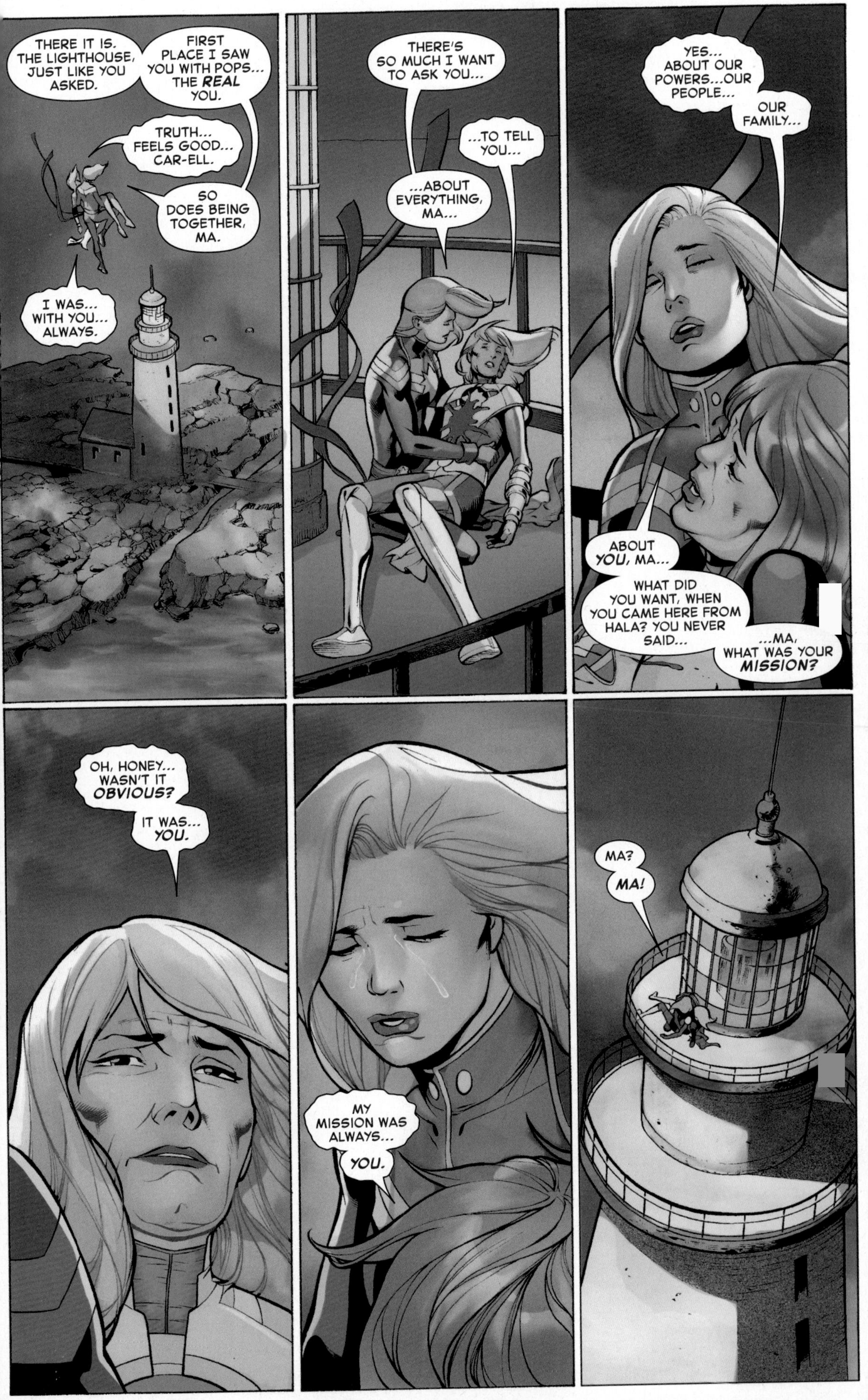
THERE IT IS. THE LIGHTHOUSE, JUST LIKE YOU ASKED.
FIRST PLACE I SAW YOU WITH POPS... THE REAL YOU.
TRUTH... FEELS GOOD... CAR-ELL.
SO DOES BEING TOGETHER, MA.
I WAS... WITH YOU... ALWAYS.
THERE'S SO MUCH I WANT TO ASK YOU...
...ABOUT EVERYTHING, MA...
...TO TELL YOU...
YES... ABOUT OUR POWERS...OUR PEOPLE...
OUR FAMILY...
ABOUT YOU, MA...
WHAT DID YOU WANT, WHEN YOU CAME HERE FROM HALA? YOU NEVER SAID...
...MA, WHAT WAS YOUR MISSION?
OH, HONEY... WASN'T IT OBVIOUS?
IT WAS... YOU.
MY MISSION WAS ALWAYS...
YOU.
MA?
MA!

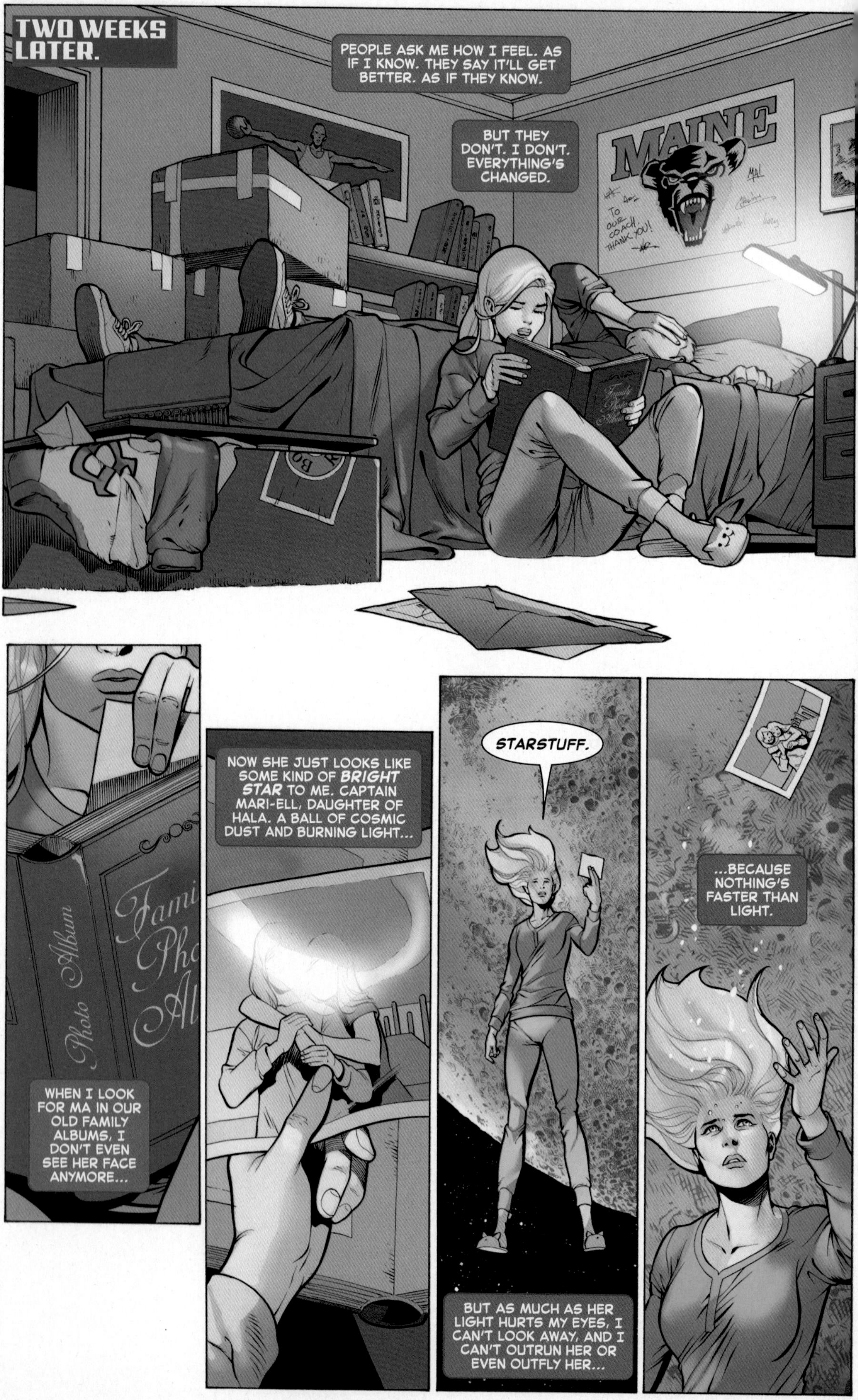
TWO WEEKS LATER.
PEOPLE ASK ME HOW I FEEL. AS IF I KNOW. THEY SAY IT'LL GET BETTER. AS IF THEY KNOW.
BUT THEY DON'T. I DON'T. EVERYTHING'S CHANGED.
MAINE
TO OUR COACH, THANK YOU!
Family Photo Album
WHEN I LOOK FOR MA IN OUR OLD FAMILY ALBUMS, I DON'T EVEN SEE HER FACE ANYMORE...
Photo Album
NOW SHE JUST LOOKS LIKE SOME KIND OF **BRIGHT STAR** TO ME. CAPTAIN MARI-ELL, DAUGHTER OF HALA. A BALL OF COSMIC DUST AND BURNING LIGHT...
STARSTUFF.
BUT AS MUCH AS HER LIGHT HURTS MY EYES, I CAN'T LOOK AWAY, AND I CAN'T OUTRUN HER OR EVEN OUTFLY HER...
...BECAUSE NOTHING'S FASTER THAN LIGHT.

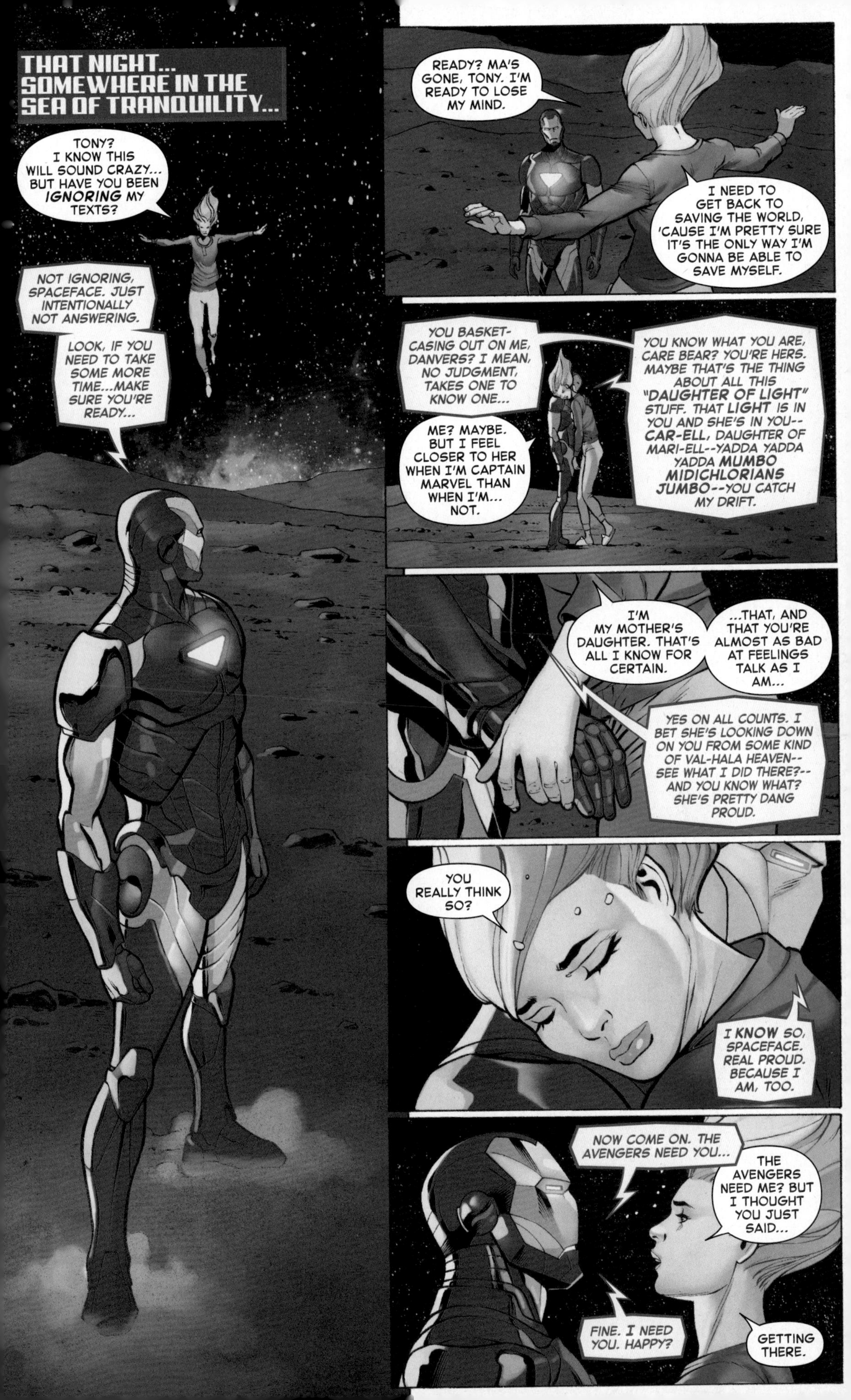
THAT NIGHT... SOMEWHERE IN THE SEA OF TRANQUILITY...
TONY? I KNOW THIS WILL SOUND CRAZY... BUT HAVE YOU BEEN IGNORING MY TEXTS?
NOT IGNORING, SPACEFACE. JUST INTENTIONALLY NOT ANSWERING.
LOOK, IF YOU NEED TO TAKE SOME MORE TIME...MAKE SURE YOU'RE READY...
READY? MA'S GONE, TONY. I'M READY TO LOSE MY MIND.
I NEED TO GET BACK TO SAVING THE WORLD, 'CAUSE I'M PRETTY SURE IT'S THE ONLY WAY I'M GONNA BE ABLE TO SAVE MYSELF.
YOU BASKET-CASING OUT ON ME, DANVERS? I MEAN, NO JUDGMENT, TAKES ONE TO KNOW ONE...
ME? MAYBE. BUT I FEEL CLOSER TO HER WHEN I'M CAPTAIN MARVEL THAN WHEN I'M... NOT.
YOU KNOW WHAT YOU ARE, CARE BEAR? YOU'RE HERS. MAYBE THAT'S THE THING ABOUT ALL THIS "DAUGHTER OF LIGHT" STUFF. THAT LIGHT IS IN YOU AND SHE'S IN YOU--CAR-ELL, DAUGHTER OF MARI-ELL--YADDA YADDA YADDA MUMBO MIDICHLORIANS JUMBO--YOU CATCH MY DRIFT.
I'M MY MOTHER'S DAUGHTER. THAT'S ALL I KNOW FOR CERTAIN.
...THAT, AND THAT YOU'RE ALMOST AS BAD AT FEELINGS TALK AS I AM...
YES ON ALL COUNTS. I BET SHE'S LOOKING DOWN ON YOU FROM SOME KIND OF VAL-HALA HEAVEN--SEE WHAT I DID THERE?--AND YOU KNOW WHAT? SHE'S PRETTY DANG PROUD.
YOU REALLY THINK SO?
I KNOW SO, SPACEFACE. REAL PROUD. BECAUSE I AM, TOO.
NOW COME ON. THE AVENGERS NEED YOU...
THE AVENGERS NEED ME? BUT I THOUGHT YOU JUST SAID...
FINE. I NEED YOU. HAPPY?
GETTING THERE.

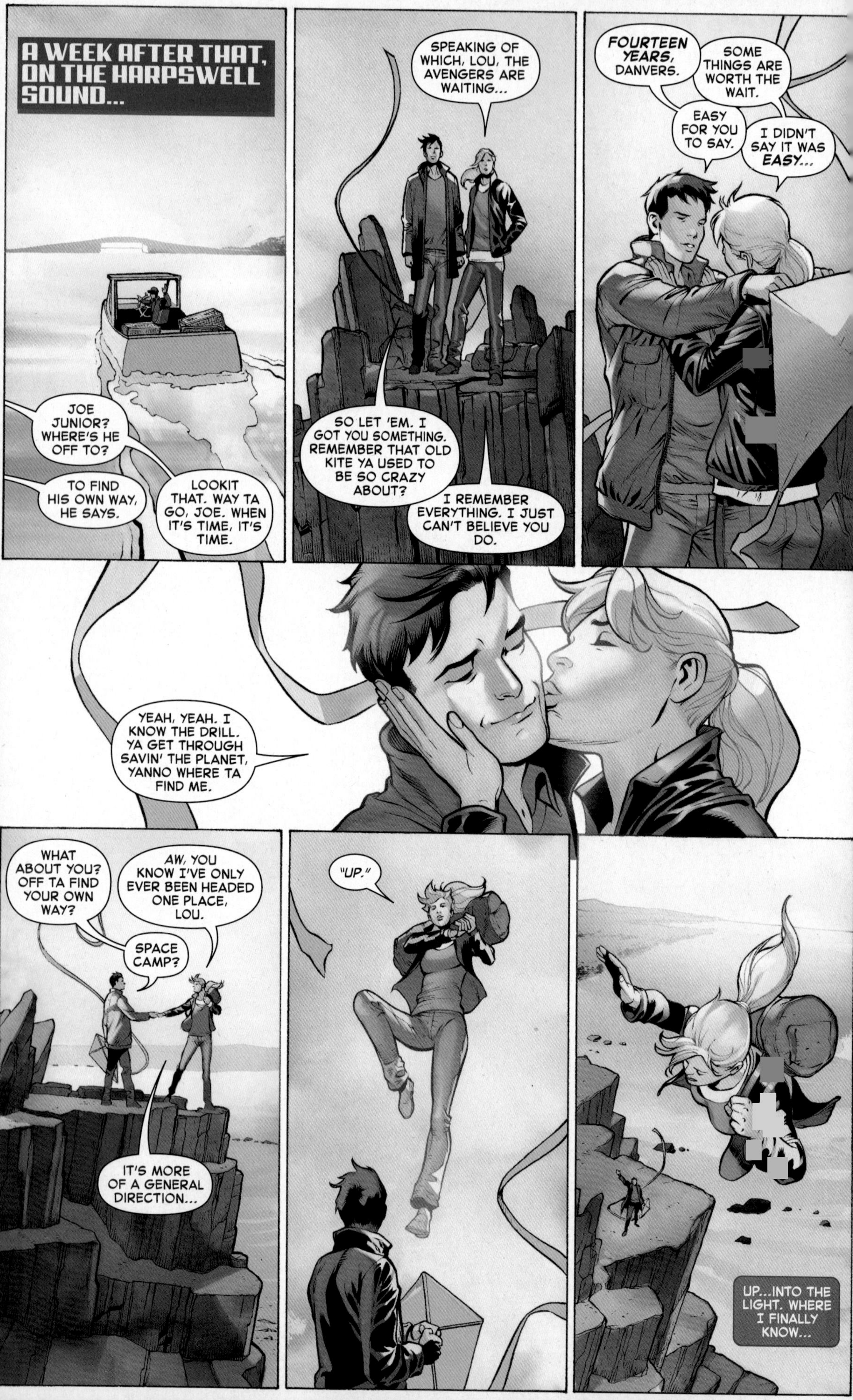
A WEEK AFTER THAT, ON THE HARPSWELL SOUND...
JOE JUNIOR? WHERE'S HE OFF TO?
TO FIND HIS OWN WAY, HE SAYS.
LOOKIT THAT. WAY TA GO, JOE. WHEN IT'S TIME, IT'S TIME.
SPEAKING OF WHICH, LOU, THE AVENGERS ARE WAITING...
SO LET 'EM. I GOT YOU SOMETHING. REMEMBER THAT OLD KITE YA USED TO BE SO CRAZY ABOUT?
I REMEMBER EVERYTHING. I JUST CAN'T BELIEVE YOU DO.
FOURTEEN YEARS, DANVERS.
SOME THINGS ARE WORTH THE WAIT.
EASY FOR YOU TO SAY.
I DIDN'T SAY IT WAS EASY...
YEAH, YEAH. I KNOW THE DRILL. YA GET THROUGH SAVIN' THE PLANET, YANNO WHERE TA FIND ME.
WHAT ABOUT YOU? OFF TA FIND YOUR OWN WAY?
AW, YOU KNOW I'VE ONLY EVER BEEN HEADED ONE PLACE, LOU.
SPACE CAMP?
IT'S MORE OF A GENERAL DIRECTION...
"UP."
UP...INTO THE LIGHT. WHERE I FINALLY KNOW...

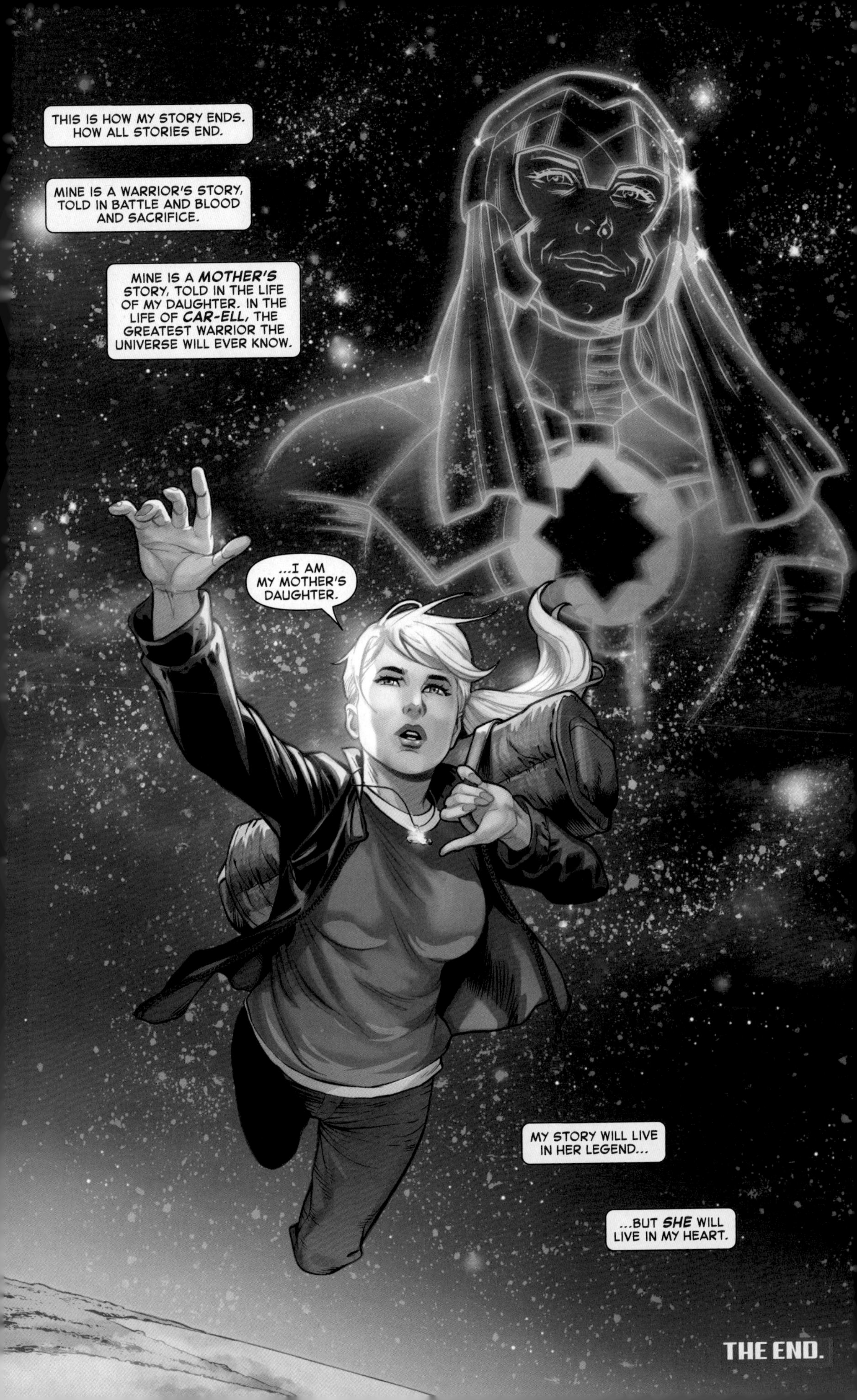
THIS IS HOW MY STORY ENDS. HOW ALL STORIES END.
MINE IS A WARRIOR'S STORY, TOLD IN BATTLE AND BLOOD AND SACRIFICE.
MINE IS A MOTHER'S STORY, TOLD IN THE LIFE OF MY DAUGHTER. IN THE LIFE OF CAR-ELL, THE GREATEST WARRIOR THE UNIVERSE WILL EVER KNOW.
...I AM MY MOTHER'S DAUGHTER.
MY STORY WILL LIVE IN HER LEGEND...
...BUT SHE WILL LIVE IN MY HEART.
THE END.

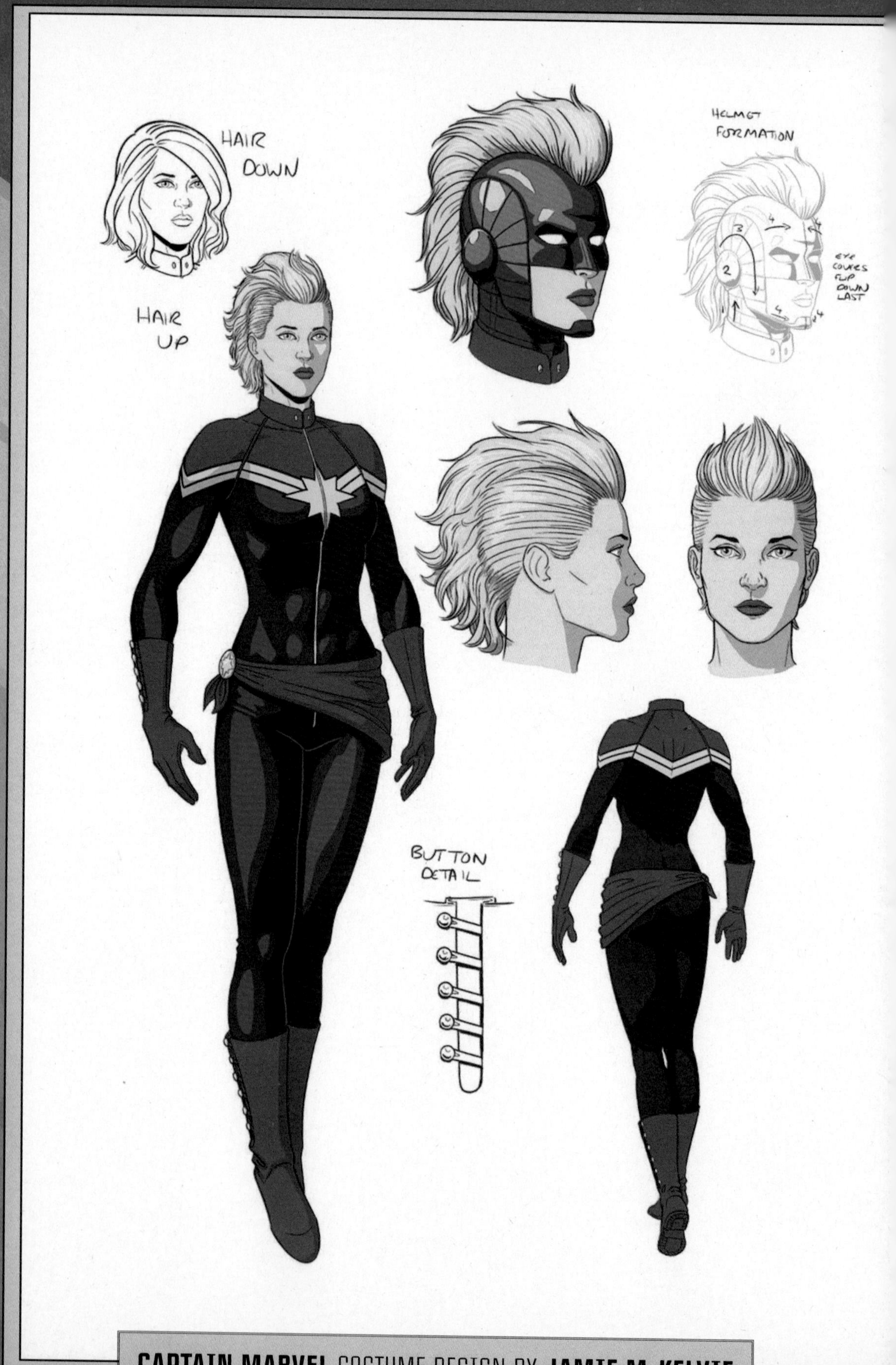
HAIR DOWN
HELMET FORMATION
EYE COVERS FLIP DOWN LAST
HAIR UP
BUTTON DETAIL

CAPTAIN MARVEL COSTUME DESIGN BY **JAMIE McKELVIE**

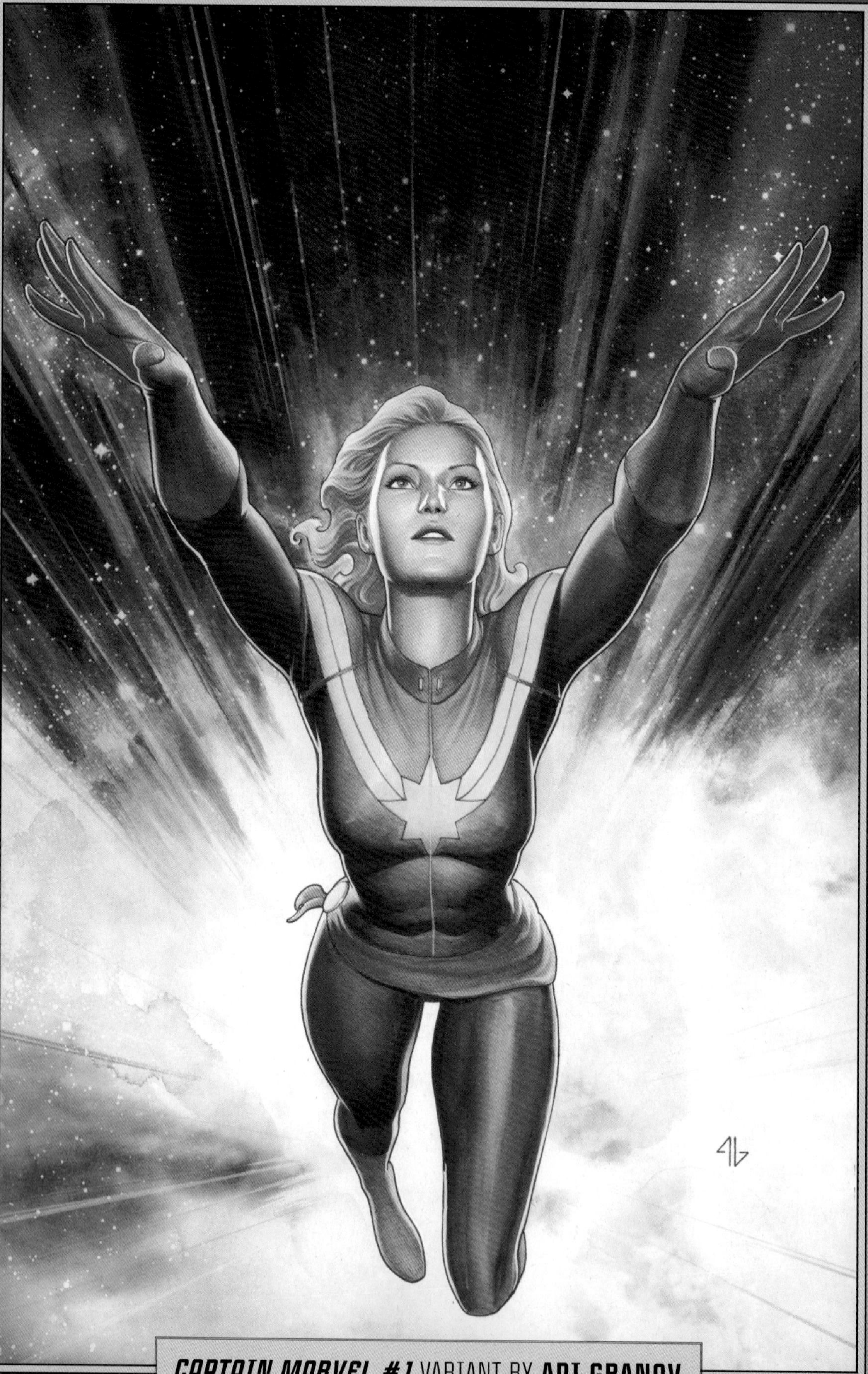

CAPTAIN MARVEL #1 VARIANT BY **ADI GRANOV**

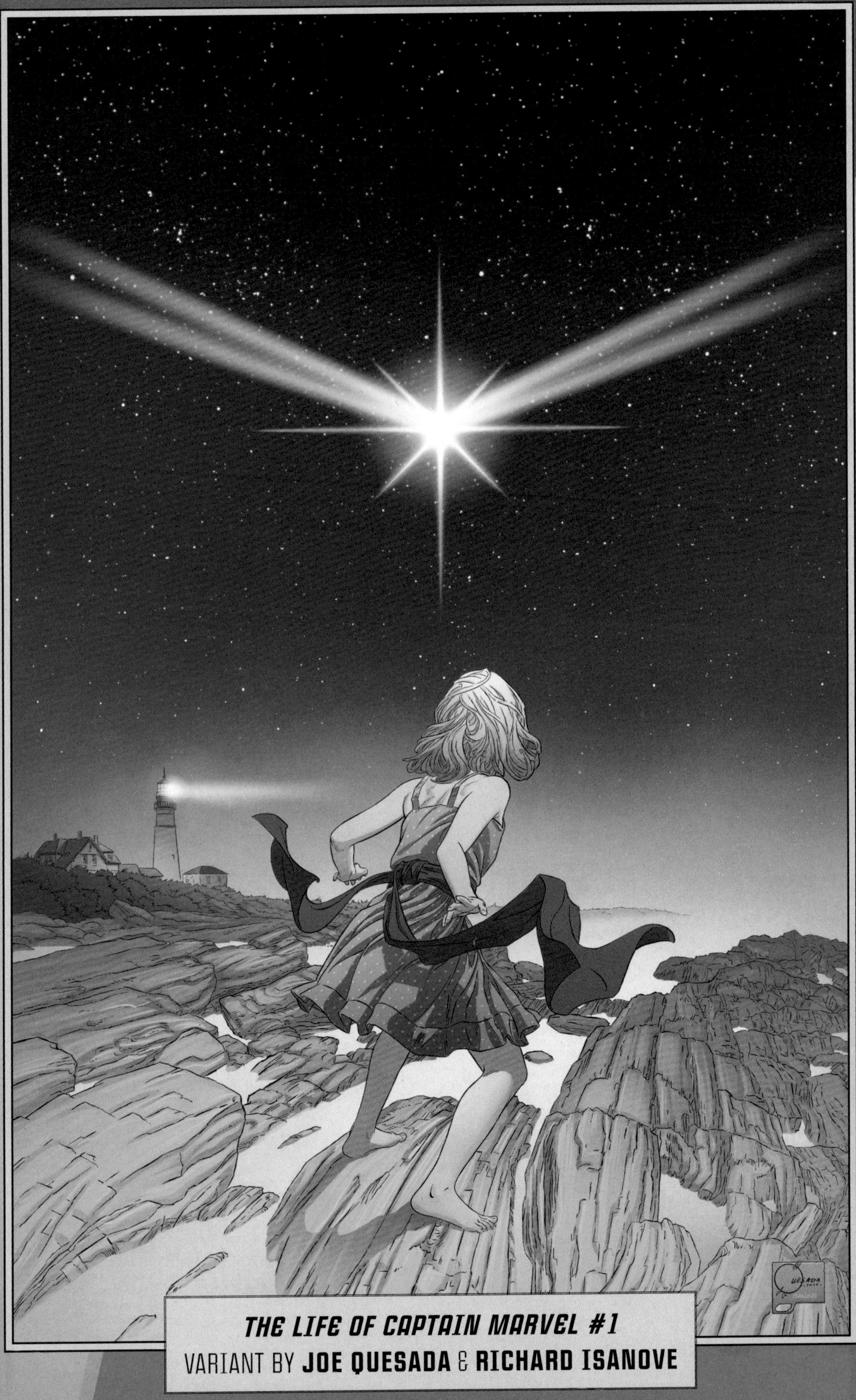

THE LIFE OF CAPTAIN MARVEL #1
VARIANT BY **JOE QUESADA** & **RICHARD ISANOVE**

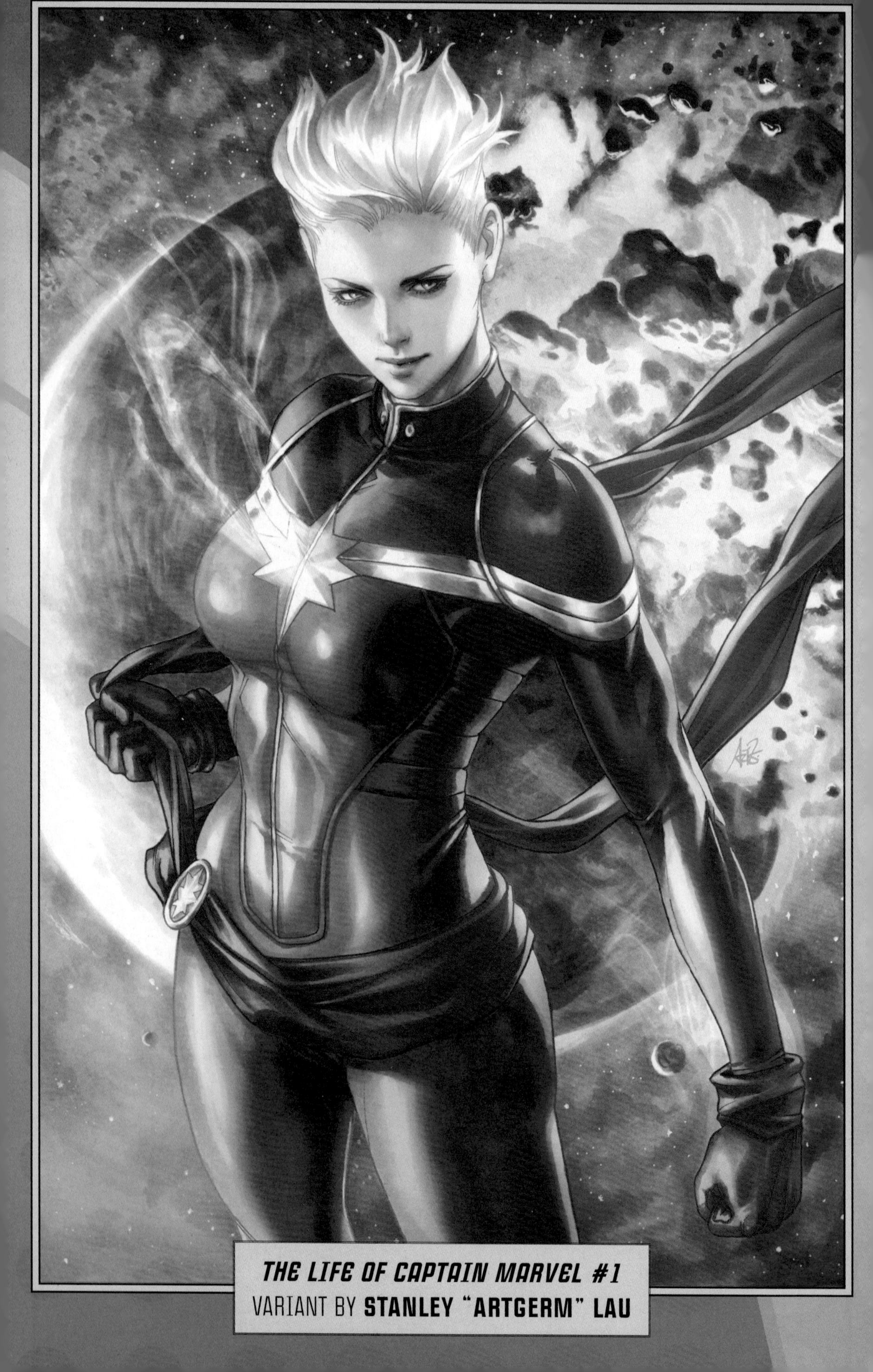

THE LIFE OF CAPTAIN MARVEL #1
VARIANT BY **STANLEY "ARTGERM" LAU**

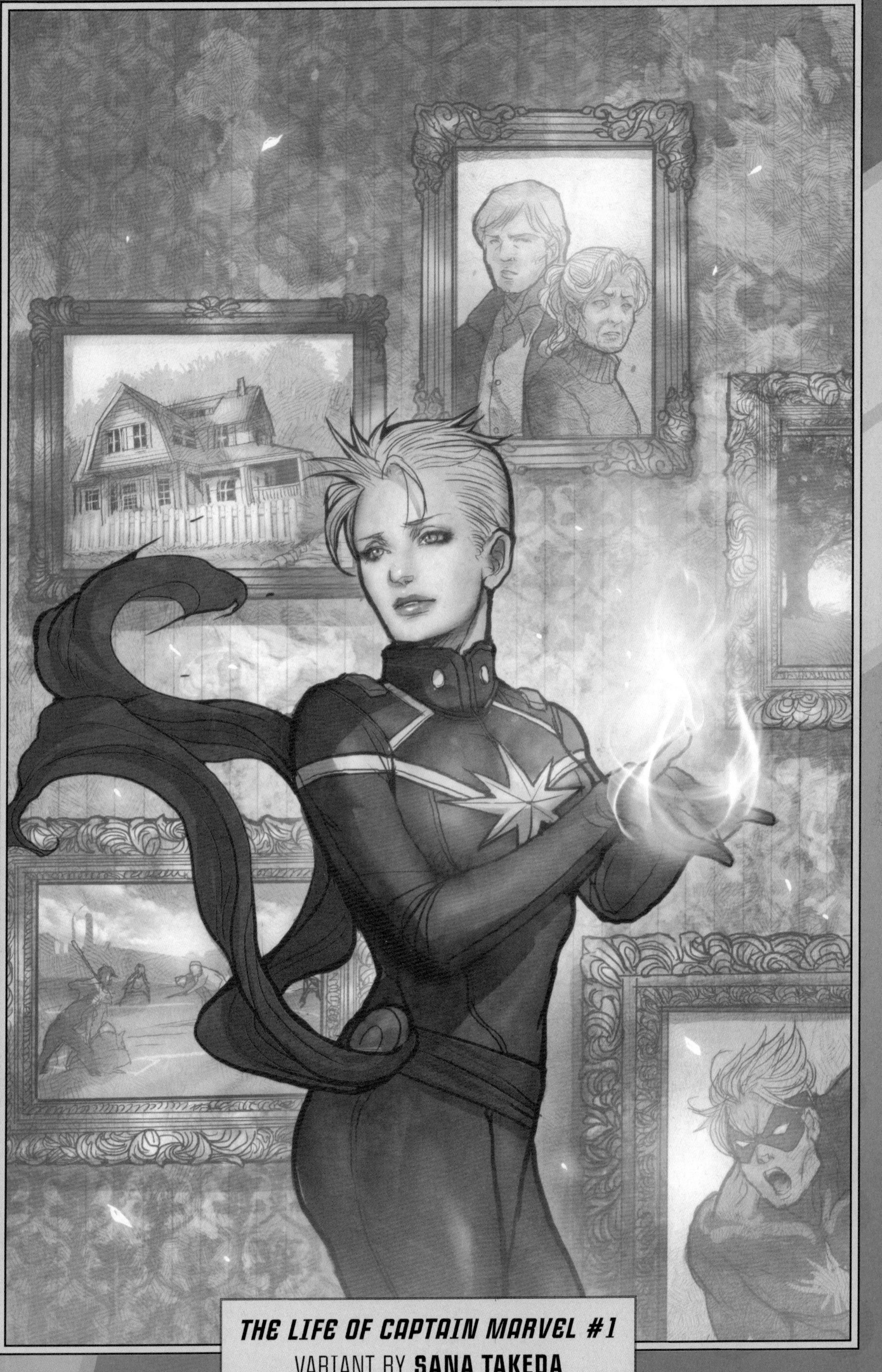

THE LIFE OF CAPTAIN MARVEL #1
VARIANT BY **SANA TAKEDA**

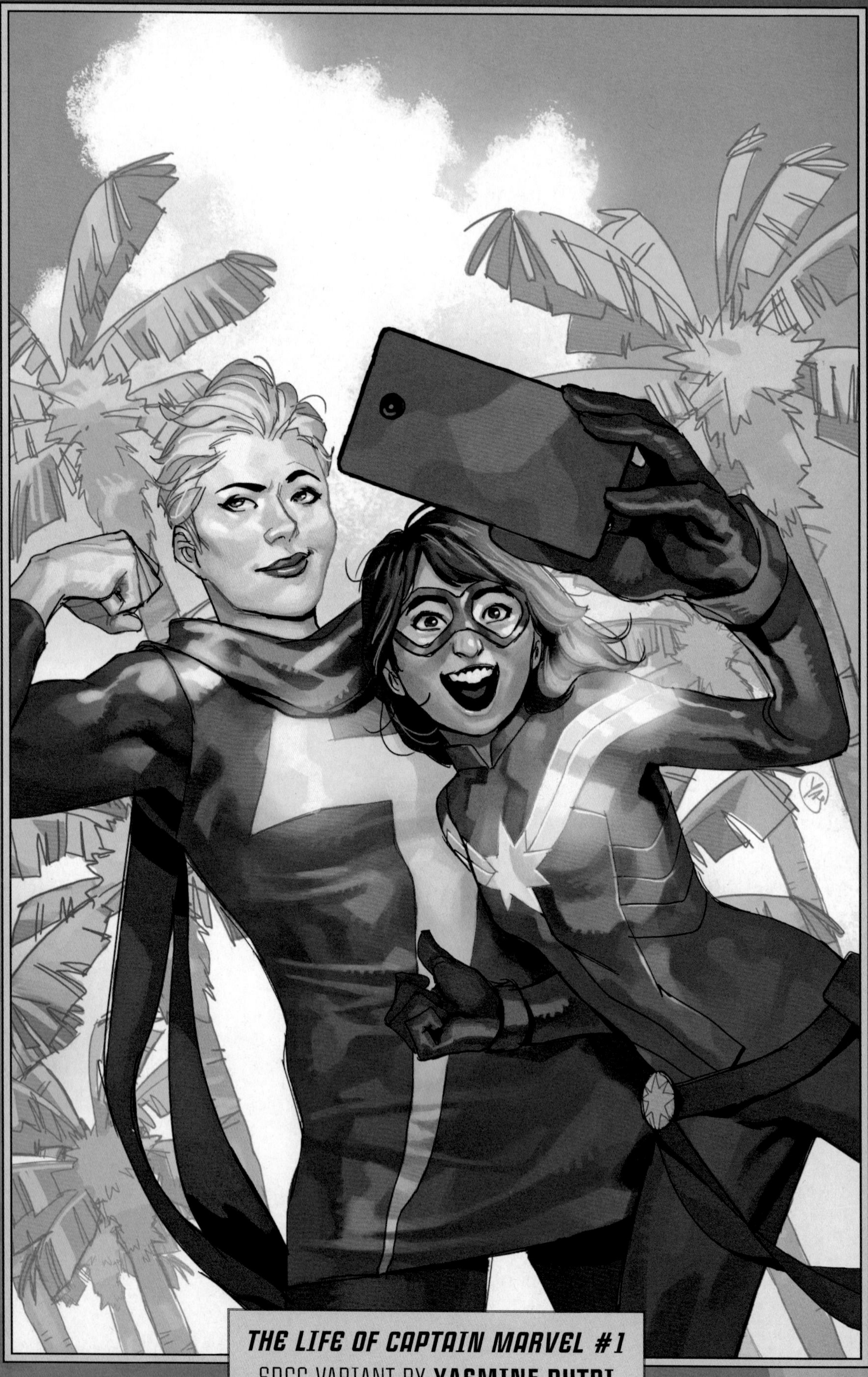

THE LIFE OF CAPTAIN MARVEL #1
SDCC VARIANT BY **YASMINE PUTRI**

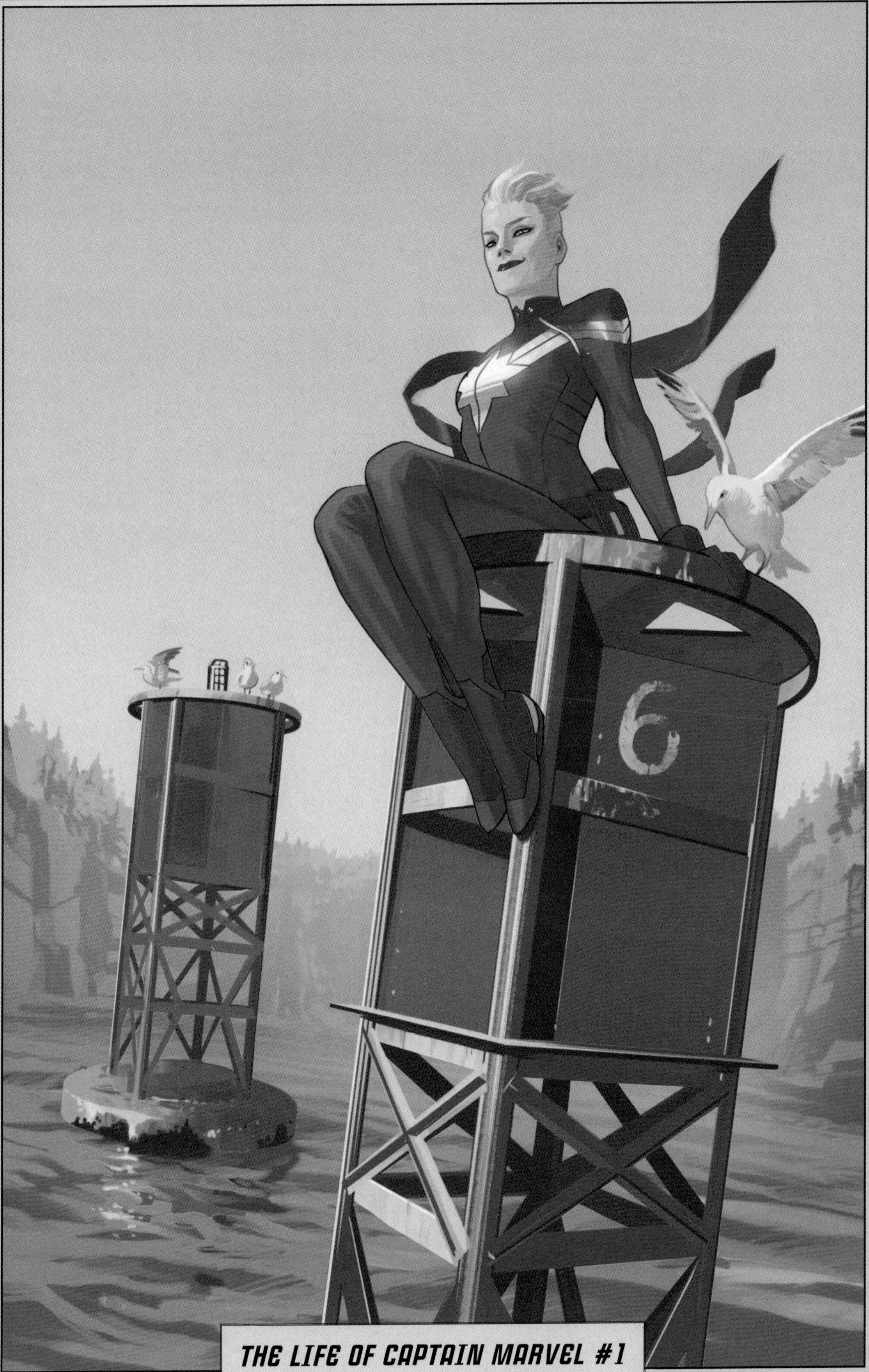
6

THE LIFE OF CAPTAIN MARVEL #1
VARIANT BY **FIONA STAPLES**

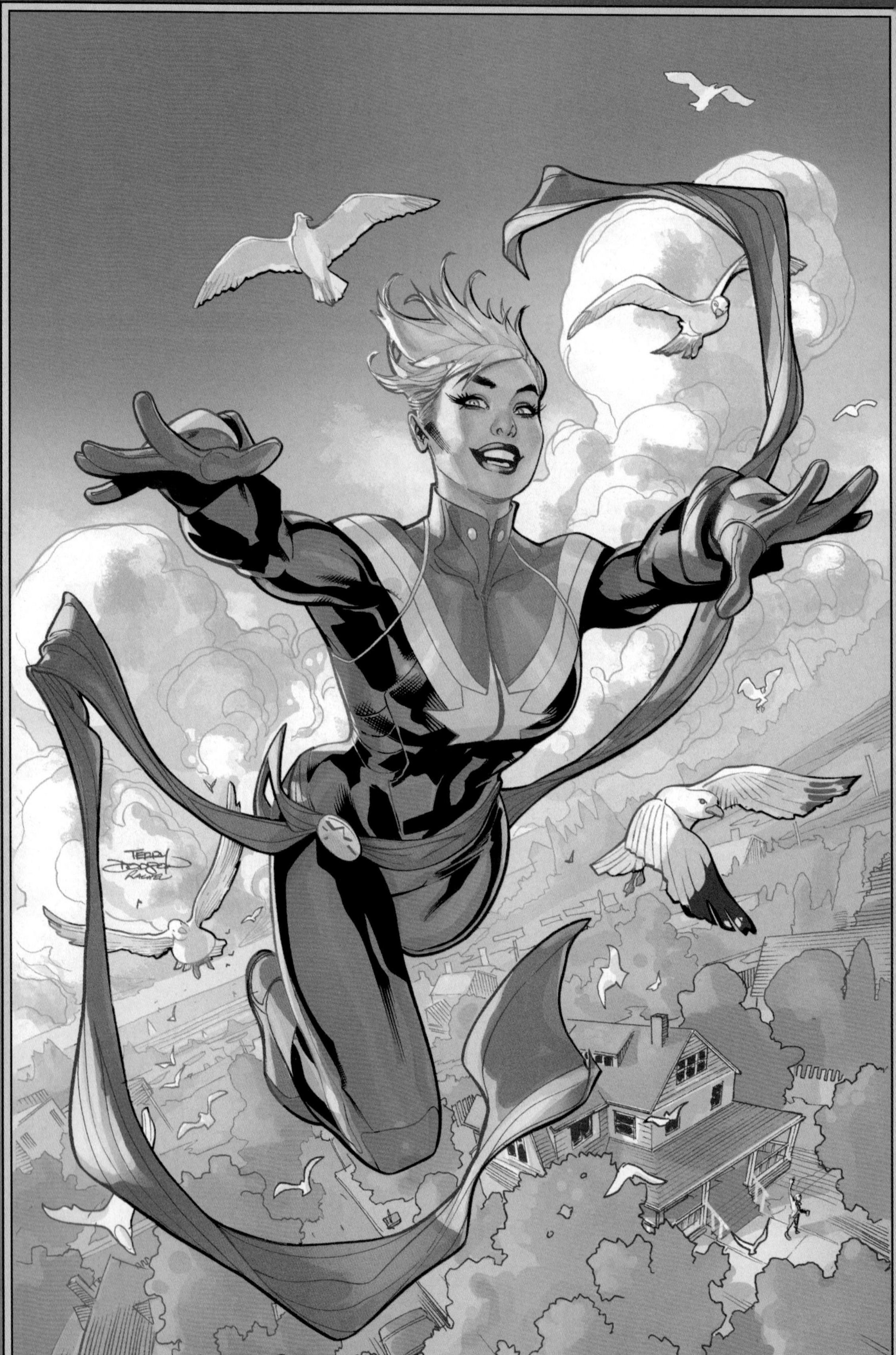

THE LIFE OF CAPTAIN MARVEL #2
VARIANT BY **TERRY DODSON** & **RACHEL DODSON**

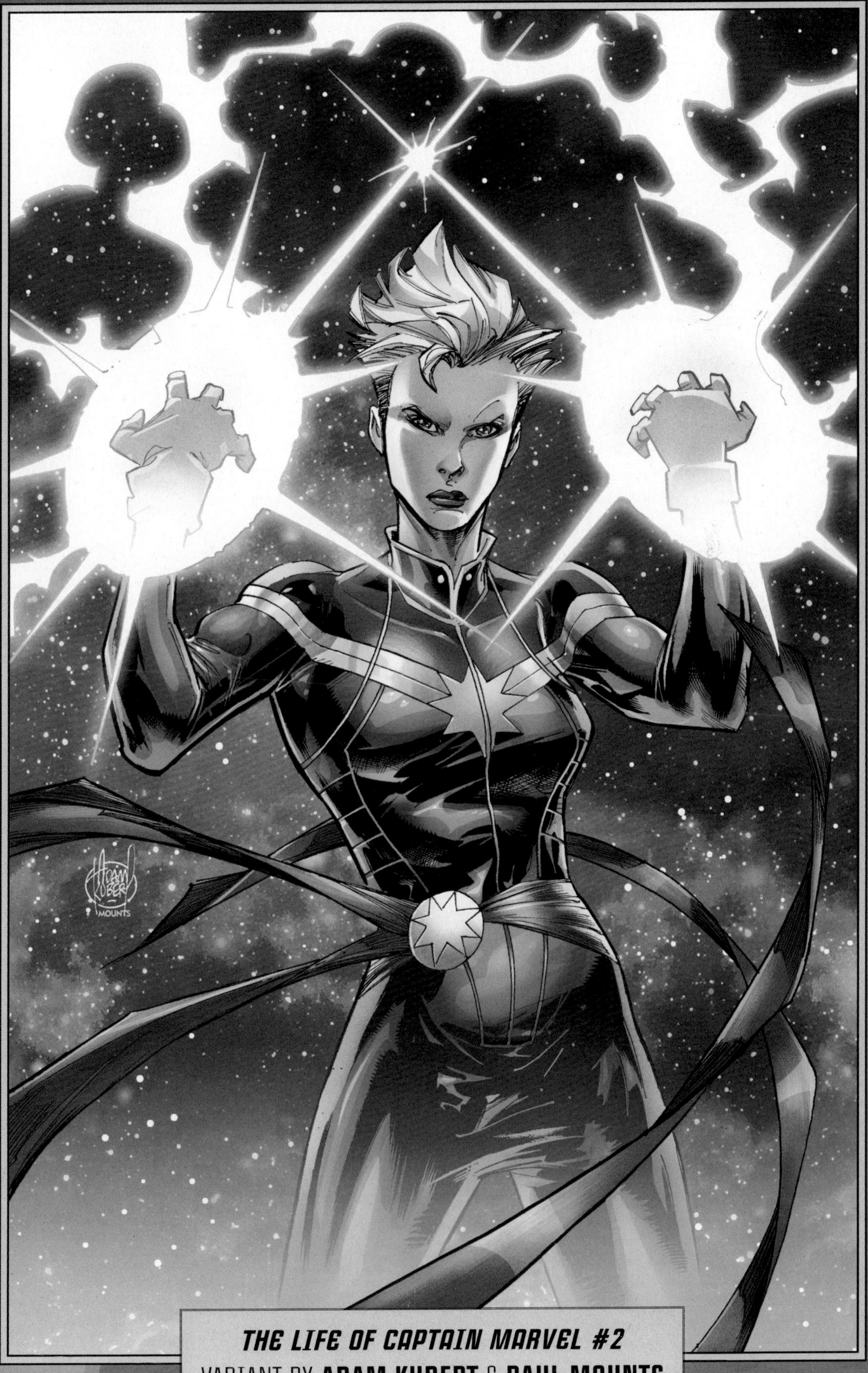

THE LIFE OF CAPTAIN MARVEL #2

VARIANT BY **ADAM KUBERT** & **PAUL MOUNTS**

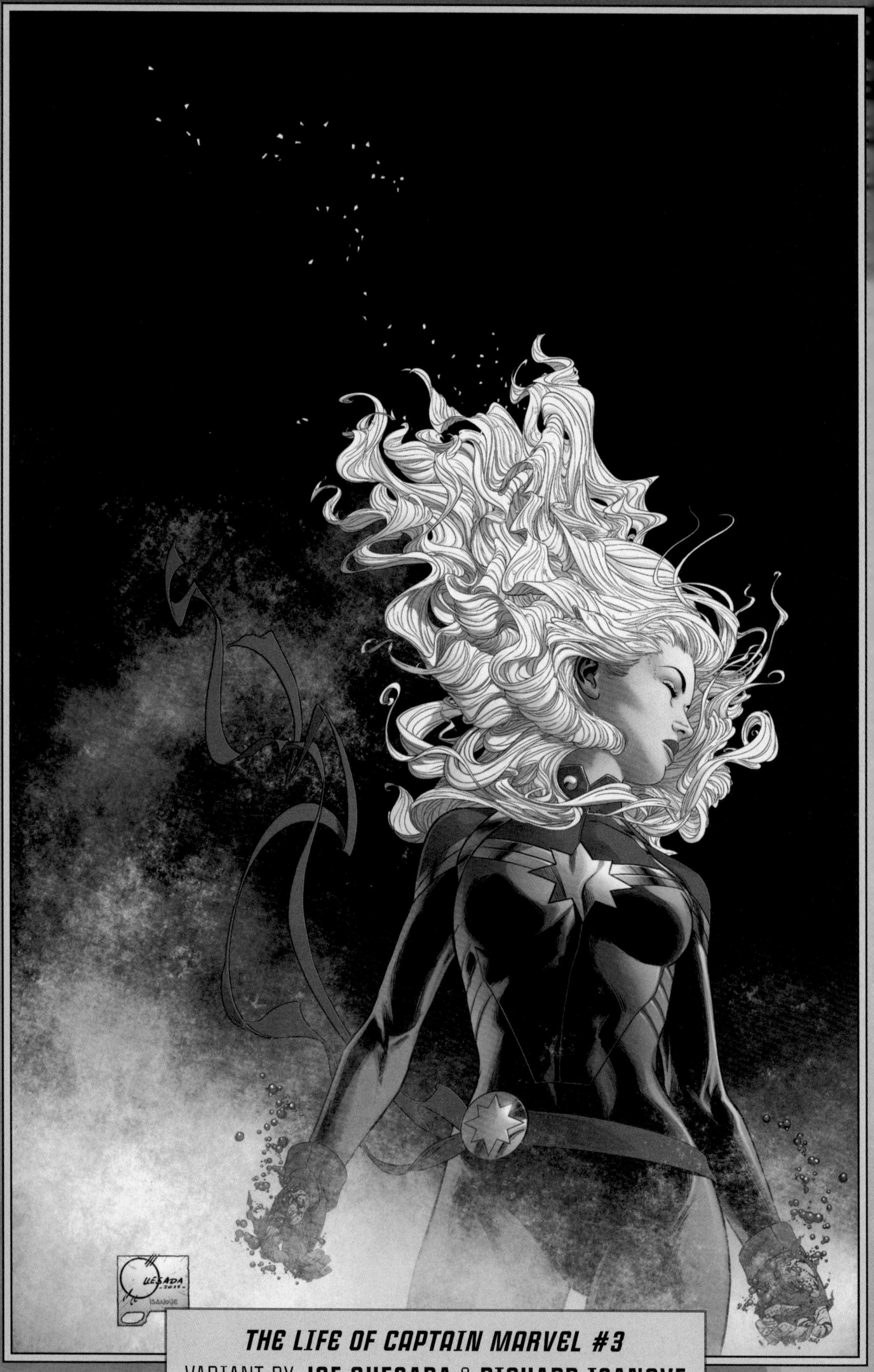

THE LIFE OF CAPTAIN MARVEL #3
VARIANT BY **JOE QUESADA** & **RICHARD ISANOVE**

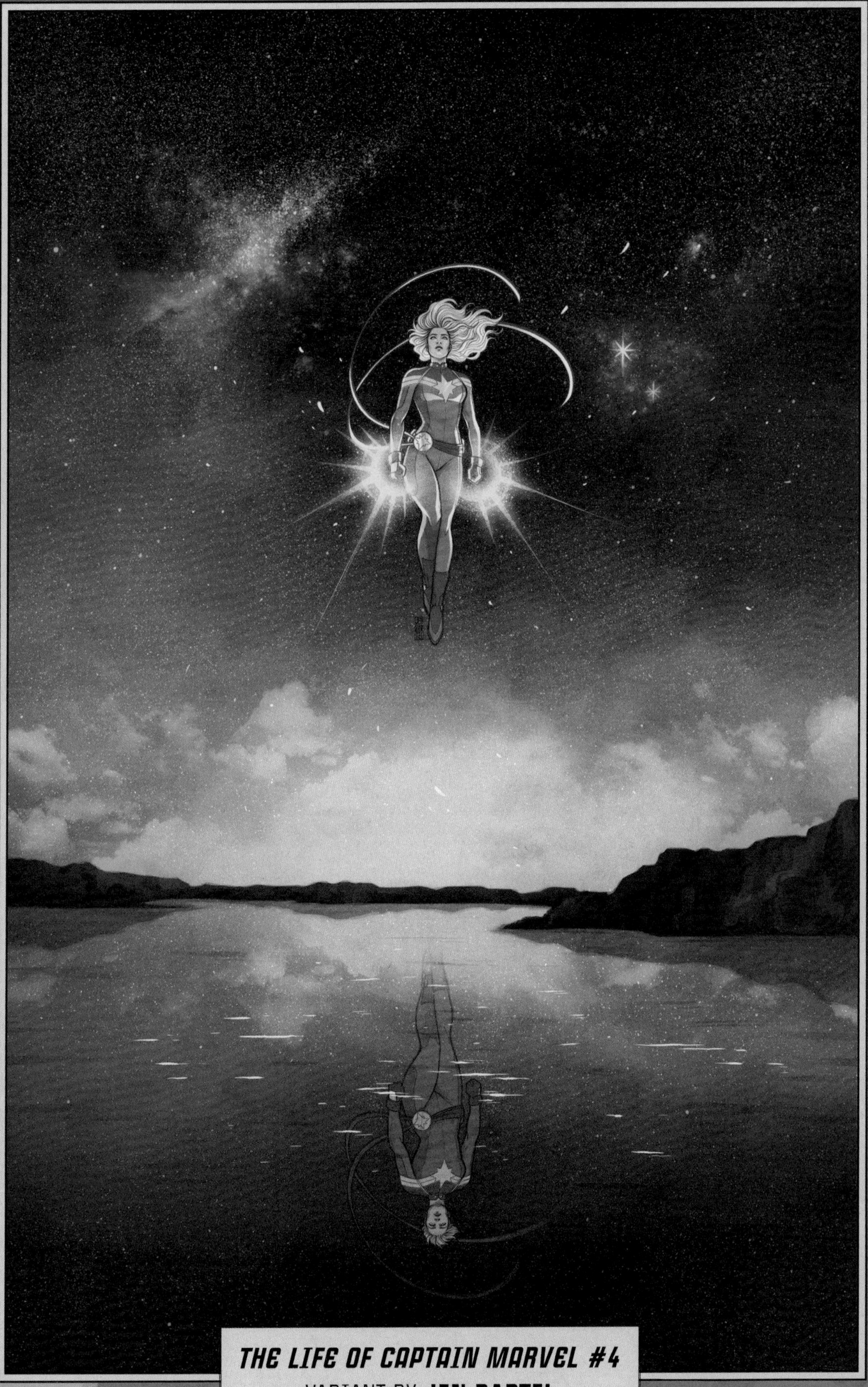

THE LIFE OF CAPTAIN MARVEL #4
VARIANT BY **JEN BARTEL**

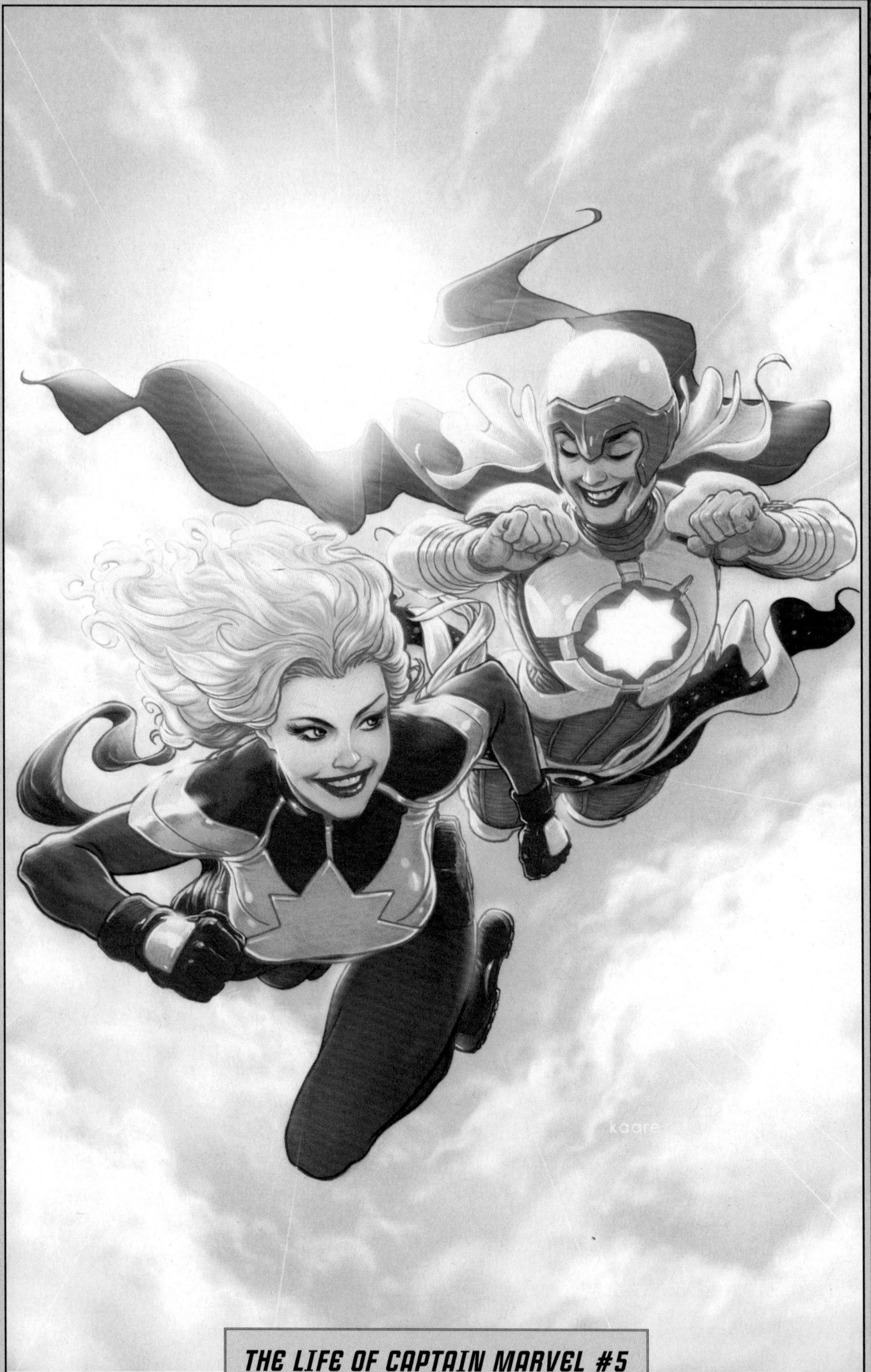
kaare

THE LIFE OF CAPTAIN MARVEL #5
VARIANT BY **KAARE ANDREWS**

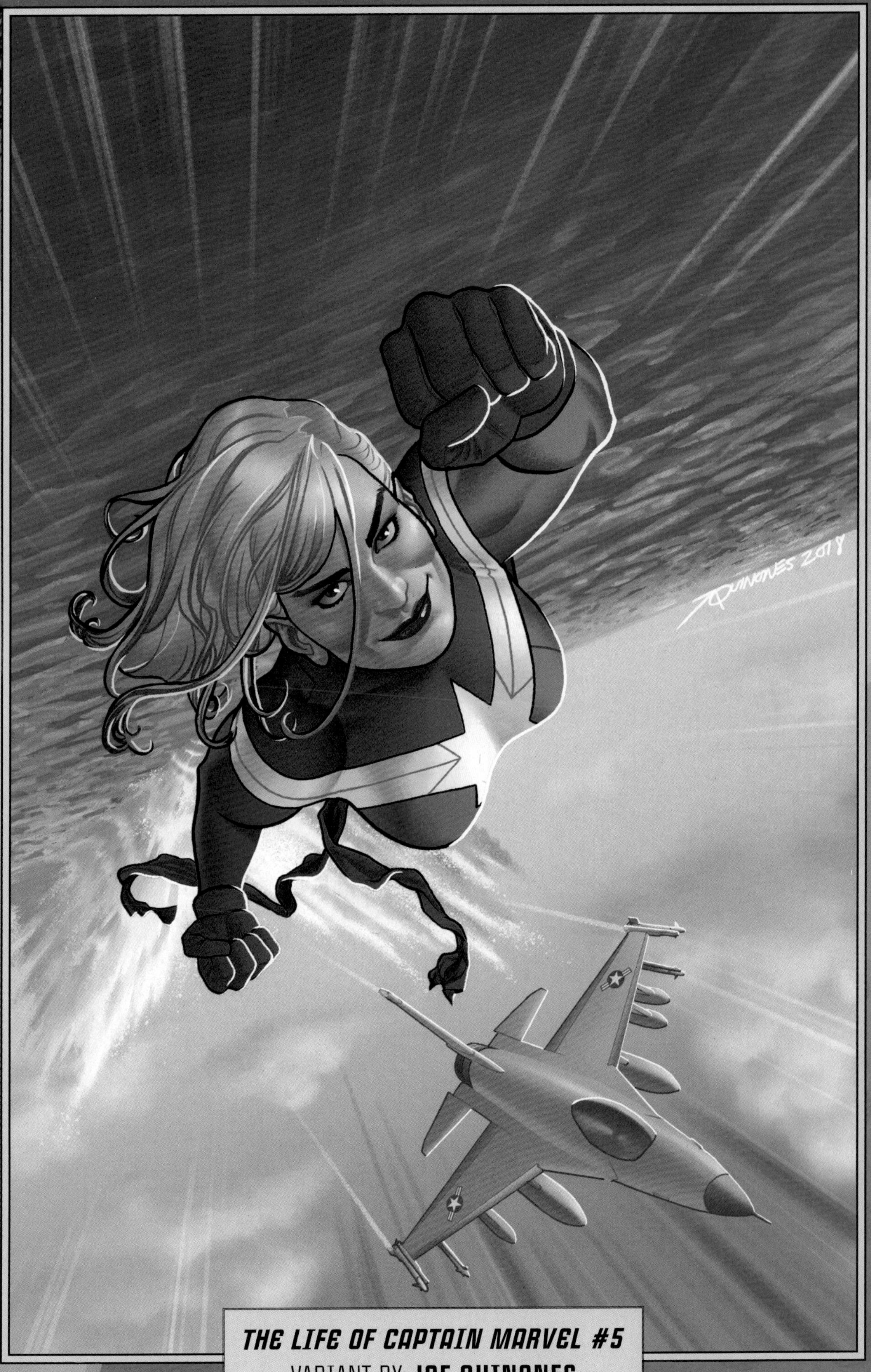

THE LIFE OF CAPTAIN MARVEL #5
VARIANT BY **JOE QUINONES**

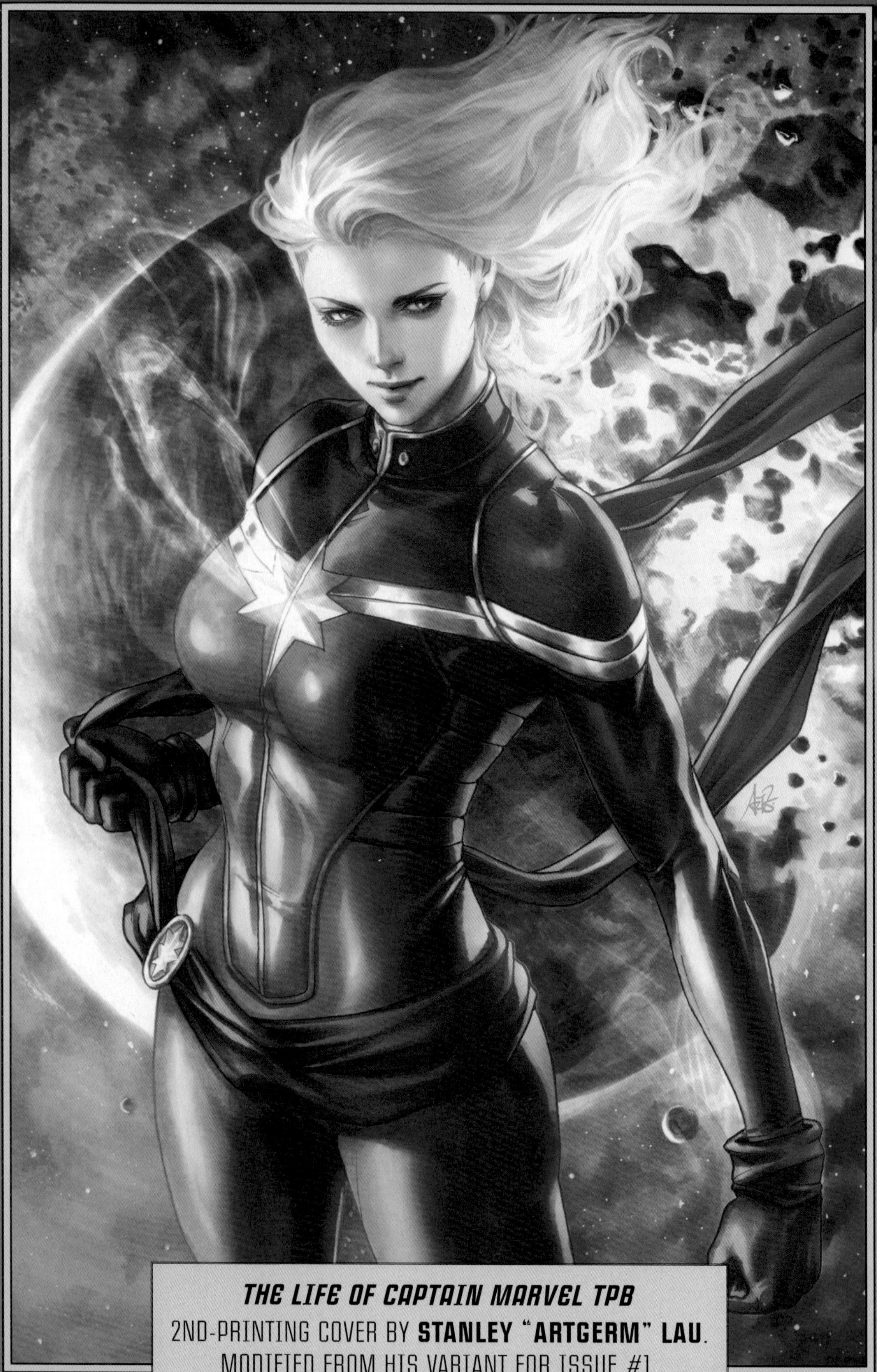

THE LIFE OF CAPTAIN MARVEL TPB

2ND-PRINTING COVER BY **STANLEY "ARTGERM" LAU**.
MODIFIED FROM HIS VARIANT FOR ISSUE #1,
THIS VERSION FEATURES CAROL WITH LONG HAIR.